LATE STALINISM

LATE STALINISM

THE AESTHETICS OF POLITICS

EVGENY DOBRENKO
Translated by Jesse M. Savage

Yale UNIVERSITY PRESS
New Haven and London

Published with assistance from the Louis Stern Memorial Fund.

Yale University Press books may be purchased in quantity for educational, business,
or promotional use. For information, please e-mail sales.press-yale.edu (U.S. office) or
sales@yaleup.co.uk (U.K. office).

Set in Sabon and Berthold City Bold types by Newgen North America.
Printed in the United States of America.

Library of Congress Control Number: 2019948653
ISBN 978-0-300-19847-8 (hardcover : alk. paper)

A catalogue record for this book is available from the British Library.

This paper meets the requirements of ANSI/NISO Z39.48-1992 (Permanence of Paper).

10 9 8 7 6 5 4 3 2 1

For Liudochka

. . . until everything is accomplished.
—*(Matthew 5:18)*

Contents

Acknowledgments

Work on this book was conducted intermittently since 1985. Over such a long stretch of time, I was fortunate enough to receive the help and advice of so many colleagues that it would now be quite impossible to name them all. However, I would like to thank the various institutions for their generous support. Fellowships at the Kennan Institute of the Woodrow Wilson International Center for Scholars, at the New York University (NYU) International Center for Advanced Studies, and at the NYU Jordan Center for the Advanced Study of Russia, as well as the John Simon Guggenheim Fellowship, the European Commission (Marie-Sklodowska-Curie Actions—COFUND Programme—FP7) and the EURIAS Senior Research Fellowship at the Institut für die Wissenschaften vom Menschen in Vienna, the Fernand Braudel Senior Fellowship at the European University Institute in Florence, and the AHRC Research Grant have all provided me with opportunities to work on the book under superb conditions and made it possible to complete this project. Financial support for my research was also generously provided by the University of Sheffield, for which I am most grateful.

Introduction

FIN DE SIÈCLE STALINISM

Preserved in the archive of the Soviet aesthetician and philosopher Mikhail Lifshits, a very close friend of György Lukács in the 1930s, is a folder entitled "Ora pro nobis" that contains notes from the early 1960s, when in the Thaw era Lifshits was contributing to the journal *Novyi mir,* whose editor-in-chief at the time was Aleksandr Tvardovskii. Within this folder is a document entitled "The Tragedy of Revolution," in which Lifshits wrote the following: "The terrible, too-easy 'fossilizing' of revolutionary lava is in its apparatus, its facilities. And then the horror of the *ready-made,* the already *done,* that which new generations find already finished and receive as compulsory, forces these unfortunates to search for some kind of desperate escape from the situation created for them, and everything that preserves and protects the results of revolution must now systematically occupy a rear guard position, must play a restraining role. It is truly a horror, unnoticed at first, but then . . ."[1]

This "then" had come after World War II. Lifshits was a man of the 1920s. For the next generation, life had already assumed a somewhat different shape, and the world at first seemed less tragic. Those of this generation who had remained true to Marxism regarded the "Great Retreat" that ensued in the mid-1930s, the turn to nationalism, and then even the alliance with Nazi Germany as tactical moves. On this subject a lively and astute member of the 1930s generation, poet David Samoilov, wrote that "we considered the beginning of superpower and chauvinist politics a tactic. . . . A tactic [that] turned out to be a strategy." Returning from the war, this generation did not recognize the country: "Power was definitively assuming Asiatic-Byzantine forms. New ideologies were required. The notorious struggle against cosmopolitanism was the 1937 for prewar-type orthodoxically Marxist ideologues. Only the most hard-boiled of them were spared. It became clear that during the war, with the arms and blood of the people, a bureaucratic state had secured a victory, an imperceptibly new state ideology had replaced the prewar one; some kind of new stratum that had come into power, for which it had fought for its own sake, needed its own new ideology, which for convenience it also called Marxism, creative Marxism."[2]

The "horror" that Lifshifts wrote about overtook Samoilov's generation. The generation gap between them confirmed better than anything else the famous maxim that in Russia everything changes over ten years and nothing changes over two hundred years. These words, attributed to Petr Stolypin, were borne out, it seems, by all of the country's subsequent history. In the first decade of the twentieth century, when the words were spoken, Russia had experienced a revolution, for the suppression of which Stolypin went down in history. In the next decade, it went through World War I and two revolutions, the latter of which swept away the former elites, changed the political system, and consolidated a new economic regime. After surviving a devastating civil war, the country entered the century's fourth decade, which was inaugurated by no lesser convulsions—collectivization, industrialization, and cultural revolution, all of which altered the country's social profile forever. The decade brought the Great Terror, unprecedented in its scope and definitively consolidating the change of the elites and the new political regime. The 1940s were inaugurated by the Great Patriotic War, which hit the country like a tornado, destroying its most economically developed part and consuming the most dynamic generation of youth. As soon as it ended, the country entered the era of the Cold War, one of yet another mobilization and unprecedented xenophobia, simultaneously developing a new imperial project and transforming itself into a world power and one of the poles of the new world order.

The following decade brought the Thaw, a new modernizing impulse that was in the 1970s replaced by stagnation. A new burst of historical dynamism in the 1980s, the symbol of which became "perestroika and acceleration," concluded at the beginning of the twentieth century's last decade with the collapse of the USSR and the "camp of socialism," the end of the Cold War, and yet another replacement of the political order and the economic system. When it entered the new century, the country engaged in an accelerating process of political counter-reforms, which were followed by economic crisis, stagnation, a new autarky, and confrontation with the West. It seems that in fact everything did change every ten years, and nothing at all changed. Nonetheless, much did change. The changes simply run deep.

The era following World War II has always been in the shadow of times far more tempestuous and hence far more interesting to historians—the revolutionary era (1920s), that of terror (1930s), or that of the Thaw (1956–64). The era of late Stalinism has gotten lost amid these historical surges like a sort of historical blank. It is perceived as a time of unprecedented political and social stability, the first such time in twentieth-century Russian history. But the depression that set in after the storm has seemed less interesting to historians.

Not without reason do historians prefer "eras of change" to eras in which "nothing happens"; it is precisely in the former that palpable social, political, and cultural fractures and shifts occur, the significance of which is defined by the longevity of their effects. At issue here are the wars and revolutions that produce breaks, but the effects of these breaks—and precisely where the subsequent wars and revolutions that produce new breaks mature—are in barely noticeable shifts, the shaping of a new routine, in the sustainability of life within these consequences. The eruption of a volcano is a short-term phenomenon; the formation of a volcano is a long-lasting process. That which determined the historical consciousness of the Soviet (and later the post-Soviet) nation for decades to come matured imperceptibly beneath the surface of the apparent lack of conflict in the postwar era.

Nations are born through the tragic events that they usually turn into triumphs. No one understood this better than Charles de Gaulle, who claimed that the future lasts a long time. In point of fact, the past lasts much longer. Victory in war was the event in which *the incipient Soviet nation manifested itself for the first time*. But this did not occur in the ruins of 1945. It took years for the tragedy of war to be transformed into the triumph of victory and for the Soviet nation to *collectively recognize itself,* during which a myth was created about the war and Soviet greatness, about an all-conquering leader and a supreme state, about the envy of the arrogant West and Russian national exceptionalism, about stolen glory and messianism. This was what constituted the essence of the late-Stalinist era. Stalin truly did take control of a country with a plow and leave it with an atomic bomb. But it is no less important that he took control of a country populated by people who had lost their own history and had been deprived of a national identity and left behind the full-fledged Soviet nation that was entirely the product of Stalinism. Stalin was the father of this nation.

History is made in eras when "nothing happens," specifically when the breaks and vivid political manifestations that occurred in the "era of changes" have accumulated political institutions and acquired their own rituals and traditions, have given rise to a corresponding political culture that is perceived as natural, have been transformed into a "way of life" and a "way of thinking" or "structures of everyday life," and have shaped a corresponding system of social relations and ties, as well as ethics and aesthetics. In other words, in order to have a long-time effect, the consequences of an "era of changes" must go through a stabilizing stage when a sort of subsidence of the revolutionary wave occurs, along with adaptation to life in the new conditions, when these new conditions are ritualized and normalized. It is in such stable periods that nations are born and history is made.

Late Stalinism was just such an era. In the most obscure years of twentieth-century Russian history this deep-seated historical process was especially intense, and it ended with the ultimate crystallization of the Soviet nation. Its post-Soviet successor is to this day experiencing phantom pains, complexes, and traumas of that era. It was precisely during that era (not before and not after) that its ideological parameters were molded. In those years much of the sediment of the 1930s had settled, and a new slurry emerged of modernized conservatism and nostalgic patriarchal sentiment, anti-Americanism and an envious attitude toward Western achievements, and isolationism and xenophobia with an aggressive international agenda.

The uniqueness of this era lies in its peculiar relationships to the preceding and subsequent periods of Soviet history. In the late 1920s it became clear that the country was entering a new era. But in the 1930s, the 1920s light still glimmered at the start of this tunnel. It was coming from the past, from behind. Turning around was not encouraged, but once turned around, one could still observe (although with great difficulty in the late 1930s) the "campfire glow" of the revolution (to use Iurii Trifonov's metaphor).[3] After Stalin's death, and especially after 1956, it was as if the door to the future had been flung open wide and the light had come out from the opposite end of the tunnel.[4] Many contemporaries got the sense that everything had started from the beginning ("purification of the ideals of revolution," "a return to Leninist norms of life," and the like). The postwar decade is in all respects unique, as *there was no light at all in it: the revolution's light had already gone out, and the light of the Thaw had not yet glimmered.*

This existence in pitch darkness was conveyed better than anyone else by the already quoted Samoilov: "The horrible eight years lasted a long time. Two times longer than the war. Long, for in fear the fictions and false faith peeled off from the soul; getting one's sight back was slow. What's more, it was hard to imagine you were starting to see, for your newly sighted eyes saw the same darkness as unseeing ones."[5] But life in this pervasive darkness did not stop. On the contrary, an intensive process of refining experience into a new historical self-awareness was at work. In precisely these years—not in the 1920s, not in the era of terror, not during the war, but specifically after it—was the shaping of the Soviet nation completed.

The postwar era differed markedly from the preceding one in that it was the quintessence and apex of Stalinism. One of its most astute contemporaries, the film and theater historian Maiia Turovskaia, wrote, "As a witness of that time, I would suggest that the 1930s were not the end product of the dictatorship and its 'golden age.' That these were, on the contrary, a transitional time, when the revolutionariness of the 1920s started to transition into the pragmatic, practical Stalinist dictatorship—the 'great terror,' as historians call it—but everyday life and culture, having undergone a radical fracturing, nonetheless resisted unification, holding on to the diversity, non-homogeneity, or multiformity that practically collapsed after the war, when Zhdanovism really set in."[6]

This transitiveness and fluidity of the 1930s, in which the repercussions of the revolutionary 1920s are clearly visible, was tied to the fact that the enormous masses of peasants who inundated the cities, ready to greedily absorb urban culture and energetically refashion it, had still not managed to comprehend it. Anyway, this culture itself was not by any means a finished thing: the 1930s were transitional also in the sense that a profound ideological break took place in them. The beginning of the decade was characterized by the powerful shift to the left that had started in the late 1920s (the end of the New Economic Policy [NEP], the rout of the "rightist opposition," collectivization, cultural revolution), while from the mid-1930s the "Great Retreat" began—an abrupt turn to the right (nationalism, traditional values, and so on) in response to the profoundly conservative values of a patriarchal mentality. Over the time that passed leading up to World War II, the masses simply had not yet managed to catch up with this turn, to grasp what was happening. When they eventually did, this coincided with the late Stalinist era, the era of "Zhdanovist" repressions, the campaign against "cosmopolitans," the "Doctors' Plot" (or "murderer-doctors" affair), and the Cold War. Hence, one might say that in the 1930s and after the war, the country lived in different cultural chronotopes.

Spatially, Soviet prewar culture was almost completely concentrated on Soviet soil. The external world—invariably hostile to it—became part of it merely through the echoes of ancient battles, through internal enemies or "smuggled-in spies and saboteurs." For the Soviet people, the postwar era became one of a real "discovery of the world." Foreign countries became part of Soviet culture in the fundamental ideological campaigns of late Stalinism—the struggles for peace and Soviet superiority, the fights against "kowtowing to the West" and cosmopolitanism. Before the war, the external world was almost absent from the Soviet imagination. But its presence there now stemmed from at least four new factors: (i) the country's new status as a superpower, which required a dynamic foreign policy, which needed a rationale and internal mobilization and, accordingly, the production of a threat and a representation of the West as its source; (ii) the new imperial status in Eastern Europe and Asia, which required their integration and, hence, familiarity with them; (iii) the necessity for an antidote to an image of foreign countries that the Soviet liberator-troops might have "uncritically assimilated"; (iv) the consolidation of the victor's image and of the sense of Soviet superiority, which energized a number of ideological campaigns of an anti-Western bent and required the constant maintenance of an image and narrative about a hostile and insidious West. All of these factors deeply imprinted the image of the West that came to the ordinary Soviet person. The fact that this "discovery of the world" was poisoned by the most acute phase of the Cold War left a deep scar in Soviet and post-Soviet consciousness.[7]

No less radical was the shift on the temporal scale. Nationalism required affirmation of preeminence, a rootedness in history, a constant narrative about grievances, injustices suffered, and glory stolen. If before the war Soviet culture had been occupied with proving its revolutionariness and newness, now the focus was, on the contrary, on its antiquity and "primogeniture." If the 1930s Soviet historical novels and films appealed to the past to demonstrate the continuity of "the people's revolutionary traditions," then now it was to prove Russian primacy in the past. In the 1930s, even after the nationalistic shift in the middle of the decade, the subject was revolutionariness and the present's ties to the past, which became the domain of historical allusions. After the war, the past became self-sufficient.

Stalinism is, pure and simple, civil war fossilized in political institutions, ideological postulates, and numerous artifacts. The late-Stalinism period was essentially the endpoint of the half-century-long process called the Russian Revolution. The post-Stalin period became a time of finding a way out of a civil war that had lasted half a century, of timid neutralization of the consequences of Stalinism (in the best times), of renewing its façade (in the worst times), but on the whole, of life on loan, due to what Stalin had created. Thus it remained, as long as the Stalinist edifice (political, economic, institutional, military, ideological, and cultural), though not fit for a peaceful life and exempt from reform, still continued to yield a return.

In all other respects, the term "Stalinism" has a right to exist as more an umbrella definition; after all, anyone familiar with Soviet culture knows the difference between the years 1927, 1937, and 1947, or 1929, 1939, and 1949, and so forth. Nonetheless, this difference is not only cultural, but also social; these are different societies. The 1933-model Soviet society, when the country was in shock from collectivization and at the peak of its industrial efforts, and the 1953 model, when a country that had already experienced the Great Terror, the Patriotic War, and the convulsions of late Stalinism froze at the threshold of the "Doctors' Plot," are different countries. The year 1946 is no less distinct from 1936 than 1936 is from 1926, no less than all three are distinct from 1956. Over ten years, everything changes.

Hence it is right to say not so much "Stalinism" as *Stalinisms,* as we look at it in a broad historical perspective, specifically as the conclusion of a revolutionary era that stretched to half a century in Russia. In fact, the Russian Revolution, if one views it as a process of intensive and forcible social, economic, political, and cultural demolition (that is, of a half-century-long civil war from 1905 to 1956), ended only with the beginning of de-Stalinization in 1956. In this broad context, late Stalinism is also, apart from all that, the end of a half-century-long development of the country. Within it is everything the country achieved, everything at which it arrived as the result of fifty years of civil war: an absolute central power and the most powerful and enormous empire in Russian history—from Berlin to Beijing—but simultaneously a rupture that three and a half decades later would lead to its collapse.

Stalinism was not only a page of history; it had its own history. It can be divided into three periods, early (1927–34), high (1935–45), and late (1946–53). Like any periodization, this is not absolute, and it has transitional periods. For example, the years 1924–27 can be considered transitional, when Stalin's leadership in the party was neither obvious nor absolute, although his political domination was growing exponentially. One can also consider the period from the murder of Sergei Kirov in December 1934 to 1936, when the Great Terror machine revved up to its full power, as transitional. The final transitional years were from 1943 to 1945, when the imminently victorious end of the war shaped the approaches that would predominate after the war but which asserted themselves definitively only in 1946. If in the first stage the dominant goals were economic (collectivization, the five-year plans), in the second, they were primarily political (the Great Terror), and in the third, the goals of nation building (preservation of the political regime, the Cold War) were ideological and mobilizational.

Early Stalinism ended with, as it was said in those years, "the construction of the *economic* foundation of socialism." Its result was the "congress of victors." Underlying the turbulent era of high Stalinism, in which the primarily *political* goals of replacing the elites (those very same "victors") were worked out, was fear. For the meantime, the only things that announced the creation of a nation were Stalin's constitution and the beginning of the Great Retreat. But fear alone is not enough for the birth of a nation. The idea of a nation is needed. It was precisely this deluge of *ideological* content of the late-Stalinism era that provided the conditions for the birth of the Soviet nation. Under the calm surface of this period (in comparison with previous ones), fear mutated into national traumas and phobias, a history of glory and grievances, and it was transformed into the ideological foundation of the Soviet nation. All three components, of course, were present in each era, although one dominated since the content and end results of each era were different. Since ideology was at the center, the problem of promoting it was fundamental, assuring the high political status of culture at this time.

Stalinism is the heart of Sovietness; the institutional, political, economic, ideological, and cultural parameters of Sovietness were all formed in it. Stalinism reached its finished form in the postwar era. In effect, all of Russian history after Stalinism (the Thaw and de-Stalinization, stagnation and re-Stalinization, perestroika and Yeltsin's market reforms, Putinism) was in one way or another a reaction to Stalinism since its instrument, subject, and object were *simultaneously* the basic products of Stalinism—the Soviet state Stalin created and the Soviet nation of which he remained the father.[8]

No less important is the generational aspect of the problem. The generation of the 1920s–30s perished in war, while in the Khrushchev era the preceding generation had already abandoned an active political life. Thus the most dynamic generation after Stalin was made up either from those whose formative years were delayed during the war or those whose youth coincided with the postwar era. These were the people who made up the demographic backbone of the active Soviet population. The generation following them (because of the demographic gap brought on by war casualties) was too small in number, which led to a significant extension of the influence of the first postwar generation, which continued for longer than a usual generation to project and reproduce its worldview, the one imbibed in the late-Stalinism era. Essentially, the Soviet era came to a close only when this generation was gone.

Furthermore, it was precisely in the era of late Stalinism that the active political careers of a whole generation of Stalin's 1920s and 1930s associates (such as Viacheslav Molotov, Lazar' Kaganovich, and Georgii Malenkov) *actually* came to an end. The period that set in after Stalin's death was the era of the promotees of the properly late-Stalinist period, one might say of the Brezhnev generation (such as Mikhail Suslov, Aleksei Kosygin, and Andrei Gromyko), which was the last generation of Soviet leaders. If one remembers that in the Stalinist system, as Stalin himself famously remarked, the cadres determine everything, then the role that the period in which this cadre revolution took place becomes clear. The new Soviet elites—the young cadres of the expanding *nomenklatura,* the party and administrative activist core, the re-educated cadres of the intelligentsia—had assimilated the principles of postwar Stalinism inculcated into their consciousness. It was just this generation, shaped and promoted after the war, that would become the last generation of Soviet leaders, replacing the generation of Stalin's comrades-in-arms. The generation that followed it, shaped and promoted in the Thaw era that replaced late Stalinism, either could not or refused to save the Soviet Union that Stalin had created.

Social sentiment, too, had changed, as compared to the prewar era; it was characterized by the population drawing closer to the regime. As A. A. Danilov and A. V. Pyzhikov note, in spite of the fact that dissatisfaction with difficult living conditions persisted after the war (as well as these conditions themselves, which even worsened), the attitude toward them changed, and "this was precisely what fundamentally distinguished the late-1940s Soviet society from that of the mid-1930s. The most interesting thing is that anti-government sentiment was now restrained not only by fear for one's fate, but also by faith in the rightness of the chosen course of development. It was not only in words that the war had united the people and the ruling party. Not by chance were expressions of dissatisfaction characterized as blather, unhealthy sentiment, false, provocational, and anti-Soviet rumors, and hostile anti-Soviet sentiment. This viewpoint was characteristic of [both] the party elites and simple people."[9]

In the 1930s the preconditions for what happened during World War II and for the fusion of the Russian and Soviet identities after it were only created. Although nationalism began to color the Soviet project ever more distinctly in the late 1930s, in connection with the need to mobilize against the external threat, it was not yet ethnic Russian nationalism but remained, on the whole, Soviet. And the 1930s era itself was quite closely tied to the revolutionary project, both politically and ideologically. Hence, prewar Soviet culture still largely preserved an internationalist model.[10] Late Stalinism, however, was already *totally* disconnected from revolution. It was a purely nationalist-state project and almost exclusively ethnically based. It was not in the 1930s but during the war and after it that the targeted and systematic inculcation of aggressive nationalism began (the mythology of the historical primacy of Russia and of historical insults to the Russian people feeding its resentment), as well as anti-Semitism, anti-Americanism, imperialism, and other key elements of late- and post-Soviet ideology. In this respect, the shaping of the Soviet nation within its basic parameters was completed in the era of late Stalinism. It is there that one should seek the sources of the majority of its manifestations in subsequent times.

After World War II, the world had changed to the point of unrecognizability. The Soviet Union's relations with the world had also undergone radical changes. The country occupied a completely different place in it, having been suddenly transformed from a pariah state into not only a superpower, but also one of the poles of the postwar world order. It was precisely the late-Stalinist era that furnished the paradigm for East-West relationships for decades to come and that became formative in all of the subsequent relations of the USSR/Russia with the world. And this paradigm applies to more than just the Cold War era. This impulse was so powerful that the inertia imposed in this time is to this day defining the relations of post-Soviet Russia with the West.

The extraordinary significance of late Stalinism is that it was the era in which the process of shaping the Soviet nation concluded with its recognition by the world. As Mikhail Ryklin shrewdly observed, "After victory in World War II, the USSR acquires a universally recognized history not tied to the dictatorship of the proletariat and worldwide revolution; the Soviet people constitute themselves as a super-ethnos and acquire (from the hands of the international community as well) a secondary legitimacy."[11] Late Stalinism became the era in which the key parameters of the new nation were set forth—the complexes, insults, phobias, and traumas, the image of the enemy, and the image of its own greatness, all grafted into it.

The birth of nations was happening everywhere in the nineteenth and twentieth centuries, and Russia was not unique in this regard. The uniqueness of its national project (and hence of its nation building) surfaces only after the 1917 revolution, which at first set the country on a completely new course, different from the general European trajectories. Before that point, the nationalist movement in Russia was completely traditional. The political and cultural elites were more than anyone else inspired by nationalism. Its rise began, not by chance, in the times of Nicholas I, in the 1840s–50s, when the Slavophiles, *pochvenniks,* Pan-Slavists, and Westernists all asserted themselves. This completely organic project was intellectually nourished by the German idealism and European romanticism with which Russia was then inspired, from romantic politics (populism) to romanticism in art.

In the early twentieth century, parallel processes begin to be politically shaped in Europe, and they reach their peak with the collapse of empires. At this time in Russia, however, a twenty-year-long collapse occurs, at the very peak of patriotic hysteria. An internationalist ideology dominates in the country from 1917 to the mid-1930s. When Stalin revived nationalism in the second half of the 1930s, the country was already different: the previous nationalism-oriented elites were no longer there, and the new elites and new masses were operating with a different political culture. The Bolsheviks had continued the imperial project. A national Russian state had not come together. Although Russian nationalism had stalled, it received an important place in the Soviet imperial project that was being intensively shaped. The unique intermediacy of this nationalism-internationalism-imperialism gave rise to a unique *imperial* culture that was *internationalist* in form and *nationalist* in content.

The derailment of the Soviet project was the logical result of the confrontational-nationalistic policy chosen by Stalin (and essentially continued, with minor variations, by all his successors). Exhausted by decades of internal fracturing, the country even after the victory over Germany could not dictate its will to the world. However, by holding the population in a perpetual state of mobilization and artificially maintaining nationalist hysteria, Stalin and his successors totally exhausted the internal potential of the Soviet nation, the life of which turned out to be, by historical yardsticks, not very long. The aggressive imperial upsurge overstrained the economy, militant state nationalism transformed the country into a real bugbear for the developed world, definitively emasculating the Soviet system of its original revolutionary content, and extinguished any impulses at all toward development, leaving behind a carcass eroded by the mass cynicism that stood in the way of the country's development, and it ultimately collapsed.

The roots of the fundamental ideo-political currents of the post-Soviet era are to be found precisely in late Stalinism. Right after World War II, the "Soviet patriotism" introduced in the 1930s was Russified and transplanted into the soil of *Russian* history. If in the consciousness of the 1920s (and partially also the 1930s) person Sovietness was *contrasted to* Russianness, then, as Danilov and Pyzhikov observe, "in the second half of the 1940s, practically the entire historical canvas of Russian history served as a peculiar reinforcement of the concept of Soviet patriotism. In the opinion of the authorities, its roots must be fed by a vivid Russian past that would establish and guarantee a continuity of sorts of the great deeds and achievements of the Russian people both then and now."[12]

Although this process began in the mid-1930s, at that time it failed to impact the consciousness of millions of people. Moreover, a significant time gap exists—for example, between the changes made in school textbooks and their consequences for the masses' consciousness; during the war, this gap was filled with concentrated nationalistic propaganda, both Soviet and anti-Soviet. This is partly why, after the war, we are dealing with a different country. Conditions of crisis led to the dominant elements of the masses' postwar consciousness—the anti-liberalism, anti-modernism, anti-Americanism, and anti-Semitism inculcated for decades in the semi-patriarchal society—being reproduced on a huge scale in the consciousness of the new generation.

In this respect, the contemporary Russian nation was molded precisely in the postwar years. Post-Soviet nostalgia for the imperial greatness of the USSR, for its invincibility and the fear the world felt for it, is by no means a product of the 1930s (the prewar myths about Soviet invincibility and greatness were dispelled during the 1941 catastrophe). It is from the postwar era. From this era, too, is the state cult of victory and the figure of Stalin-as-conqueror in war, before whom the great powers "tremble." The nostalgia for the USSR has a quite precise chronological localization: it is nostalgia for the postwar era, for *late Stalinism,* when the Soviet Union was "feared and respected." The sources of this nostalgia are also late-Stalinist: the future-orientedness of prewar Stalinism was completely played out, the attractive image of the future had not taken shape, and the present was replaced by the political improvisations of the next autocrat.

THE POLITICS OF AESTHETICS AND THE AESTHETICS OF POLITICS

This book was conceived so long ago that when I first sketched its outlines in April 1985, the very word "Stalinism" was taboo in the USSR. Even the phrase "Stalin era" was not used; the de-Stalinization brought by perestroika was still at least two years off. But it was not simply the words that were taboo. Soviet history was structured in such a way that its fundamental collision remained invisible; instead of the Stalin era that was formative of the Soviet nation and the nerve center of twentieth-century Russian history, there were isolated "periods" (collectivization, industrialization, "the postwar recovery of the economy," and so forth). Since there was no Stalinism, there was no Thaw either. Without the Thaw, there was no Brezhnev re-Stalinization. Standing all by itself was the Twentieth Party Congress (with no mention of Khrushchev's "secret speech"!), which adopted the resolution "On Overcoming the Cult of Personality and Its Consequences" and thereby, as it turned out, "reestablished Lenin's norms of party life," as many said at the time. Stalinism has been (and even now is most frequently) associated almost exclusively with the 1930s—the era of the Great Terror and the Gulag. Such a view has become so widespread that researchers of Stalinism rarely venture beyond the 1930s, and if they do, most of the time they find nothing new there, assuming what they see is merely an extension of the 1930s. From this perspective, the postwar decade looks like an incomprehensible and uninteresting episode; Stalinism came together in the 1930s, and the Thaw that began in 1956 was completely focused on rehabilitating the victims of the Great Terror. The war was simply situated between these points and regarded as an event of either military or international history.

The picture began to change after the collapse of the USSR. The revolutionary era receded to the background, and Stalinism was finally understood as a central event of twentieth-century Russian history. This change is explained by the fact that with the end of the Cold War and the ideological showdown of two systems, the view of the October Revolution became soberer. Interest in Stalinism also stimulated a reevaluation of the postwar era. Over the last quarter-century, important archival documents have been published, and the work of both Russian and Western historians has shed light on many pages of the history of late Stalinism.[13] Above all, this is research on the key events and campaigns of these years, such as the anti-cosmopolitan campaign in science, the Jewish Anti-Fascist Committee trial, the "Doctors' Plot," Lysenkoism, and the "Leningrad affair."[14]

Nevertheless, late Stalinism (although this term is not used) as a discrete era has thus far been investigated only by political historians[15] and international relations historians (mainly Cold War specialists).[16]

In time, interest in the social and economic history of this period has also awakened.[17] The result is a situation that I would call positivist dystrophy; due to the methodological limitations of a narrowly fact-driven approach and the disciplinary insularity of various divisions of historiography, the corpus of documents and knowledge accumulated does not produce breakthroughs in either an understanding of this period that is in so many respects crucial or its interpretation.[18]

Historians of *Stalinist culture* have primarily studied the 1930s. Only a few books have been written about the culture of late Stalinism, and they are all limited by the material—either the work of a single author,[19] or a single event,[20] or a particular institution,[21] or one type of art or science.[22] The problem is that narrow specialists rarely venture beyond the boundaries of their own material into historical generalizations, and historians who address culture, since they are not specialists and therefore lack the corresponding analytical skills, do not undertake to examine it. The result is that no integral picture of the era in its diversity and significance has emerged.

Since Stalinism was a personalist regime, many of its complexes and traumas were projections of Stalin's own complexes and traumas, accumulated in the course of his struggle for power, and of his imperial ambitions. He inflicted them on the country, just as any autocrat transforms his personal complexes into a national agenda (such a link can be easily traced in Putin's Russia). As Samoilov noted in his memoir, Stalin "managed to infect the whole country" with the "severe, senile illness that exacerbated his natural suspiciousness and cruelty"; as a result, "We lived by a persecution complex and a delusion of grandeur."[23] But since the era was not just about the Cold War, but also about nation building, the role of culture was enormous. Though secondary for foreign policy, it was indispensable for the audience at home.

The historiographic picture presented here reflects the dynamics of historical scholarship in the second half of the twentieth century. Before the "new left" historians emerged in Western historiography (including Sovietology), political history dominated. In the 1960s, it was supplanted by social history. In recent decades, however, as a result of the weakening of the 1960s impulse and the departure from social history in its most rigid sense (the study of social structures such as social classes), the so-called cultural turn occurred, which is frequently described as a shift from the social history of culture toward a cultural history of the society. The post-modernist shift to "soft," flexible, pliant, fluid, and fragile sociocultural forms and constructed identities (historical, class, gender, national, political, or individual) was fed by the works of Michel Foucault and Jacques Derrida, Jean Baudrillard and Guy Debord, Pierre Bourdieu and Michel de Certeau.[24] Alongside the phenomenon Zygmunt Bauman called "liquid modernity," the "cultural turn" was also defined.[25] Sovietology, however, by virtue of its specific position, landed (as was the subject of its study) in a situation of developmental catch-up; its belated transition to social history coincided with a decreasing interest in it in Western historiography. As a result, the shifts toward social and cultural history in Sovietology overlapped.

This dynamic in historiography had serious consequences for understanding the very object of study; the historical sequence transitioned into the hierarchical one. By the logic of post hoc ergo propter hoc, there arose a notion that there is a political history *beneath which* social history happens, and *beneath that* is where cultural history is situated. In reality, however, the very fact that social historians had turned to culture is tied to a realization that a gap had formed between social and political history and that culture was the lost link that had to be restored in order to complete the chain. Cultural history is situated *between* social and political history.

Cultural history is not a supplement to the "main" (political, social, economic) history, not a vignette, not a few lines at the end of a historical narrative. Culture is the basis of sociality, no more and no less than a symbolic system of conventions, limitations, and norms. A person is shaped in society, which is manifested as a system of restrictions and mechanisms of control and normalization, and he or she functions in it. In other words, sociality is regulated and realized through law. But bare law is no more and no less than pure coercion, and to become a reproducible norm, to be legitimate, morally and ethically justified, and socially recognized and universal, it must manifest, as Terry Eagleton suggests, in the guise of culture, which in a broad sense (education, media, the arts, and so forth) is no more and no less than *the vestments of law.*[26]

Stalinism, as the culture of permanent civil war, was a militant culture constructed in such a way that the repressive aspect of law in it was revealed. But even a mobilizational culture cannot exist on pure violence (or the threat of it). The role of culture in this is huge since war exacerbates and brings into a state of mobility all the aspects of life that in peacetime seem more or less fixed: reproduction, legitimacy, moral constants, social unity. In wartime conditions, all of this ceases to be evident; it requires renewal, affirmation, and consolidation.

The culture of late Stalinism is unique in that it is the culture of a unique war: a cold war that was positioned as a war against external "enemies of peace" was waged *within the country;* it was a war that could only metaphorically be called a war since it was predominantly an ideological one (for example, the propaganda of Soviet peaceableness was far more successful inside the country than outside it; the longer it went on, the more the main audience of the "fight for peace" became Soviet citizens themselves since the external audience was extremely limited). In it, there could be no distinctions between the external and the civil wars; what happened in the international arena was subjected to swift ideological translation inside the country, and the international situation itself was accordingly engineered for internal consumption. In this war, paradoxically, there could be no distinctions between an active phase and a "truce" since it knew neither the former nor the latter.

If after the first Russian revolution a period of normalization (called a "period of reaction" in Soviet historiography) came; if after the 1917 revolution and the civil war a period of relative social peace set in (NEP); if after the paroxysms of the first five-year plan a short Stalinist thaw happened; and if after the Great Terror there was a short-lived period of new pacification, then after the Great Patriotic War the state's policy was aimed at undermining normalization and "sentiments of self-complacency." This was the result of the duality of the late-Stalinist era. In terms of internal politics, the postwar era was the nirvana of Stalinism; never before had the regime been so solid, Stalin's power so absolute, and society (nor ever after) so homogeneously Soviet, when even slight deviations from the official line were purely Soviet and system-internal. In terms of foreign policy, on the contrary, Stalin's regime had never had to solve such complex problems (one should not confuse these problems with military ones!), nor had the world seemed so volatile as it did in those years. For the first time after the revolution, the country became a superpower and one of the key world players, engaged in building the Pax Sovietica both "from Stettin in the Baltic to Trieste in the Adriatic" (as Churchill said) and in Asia, from the Near East to China and Korea.

As distinct from the notions cultivated in the Russian emigrant milieu and still widespread in Russia to this very day of Bolshevik ideology and the Soviet political model being "imposed" and "superinduced," of their being alien and "inorganic," my premise is that Stalinism was the Russian national form of a universal phenomenon—the reaction of a patriarchal society to the process of modernization. As such, it was simultaneously a political form of modernization—that is, the transition of an agrarian society into an industrial one—and a form of resistance to this process. Its instruments and resources were socialist ideology, Marxism, the myths of Bolshevism and Leninism, and, of course, "the party of a new type." But at the heart of Stalinism lay the product of Russia's centuries-long history: Russian political culture. As Mikhail Ryklin observed, "The Soviet authorities did not invent their ideologems but drew them from the subconscious of simple folk."[27] In this respect, political, social, and cultural history are inseparable. They form a single semantic field.

History is meaning. But too often the history behind events is not seen in traditional historical narrative. To understand it requires an expanded understanding of culture, which in the twentieth century was politically instrumentalized in an unprecedented way. As Jeffrey Schnapp has shown in his pioneering studies of Italian fascism, any type of revolutionary culture—Fascist, Nazi, or Communist—strives to break away from the cultural isolation of the period preceding the revolution.[28] In the process of producing new subjects, new citizens, and mass societies, it not only expands ever newer realities and absorbs them, but also undergoes a full spectrum of transformations itself—from resistance to autonomy and from autonomy to instrumentalization.

As such, culture is vitally important to dictatorial regimes; as essentially the only means of constructing reality, of the regime's production and the masses' consumption of its own image and legitimacy, it is the universal weapon of political power, a necessary object of centralized planning and coordination. It is a means of reaching, coopting, or resisting political subjects and a domain of concepts and images that must be under state control. For all these reasons, the culture of modern dictatorships, including Stalinism, goes beyond the boundaries of its previous existence in courts and salons, galleries and theaters. It goes out into public squares, schools, sports arenas, and television—the beloved spaces of mass societies—where it interacts with print and visual culture and communications technologies. Without this necessary interaction, the history of these states, societies, and their institutions cannot come about. This aspect of the interaction of the aesthetic and the political in twentieth-century totalitarian regimes has been studied in depth and for a long time in works about nazism and fascism but has been mostly ignored by researchers of Stalinism.[29]

POLITICS AS WORK OF ART

This book can be regarded as a cultural and intellectual history of the era in which the shaping of the Soviet nation was completed, also meaning the era when the mental and cultural dominants that determined the character of Russia today were definitively affirmed. But this history is told here in a special way: through the products themselves of cultural and intellectual history. Literature has the genre of critical biography—an anti-apocrypha but at the same time a biography of an artist or thinker revealed through an analysis of his or her works. This book is an attempt to write a critical biography of an era.

This is not a story *about* the history of late-Stalinist culture but an attempt at reading history *through* its cultural texts. It is not a historical narrative but a close reading of cultural texts (of literature, theater, cinema, art, music, scientific and historical texts, popular literature, and the like), through which history reveals its internal logic. I try to avoid traditional historical narrative because in such narratives the system of argumentation is constructed from a chain of events and actions that are non-textualized (or textualized only in archives).

An archival text as merely a witness to particular actions seems to me not self-sufficient, partly because the functions of official party-state documents and mass media (with which historians in an overwhelming majority work) are boiled down to leveling the changes of the political course. Designed to demonstrate the "inalterability of the course," loyalty, and "the unwavering adherence to a single true teaching," official discourse fulfills a stabilizing function. Hence, political transformations of a regime, ideological fluctuations, and massive metamorphoses of worldviews are most often discernible at the margins or beyond the boundaries of this discourse (and, accordingly, of the document)—where they are aestheticized, come into contact with art, and spill over into it. An ideological message did not transform into a fact of mass consciousness directly from Agitprop's resolutions. In order to "take hold of the masses," it had to be implemented in the media and aestheticized. This is the only path to mass assimilation and individual interiorization.

It was precisely through art that Stalinism communicated the new agenda, gave the new political course form through media, and inculcated the new ideological modulations. It was art that made them the property of mass consciousness. This is why art should be viewed not simply as some kind of illustration or appendix to political, social, or economic history (as culture is most often viewed), but also as one of the most significant (and often the only) indicators of the dynamics of mass consciousness. However, one can read this message only in texts, in culture. It is through the prism of Soviet art that one can trace the political and ideological transformation of the Stalinist regime from revolutionary international utopianism to conservatively patriarchal national Bolshevism.

This determines the key role of the cultural text. Its self-sufficientness contains enormous semantic and explanatory potential. An archival text can shed light on particular events, but it cannot conceptualize them. This is the work of the historian. As opposed to an archive, a cultural text contains in its concentrated conceptuality not just traces of the past, but also an integral picture of how people thought and imagined things in a particular moment of the past. This is what adds an important dimension to history. In addition, history reveals itself to us in the form of a cultural text. Fredric Jameson noted in *The Political Unconscious* that "history is *not* a text, not a narrative, master or otherwise, but that, as an absent cause, it is inaccessible to us except in textual form, and that our approach to it and to the Real itself necessarily passes through its prior textualization, its narrativization in the political unconscious."[30]

Ideology also invokes narrative. But textualization and narrativization are the arena of *cultural* production. On the other hand, power itself can be defined as the capability and possibility of producing narrative; producing a text is, after all, a means of exercising power. In an authoritarian state, and even more so in a totalitarian one, concentration of power is the concentration of the capability for narrative, the monopolization of this capability. These narratives are not simply acts of direct political action in the form of political speeches, editorials that make a political point, or slogans. The most functional of them are those that go beyond the boundaries of the purely political genres and appeal to the sphere of the political unconscious and the imagination. Such narratives have a life of their own, weaving themselves into the complex mosaic of cultural and mental associations that are based on the historical and cultural memory and experience of various social groups. It is through them that the content of official ideology becomes naturalized and universalized. These are the narratives that fulfill the legitimizing function. Power is thus exercised as power over the imagination, through control over the production and consumption of signs and images of reality—through culture.

When the conversation turns to the aestheticization of politics, we have to deal with three components: direct political action, ideology, and culture. It is cultural texts that are the necessary medium that translates ideological imperatives into political actions. However, historians often stop short at ideology when studying politics. The explanation lies at the surface: as distinct from the language of art, the language of ideology is less specialized and hence accessible to political historians.

Various definitions of ideology ultimately reduce it to a means that a state uses in "*promoting* beliefs and values congenial to it; *naturalizing* and *universalizing* such beliefs so as to render them self-evident and apparently inevitable; *denigrating* ideas which may challenge it; *excluding* rival forms of thought, perhaps by some unspoken but systematic logic; and *obscuring* social reality in ways convenient to itself."[31] Hence, even historians sensitive to culture can conclude that ideology supposedly "serves as both ends and means, not only defining political objectives and worldviews, but also acting as a vehicle for the realization of these objectives."[32] In fact, however, ideology is merely a set of ideas that (in order to become a part of or even a motive for political action) must be rooted in the masses' consciousness and interiorized. A process of indoctrination is not limited to mere propaganda. Reading newspapers does not alone transform the masses' consciousness or mobilize society; it is not enough. To be effective, this process needs a *transformation of reality itself*. Although newspapers play an important role in such a transformation, they do not act directly on the sphere of the imagination, much less on the unconscious.

As Frank Ankersmit has shown in his work (especially in *Aesthetic Politics*), the political sphere cannot be understood without an aesthetic perspective since it is based on aesthetic modi, tropes, and figures.[33] The political dimension intersects with the aesthetic one since "political reality is not something we come across as if it has always existed; it is not found or discovered, but made, in and by the procedures of political representation. The cliché about the creation of a new fact can be taken literally here" (48). This new fact is located at the boundary between politics and aesthetics. Like art, politics is permeated with metaphor and false mimeticism. Political representation functions with practically the same laws as art; after all, like art, it "is making something present that is absent" (45).

The role of aesthetic representation in shaping the political field is exceptional: it generates power itself. As Ankersmit observes, "The political reality created by aesthetic representation is essentially political *power*. The aesthetic difference or gap between the represented and his or her representative is the origin of (legitimate) political power, and we are therefore justified in assigning to political power an *aesthetic* rather than an *ethical* nature" (49).

The issue here lies in the fictiveness or constructedness of the very foundation of the political in the modern era. The very notion of popular sovereignty has been "a most useful conceptual asset in the struggle since the seventeenth century against absolutist political theories. Certainly the notion has been a most valuable and effective fiction in this struggle—but we should never forget that it is and will always remain a fiction" (54). The entire political sphere is permeated with this fictiveness.

However, the disintegration of the political and the aesthetic has, in turn, a political dimension. After all, "purely political history" essentially bases itself on a mimetic theory according to which a "real" connection exists between the holder of supreme power and the institutions of this power—that is, the state. And in this lies, as Ankersmit observes, the greatest contribution of mimetic theory, from the viewpoint of the state itself: "It helps the state to make itself invisible, to obscure the nature and the extent of political power as much as possible and to assume without opposition the Leviathanistic dimensions that it has acquired in the course of the last two centuries. Mimetic political power tends to become invisible, and therefore uncontrolled, power; aesthetic power, on the other hand, is clearly visible, recognized as such. In this way it keeps alive at all levels, from the mind of the individual citizen to the collective 'mind' of representative institutions, the desire to control and to check collective power. Mimetic representation paralyzes political control, aesthetic representation stimulates it while at the same time creating political power" (55).

The disciplinary antagonism of political and cultural historians is a particular case of the triumph of the mimetic concept of the state; it is assumed that the former study "real history" while the latter study what is interesting to neither historians nor literary and art specialists. In fact, however, the aesthetic dimension of politics allows one to restore the lost link and, as Ankersmit says, to return to an aesthetic understanding of the political. If this book serves to resolve this issue in working on an understanding of Stalinism, I will consider my task complete.

In Walter Benjamin's famous call to counter the Fascist aestheticization of politics with the Communist politicization of art, the mirroring that this contrast suggests is imaginary since in the two halves of the formula, politics is primary. And it is not aestheticized through the politicization of art. On the contrary, the politicization of aesthetics is accompanied by its depoliticization.

Aesthetic politics is possible when politics—along with power—is alienated, a situation that is inherent to the nature of a dictatorship. And this is just the sort of aesthetics that we deal with in Stalinism. The depoliticization of aesthetics is a prerequisite for the aestheticization of politics. This is why political poetry, political theater, and the like die out in Socialist Realism. For aesthetic politics, only a depoliticized aesthetics works. Not coincidentally did Benjamin see war as the ultimate triumph of such politics, where "art for art's sake" triumphs— destruction for destruction's sake. It is not only fascism and nazism, with their programmatic militarism, that find their consummation in aestheticized politics—it is also Stalinism, as an institutionalized form of civil war. In conditions that are highly specific to a dictatorship, politics, in order to be effective, is realized through various modi and tropes that are often ignored or else taken to be some sort of "ideological accompaniment" of politics. However, in attempting to analyze Stalinism's political tropology, I took note that its modi coincide with those of Socialist Realist aesthetics. Modi realize themselves through a system of tropes to which particular figures and genres correspond. These aesthetic modi, tropes, and figures of late-Stalinism politics are the subject of this book.

In late Stalinism (and in this it is by no means unique) we are dealing with politics that plays by the rules of aesthetics. In early Stalinism the aesthetics were not yet those of Socialist Realism. They were the revolutionary/avant-garde aesthetics of *Sturm und Drang*. In high and late Stalinism, the only possible aesthetics remaining were those of Socialist Realism. However, neither in the second half of the 1930s nor even less so in the war years could Socialist Realism become a full-fledged matrix for politics since toward the second half of the 1930s it had not yet fully come together, and during the war it was marginalized by the urgent tasks of mobilization. Only after the war did politics begin to play by the rules of Socialist Realist aesthetics. And the reason these politics were so successful is that they were, in essence, artistic.

The official definition of Socialist Realism was given for the first time, as is well known, in Andrei Zhdanov's introductory speech during the opening of the First Congress of Soviet Writers in 1934, where he worded the definition almost to the letter of what went into the text of the Charter of the USSR Union of Writers, adopted at this congress: "Socialist Realism, as the fundamental method of Soviet artistic literature and literary criticism, demands of the artist a truthful, historically concrete portrayal of reality in its revolutionary development. Furthermore, the truthfulness and historical concreteness of the artistic portrayal of reality must be combined with the goal of ideological transformation and education in the spirit of socialism." Only a few words of Zhdanov's speech were left out of this definition; he had said "the goal of ideological transformation and education *of the working people* in the spirit of socialism" and had also stated that "revolutionary romanticism must become a component of the literary work, for the entire life of our party, the entire life of the working class and its struggle, lies in a combination of the most rigorous, soberest practical work with the greatest heroic spirit and immense perspectives."[34]

It is not difficult to distill the key principles of this doctrine:

1. Transformation of reality ("transformation . . . in the spirit of socialism");

2. Historicism ("historical concreteness");
3. Ideological conscientiousness *[ideinost']* ("ideological transformation");
4. Party-mindedness *[partiinost']* ("education in the spirit of socialism");
5. Popular spirit *[narodnost']* ("education of the working people");
6. Revolutionary romanticism ("portrayal of reality in its revolutionary development," "revolutionary romanticism must become a component of the literary work");
7. Realism ("the most rigorous, soberest practical work");
8. Portrayal of life in the forms of life itself ("concreteness of the artistic portrayal of reality"); and
9. Truthfulness ("truthfulness . . . of the artistic portrayal").

The reader is given not only a list of the basic parameters of Socialist Realism, but also the structure of a book.

The main distinguishing function of Socialist Realism is *transformative*. This is not the art of depicting the world but of *changing* it. Much of this comes from the avant-garde; Stalinist culture extended its life-building project, understanding art not so much as the shaping of individual works of art as the shaping of the social milieu in which people live. However, one should not overestimate the role of the avant-garde. This function was incorporated into the new method by the tradition of social education that had been part of all earlier Russian literature (a tradition that the revolutionary avant-garde forerunners, too, had been a part of, with their ideas of radically transforming the world), as well as by the Marxist concept of new superstructures as changing and not only explaining the world, and, finally, by its founder, Maxim Gorky, who viewed culture as a "second nature" and the goal of art as the creation of a "second reality." This transformative function can be described as one of *de-realizing* reality. After World War II it manifested itself most obviously in the regime's fundamental politico-ideological task: reshaping the traumatic *war experience* into the heroic-romantic *history of victory* and replacing revolution with victory as a focal point of Soviet history and as the basis of the creation myth of the nation. In this respect, Stalin ceased to be not only "Lenin's faithful student," but also "the Lenin of today"; the very concept of "two leaders" receded into the past, and a new reckoning of time began. Scorched by revolutions and civil war, the ravages of collectivization and accelerated urbanization, and the Great Terror and the horrors of war, the Soviet nation was entering a condition of normalcy. By examining in chapter 1 the poetry from the first year after the war, the theme of the Leningrad blockade, and the postwar films about the war, we will see how this process passed into postwar culture.

The transformation we have noted required a change to the image of the past. Refashioning the past became an urgent task for the regime. For this to be a "usable past," a new basis of legitimacy had to be forged, and a definitive shaping of the new Soviet nation had to take place. The Socialist Realist principle of *historicism* takes on a decisive significance. "Historicism" means an image of the past as the regime would like to see it. Although Stalinism repudiated the formula of the leading Marxist historian, Mikhail Pokrovskii, that "History is politics projected into the past," Stalin proceeded from an assumption that politics was history projected into the present. And since politics was Stalin's exclusive prerogative, the content of historicism was in every case determined by him, in accordance with the current political goals. This was true in the 1930s and during the war. But after the war, Stalin no longer needed comparisons or historical metaphors. The time had come to change the key trope. Synecdoche came to replace allegory, and metonymy took the place of metaphor. The era of metonymic replacement set in. If Ivan the Terrible had been an allegory for Stalin, then the Stalin of Mikhail Chiaureli's films was no longer an allegory. He was a metonymic (substitutive) figure. In chapter 2, we will see that the 1946 criticism of Sergei Eisenstein's and Vsevolod Pudovkin's films about Ivan the Terrible and Admiral Nakhimov were linked precisely to this substitution; the status of the country's newly most important director, Chiaureli, was defined by it.

Changes to the historical narrative were part of the wider process of reformatting the representational regime for Soviet reality. As chapter 3 will show, this reformatting was the main goal of the three Central Committee resolutions adopted in August 1946 regarding the most popular—and therefore most important to the regime—forms of art: literature, cinema, and theater. These resolutions are usually considered to be the starting point of the "Zhdanov era." What united these resolutions was the theme of the present day. One of them talked about an inaccurate portrayal of the postwar Donbass in the second part of Leonid Lukov's film *A Great Life;* the second one demanded that a stop be put to the domination of foreign plays on the Soviet stage and that Soviet plays about the present time be created; and the third pointed out the dangers of both "detachment from life" (in the poems of Anna Akhmatova) and a too intent (satirical) close look at it (in the work of Mikhail Zoshchenko). "Communist conscientiousness" [kommunisticheskaia ideinost'] was called upon to replace the nineteenth-century concept of "tendentiousness." Attention paid to these resolutions has always focused on films shelved or sent back for reworking, plays removed from the repertoire, and books removed from libraries and taken out of production, but the resolutions were not simply censorial; they were also actions that definitively affirmed the "Grand Style" of showy Stalinist art that was their direct result. Without the 1946 resolutions, "varnishing" and "conflictless" literature and art would not have become dominant. These resolutions created the conditions for producing plays and other spectacles, novels and poems, and films that all differed strikingly from the condemned ones and that to a far greater extent determined both the development of Soviet art and the Soviet politico-aesthetic project as a whole for years to come than what the resolutions censured. The culture-generating potential of these resolutions, which affirmed "ideological conscientiousness" in 1946, turned out to be enormous. All postwar Soviet art takes its principles from them, the art whose summits would be the "conflictless" plays that filled the Soviet stage, *Kuban Cossacks* in cinema, *Cavalier of the Golden Star* in literature, the canvases of Aleksandr Laktionov and Dmitrii Nalbandian, the cyclopean monuments of Nikolai Tomskii—the most famous exemplars of "varnishing art." It was in just this art that Socialist Realism would achieve its finished form.

An explicit *party-mindedness* is intrinsic to Socialist Realism. This is what remained in it from the political art from which it originated, and it should not be confused with tendentiousness (or "conscientiousness"). "Party-mindedness" is not a matter of content but a *modus operandi,* an ability and willingness to change in response to an impulse imposed from the outside, a principle of direct political action. To be party-minded, an individual's position must be flexible since the party's position is always political. Stalinist decisions and Stalin's own texts were absolutely opaque and thus generated vagueness, fear, and anxious suspense. In the hands of the artist-leader, the laws of dialectics turned into those of a thriller. In Stalinism there were no other rules except party-mindedness (read here: dialectics), which in politics is merely a principle of arbitrariness and, hence, a key principle of terror. Party-mindedness was thus an ideal instrument of control. Dialectics constitutes its very essence and hence is most fully manifested in the sphere of ideology, particularly in Stalinist philosophy, which was the product of the ideological apparatus. The party-mindedness of Soviet philosophy can be understood as a principle of the link between the Marxist philosophical tradition and party institutions, in the same sense that the party-mindedness of Soviet art was the principle of the link between the ideological institutions of the state and aesthetic practice. Similarly to how Socialist Realism was by its form an aesthetic practice but by its functions an ideology, Soviet philosophy was also functionally an ideology. In other words, it was not that ideology was a product of "Marxism-Leninism" but, on the contrary, "Marxism-Leninism" itself became the product of a mutation of ideology. Philosophy was transformed into an ideological machine that not only unceasingly produced legitimizing ideological language, but also updated it. For the exchange of politically current versions of "Marxism-Leninist theory" to go smoothly and, whatever the turnarounds, legitimately, the principle of party-mindedness was needed. The theme of party-mindedness became central to the battle that had broken out on the "philosophical front" and reached its apogee in 1947 in the course of the "philosophical discussion" that is examined in chapter 4.

The effectiveness of these politico-ideological transformations is assured by the accessibility of propaganda. If it is true that propaganda is the conscious manipulation of the unconscious, then the shortest path to it is art, as its most important and effective instrument. *Popular spirit,* a key category of Socialist Realism, produces the image of the people as the regime wanted to see them. In this sense, "popular spirit" is the mirror of the regime. Constructing an image of "the people," it was in fact constructing itself. This function emanated from the very nature of the regime; the Soviet bureaucracy could not talk about itself in any other way than in the form of a discourse about the social whole (the people, society, common interests), and this was the only form of universalizing its own interests available to it.[35] The staged articulation of "the people's opinion" was the regime's only form of representation. "Popular spirit" as a key characteristic of Socialist Realism gained a new momentum in 1948, during the campaign against "formalism" in music. The "realistic trend in music" that Zhdanov fought for was not so much realistic in style as in function; it was about extreme pragmatism and realism as the regime's aesthetic strategy for articulating the intentions of the masses. The aesthetics produced as a result can be called (by analogy with *Realpolitik*) *Realästhetik*. What set this campaign apart was that while seemingly focused on a theme so specific as popular spirit in music, it was extended to theater, cinema, and literature as well. In chapter 5 we will see how "popular spirit" was given life in various media, how it was transformed from an "aesthetic category" into an object of aestheticization. Stalinism responded to the "politicization of aesthetics" in revolutionary culture not only with the "aestheticization of politics," but also the aestheticization of aesthetics itself.

In asserting its identity and returning to a traditionalist utopia, the young Soviet nation required romantic popular spirit in music, but not just because this type of music was "accessible to the people." *Romanticism* was a component from the very beginning of Socialist Realism, which proclaimed "life in its revolutionary development" as its object. Socialist Realism absorbed revolutionary romanticism (a vivid trend in early Soviet art) into itself, transforming it into what I would call *state romanticism,* which assumed its definitive shape in the late-Stalinist era. As opposed to traditional romanticism, which had affirmed the conflict between a dream and reality, tragedy, pessimism, individualism, and the death of the ideal (which was always viewed as being in the past), this new romanticism affirmed the triumph of the dream, collectivism, the heroic spirit, historical optimism, and the victory of an ideal that was always situated in the future. It was most vividly manifested in the assertion of variability and the denial of heredity in Soviet biology. Socialist Realism materialized phantasms and agronomic miracles produced by the magical science of the "people's academician," Trofim Lysenko. As the aesthetics of a regime that had long since lost any and all ties to its Marxist enlightenment roots, Socialist Realism showed itself to be consonant with a romantic reaction to Enlightenment rationalism. As opposed to romanticism, which counterposed the cult of nature to the Enlightenment cult of reason and the idea of a *return* to roots to the Enlightenment idea of *progress*, Socialist Realist revolutionary romanticism combines one with the other by dialectically asserting the idea of *progress* through the Great *Retreat*. All these aspects of political romanticism are examined in chapter 6, which focuses on the 1948 campaign centered on the biological theories of

Lysenko, Ol'ga Lepeshinskaia, Gevorg Bosh'ian, and others, mainly on how these theories were revealed in science fiction novels, plays, films, and popular science literature.

Radical theories such as these thrived in the Stalinist era not only in the natural sciences, but also in the humanities disciplines. The predominant theory in linguistics was that of Nikolai Marr. It was a rebellion in a romantic-revolutionary spirit against positivist science, and this rebellion was led by none other than Stalin. A romantic Lysenkoist in 1948, he spoke as a realist anti-Marrist in 1950. The switching of roles was neither opportunistic nor random. A comparison of the two major ideological campaigns in the late-Stalinism era—in biology (1948) and linguistics (1950)—that Stalin himself initiated and then participated in quite directly and fervently indicates that *realism,* along with revolutionary romanticism, remained a principal balancing element in the politico-ideological project of Stalinism, a project based on dialectical counterweights necessary for the political instrumentalization of the ideological campaigns in the various sciences. The objective of these campaigns were the urgent political signals that Stalin sent to "the city and the world." Speaking out against the Marrist concept of "linguistic revolution" as a sort of "explosion," Stalin manifested a clear understanding of the logic of historical realism: if in the case of 1917 Russia the transition from an old qualitative state into a new one did in fact take place by means of an "explosion," then this implied several things. First, this could not lead to anything "qualitatively new" (the product of explosions is ruins, and Stalin was a restorer). This "new state" (or "new quality") itself was suspect: Russia remained a country with a political culture that completely corresponded to the Soviet historical experience, which Stalin also understood perfectly. Second, neither the society nor its political elites (the Soviet bureaucracy) were ready for profound social modernization (even the limited industrial modernization turned out to be extremely superficial). Finally, a real "transition to a new state" is possible only by the paths of "gradual and lengthy accumulation of elements of the new sort . . . by means of the gradual dying out of the elements of the old sort"[36]—that is, by evolution, and hence necessarily (as post-Soviet experience also attests) within the confines of history. The advent of communism was delayed. The arguments surrounding Marr in both the early 1930s and the early 1950s revolved around his "Marxism." His "new theory of language,"

proclaimed at the cusp of the 1930s to be a true embodiment of Marxism in linguistics, was in 1950 cast down from the Marxist pedestal by
the chief ideological judge. This political dimension of the "discussion
about language" comprises the subject of chapter 7.

The stylistic shape of this realism was embodied in the principle of
verisimilitude; conventionality was alien to Socialist Realism, which
is based on "portrayal of life in the forms of life itself." The real-life
experience of war presented for various reasons a substantial threat
to the regime and hence was subject to transformation and substitution. This was a complex, multistage process. At each stage, there was
a modification of experience through squeezing it out and replacing
it without verification, which had to be compensated for by emphasized verisimilitude. The experience of contact with the West was transformed into a simulation of an *inferiority complex* ("kowtowing"),
which had the goal of refashioning Soviet national narcissism through
the construction of a *superiority complex* (expressed in a "feeling of
Soviet national pride," the supposed proof of the "preeminence of Russian science," and the like) and the development of immunity against
any forms of political disloyalty. Among the guises this disloyalty could
take was "rootless cosmopolitanism," which was nothing more than a
projection and point of rejection and which completed the process of
degenerating narcissism into paranoia, the last stage of refashioning
(that is, alienating) the experience of the encounter with the West. The
main thing that united these stages was the principle of fabrication: the
"harmful" social symptoms are falsified since "kowtowing" and "cosmopolitanism" were symptoms not so much of societal trauma as of
Stalin's own. Extrapolation of these false symptoms onto all of society
required a profound deformation of both current political events and
history. The Socialist Realist "portrayal of life in the forms of life itself"
proved to be an adequate stylistic shape for this strategy, which was
realized in various ways in the different genres. And if the results of
these representational efforts looked implausible, it was by no means
because any means of fantasy or forms of conventionality were used
in them but because Stalinism was based on conspiracy theories; any
reflection of its reality came across as completely distorted, as fantastic as the fictitious world of conspiratorial paranoia that permeated
it. The fear of a nonexistent conspiracy that lay at the heart of this
paranoia required confirmation and found it in the rationalization and

dramatization in which the conspiracy theory supposedly materialized. The resultant parallel reality seemed distorted, dislocated, and twisted. Its "truthful portrayal" in the forms of "life itself" merely made these deformations more severe and explicit. Immersed in conspiracy theories, Stalin was simultaneously the manipulator and victim of his own manipulations. In the instances that we will examine, the issue is the use of a *conspiracy theory* as a sort of screen for *a real conspiracy*. So it was, beginning with "American spying" for Soviet discoveries at the very height of the most extensive Soviet espionage operations in the West (1946–48) and ending with the fabricated "Doctors' Plot" (1953), a conspiracy organized by Stalin and based on accusing the doctors themselves of a conspiracy. Chapter 8 analyzes how the masses' and individual experience were refashioned and the view of the world was structured in postwar Soviet art (in patriotic plays, biographical films, anti-Semitic pamphlets, and other genres) in the very period when the complexes and traumas of the nation that emerged after the war, its worries and phobias, illusions, the conceptions of its own greatness and messianic role were all harmonized into the Soviet nation that was to persist for so many years to come.

Nonetheless, Stalinist art could not completely de-realize life. Reality found an escape, paradoxically, in Soviet Cold War art. This oxymoron is like a magnet, in which the effect of attraction is tempered by the effect of repulsion. In a real oxymoronic coupling, the superpowers remained in a state of "cold war" because they did not want war and, at the same time, they "fought for peace"—by waging war. It was an imaginary war *par excellence*. The uniqueness of cold war is in its oxymoronic nature; if traditional war is a system of actions aimed at a forceful break of the status quo (even if one of the sides is fighting to preserve it, the other [or others] is fighting to change it), then cold war is a war in which *both* sides are fighting for the same thing: the preservation of the status quo. In other words, *the goal of cold war is the preservation of peace*. But if the goal of war is preservation of the status quo, then the "fight for peace" is essentially a form of war propaganda. The ideology and art produced by the Cold War, as the product of war propaganda, were patently false in one respect and just as strikingly true in another. False at the informational level, they were true in that they reflected better than anything else Soviet traumas, complexes, misperceptions, and phobias, the real political aspirations of the regime and its refashioning of ideological directives. Similarly to how Soviet art was a reflection and extrapolation of ideological fantasies onto every-day Soviet reality, Cold War culture was a projection and displacement of its own image. In this sense, Soviet art was thoroughly truthful. With it, we deal with Socialist Realist mimesis. In examining Stalinist texts having to do with foreign policy and international journalistic writing, poetry, and film in chapter 9, we will see that similarly to how the film *Kuban Cossacks* was a reflection of the ideological fantasies of Soviet daily life, the culture of late-Stalinism Cold War culture reflected the Other, which was essentially the most fitting image of the Self, and in this sense was thoroughly mimetic. This incessant process of modeling the Self through the image of the Other allowed for not only "material-izing" the fantasy of one's own phantom greatness and peaceableness, but also smoothing out the trauma of the incessant war that continued in Russia right up to Stalin's death.

Thus, while sticking to a chronology, we have endeavored to align the political constants of the late-Stalinism era with the categories of Socialist Realist aesthetics, which allows us to create a conceptual frame in which the seemingly contradictory and multidirectional iso-lated historical events find a logic and an explanation and acquire an interconnection and internal historical meaning.

Late Stalinism, which seemed an era of immobility and fossilization, exerted an enormous influence on the shaping of the Soviet nation and was held up on a complex balance of interdependent and mutually supporting principles: Marxist class awareness and rabid nationalism, revolutionary prometheanism and sober pragmatism. One campaign replaced another, with each successive one apparently contradict-ing the previous one, but not one of these contrasts in fact abrogated any other; on the contrary, they all supported each other. This politi-cally flexible and dialectically mobile system of internal supports and counterweights was what made the system created by Stalin near the end of his life so durable and so effective.

The explanation for this should be sought in the fact that in late Stalinism—after half a century of the paroxysms of terrible wars, social cataclysms, the economy collapsing and then taking off—the Russian Revolution came to a close, the institutions of the new state were con-solidated, as was the Soviet nation, with its fantasies of its own great-ness and "primacy"; its aspirations to a messianic role and conviction of its absolute moral superiority; its aggressive nationalism and imperialism; its resentment of and implacable resistance to the haughty West; and its deeply rooted authoritarianism, statism, paternalism, and anti-liberalism. With this legacy, the country entered a period of relatively peaceful development. Although this legacy was more than once modified, rejected, and newly affirmed, its fundamentals were never overcome. And, ultimately, it lay at the heart of the post-Stalinist, late-Soviet, and post-Soviet imagination. It is precisely where contemporary Russian society looks for the "spiritual ties" *(skrepy)* for creating a nation that is more and more reminiscent—politically, ideologically, economically, and institutionally—of that same late-Stalinist society, though in a somewhat mitigated and modernized form. Immersing itself in a comforting nostalgia for "Sovietness," exchanging one state religion/ideology for another, Russia continues to preserve deep-seated features of the Soviet identity, drifting into the past and producing ever newer versions of late, but by no means extinct, Stalinism.

1 Victory over the Revolution
A Transformed War

ABOUT THE PEACE THAT TRANSFORMED WAR

Usually, the pivotal events that serve as the reference points of a political nation's creation myth are those that replace the sociopolitical structure (revolutions, wars, political upheavals), resulting in not only the establishment of a new regime but often the birth of a new nation. Such were the Petrine reforms (1696–1725) in Russia, the American Revolution (1775–83), the French Revolution (1789–94), and the creation of the Turkish Republic in 1920–24 and that of West Germany in 1949 (among others).

After the Russian Revolution, the Soviet nation was shaped around the October myth, which became its central legitimizing event.[1] As time went on, however, the deformations of the goals it proclaimed became so obvious, the people who had effectuated it so discredited and unsuitable to the new political reality, the culture that engendered it so distinct, the new ideological vector so obvious, and the "Great Retreat" so apparent that the revolution in its former political connotations became more of a burden than a basis for "useful history." Although Stalin's *Short Course* on party history decisively "Stalinized" the revolution and rewrote it in such a fashion that Stalin appeared at its center, this event *preceded* the Stalin era, which began in 1929. This was also when the shaping began of the Soviet nation, properly speaking, a process that took on a purposeful nature in the mid-1930s.[2] The sheer fact of rewriting the October Revolution into the 1930s bore witness to its location beyond the boundaries of the history of the new nation and to its retrospective adaptation into its central event.

Only in victory did the Soviet nation at last discover the myth of its founding. Since the Stalinist revolution cardinally changed the politico-ideological and sociocultural landmarks of October 1917, it was finally transformed from the main "constituent event" of Soviet Russia before the war into the central event of the *prehistory* of the Soviet nation. The latter, as the product of Stalinism, now acquired an adequate focal point; the myth of its founding was combined with the fundamental legitimizing event of Stalinism and the culmination of its triumph—victory in war. Furthermore, since fascism was the absolute universal evil, its conqueror emerged as the extreme of absolute good, giving the Soviet regime not only internal legitimacy, but also worldwide justification. There was so much of this potential in victory that, once it became the central event built into the system of memory production in the USSR, it preserved its status as the main "constituent event" in the new, post-Soviet Russian history as well.

It might seem, however, that the subsequent fate of the victory myth bore witness to the reverse; Stalin did not like remembering the war, and the May 9 "Day of National Triumph," which was proclaimed a work holiday, soon lost its exclusive status. By December 1947, a resolution of the Presidium of the USSR Supreme Soviet announced that "the day of May 9, the celebration of victory over Germany, is considered a work day" (tellingly, the "national triumph" was no longer mentioned). About this, Richard Overy wrote pointedly that Stalin "wished after the war to restore his personal power, after several years of depending upon the loyalty and competence of others"; and to do so, it was quite enough to force into silence anyone who directly or indirectly contradicted his favorite narrative about himself as the "architect of victory."[3]

But since no one from Stalin's circle called his role as the "architect of victory" into question, what we are dealing with is a widespread representational aberration that sometimes prevents even specialist historians from understanding the specifics of the turnaround that had taken place. We will provisionally designate this as *the transition from War to Victory*. Stalin truly did not like remembering the war. *But War and Victory in War* are not the same thing. The focal point and basis of the founding myth of the Soviet nation was *not War but Victory*. When the outcome of the war started to become ever more clearly defined, the Soviet ideological machine (the press, literature, cinema, and the visual arts) began to divorce the real experience of the war (in which it had been immersed before 1944) from the imminent victory and subsequently to purposefully replace the War itself with Victory. Socialist Realism, at the heart of which lay the function of "transforming the world," was an ideal instrument for derealization of the war experience and its transformation into the history of victory. Before one's eyes, experience began to be replaced with a prosthetic historicization. To the same extent that Stalin did not need war itself, he did need victory. Accordingly, War as a tragic experience of losses was transformed into a heroic path to Victory.

In this respect, Stalin's interpretation of the war in essentially his first public act after its conclusion is crucial, in a speech given on February 9, 1946, at the pre-election meeting of electors of the Stalin Electoral District. Here he declared, "Our victory signifies most of all that our Soviet social structure has triumphed, that the Soviet social structure has successfully withstood the ordeal in the fires of war and has proven its absolute vitality."[4] Here Stalin spoke outright about victory, but even when speaking about the war, he spoke about its result: "The war showed that the Soviet social structure is genuinely a national structure, arising from the heart of the people and enjoying their mighty support, that the Soviet social structure is an absolutely vital and stable form of the organization of society."[5] Of course, it was not war—with its sufferings, sacrifices, and devastations—that showed all of this, but precisely *victory in war.*

But interpreting victory solely as the triumph of the "Soviet structure" was not enough; it was proclaimed the principal *proof* of its vitality and, hence, its legitimacy. Furthermore, victory was retrospectively a confirmation of the rightness of the entire course of Soviet history, a justification of all preceding Stalinist policy; the country had managed to triumph in war thanks to the "material capabilities" it had available. So when Stalin asks, "What policy enabled the Communist Party to provide these material capabilities in the country in such a short period?," he is able to answer, "the Soviet policy of industrialization of the country," "collectivization of agriculture," and so forth.[6]

The end of the process of shaping the Soviet nation became possible only thanks to victory. Tellingly, in the historical periods when liberalization began and society was again presented with a modernizing vector of development, the victory cult dramatically weakened. Thus it was in the Khrushchev era, when not only was there a dethronement of many Stalin myths, but also a cultivation in society itself of other values—"a return to Leninist values" and to "the revolution's ideals"; optimism for an attainable "bright future" (communism promised in twenty years); "peaceful competition" with "the capitalist world"; and the visible successes of modernization (such as space satellites, manned space flight, and the first Soviet atomic-powered vessel).

But when it became clear that the grandiose plans for the building of communism "in the lifetime of this generation" were unattainable and the Brezhnev "stagnation" arrived to replace the future-oriented outlook of the Khrushchev "Thaw" era, the victory cult gradually returned in an even more institutionalized form. And this is tied not only to a change of generations, but also to an estrangement of the ideological device; in essence, there was a return to the Stalinist victory cult—*an institutionalized memory of the war* that was less and less connected to the real experience. Just half a year after Khrushchev's removal, on April 26, 1965, a decree of the Presidium of the USSR Supreme Soviet declared that henceforth May 9 would be a vacation day in honor of the Soviet people's victory in the Great Patriotic War. This brought with it the creation of a host of new rituals. Among these were the Victory Parade in Moscow's Red Square and the formation of places of ritualized memory of the war, the erection of monumental memorials throughout the country (suffice it to recall the opening in 1967 of two of the most impressive of these, imbued with the greatest symbolic status: the Tomb of the Unknown Soldier at the Kremlin Wall in Moscow and the cyclopean complex The Motherland Calls! on Mamayev Kurgan overlooking Volgograd).[7]

However, with the beginning of Gorbachev's perestroika (which was positioned as "a continuation of the revolution") and "acceleration," the victory cult was coming to naught until it practically disappeared in the 1990s, when official ideology was in a state of anabiosis. In this period there was a decisive dethronement of the myths about the war, practically all of which had been created in the Stalin era. Made public, for example, was the total number of deaths in the war (close to the actual figure), and truths were revealed about the thitherto carefully concealed secret articles of the Molotov-Ribbentrop Pact and the massacre of the Polish officers in Katyn, as well as a majority of the heroic myths created in 1941–45 by wartime journalists.[8]

In the Putin era, when "stability" again became a supreme value, the Victory cult returned, no longer as simply one of the main cults but in fact the *most significant* and *only* state cult (since the Revolution had not only lost any founding status whatsoever, but had also turned into a bugbear) and in an even more striking form—with aggressive battles against "distortion of history." While the masses' attitudes in late- and post-Soviet Russia—from Gorbachev's time to Putin's—have undergone enormous changes, with respect to the status of victory they have remained unchanged. The oft-posited question "What is left of the twentieth century?" has evoked the most polarized evaluations: prerevolutionary Russia, Nicholas II, the October Revolution, collectivization, industrialization, the Great Terror, war, the Thaw, "the prosperity of stagnation," perestroika (not to mention polarized opinions of political leaders from Lenin and Stalin to Khrushchev, Gorbachev, and El'tsin). The evaluations of events have changed massively over the past three decades. And only one event has remained impervious to the changes in political attitudes: victory, which writes off the cost of incompetent leadership at the start of the war, Stalin's faith in the agreement with Hitler, the loss of tens of millions of human lives, unheard of devastation, and the like. Nothing "sacred" or "untouchable" has remained of the twentieth century except the 1945 victory. Similarly to how sociological surveys (which invariably grant the victory first place among the outcomes of the twentieth century) are practically the only process of legitimization in contemporary Russia, victory itself has become the fundamental legitimizing event of the new, post-Soviet Russia. Furthermore, the creation of the new nation is proceeding through it: the enemy's image is shaped through the former wartime enemy, as the country is again surrounded by the same old "Fascists"—from Ukraine to the Baltic states—supported by the Western plutocrat adversaries of Russia. The post-Soviet situation, in which victory is ultimately transformed into the *only* event of twentieth-century Russian history that cements national unity, is a direct projection of the postwar situation.

The institutionalization of the victory cult in Stalinism, its ritualization in the Brezhnev era, and the aggressive defense of "historical truth" in Putin's Russia are supposed to conceal its replacement of the revolution, and then the replacement of war by victory and the experience of the war by the modeled memory of it.[9] These modifications were set down in the last years of the war and the first years of peace, in the era of late Stalinism, defining the entire subsequent legitimating matrix operating in Russia for more than seven decades—just as long as the Soviet Union itself lasted. Hence, they require close attention to the ideological and aesthetic practices used at the end of and immediately following the war. Memory that displaces experience is the product of historical manipulations, is shaped in myth, and undergoes subsequent musealization. Hence, tragedy is replaced by the heroic, realism by romanticism, and narrative by symbolism. Experience, memory, history, myth, museum—these are all steps of the monumentalizing of war, its reduction to victory with the subsequent transformation of victory into a symbol of national greatness, as the basis of the greatness of the leader.

THE RETURN FROM EXPERIENCE TO HISTORY: THE POETRY OF THE FIRST POSTWAR YEAR

The central theme of poetry in the first year after the war was *the return from the front*. This theme was paid homage by poets from all different trends, generations, and schools—Il'ia Sel'vinskii and Aleksandr Prokof'ev, Pavel Antokol'skii and Mikhail Svetlov, Mikhail Lukonin and Aleksandr Tvardovskii, Semen Gudzenko and Aleksei Nedogonov, Vera Inber and Mikhail Isakovskii. If the other themes of Soviet poetry that year—for example, about the "atrocities of the invaders," the "destroyed cities and burnt-down villages," and the imminent "resurrection of the country"—receded to the background, being still connected to wartime, then the elements of postwar consciousness accumulated precisely in the theme of return: intense grappling with the meaning of things seen beyond the earlier hermetically sealed border, active experience of one's own "heterogeneity" in an alien and aggressive space, the processing of experiences from 1941–45—all of this was the reality that largely defined the structure of artistic consciousness at a fundamental moment—in a tense search for *new support for a corrective of Soviet identity that could encompass the experience of the war*. This was an experience that by no means fit into the ideological framework of prewar Soviet identity. "We pass the night on the old border, / which we can no longer see. / And somehow we can't sleep / in the hills of the former frontier. // We sense the entire planet / and its every turn. / Erasing borders worldwide, / freedom advances westward. . . . // We will still have to pass the night / on the old boundaries, more than once."[10]

"We sense the entire planet" in Gudzenko's *Transcarpathian Verses* is not a metaphor, but rather the new reality: one "can't sleep" on the former frontier because of the realization of the unprecedented and abrupt end to the former isolation, insularity, and lack of boundaries within one's own space, when the impenetrable borders not only begin moving, but are also revealed to be penetrable. This is how the generation returning from the war apprehended reality, and since it was at the center of postwar poetry, the self-awareness of this generation became the defining one. This generation of poets was extraordinarily diverse. The main thing that determined the short period of its unity in the first postwar year was *the focus on the existential problems brought on by the lived experience of war.* By comparison to prewar poetry, which was immersed in the stylistic conventions of heroicism, "romanticism," and populism or had not yet fully surmounted its avant-garde features; by comparison to wartime poetry, focused on mobilization and propaganda in a range from strident intimacy to almost hysterical naturalism; and by comparison to post-1946 poetry, which was settled into the normative memory of the war, the poetry of 1946 had fallen out of history, out of the still unfolding narrative. It was focused on themes supposedly closed off forever in Soviet poetry—problems of identity, existential questions, sense-making of an experience that still lacked a language of description and had yet to find its own expression.

Of course, the recasting of experience into history was not merely part of some sort of "political assignment" that Soviet poetry was following. Its reasons were to be found in the exceptional trauma of the war experience: the process of reworking personal experience into collective experience, the process of its transition into memory with a simultaneous folding of memory into history, was most often a means of taking away the pain. The social demand, both from below and from above, was for just this sort of therapeutic process. But since the wartime generation of poets was for the most part already genuinely Soviet, the conventions of memorialization inculcated in it in the 1930s were the track onto which this poetry naturally and almost unconsciously rolled.

"In all that's dear in the doleful world, / there is, beautiful, news about you. / For us, wider than others' forests / our gardens bloomed and will bloom again!" Thus Aleksei Reshetov addressed the Russian land. Other authors exchanged this motif for active rejection of foreign space: "There is no joy in a foreign land. . . . / The bird cherry bush, anxious, / blooms through cement. / No houses there—just jails, / which frighten flocks of birds. // And no matter where you cast your eyes, / every stone is watchful. / I'm used to wandering the garden, / where nothing frightens us. // I'm used to such spaces, / where there's no limit to yearnings, / so here, in the dark of night / I often dream of my boyhood home. // I see the garden, where you, in the mist, / sang songs about happiness to me, / where neither in thoughts nor in desires / is a man limited." Characteristically, this poem by Ivan Baukov transfers borders and spaces into the center of the "poetic meditation" (compare his 1945 poem: "Talk about anything you like, / As long as it's about Russia").

Also at this extreme is the quite complete disappearance of the foreign from the author's horizon, as in, for example, Lukonin's "Prologue," where the voice of a powerful, borderline erotic, patriotic feeling is heard: "At seventeen, overcoming a vague unease, / I whispered in the cold ear of a girlfriend, / 'It's good we were both born in Russia, / else we might not have met each other?!' / I have loved Russia like a mother, / loved her like they once love a sweetheart . . . / like they love water when dying of thirst." This idea was maintained at all levels, even down to children's literature. Inber, for example, writes a poem about birds flying south—"our starlings," sparrows, "French titmice, Belgian goldfinches, Norwegian loons, Dutch pochards"—but despite the warmth and colors of the south, "the sparrows pine for a tiled roof." The poem ends with the song of a young starling, returned to Mozhaiskii Roadway: "Whatever roads might lead to wherever / the world over you'll find nothing dearer than your native land." Tellingly, the topic everywhere here is the "native land" and the "native strand"—Russia, whose rehabilitation took place during the war.

There was also a rehabilitation of "Slavic brotherhood" during the war years. The poem "Nazdar!" by Ukrainian poet Leonid Vysheslavskyi paints the following picture: "Elegant crowds. Fanfares and flags. / We ride under the sky of triumphant Prague. . . . / The stirring sounds of a popular march, / 'Nazdar!' and they wave at us, welcoming. / I hear

'Nazdar,' this first Czech word, again, like an echo. / At first seeming strange to me, / now it seems a motto of Slavic brotherhood."[11] Here "Slavic brotherhood" serves as an attempt at adaptation in a foreign space, even union with it. But even in this Slavic world, adaptation had its limits, which were precisely designated by Isakovskii in the poem "Where are you, where are you, brown eyes?," which became a popular song: "Let's remember the brown eyes, / the quiet talk, the sonorous laugh. . . . / The country of Bulgaria is good, / but Russia is the best of all." How unexpectedly explosive the theme of return from the front proved to be is attested to by the excesses indicating its boundaries and the direction of its development. The poetry of war was the poetry of experience. The poetry of return from the front became the poetry of return to history, the poetry of transcending experience and exchanging it for memory. Experience, insofar as it is pure trauma, is difficult to manipulate; memory is possibly easier. The memory of the war becomes the machine for wiping out experience and replacing it with history. Although this experience is irremovable (and would return to literature in the Khrushchev Thaw era), postwar literature would purposefully engage in anesthetization of experienced trauma. Most of all this meant refusing to depict what wartime Soviet poetry and prose, drama and journalism, cinema and documentary, had consisted of: descriptions of "the atrocities of the German Fascist monsters" and the sufferings of their victims. In the course of literally one year, the literature of war became ideologically unacceptable.

There were, of course, political reasons for this as well. For example, the necessity of forming some sort of constructive policy regarding occupied Germany required reining in the powerful current of anti-German propaganda in which Soviet poetry from Ilya Ehrenburg and Konstantin Simonov to Surkov and Isakovskii had engaged throughout the course of the war. Just as in 1941 one had been obliged to forget "proletarian internationalism" and be guided by Ehrenburg's slogan of "Kill the German!," now it was again necessary to separate Germans from Fascists. Thus, in response to Ehrenburg's article published in the April 11, 1945, issue of *Krasnaia zvezda*, "Enough!," *Pravda* featured a response article from Agitprop head Georgii Aleksandrov, "Comrade Ehrenburg Oversimplifies," where it was explained that one must not depict Germany as one "colossal gang." This meant that one had to progress to a more "constructive" representation of the war—in other words, to engage in a corrective of experience. The war was becoming the past, the lot of history, which meant that it was transitioning fully into the management of Aleksandrov's agency.

Until August 1946 the experience of the war found an outlet in the pages of the Soviet press. It was already being called the "memory of the war," but the *war* in this was also being intensively replaced by victory in the poetry of return. This backdrop explains why Antokol'skii's poem "Memory Is Not Eternal," on the very theme of memory and the experience of suffering, sounds so dissonant. The theme of suffering had not yet been officially forbidden, nor had anti-Semitism yet become public, so Antokol'skii was writing about the Holocaust, although in a purely symbolic way, resorting to euphemisms. Addressing his contemporary, he calls him the "coeval of a terrible century": "you, the man of the forties, lashed by memory like a scourge." This memory is not history and is not nostalgia for Russia, but rather the raw experience of pain. Antokol'skii's "man of the forties," in a world of "massacres and raids," has ended up in the ruins of history, beyond the limits of the humanist tradition and of humanity itself, having practically returned to an age of barbarism: "Well, look around more clearly after this, / Heed the underground voices! / You yourself are the scrap from the savage's repast, / You yourself are tanned in shreds of skin." The point of reference is the tragedy of the European Jews, which is formed as the theme of memory of the endless millennia of suffering that recedes ever more distantly into the past: "The traces are lost in millennia-long / wanderings through burnt-down cities. / In sands beyond Babii Yar, in black gossip, / In black markets, in ramshackle furniture, but there // Projectors rummage along the horizon / They slither through ditches, crawl along bridges . . . / But somewhere they burn, dismember, mangle, and fry, / They rot behind rusty wire, but there // There are not even traces, neither in Europe's cities, / Nor in one of the imagined planets, / Nor in the black thickness of Earth's belly, / Nor in heaven, nor in hell, nothing more of them remains." The repeated "but there" at the ends of verses immerses us deeper and deeper into the past, which materializes in a terrifying symbol of the present—experience, which in 1946 has not managed yet to become history or even memory: "There lie the bars of Danzig soap, / Which was cooked up from bones and sinews. / There someone's life has soared upward on two wings / And ended, so that I might live in the world." Antokol'skii does not historicize the just-dying-down war, nor even less its victory, but rather the horrible experience of destruction, which immerses him into the millennia-long history of the Jews: "Forgive me three centuries of delay / and three millennia of muteness!" However, this is not an epically impersonal world but one that is profoundly personal. Pictures of suffering literally permeate the entire poem: "the scum drove you with rods ... through the maze of Warsaw's streets"; "the stinging gravel, bone-crushing earth, has bloodied your tender legs"; "the spiteful crone has chopped [your] life in half, croaking 'Stop! Don't move!'"; "clods of damp earth came right up to your throat at those frightful gates ...'"; "your child, having pierced forever / With immortal lips your teat, / Can't see through his drowsy eyelids, / How green and tall this stem is. // The trumpets have grown hoarse. The strings are played out. / The bows have broken in the fiddlers' fingers. . . . // Wake up, child of the burnt-down people! / Gas, or the whip, or a draught of lead, / Damsel, arise!"

This poem amplifies the images of wartime poetry, its motifs, tropes, and stylistics, at a time when they were being emphatically and consistently washed out of the poetry of return. This process is a consequence of the change in the status of war, which was growing into the laurel of victory. What Antokol'skii here calls memory ("Memory is not eternal") was essentially the language of wartime poetry—that is, the language of trauma, whose function was to inflict pain. It was just this memory that the poetry of return from the front strove to spare the reader. But Antokol'skii's voice resounds "over hundreds of years, over hundreds of thousands of versts," in an outright refusal to forget the past and its pain. In fact, he equates this forgetting with betrayal. But the sense of an unspoken but powerful impulse is such that it transforms these verses into meta-poetry. The last part of this three-part poem consists of two verses that answer, as it were, the question of why the poem was written—why memory is necessary and why forgetting is inevitable: "How desperately, how cruelly / Time is carried across the years. / But the continuous drone of its flowing / Resounds. REMEMBER FOR EVER. // It corrodes the stone with every drop. / But once you step out on the path—/ Even more desperately, more cruelly / It resounds: FORGET, FORGET, FORGET." Here the years are experience, and the flow of time is history, which ultimately triumphs; at the cost of forgetting, a person is saved from the pain of experience. This poem was published in the seventh issue of *Znamia* for 1946. When this issue reached readers in August 1946, another era—Zhdanov's— was on the threshold. Soon, the ninth issue of the journal reprinted the resolution of the Presidium of the Executive Board of the Soviet Writers' Union, adopted September 4, 1946, which was a response to the party Central Committee's decree "On the Journals *Zvezda* and *Leningrad*" and which stated that "pessimistic attitudes agitatedly slip through" in Antokol'skii's poem.

The poetry of return from the front was drawing near to the advent of the new era. It brought not only forgetting of the war, but also forgetting of the experience of being abroad. However, instead of the "song of the young starling" rejoicing in the return to Mozhaiskii Roadway, completely different motifs sometimes broke through in it. Gudzenko, whom we quoted above, especially frankly expressed the "alien attitudes" against which the decree about the Leningrad journals was directly aimed. In the poem "We will die not from old age, but from old wounds. . . ," he writes about a soldier returning from the war: "He'd seen so many cities, ancient cities. / He is ready to talk about them, and even to sing. . . . / But he also has a wish. Can you understand it? / He wants to know what happened here while we were there." The very posing of such questions was no less challenging than the readiness to sing about the foreign cities seen. Gudzenko, who did in fact die from his old wounds in 1953, sang this song through the mouth of this soldier: "O what cities I have been in! Couldn't begin to count them. / O the castles I've slept in! You could only dream of them. / O the joy I served with! Firing was not firing. / O the freedom I consorted with! / Don't touch the memory." Exactly a year later, the All-Union Conference of Young Writers had literally the following to say about this reminiscence of the former freedom: "What can one find in these lines but aestheticism, shallow thinking, and the vulgar savoring of the 'charms' of the bourgeois West?"[12]

As it became less and less suitable for the creation of a new "useful past," the war experience was subject to further reworking and replacement.

A BLOCKADE OF REALITY: THE LENINGRAD THEME IN SOCIALIST REALISM

What would later become known as "the Leningrad theme" emerged within Soviet war poetry from the first months of the war and differed little from the basic tendencies of that poetry. The majority of it was completely in keeping with the traditions of Socialist Realist heroics.

The historicization of the defense of Leningrad in the first period of the war also takes its beginnings from the conventions of the preceding period. It was incorporated into the general tendency of a historicizing discourse that was supposed to resurrect the ghosts of the great heroes of the past who had risen to the defense of the Fatherland. But the hallmark of the Leningrad historicizing discourse was that it referenced not heroes such as Mikhail Kutuzov or Aleksandr Suvorov but rather Soviet history, since in the Soviet ideological space Leningrad was the "cradle of revolution" and its prerevolutionary "useful past" was tied almost exclusively to culture (as opposed to Moscow, which was tied not to tsarism, like Petersburg, but to patriotism—Kuzma Minin and Dmitrii Pozharskii, the 1812 Patriotic War, and so on). In one of the first works that signified the birth of the Leningrad theme (and which was canonized in this regard by the highest Stalin Prize, First Class, for 1942), Nikolai Tikhonov's poem "Kirov with Us" (1941), the historical depth is quite shallow: the end of the 1920s and the beginning of the 1930s, of which Sergei Kirov, Stalin's party leader in Leningrad, is the symbol.

However, historicizing strategies, like the other conventions of Socialist Realist heroic style in war conditions, demonstrated their complete ineffectiveness and hence were subjected to replacement through a sort of baring of the device. Even in the early period of the war, the literature about the Leningrad blockade reveals a thematization of heroism; heroism is transformed into the central theme. This literature engages in scaling down conventional Socialist Realist heroics. Nikolai Tikhonov's "Leningrad Stories," written during the first winter of the war, are typical in this regard. The stories were published in March 1942 as a collection called *Traits of the Soviet Man;* each of the ten stories reveals a new "trait." But the stories were intentionally humdrum, and the more trivial they appeared, the more elevatedly what they depicted was supposed to be apprehended by readers. The stories demonstrate not only the "non-heroism" of their heroes, but also the intentional non-heroism of their actions; their behavior is not heroic but rather *natural*—they behave as they would in peacetime. Heroism is not something extraordinary; it is merely an extension of the natural behavior of a Soviet person.

The absence of "external heroics" (that is, of the conventional heroism of the 1930s) was supposed to bring what was described closer to the reader, to make the common experience of the war intimate and personal. This "lyricization," it would seem, was supposed to intensify the feeling of the tragic. But the picture of the blockade's reality was supposed to figure as "harsh," not tragic. Thus, in the principle of de-accentuating heroics one can easily read strategies not so much of de-heroicizing as of taking away the sense of the tragic.

Heroic style was the result of the breakdown of the mythological model of the world that combined with myth and ritual the presence of immortal gods and mortal demigods—heroes through which "art asserts the immortality of the mortal—a new, nonmythological, personal form of immortality: to attain immortality, one need not be born immortal but rather became a heroic *personality* by performing—although at the cost of one's own death—a *heroic feat* as an act of free acceptance of necessity."[13] This act encompasses a *complete merger of personality with the social role*. Historically, the tragic was the product of the crisis and disintegration of the heroic. Personality in it was *broader* than the social role. In the tragic, as Mikhail Bakhtin said, "the authentic life of personality is accomplished, as it were, in the point of this non-coincidence of a person with himself, at the point of his *escape* beyond the bounds of everything he is as a material being."[14] If "in heroic antiquity (pre-reflexive heroic style) the self-determination of the hero from within and the completion of it from without are practically indistinguishable" and this self-determination itself "is wholly reducible to the acceptance of external completion (fate) and does not assume choice,"[15] then a tragic personality finds itself in disharmony with a predetermined choice and social role and performs an act of self-determination.

Thus the matter stands in traditional aesthetics. For Socialist Realism, the concession to tragedy was forced, called for by the demands of mobilization, and therefore particularly limited. According to Socialist Realism, the tragic depends completely on the heroic: "In the art and aesthetics of Socialist Realism, the tragic functions as one of the particular instances, as one of the manifestations of the heroic." From the assumptions that "the death of the heroic is not a necessity internally situated in heroism itself" and that "heroism is most often rewarded with victory, with the hero's triumph," the conclusion was drawn that "heroism is tied to a certain risk with overcoming difficulties and dangers, [and] the tragic is a particular instance and one of the concrete forms of manifestation of the heroic."[16] Hence, "in the aesthetics of Socialist Realism, the tragic becomes one of the particular manifestations of the irreconcilable struggle of the nascent, the new, against the obsolescent, the old. In our art the tragic reflects the heroic death of individual proponents of the new and progress in their irreconcilable struggle against the old, the obsolescent, against the doomed but still strong opponent[;] it reflects the death affirming the invincibility of the new, its ultimate victory, its inevitable triumph."[17] The tragic is not simply the heroic. Essentially, it serves it: "In the literature and art of Socialist Realism, the tragic is not only newly optimistic, not only full of high proletarian humanism, the invincibility of the new and one of the particular instances of the heroic[;] along with this, it is one of the spiritual sources of the victory of the new, one of the means of inculcating the heroic features of character."[18]

The transformation of literature into a state institution in the 1930s sharply reduced its potential to be a domain of individual expression, personal experience, and private memory. Immersed in singing festive hymns to happy Soviet life, endless glorifications of "the creator of happy Soviet life" and the joyous "poetry of creative labor," Soviet literature was unprepared for a defensive war, painting the future battles as marches "on the enemy's territory" and its defeat "with little blood and a mighty blow"; but it also had no idea how to describe whole strata of political, ideological, and psychological collisions; uncontrolled emotions and unpredictable reactions to events tied to defeat; the prospect of one's own death and the massive loss of lives; the losses of loved ones; violence; suffering; hunger; victimization; the destruction of an entire way of life; and everything else that was rained down on the country in June 1941 and caught the Soviet ideological apparatus by surprise. But the restructuring of this apparatus began right away, and a host of established ideological schemas had to be changed on the fly. The process of *humanizing ideology* began.[19]

What had to be reexamined most of all were the former heroic conventions, which, given their 100 percent "ideological restraint," were totally ineffective when the main task of art became mobilization. Heroic style, which affirmed the harmonious convergence of personality with its social role, was not oriented toward the reality of the war, which required working through the existential problems that had unexpectedly faced everyone. There had to be a response to the appearance of fears and physical sufferings, a consideration of the whole sphere of personal experiences that was so remote from the "living man" of Socialist Realism, all of whose complexities boiled down to the problems of family and production. In prewar Soviet literature, "a grasp of the situation of the contemporary person was substituted by rhetorical-ideological projection, which had the goal of shaping and maintaining a new—specifically Soviet—collective identity." Il'ia Kukulin calls this projective and at the same time psychologically limiting function of Soviet literature "the rhetorical reduction of the subject."[20]

Subject most of all to this reduction were uncontrollable and unpredictable experiences: fear; physical and psychological discomfort (pain, hunger, cold); the feeling that the whole prewar picture of the world was collapsing; and aggressive manifestations of "animal" origin in a person in extreme circumstances (just as frequent as heroism). The peculiar wartime anthropology was also shaped by a new sensation of physicality; the body of a person in war or on the home front was pained and burdensome and at the same time was perceived as part of a single suffering collective body. During the war, all these factors were sharply redoubled due to state pressure on all segments of society, which amplified many times the burden of war itself: terror and coercion on the front (from political departments and retreat-blocking detachments) and at home (deportations of ethnic groups, "preventive arrests," arrests for "defeatist conversations," and the like), and repressions of prisoners of war and people living in occupied territories.

The collision of mobilizational goals, the new reality, and aesthetic conventions overturned before one's very eyes created a new situation of "discomfort" writing. Its emergence transformed the history of Soviet literature about the war into a history of the adaptation of *emotionally* uncomfortable experience to a new basis of Soviet identity and a history of repudiating experience that was *existentially* uncomfortable. This separation allows us to understand the nature of the mobilizational goal of Soviet wartime literature, which consisted of blocking the existentially uncomfortable sense of self at the cost of broadening the zone of emotional discomfort. The latter required rejection of earlier heroic conventions that were altogether alien to any discomfort at all, but it did not permit a fundamentally new aesthetic for the depiction of war to come together. It is true that "with this change of optics, it turned out to be fundamentally important to fix the everyday 'trivial' sensations, the very fabric of everyday perception of the world. . . . A consequence of this relationship toward the reality described is the de-ideologicization of the text."[21] However, the function of this writing was above all to *blockade reality*, and this was just what the new humanized aesthetics of Socialist Realism boiled down to.

A byproduct of tragedy thus treated was that experience was made more intimate. Having unlearned to speak to the reader without the mediation of Socialist Realist conventions, literature turned to the diary form. No single trend (current, theme) in Soviet literature gave rise (proportionally) to such a quantity of diaries. Furthermore, it was diaries, specifically, that accounted for the central part of the corpus of significant *literary* texts on the "Leningrad theme." Some of them were canonized in Soviet literature (Vera Inber's *Almost Three Years [A Leningrad Diary]*, for example, as well as her long poem *The Pulkovo Meridian*—essentially a diary in verse—were awarded the Stalin Prize). Ol'ga Berggol'ts's *February Diary, Leningrad Poem, Leningrad Speaks*, and *Day Stars* were all sustained examples of an emphatically diaristic form. The appeal to authentic experience, transforming a literary text into a document, allowed the writer to make the very process of molding this experience explicit. Soviet literature reworked experience into history, at the same time transposing tragedy into heroics and developing new conventions of heroic narrative. This process of adapting traumatic memory within the framework of Soviet rhetorical models was a most significant stage in the process of replacing War with Victory.[22]

The first type of writing (we will call it *the narrative of ideological discomfort*) is so similar to prewar narrative that it seems not to have departed from it. This writing simply ignores emotional discomfort, being completely immersed in ideology. Exemplary texts of this sort are the wartime diaries of Vsevolod Vishnevskii. Above all, what draws one's attention is the almost complete absence in them of the difficult everyday life of the blockade, which filled (for example) Inber's and Berggol'ts's texts. Vishnevskii is completely engrossed in idle discussions of geopolitics. He devotes many pages to discussion of "the strategic prospects of the position of the English" in North Africa, views on the imminent opening of a second front, problems with the production of ordnance, details of military operations, the situation in the Far East, and so forth. A career military man turned dramatist, he, like a frustrated strategist, discusses the role of Russia after the war, devises plans for the occupation of Germany, and ponders the postwar makeup of the world and the problem of zones of influence after the war. Well received in the offices of major military commanders, Vishnevskii talks about everything like an initiate. Such notes color Vishnevskii's wartime diaries for the end of winter 1942, when Leningraders were dying from hunger on the streets and rations had gone down to 125 grams of bread per day. It would seem, however, that Vishnevskii totally fails to notice this "emotional discomfort," as if the burden of the blockade did not involve him. He mentions in passing, as if about something insignificant, "For dinner today they gave us a cup of vodka, soup made from dried American (disgusting) meat, and rice." Or, in another place: "Last evening the whole group drank tea. . . . There was cheese, bread, and jam on the table. . . . Jokes, witty remarks." And just afterward: "During the night I read about Mayakovsky. Worrying thoughts about art."[23] Such a diary might have been written in Moscow or Sverdlovsk, or anywhere at all.

As a highly placed propaganda writer, Vishnevskii lived in a parallel reality carved out of geopolitical fantasies. His authorial self was completely dissolved in the propaganda narrative that he had spent his whole professional life producing and, during the war, doing so exclusively and tirelessly. He did not simply "believe in" the speeches that he gave in meetings in the military units; for him, a different reality simply did not exist. He did not have to be compelled to subordinate his opinions to some sort of "correct" line. He was himself engaged in an unbroken quest for this line, continuously adjusting his own opinions to it. His diaries describe, seemingly, a perpetually changing series of conferences, meetings, discussions, political information sessions, tea drinkings, work with delegations, changes in quarters, conversations with various ranks of military commanders, discussions of what the American newspapers were writing at the moment, and so forth. It is often hard to discern where a diary entry ends and the narrative stream begins—the actual eruptions of the ideological lava. Not surprisingly, a person who spends entire days speaking in meetings speaks the very same language even in his diary. But what is interesting is his complete detachment from what he observes all around himself. In the entries he made in even the most horrible days of the blockade, there is not even a hint of human feeling.

If this kind of writing does not specify any details, dwelling entirely in the space of ideological abstractions, then the opposite extreme— writing totally immersed in everyday existence, fixing mundane details and the minutiae of living—can be called *emotional discomfort* writing. The texts of Vera Inber can serve as an exemplar. If Vishnevskii's diaries are situated outside the everyday reality of the blockade, if Berggol'ts strives for journalistic and lyrical generalizations, then Inber's diary is totally dedicated to a continuous recording of everyday life and a constant presence in it. Among the very few who would make it through to the end of the blockade was Lidiia Ginzburg, who focused on the existential problems of everyday blockade living. In Vishnevskii's world, such issues simply did not arise. His writing is maximally comfortable (to the extent, of course, that wartime writing can be comfortable at all). Everyday life flies into his world of propagandist-ideological phantasms as muffled, distant sounds. Inber's writing, on the contrary, is emotionally uncomfortable, but she deliberately avoids any complex questions at all that have political or ideological implications, not to mention existential themes. Berggol'ts comes closer to these themes than Inber does, indicating their boundaries and only sometimes attempting to cross them. Ginzburg is the only one to concentrate on them, situated entirely beyond their boundaries; for her, the situations of daily life are merely a point of departure. Managing to rise to reflection, to break through the blockade of rhetoric of battle and victory, Ginzburg in her *Notes of a Blockaded Person* became "one of the most anti-utopian and non-ideological authors in twentieth century Russian literature."[24] This was largely achieved on account of a strict selection of material, much stricter than with Inber or Berggol'ts, who had subordinated this to its rhetorical aims. With Ginzburg, on the contrary, as Irina Paperno so astutely observed, "Biographical fact and raw emotion have no place on the pages of Lidiia Ginzburg's disciplined notebooks, which are filled with carefully crafted situations, maxims, and reflections; but the notion of intimacy, history, and the catastrophic quality of experience that mark other memoirs are present."[25] This is why these texts in Soviet times were excluded from the public domain.

Here we see four models of processing experience: displacement (Vishnevskii), fixation and rhetorical generalization (Inber), testing boundaries (Berggol'ts), and problematizing (Ginzburg). The modes of writing differ in the degree of departure from reflection into the rhetoric of battle and victory and in the degree of refusal to process experience, as the forms of this departure also differ. In every case the goal amounts to avoiding meeting the war face to face—think, but don't analyze; look, but don't see; experience, but don't generalize. These are strategies of intentional self-deception. Vishnevskii's and Inber's are two different strategies for de-realizing war. The third model is based on an attempt to go from the boundaries of emotional experience to the existential, but as it is constructed on constant self-control and self-limitation, it fixes only discomfort and frustration from one's inability to complete the work by attaining existential themes. Only Ginzburg succeeds in writing existential discomfort.

Inber's blockade texts are interesting as a polar opposite to Vishnevskii's; her experience of the events surrounding her is very personal. Inber's diary, *Almost Three Years,* published in 1946, was at the same time the history of her writing in 1941–43 the long poem *Pulkovo Meridian,* which started to be published in 1942. The Stalin Prize that consecrated the theme of the Leningrad blockade was by no accident awarded to both these books in 1946. The diary and the poem complete each other: the diary details, and the poem generalizes. The diary is full of shockingly precise details that are intensified by the image of the author—an exceptionally civil person, unaccustomed to and unadapted to the severities of wartime life. This imbues the endless descriptions of death from hunger, cold, and illnesses with an especially vivid contrast. Inber's daily life, of course, as the wife of one of the medical bosses in the blockaded city, was far from ordinary. There are almost no generalizations in her diary. This, it would seem, is an exceptionally private document. Meanwhile, the very fact that it was almost immediately published removes the boundary between the personal and the public, sweeping aside the defining characteristic of a diary—its privateness.

But the main thing is that the diary, which fixes everyday events, is directly linked to the poem, the work on which (the process of writing, revising, public readings) became practically a life's work for Inber during the days of the blockade. This link is not merely event-driven. The poem squeezed out of everyday life the concepts that Inber was able to extract from it, transforming everyday life into a press cake. The departure from reflection into the rhetoric of battle and victory and the rejection of processing experience are so complete here that they diverge even as to genre. Everyday life/diary and generalization/poem do not meet. The poem takes shocking details and the sequence of events from everyday life, essentially constituting a parallel diary. But in actual fact, it is a matter of escaping actual experience that is still being felt, has not yet grown cold, which is declared to be the past. Everyday life congeals into history before it even sets in. Victory in war here is at the same time victory over experience. It was no accident that *Pulkovo Meridian* became a canonical war-era text of Soviet literature; it is a complete collection of the conventions of wartime literature in which a mechanism is established for restraining writing within a framework of emotional discomfort aimed at mobilization but not at formulation—or even less, a working through—of the existential questions raised by the conceptualization of experience. Hence, these conventions are at the same time a mechanism for its subsequent erasure.

Inber began writing the poem in October of 1941 and finished it in November 1943, by which time not a trace remained of the writing of tragedy. The still unliberated city is portrayed in the final chapter as returning to life after two years of the blockade, and the author is gladdened by the appearance of "birds and little children" who "are again chattering in Leningrad's nests." Heroic spirit and optimism are powerful tranquilizers. But the cost of taking away the pain is a rejection of dealing with the problems of experience and, ultimately, a rejection of experience itself.

One of the very few who tried to publicly test the boundaries of adapting experience to Soviet identity was Ol'ga Berggol'ts. Her poetry occupies quite a unique place in the literature of the Leningrad blockade because her status was itself ambivalent, combining true party-mindedness with dissidence.[26] Her poetry combined these seemingly mutually exclusive principles. This has most of all to do with its expression of uncontrolled experiences, unexpected feelings, and impossible emotions. In the literature wholly devoted to the war and mobilization (and Berggol'ts engaged in this throughout the blockade, speaking on Leningrad radio and actively participating in the work of propaganda institutions in the besieged city), Berggol'ts in September 1941 suddenly speaks not of revenge and hate but of love: "Never have I with such strength / as in this autumn lived. / So beautiful I've never been, / so in love." Her perception of what was happening is unexpected, her reactions paradoxical, and her break with Socialist Realist conventions is demonstrative: "I don't know what has happened with me, / but I tread the earth so lightly / as I have not for so long, so long ago. / And all of terra firma is as dear to me, / as my song is pure and lofty. . . . / Is it not because death is entering the city, / and new love is close at hand?" The ability to talk about love in 1941 was akin to the right to talk about freedom in 1942: "In mud, in gloom, in hunger, in sorrow, / where death dogged your heels like a shadow, / we were so happy, / we breathed such boisterous freedom, / that our grandchildren would envy us."

Berggol'ts manifests the humanizing of ideology by her emphasis on the profoundly personal connection of the city's defenders with on-going events and their growing larger and closer. The poem's call for the defense of Leningrad is made maximally intimate. This strategy is aimed at justifying the right to speak about the tragic experience of the war without the descriptiveness and naturalism that are calculated for a direct mobilizational effect. This shaped the specifics of the Leningrad theme: its authors are not witnesses but rather participants. Actually, participation itself was the basis of the heroism of those "remaining in Leningrad." As Ginzburg wrote on this subject, "this affiliation in and of itself became an inexhaustible source of the feeling of self-worth, a source of pride, of justificatory concepts, and in particular, of a sense of superiority over those who had left." She adds, though, that a complex mechanism of forgetting stood behind this "heroism": "Everyone almost naively and almost honestly forgot a great deal—they forgot how they had hesitated whether to leave or not. How many remained for very personal and incidental reasons, how at times they regretted the fact that they stayed, how they evaded defensive work, how they lost their human aspect." As a result, "what was an instinct for self-preservation and an obscure manifestation of the overall will for victory they now see as much more refined and conscious. And they see it with the addition of a heroic self-perception that they didn't have at the time."[27]

Survival itself turned out to be heroism. Berggol'ts would write precisely about this in *February Diary*: "I was never a hero, / I hungered for neither glory nor reward. / Breathing only breath with Leningrad, / I didn't play the hero, I just lived." This was the assertion of a very personal right to articulate experience and an important part of her poetic identity. It was a powerful brace in her justification of the right to assert that "for our sufferings one won't find / a measure, nor a name, nor a comparison," at the same time avoiding describing them. What Berggol'ts describes is not the horrors of the blockade themselves, but rather survival of them—the experience of them itself.

Berggol'ts's main work in the blockade years was with the Radio Committee.[28] Her book *Leningrad Speaks* collects her numerous speeches given in this capacity. The transformation of normalcy is interesting in them, in the process of constantly rewriting the past in light of the present. Most of all, this has to do with a new experience and a rethinking of the prewar past, which is idealized. Against the backdrop of endless stories of suffering and death, the accounts of the miracles of mutual aid were supposed to show that "despite the enemy's attempts, by means of horrible trials, to disunite us, make us quarrel, throw us against each other, we have, on the contrary, banded together, become a single labor collective, a united family." It was specifically during the war that there was a radical reevaluation of prewar life, against whose "backdrop" what was happening was perceived.

The psychological aspect of this *shared* experience is also significant. It is after the war that *lived experience* appears—a *shared legitimate experience* that did not exist before the war. All of prewar Soviet collective experience had seemed a chain of festival ascent and endless triumph, while the experience of trauma remained strictly individual. Now a *shared* experience of trauma had emerged. In light of the prewar experience, this was the experience of war.

Leningrad Speaks is a book by a military political worker, which is essentially what Berggol'ts was during the war. Her speeches made in the course of the three years of the blockade, presented in the volume and restrained in the genre of chats with Leningraders, are a testament to the enormous therapeutic efforts undertaken by the regime to relieve pressure and at the same time to mobilize the city's population. Berggol'ts is in this respect similar to Vishnevskii. But at the same time she dwells in the everyday life of the war; she domesticates ideological abstractions, tearing apart the closed ideological circle and moving beyond it to existential problems. In this respect, she is incredibly remote from Vishnevskii. Both these tendencies constantly battled each other within blockade literature and were forever preserved in it.

In one of her talks, in December 1943, Berggol'ts confessed: "I would be lying if I said that I am not terrified now. I would be lying if I said that it doesn't matter to me. No, a sort of anguish, similar to a feeling of profound loneliness, grips my heart and drags it downward, as it were. . . . This is probably the anguish of a human in inhuman conditions. It is stronger and more terrifying than fear. There are moments when I want to just lie down on the floor, with my face in my hands, and start to groan because of this profound anguish dragging my heart down, because of the pain for those who are now dying. . . . But I will not allow myself to do this—I wrote you about that night; I want you to know about that night, the twentieth of December in Leningrad—alas, about one of hundreds." These stridently honest confessions, these flashes of sincerity, are in sharp contrast to the officious narrative that permeates these texts. But the stories in her book show how the blockade theme was transformed after the war.

Leningrad Speaks came out in its first edition in 1946 as a *documentary* book, with the subtitle "A Collection of Radio Speeches Made from 1941 to 1945." In 1967, Berggol'ts would not only remove the subtitle, but would also write a long, lyrical introduction and add two essays at the end—"Forever Young" (from 1957) and "Lenin's Call" (from 1959). This new "frame" dramatically changed the accents since these additions differed thematically and stylistically, as well as in their ideological function, from the basic corpus of the texts. The original corpus was devoted to everyday existence during the blockade, while the introduction and the added essays were either reminiscences about her time working for the Radio Committee or were about events that took place after the war. The basic texts were in a conversational, journalistic style—radio broadcasts addressed to an "interlocutor" listening to the radio—while the material later added was strictly literary, executed in a lyrically reminiscent register and lacking in mobilizational passion. The broadcast of the texts had been suggestive and mobilizing, while the added texts made the work a finished memorial. The reworking of the book had the goal of *historicizing* the blockade, incorporating it into the new historical matrix. And this is where Berggol'ts unwittingly gives away the key to her writing. In 1967, pell-mell referencing of revolution with anti-Stalin rebelliousness was in fashion.

The first occasion for referencing revolution in Berggol'ts's book was presented by Vishnevskii. Recalling the atmosphere of those years, she declares the following:

> When it comes to the style of meetings and recruitments, then a Leningrader living in the city in the blockade days will never forget Vsevolod Vishnevskii's passionate radio addresses. Radio in particular, whose vagaries—sound, voice, timbre—was what fully conveyed to everyone his inimitable intonation of a Baltic sailor from the *Aurora* era, the era

of storming the Winter Palace and of civil war; that intonation, that manner that in and of itself was a still-living link to the revolutionary history of Piter-Leningrad. And this manner, after all—this Baltic bravado, this selflessness of a "little brother"—had already once justified itself magnificently in the October Revolution days, in the civil war, and now it was again heard, alive, authentic, dear to one's heart! Only now the Baltic "little brother" had become very much a man, grown rough, and his passionate, at times incoherent speeches were so reassuring and so necessary then, in the autumn of forty-one precisely, in the desperate days of the onslaught, and precisely for the city that not only preserved traditions but lived them."

Vishnevskii is here a symbolic figure, signifying the link with October, the "spark of the bonfire" of revolution.

But there is a completely different, if not to say contradictory, line that arises in Berggol'ts's supplements in the 1960s. She recalls not only Vishnevskii, but also one more speech in the *Leningrad Speaks* broadcast:

[a speech] made at the end of September 1941, during the most severe artillery and air attacks, by Anna Andreevna Akhmatova. We recorded it not in the studio, but in the writers' house . . . in M. M. Zoshchenko's apartment. As if for spite, there was a horrible shelling, we were nervous, and it took a long time to get the recording started. I took down Anna Andreevna's short speech from her dictation, which she later corrected herself, and this piece of paper—also yellowed already—I have carefully preserved up to this very day, like the little rough draft of Shostakovich's speech. And if up to this very day, after twenty-odd years, I can still hear Shostakovich's muffled and wisely peaceful voice, and the sometimes high, sometimes passionately low voice of Vishnevskii, then I also cannot forget how just a few hours after it was recorded, there arose above the darkening, dark-golden Leningrad, which had grown quiet for a minute, the deep, tragic, and proud voice of the "muse of weeping."

Berggol'ts reproduces Akhmatova's speech in full in her book. It seems that she wants to speak simultaneously as Akhmatova and Vishnevskii. The drama of this incongruity permeates all of her writing.

Berggol'ts was almost the only writer who, in parallel to the belles-lettres line, continued the Leningrad theme after the war in the lyrical-diarist mode. The theme of memory would remain central for Berggol'ts and would find its warrant in perhaps her most famous line, written for the memorial at Piskarevskoe Cemetery in 1959 but becoming a symbol of the memory of the war for many decades, reproduced on countless monuments throughout the country: "No one is forgotten, nothing is forgotten."

But if there is a "useful past," then there also should be a "useful aesthetics" that creates this past. As a coherent narrative, history is always linked to harmonization and to a heroic style based on harmony and on a convergence of personality and social role. Tragedy, by contrast, is linked to disharmony. History is linked to reconciliation and thus to a prohibition of tragedy, which is linked to revolt and exaltation. This is why there are many more monuments to heroes than to victims, and the history of art and literature gives us an endless gallery of heroes and is much more sparing of tragic subjects, which by no means were fewer than heroic ones in the past. The explanation is that tragedy is the lot of the conquered, and history is written by the victors, who have no reason to be ashamed of self-acclaim as they appear in the heroic halo. One could say that heroics is the aesthetic agent of history and tragedy that of the present.

The sincerity that Berggol'ts maintained is permeated with tragedy. In the tragedy "Loyalty" (1946), which deals with the defense of Sevastopol, she emphasizes this link: "*From heart to heart.* / Only this path / have I chosen for myself. It is direct and terrible. / Impetuous. You cannot turn from it. / It is seen by all and unadorned by glory. // I speak for all who perished here. / In my lines their muffled steps, / their eternal and hot breath. / I speak for all who live here, / who went through fire, and death, and ice, / I speak like your flesh, o people. / By the right of shared suffering. . . . // See, I have become many-faced, / and many-souled, and multilingual. / But I am myself am sentenced—by myself / to remain in different faces and souls, / and in someone's grief, in another's joy / to hear my own secret groaning and secret whispering."

Here she speaks of *collective tragic experience,* the past. And although Berggol'ts's work has a great deal of heroic spirit and official optimism, it is just these tragic Akhmatovian intonations that set her apart among the blockade poets. Very few artists managed to retain these intonations. Besides Akhmatova, there is perhaps only Shostakovich. One should not confuse them with the minor key by seeing their flashes of light as an inevitable tribute to heroic spirit. The finale of Shostakovich's "Leningrad" symphony is written in C major. But it is by no means a theme of imminent victory, nor is it a triumphant ending. One hears in it that same tragic theme of invasion. It is an affirmation of tragedy in the present. For the tragic worldview, the future is the present that has become the past. It does not lose its tragic quality.

This is exactly what Berggol'ts's *Day Stars* is about. This book, written in 1959 and giving rise to a whole trend in post-Stalin literature—one of the most full-blooded, the so-called lyrical prose—was essentially the summation of the author's reflections on the blockade, the main event in her creative biography. Although a significant part of the text could not be included in the book because of censorial pressure, the lyricization of trauma in itself was a revelation to the Soviet reader. The experience of war and the blockade was an existential experience, any outlet for working with which was hermetically sealed in Stalinist literature. As sealed as was an outlet to the document. Lyrical prose was akin to a document since it fixed and documented personal experience and was intent on the destruction of history as a conventional narrative. But there was also another topical dimension. As Mikhail Ryklin observed in the context of a completely different documentary project—the "Black Book" that preserved the experience of the Holocaust—"this narrative was endowed with a lyrical quality by the Stalin era's drawing to a close, when the need to displace enormous blocks of social memory was pure and absolute. The crimes of the Nazis were greater than the crimes of nazism; they were also a metaphor for the numerous crimes about which one must not speak (not only because this was forbidden, but also because there was no language in which this could be done); as a phenomenon that had come to a close at that time, nazism was for its Soviet victims a narrow little window into the world of history. It had committed crimes that had already acquired a literal named significance."[29]

Berggol'ts became famous for her stirring and passionate fight against conservative criticism in defense of "self-expression." It was exemplified in her article "A Conversation about the Lyric" (1953), which came out right after Stalin's death and provoked a boisterous discussion, then "In Defense of the Lyric" (1954), and, finally, her speech at the Second Congress of Soviet Writers (1954) against the most orthodox Soviet poets, Nikolai Gribachev and Anatolii Sofronov, defending the artist's right to creative freedom. But the very concept of *Day Stars* was profoundly dualistic with respect to the idea of self-expression. The image itself of Day Stars, reflected only in the deep wells of memory, is a symbol of a very personal and simultaneously collective experience in collective memory. The author's personal experience became collective because "the Soviet person, with his titanic biography, not only wants to share his spiritual experience . . . not a 'mute confession,' not a tongue-twister, but [also wants to share] through the Main, Great book of his writer. More than that, he wants to create this book with the writer, with the writer he wants to be the hero of this book, whose soul is thrown open, to the very depths, open to the people; that is, he wants to be the hero of 'the confession of the son of the century.'" At the end of *Day Stars* Berggol'ts addressed the reader directly: "I have opened my soul to you . . . with all its shadows and light. Glance into it! And if you see even a part of yourself, a part of your journey, this means you have seen Day Stars; it means they have lit up in me; they will flare up in the Main book that is always ahead, that you and I are constantly and tirelessly writing."

Self-expression hinged on the transformation of the author into a medium of collective experience, his or her personal experience being declared as collective. This collectivization of personal experience was, of course, an aesthetic gesture. Valentin Kataev in *My Diamond Wreath* admitted outright that he "couldn't stand" memoirs. Memory assumed its primordial function—opposing history. Berggol'ts's work from the end of the war fixed the opposition of experience to the practices of historicization and memorialization. The latter appeal to the facts of everyday life, the details of living, and, ultimately, to emotional discomfort, while experience is tied to "the memory of feeling," to trauma and pain, and feeds existential discomfort.

But this experience was to undergo rigorous trials immediately after the war. The return of earlier ideological and aesthetic conventions began to be felt in literature from the middle of 1943, immediately after the turnaround in the war; lyricism, tragedy, and experience begin to be replaced by epic, heroism, and history. In 1946 the series of famous "Zhdanovist" resolutions would be necessary, completing and legitimizing this transition that took three years, from 1943 to 1946. But in the meantime, critics were seeking a synthesis of both principles. Symptomatic in this regard was Lidiia Poliak's article in the September–October 1943 issue of *Znamia*, "About the 'Lyrical Epic' of the Great Patriotic War." "Great historical epochs," Poliak wrote, "give birth to large-scale art, national art, the art of heroism . . . a heroic epic." The peculiarity of the heroic epic of the war is that it is "lyrical through-and-through. Poetic terminology should include such at first glance paradoxical definitions as 'lyric epic' and, on the other hand, 'epic lyric.' . . . The birth of a socialist lyric has already enabled the erasure of the borders between the epic and lyric poetry." Poliak went on to say that "the lyricism of epic narrative, as it is from the other side, the epic tone of lyricism, is a characteristic feature of our poetry, the poetry of the patriotic war," and precisely because of this, "'the personal' has ceased to be heard in poetry as something 'unworthy' or forbidden. Soviet poets of our times have been liberated from the ascetic shackles, from the iron fetters with which they hampered themselves in the recent past. The Great Patriotic War amplified, emphasized, and filled with new content the patriotic feelings of the Soviet person and thereby decisively removed the contradictions between personal interests 'of one's own' and the interests of the nation, the people, and the motherland. In the poetry of our times, the call to defend the motherland is simultaneously a call to defend personal, individual human happiness. And revenge for personal misfortune merges with revenge for the misfortune of the people."

From this followed Poliak's conclusion, which was a defining one for the succeeding era of "conflictlessness": "The conflict between the private and the public is ceasing to exist." There also followed a demand for a return to the Socialist Realist hero: "There is a certain insufficiency in the poetic epic of our times. . . . The heroic epic of the war years is 'hero-less.' . . . Soviet poets have yet to create the heroic exemplar of the warrior-person that could become part of the gallery of immortal poetic monuments of the era. . . . The lyrical image of the poet, his poetic self, displaces the figures of individual heroes. . . . Soviet poets can and should create the image of the people's hero." Analyzing the poems of Inber, Tikhonov, Berggol'ts, Antokol'skii, and Margarita Aliger, Poliak formulated demands for the depiction of such an epic hero; the poets whose work she was addressing "do not endow the image-character with any individual peculiarity, and without this an authentic, realistic image is inconceivable. . . . The inadequacy of the contemporary poetic epic lies in this absence of distinct, figurative, three-dimensional figures with their own unique biographies and natures, unique destinies, and heroic acts and deeds."[30] The problem itself of the epic and the aesthetic program to create it that were worked out in this article belong to the postwar late-Stalinist culture.

The aesthetic principles according to which the templates of the "panoramic-epic novel" about the war would be prepared after the war were formulated here. Hence, Soviet critics immediately after the victory began to demand a return to Socialist Realist epic-making writing, repeating almost verbatim what Poliak had said in 1943. "The time has come now," Lev Subotskii wrote two years after Poliak, "for a profound and comprehensive conceptualization of the real-life material accumulated by writers over those years on the battle lines and the home front, a screening out of the incidental and secondary, and a selection of the main and typical things. The mass reader is no longer satisfied by a hero without a biography, without a clear human nature; he wants a variety of attributes, a wealth and diversity of the person's ties to reality, a tight interweaving of historical events with the destinies of their creators, a broad artistic canvas that would accommodate the image of the great leader of the new world, the military leader of their victories, and the image of the rank-and-file soldier of our armies."[31] This is the ready-to-use template of the "panoramic-epic novel" that became the metagenre of Soviet literature after the war. The fundamental collision of the new epic, the leader (commander) and the masses ("rank-and-file soldiers"), had come into war literature from the 1920s, but it was engendered, of course, not only by literature. Typical in this respect was the three-day discussion in December 1944 in the Writers' Union entitled "The Image of the Soviet Officer" (addressing this theme at the end of the war was itself indicative).

Aleksei Surkov noted that "the war has taught, and thoroughly, a particular group of people from literature who ended up in the press of the army and at the front a realistic attitude toward events, a realistic attitude toward what happens every day in the place where history takes its basic steps" and that "war has taught us to speak, when necessary and when this is called for by the very nature of a developing struggle, in a direct and coarse manner." He further noted that "before the war, it was rare that any of us could imagine you could say that people with a red star on a garrison cap or service cap were not all heroes, that there were cowards among them. The war taught us that we can and should speak frankly, straight to their faces, to the people who have quite often been covered in blood, blocking the road to the east with their own lives, about the old women, younger women, and children who see them off in silence, see them off as they go east, with sorrowful and indignant looks. The war taught us a realistic attitude to what happens in life, and thereby opened a path for us to the reader's heart."[32]

But the war was drawing to a close, and with it the blockade of reality also intensified, a blockade that had always been a supremely important strategy in wartime propaganda, a part of which was wartime literature. The "bodyguard of lies" (as Churchill famously said) that safeguards the truth during wartime was almost the only force that did not sustain losses. But literature, on which the functions of showing and retranslating the war onto all of society were imposed, was also supposed to fulfill the functions of wartime censorship along with the regime—to measure out and supply the dose of "the truth about the war." "Millions of people are battling on the front. Millions are working in the rear. The Urals steel founder or the team leader on the Kazakh *kolkhoz* can possibly never see the Germans or hear the artillery bursts, but they nonetheless know the truth about the war. . . . The sons and daughters of the warring people, on the front and in the rear, have a common experience, common ideas, concerns, and aspirations. This is why even the truth about the war is not only one for us— identical for those who were and were not in battle. Stalin's orders and the communiques of the Soviet Information Bureau are full of 'plain truth, truth beating straight to the heart,' as are all our agitation and propaganda." Thus wrote Evgeniia Knipovich in the article with the telling title "The 'Beautiful' Untruth about the War," where its author sharply criticized the short stories of Konstantin Paustovskii, Veniamin Kaverin, Lev Kassil', and Boris Lavrenev.[33] Propaganda here is openly called "truth." Its straightforward aim is to create what is fundamentally impossible—"common experience, common ideas . . . for those who were and were not in battle."

At the end of the war, two opposite tendencies surfaced: one, the mobilizational inertia of wartime literature; the other, a return to the former heroic conventions. Thus, all the journals rose up in concert "against the attempts of certain writers to embellish and romanticize the difficult existence of the war." *Oktiabr'* printed Berggol'ts speech at the 1944 February Plenum of the Soviet Writers' Union, in which she condemned the falsely romantic spirit of several of Paustovkii's short stories (especially his "Leningrad Symphony").[34] The "'beautiful' untruth about the war" became the object of quite a few critical articles. In his review of Vladimir Beliaev's *Leningrad Nights,* Aleksandr Prokof'ev criticized its "hackwork, all the more intolerable as the author tied it to the themes of his great and beautiful city";[35] Bella Brainina rebuked Valentin Kataev for being idyllic when depicting "the harsh wartime life of the people";[36] A. Matskin demanded an end to "literary 'confection-making'" and "masters of trifles";[37] and M. Gel'fand railed against writing for literary effect, complacency, and "trivialization of reality."[38] This, as sanctioned by the regime, was the "struggle against conflictlessness and varnishing [reality]," which every time aimed to mobilize the masses. All of this was receding into the past, an example of which was the fate of the "Leningrad theme."

The "Leningrad theme" became powerful fuel for debate, and the Leningrad division of the Soviet Writers' Union held a discussion about it in April 1945. This discussion brought to light divergent vectors in the determination of the true balance of "the truth about the war." As the situation changes, so do the demands made of literature and, along with that, the threshold of "truth." On the one hand, the principles of wartime literature continue to operate, and on the other, the conventions of terror-inducing naturalism that are basic to it are replaced by "peacetime" practices of control and normalization. In literature, this means a fight against "naturalism" and a transition from depicting the sufferings and horrors of war to making war itself epic and heroic. The practices of erasing experience are replaced with those that change it into history and epic.

One symptomatic speech in the discussion of the "Leningrad theme," reproduced in the journal *Leningrad,* was that of Pavel Gromov, who was distressed that "authors try to grab the reader's attention by describing pictures of the hunger and deprivations that fell to the lot of Leningraders" and draw "a picture, calculated for its effect, of all sorts of naturalistically rendered details of everyday Leningrad life. Authentic art has always kept aloof from naturalism." Accordingly, one should not "chase after verisimilitude of the everyday" but rather "give a large-scale, generalized picture of the whole" since readers and reviewers "are not interested in particulars, no matter how striking they might seem, but in the intensity of the Leningrader's higher feelings, the passion of the Soviet soldier, the courage of the Soviet person." In Gromov's opinion, Vera Inber did not understand this when she vividly described the horrors of blockade life in her *Leningrad Diaries:*

"To what purpose these clinical descriptions? What do they provide, and to whom? It is not at all a matter of the artist's being obliged to conceal anything—No. Write about anything you like, but you must have generalization, a conceptualization of events, and not simply a conglomeration of shocking details. . . . The book has no atmosphere of the era; one cannot tell where, when, and to what kind of people the events described happened. There is no history in Inber's diaries. Time comes into them in trivialities of daily life, 'horrible' details, and not in the historical peculiarities of the psychology of the Soviet person educated by the new social structure." Gromov was partly correct: the "intensity of . . . higher feelings" was displaced into *Pulkovo Meridian*. But this is not what the critic had in mind. His attacks on "naturalism" were aimed at the experience of the blockade itself. Also speaking in May 1945, at the Tenth Plenum of the Soviet Writers' Union (a speech also reproduced in *Leningrad*), Aleksandr Prokof'ev used the same condemnatory tones about Berggol'ts, who in her *Leningrad Diary* "forced you to hear in her poems exclusively the theme of suffering tied to the countless calamities of the citizens of the besieged city." One and the same discourse, the same system of arguments and rhetorical figures, crops up in Socialist Realism every time a transition to "epic" begins, which is always linked to a change in the threshold of "plain truth."

Repeating Lidiia Poliak's reasoning about the "lyrical epic" almost verbatim, Gromov advised writers "not to fear poetic generalization, poetic conventionality" and to "think more about the poetic, inner meaning of the phenomena depicted. The goal of a work of art on the Leningrad theme should be a mapping, an artistic portrayal of the unyielding soul of the Leningrader, contrasting his strength, tenacity, and selflessness, the authentic patriotism of the Soviet person, to the enemy's blockade." Thus, before one's very eyes the "Leningrad theme" was transformed from a person's struggle to live (as it was interpreted in the war years) into "the theme of the historical uniqueness of a new person able to endure any difficulties and deprivations in the name of the lofty idea of Soviet patriotism that inspires him."[39]

After the war, when the industrial novel again comes to the foreground, the blockade theme not only recedes to the background under the pressure of literature about "peaceful everyday life" and "restoration," but is also deliberately washed out of the war narrative. Telling in this respect is the collective anthology of essays *Leningraders* (1947) written by seventeen Leningrad writers. In these essays about all kinds of Leningraders—party workers, laborers, engineers, shipbuilders, teachers—the blockade theme is a distant shadow. If the war comes up (and it does only in a few of the stories), it is, as a rule, in stories about "heroic feats of labor." There is no mention at all about suffering, hunger, cold, or the massive loss of life, despite the book's being written so soon after the blockade was lifted, when the traces of destruction were still visible everywhere and the consequences for the city's inhabitants, a huge number of whom had died during the blockade years, were still devastating. The authors (many of whom had themselves lived through the blockade) wrote about this time as if it were an episode that could almost be ignored. If the blockade was mentioned at all, it was only in the inhabitants' participation in the heroic defense of the city. The theme of suffering had become taboo.

The subsequent rejection of the blockade theme was tied not only to the "Leningrad affair" (repressions, the destruction of the museum of the city's defense, and so forth), but also to the dynamics of the representational strategies of Socialist Realism after the war, a result of which was that the war theme as a whole lost its suggestive characteristics and took on entirely different functions—those of monumentalization and heroicization. The source of these changes was, in fact, the replacement of war by victory. Once the latter acquired the status of the fundamental legitimizing event of the Soviet era, it led to war being regarded as the history of victory. If the history of war, which was dominated by a theme far from that of victoriousness—suffering—had a low ideological coefficient and was the experience of pain, then the history of victory was a state enterprise. Without doubt, everything that had to do with any sort of particularization of suffering became unacceptable in this perspective—be it the theme of the Holocaust or that of the blockade. Stalinism refuses to recognize not only uncontrolled individual experience, but also any kind of particularism. Only in two cases was it allowed, and these were explained by the extraordinary circumstances of the war. And in both cases it ended tragically: the Jewish Anti-Fascist Committee was annihilated and the theme of the Holocaust, along with the "Black Book," became taboo, and any mentions of civilian suffering during the Leningrad blockade were heavily downplayed, and the "Leningrad theme" was laid to rest. In both cases, the subjects of the particularity were disliked by Stalin:

Jews and Leningrad. The experience of trauma—that is, the experience of the war proper—lost its language and was no longer capable of representation.

THE WAR MUSEUM: VISUAL STRATEGIES FOR THE REPRESENTATION OF VICTORY

The shift in the perception of what was happening in the second half of the war was aphoristically formulated by Aleksandr Tvardovskii in *Vasilii Terkin:*

> A different time, different dates.
> Labor is divided since ancient times:
> Soldiers surrender cities,
> Generals conquer them.

This change in perspective (to a different time and different dates) at the threshold of victory brought into Soviet art new main characters as well: the era of "the generals' optics" had arrived. Cinema during the war period had not a trace of this optics since its main function (as that of literature and the other arts in the time of war) was mobilizational; by depicting heroic deeds, it stimulated their production; by portraying a horrible enemy, it shaped hatred for it; and by painting a picture of the villainies of the invaders, it called for revenge. At the end of the war and after it, art had no need of any of this since war was transformed into the new founding myth of the Soviet nation. Accordingly, the aim of art (including cinema) became something else as well—the retranslation of the new status of the regime, which no longer required the previous legitimization. The consolidation of this status and the development of new strategies to confirm it were turned into the fundamental ideological goals of late Stalinism; the stamp of this novelty lies on all the "artistic production" on this era. We will subsequently attempt to trace how the solidification of the new principle of legitimacy through victory took place in the themes and semantic-mythological blocks of postwar cinematic production, where this process was the most visible.

The idea of a cinematic epic of the Great Patriotic War arose at the very end of the war and focused not so much on heroic biographies as on military operations, central to which was the biography of a single military commander and strategist: Stalin. The people surrounding him had no biographies. Naturally, the list of cinematic battles approved by Stalin did not include the early disastrous period of the war, but the operations from the battle for Stalingrad up to the Berlin operation were part of the epic. This cycle of "artistic-documentary films" consisted of "ten blows" designated by Stalin in the first part of his November 6, 1944, report entitled "The Twenty-Seventh Anniversary of the Great October Socialist Revolution" and given at the triumphant session of the Moscow City Soviet, where he set about historicizing the still unconcluded war as the history of victory, excluding its beginning stages. This was when the planning began for the films about the greatest victories of the Patriotic War: Stalingrad, Leningrad, the battle for Crimea and Belarus, the taking of Königsberg and Berlin. However, only three of the "ten blows of Stalin" managed to get made. This was a new cinema.

The war films talked about the battle lines, the home front, and the "temporarily occupied territories" but without specifying exact places, events, or people. These were invented stories of suffering and heroism, but they were very personal, appealing to the personal experience of the viewer and therefore mobilizing and forceful. After the war, Soviet art set about transforming the war into a "useful past," and therefore it needed a genre that would freely combine historical fantasies with references to real historical events and people.

We will call this process *the musealization of war*. A museum is an ideal milieu for producing a "useful past." This sort of past is tightly linked to an interpretation of experience, sifting it "through an artefactual history which partly obscures the social relations and struggles which underlay that past"; this history is based on an understanding of the past "through pastiched images and stereotypes, which convert that past into simple narratives and spectacles" and on "the belief that history is turned into heritage and made safe, sterile and shorn of danger, subversion and seduction."[40] It is here that the strategies of musealization prove decisive.

A museum presents not only a finished past, but also one that is transformed into spectacle. The transition of the past into pure representation and display has historically been linked to nation building. As Tony Bennett observes in *The Birth of the Museum,* museums have always played an important role in the creation of nation-states; in them, "the recent past was historicized as the newly emerging nation-states sought to preserve and immemorialize their own formation as a part of that process of 'nationing' their populations that was essential to their further development."[41] Political instrumentalization dramatically altered the nature of the museum. As Bennett wittily observes, in the museum, "it had initially been envisaged that the past was to be preserved *from* development, [but] it is now typically preserved *for* it."[42] But it was for development of a special sort.

If earlier the legitimacy of the regime was based on the idea that Stalin was the pupil, confidant, and successor of Lenin, then Stalin as victor and savior of the country no longer needed these titles to prop him up. The evolution of Stalin's image reaches its apex in the postwar "artistic-documentary" film. In the 1930s "historical-revolutionary" films (such as *Lenin in October, Lenin in 1918,* and *The Great Glow*), Stalin had been presented as Lenin's pupil, and later, in *The Vow,* as his only successor. In the wartime films, Stalin was *not associated at all* with Lenin. He was finally becoming self-sufficient. Legitimization through comparison came to an end. Metaphor became unnecessary. The era of metonymy had arrived; the *comparison* of objects was being replaced by the *substitution* of one object by another. And it was the strategies of musealization that corresponded to this shift in postwar Stalinist culture.

To the extent that "postwar state policy in the area of cinematography was above all meant to exclude and substitute for the ethical and therefore aesthetic experience accumulated by society in the war years,"[43] postwar art was not simply a quantitative expansion and continuation of the ideology of "national Bolshevism."[44] A postwar film about the war was something completely new in comparison with prewar filmmaking. At its core lay a new goal: "by rejecting the real historical experience of the war period and declaring it nonexistent, [the goal was] to contrast a new myth to it. . . . At the center of [this myth] is victory in the Great Patriotic War, achieved thanks to the perfection of the state mechanism created by Stalin."[45]

The epic sweep supposedly inherent in the "artistic-documentary film" arose as a byproduct of the aggressive transformation of the real war experience, which had still not been fully processed by its participants but was already being mercilessly reworked into epic. This process would bide no delay; the change in the status of the legitimacy of the regime emanated from the results of the war and had to be fixed hot on their heels, imprinted in still flexible memory and spilling over into the indisputable narrative of victory, whose political dividends Stalin had to reap right away. Victory had to overshadow the war, to stamp into the still fresh and incomplete image of the past a new explanatory matrix—that is, to reformat this experience.

Since these "documents" completely reversed the picture of the just ended war, the new genre was not subject to description but only to justification. It was stated, for example, that "the artistic-documentary genre is a qualitatively new aesthetic category, a new stage, a new phenomenon in the art of Socialist Realism. The concept of the new genre is defined not in scholastic arguments about the essence of the new genre but rather in a lively process of solving the important and complex ideological-creative task facing Soviet cinematic art."[46]

No matter what the new genre touched, it all petrified into a majestic pose, swelled with epic juices, and became surfeited with historical significance, and all the "secondary participants" of the events (as well as the events themselves that were not completely victorious) were replaced with victories and commanders over whose collective intellect and will the genius and will of Stalin hovered. And if as a result what was "truthfully depicted" on the screen contradicted the viewer's experience, this was merely because these films "sought to capture life itself not in its external relation but in its internal one, to reveal the moving forces of the historical process, to show the link between events and individual human destinies, in no way and never deviating from the actual course of history—all of this has indeed become the internal basis of the drama of the artistic-documentary film."[47] In other words, the correspondence of what was seen on the screen to experience was by no means part of "truthful depiction." And, in fact, the stated goal of these films was to show the viewer the "*truth of history*." Poured over into life, it was concealed from the eyes. And this was what these films *created* (and by no means reflected!) "truthfully." The truth of history was that victory was attained thanks to Stalin's genius. And here Soviet art had to follow the path trodden in European medieval art.

As Louis Marin indicated in *Portrait of the King*, the history of a king's life and deeds (both personal and historic) is always laid out in full accordance with the history of the state. The result is a history that "admits of no remainder ... [and] is also a space of total visibility and of absolute representability."[48] To suppose otherwise would be to "admit a 'corner' of the royal universe where a kingly act, word, or thought would not be representable, would not be praisable, would not be sayable in the form of narrative-praise.[49] This would mean thinking of the unthinkable—absolutism that is not absolute; the story of the king cannot be represented any other way than as history, in which the king is simultaneously "the archactor of History and the metanarrator of his narrative."[50]

The link that Marin established between absolutism and the strategies of historicization used in it can be considered universal; after all, "to see the historical event at the place of the king, to be placed in this, supreme—or almost—position, is to see the coming of History itself, since the king is its unique agent. And since the gaze of the absolute master sends the light that gives sight and produces what is to be seen, to be present at his side is to participate in his gaze and to share, in a fashion, his power: to double and substitute for him in the narrative-to-come that this past presence not only authenticates but permits and authorizes."[51]

The new representation of war is a striking example of how this optics operates. The Soviet spectator was transformed into a participant of Stalin's "theater of absolutism" by being himself included in the new spectacle, which, having little in common with reality, was constructed in accordance with the logic of the historical representation of power: "A history that would be the accomplice of absolutism must see the king everywhere and in everything, the moving force of all that happens, and it must tell the story of history as the unfolding of the monarch's self-originating activity from the monarch's point of view. Since this is the source of all illumination, it offers the only vantage point from which history's unfolding can possibly be understood."[52] Hence, it is no surprise that these films challenge the spectator's memory and experience. Their action unfolds

in a space demonstratively contradictory to the masses' experience . . . that is, however, declared to be the only historically accurate one. Photographed with a moving camera from a bird's-eye view, the crowd scenes of many thousands with a barrage of military equipment and pyrotechnical wonders were designed to demonstrate to the mass spectator the point of view of the leader, which was fundamentally inaccessible to [that spectator]—the leader being the only one who holds the fullness of truth at each historic moment. . . . But the rank-and-file spectator is supposed to find his own place in a crowd scene, which is fundamentally indivisible into separate faces. Obviously, the very sensation of participating in the sweep of the action unfolding on the screen is designed to serve as compensation to the masses' perception for this vivid sensation of the utter smallness of their place—and experience—in the system."[53]

In prewar films Stalin figured as a strictly *historical* person—either as the organizer of revolution, or the organizer of victories in the civil war, or the favorite pupil and closest confidant of Lenin. But now he had to appear in his *current* capacity of leader and organizer of the war. A strictly representational problem was resolved: for the first time, the spectator got the opportunity to venture into the holy of holies— Stalin's office in the Kremlin—to see the war through Stalin's eyes, to hear how he had led and interacted with legendary marshals, and to see how the headquarters of the High Command operated. In other words, the spectator got the opportunity to see the secret of Stalin's power. The problem of the legitimacy of this power disappeared with the beginning of the victory phase of the war.

These films offered not a "documentary" demonstration but a "documentary-artistic" one. The films tell the story not so much of how Stalin actually managed the war as of how he wanted to appear in the role of "supreme commander of all times and peoples." Film reviewers untiringly emphasized the "documentary quality" of these films, which was supposed to assure their "historical truthfulness." But if the films did in fact reflect anything truthfully, it was the official historical narrative. It was a docudrama of a very specific kind: a dramatized version of a ready-made ideological text rather than of real events. Immediately after the war a revised *Short Biography* of Stalin appeared, equal in status to his *Short Course on the History of the Communist Party*, with pages added (and personally edited by Stalin) about the leader's pivotal role in the victory.

Film critics would occasionally acknowledge that these films did not so much *reflect* reality as they *transformed* it in accordance with the new historical narrative: "The authors of the film *The Fall of Berlin* were faced with a difficult and honorable task. The facts of history had happened, but history itself had yet to be written. Witnesses to and participants in great events, they also had to be chroniclers. Scientific analysis in their labor had to be combined with artistic reflection of the world; historical study had to result in artistic generalization."[54] As if not noticing the gap between the "facts of history" and "artistic generalization," the critics asserted that films like *The Vow* and *The Fall of Berlin* "preserve for posterity the living, undying spirit of the time, obviously in artistic form, and depict in living realistic images the development of historical events. The spectator as it were relives what happened, becomes a participant in it, and gets an impression of the events transpiring that is at times more vivid than he could get by resorting to detailed historical study."[55] And this despite the fact that what was depicted on the screen—mainly Stalin's Kremlin office and the army headquarters where generals and marshals argued—had nothing in common with what the spectators had experienced during the war.

But even though he was the only individual on which the action of these films was focused, Stalin was devoid of any individuality whatsoever. This was a matter of deliberate principle. Mikhail Romm's account of his conversation with Aleksei Dikii, who played Stalin on screen, is widely known:

> I ask Dikii, "Why do you talk without looking at the person you're talking to? Why are you so arrogant that you aren't even interested in that person's opinion?"
>
> Dikii answered: "I'm not playing a person; I'm playing a granite monument. It is meant for the ages. A monument has no place for little smiles and that sort of everyday rubbish."[56]

The rejection of such "everyday rubbish," such as a physiognomic resemblance to Stalin or Stalin's accent, was what determined the leader's own choice of Dikii for the role; Stalin had concluded that Mikhail Gelovani, who had played him in practically all of the prewar films, "suffer[ed] from a national limitation" and was not quite right for the image of a "Russian" leader. Stalin told Minister of Cinematography Ivan Bol'shakov that "Gelovani has a strong Georgian accent. Do I really have an accent like that? Think about a suitable actor for the role of Comrade Stalin. Best to get one of the Russian ones."[57] Ultimately, the choice of Dikii was made. The cinematographic image that he created of the leader, according to Stalin's own review, showed that "Comrade Stalin belongs to the Russian people and to the great Russian culture."[58]

Dikii did not conceal the fact, even from the leader himself, that he was not playing him but rather "the image of Stalin." The actor Evgenii Vesnik, who was a friend of Dikii's, retold his friend's own account of a conversation with Stalin. Stalin supposedly told Dikii that he had personally chosen him for the role after reviewing twelve actors' auditions because he had no accent at all and, for that matter, no external resemblance to Stalin. After telling Dikii that he "looked powerful in this role," Stalin asked him why he did not use the characteristics that all artists used—an accent or an external resemblance. Stalin was pleased by Dikii's answer: "But I, forgive me, was not playing you. I was playing the people's impression of the leader."[59] If it was true that Dikii was playing "the people's impression of the leader," then we can say that the director filmed *the leader's impression of the people (and of the war).* And this dual perspective makes late-Stalinist war films particularly interesting. They reflect not so much the leader as his impression of himself and of the "simple people" for whom the film is intended.

The main character of *The Fall of Berlin* (dir. Mikhail Chiaureli, 1949), the steel founder Aleksei Ivanov, is just such a "simple person," changed beyond recognition. An exemplary poster hero, devoid of will, initiative, and any independence whatsoever, he does not change in any way despite having gone with the troops all the way to Berlin; in the film, he exists exclusively for a meeting with Stalin. When he finds out that Stalin is summoning him, the hero of *The Fall of Berlin* panics: "I won't go. . . . I can't even imagine: how am I going talk to Stalin!" The factory's director tells him, "You have to talk to him! . . . Alesha . . . they'll talk to you! Just listen, and keep your wits about you." Essentially, Ivanov is playing a *spectator of the film,* a construction of the film's authors' whose voice and experience have no significance whatsoever because "They'll talk to you!"

Ivanov is a big, clumsy bumpkin with a halting glance whose 100 percent Soviet correctness is emphasized by his peasant manner, impulsiveness, folkloric directness, and folksy simplicity. The actor portraying him, Boris Andreev, had mastered this character type of the "state's child" back in the era of prewar and wartime films. The living incarnation of the "glorious tribe of Stalin's sons" and of the homogenized image of the "masses of the people," he is a completely conventional figure. The sheer fact that he was "a man of the state's birth," since he was born on November 7, 1917, and his "commonplace" surname worked to endow this image with conventionality (even down to the fact that, like a fairytale *bogatyr'*, after suffering a concussion, he spent three months in a hospital without waking up). Nominally the "main character," he appears in various battle scenes leading the soldiers behind him with the words, "For the Motherland, for Stalin!" and forging ahead among the corpses of the fallen enemies, engaging in hand-to-hand fights alongside the soldiers until the victory banner is raised above the Reichstag. His ideological function is to be staggered by the greatness of Stalin, whom he meets before the war and in the victory days in Berlin. This "eternal child of the state" is presented as infantile, direct, and comically simple.[60] However, Chiaureli's characteristic tendency toward exaggeration and his lack of a sense of proportion played a cruel joke on him. The ideological schema of the film was so obtrusively straightforward that the line beyond which the "simple Soviet person," Ivanov, turned into a self-parody was crossed, and it displeased many viewers.[61] Of course, their voices did not make their way into the press, where there was no shortage of reviewers wanting to express their delight with the "truthfulness" of these films.

The father of the new genre was one of the most flamboyant directors of Stalinist cinema: Fridrikh Ermler.[62] This was not his first contribution to the development of totalitarian cinema. His *The Great Citizen* was a real discovery, a result of the evolution of the historical-revolutionary genre and an apex of tradition; the screenplay, edited by Stalin and created at the same time as the 1936–38 show trials, brought the viewer into the world of Stalin's paranoia and into his logic for justifying the Great Terror, the founding event of which was the murder of Sergei Kirov. After it became one of the exemplary products of the Great Terror era, the film was awarded one of the first Stalin Prizes. Then Ermler made his next well-timed discovery; he succeeded in divining Stalin's still unspoken political order, as if foreseeing what Stalin would want to see after the war.

In *The Great Turning Point* he used the very same techniques of vagueness and translucence as he had in *The Great Citizen*. Both films feature easily recognizable (although unnamed) historical characters (Kirov and the opposition leaders in *The Great Citizen*; in *The Great Turning Point*, the commanders who led the battle for Stalingrad; Ermler himself later named Vatutin, Malinovskii, and Tolbukhin, although Murav'ev is easily identified as Zhukov and his adversary

Klaus as Paulius). A secret lies at the heart of the plots of both films (a conspiracy in the first case and the secret preparation of a decisive offensive in the second). Central to both films are key historical events that are unnamed but easily guessed (the murder of Kirov, the battle for Stalingrad).

Like *The Great Citizen*, *The Great Turning Point* is less action than verbal arguments merely accompanied by actions. One could say that *The Great Turning Point* was a curious sequel to *The Great Citizen*, a film in which Ermler synthesized the basic techniques of totalitarian cinema, creating a film-cum-party-meeting seemingly devoid of any entertainment value whatsoever and bogged down in endless discussions/battles of the party with the opposition. In applying the very same techniques to new, up-to-date material, Ermler contaminated two genres: the historical-revolutionary film and the war film. Thus a new genre arose. Conceived as the story of a hero (the screenplay was titled "General of the Army"), the film turned out to be the story of a battle. It was no accident that the focus shifted from a character to a strategy; there was one real character in it (as would later become the norm of the new genre): Stalin. All the rest were merely a retinue. Accordingly, what became central was an event whose unfolding could reveal the history of (Stalin's) strategic thinking. The drama and dynamics of the plot grew out of the inner dramatic potential of the strategic situation of war. A military operation, the archetype of which was the battle for Stalingrad, became the center of the film.

The film's main character, army general Murav'ev, carries a glint of Stalin's strategic genius. He is not only privy to Stalin's scheme, but is also charged with carrying out his plan. Although everyone around him, including his far more experienced and senior comrades-in-arms, respects Murav'ev, he thinks of himself as merely carrying out the will of him whose name is not spoken: "Correctly evaluating and using the situation as it develops, extrapolating a fulfillable goal from it . . . any talented military leader knows how to do this. But only a genuine military leader sets a goal and himself creates the situation he needs. And we have only one such military leader."

Ermler conceived *The Great Turning Point* before his film *She Defends the Motherland* (1943), a typical wartime film that cried out for vengeance. But the new film, although it was filmed during the war, was in every respect a postwar product. It was addressed to a country that was now something different: "The film no longer anticipated a country surprised by a sudden attack, summoning its people to resistance by any means, but a country advancing to a decisive, imminent victory. Accordingly, in this second film the accent was not on hatred for the enemy, not on the battle call, but on the assertion of the authority of the battlemaster, the leader, the military and political commander."[63] This was a turnaround from the images of the simple folk whose backs had borne the brunt of the war to images that "personified the confident and reliable force that conquered German fascism."[64] For the meantime, this was merely an apologia for the will of the infallible commander, but one could easily detect the infallible Stalin behind him. Not surprisingly, Soviet film critics allotted Ermler's film a place "among the sources of the war epic in our cinema."[65]

The screenplay, "General of the Army," written by Boris Chirskov in 1944, was shot into a film in tight deadlines; *The Great Turning Point* came out in January 1945, and was awarded the Stalin Prize, First Class. Receiving this highest praise was no accident. The idea of portraying military actions as the result of generalship was deservedly understood and appreciated by Stalin. The film became the template for the "artistic-documentary" genre. In it the battle for Stalingrad was shown "not from the trenches but from above, from headquarters, from which one could see the whole grandiose sweep of the operation that decided the fates of divisions, corps, and armies. The characters in the script are generals who command large-scale formations. The fate of the besieged city depends on which plan of action is taken and how it is worked out in the headquarters of the front."[66]

"Almost all the action is confined to generals' offices and bunkers, almost all the dialogue hinges on one and the same theme of a military-operational nature; there is not a single female role in the picture; and a map lying on a Soviet commander's desk all but plays the role of a main 'character.'"[67] How could such an unentertaining film become successful? "The viewer sees people bent over maps, plans, and communiqués. Only maps, plans, and communiqués, meetings of formation commanders, discussions of the enemy's intentions and ways of defending the city. . . . How could a strategic problem become the subject or art?" the film critics asked, trying to understand the reason for the film's success.[68] In part, success was assured by the fact that those whose world was hidden from the mass viewer were in action on the screen. Soviet war cinema had mainly related the deeds and sufferings of simple people—soldiers, partisans, peaceful civilians, workers on the home front. But here, for the first time, the work in the headquarters and the everyday life of military commanders was revealed. This all piqued an understandable curiosity.

Such an unusual plot was born of a goal. "We could discern the plot we needed in the defensive operations, full of drama, and in the completed models of the offensive operation," Ermler wrote when explaining how the screenplay, which originally had concentrated on the hero, was refocused on the event.[69] This allowed the scenes of staff meetings and debates over maps—absolutely devoid of entertainment value—to bring the dynamics of the unfolding war situation itself to life. Ermler wanted to show that a seemingly boring situation is full of life and internal drama, risk, emotional tension, and even excitement. He intentionally steered clear of any warm and diverting motifs and touches whatsoever.

Sidestepping any fleshing-out of the events depicted, Ermler and Chirskov transformed a specific battle into almost a symbol, a sort of matrix for films yet to be made, revealing a formula for a new genre. This is why the film not only told the story of the "great turning point" in the war, but was itself also a "great turning point" in the representation of war. We could call it *headquarters cinema*. The just ended war now had to come across in this fashion. Now it was a war of thought and of commander-thinkers and the unnamed commander-in-chief, Stalin. Thus the "artistic-documentary film" was born.

The notable French film critic André Bazin, who first analyzed the phenomenon of Stalin on-screen, drew attention to the fact that in Vladimir Petrov's *The Battle of Stalingrad* (1949) "tranquility, an atmosphere of being deep in thought, in seclusion, are contrasted to the hysterical environment of Hitler's general staff."[70] According to Bazin, this atmosphere was derived from a peculiar optics of the war:

> It is as if you are following the course of the operations from onboard a helicopter out of reach; the battlefield appears before you in the broadest view imaginable, and you haven't the slightest possibility of judging not only the fate of the military subdivisions, but even their redeployment and orientation. Thus the whole sense of the military operations becomes clear only because of the supplementary commentary, enlivened with the help of a multiplicity of maps, and, most of all, thanks to Stalin's thinking out loud.

And this is what results: below is the apocalyptic chaos of the battle-field, but above it is a unique, all-knowing intelligence that puts this pseudo-chaos into order and guides it in the only correct way. And be-tween these extremes is—nothing. No intermediary link in the chain of history, not a single frame telling about the psychological and intellec-tual processes that determine the fate of people and the outcome of the battle. It is as if there is a direct link between the stroke of the genera-lissimo's pencil and the soldiers' self-sacrifice or, at least, that the inter-mediary mechanism has no meaning whatsoever; it is no more than a transmitting link, and therefore analysis of this stage can be omitted.[71]

This disposition of the "artistic-documentary film" grew out of a strictly mythological picture of the war. Ultimately, these films tell the story of victory, not of war, and therefore not the story of those who "surrendered cities" (soldiers) but of those who "conquered" them (generals) and, more specifically, the generalissimo (Stalin). The aim of these films is to put "Stalin's blows" of liberation on the screen. Every strategic operation ("blow") emanates from the preceding one and, in turn, is linked to the conception and execution of the following one. This teleology of war is constructed by backdating. The exposition of Igor' Savchenko's *Third Blow* (1948) is the second blow (the libera-tion of right-bank Ukraine) since only after it did the "third blow" (the liberation of the Crimea) become possible. And toward the ending, the theme of the next blow emerges, the prerequisites for which were cre-ated by the success of the third blow; and so on it goes.

According to these films, war is the product of planning. The con-cept of planning is crucial here. Everything in these films is intended to prove a proposition formulated in the *Short Biography* of Stalin, which he edited himself: "With the perspicacity of genius, Comrade Stalin guessed the enemy's plans and thwarted them."[72] *Planning* and *fore-sight* belonged *personally* to Stalin. He no longer needed "the found-ers of Marxism" or references to Lenin. Stalin himself now became the only source of action, the chain of which goes from the people to their leader. The latter's will is transmitted to the army through the commanders. This movement was precisely formulated by one of the leading film critics of the Stalin era, Rostislav Iurenev, when he ob-served that in *Third Blow* "the central image of the film is the image of Generalissimo J. V. Stalin. The people's leader executes the people's will for victory. A strategist, a commander, dictates his will to the army. . . . Stalin aims the strike. The strike is carried out by the commanders of

Stalin's school: Voroshilov, Vasilevskii, Tolbukhin. . . . The leader's plan is clear to them, and they find the means to carry it out.[73]

History is narrated here as if it had not yet happened, while the basic premise of these films is the viewer's knowledge about everything that had happened. Stalin "foresees" something that, in fact, took place long ago. And if in *The Third Blow* the battle and headquarters scenes were balanced by bringing in fleshed-out characters among the rank-and-file and junior command staff, then in *The Battle of Stalingrad,* by the director's own admission, "the main goal, the most crucial and honorable one, was to create with the means of cinematic art an image of the leader of the Soviet people, the genius commander, the great thinker, the unsurpassed military organizer and strategist, Comrade Stalin, unmasking with eagle eyes the enemy's war plan. We had to use the resources of cinematic art . . . to reveal the wisdom of Stalin's strategic plan."[74]

The Battle of Stalingrad was the second treatment of the Stalingrad theme after a short time interval. But if in *The Great Turning Point* the battle for Stalingrad remained unnamed—although "from the very first frames of the film the viewer recognizes the heroic defense of Stalingrad and hence knows in advance what will happen next" and "the whole world knows this now"[75]—then in Petrov's film "Stalin's blow" was clear from the very title of the film. If Ermler had faced the task of "revealing not the plan itself but the behavior of people immersed in a still palpable atmosphere of secrecy, people who, with the exception of Murav'ev, act as if with tightly closed eyes,"[76] then for the authors of *The Battle of Stalingrad* the task was precisely the revelation of the plan as the result of Stalin's genial foresight, and thereby a real historical event verifying this divine gift of the leader was transformed into a story of the fulfillment of his foresight.

The idea itself of history as foresight is based on a contradiction in terms since foresight is a victory over history. History "foretold" in advance becomes literally *predictable* and loses the element of the unexpected. Its filming is therefore deprived of a sense of plot. The film turns into a curious baring of the device. Since a story must be told to a viewer such that it is motivated, a number of buttressing scenes are created, which help the characters to express themselves (and, in fact, to clarify the plot for the viewer). This is not so much sound film as it is visual radio; without sound, these films are totally incomprehensible. In them, the characters only talk (and occasionally shoot). One would be justified to call this the *parquet-battlefield* genre.

The historical optics of this genre transform the present into the past, from which Stalin looks into the future, which appears to the viewer as the past. In order to produce this yesterday's future that Stalin looks into, the director must look intently backward. But even this does not allow him to achieve the sacred goal: to convince the viewer that "what happens there on the battlefields, is here, in the working office of the High Command, constantly subjected to analysis and generalization."[77] On the contrary, Stalin here is the only one who has a voice and is a subject. All the others are merely instruments of his will, and the events themselves develop in order to confirm Stalin's correctness and the accuracy of his "foresight."

But if in *The Battle of Stalingrad* the new concept of war is cast into the shapes of parquet war cinema, then in *The Fall of Berlin* it takes on the shape of a perfected myth. Created as a seventieth birthday gift for Stalin, the film piqued the lively interest of the leader, who was acquainted with Petr Pavlenko's screenplay. As the undoubted apex of the Stalin cult in cinema, this film is interesting for its genuinely barbaric straightforwardness.

Stalin assumes the form of a messiah in *The Fall of Berlin*. In the widely known final apotheosis of the film, Stalin, when he flies to the prostrate Berlin, dressed in a blindingly white tunic, descends like an angel from the heavens to the crowds of people awaiting him. They represent all peoples, and they praise the savior of humanity in every dialect. The exultant crowds welcome Stalin, and over all this thunders the song "We go behind you to luminous times by way of victories." The scene of the "descent from the heavens" (as if reproducing the corresponding scene from *Triumph des Willens*) and the exultant crowds praising Stalin in all the world's languages impressed Stalin. The perfected mythology of *The Fall of Berlin* literally anchored the film's plot, and the "descent from the heavens" was the scene that transferred the action into "spaces of exultation."[78] Chiaureli had a penchant for such scenes. In *The Vow*, for example, he moved the scene of the vow to Red Square so that "the revelation of the leader to the people" would be especially striking. The ending of *The Fall of Berlin* is of the same order:

> Victory in the Great Patriotic War is indeed considered a real conclusion of the "final battle" that results in the enemy of the human race being cast down, an ideal world order coming to reign, and thus time coming to an end. . . . The real fulfillment of the ideal is possible only after a "final battle," which is why the prewar idyll occupies such a significant place in

the films of both Chiaureli and Pavlenko. Berlin in them is in equal measure the real-world capital of an enemy state and the name of a world of evil. Hitler, in turn, is both the antagonist of Stalin and his comic double, especially fussy and pompous in contrast to the monumental, laconic Supreme Commander. And this comical, tricksterish fussiness, and the Führer's staying exclusively underground, invariably so in the Soviet films of this period, gives rise to an association with the enemy of the human race in the literal sense—that is, with the devil. The ending of *The Fall of Berlin,* famous at the time for its disdain of the historical facts, can be regarded as conceptually irreproachable. The destruction of Hitler in his bunker-lair opens the path to freedom from captivity for prisoners of all nationalities (by the logic of the narrative, the prison camps, too, are situated right there in Berlin). The martyr-peoples are thereby rewarded for their righteousness. Accordingly, at that moment Stalin descends from the sky in snow-white clothing over the welcoming faces and heralds the advent of "peace in all the world."[79]

This is no longer the Stalin of the 1930s films. After the war, the symbolic order that affirmed the foundations of the new legitimacy changed. Pointing out the signs of Stalin's astuteness in postwar films, Bazin asserted that "we are distinctly given to understand that Stalin possesses characteristics that you wouldn't call psychological, but rather ontological: these are omniscience and invulnerability."[80] But the critic did not associate this with the change in the status of the Stalin regime and with the dynamics of the change in the foundations of his legitimacy after the war.

Meanwhile, Stalin promoted the image that had become a new basis of legitimacy: that of the genial commander who had won the war and saved the country and the world. This image not only had nothing to do with reality, but was also itself the product of a new reality that Stalin created and dwelt in, seeing in these films a reflection of *his* ideal picture of the war and *his* view of how it should go down in history (that is, "the truth of history"). At the same time, he drew information about the war from these films. *His* experience and *his* views were actually reflected *truthfully* in them. These films were the main material witnesses of Stalin's genius and of the new "truth of history" that came to replace the experience of the war, an experience that underwent complete de-realization in them. This elemental mass traumatic experience of pain, loss, dispersion, and death that failed to coincide at all with Stalin's experience was displaced, denied any sort of representation whatsoever, with practically no impingement into the public sphere. The real goal of these films was to neutralize and suspend it in a sphere of muteness.

*

On June 25, 1945, Aleksandr Dovzhenko, the author of *Ukraine in Flames,* wrote the following in his diary:

> Yesterday I was at the Victory Parade in Red Square. There were troops and ordinary folk standing in front of a great mausoleum. My beloved field marshal Zhukov read the triumphant and redoubtable Victory speech. When he mentioned those who fell in battles, in enormous numbers unprecedented in history, I took off my hat. It was raining. Glancing around me, I noticed that nobody else took their caps off. There was no pause, or a funeral march, or a silence. One or maybe two phrases were spoken. It was as if the earth had swallowed up thirty, if not forty million victims and heroes, or that they hadn't lived at all; they weren't mentioned. . . . It made me sad, and I was no longer interested in any of it. . . . At the mention of their glorious memory, their shed blood and torture, [the people on] the square did not kneel, did not reflect, did not sigh, did not remove caps. That's probably how it should be. Or maybe not? Else, why did nature weep all day? Why did tears flow from the sky? Were they not giving a sign to the living?[81]

In this world of the living, Dovzhenko found no place for himself. But a country of many millions, not only Dovzhenko, had to come to terms with this new reality, this *for-show war.* The war had been a real, years-long experience for millions. But victory had no history. It was an outcome. The substitution of one with the other—the transformation of the war's history into that of the victory—presupposed a completely new optics. This change of optics was traumatic. After all, if one remembers the war through the prism of the Leningrad blockade or the Holocaust, then it is not so much victory that comes to the foreground as the enormous catastrophic loss of life. A colossal effort was required to adopt a different optics than Dovzhenko's (and, one might add, Lidiia Ginzburg's and that of the authors of the "Black Book").

As Maurice Halbwachs demonstrated, history is opposed to memory as the dead is to the living; history begins when collective memory dies, when it "fades or disintegrates." But Halbwachs linked this process to the fading out of social groups for which past events had been personal experience.[82] The twentieth century proved that historicization can follow right on the heels of events and, regardless of the presence of the bearers of living collective memory (and despite their active participation), can begin to create a parallel reality, distorting both personal and collective memory, forcing these who remembered to adapt to a promoted version of the past, to a historical narrative, if not to be silenced altogether. History no longer waits for its living witnesses to disappear; it bears false witness in their presence. As Stalin would say, it "lies like an eyewitness." History buries memory alive. Due to the influence of official art about the war in post-Soviet Russian society, as Lev Gudkov observed, "the non-victorious, non-state side of war, and all its gravity and human terror, have disappeared into a sort of 'subconscious' of society (the 'blind spot' of its official memory)."[83]

2 From Metaphor to Metonymy

The Political Tropology of Historicism

VISUAL FIGURES OF IDEOLOGICAL SPEECH: PUDOVKIN'S "FRIVOLITY"

While recovering from a heart attack, Sergei Eisenstein heard about the Central Committee's resolution "On the Film *A Great Life,*" the main object of criticism wherein was Leonid Lukov's film about postwar Donbass and which in passing criticized the second part of his own *Ivan the Terrible,* and he reacted with genuine surprise: "What does Lukov have to do with it?"[1] This reaction might seem even stranger given that ten paragraphs of the resolution were devoted to Lukov's film, while there was *one sentence* in it about Eisenstein's. Nonetheless, Eisenstein's reading of the situation was on point and grew out of his deep understanding of both the nature of the Stalinist regime and Stalin's political psychology as a power maniac; the main thing that provoked Stalin's ire was not an inaccurate depiction of the postwar reconstruction in Donbass but rather the second part of *Ivan the Terrible.* So what did Lukov have to do with it?

Stalin's ire arose from the fact that having given Eisenstein such a delicate assignment as to create a film about Ivan the Terrible and thus having embarked on a sort of trusting relationship with him, he had been deceived; the commission was based on a mutual understanding by both sides of the problems facing them. But the supplier had mocked his client. *Ivan the Terrible* was conceived by *both* as a historical allegory, a genre that Soviet historicizing art had begun to churn out at this time. Only here the stakes were incredibly high; it was not a question of an allegory of some specific event (as in the film *Kutuzov*, which was supposed to explain the retreat at the beginning of the war as the strategic brainchild of a great military leader), nor of any specific historic situation (as in *Aleksandr Nevskii*, where the prewar geopolitical realia could be easily discerned), nor of a current political propaganda task (as, for instance, in *Bogdan Khmel'nitskii*, which inflamed anti-Polish hysteria by postulating the brotherhood of Ukrainians and Russians). *Ivan the Terrible* was created as an allegory of Stalin's regime as such— of its validity and, hence, its legitimacy. Stalin's resolution regarding Eisenstein's screenplay on September 13, 1943, "Ivan the Terrible, as a progressive force of his time, and the *oprichnina* as his efficient instrument, did not come off badly," should be interpreted not so much as the leader's gesture of approval (as it usually is read) but as a dictum; in two explanatory constructions Stalin formulated the concept of the film and, hence, the concept of his regime. Accordingly, it was no accident that this resolution was granted the status of state importance: Ivan Bol'shakov included it in a special album of the records of Stalin's decisions.[2]

Thus, the first part of the film, which circulated widely in the country's cinemas, could not be interpreted as anything but an apologia for Stalin's dictatorship. The client was still satisfied, and on January 26, 1946, Eisenstein was awarded the Stalin Prize, First Class. But a week later, on February 2, a few hours after finishing the montage of the second part of the film, the director was hospitalized with a massive heart attack. It is not hard to imagine what caused it; having transformed Ivan's "progressive" dictatorship, its "efficient instrument" and "great Russian tsardom," in which the triumph of Stalin's great power and the brilliance of the great Stalinist project were supposed to be discerned, into a true witches' coven of the forces of infernal evil that took possession of a tsar sinking into paranoia, Eisenstein had every reason to expect a most unpredictable reaction from Stalin.

This reaction ensued without delay. Real fury is plain in the resolution of the Party Central Committee Secretariat of March 5, 1946, dictated by Stalin and short as a shot, consisting of two points: "1. Declare that the second part of the film *Ivan the Terrible* (Eisenstein's production) does not stand up under scrutiny, in view of its anti-historicism and anti-artistic nature. 2. Prohibit the release of the film to the public."[3] Right after viewing the film, Stalin blurted out to Bol'shakov: "It's not a film but some kind of nightmare! During the war, we kept our hands off, but now we'll get at all of you." Filmmaker Grigorii Aleksandrov asked Stalin "as a person attentive to people and their misfortunes . . . not to make a final decision about the film until its author is finally well."[4] But Stalin made good on his threat: from March to August of 1946, the short resolution mushroomed with more and more claims about more and more films until it spilled out into the resolution "On the Film *A Great Life*," with its criticism of Eisenstein reduced to the one remaining sentence.

To submit a film like *Ivan the Terrible* to Stalin's scrutiny was a suicidal step. But as a radical artist, Eisenstein essentially played the role in life that he depicted on the screen. In his precisely titled essay "A Double 'Mousetrap,' or Suicide by Film," film director Vladislav Tsukerman pointed out that the whole plot of *Ivan the Terrible* is constructed on a chain of trap scenes. "Time and again, the characters set traps for each other or fall into their own traps or someone else's." Two of these scenes, "The Fiery Furnace" and "The Feast of the Oprichniks," are not only constructed around theatrical representation, but also comprise in terms of time over half of the second part, and almost all the other scenes are linked to these two.[5] But the scenes in the first part of the film are of the same type of theatrical representation—those of the coronation, at Anastasiia's tomb, and in the Alexandrov village. The first is purely ceremonial, transforming all those present into spectators; the second, a discussion of a trap; and the third, the filming itself of a trap. These are key scenes, on the conceptual level, of the transformation of the tsar into a leader.[6]

Now Stalin, who had approved the screenplay, found himself in a psychological trap. Availing himself of the status of most official Soviet film director (just then confirmed by the Stalin Prize, First Class), Eisenstein ultimately decided to lay bare the device of the allegory, forcing Stalin to publicly acknowledge himself as the Ivan of not only the first part, but also of the second. What happened next is well known: "The second part was ordered destroyed, and with it the screen life of the first part was also cut short. The complete and decisive catastrophe was official, businesslike. And—the moment of supreme creative triumph, the complete and decisive moral victory of the artist: one of the 'proto-types' recognized himself in the type and could not stand this spectacle, went to pieces, buckled, gave himself away, publicly acknowledged, and in an oblique form, the truthfulness of the portrait and was frightened of the power of its influence."[7]

The allegory exploded into the face of the one who had commissioned it. The scandal from the second part of *Ivan the Terrible* signified a demonstrative rejection of metaphor. The era of metonymy was setting in.

After the war, films about historical figures and military leaders continued to be made and planned for release. However, figures from Russian science and art now dominated in historical films. Military leaders and state figures, which had filled the screen on the eve of and during the war, receded to the background. Only two such films were made after the war, and they were about naval commanders. One of them, *Admiral Nakhimov* (1945–46) opened the late-Stalinist era, and the other, Mikhail Romm's *Admiral Ushakov* (1953), brought it to its close. These films were called "historico-biographical," but this designation was internally contradictory. Historical films were of course also biographical, just as biographical ones were historical. But the difference between them is not so much plot-related as structural, and the main thing is the functional difference. The difference between Pudovkin's film about the military leaders Minin and Pozharskii (1939) and the one about the "father of Russian aviation" Zhukovskii (1950) lay not so much in the professions of their heroes (political figures and military commanders in the "historical films" predominantly of prewar cinema; figures from science and art in the postwar "biographical" films). The difference was the result of a change in the genre structure underlying them, which itself was a consequence of a change of functions: a transition from metaphorical structures to metonymic ones arose from the fact that a film had to become less a history textbook that illustrated through allegory and more a current political document.

Historical films of the 1930s were allusions; one was supposed to discern the similarity in the historical persons to present-day heroes and villains, to see similar historical situations. A biographical film was not a metaphor. The function of the Russian "discoverer of radio," Popov, or of "the father of aerodynamics," Zhukovskii, in their eponymous films cannot be reduced simply to their being similar to someone.

Their function was to *produce* a Russian birthright and primacy in the history of science, to *testify* to them. Thus the film *Aleksandr Popov* (1949) becomes an "artistic *document*," a "factual *testimony*," and "substantial *proof*" that a Russian scientist invented the radio. This is not a metaphor but rather a historico-scientific metamorphosis. Furthermore, there is a step outside the boundaries of poetic tropology here and, essentially, beyond the boundaries of art as such. And at the heart of this metamorphosis lies not a metaphor at all but a synecdoche. The birthright of Russia in the invention of the radio, after all, is also merely a part instead of the whole: of the primacy of Russia in practically everything. And, more broadly, the primogeniture of Russia as such.

It is telling that the "Zhdanov era" began with cinema. Indeed, it was at a Central Committee conference about cinema issues, on April 26, 1946, that Zhdanov proclaimed the five-year plan that had begun after the war an "ideological" one.[8] Nor was it coincidental that the issue of history, essentially, was at the center of the discussion regarding cinema. As we have seen, the reworking of the past, the transformation of lived experience into historical narrative, had become a vital concern of the regime. A new base of legitimacy was supposed to be forged in this process, and in it the ultimate shaping of the new Soviet nation took place. Whether the experience of war would become the experience of victory depended on how convincing the newly written history would be. The forging of experience into history required a rejection of earlier aesthetic conventions. And this is where we encounter one of the key principles of Socialist Realism: the principle of historicism.

To be fit for current political needs, historicism had to become part of Soviet aesthetic doctrine, part of the system of flexible, dialectically contradirectional principles of Socialist Realism, and to become a hybrid of "the truth of life" and "revolutionary romanticism": "The historicism of Leninist teaching is a scientific conceptualization of actual historical reality based on a correlation of man with history. Reality is regarded as a logical continuation of the historical process in its constant development and rush into the future, from whose positions the leading tendencies of the present time are determined and evaluated."[9] This formula, by the familiar dialectic of Socialist Realism, is also true in a backward reading; if "the leading tendencies of the present time" are determined and evaluated from the viewpoint of history, then the past, too, should be determined and defined from the viewpoint of "the leading tendencies of the present time," quite definitely: "Socialist historicism is the artistic conception of life from the standpoint of the Communist ideal, the determination of the leading tendencies of an era that facilitates a vivid reproduction of life in its historical perspective and historical retrospection, which bring the writer to create an image of the time and the typical hero of the era."[10] In brief, historicism is an image of the past as those in power would like to see it here and now.

Here we are dealing with a new redaction of Mikhail Pokrovskii's formula: history is politics toppled into the past. We would not err, then, if we said that politics is history toppled into the present. And since politics was Stalin's exclusive prerogative, the content of historicism was also determined by him, every time. According to official doctrine, Socialist Realist historicism constitutes "a profound understanding of the rational connection of the phenomena, process, and perspectives of social development from the standpoint of scientific socialism. Knowledge of the logic of history elevates the artist to the level of genuine artistic freedom—freedom from prejudices and delusions. Seeing the world in its real logic means acknowledging oneself as a force capable of judging truthfully about this world and influencing the process of improving it."[11] This means truly divine knowledge, and only Stalin could possess such historicism.

Although the production of historic films was an exemplary Soviet enterprise for the making of politico-historical allegory-metaphors, it remained a typical product of Stalin's megalomania. Having completely given himself over in the 1930s and 1940s to historical cinematography, Vsevolod Pudovkin stated in 1945 that the flowering of the Soviet historical film was essentially the main accomplishment with which Soviet cinematic art had arrived at victory. This was a result of the fact that, as Pudovkin put it, "the course of development of national consciousness has elevated these themes as being the main, most interesting ones."[12] And in fact, these films, made in a relatively short period of time— Eisenstein's *Aleksandr Nevskii* (1938) and *Ivan the Terrible* (1944–46); Pudovkin's *Minin and Pozharskii* (1939) and *Suvorov* (1941); Vladimir Petrov's *Peter the First* (1938) and *Kutuzov* (1943); Mikhail Chiaureli's *Georgii Saakadze* (1942–43) in Georgia; Amo Bek-Nazarov's *David-Bek* (1943) in Armenia; and Igor Savchenko's *Bogdan Khmel'nitskii* (1941) in Ukraine—were each, individually and together, collectively, significant phenomena in Soviet cinema (and in Eisenstein's case, in world cinema). However, Pudovkin would go on to an idea atypical of an artist:

> We hope that in time historical films will not be shown only in cinemas. They constitute a systematic course that we could show in schools.
>
> Our dream is to make films such that they are not put in an archive after the picture has had success and its run on the screens, but are put in a film library, just like they put a history course or a historical novel on the shelves one volume after another, so that afterward, over long periods of time, their success and significance is not used up but, on the contrary, is increased.
>
> I think the tighter the link between films is, the sooner and easier this will happen. *Aleksandr Nevskii* or *Ivan the Terrible* will be even more valuable when new films appear on the screen that will let them be made the first series of a "History of Our People" multiserial film.[13]

Film here loses the status of art as it is transformed into an endless historical serial and, essentially, a thematized ideology, since this written and filmed history is supposed to not only replace the old one, but also to fill all the space of the constructed past to its limit. The idea of totally appropriating this space and swallowing up any enclaves of autonomy through the production of a prosthetic, screen-created (in the outright sense and in the abstract) memory became the radical extension of the 1930s historicizing project. This idea of total history took hold of everyone—from the main film bureaucrat Bol'shakov to the classic filmmaker Pudovkin.

But right after the Central Committee's resolution criticizing Pudovkin's and Eisenstein's historical films, Bol'shakov spoke out against too much engagement with historical themes in particular in the national studios: "The overweening obsession of the national film studios with showing the life of the past and not showing the contemporary life of our people has been reflected very harmfully in the conditions of national cinema. The Soviet people want to see not how the tsars or the Huns lived but rather the contemporary life of their republics; they want to see what Soviet power has given the peoples of these republics and how their culture and economy have grown."[14] Suddenly, what had been encouraged in 1945 became unacceptable in 1946. The reason for this volte-face was that the optics had changed, completely transforming the historical film.

Stalin personally managed the historical film industry; he not only drew up the lists of characters for future films, but also personally determined the directors that would make them; he familiarized himself with the screenplays, approved the principal actors, and received the finished products. As the well-informed Konstantin Simonov recalled, Stalin "programmed nothing as logically and systematically as future films, and this program was tied to current political aims, although the films that he programmed were almost always, if not always, historical ones. . . . This can be traced by the figures that he promoted for films: Aleksandr Nevskii, Suvorov, Kutuzov, Ushakov, Nakhimov. It is nonetheless telling that at the height of the war, when the Suvorov, Kutuzov, Ushakov, and Nakhimov medals were established as commanders' medals, it wasn't those who stuck most in the people's memory—Kutuzov and Nakhimov—that were put in first place, but rather those who led the war and won brilliant victories at the frontiers of Russia and beyond them."[15]

Shaping national identity through the transformation of history into an onscreen image that was constantly adapted to current political needs is doubtless one of the most effective components of Stalin's politico-aesthetic project. The "historico-biographical film" reaches its apogee in 1952, when a decision was made to *again* produce films about the great figures of the past that had already acquired an "onscreen life" in the films of the most eminent Soviet directors and screenwriters. *Iskusstvo kino* published in its January 1953 issue Bol'shakov's article "Tasks for the New Year," which announced that new color films would be produced in 1953 about Ivan the Terrible, Aleksandr Nevskii, Peter I, and Kutuzov. This decision was motivated by the fact that the films made about them had been released many years prior. On the one hand, the successes of Soviet historical science now allowed for a fuller and more vivid "illumination" of the country's history, the life of the great commanders and figures of state. On the other, cinema had meanwhile been enriched by color. Accordingly, Bol'shakov promised, work would be undertaken in 1953 also on films about Dmitrii Donskoi, Tchaikovsky, the artist Kramskoi, the Albanian national hero Skanderbeg, and the liberation of Bulgaria from the Turkish yoke. Not a single film was planned about the history of the revolution, and even contemporary themes had a secondary place in the thematic plan. The very idea of "re-shooting" films already made, so it seems, bespeaks the realization of Pudovkin's idea of a "textbook of history"; film here is transformed into a visualization of a historical narrative. This was also tied to the transformation of the genre itself. To understand what happened with Soviet historical film (and historicizing Soviet art as a whole) we must examine the concept of the "historico-biographical film" itself more closely.

For this we should start with the peculiarities of Stalin's mode of self-representation. Stalin not only distinguished the personal from the political in public representation, but also logically constructed his own image on a complete compartmentalization of these two spheres. Thus thinking and talking about himself in the third person became not only a grammatical habit, but also a peculiarity of his thinking. Konstantin Simonov, who had met Stalin more than once, wrote a striking passage in his novel *They Are Not Born Soldiers:* "For years he had that set expression, carefully developed, that in the presence of these people should be on the face of 'Comrade Stalin,' as he had long since called himself in his mind, and sometimes out loud as well, in the third person."[16]

This duality was a deliberate representational strategy of Stalin-as-politician that allowed him to depersonalize his own decisions. The Stalin speaking in the third person was necessary to mask the first-person Stalin who was in fact that very power that through the exposition of his own word and his own history and of the production of his own image imposed his will. The reduction of the "historical person" to a "human person" was from this perspective a laying bare of the device, an encroachment on the very nature of power, putting its legitimacy in doubt. This became totally unacceptable after the war, when the image of the "loyal pupil of Lenin" that Stalin had himself created in the '20s and '30s became too narrow for him, when he required a new basis for a legitimacy that would not need any ideological and historical supporting allusions. He no longer needed an *other* Other in the form of Lenin or "Marxism-Leninism." Only the third person remained. Aimed at its defense was the Central Committee's resolution about Pudovkin's film *Admiral Nakhimov*, which stated that Pudovkin had "frivolously" and "irresponsibly" dispensed with the historical facts and without the necessary seriousness had shot a film with balls and dances about the personal life of the admiral instead of depicting historical events.

Stalin's displeasure with *Nakhimov* had been programmed back in 1940. Pudovkin was told that Stalin said, after seeing *Suvorov,* "They've made a good film about Aleksandr Vasil'evich Suvorov, and now they ought to make a film about Suvorov the military leader."[17] What in 1940 sounded like a good-natured joke (*Suvorov* would be awarded the Stalin Prize, First Class, in 1941) in 1946 had grown into a strict political demand, and the cardinal defect of *Admiral Nakhimov* was pointed out unambiguously: "The baseless attempt to define a hero in trivial and invented episodes instead of important historical events is a distortion of historical truth and of the heroic image of Nakhimov."[18] Although the director was above all interested in personality and psychology, no exploration whatsoever of the personality or psychology of the historic personage was now permitted (and such an exploration was exactly what Eisenstein was accused of with respect to the second part of *Ivan the Terrible*). Echoing the resolution, critics pointed out that "achieving a biographical image of a remarkable person is possible only by using the basic facts that comprise his biography, operating boldly with significant historical events, and not detouring into trivial quests for amusing and original little episodes."[19]

The internal contradiction of the "historico-biographical" genre in the case of *Admiral Nakhimov* reached its limit. This contradiction can be formulated as an opposition: history against biography. What was demanded of Pudovkin was realized in an extreme form in an "artistic-documentary film" about the war in which Stalin, whose biography could in fact be nothing but history itself, was emptied of any individuality whatsoever as a historical person and became history personified.

The situation with Nakhimov is interesting for its quest for a balance between the personal and the public. The screenplay adopted for the production, by Igor' Lukovskii, focused on biography and above all imagined Nakhimov as a person. Pudovkin fully realized this when, speaking two years before the resolution (February 4, 1944) at a discussion of the screenplay by Mosfilm's Artistic Council, he talked about the kind of Nakhimov he was creating with Lukovskii's work: "Personally, Comrade Lukovskii and I are convinced that the screenplay now accentuates the human aspect of Nakhimov. The character of Nakhimov has come alive, but it is basically achieved in his interactions with all kinds of people in his purely everyday life."[20] What is more, neither Pudovkin nor his colleagues saw anything wrong with this. Speaking about the screenplay at the Plenum of the Writers' Union

(February 5–8, 1944), Ivan Astakhov said, "The biggest success is that by the direction the studio chose in its work and indeed is striving for to reveal the character most fully and profoundly, not superficially, as was earlier thought best for description of purely anecdotal situations, they have successfully created a living image of our naval commander Pavel Stepanovich Nakhimov, who plays the part of the main hero in the screenplay."[21]

During the discussion of the film on the eve of its release on February 13, 1946, colleagues in the Artistic Council of the Committee on Cinematography took rather different views of the film. Some (Boris Babochkin and Nikolai Okhlopkov) spoke of "an extraordinarily important work of cinematographic art" and "a most important work of a great director." Others, however, saw quite a number of flaws in the film. Sergei Gerasimov, for example, although noting that "the master Pudovkin" was evident in it and that it was "significant, memorable, stirring, and passionate," stated that Nakhimov "was shown in monotone by the director. Just as he stood like a medallion at the very beginning, he moves medallion-like throughout the film."[22] Ivan Pyr'ev, on the contrary, declared that he was not shown "who Nakhimov was, what kind of man he was, what kind of relationships this person had with the seamen, sailors, and ordinary people around him, and how he educated and taught these sailors, and why he was so beloved that people could give their own lives just for his sake. What kind of secrets were held by this admiral who has become immortal and in whose honor a medal bearing his name was created during the Patriotic War? This did not come across. It is a vacuous screenplay, and it amazes me that this could happen, that a screenplay could survive in such a form all the way to filming without being critiqued." Representing the editorial board of *Pravda*, Major General Mikhail Galaktionov likewise stated that "the greatness of the events and of the person depicted in it did not come across."[23] And another member of the Artistic Council, Major General Nikolai Talenskii, formulated his accusations in roughly the same way that Stalin would formulate his after seeing the film: "It is not enough to show a good admiral. One ought to show his historical significance for Russia, for the Russian fleet, in its full breadth. And one can raise accusations against the film above all from this viewpoint. Russia is absent from the film. The whole historical epic of Sevastopol and the historical events connected to all this are taken in isolation, on their own, which diminishes the historical-cognitive and educational significance of Nakhimov's feat."[24]

The screenplay raised serious doubts from the very beginning. The verdict pronounced on Lukovskii's work on February 2, 1944, by Sergei Sergeev-Tsenskii, author of the epic novel about the 1854–55 defense of Sevastopol, *The Ordeal of Sevastopol,* contained a complete eight-page hammering of the screenwriter's work, from indications of gaffes in everyday detail and historical inaccuracies to accusations of banality and melodrama. In concluding, Sergeev-Tsenskii wrote: "Is this how one ought to regard the task of reproducing the image of Nakhimov onscreen for millions of Soviet people, the way this screenwriter did? I must say with all resolve that this task was carried out in slipshod fashion and even disgracefully slipshod. I would be committing a crime if I approved this concoction and said it could be filmed."[25] Central Committee Secretary Aleksandr Shcherbakov's resolution to Bol'shakov asserted that "You must consider the series of criticisms that I told you about on the phone."[26] This referred to the very criticisms that Stalin had formulated after seeing the film—about the necessity of showing the Russians' victory in the Battle of Sinop "when a whole group of Turkish admirals were taken prisoner, along with their commander"— and had immediately conveyed to Pudovkin. A few months later, these criticisms were formulated in a closed resolution of the Central Committee Secretariat that was hammered out in April 1946 and adopted on May 11.[27] By the time the film was criticized in the open Central Committee resolution about the film *A Great Life,* in September 1946, Pudovkin had practically finished his reworking of the film.

Be that as it may, the attitude of both the Ministry of Cinematography and the Central Committee to this work was completely sympathetic. This was certainly the case at a Central Committee conference on cinema issues held April 26, 1946, where the 1946 thematic production plan for art films was discussed. In attendance were Central Committee Secretary Andrei Zhdanov, Agitprop head Georgii Aleksandrov, Minister of Cinematography Ivan Bol'shakov, and filmmakers Grigorii Aleksandrov, Amo Bek-Nazarov, Ivan Pyr'ev, Sergei Gerasimov, Iulii Raizman, Aleksandr Ptushko, and Mikhail Romm, among others (forty people in all had been invited). Here Zhdanov declared: "We heartily welcome the *Nakhimov* film. . . . This will be one of the best films, and for it to be our *Lady Hamilton,* it would be best to refine it so that it becomes a masterpiece. *Admiral Nakhimov* has the possibility of the kind of finish that would enable the film to stand at the level of the classic works of Soviet cinematic art."[28] It was no accident that the new version of the picture was awarded the Stalin Prize, First Class, the following year.

Thus it is beyond doubt that the criticism of *Admiral Nakhimov* in the resolution regarding *A Great Life* was included in order to refocus the criticism of Eisenstein's film, as if his *Ivan the Terrible* was the result of the same "ignorance"—not of a deliberate sabotage of Stalin's clearly expressed will and not of a subversive strategy of the director aimed at shattering existing historical allusions, but an "ignorance of the facts" and "unscrupulousness." Thus the criticism of *Ivan the Terrible* followed that of *Admiral Nakhimov* as a continuation of the condemnation of those same "major faults." And had Eisenstein not spent these months in 1946 recovering from a heart attack in the hospital, he would not have asked, "What does Lukov have to do with it?" but "What does Pudovkin have to do with it?"

THE END OF THE ALLEGORY: EISENSTEIN'S TRAP

Stalin and Eisenstein had one thing in common: for both, allusion remained the main artistic-political trope, a code, based on a metaphor, for encoding and decoding a subtext. Eisenstein spent his entire creative life producing such metaphor-allusions, frequently multileveled and extraordinarily complex ones, and he had few equals in this in world cinema. Likewise, Stalin had few equals among politicians who were so immersed in the paranoid decoding of subtexts and hidden intrigues of open and secret enemies.

Ivan the Terrible, like *Aleksandr Nevskii* before it and like essentially all the historical films of the time, was a film/allusion. It stood out from the flood of historical films because the allusion was too politically mired and directed at the most sensitive aspects of the regime, having basically become an analysis of the nature of Stalinism. Any change of the accents transformed the allusion into a challenge. Eisenstein's film is a sort of screen adaptation of Machiavellian fantasies projected onto sixteenth-century Russian history and simultaneously of Stalinist terror. As Bernd Uhlenbruch observed, "After the victory over Hitler, it was historically proven that Stalin had succeeded in completing

Groznyi's work. Instead of now creating a historical parable of the apotheosis of Stalin, Eisenstein filmed, in part two, a cryptogram of the internal state of the Party in the 1930s and 1940s."[29] Meanwhile, the status of the central character was such that it could no longer be read as anything but an allusion. As Maureen Perrie stated, Ivan the Terrible "had become [so] identified with Stalin by the late 1940s . . . that criticisms of [Ivan], however mild, might be read as an allegorical attack on the Soviet leader."[30]

In February 1946, writer Leonid Sobolev summarized the task facing the director very accurately: "We must somehow bring our people closer to understanding Ivan the Terrible and loving him, because this historical character did much good for the state. . . . We must love the *oprichnina* because people in the name of great progressive good did very good things."[31] Eisenstein understood his task in a similarly allegorical way; accordingly, he set himself the goal of dehistoricizing the main character (as Pushkin had done in *Boris Godunov*) in order to elevate the subject above everyday historical reality and political exigencies to the level of "the tragedy of power." Nonetheless, the allegorism of Soviet historical films was the product of a very complex balance between plot narrative and visual image; it could not tolerate too strong a historicization (since it must leave space for historical allusions), but it also could not endure de-historicization (since "generalization" through symbolization too strongly obscures the aspects of "historical reality" that must not be articulated; even interpreting these aspects becomes an act of dangerous dissidence).

Eisenstein intentionally used this internal logic of historical analogy in order to discredit the Stalinist conception of power. He rotated allusion's binoculars such that it was not figures from the past that came to the foreground but rather present-day people wardrobed into historical costumes. Iosif Iuzovskii related his conversation with Eisenstein, in which the latter conveyed what Zhdanov had told him about Ivan the Terrible:

> "History is a lesson, and the people must comprehend this lesson. Whoever doesn't understand will understand. Allusion, or analogy, is the film's goal, so that everyone can be recognized," Eisenstein summarized. "Everyone everywhere must be recognized, [so] I will not be wandering into remote antiquity to drag some character or another out of it; on the contrary, I will take on contemporaries and will be dragging them

into remote antiquity. After all, they told me analogy, and you know, it's an entertaining task for an artist; I think—analogy, analogy; I walk around—analogy, analogy; I look around—analogy, analogy. All my acquaintances and all the faces I know, the faces everyone knows, are transformed in my imagination; their clothes, gait, and movements are changed, even their exterior is modified or altered accordingly, but they themselves remain as they are."[32]

An exhaustive interpretational model for reading Eisenstein's film was provided by the classic writer of Soviet drama, Vsevolod Vishnevskii, in a comprehensive review in *Pravda* on the occasion of the film's being awarded the Stalin Prize, First Class.[33] The film itself was of course "an immense, talented, and gladdening contribution to the cause of learning about Ivan's era and Ivan himself," and "through powerful, vivid artistic means the film in a historically correct way reveals the content of the era, the image of Ivan the Terrible as a progressive figure of his time." The boyars were reactionaries and traitors, tearing the country apart into separate principalities and prepared to betray it. Hence

Ivan's passionate and terrible fight against the state's internal ulcer—against the boyars' opposition. They pass before our eyes—these representatives of 200 well-born, titled families—scions of appanage princes, these rebels who again wanted to tear the state into little pieces, into appanages and estates, to weaken it. Here they are—haughty, arrogant, greedy—ready at any moment to betray their motherland to satisfy their own selfish interests. . . . They don't move a muscle when Tsar Ivan, ill, standing at death's door, and melancholy about the fate of his motherland, begs them to understand the interests of a common, united Russia. They turn away, stay silent or hiss spitefully, cooking up plots, [these] two-faced traitors, writers of "petitions" and letters to German and Polish-Lithuanian princes and *pans*. And our viewer comes to understand why Ivan hacked off the heads of these reactionaries and destroyers of Russia and where the flood of slanderous accusations against him came from and why it was so torrential. . . . Ivan wages a relentless war against the greedy and insidious boyar world that tries to crush the tsar with its tight circle and make him submit to the old order and to the feudal boyars. Ivan the Terrible threw ideas in the face of this whole camp about a unified, centralized tsarist regime to which all must submit in the name of higher interests.

All of this arises from the fact that "Ivan lived a lofty idea of the state." The "positive heroes" of the film are a reflection of these "lofty ideas"—"simple people, 'zemstvo' people, rank-and-file newly titled gentryfolk—Basmanov and his son, Maliuta Skuratov and others who serve Ivan's cause devotedly and tirelessly. It was from the people of just these strata that Ivan created the *oprichnina* and the reliable command cadres of the army. It was in the name of the state cause of great Rus' that Ivan implemented a number of reforms." Thus "the film reveals the very methods by which Ivan consolidated the new social bases."

World War II moves to a victorious apotheosis, and therefore Eisenstein's film is a direct projection of the victories of Soviet arms since, as Vishnevskii says, the army created by Ivan is

> an authentic, well-armed and sizeable army with the best artillery in Europe, an army that with just a few attacks routed the entire khanate of Volga, took Kazan and Astrakhan, impelled the states of the Caucasus to establish relations with Moscow, subordinated with its advance on the Urals the Siberian khan Ediger, and forced Europe to sharply change its assessment of Russia. The viewer will see our stern warriors and will see our silent gunners at the enormous Russian cannons and will understand why the Europeans held Russian might in high esteem and thought that Ivan could raise the most sizeable army in the world.

It is hard not to recognize this army as the prefiguration of the conquering army in World War II, just as it is impossible not to see a projection in the film of the new geopolitical realia of postwar Europe. After all, "on the Baltic coast Russians stood together with Estonians and Latvians even before the emergence of the Livonian Order (thirteenth century). The fortifications of the Polotskian princes on the Western Dvina and the shores of the Gulf of Riga and further south (Koknese and others) were long-standing Russian frontier fortifications from ages ago." How could one not recognize the genius-strategist Stalin in how "Ivan anticipated with genius the enemies' intentions, and by a northern route across Arkhangelsk established friendly ties with England, which were followed by ties with Holland as well, consolidated a century and a half later by Peter I"?

Ivan the Terrible is, besides a historical allusion to the internecine party struggle in the Great Terror era, a sort of screen adaptation of the *Short Course,* and thus "ominous shadows fall on the walls of the Kremlin's front rooms and passages. The conspirators get further and further inside." The personal dimension emerges here as well: "Ivan's wife, the tsarina Anastasiia Romanovna, becomes a tragic victim. She had learned by chance about Kurbskii's ambitious plans but had kept quiet, had hidden the truth from her husband, and fell victim to those same confederates of Kurbskii." This recalls Stalin's wife, Nadezhda Allilueva, who had committed suicide, a "betrayal" that Stalin could not forgive. And so "grief, terrible grief befalls Ivan. Heavy doubts weigh down and suffocate his soul, which is lonely and suffering agonizingly. His old friends are gone. . . . And then, at the minute it seems everything will go dark, the soldiers and state guards stand together with the lonely Ivan." One need only compare these passages with how Svetlana Allilueva described Stalin's sufferings after his wife's suicide to see how transparent the allusions in these scenes are.[34] How strong these profoundly intimate parallels are was attested to by Vishnevskii's style, permeated with an uncharacteristic eroticism: "New forces surged from the depths of Ivan's great soul. We see how the tsar's impetuous energy abates. . . . We are present for the birth of his new, grandiose projects and his unexpected moves, far-sighted and purposeful."

This whole theater of allusions encoded into the first part of the film was demonstratively demolished by Eisenstein in the second part. Nonetheless, the fundamental thing that turned the events surrounding *Ivan the Terrible* into a political scandal was, as one might imagine, not so much the dissident "dragging out" of all sorts of unexpected allusions as it was the creation of a situation in which one had to say things that should not be said in order to put the criticism into words. Eisenstein pushed the boundaries of the "analogies" and historical boundaries that had been ordered such that they not only produced an effect opposite to the one expected, but also created a situation in which viewers found themselves obliged to fill in what had been left unsaid. In other words, allusion became fatal. One must not read *this kind* of Ivan as an allusion.

Iuzovskii related how Eisenstein exulted when he told him that he saw a hint of *Boris Godunov* in the film:

God, is this really obvious? What luck, what luck! Of course, Boris Godunov: "It's already my sixth year ruling in peace, but there is no happiness in my soul." I couldn't make a film like this without Russian tradition, without the great Russian tradition, the tradition of conscience. One can explain violence, can make it law, can rationalize it, but one must not justify it; you must have expiation, if you're human. . . . So that's it—the motif of expiation, and not of doubt; not Hamlet—the

European tradition—but Boris Godunov—the Russian one. But I imagine how J.V. [i.e., Stalin] bristled. How? He embodies the triumphant victory over the conquered enemy, but I force him to reckon with this in that "there is no happiness in my soul"; yes, no happiness, exultation, or strength. I understand his anger from this dissatisfied hint, this rebuke. . . . He was offended that they suspected him of weakness, but this isn't weakness.[35]

Eisenstein, of course, was dissembling; he understood that these innocent hints were by no means what caused "J. V." to be "offended." One need only read the works of Stalin as polemicist (against the Mensheviks before the revolution or the opposition in the 1920s or his angry speeches at the murderous Central Committee plenums in the latter 1930s) to be convinced of his rare ability to detect the most improbable political "distortions" and "mistakes" in his opponents, his capacity for the most recherché casuistry, and his inclination toward the most warped suspicions. No, Stalin was not "offended." He simply read the analogies embedded in the film quite accurately—those that his contemporaries were afraid to acknowledge. In his diaries Vishnevskii records a conversation with Aleksandr Dovzhenko about the second series of *Ivan the Terrible*. Dovzhenko says, "Some hints, parallels with the present time. . . . It's odd, Vsevolod. . . . Either Eisenstein is naïve or . . . I don't know. But a film like this, with this kind of Russia and Kremlin, would be an incredible provocation against us. And that concluding monologue about the right of tsars to amorality. . . . Ivan speaks into the lens. . . . From the author. . . . Something's not right here."[36]

This fear of the need to articulate what both the interlocutors of course understood (and what they understood, no doubt both Eisenstein and Stalin also understood) was in fact the fundamental blast effect produced by the film. Eisenstein did everything he could so that his own attitude to the tsar and the boyars' opposition stayed ambiguous and indistinct. As Uhlenbruch observes, "Eisenstein's films and his self-criticism are excellent examples of subversion. In the film itself, it is the refusal of a second interpretation, the questioning of motives by which the viewers and censors are irritated."[37] Sergei Gerasimov articulated this issue more harshly than anyone else during the discussion of the film at the Artistic Council: "And who is Ivan? A clinical petty tyrant, a sick man hungry for blood, or a statesman struggling to free Russia from the boyars' heresy and elevate it to high levels of statesmanship. There is still a serious doubt as to whether this film is about what we all expected."[38]

In the course of the campaign against the second part of the film, it became necessary to articulate these serious issues most assertively. Eisenstein's colleagues had to admit in the closed discussions that he had created not the historical legitimization of Stalinism that had been ordered and consequently was expected but instead a "tragedy of power." In this all the critics were forced to construct their debate with Eisenstein according to the principle of demonstrating the disconnect between what he *supposedly* was striving to depict (the progressiveness of the tsar and the *oprichnina* and the like) and how the film "came across" in his treatment ("because of naïveté" or "unintentionally," as his well-wishers stated, or "because of ignorance," as the Central Committee resolution declared). Nonetheless, it is clear that the film "came across" as precisely what a director who suffered from neither naïveté nor inexperience wanted.

The rhetoric for condemning the film under these conditions could not be constructed in any way but by contrasting "what was supposed to be" to "what came out." The result was that precisely the historical reality that official myth assiduously strove to conceal was the one that was laid bare. This happened not only behind the scenes, but also publicly. Critic Rostislav Iurenev wrote the following:

> They tried to convince us that Ivan's politics were progressive, but there are no politics in the film, unless you consider the palace intrigues to be that. They tried to convince us that the fight against the boyars was of a social and political nature, but the explanation of this hatred and this struggle was given in a psycho-physiological way; Ivan's childhood is depicted, when he, a pale, sickly, and nervous boy, as if he had just descended from an icon, was frightened and tortured by the brutish boyars, planting cruelty and eternal hatred for themselves in his heart. They tried to convince us that Ivan's state apparatus was progressive, but they showed the oprichniks raving in masks, drunk, bawling songs about murders, about blood, giving themselves airs in red monks' garments, then in black ones. Finally, they tried to convince us that all of Ivan's thoughts and feelings were focused on the people. But what do the great Russian people have in common with the horrible and wretched psychopath that Ivan was portrayed as in the second part of the film?[39]

The first part of Iurenev's construct ("they tried to convince us that") sounds equivocal, as if to say that someone—not Eisenstein—tried to convince them of Ivan's positive aspects, while the film showed something completely different. It would be hard to come up with anything more destructive to an apologetic mythology based on the removal of all sorts of contradictions in the image of Ivan the Terrible than this very contrasting construction at the very same moment that the apologetic plays of Aleksei Tolstoi and Vladimir Solov'ev were being performed in the country's most prestigious theaters (including MKhAT, the Malyi, the Vakhtangov, the Leningrad theaters, and many provincial ones), when the historians' books (those of Robert Vipper, Ivan Smirnov, and Sergei Bakhrushin) with apologias for Ivan were being issued in multi-thousand printings, as well as apologias in articles in the central newspapers and in literary works from Valentin Kostylev's three-volume novel to Il'ia Sel'vinskii's "poetic tragedy."[40]

The first to be caught in the trap set by Eisenstein was not, however, Stalin but rather the Artistic Council of the Ministry of Cinematography, where the film was being discussed. The first part of the film, which as everyone knew Stalin had ordered for Eisenstein to make and had just been awarded the Stalin Prize, First Class, furnished the optics for the appraisal of the second part, and "since no one any longer doubted that the first part was a story about both Stalin and his dictatorship, to claim that the second one was about something else was simply impossible."[41] Hence, even having understood the intention of the second part, Eisenstein's colleagues found themselves in an extremely dangerous situation: "Could they really even put this into words out loud, not to mention openly discuss it, accept it, or repudiate it? In any case this meant risking Eisenstein's life, fatally, and putting themselves into the extremely dangerous position of unwilling witnesses to an audacious blasphemy that was unacceptable even in thought, even in the subconscious. Only one thing remained for those who did speak—to compare the execution with the order and to do this harshly or gently; this was the choice for each. And let us grant them their due: they expressed their rebukes rather guardedly."[42]

Eisenstein's subversive strategy was based on intentional ambiguity and the obvious disconnect between the assignment and the execution of it. One of the most officious Soviet writers, Leonid Sobolev, during the discussion of the second part could not help suspecting Eisenstein of intentional deviation from Stalin's order: "Although Ivan swears that he does everything in the name of the people, in the name of the future, in the name of reaching the Baltic, I see something else: that this man keeps himself on the throne and wants to hack his enemies through. . . . When Basmanov says, 'Burn the palaces,' this destruction is not in the name of the people, not in the name of the historic future, but in the name of the sadism inherent in people: they like killing, burning down palaces."[43] This is exactly what Stalin felt, too, when he compared Eisenstein's oprichniks to Ku Klux Klansmen. But the "explanation" (and, along with it, the justification) of Russian history (through sacrifices and tragedy) coming from the film was also already called into doubt by Eisenstein's contemporaries. During that same discussion Ivan Pyr'ev remarked in this vein, "As a Russian, it is hard for me to watch a film like this. I cannot accept it because it makes me ashamed for my own past, for the past of our Russia, ashamed for this great sovereign, Ivan, who was the uniter and first progressive tsar of our Russia."[44] Less experienced viewers than Pyr'ev, like Boris Chirkov, were completely depressed: "This film made a horrible, depressing impression on me. Not only because I didn't see these people as alive [but] as stone blocks moving around. I was scared for people. Such horrible people not only used to live, but they continue living. I was scared for humanity. This was very depressing to me."[45]

Under the circumstances, the mildest possible accusation was the "un-Russianness" of the film—a serious enough charge at the time, but nonetheless much milder than an accusation of "anti-Sovietness":

Mikhail Romm: "This is all somehow un-Russian. It is a sort of disguised Spain transplanted to Moscow. . . . The Play of Daniel is depicted strangely, somehow: some sort of Chinese in makeup, some sort of buffoons, playing Chaldeans."[46]

Leonid Sobolev: "This is not a Russian film. It was the same in the first part. There is nothing Russian in it. . . . Strange as it may seem, the only person I feel is Russian is that blockhead, the cretin, Vladimir Staritskii. Ivan the Terrible is un-Russian."[47]

Ivan Pyr'ev: "From this film it is unclear to me why the boyars are accused of being on the side of foreigners, that they are ready to betray their motherland to foreigners, and so forth. You can't see this from the film. On the contrary, judging by how Ivan and the oprichniks behave, how they are dressed, how they conduct themselves, the kind of makeup they have on, what their behavior is like, and the kind of milieu they in-habit, I could instead accuse Ivan and his oprichniks of having betrayed themselves to foreigners because they don't behave like Russians but like some sort of Jesuits . . . , and Ivan is the grand inquisitor who heads this *oprichnina*. I justify and completely stand behind the boyars that were beheaded, these bearded Russians good and bad, because it isn't shown why they are bad; I don't see anything—no actions taken against the Russian state—to blame them for. So I stand behind the boyars, behind Vladimir, because there are features of a real person in him, at least glim-mers of this real person."[48]

"Meanwhile, all these people who follow Ivan, led by Maliuta, have nothing human, kind, or good in them (no matter what century this might have been in, but coming from Russian people). . . . The tsar does not look like a progressive tsar in it, but merely a grand inquisitor who has gathered around him these awful young people who are similar in their behavior to fascists in the sixteenth century."[49]

The audience responded to Pyr'ev's last comment with laughter. Nonetheless, the mood among those discussing the film was quite gloomy. Everyone understood that it was not simply a matter of a dis-ruption of Stalin's order or a specific campaign to rehabilitate Ivan as a "progressive tsar." By "laying bare the device," Eisenstein had essen-tially turned inside out Soviet film's supergenre: the historical film, con-structed on allusiveness, which fulfilled important politico-ideological functions. It was no accident that the historical films that came after *Ivan the Terrible* were almost exclusively about composers, writers, and scientists; these films could not wrestle with the political problems that were treated in the films about tsars, national leaders, and military commanders.

Eisenstein understood the task better than anyone; *Ivan the Terrible* was supposed to present the most horrible figure of the Russian Middle Ages and his bloody "historical undertaking" as "progressive." And in his doing so, the bloodiest regime in the "history of the all-Russian state"—that of Stalin—was also supposed to acquire supreme histori-cal legitimacy. "They told me to make a film not for the sake of the past but for the sake of the future; it is not the present era that should explain the bygone one—what do we have to do with it!—but let the bygone one serve the present, serve not for fear, but for conscience; but if need be, let it be for fear as well, if your conscience is fragile and you are so finicky! Get it?"[50] This is how Eisenstein explained it to Iuzovskii. If one continued to interpret the film allegorically (and there was no other way to interpret it), then it essentially presented the viewer a Soviet Middle Ages led by a bloody autocrat. Such comparisons were fatal. This problem was summed up unexpectedly precisely by a member of the Artistic Council, Major General Galaktionov: "The diamond turned out black. The film includes elements of 'Dostoevskyism.'"[51]

The device the director used to achieve his goal was *completion.* The Stalinist historical concept was based on a balance of internal contradictions that were laid bare in literally each new historical film or novel. *Ivan the Terrible,* about which its author wrote that he had striven to show the "contradictions," turned out to be the least contradictory of all of them. Leonid Sobolev neatly summed up what was obvious to everyone: "Although Ivan swears that he does everything in the name of the people, in the name of the future, in the name of reaching the Baltic, I see something else: that this man keeps himself on the throne and wants to hack his enemies through."[52] While in other films the motives for the behavior of the characters and the social groups they represented were absolutely opaque and the political significance of a power struggle was gauzed over by a struggle for a "great undertaking," in *Ivan the Terrible* the motives for its characters are crystal clear. Yes, Ivan constantly talks about a "great undertaking," but it is obvious that this "undertaking" is not the one that preoccupied the tsar, Eisenstein, and the film's chief spectator, Stalin.

A Stalinist historical narrative unhappily tolerates a lack of contradiction. Without assertions that contradict each other, the ideological system ceased to be dialectically flexible; that is, it became politically nonfunctional. Thus a simple glorification of the tsar with a consistent elimination of any traces whatsoever of class or revolutionary rhetoric became politically meaningless, if not to say dangerous.

And, in fact, the officially stated task for the making of *Ivan the Terrible* was to substantiate the "historical progressiveness" of absolute monarchy. Eisenstein brings the idea of absolutism to its logical conclusion. The inner subject of his film boils down to the transformation of Ivan: at first he proclaims himself *tsar* (the coronation), then is transformed into *the people's tsar* (the scenes by Anastasiia's coffin and in the Alexandrov village), then into *head of the oprichniks* (after the Play of Daniel scene), and, finally, into a *leader* situated above ritual and the people, controlling the state's punitive apparatus (the oprichniks' feast) and shedding "royal blood." And it was *leader* Ivan that could speak his "bad" speech directly into the camera, the "concluding monologue about the tsars' right to amorality" that so frightened Dovzhenko.

Eisenstein shows how the collapse of Ivan's "great historical undertaking" resulted in his fight for absolute power. Thus historical allusion creates a projection not so much of Ivan's "historical accomplishments" as of the Time of Troubles that ensued after his reign; Boris Godunov, who stood at the roots of this time, finally articulated ("through Pushkin") this tragic paradox.

The Godunov theme is dissolved in the logic of the plot's development but nonetheless makes itself felt most distinctly at precisely the end, in the feast of the oprichniks. In his film about Pushkin that never came to fruition, Eisenstein had intended to transform Godunov's monologue into a "nightmare in color."[53] The scene of "buffoonery" and "cursed fornication" turned out to be just this sort of "nightmare in color." The precision of the hit is emphasized by the reaction of the chief spectator: as noted above, Stalin's first reaction to the second part was, "It's not a film but some kind of nightmare!"

But here there is another unexpected parallel as well: the 1946 production of Mussorgsky's opera *Boris Godunov* in the Bolshoi Theater turned into a heated discussion of the concluding "Near Kromï" scene. The discussion turned on the content of the scene, in which the people exalted the Pretender, a portent of the Time of Troubles. The "antipatriotism" of this scene forced the Bolshoi Theater to cut it, a move that Agitprop supported. *Pravda,* however, rose up in defense of the scene (a rare instance of a discussion engaged in between Agitprop's newspaper, *Kul'tura i zhizn',* and the Central Committee's *Pravda*), maintaining that peasant uprisings were spontaneous and that various adventurists had easily deceived the peasants.[54] The result was that the scene was reworked and restored to the production, and crowd scenes were added as well. (The premiere of the new variant of *Boris Godunov,* including this scene, was in 1948, and the production was awarded the Stalin Prize, First Class.) However, the depiction of the "cursed fornication" at the end of *Ivan the Terrible* is almost a mirror reflection of Mussorgsky's "peasant uprising": Ivan/Pretender; Vladimir/Iurodivyi; Vladimir's "coronation"/the "glorification" of the boyar; and, finally, Ivan's refrain "Burn! Burn! Burn! Hey! Hey!" and the people's chorus in the opera, "Hey! Strangle him! Crush him!"

Eisenstein demonstratively introduces this parallel; referring to another cultural text that gives the film a different highlight was a typical allegorical device of his. An almost conspicuous reference to, if not to say a quote from *Boris Godunov,* changes the very end of *Ivan the Terrible,* where one can almost hear Iurodivyi's lament over all the action: "Flow, flow, bitter tears, / weep, weep, Orthodox soul. / The enemy will soon come and darkness set in, / blackest of darkness, opaque." The direct result of Ivan's reign thus becomes not the greatness of his empire but its collapse—the Time of Troubles, which lays bare the tragic import of the events. Against the backdrop of the grandiose-sweep "Near Kromï" scene and Iurodivyi's song, the ending of *Ivan the Terrible* becomes even more politically subversive, taking on the significance of not only a gloomy prophecy, but essentially of a historical appraisal of the Stalin regime.

However, the events of 1946 were less about history than about the present time; after victory in the war, the problem of legitimacy through historical allusions lost its urgency for Stalin. In his political biography of Stalin written in those years, Isaac Deutscher pointed out the following:

> It was no longer good patriotic style to evoke the names of Kutuzov, Suvorov, Minin, and Pozharsky. It was no longer fashionable to glorify the great Tsars, Ivan the Terrible and Peter the Great, whom historians and writers had just treated with more reverence than discretion as Stalin's spiritual forebears.... In part the new turn was probably a genuine reaction from the surfeit of wartime nationalism. In part, it may have been dictated by Stalin's personal considerations. In 1941–43 he could still be flattered by comparisons between himself and Peter the Great and take pride in analogies drawn between the two Patriotic wars of 1812 and 1941. Mounted on ancestral shoulders he gained in stature. As victor he has no need for all that. The Peters, the Kutuzovs, the Alexanders looked like pygmies in comparison with him.[55]

As far as Eisenstein's film was concerned, the situation was quite clear. As Uhlenbruch observed,

> After the victory over Hitler's Germany, the immediate past had much artistic material to offer. The system had legitimised itself internally and no longer needed historical parallels. . . . The dilemma of history, into which the Stalin culture had manoeuvred itself during the years of foreign policy conflicts, becomes clear after the end of World War II. As seen from the chronology of events, Eisenstein's fight to save his *Ivan*

Grozny is an outdated battle retreat. A true, vital interest was evident in the first part of the film, whose mistakes could be easily pardoned. The second part had to disappear into the archives, not only because of its mistakes, but also due to official indifference. The Stalin cult in the post-war period no longer needed a historical metaphor. In films such as *The Battle of Stalingrad* and *The Fall of Berlin,* Stalin himself appeared on the screen.

After the victory over Hitler's Germany, the historical dualism could be abandoned in which Soviet history and its perfecter, Stalin, had positive prefigurations in the past history of Russia. The model of the early 1940s was discarded after 1945. If past history up to that point was to have been read as a result of prerequisites, which one could interpret "ex post" as prophecies of redemption—in the Old Testament too there were nearly redeemed persons—then Soviet culture found itself now, after 1945, in the state without history, focussing on the present and on the latest war events.[56]

Eisenstein ended up in the very epicenter of this historic shift. As one of the main creators of the focal point of the revolution, a directly contradictory role was prepared for him in his last film—creating the focal point of counterrevolution. He fully realized this tragic collision when he brought the direct reference to *Battleship Potemkin* into *Ivan the Terrible.* The parallel, noted many times in the literature about Eisenstein, is the two ribbons of humans; in *Battleship Potemkin,* it is the endless human chain on the pier, and in *Ivan the Terrible,* it is the religious procession to Alexandrov village at the end of the first part.

But by having turned Stalin's concept of *Ivan the Terrible* inside out, Eisenstein rewrote the ending of his own life written by Stalin.[57] Accordingly, before any resolution had been adopted, in the hospital after his heart attack in the winter of 1946, forty-eight-year-old Eisenstein would tell Sergei Prokofiev, "Life is over; a postscript is left."[58] The postscript was the Central Committee resolution—a testimony to Stalin's powerlessness and undisputed proof of Eisenstein's final victory.

FROM ALLEGORY TO SYNECDOCHE: CHIAURELI AS THE NEW EISENSTEIN

When the accusations against Soviet cinema reached critical mass, Stalin gave a speech on August 9, 1946, at the Organizational Bureau of the Communist Party Central Committee. Although the speech was centered on the second part of Leonid Lukov's film about Donbass, *A Great Life*, the real target was Eisenstein's *Ivan the Terrible*, the criticism of which Stalin saved until the end of the speech. Calling the film an "abominable thing," Stalin contended that Eisenstein "digressed completely from history. He depicted the oprichniks as the worst sort of rogues, degenerates, something like the American Ku Klux Klan. . . . Ivan Groznyi, a person with will, with character, comes across like a spineless Hamlet in it. This is clearly formalism. What business do we have with formalism? Give us historical truth. Study requires patience. But some people are not patient enough, and thus they cobble everything together and present us with a film: here, eat it up, it has Eisenstein's stamp on it." In the Organizational Bureau's resolution published a month later, "On the Film *A Great Life*," Stalin's phrasing—about the "progressive army of oprichniks" portrayed "as a band of degenerates like the American Ku Klux Klan" and about Ivan appearing to be "something like Hamlet"—was preserved.[59] However, this was not followed by any further repressions; furthermore, all the criticized directors were given the chance to make corrections (which cannot be said about the fallout of another issue scrutinized at the same meeting, regarding Anna Akhmatova and Mikhail Zoshchenko). The reason for this relative mildness, one might assume, is that Stalin had lost interest in the theater of historical allusions.

In that same month that *Ivan the Terrible* was publicly condemned, August 1946, Mikhail Chiaureli's new film, *The Vow*, hit the screens. In it, Stalin was given legitimacy straight from the hands of the Soviet people—without any historical allusions whatsoever. Working during the war in parallel with Eisenstein on the historical film *Georgii Saakadze*, Chiaureli was executing Stalin's order, though on a lesser scale than Eisenstein, but keeping in mind that it was about a figure from the *Georgian* Middle Ages who was in Stalin's view extremely significant.[60] As opposed to *Ivan the Terrible*, Chiaureli's film was acknowledged a success. It was awarded two First Class Stalin Prizes, in 1943 and 1946, for each part separately.

Then, when the maker of *Ivan the Terrible* fell into disfavor, Chiaureli was directly compared to Eisenstein (not to the latter's advantage, of course). Thus Sergei Gerasimov ascribed to the maker of *The Vow* the accomplishments that had long been assigned to Eisenstein in film history. For example, he asserted that in *The Vow* "the language of cinema is applied with boundless freedom and convincing power" and that this "decisively confirms Soviet film as a completely independent distinct type of art that not only synthesizes other types of art, but also freely combines differing genre attributes under the badge of a united sense of political purpose." He argued that "the innovation of *The Vow* is defined by the fact that its authors understood their task not as chronicling or objectivist registration of the events of their era, not as invention of formal devices, but as active struggle, using the means of art, for the great goals of the Soviet people, for communism."[61] In 1950, references to "formal devices" in film were uniquely applied to insinuations about Eisenstein (suffice it to recall Stalin's reaction to *Ivan the Terrible*: "This is clearly formalism. What business do we have with formalism? Give us historical truth.")

If Eisenstein's colleagues allowed themselves such comparisons, then we should not be surprised that Chiaureli's official biographer, Iosif Manevich, saw *The Vow* as a new *Battleship Potemkin* and stated that the "innovational significance" of Chiaureli's film was that it "broad-ened the framework and boundaries of cinematic art by proving that it is quite capable of the themes and dimensions of narrative that had been thought accessible only to epic prose and the novel." It was just this epic quality of the film, which became a sort of screen adaptation of the *Short Course,* that Manevich saw as the advantage of Chiau-reli's extensive method. He recalled Eisenstein's words about how *Battleship Potemkin* had been created: "The story about how *Battle-ship Potemkin* was born from a mere half page of the vast screenplay of *The Year 1905* is rather well known. Sometimes in the bins of a creative archive you stumble across this giant of diligence, who with a sort of atavistic greed has absorbed into his countless pages the whole im-mense sweep of the events of 1905. You marvel at how two people, not deprived of their quick wit and possessing professional habits, could for a second imagine that all of this could be filmed and shown, and in a single film to boot."[62]

If "the experience of *Battleship Potemkin,* which succeeded in con-veying the zeal of the revolutionary uprising of the masses in a single episode from the 1905 revolution, was in its time a gigantic innovative leap that moved all our cinematic art forward" and "became part of the arsenal of cinematic art," then after the release of *The Vow* "no one doubts that a film can be created in which the immense events of the 1905 revolution are shown with the kind of simplicity that seemed for Eisenstein to be unattainable in cinematic art."[63] *Potemkin* became an inimitable synecdoche; in a single episode from the first Russian revolution, Eisenstein managed not only to fit in the might of all three Russian revolutions, but also to create a symbol of revolution as such. This metonymic intensiveness of the image made his film immortal. Chiaureli's strategy, on the contrary, was extensive. In both *The Vow* and *The Fall of Berlin,* he followed a path of descriptive aggravation.

The Vow is a film-synecdoche; within it is concentrated the country's history after Lenin's death right up to the victory in World War II, presented as the history of the continuous accomplishments of Stalin, his bringing to life the vow he made over Lenin's coffin. The country's history is embodied in the Petrov family, whose members represent Soviet society. The fate of the father—a Bolshevik worker sent into the countryside and killed by kulaks—gives life to the "escalation of class struggle" in the era of collectivization. The older son, Aleksandr, typifying the "national intelligentsia," qualified as an engineer, actively contributes to the five-year plans, and in the war years brings a tank from his factory to the front and dies in battle. The daughter, Ol'ga, becomes a victim of saboteurs who set fire to a factory (accordingly, her death bears witness to the "escalation of class struggle" in the era of the five-year plans). Finally, the mother, Varvara Mikhailovna, symbolizes the Motherland. At a reception in the Kremlin, we see her sitting at the table with her children and grandchildren alongside leaders and the main heroes of the 1930s—the Stakhanovites and Papaninites— and the other characters of the film that embody the "friendship of the peoples"—a Ukrainian, a Georgian, and an Uzbek.

Although the critics insisted that "any sort of schematism is alien to *The Vow,* an epic work,"[64] Chiaureli's film is literally woven together, scene after scene, from complete and utter "performed" ideologems, each of which is consistently a metonymical image. Thus, following a scene in which Stalin, suffering profoundly from Lenin's death, is taking a walk through a park in an icy wind, is a scene on a bench in Gorky. The famous bench, which everyone knew from reproductions, was a reminder of Lenin's friendship with Stalin (one of the most famous photographs of Lenin and Stalin together was taken with them on this bench, during Lenin's illness). The screenplay specified a conversation scene following this (reminiscences about Lenin). But Chiaureli took the dialogue out, leaving the now empty bench since "its appearance in a montage phrase in a certain visual and musical context gives rise to so many associations that there is no need for explanations."[65]

Montage setups like this one follow one after another—for example, a scene in Stalin's office, where after Lenin's death he draws his profile and Lenin appears to come to life, and in the corner of the office his documentary image appears. Appearing before Stalin, it is as if he transmigrates into Stalin's body. The metonymy grows into metamorphosis. The transformed Stalin refuses to write an obituary for Lenin: "People like Lenin do not die. He is alive and will live among us forever!" Having said this, he goes out to the crowd of thousands awaiting him and utters the words of his vow to fulfill Lenin's legacy. This scene, executed in an operatic style, is a sort of echo of the scene in Alexandrov village at the end of the first part of *Ivan the Terrible,* where the tsar goes out to the bereft people and acquires a new legitimacy.

The fusion of different genres—obituary and oath—is also interesting here. An obituary confirms the death of a hero. An oath, on the contrary, is tied to the idea of the postmortem life of his undertakings. But as Ursula Iustus demonstrated, the cult of Stalin was constructed on a utilization and instrumentalization of the Lenin cult, when it had lost its independence and become merely a function of Stalin's cult. Mourning the death of Lenin freed up, as it were, the space Lenin had theretofore occupied in the poetic, political, and mythological spheres for the advent of a new leader. It also emphasized the definitive loss of the beloved father and leader, a loss that worked toward the legitimization of Stalin's ascent to power. The cult of Lenin's immortality and eternal life was transformed into the cult of his death. Lenin was no longer among the living.[66] In the oath scene, Varvara Mikhailovna, who has brought to Moscow a letter addressed to Lenin, without a second thought hands it to Stalin with the words "Today you are our Lenin."

The Vow is the first historical film in which Stalin figures as a main character without Lenin. In the beginning of the film, he is "Lenin today." At the end of it, as a victor in war and the savior of his country, he is fully self-sufficient.

Remarking on the "peculiar transcendence" of the onscreen Stalin, André Bazin observed that when depicted in this way, he does not seem, nor can he seem, either an exceptionally clever person or a leader "of genius"; "It is the lord god himself, transcendence incarnate. This is what makes it possible to create his onscreen image in parallel with his actual existence."[67] This, Bazin notes ironically, expresses by no means a "superpowered manifestation of Marxist objectivity, nor a supplement to the art of the principle of historical materialism—absolutely not, because now it is a matter, we might say, not of a person but of a sort of social hypostasis, a transition to transcendence—that is, of a myth" (163).

This hypostasis—that is, the materialization of a sort of ideal substance, endowing it with concreteness—is the product of metonymic replacement. In turn, it is linked to a change in Stalin's status as a source of legitimacy, thenceforth needing no sort of buttressing at all. Bazin put his finger precisely on Stalin's peculiar "completion" in these postwar films: "Making Stalin the main character of real historical events, a person who determines their course (admittedly, with the people's complicity) despite Stalin's being an active character to this day, means tacitly assuming that henceforth he is not subject to a single human weakness, that his life has already acquired an ultimate meaning" (163).

But by being completed and acquiring ultimate meaning, Stalin's life became consistent with history itself. The fact that Stalin is not just one of the characters in a historical film (as he was in the prewar historical-revolutionary films) but is now the "mainspring of the drama" brings with it the necessity that "his biography be literally identified with History, that it share its suprapersonal nature" (163). Bazin viewed the sensation of the absolute permanence of Stalin's position as the hero of biography in postwar Soviet films as a confirmation not only of his immortality, but also of something much bigger:

> Here it is not a question of Stalin's possible death, being turned into a statue during his lifetime, but rather of the exact opposite: the end of History, or at least the completion of its dialectical development in the socialist world. The mummification of Lenin, the creation of the mausoleum, and Stalin's "Lenin lives" obituary all proclaimed the beginning of this end. However, the embalming of Lenin's body is symbolic to no less a degree than the mummification of Stalin in cinema. This mummification signifies that nothing coincidental, nothing relative is left in Stalin's relationship with Soviet policy, and if we take this to its logical conclusion, nothing of what is usually called "human," which is the asymptote:

Mankind and History—in this case, the foregoing stage. And Stalin is in fact embodied History (166).

However, in adducing examples of Stalin's amazing transformation into a prophet and the savior of the country, Bazin contradicts himself when he states that "in all these films Stalin figures as a true allegory" (166). Bazin references the scene in *The Vow* where, after Lenin's death, Stalin wanders through the snow, completing a pilgrimage to the place of their last meeting to give himself over to meditation once he sits on the sacred bench. Then the ghost of Lenin appears in the snow, and the voice of the dead emerges. Bazin goes on, in reference to this scene:

> Fearing that the metaphor of the mystical coronation alone and the passing along of the tablets with the commandments will not be enough, Stalin lifts his eyes to the heavens. A ray of sunlight breaks through the fir branches, falling on the brow of the new Moses. As you see, all things are in their places, right up to the tongues of fire. Light falls from above. It is remarkable, of course, that Stalin is the only participant in this Marxist Pentecost, while there were twelve apostles. Then we see him, slightly stooped under the weight of grace that has cast itself down upon him, returning to his comrades—people from whose ranks he will hence notably stand out, and now not just owing to his erudition or genius, but mainly because he carries the God of History within himself (167).

Nevertheless, there is nothing metaphorical in this scene. The matter stands exactly opposite: the Soviet Moses is created not allegorically but through synecdoche. After all, Moses acting as Stalin is an undoubted allegory, but Stalin acting as Moses is metonymy: Stalin essentially "replaces" Moses. This metonymic transformation is the product of a new symbolic order to secure a new legitimacy. In the Stalin films, Bazin goes on to say, again contradicting himself, that "the idea of the superiority of Stalin's genius is devoid of any metaphor and opportunism; it has a purely ontological nature" (167).

As he was a film critic, Bazin sought the reason for this not in a change of the mode of legitimization but in the very nature of film, which "imposes itself on our consciousness like something strictly corresponding to reality" and is "inherently beyond controversy, like Nature or History" (168). Nevertheless, nature and history are inherently different things. As opposed to nature, history is the output of ideological production. And Chiaureli was a true master of this production.

The status of an all-powerful film director patronized by Lavrentii Beriia, a participant in the nighttime repasts at Stalin's dacha, was unattainable in Soviet cinema. The honoree of five First Class Stalin Prizes, from 1941 to 1950, Chiaureli became a key figure in the creation of the postwar Staliniana. Specializing exclusively in films about the leader that were personally supervised by Stalin, he was beyond criticism. A discussion of his films usually turned into a flood of glorification, as if it were pouring out of the films themselves, which were made up of crude flattery. During a discussion of *The Vow* by the Artistic Council of the Ministry of Cinematography, on June 14, 1946, colleagues said that "Chiaureli has created a monument to a great life, a great country. This film makes an enormous and a profoundly moving impression" (actor Boris Chirkov);[68] that the image of Stalin was particularly successful: "The film touches your soul. Again, a sort of spirit-level standard, a ceiling, has emerged for which we, too, ought to strive. The whole range of portraits that he [Gelovani, the actor playing Stalin] creates is simply amazing. . . . We have gotten used to understanding Stalin in this way" (Gerasimov);[69] that "Stalin's image is simply sculptured by Gelovani in it; he is extraordinarily expressive and makes a strong impression" (Pyr'ev);[70] and that "the real Stalin is shown in it. At least, that's how I imagine Stalin. That's how I've always felt him to be, and still do" (composer Vladimir Zakharov).[71] And actor/director Nikolai Okhlopkov declared that he was simply incapable of "conveying [his] excitement and not blurting out the overwhelming great feeling that you are left with after seeing this film. We are dealing with a genius phenomenon. I don't think we can even appreciate the enormous culturedness and supreme mastery of the director at present. . . . I consider this a thing on par with Beethoven's *Heroic Symphony*. I'm convinced that this film will live forever."[72]

Comparing *The Vow* to a symphony was not simply exaggerating. Chiaureli himself wanted to see his film as such. Back in 1940, talking about his intention to wrap up filming of *The Vow,* he said the film would be executed "in the style of a historical epic with elements of the symphonic form, which the theme of the oath demands, as it suggests the necessity of elation, pathos."[73] Thus, when the film came out, the critics found that "the dramatic composition of *The Vow* resembles the structure of the symphony, the sonata form in which all the great musicians have expressed the most profound philosophical ideas, thanks to which they achieved the greatest emotional effect."[74] Nonetheless, the film consisted of "a series of poster-episodes that accentuated one or another event of state-level importance. The characters, too, express their attitudes toward these events in just such a poster-like fashion. Despite the external drama of the circumstances and twists of fate, the schema-images are extremely cold, emotionless."[75]

Attempts to elevate the "artistic-documentary" genre were made more than once and, no doubt, were tied to its main character. After the success of his completely allegorical historical film *Georgii Saakadze*, Chiaureli understood that allegorical restraint and allegorical technique were no longer required. The demand was for outright mythmaking that assumed resorting to the simplest visual executions that turned his films into absolute political kitsch.

Appealing to the masses' taste was part of Chiaureli's program as far back as the times of his prewar film, *The Great Dawn*. Critics explained this by saying that since "re-creating images on the screen of the leaders of the victorious revolution, the geniuses of humanity Lenin and Stalin, is an extremely difficult task," the former canons of drama could not serve as a basis for such a re-creation. Thus Chiaureli turned to "the type of images that were created in the people's revolutionary era" and "revealed the people's concept of Lenin and Stalin that came out of the folk narratives about the great leaders. In the structure of its images lives the theme of the inviolable friendship of the leaders that was celebrated earlier in the people's creative work. . . . The way that popular creativity portrays Lenin and Stalin is how the film depicts them."[76] The appeal to "popular creativity" was supposed to serve as a justification for the aesthetic of the ideological primitive that Chiaureli had mastered to perfection by creating films addressed to the most undemanding audience.

If "simplicity" made them functional, then "sublimity" was achieved by the accompanying discourse of the obvious imperfection of the images (primarily, of course, the image of Stalin). The director awaited the arrival of an artist who would create a full-fledged image of the leader. This image would be grandiose, as grandiose as the figure of Stalin itself was:

We know without a doubt that a true artist will come from the heart of the people, who will be up to this grandiose task. . . . Our timid preliminary attempts will give him nourishment, will serve as impulses for the creation of a finished canvas, a true masterpiece, a jewel of world art. And all our artists—sculptors, masters of the brush, poets, musicians, dramatists, actors, and directors—must carry on this preparatory work, not just from one instance to another, but constantly, day in and day out, for this is one of the chief tasks of contemporary art. Through monumental canvases we will be able to tell humanity in the most exhaustive, moving, and profound way the story of the remarkable, blindingly bright happy days of the era of the great Stalin![77]

Stalin's performers, too, developed this theme onscreen. Actor Mikhail Gelovani said that while he was working out his portrayal of Stalin in *The Vow,* he understood that "the image of Comrade Stalin—a leader and statesman, commander and war strategist, and our era's man of genius—is so complex, many-sided, and majestic that to plumb its depths is beyond the powers of the most talented actor, even more so in a single acting role."[78] He was seconded by another performer in the role of Stalin, Aleksei Dikii: in this job "the sense of perfection in the role never comes, nor can it come. In every such work for the screen or stage, you manage perhaps to find just some new tint, another authentic touch of some sort to portray the great character. But our art has still not created a perfect image of our leader." There remained only the endless process of approximating it. Dikii added, "Granted, we are still not doing this fully, we are only chalking out the paths to creating a future masterpiece. But breaking out into new untrodden paths, boldly laying them out for travelers of the future—this is exactly what the sacred duty of the Soviet artist-patriot is."[79]

The theme of the artist's powerlessness to capture a leader's greatness emerged back in the 1920s in Leniniana and was shrouded in the literary raiment of Oriental grandiloquence in 1930s Staliniana. But the Stalin cult before the war was constructed with either historical allusions or references to Lenin. Under the new conditions it had to find internal foundations. Chiaureli was undoubtedly one of those who came closest to solving this problem. With access to the "sitter," he found himself in a unique position. His descriptions of the creative process of working on the image of Stalin are full of mysticism:

Many Soviet artists have not even once seen Comrade Stalin, chatted with him, heard his voice, seen his eyes, his warm smile, or felt the squeeze of his hands. But in the simplicity of his words is the wisdom of the ages, in his eyes the light of genius, in his gestures calm self-confidence, and in his manners, the simplicity of a great man. How can you show the greatness of this simplicity in art? Here we have a man who grasps with a philosopher's thinking the whole complexity of the organism of the universe and of our world, the relations among the classes, societies, and states—a man who did the impossible, a master of the great ideas and of the unusual moving force of history. . . . Involuntarily, you start to think that Stalin is bigger than a person, but this thought is from the inability to understand that everything great is simple. . . . No! But still, he stands out from ordinary people, even externally! I have watched his hands at length, followed his every move, tried to imprint in my mind the tiniest detail of his face, gestures, every line, big and small, of his face, his facial expressions, and manner of speech. And all the while I couldn't shake the thought that subconsciously I was striving to bring the image of this great man "down to earth," as it were. . . . But at that very moment I remembered the grandeur of his works [deianiia] and again sensed that everything about him was extraordinary: his hands, his eyes, his smile.[80]

But then the knowledge that Chiaureli acquired in the Tiflis school of painting and sculpture comes to his aid. Running through a list of master artists of the ancient East, Egypt, Greece, and Rome—names from Michelangelo and Leonardo da Vinci to Velázquez and Goya—Chiaureli comes to the conclusion that none of them has left us a real path for revealing Stalin's image. And this is understandable: "None of the artists of all times and nations have been faced with the task of creating such a magnificent image as are we, the art workers of the country of the Soviets. . . . We are the first to have glimpsed the world's genius. His name is *Stalin*."[81] In this world there was no longer a place not just for Ivan the Terrible, but even for Marx and Lenin.

On May 20, 1946, Andrei Zhdanov, Georgii Aleksandrov, and Ivan Bol'shakov sent Stalin a memorandum about the production plan for artistic films in 1946–47. The memo mentioned in particular that "two films on themes from the history of the Soviet state and the life of the peoples of the USSR will be released: *The Vow*, about the fulfilling of the great vow of Comrade Stalin, made by him at the tomb of V. I. Lenin, by the peoples of the Soviet Union, and *Light over Russia*, about the origin and bringing to life of Lenin's GOELRO plan."[82]

Let us note this awkward phrasing: the vow belongs to "Comrade Stalin," but it is "the peoples of the Soviet Union" who fulfill it. There is a remarkable dialogue between Stalin and Varvara Mikhailovna that takes place at the end of *The Vow:*

> Stalin: I thank you on behalf of the Motherland.
> Varvara Mikhailovna: Like we thought, Joseph Vissarionovich, we had it our way. We're still standing. We kept our vow.
> Stalin: Yes, we did. And all because you and a million other Soviet mothers raised outstanding sons. The blood shed by our people will yield a great harvest.

This short dialogue is striking for its abrupt and unexpected shifts of subjectivity. In the pronouns it uses is an entire system of collateral subordinations: like a synecdoche, where the part replaces the whole, the pronoun replaces the name. And this is what creates semantic tension: Stalin is the people, but he is simultaneously the people's medium, and thus he speaks on behalf of the Motherland. Although the heroine says, "Like *we* thought" and not "Like *you and I* thought," it seems that the "we" who kept the vow (*"we* had it *our way. We're* still standing") are both Stalin and Varvara Mikhailovna. But it follows from Stalin's reply that he-as-father is not part of the multitude, that it is not "the generation's vow"; the ones who have kept it, kept the covenant, are the mothers (*"you and a million other Soviet mothers"*) and their "outstanding sons." The absence of a mention of "fathers" here is remarkable. Although Stalin makes the vow *on behalf of* the People, it is the People who fulfill it.

In this respect Stalin is similar to Ivan the Terrible, transformed from "the people's tsar" into the leader. In the postwar films about the war, on posters, and in paintings like Fedor Shurpin's "Our Motherland's Morning" or the grand canvases of Mikhail Khmel'ko, Dmitrii Nalbandian, Aleksei Shovkunenko, Iurii Kugach, and others, Stalin is just as alone as Ivan. But the difference between Eisenstein's Ivan the Terrible and Chiaureli's Stalin is that the former was *an allegory of Stalin* and the latter *a synecdoche of the People and of History itself.* There was nothing ontological in the former; he was essentially an ideological puppet that could be encoded and decoded in various ways. The latter was pure transcendence and assumed not only no *difference* of interpretation, but even any interpretation at all, but rather mere contemplation. This is why, when Eisenstein's colleagues said that "in both the Kazan campaign and the fight against the boyars' revolt, as well as the fight against the interventionists, Ivan the Terrible embodied the aspirations of the people of his time," they were talking not so much about Ivan as about Stalin, through whom they viewed the tsar; Ivan was the embodiment of "the people's aspirations" to the extent that he was an allegory of Stalin. The representation of the leader before the war was constructed on allegory, when Stalin was conceived as the best and most faithful pupil and successor of Lenin's undertaking, or, as Henri Barbusse said, "Lenin today." Stalin purposely revived the model of legitimacy familiar in Russia with a god in the face of Lenin and a tsar in the form of himself. However, after the war Stalin's status did not simply rise to the level of Lenin's; it surpassed it. That Stalin no longer wished to be merely the "faithful pupil" is attested by this remarkable fact: in 1949, when celebrations were being planned on the occasion of Stalin's seventieth birthday, Georgii Malenkov suggested establishing an Order of Stalin, but Stalin decisively rejected this idea. This could be explained only by the necessity in such a case of determining which of the two awards, the Order or Lenin or the proposed Order of Stalin, was higher in the hierarchy. Stalin thought it politically inappropriate to openly place himself above Lenin, but he definitely did not want to be second.

Here we should mention what happened to the second of the films named in the letter of Zhdanov, Aleksandrov, and Bol'shakov, Sergei Iutkevich's *Light over Russia* (1947), based on Nikolai Pogodin's screenplay. Stalin took an immediate dislike to the film since he was no longer happy with the very idea of depicting any event in the country's history in which his own role was not a defining one. The Central Committee's verdict after seeing the film stated outright that Stalin's part in the creation of the GOELRO electrification plan for Russia was not shown enough, and the scenes with Lenin in them were artificial and superfluous—"They have a 'false democratism' in them not characteristic of Lenin." In fact, what Stalin did not like was that Lenin's GOELRO plan was not credited to Stalin in the film. Nevertheless, in hopes of saving the film, its author set about correcting it, and then "in one of the main scenes where Krzhizhanovskii was showing Lenin a picture of 'Hydrotorf,' where Lenin's electrification plan was essentially germinated—a scene, by the way, that was widely known from the reminiscences of contemporaries—Krzhizhanovskii stood aside for Stalin."[83]

But even this did not save the film; Stalin categorically refused to be in Lenin's shadow any longer. It would be hard to disagree with Evgenii Margolit and Viacheslav Shmyrov: "The reason behind Stalin's rejection of the film is obviously its discrepancy with the historical-revolutionary myth in the postwar period. The pretentious parity of the leaders emphasized in the historical-revolutionary films of the prewar era was after the victory over Germany once and for all transformed into the formula 'Stalin is Lenin today,' which found a direct onscreen embodiment in Mikhail Chiaureli's film *The Vow* (1946) and an indirect one in a series of epics about Stalin's role in the battles of the Great Patriotic War."[84]

Be that as it may, historicization was one of the fundamental ideological and aesthetic strategies of Stalinism beginning in the mid-1930s.[85] Its go-to device was still allegory, in which ideological content found a vivid expression and a way to the mass consumer. The viewer looked at Ivan the Terrible but was supposed to see Stalin; interpreting the retreat to Moscow as a deliberate "enticement" of the enemy deep into the country with the aim of destroying it, the viewer was supposed to see Kutuzov's tactic as a "military maneuver"; looking at Nakhimov, that viewer saw Stalin's relationship with ordinary soldiers, his "concern for the people," and so forth. Soviet prewar and wartime art produced allegories like these in commercial quantities.

After the war, a metonymic mechanism (primarily through synecdoche) of producing political imagery came to replace metaphorical and allegorical images. As distinct from metaphor, based on replacing words "by similarity," the metonym replaces words "by contiguity," when a part replaces the whole, or vice versa. The triumph of synecdoche was primarily the triumph of the symbolic and the ideal over the concrete and the real. This victory constricted freedom of the imagination by producing endlessly similar images. Thus all the "progressive" tsars and great military commanders, from Aleksandr Nevskii to Georgii Saakadze and from Ivan the Terrible to Peter I, were allegories of Stalin. But symbolism, which was connected not by similarity but by contiguity, required inductive-deductive reasoning; seeing a leader's vow as the symbol and code of practically all of subsequent Soviet history, and seeing history itself as the development of the political magic pledged in the vow, was more difficult than recognizing Ivan the Terrible as Stalin.

Metaphor (allegory) compares and points out something in actual reality with the aim of recoding this reality; seeing the actions of the oprichniks, the viewer of *Ivan the Terrible* was supposed to understand the justifiability and even necessity of state terror (as Stalin had told Eisenstein), but the biographical film about Aleksandr Popov did not just imply that Popov, and not Marconi, had invented the radio. It told a story of Popov as the true inventor of the radio, *transforming* him into an inventor. *It changed reality.* The mechanism of this change can be likened to the mechanism of metonymic substitution.

If the reality in question was lived experience (as in the case of the war that had just ended), a remaking of this kind required a serious restructuring of the mechanism of social memory. This was exactly the framework into which individual memory was integrated, memory that could differ dramatically from the constructed "general picture" of the past. Nonetheless, the two could exist in parallel without contradicting each other. It was another matter with the spheres in which the past had no individual dimension, the spheres of "pure history" (as in the case of party history). Here the production of ideological reality was less painful. However, its influence was much more profound since it was directed not so much at memory as at the collective imagination that shaped political consciousness.

3 Three Resolutions about Beauty

Ideological Conscientiousness as Device

THE HOT AUGUST OF '46

Sergei Eisenstein was mistaken to assume that the Central Committee resolution that contained the name of Leonid Lukov's film *A Great Life* had nothing to do with Lukov and his film. Stalin was no less interested in the present than in history. An era of imperial historical stasis had set in, demanding a change of representational strategies and a visual culture that was new in comparison to prewar and wartime art. Sensitive to shifts of this sort in the sphere of political representation, Stalin concentrated on this problem with extraordinary attention.

Although the three Central Committee resolutions that are usually associated with the beginning of the Zhdanov era were brought to their final form in the course of three weeks (the resolution on literature was published on August 14, the one on theater on August 26, and the one on cinema on September 4, all in 1946), they were essentially conceived all on the same day—on August 9, 1946, at a session of the Central Committee's Organizational Bureau (Orgbiuro). The significance that Stalin ascribed to this action is attested by fact that this Orgbiuro session was the *only one* in the last fifteen years of Stalin's leadership of the country that was held under his direct supervision. Three issues were examined at this session: the journals *Zvezda* and *Leningrad,* the

second part of the film *A Great Life,* and measures to improve the repertoire of drama theaters. Although the resolutions were in fact made in
a single day, they had been readied in the Central Committee apparatus
for a much longer time; the one on literature had been in preparation
for at least three years (beginning in December 1943, when complaints
in Central Committee documents about literary journals, and in particular Zoshchenko's story "Before Sunset," began to be expressed); the
one on theater, between four months (if counted from April 2, 1946,
when the anonymous letter received in Beriia's office was forwarded
to Agitprop head Aleksandrov) and six months (if counted from the
receipt of this letter by Beriia's staff on February 3, 1946); and the one
on cinema, over five months, from early March, when Stalin saw the
second part of *Ivan the Terrible.*

These three resolutions are usually considered political triplets and
regarded as a single bloc ("the 1946 Zhdanov resolutions"), but they
were very different. This is not simply because they concerned different art forms (although the most popular and the most important to
Stalin)—literature, cinema, and theater. It is because the resolutions
represent three different institutional modes of Stalin's cultural policy: the personal-volitional (on cinema), the procedural-bureaucratic
(on theater), and the *nomenklatura*-battling (on literature). Of course,
all the elements of the decision-making system were at work here; in
each instance the initiative and will of Stalin, the personal stakes of the
participant-beneficiaries, and adherence to the bureaucratic and ritual-
ideological procedures were all required. Nonetheless, as we shall see,
the dominant impulse in each case was also different.

Each of these resolutions activated various aspects of cultural production in a different way. If the one on cinema set the required parameters for the new regime of the representation of reality in art, then
the one on theater demanded not only the creation of plays about the
present time "in reverse" (complaints about the censured plays gave an
idea about what the authorities did not wish to see as "scenic reflection
of the present time"), but also rejection of the "dominance" of foreign
repertoire, creating the conditions for a curious "ideological import
replacement." The resolution on literature completed this shift, relying
on the ideological and aesthetic aspects of the required transformation;
it established new parameters of literary-critical discourse ("the fight
against ideological emptiness" became a theme of criticism over all the

following years) and brought a historical dimension into it (criticism of decadence, the "Serapion Brothers," and so forth).

What united all three resolutions was the theme of the present time. Not by chance was the resolution on cinema titled with reference to Lukov's work as "On the Film *A Great Life*," and it touched upon historical films only in passing; ten paragraphs were dedicated to Lukov's film about postwar Donbass and then only one to Eisenstein's and Pudovkin's historical films. The resolution on theater repertoire noted the dominance of foreign plays and demanded that Soviet plays about the present time be created. Finally, the resolution on literature referred to the unacceptability of both "detachment from life" (Akhmatova) and a too intent (satirical) drawing near to it (Zoshchenko). All the resolutions implicitly demanded one thing: the creation of works of art—literary, theatrical, and cinematographic—about the present, executed in a new, "varnished" manner.

This last point should not be taken as *only* deliberate falsification, but also as the consequence of Stalin's optics, with which too much was bound up, given the personalist nature of the regime. Ultimately, as Evgenii Margolit so keenly observed, "Practically the only addressee of the country's cinematic production on the cusp of the forties and fifties was a single person: Stalin."[1] We should remember that this "single person" was detached from the reality beyond his dachas and the Kremlin.

Except for vacations—from one government facility to another in a special train—Stalin did not travel about the country, visit factories or kolkhozes, or meet people other than his own security guards and associates; he had no idea how the masses lived. Except for the newspapers that portrayed an extremely sugar-coated life, the reports of the secret police, and the statistics that likewise affirmed the picture that he expected, his window to the world was in the films, books, and plays about the present time. All together they were supposed to create some sort of unified picture for him. Anything that could cause cognitive dissonance and destroy this harmony was consistently deleted.

As a result, Stalin's picture of what should be and what was were resolutely merged. Hence it is unsurprising that he not only liked novels like *Cavalier of the Golden Star*, whose author received three Stalin prizes (for each of the novel's parts separately!), but also took them to be reality. For example, after his first viewing of *Kuban Cossacks*,

Stalin had no doubt that what he saw in it was reality: "So, things are going pretty well with our agriculture, after all. . . . I always knew that our folk in the countryside live very well!" This was his comment when he suggested that Pyr'ev's film be renamed from its original title, *The Merry Fair,* to *Kuban Cossacks.* The renaming is significant: the first title pointed to the fiction of what was depicted and to genre identification, while the second appealed to reality.

For decades, experts in literature, theater, and cinema have studied the negative—prohibitive and censorial—consequences of these resolutions: films shelved or sent back for remakes, plays removed from the repertoire, books yanked from libraries and stopped in production. But there is another aspect of these political actions that is not well enough understood: these resolutions not only blocked certain things, but also opened a path for others. They definitively affirmed the "Grand Style" of showy Stalinist art that had only been taking shape before the war—the lurid imperial style of Moscow skyscrapers, the baroque pompousness of postwar metro stations, the Stalinist style of luxury, and impassioned populist poetry, which were all the direct result of the 1946 resolutions. Without them, varnishing "conflictless" literature and art would not have become dominant. These resolutions created the conditions for producing plays and other spectacles, novels and poems, and films that all differed strikingly from the condemned ones and that to a far greater extent determined both the development of Soviet art and the Soviet politico-aesthetic project as a whole for years to come than what the resolutions censured. They were not only censorial resolutions. Their potential to engender culture was enormous. In fact, all postwar Soviet art takes its principles from them, the art whose summits would be the "conflictless" plays that filled the Soviet stage, *Kuban Cossacks* in cinema, *Cavalier of the Golden Star* in literature, the canvases of Aleksandr Laktionov and Dmitrii Nalbandian, the cyclopean monuments of Nikolai Tomskii—the most famous exemplars of "varnishing art." It was in just this art that Socialist Realism would achieve its finished form.

THE GREAT LIFE OF MINERS OF THE DON

The adoption of the resolution on the second part of the film *A Great Life* was preceded by a discussion and Stalin's speech at the session of the Orgbiuro held on August 9, 1946. The initiative to discuss films was Stalin's own. It did not originate from his entourage, nor from the Central Committee apparatus, nor from film-industry functionaries. It was Stalin's reaction to Eisenstein's "high-handedness" that upset him, Pudovkin's "frivolous and ignorant" approach to the historical figure, and what he saw as Lukov's "distortion" of the picture of reality. All three of these things hit Stalin personally; what Eisenstein allowed himself to do with Ivan the Terrible raised doubt about the historical and symbolic legitimacy of Stalin's regime; how Pudovkin portrayed Nakhimov presented a historical figure as too intimately human, creating an unacceptable perspective for the representation of Stalin in the present and the future; and how Lukov depicted the Donbass stripped from the Stalinist picture of reality the harmony upon which the Stalinist propaganda of the achievements and efficacy of the Soviet system was constructed. Stalin ascribed all of this to "ignorance," "frivolousness," "formalism," and "slapdash work." (One had been too lazy to study life; the second studied history unscrupulously; and the third, instead of offering a full-fledged depiction of history, decided to limit himself to "a depiction of two or three paper ships, while the rest was dances and encounters of all sorts,"—the way a Zoshchenko character would talk about films.)[2]

In each instance Stalin reacted angrily and initiated repressive actions for each film. The Secretariat of the Central Committee's resolution of March 5, 1946, "On the Second Part of the Film *Ivan the Terrible*," banned the film as being "anti-historical and anti-artistic," and the same body's resolution of May 11, 1946, regarding *Admiral Nakhimov,* stated that "there is disdain in the film for historical truth."[3] Then the resolution regarding Lukov's film was adopted. But if the two earlier resolutions were secret, this third one was public.

A comparison of two documents—the transcript of Stalin's speech during the Orgbiuro session and the text of the resolution—shows that, on the one hand, the resolution is faithful to Stalin's speech (it literally repeats all the phraseology of the speech), but that, on the other, it is an obvious change of the object and proportions of criticism. Stalin's speech dealt with three films—those of Pudovkin, Eisenstein, and Lukov (in exactly this order). In his speech, Stalin spent the same amount of time on Pudovkin's film as on Eisenstein's, but the amount he allotted to Lukov's film was exactly the same as for both the others put together. A reading of the transcript plainly shows that Stalin had a lively interest in all the films, and although he was most upset by Eisenstein, he decided to unleash his wrath on Lukov, evidently supposing that too harsh a public criticism of Eisenstein and Pudovkin would be counterproductive.

The accusations of "calumny" and "slander of Soviet reality" that Stalin rained down on the second part of *A Great Life* became the program for conflictless art for years to come. Portraying reality as it was meant merely pandering to the tastes of the "undemanding viewer." What Lukov depicted, as Stalin declared, was "of course, not a great life." It was simply life. Not art, but photography, "objectivism." Catering to the tastes of an unexacting audience meant following the lead of "outdated," "vulgar," and "philistine" trends. In the resolution, all of this would be called a "propagation of outdatedness, lack of culture, and ignorance," which results in "a false and distorted portrayal of the Soviet people." The epithets are laid on: the Soviet people are portrayed as "lowbrow," and the songs and romances in the film are "vulgar." These same epithets were used also in the resolution regarding the Leningrad journals, applied to the "vulgarian Zoshchenko." Thus, ridding films of accordions, restaurant songs, drunken binges, "gypsy traits," "vulgar romances," and "romantic adventures" was the first step toward "ideologically conscientious art."

This art is not like reality but is precisely what makes life "great," corresponding to that higher reality in which Stalin already lived and whither he summoned artists who were still torn between the viewer-consumer and Stalin-the-consumer. Stalin called on them to break definitively with the viewer, declaring that they "live among golden people, among heroes" but "cannot portray them as they ought to, but must inevitably sully them." But how did Soviet artists "sully" the Soviet people? By "attributing . . . outdated attitudes" to them. Stalin does not deny that "workers did have such attitudes in the first years of Soviet power, when the working class first took power. They did, but this was not right." But then he immediately declares, "How much time has gone by since then! The country was raised to an unprecedented height with the help of mechanization." But in the film, "What kind of reconstruction does it show, where not a single machine is seen? Everything is the old way. People simply haven't studied the facts and don't know what reconstruction means in our circumstances. They have confused what took place after the civil war in 1918–19 with what is tak-

ing place, say, in 1945–46." The directors did not know the changed life
and, due to inertia, continued to pander to "outdated" tastes.

Lukov had filmed the Donbass all his life. All of his films, beginning
with *Italian* (1931), were about the region. The most famous of them
were *A Great Life* (1939), *Aleksandr Parkomenko* (1942), and *This
Happened in Donbass* (1945). His films were about prerevolutionary
Donbass, the region in the first five-year-plan periods, and Donbass
during the war. No one knew Donbass better than he. But he, born
and bred in Donbass, having spent his youth there, working as a journalist and then a film director, did not know Donbass the way Stalin
did. And Stalin's inner sight was true, whereas the director's knowledge
was false.

The screenplay's author, Pavel Nilin, and Pyr'ev, who was the deputy
chair of the Ministry of Cinematography's Artistic Council, grasping
at the straw offered to them, laid the emphasis on the fact that the
screenplay had been written when Donbass had just been liberated, but
now it was already 1946, and over that time everything had supposedly changed to the point of unrecognizability (since without this explanation, the catastrophe would have to be acknowledged as the bad
intention of the authors, which brought a direct threat with it). It came
to light that the authors had been unable to see "life in its revolutionary development," that Donbass had literally over a year changed so
as to be unrecognizable (everything was being done by new machines
instead of manual labor, and so forth). A mistake like this was assessed
as professional, not political. But then one of the representatives of the
Ministry of the Coal Industry of the USSR Western Regions attending
the Orgbiuro session, a certain Savchenko, gave a speech. He was inex-
perienced in politico-aesthetic politesse and, judging from what he said,
the authors were guilty of just the opposite:

> You must not show the reconstruction of Donbass with such levity, as
> is shown here. Everything proceeds too easily. First, the ruined Donbass
> is not shown. When we began the reconstruction of Donbass, there was
> not a single headframe (and a headframe is the most basic thing for a
> mine).[4] All the headframes had been blown up and destroyed. But the
> film shows the reconstruction with ready-made headframes. And it gets
> worse. The film shows that the headframes had remained in the mines.
> They make it seem like the mines had been blown up, everything had
> exploded, but the headframes were still there.
> Stalin: People will laugh at this. . . .

When showing the theme of reconstruction, you have to show the extent of destruction of the Donbass, but what they end up with is an episode, not a film. They show a mine, but it's not even destroyed. They show mines that don't even exist. . . . You have to show how people go down into the mineshaft, how miners work in water, not to mention being knee-deep in water. They do show people standing in waist-deep water, but, in fact, when there is a huge rainfall in the shaft, there are usually pumps there that pump out this continuous rain, but the film shows a lot of space, a lot of light. This doesn't make sense. If you show this to miners, they'll say an artist drew this and they filmed it on a motion-picture stage.[5]

So it emerged that either the filmmakers had embellished everything, which directly contradicted everything that Stalin and Zhdanov had told them about the film, or else the latter knew what life in the Donbass was like a great deal better than the workers in the Ministry of the Coal Industry of the USSR Western Regions did. One would have to laugh at this and not at what Stalin conjectured.

Hence Stalin transitioned to the recommendations for remaking the film. Each new suggestion ended with the words, "This must be thrown out." For example, "People living in horrible conditions, almost outdoors, or an engineer in charge of a mine doesn't know where he can sleep—all of this must be thrown out. This perhaps really does occur here and there, but this is atypical. We built whole cities in the Donbass, but it was all blown up." It is obvious how difficult it was for Stalin to combine the real with the imagined. He declares the reality depicted in the film "atypical," but then immediately justifies himself, as it were, conceding that it "*perhaps* really does occur *here and there*" since "we built whole cities [that were then] blown up." But if they were blown up—and not perhaps, but in fact, and not here and there, but everywhere—then how can what the film showed be "atypical"? Having enumerated everything that was "atypical" and that "must be thrown out," Stalin raises the question, "What is left, then?" He hesitates as to whether he should allow a remake of the film:

Stalin: If it's possible to repair it, then please do so. But it will be very difficult; you'll have to turn everything over. It will essentially be a new film. . . .
Pyr'ev: I think we can repair it. . . . We have to produce and make a film about the reconstruction of the Donbass.
Stalin: But what will be left of this film?[6]

What was to remain was truly "a new film," *Miners of the Don.* Lukov's path to making it was torturous. The director's speech at a meeting in the Ministry of Cinematography several months after the resolution regarding his film was adopted gives us some idea of how the breakdown of optics had progressed and how a new representational mode in Soviet art had been established.

But how was one to film the "new Donbass" that was so vividly described in the resolution but that did not exist in reality? Straight to the point, Lukov admits that what he is determined to bring to the screen is . . . a plan:

> We have examined the current plan for the future reconstruction and development of the Donbass, and we discovered it only after what had happened when we turned to the materials. In fact, the Donbass was reconstructed not at the expense of tiny mines but according to a grand designed plan by which the mines not only were returned to their former prewar scale, but also increased their effectiveness and are being built on the basis of high technology and the introduction of a new working method in these mines, which allows for extracting more coal with less labor.[7]

And so it becomes clear to this director, who knew the Donbass better than anyone else, that "in light of these facts our film is absolutely false, for it shows only crude, muscular labor. If we had carefully examined the five-year plan for developing and reconstructing the Donbass, if we had attentively delved into the figures that show the future growth of the Donbass, then we would have had to see the absolute inconsistency between what was in the screenplay and what is actually happening, in real life." The idealistic mock-up of the future—a plan, figures, and future growth—is here called "facts": "what is actually happening, in real life." From this perspective, the heroes of the second part of *A Great Life* do not exist: "In the real life of the great Donbass there are no such people. The sort of people who engage in idle chatter instead of work do not exist. [Nor do they engage in] drinking bouts for any reason at all or no reason at all, in melancholy songs accompanied by a guitar."[8]

At the beginning of *Miners of the Don* there is a long flashback in which contemporary miners are compared to how they were portrayed by the prerevolutionary artist Nikolai Kasatkin—gloomy people, exhausted from labor, covered in coal dust and soot. All this was supposed to contrast with the contemporary (1950) model miners. The action of the film flows into a palace of culture, where miners—all wearing elegant black uniforms with gold stripes and medals—arrive on their "Victory" and ZIS cars to huge, bright, two-story halls with pompous chandeliers and orchestras, where the tables are covered like those in *The Book of Delicious and Healthy Food* and champagne sparkles in crystal glasses. Or it flows into bosses' offices spacious as gymnasiums, with wood paneling, plush curtains, bookshelves on every wall, and deep leather sofas and chairs, always against a backdrop of huge portraits of Stalin. Or it flows into mines like Moscow Metro stations—with plastered tunnels lit by neon lamps, where the miners travel in special coaches. Or it flows into the miners' houses, which are like manors—with huge bright spaces more like halls than rooms, with gardens under the windows, with pergolas and verandas on which, like Ostrovskii's merchants and their wives, the miners and their wives sit solemnly and, while taking their tea and hors d'oeuvres, extol the virtues of the jam made from heavenly apples.

Nonetheless, a comparison to Kasatkin's pictures in *Miners of the Don* seems completely superfluous here; Lukov did not have to look back into the nineteenth century. The point of repulsion could have been the second part of *A Great Life,* with its drinking, sooty miners, coarseness, lack of discipline, cursing, filth, poverty, and devastation. All of this had disappeared somewhere in the time that had passed since 1946. What Lukov brought to the screen was not so much Boris Gorbatov's screenplay as the Central Committee's resolution.

The basic complaints about the second part of *A Great Life* were formulated in the resolution, beginning with "The film depicts only one insignificant episode in the first onslaught of the reconstruction of the Donbass, which does not give the correct impression about the real sweep and significance of the work done by the Soviet state. . . . The main attention was devoted to a primitive portrayal of all sorts of personal experiences and everyday scenes."

What was being depicted now was not an "episode" but a real technological revolution in the mines and in all of the Donbass. A central event in the film is the introduction of a coal-heading machine into the system, which completely mechanizes the miners' labor. Mining coal is transformed into "contemporary industrial production," where miners are not needed but engineers are, on a massive scale. Hence the main attention is devoted to the introduction of new technology and training. Personal experiences are reduced to whether or not one should go study or continue giving a 300 percent fulfillment of the plan.

"At the level of technology and production culture," the resolution continued, "[A Great Life] reflects more the reconstruction period of the Donbass after the end of the civil war, not the contemporary Donbass with its advanced technology and culture created over the years of the Stalin five-year plans." But central to the new film was the most modern technology and a production culture of the sort in which the workers go about the mines practically in uniforms. Everyone talks only about professional perfection; not only have the picks and jackhammers disappeared, but so also have the holers and horse transports; now tunnelers turn into mechanics, mechanics into technicians, technicians into engineers, and engineers into mine managers.

Another fault of the previous film, the resolution stated, was that "the business of reconstructing the Donbass is portrayed as if the workers' initiative in reconstructing the mines not only found no support on the state's part, but was also carried out by the miners despite the resistance of state organizations. . . . In this respect, party workers are portrayed falsely in the film." But now the screen was full of leaders: the mine's manager, the director of the enterprise group, the secretary of the regional party committee, the minister of the coal industry, and, finally, Stalin himself, surrounded by Politbiuro members. Stalin personally initiates the creation of the cutter-loader, and the whole film essentially tells how this decision is brought to life. The plot of this exemplary, conflictless, varnished film rolls along the well-worn rails of the industrial play. The critics joyously declared that "The film *Miners of the Don* has no negative characters in it. The film's heroes lead the struggle for bringing in the most perfected technology, which changes their labor and everyday life to the core and brings them into new relations among themselves. The film *Miners of the Don,* which truthfully reflects our contemporary reality, is romantic, focused on what tomorrow brings."[9]

Another defect of *A Great Life* was that "the film talks about the war, which was at its height in this period, as the distant past." But in *Miners of the Don,* with the action moved four years ahead, the war is not mentioned at all, as if it had never happened. Such an abrupt change of the historical perspective is tied to the fact the war was supposed to justify "backwardness," but with the replacement of "backwardness" with an unheard-of prosperity, any mention of the war would merely intensify the inauthenticity of what was depicted.

In *A Great Life,* "The massive promotion of technical workers with backward views and attitudes to leading posts was shown completely without motivation, and wrongly so. . . . In the film's conception, the very best people are habitual drunkards. . . . People serving in the German police appear to be the basic heroes of the film." But the heroes of *Miners of the Don,* it would appear, have gone through the screening of an HR department. At the center of its narrative is the family of Stepan Nedolia, which represents a whole dynasty of miners. His elder son, Pavel, is a party organizer in the mine, and his other son, Vladimir, is the manager of the leading production area; his daughter Lida is a dispatcher. Towering over them is the father, who, in the words of one critic, "comes across as a living monument, embodying the most characteristic features of those who are miners by birth."[10] Surrounding this "monument" are warmly enthusiastic crowds of workers, wise party leaders, and old men moved to tears, regretting that they have lived their whole lives before life became so beautiful.

Finally, the resolution condemned *A Great Life* because "the artistic level of the film . . . does not stand up to criticism. Separate frames of the film are scattered about and not tied together by a common concept. . . . Awkward roles are imposed on the artists, and their talent is focused on portraying primitive people and everyday life scenes that are dubious as to their nature." But now *Miners of the Don* brought a curious rendition of *Kuban Cossacks* to the screen, like a coat turned inside out, but in a miners' setting. Lukov's film, which came out right after Pyr'ev's comedy, was perceived by viewers as a direct continuation of the latter, only now in a serious mode. Lukov used the same corps of actors that Pyr'ev had used in *Kuban Cossacks:* Sergei Luk'ianov, who had played the kolkhoz chairman in it, now played the regional committee secretary for Lukov, and the couple in love—the lyrical Klara Luchko and her ill-starred suitor, played by Andrei Petrov— also migrated to Lukov's film. Lukov even brought over the typically Pyr'evian "correct" *chastushki* (only now on the miners' theme) into his film for these lovers: "Oh, how old my boyfriend's gotten / Using the hammer and the shovel. / Start using the cutter-loader, miner, / And propose to your girlfriend then." On the other hand, a key figure of "pre-varnishing" Soviet cinema from *A Great Life,* Petr Aleinikov, remained in *Miners of the Don*. But if in *A Great Life* he embodied the jovial, folksy nature of a sort of instigator inclined to drink, buffoonery, and unpredictability but still a sincere "simple fellow," then in *Miners of the Don* he merely smiles foolishly and, stuffed into a uniform, demonstrates an exemplary conscientiousness and discipline for labor. Even the characters' manner of speaking has changed; instead of the lively speech of *A Great Life*, "correct" theatrical speech pours from the screen in *Miners of the Don*.

Miners of the Don was recognized with a Stalin Prize (although Second Class) and later with another prize at the film festival in Karlovy Vary. Lukov worked for four years on the picture that was initially titled *The Battle for Coal* before coming out as *Miners of the Don*. And if the film was a success (to which the Stalin Prize attested), then this was thanks to the new way of working, as Lukov declared it: "Learn your material! This is the main thing." He explained what this meant: "When you approach the study of contemporary material, especially our Soviet reality, which is moving ahead at a literally stunning pace, you have to know not only what already exists, but mainly to firmly grasp the laws of society's development in order to draw a reliable, precise conclusion, to choose the most typical, so that you aren't left behind a rapidly developing life the moment the work is finished. Thus, when studying the present world, it's important not only to confirm what exists, to recognize what is happening; you [also] have to see the main thing: the future."[11] This is just how Lukov did his work on *Miners of the Don,* by looking into the future.

The dilemma that a Socialist Realist artist had to resolve was how to fit mimetic features with "the revolutionary development of life." The future was encroaching in so headlong a fashion that it swept reality from its path. As a result, the Socialist Realist artists found themselves in constant danger of remaining behind the still-unarrived "tomorrow," incapable of capturing the changing face of reality.

The only means of verifying what was "reflected" turned out to be the testimonies of contemporaries, including the authors themselves. The latter were convinced that since "the slightest inaccuracy would irritate the miners, the tiniest untruth would shake their faith in the whole work," "only a pure alloy of our diverse life should be the source of the film." This alloy of dream and reality might raise questions among viewers: "'Is the Donbass really like this?' people who never were there ask, surprised." The filmmakers affirm that "we shot everything with a chronicler's exactitude." The chronicler's exactitude of filming a nonexistent coal cutter-loader and other such technology, or mineshafts wide as avenues, lit by neon lamps, can cause cognitive shock only in an unprepared viewer. On the contrary, "their own viewer" readily recognizes the already-arrived tomorrow. The miners "recognize in the film the places where they live, work, and have fun, recognize familiar people, and not only in the images created by actors but also in the literal sense of the word, they recognize their own acquaintances, the remarkable people of the Donbass, and many discern themselves on the screen."

Having been burned once for "calumny," this time Lukov spared no bright colors in depicting "achievements" and the joyous toasts in Stalin's honor. Celebrations, festivities, and jubilees follow one after another in the film. The film opens with glorifying words and closes with them. Even the extremely well-disposed "pronouncement" of the Ministry of Cinematography's Artistic Council on the film noted that "as a whole, the film leaves an impression of a certain 'smoothing out.' Too many celebratory episodes and festive meals."[12] Even one of the most officious Soviet film critics, Rostislav Iurenev (granted, in the perestroika years!), wrote about *Miners of the Don* that "this work can serve as a model of varnishing, insincerity, and timeserving. The miners in it live in cottages reminiscent of exhibition pavilions. The mine tunnels are like metro tunnels. The coal cutter-loader that the main hero-innovator introduces is like a concert grand piano. Conflicts, as the Zhdanovist concept says they should, occur between good and even better people. The old miners affectionately yield their places to the young ones. The young ones become inventors and engineers. A veteran miner, when he is retiring, is given a huge house in which there is a magnificent banquet with loyal subjects' toasts and decorous singing of songs without, of course, the tavern's melancholy. . . . Poor Lukov!"[13] In 1946, Soviet film critics did not yet possess a language to describe such a radical aesthetic practice.

On the one hand, as Iurenev wrote, "the viewer coming to the cinema to learn, to come to know reality, requires from his art a faithful and full, comprehensive depiction of life."[14] The singular "viewer" to whom the film critic refers here is not a figure of speech; ultimately, the only viewer-addressee of Soviet cinema was Stalin, who in fact "came to know reality" in the movie theater. All other spectators had many other opportunities for such an acquaintance with reality.

On the other hand, even the most experienced masters of Soviet film dared to call this "life." Typical in this respect were the complaints made by Sergei Gerasimov in an August 19, 1946, session of a commission drafting a resolution regarding the reform of the Ministry of Cinematography's Artistic Council (after the Orgbiuro's session but before the publication of its resolution): "People look around at some sort of empirical reality and at practice, completely forgetting about goals, about tendencies, and stomp around the bush."[15] The mention of *goals* provides the key to understanding exactly what the Central Committee resolutions demanded from art, and particularly from cinema.

Only toward the end of the Stalin era, at the exact time when the "struggle with conflictlessness" began, was film criticism finally able to formulate these aesthetic requirements of Socialist Realism. The eminent Soviet aesthetician Aleksandr Burov explained them as follows: "In the Central Committee's well-known resolution regarding the film *A Great Life,* the filmmakers' ignorance of the material they depicted, the fact that they had not learned the reality they had undertaken to depict, was indicated as a decisive reason for their failure. This means that the filmmakers approached the matter not totally conscientiously, without a clear and keen understanding of the objective before them. The film *Miners of the Don,* with a different approach to the theme, with a clarity of understanding of the objectives that the very same director observed, is a success of Soviet cinema, for it portrays the life of today's Donbass in [its] sweeping development, with its new technology and new people."[16]

Thus, a correct solution is the result of a true understanding of the *objective.* Only this understanding allows for the creation of a "conscientious" work. The "idea" (like art itself) is strictly functional here. Harking back to Konstantin Stanislavskii, Vsevolod Pudovkin talked about such an understanding of "conscientiousness as a creative principle." In answer to what he understood "high art" to be, Stanislavskii said, "It is the kind of art in which there is a *super-objective and continuous action.* And bad art is where there is no super-objective nor continuous action." From this Pudovkin drew the following conclusion:

What Stanislavskii provisionally calls by the abstract term "super-objective" has become for us a quite concrete part of practical social action. When I was working on the first version of *Admiral Nakhimov,* I suffered from failure, and the party explained to me the incorrectly understood and hence also incorrectly executed "super-objective" of the film. In dealing superficially with the main goal—showing the people Nakhimov as the great admiral who determined the development of the Russian navy for many years to come—I got sidetracked with inventing details of his private life that actually didn't exist only because I wanted to make the picture externally interesting. We decided to do the full remake of the film not through specific minor corrections but by turning around the direction of all the film's action as a whole. Not only did we discard the scenes that were no longer needed; we also shot completely new ones that cardinally changed the image of Nakhimov, and ultimately we succeeded in correctly establishing and resolving the "super-objective."[17]

And the objective truly was achieved, the proof of which was the new ("conscientious") version of *Nakhimov,* which won a Stalin Prize, First Class.

Let us now return to Socialist Realist theory: "Conscientiousness *[ideinost']* in the creative work of a Soviet artist in the Socialist Realist method comes out in a new and higher quality. The conscientiousness of Soviet art is Communist conscientiousness; it is based on the Marxist-Leninist theory of scientific communism and hence on scientifically grounded social ideals." This allows the Soviet artist to "catch reality in its revolutionarily progressive development."[18] "Communist conscientiousness" lies at the heart of the principle of party-mindedness (that is, it justifies why an artist must follow the party line). In other words, "conscientiousness" is a sort of set of party eyeglasses that correct the focus of reflecting, selecting, and conceptualizing material from life.

In late Stalinism "the postwar present becomes a synonym of eternity." Accordingly, late-Stalinist art is one of the endless *perfecting* of what is already beautiful and perfect, resolved in the "conflict of the good with the better and of the better with the excellent."[19] In this regard, it is hard to find a more telling example to explain its specifics than a comparison between *A Great Life,* buried by a Central Committee resolution, and *Miners of the Don,* given birth by the same. The blow dealt to the second part of *A Great Life,* one of the first postwar films about the present time, and the dangers of being accused of "denigrating Soviet reality" led to the abrupt dwindling of contemporary subject matter in postwar cinema, remaining in almost nothing but screen adaptations of contemporary Soviet literature that was "approved" by Stalin Prizes (Aleksandr Stolper's *Far from Moscow,* Iulii Raizman's *Cavalier of the Golden Star,* Pudovkin's *The Return of Vasilii Bortnikov,* and the like) and musical comedies (Pyr'ev's *Tale of the Siberian Land* and *Kuban Cossacks,* Grigorii Aleksandrov's *Spring,* and others).

THE THEATER OF ABOLISHED REALITY

Akhmatova's lines, "If only you knew what trash gives rise / To verse, without a tinge of shame . . . ," apply to more than poetry. The Central Committee resolution "On the Repertoire of Drama Theaters and Measures to Improve It" had its genesis in, of all things, an anonymous denunciation that arrived on February 3, 1946, in Beriia's office. Two months later, on April 2, the letter was forwarded to Agitprop head Georgii Aleksandrov.

The letter was an extensive analytical report that ran to forty-two(!) typewritten pages.[20] It was a competently constructed document, clearly written by someone who knew well the workings of not only the theaters, but also the Committee on Arts Affairs from the inside, had extensive information at his or her disposal, worked adeptly with statistics, and understood how the bureaucratic mechanism of clearing plays and other productions functioned (the relevant financial aspects, for example). It was precisely this letter that became a source of the discourse about the absence of plays on contemporary Soviet subject matter: "The theaters' repertoire is structured as if our country had a past but no present" (131). The author placed the blame for this on the state's organs of control: "The noticeable decrease now in the number of plays on Soviet themes is explained . . . by the deliberate policy of the Committee on Arts Affairs, which shifts productions of classical works to the foreground" (135). The author declared that "our theater has become apolitical to a significant degree" (129), as if "the times when the reactionary theory of 'pure' art held sway in art had returned" (130).

The document frankly had an "insider" feel. Although it criticized the Committee on Arts Affairs, it was indirectly aimed at Zhdanov, under whose direction cultural institutions fell. If we recall that it had passed through Beriia's office, then it is easy to suppose that this letter was ordered from its author by somebody acting in the interests of the Beriia-Malenkov dyad. Zhdanov could not bear any direct responsibility for the situation in the theater; "his" cadres (as in the case of the Leningrad journals) were not implicated in this. It was merely an additional step aimed at discrediting the propaganda-ideology leadership. Meanwhile the bureaucratic machine had been set in motion since Agitprop could not let drop a letter that had come from Beriia. The audit that began on June 24, 1946, gave rise to the analytical memorandum titled "On the State of the Drama Theaters' Repertoire," which was signed by Aleksandrov as the head of the Central Committee's Department for Propaganda and Agitation, his deputy Aleksandr Egolin, and the head of the department's Arts Division, Polikarp Lebedev.[21] Largely echoing the conclusions drawn in the anonymous letter, as well as its examples, this document served as the basis for the Central Committee's future resolution.

Utilizing the same statistics as the anonymous letter's author, these leaders of Agitprop pointed out the abrupt decline in quality of the plays then being staged in Soviet theaters. If in 1943 the most widely performed were Konstantin Simonov's *Russian People,* Leonid Leonov's *Invasion,* and Aleksandr Korneichuk's *The Front,* then in 1946 dozens of theaters throughout the country were putting on "kitschy" plays "devoid of a message," such as Vladimir Mass and Mikhail Chervinskii's *Somewhere in Moscow,* Mikhail Vodop'ianov and Iurii Laptev's *Forced Landing,* Aleksandr Gladkov's *Bygone Days,* and Nikolai Pogodin's *The Ferrywoman.* Many of the authors were not so much dramatists as feuilletonists or essayists, or even people who had no direct connection with the actual writing (Vodop'ianov, for example, was a pilot), who "had got the hang of 'coming up with' entertaining plots and endow[ed] their invented characters with vulgar argot, provincialisms, and trite little expressions that disfigure[d] the Russian literary language. . . . They do not have a single vivid and truthful character in them" (177).

The plays pointed out in this document would be enumerated in the Central Committee resolution, which declared that in them "the Soviet people are portrayed in a deformed, caricatured form as primitive and uncultured, with philistine tastes and manners." The resolution banned not simply the particular plays, but also the trend of mass culture as such. The selection of plays named in the resolution provides a clear idea about the sort of drama that must not be offered on the Soviet stage. Hence it is worth taking a closer look at them, the more so since when they disappeared from the repertoire, they were never examined.

Above all, many of them were lowbrow comedies of dubious quality. This is unsurprising since during the war many plays had been created for theaters on the front. Accordingly, these plays were not only thematically tied to various sorts of wartime situations, but also came down to the level of "soldiers' humor." Typical in this respect was the "frontlines life comedy" *Birthday,* which was running in thirty-four of the country's theaters. This play was so popular that it was adapted to the screen at the same time (as the film *The Busy Estate,* which was joined by comedies such as *The Aerial Driver* and *The Heavenly Slug,* which were also filmed at the time). They were essentially vaudeville. The jolly war that they depicted, where comic and chipper soldiers appeared and theatrical passions erupted, was no longer needed. But along with the war plays, plays about peacetime life, written in the same vaudeville style, also became superfluous, like *Forced Landing,* in which a girl dressed as a man appears in the role of a tractor driver. The ruse is revealed. A pilot falls in love with her as a girl, but the girls who fail to guess her gender also fall in love with her, believing her to be a young man. The whole play consists essentially of endless courtships and vaudevillian romantic misunderstandings.

These plays were the epitome of the most lowbrow mass culture, which was, nevertheless, in great demand. They stood out not only for their colloquialness, but also, as the resolution noted, for their "vulgar argot, provincialisms, and trite little expressions." The following is a characteristic dialogue, this one between two girlfriends in *Forced Landing:*

Frosia: Just have a look in the mirror. Your whole mug's swollen up.
Niushka: What a primitive opinion you-all have. Of course. Do you really understand anything? You've not even read *Anna Karenina.*
Frosia: What do you mean, didn't read it? I read *Anna.* That's the one threw herself under a train.
Niushka: And what made her do that?
Frosia: She's a stupid woman. You saw who she was chasing after. But since that's the way it was, her real-life husband couldn't do anything about it, like him, the officer guy. . . . What's his name, Voronin?

Niushka: Vronskii, fool!
Frosia: You're the fool.

This play was running in seventy-four(!) theaters around the country and was fourth in the repertoire in the number of performances. The historical version of such a plot, but with a woman dressed many times as a man, was represented by the comedy *Bygone Days,* which was playing in forty-five theaters.

Another variety of the genre was the review *Somewhere in Moscow,* which was playing in 117 of the country's theaters (third place in the repertoire). Its main character is Lieutenant Mel'nikov, who is searching in Moscow for the girl who saved his life on the front. As the play progresses, he ends up in three different apartments by mistake, ends up in laughable situations, and finally finds the girl. Comedies like this were viewed as vulgar, lacking in message, and indulging "backward tastes."

Relegated to the ranks of "lightweight escapist plays" also were cloak-and-dagger plays in which the cunning schemes of rogues stealing canned goods in factories during the war were unmasked. Such was the satirical comedy *Extraordinary Law,* which was running in sixty theaters. Although satirical, police-driven plays of this sort about "plunderers of socialist property" were quite popular—they unmasked profiteers and thieves, the law triumphed, and the rank-and-file viewers' sense of social justice was satisfied—they were now considered "lowbrow" and had the defect of being "light entertainment." They had too little "conscientiousness" and too few party-minded protagonists, and they overemphasized the negative aspects of Soviet reality (even if these aspects were the exception). As always, mysteries and plays about spies enjoyed huge popularity with mass audiences, such as *Window in the Woods,* which was having a successful run in many theaters.

The main characters in these plays—comedic misfits, rogues, and amateur detectives—attracted their audience in different ways. What united them was that they all were typical characters from popular culture and, as such, were unfit for "conscientious" art. Although they were woven into Soviet themes (albeit "politically unbalanced" ones), they were subjugated more to the logic of genre than of ideology. But attempts to politicize the popular genres ended with predictable flops. The characters lacked the discipline required by the plots; they were too individualized and too "unbridled," and they operated without regard for ideological conventions.

In short, the drama theaters' postwar repertoire enumerated in the Central Committee's resolution was an exhaustive collection of "incorrect" plays. And if the resolution failed to explain exactly what the new Soviet theater should be like, it gave a comprehensive idea of what it should *not* be.

Two years passed after the resolution was adopted. One could sum up what had happened in the interim. The situation of the repertoire had changed very little. However, there was a radical change in the theaters themselves. According to G. Shtein, author of an article in the journal *Teatr,* "It seemed such a short time ago that there were lines at the theater box offices and that before the beginning of the shows, administrators hid in the wings from people who refused to believe there were no seats left; but for more than a year now, these same administrators, and others besides, are bending over backward to find different ways to draw audiences to the theater."[22] Even after prices were reduced, "attendance and receipts have not risen at all." Shtein tried to account for this by the unexpected growth in audiences' demands: "The fact that recently in Tula there were 150 spectators at the sixth performance of the comedy *Taimyr Calls You* must be explained not by supposing that the performances there were good before and now they are bad . . . but solely by the fact that alongside the growth in the real value of the ruble, viewers' demands of the theater have also grown precipitously."[23]

Nonetheless, the abolition of ration cards was not the only issue. If in 1948 the auditoriums were empty for the most popular comedies of the postwar repertoire, then what about the plays about kolkhoz and industrial life, in which there had never been any interest? It turns out that the problem was not the plays themselves but the productions. Shtein continues: "When staging Soviet playwrights' plays devoted to portrayal of contemporary Soviet reality, our theaters still too rarely observe the kind of passionate interest in them that, for example, MKhAT did when it so brilliantly produced its contemporary Chekhov's *Seagull* on its stage, which had flopped in Petersburg."

If even the metropolitan theaters were unprepared for the invasion of Soviet *Seagulls,* then the picture at the periphery was completely depressing. Shtein cited the example of the Saratov Drama Theater, where one foreign play provided 70 percent of ticket sales, the play running fourteen times a month (out of the total of thirty performances), while four plays by contemporary Soviet playwrights played seven times and provided 14 percent of receipts. In his words, this was "the typical situation everywhere." But the conclusion drawn by the critic did not at all follow from the situation he described: "It can all be explained by the quality not of contemporary plays but of theaters' productions. That is, the theaters stage good plays badly."[24] In one and the same theater, productions of foreign plays had much greater success than productions of native authors' plays, among which Chekhov plays did not appear.

Three more years passed after the adoption of the "historic resolutions," and then the Committee on Arts Affairs presented a report and an action plan to the Central Committee. The voluminous memorandum attached to this report, authored by Vladimir Kruzhkov (head of the Central Committee's Literature and Art Division) and Dmitrii Shepilov (first deputy to the head of the Central Committee's Department for Propaganda and Agitation), was sent to the Central Committee secretary, Georgii Malenkov. Its authors wrote that very little had changed in playwriting and theater. Although they stated that theaters were showing "works successful from the standpoint of ideas and artistry, which correctly reflect the life of the Soviet people," and that "the drama theaters' repertoire has been enriched by works on the subject of the working class and kolkhoz village life in the postwar period,"[25] when it came down to specific plays and theaters, the picture was bleak: "an unsatisfactory state of playwriting. Playwrights at present are left to their own devices" (3); "uninteresting, recurring conflicts," "unconvincing and sketchy characters," and "monotony of genre" (4).

The country's main drama theaters—MKhAT and the Malyi—were cited as examples of the flaws mentioned. In MKhAT, the only production on a contemporary subject staged in 1951 was Sergei Mikhalkov's *The Lost House*. The production, however, "came off as defective": Mikhalkov's play "interprets the issue of the morale of the Soviet people in a petty way, from a philistine perspective" (6). Hence "the production came off as devoid of the truth of life" and was removed from the repertoire. A second play contemplated for staging, Aleksandr Kron's *The Party's Candidate*, as it "incorrectly reflect[ed] the life of the factory collective, was subjected to criticism in the party press" (7). Accordingly, work on it was suspended. MKhAT had no other plays on contemporary subjects. "As regards repertoire for the future, hopelessness prevails in the theater. MKhAT has no repertoire plan for 1952, and is experiencing a period of stagnation in its creative activity." It turned out that "MKhAT's serious trouble with repertoire is explained mainly by the fact that the theater does not work with playwrights. Stanislavskii and Nemirovich-Danchenko's traditions of working with Chekhov and Gorky are forgotten" (7).

Without offering advice as to where Chekhovs and Gorkys might be found, the Agitprop functionaries themselves undertook the selection of plays worthy of MKhAT. But it was immediately apparent that all the plays they examined were defective. One had "serious limitations"; another had "major limitations that decrease the conscientious and artistic qualities, [and it is] overburdened with superfluous scenes"; a third play (August Jakobson's *At the Border of Night and Day*) "should not be recommended for staging at MKhAT" at all since "the role of the Communist Party in the fight for peace is not revealed." Thus, the Central Committee division's recommendation boiled down to the following: "Task the Committee [on Arts Affairs] and the MKhAT management with discussing the possibility of staging Kondrat Krapiva's play *The Larks Are Singing* at the theater." This play, "about kolkhoz construction in its current phase, reveals the significance of an issue as important as the correct allocation of natural and monetary income in the kolkhozes" (7).

As far as the Malyi Theater was concerned, its situation seemed even more hopeless to the overseers from the Central Committee. The majority of the productions it had staged over the five years since the Central Committee resolution were "weak." Only one play on a contemporary subject had been staged in 1951, *The Lutonin Family,* which "because of the play's weakness has not become a meaningful event of theatrical art." The theater was now "in a dead end of repertoire," and all the plays targeted for production were severely criticized. The play *Nastia Kolosova* "is already readied by the theater and included in the repertoire. Judging by its artistic merits, the production is not a theatrical contribution to a development of the kolkhoz theme." A second play was "an artistically weak work." The author of a third play "has failed to reveal the great and complex theme in an artistically convincing way," hence "the play should not be staged at the Malyi Theater" (8).

All of these defects, which were "the consequence of the playwrights' unsatisfactory work," were ascribed to other theaters as well. The report recommended "changing, on the part of the Writers' Union and the Committee on Arts Affairs, the methods of managing the work of playwrights and requiring them [the union and the committee] to implement constant conscientious leadership of the creative work of playwrights and theaters" (9).

Thus, the theaters were initially guilty. Afterward, blame was laid on the playwrights. But the problem was actually in the aesthetic program of "conscientious theater" *(ideinyi teatr)* itself that had been imposed by the Central Committee's resolution. It had resulted not only in the disappearance from the repertoire of the Soviet and foreign "light" plays, but also in the large-scale production of new "conscientious" ones. The Central Committee resolution was a typical censorial document, but in proscribing, it was above all aimed toward the creation of new plays and demanded that the Committee on Arts Affairs and the board of the Soviet Writers' Union "concentrate [their] attention on the creation of contemporary Soviet repertoire."

This sort of repertoire assumed the creation, figuratively speaking, of *Miners of the Don* instead of the second part of *A Great Life*. To this end, the Committee on Arts Affairs was tasked with "annually staging in every drama theater no fewer than 2–3 new plays of high quality with respect to ideas and artistry on contemporary Soviet subjects."[26] This in turn required a massive production of new plays. Accordingly, the resolution made provision for countrywide competitions for the best contemporary Soviet plays, to be jointly run by the Committee on Arts Affairs and the board of the Soviet Writers' Union.

But the resolution led to more than a quantitative growth in plays. It consolidated the Soviet "conflictless drama," introducing new genres, types, and conflicts. This drama was distinguished by a peculiar style, and it developed in a specific discursive space. It was populated by unheard-of characters, the likes of which neither prerevolutionary theater, nor revolutionary-era drama, nor the post-Stalin era knew. Stalinist conflictless drama was aesthetically unique.

On April 7, 1952, *Pravda* issued an editorial titled "Overcoming the Lag in Dramaturgy," which stated that "the strength of Soviet drama is in its real-life truth" and that accordingly it "must show real-life conflicts, without which there is no drama"; it declared that "we must not be afraid of showing defects and difficulties" and proclaimed that the source of dramaturgy's "backwardness" was "the notorious theory of conflictlessness."[27] But it was unclear what kind of theory this was; where, by whom, and when it had been formulated; and how such a harmful theory could have dominated theater after so many of Stalin's cleansings (suffice it to recall the campaigns to canonize the Stanislavskii system and the "MKhAT realistic method," the persecution of Meyerhold in the latter half of the 1930s, the 1946 resolution we have examined, or the late-1949 campaign to exterminate the "cosmopolitan theater critics").

The originator of the pernicious theory was soon revealed to be the regime-pampered dramatist and Stalin Prize winner Nikolai Virta, who in his review of Sergei Gerasimov's film *Country Doctor* had declared that Soviet life "does not allow the conflict between the remnants of capitalism in the people's consciousness and the Communist consciousness to *grow into* a complex, protracted dramatic collision."[28] This quote migrated from one article to another, and the "battle against conflictlessness" turned into an unrelenting campaign that gripped all of Soviet art in 1952. Critics and playwrights (and prose writers and poets right behind them) vied to be the first to convince each other and readers that they had noticed the harmfulness of this "theory," as if they had not been writing absolutely the same thing as Virta had for many years.

The term "theory of conflictlessness" emerged in 1952 during Stalin's preparations for a new wave of terror, at the same time as calls for a revival of satire and the emergence of Soviet "Gogols and Shchedrins." It was unmasked as an "anti-party" and "anti-national" theory. To counter it, Stalin's speeches were quoted—those about the necessity of criticism and self-criticism, about the fact that development always occurs "as a struggle"; it was asserted that "the struggle is between forward-looking people and people alien to our society, and not between 'good and better people' as the poor excuses for critics tried to claim when they devised the notorious theory of 'conflictlessness.'"[29]

Meanwhile, as I have written elsewhere, Socialist Realism did not simply *portray* "life in its revolutionary development; [Socialist Realism] produced it [this life]."[30] And, in fact, if Soviet literature in the 1920s told stories about the unconscious masses (or particular representatives of them) who under the influence of the party's protagonists (commissars or party organizers) were reforged into conscientious builders of socialism, then mature Socialist Realism, as if having made the journey of reforging alongside Soviet society, depicted a by then completely different country. Reforging was the basis of the conflict, and the "remaking of human material" was the subject of early Soviet literature. But in the era of late Stalinism, what the Soviet viewers saw on the theaters' stages was the already reforged country that had passed through the crucible of Bolshevik re-education. One of the products of this harmonized society was indeed the conflictless play.

Industrial and kolkhoz plays were transformed into a sort of Socialist Realist *commedia dell'arte*—with a stock collection of masks, characters, and gags. It was as if the characters had arrived from prewar drama, but they were unrecognizable. For example, the cultural level of the workers in them was simply incommensurable with what the viewer saw in 1920s and early 1930s plays from the era of cultural revolution and the struggle for "culturedness." By now, culture had become part of their everyday life. In the play by the Tur brothers and Ivan Pyr'ev, *The Lutonin Family* (1950), a young working-class couple is getting ready to go out. When the girl's mother asks the young man where he wants to go, he answers "To the Tchaikovsky Hall, Angiia Vasilev'na. To a concert. I really love music. They say it cleanses your soul." The ironic overtones of such responses—as if they came from Zoshchenko's "cultured" characters—no longer penetrate this world. But such refined tastes are not just characteristic of young workers. The artistic preferences of old workers are also far from any hint of "vulgarity." The following dialogue is heard between two such workers in Vadim Kozhevnikov's play *The River in Flames* (1950):

> Gusev: Maybe I should play a record for you? (*Flips through the records.*) Do you want to hear a foxtrot from abroad?
> Sukhov: No.
> Gusev: But why not?
> Sukhov: That's for mangy people.
> Gusev: Want to hear some Vertinskii?
> Sukhov: Play the funeral service for yourself, but I don't need it yet.

Workers such as these, of course, cannot watch the second part of *A Great Life;* the "vulgar romances" and "gypsy traits" would offend their ears. In the world that the workers in these plays inhabit, high culture has become a part of a high standard of living. In Iulii Chepurin's play *Conscience* (1949), the buoy keeper Zakharych tells about the gift he received from his daughter, a quality control inspector in a factory: "I have a boat now with a motor. Iul'ka gave it to me for my birthday. I pulled the cord, put on the gas—and could have gone to the end of the world! Instantly! These are the kinds of gifts they've started giving." In the same play, the mistress of the house complains to her guest—a Hero of the Soviet Union—about her son: "My son's about to build a garage. . . . He's decided to buy a car." Her husband tells about the family's worries: "I'm suggesting planting a couple of apple trees here. But Maksim insists on a pergola. It will hide the view of the factory, how could you not see that! . . . I suggest planting some raspberries come fall, but Maksim fights me for space to plant flowers. Conflict again." The lady of the house laments, "They have the conflicts, but I have to take the rap. You can't get either one to crawl out of the factory, and I furnish the beauty by myself." The workers' lives in Stalinist plays are full of just such conflicts over "beautification." Apple trees versus a pergola, raspberries versus flowers. . . .

The Soviet industrial play, just like the industrial novel, was the product of revolutionary culture. However, as the working class was losing its class distinctiveness by blending into the boundless masses of peasants and its leading political role in the Soviet "state of all the people," it was becoming de-realized in art. The process of consolidating the "new class"—the Soviet bureaucracy—proceeded in parallel to this. This class did not have sufficient ideological legitimacy and needed representation. The most effective genre forms for these goals turned out to be ones that already existed but had been deserted. Among them was the industrial play.

Critics turned their attention rather late to the turnaround that had occurred. In mid-1952, Efim Kholodov wrote: "If at the end of the evening shows you gathered up the characters from all the Moscow theaters into one hall, very likely amid the crowd of Spanish grandees, American businessmen, long-bearded merchants, noisy students, and bungling directors, it would be extremely hard to find simple working people—the main characters from our life."[31] Even Anatolii Surov, who himself was practically a legislator of such plays, found himself distressed in 1953 that "the problem of endless encounters with directors, managers, bosses, chairmen, and party organization secretaries, all presented in variations on a theme, has one very important aspect: Soviet playwrights' insufficient attention to the image of the simple Soviet working man. . . . [The characters] that collide and fight are assorted . . . 'bureaucratic' types, detached from the people, knowing neither their life nor their aspirations."[32]

Meanwhile, these plays did reflect a quite real collision. Though ending up in the position of a superpower after the war, the Soviet Union fell into a paradoxical situation. On the one hand, this role was too much from the very start for a country bled dry by war and with an inefficient economy, and once it embraced the role, the country with each passing year got bogged down deeper in the defects of its structurally inadequate sociopolitical order and its abnormal economic structure. On the other hand, the preparations for the war, the victory in it, and postwar reconstruction all created a false impression of the economic effectiveness of a planned state economy. But above all, the war had shaped a new elite. The wartime director—the authoritarian type of manager focused on fulfilling assignments at any cost—became the exemplar of a Soviet boss. This was a peculiar social type: a freakish, psychologically complex hybrid of a bureaucrat, a reporting officer, and an adventurer. Even if a Soviet play wanted to avoid any conflicts at all, if it had such a central character—simultaneously strong-willed and power-hungry, cynical, and convinced of the rightness of the Soviet order—it would be unable to do this. This was how the new type of play emerged that dominated the Soviet stage, in which the bureaucrat-hero engaged with "simple folk." These are the relationships that the Soviet bureaucratic-industrial play depicted.

There was only one class in the Soviet country that possessed plenary powers: the *nomenklatura*. The struggle for power was the main professional activity of this class. This struggle was most often hidden but no less bitter because of that. It was just this struggle, flowing through the social capillaries, that set the *nomenklatura* machine in motion, with its all-encompassing system of internal dependencies, subordinations, and tyranny on its various levels. Literature engaged in camouflaging this real struggle, passing it off as anything but what it was in reality—as a struggle to fulfill the plan, to introduce new technologies, or to raise the level of educational work.

In fact, this simulation was what provided work for the enormous army of Soviet playwrights. These plays were mass-produced in the

Soviet Union since the plays did not linger in the repertoire; the same play could run in dozens of theaters throughout the country in one season, only to disappear without trace in the following one. The quantity of these plays is attested by the fact that the playwrights' section in the Moscow Writers' Organization alone in 1953 counted eighty members. Many provincial theaters worked with local authors, who structured their plays around local material to ready-made templates from the capitals, only with bureaucratized bosses of lesser calibers.

"A LEAD PEA FROM THAT SECRETARY"

The Central Committee's 1946 resolution concerning the journals *Zvezda* and *Leningrad* went down in the history of literature and Soviet culture as a model of the Soviet regime's crude administration and prohibitive policy concerning art and as one of the most somber chapters in the creative work of Akhmatova and Zoshchenko. In the eyes of the party leadership, authors subjected to ostracism were unreformable, but since they had no institutional power, they presented no threat. But the "threat" from their creative work was deliberately exaggerated in the resolution. As we learn from the transcript of a debate in the Orgbiuro[33] and from the detailed notes of two Leningrad writers who participated in the debate, Dmitrii Levonevskii[34] and Petr Kapitsa,[35] Zoshchenko and Akhmatova ended up at the center of the campaign by chance; neither had given offense for anything in the summer of 1946 (and even Zoshchenko's short story in *Zvezda*, "The Adventures of a Monkey," was being reprinted for the fourth time when this appearance in the journal elicited Stalin's obviously exaggerated reaction). However, the choice of victims was not accidental. Authors respected in the writers' community with long-standing reputations were subjected to attack as a warning to the rest.

These resolutions actually were a signal of preserving the status quo, of a return to the norms established before the war. It was a sobering cold shower for the few who were hoping for some sort of "ideological relaxation." In this respect, they played an important stabilizing role. Although they unburdened writers of any liberal illusions, their influence on writers' moods should not be exaggerated. There were few dissidents among them.[36] And despite the fact that they could have taken this as an attack on freedom in creative work, the overwhelming majority of writers, who had long since grown used to the Soviet conditions of "literary work," regarded the resolutions as a *positive* signal that affirmed their status as high-ranking state functionaries and that of the Writers' Union as an important political institution. This status needed affirmation after the war, which had shaken up many institutions established in the 1930s. Petr Pavlenko best expressed this mood in a letter to Vsevolod Vishnevskii dated October 7, 1946: "What's good about the Central Committee's decisions is that they officially recognized us as service class people, statesmen! It's about time!"[37]

Ultimately, it was to just this "mass of writers" that the resolutions were addressed in the first place. Writers such as Pavlenko and Vishnevskii, writer-functionaries, were in Stalin's mind exactly the ones who defined the process of literary production. The rest were a voiceless majority who had no influence. The best idea about the atmosphere then prevailing in Soviet literature is provided by a wide-ranging analytical report about the state of literature and art in the USSR written by Isaiah Berlin, who after the war was in Moscow as a British Embassy official and became one of the important characters in the drama that played out in 1946. As it happened, his account was the last detailed sketch of the state of culture in the USSR on the eve of the 1946 resolutions' adoption. Berlin wrote that the regime need not worry about problems going forth since "contemporary Soviet culture is not marching with its old firm, confident, or even hopeful step; there is a sense of emptiness, a total absence of winds or currents. . . . Certainly the present aspect of the Soviet artistic and intellectual scene suggests that the initial great impulse is over, and that it may be a considerable time before anything new or arresting in the realm of ideas, as opposed to steady competence and solid achievement firmly set by authority within the framework of established tradition, is likely to emerge from the USSR."[38]

A keen and well-informed observer, Berlin had precisely characterized the state of profound anabiosis into which Soviet culture had sunk as the result of the exhaustion of the revolutionary impulse. From his account, written just a few months before the Central Committee adopted the resolutions, it would be hard to predict a storm brewing that was just about to erupt onto Soviet culture. It seemed that there was simply nowhere from which it might come; Soviet culture had entered an immobility phase. But a stimulus was needed to make *Kuban Cossacks* and *Cavalier of the Golden Star* into exemplars of "steady competence and solid achievement firmly set by authority within the framework of established tradition." And that is exactly what the 1946 resolutions were. They resulted in not only a censorial and ideological clampdown, but also a golden age of Socialist Realism.

Berlin saw no signs of any independence whatsoever (let alone disobedience) of intellectuals and artists. But Soviet literature was for Stalin paramount as an instrument for mobilizing efforts to uplift the ruined country and in the incipient showdown with the West. And since his understanding of art was politically utilitarian and purely bureaucratic, he saw the issue as restoring control over the ideological sphere, which, as it seemed to him, had become unsteady during the war. A return of political orthodoxy was a signal of such a restoration. And the cruelty, outright callousness, and intemperance that accompanied it were supposed to signal complete control over the situation. These actions manifested more a demonstration of power than the urgency to vex any sort of intelligentsia revolt that could occupy any place in Stalin's paranoid consciousness. However, the fact that he solved the problem with literary functionaries proved that he continued to view art more as an institution and an instrument of political influence than as individual artists and intellectuals with the vague moods, sentiments, and expectations they supposedly had.

Of the three resolutions, unquestionably the most resonant one, which signified a true historical turnaround and for many years to come defined the ideological course that the country had to follow from that point on, was the one titled "On the Journals *Zvezda* and *Leningrad*." This is only partly tied to the fact that the resolution was aimed at high-profile Soviet writers; much more important was the fact that it was precisely where Stalin's will came together with the interests of his inner circle. Moreover, this resolution impacted all the Leningrad institutions and was accompanied by Zhdanov's blistering speeches.

The resolution regarding literature was assured the greatest influence by virtue of the very status of literature in literature-centric Stalinist culture. Unsurprisingly, this resolution specifically has also been the most widely studied—both in terms of its consequences for its direct victims, Akhmatova[39] and Zoshchenko,[40] and in terms of influence on the development of Soviet literature as a whole.[41] Nevertheless, the fundamental role of these resolutions was that they became the cornerstone of the aesthetics of radical Socialist Realism and paved the way for its full implementation.

The resolution concerning the Leningrad journals is also interesting because it reveals the functioning mechanism of Soviet culture in the Stalin era. It is exemplary of the bureaucratic *nomenklatura* process of decision making. The prerequisite, as always, was the will of Stalin. But the directive itself, and the forms assigned to its workings, were the result of maneuvering by two main figures battling for influence: Malenkov, who had fallen into disfavor at the time, and Zhdanov, who was quickly gaining bureaucratic clout. Standing behind each of them were insider clans of apparatchiks, entire parties of the *nomenklatura*. Malenkov, who had held responsibility in the Central Committee for ideological issues during the war, had done everything he could to weaken the positions of Zhdanov's prewar protégés (especially Aleksandr Shcherbakov, who was in charge of literature), and he had personally initiated the 1943–44 campaign against Zoshchenko. Zhdanov was forced to accept this challenge. And in every instance this meant particularly aggressive attacks on writers, who were supposed to be the lightning rods taking Stalin's wrath off Zhdanov's cadres.

The Central Committee's 1944 decisions about literary journals had essentially laid the groundwork for the 1946 campaign. It is interesting that it was at just this time that *Zvezda* and *Leningrad* were excluded from a list of journals that Agitprop had preliminarily censored. As Denis Babichenko notes, "Malenkov understood perfectly well that literary journals that remained outside the control of [Agitprop], that is, in an exceptional position, would provoke obligatory reprimands with the very first error they made."[42] And that is exactly what happened. We might also question how accidental the reprint of Zoshchenko's "The Adventures of a Monkey" was (the story that raised Stalin's hackles) without its author's prior agreement.

As Vitalii Volkov has shown, the campaign against Zoshchenko's tale *Before Sunrise* in 1943 was the start of "a multi-move strategy that Malenkov played against Zhdanov."[43] The 1946 resolution became a part of this strategy, when Malenkov was battling Zhdanov's protégés (above all Aleksei Kuznetsov), who had squeezed him out in Moscow. It is even stranger that these resolutions came to be called "Zhdanovist" (especially the one concerning the Leningrad journals since it was accompanied by, as we have noted, his blistering speeches). But in actuality, the last resolution was particularly harmful for Zhdanov. As V. I. Demidov and V. A. Kutuzov have written, "But what use

did Zhdanov have for a huge scandal surrounding the party organization and cultural stratum that he personally—for eleven years!—had
shaped and fostered? . . . After all, did his political authority not also
suffer?" Without access to the documents that had at the time yet to be
published, they concluded, "It seems that there was some third person
involved, besides Stalin and Zhdanov, who had escaped our inquisitive
gaze."[44] The later declassified Orgbiuro transcript leaves no doubt that
this third person was Malenkov.

All of Malenkov's interventions and retorts demonstrated his obvious desire to reduce the discussion of the Leningrad journals to a
denunciation of the Leningrad party authorities who had confirmed
Zoshchenko as a member of the editorial board of *Zvezda*. As a result, he succeeded in drawing Stalin's attention to the "crude political
mistakes" of the Leningrad party leaders, and this was reflected in the
resolution. During the discussions at the Orgbiuro, Malenkov talked
about nothing else—not about the journals, nor about any other works
and authors being discussed/condemned, but every time about the fact
that Leningrad party leaders had "sheltered" Zoshchenko when he was
being criticized in Moscow. And it was precisely Zhdanov's desire to
deflect the blow (or soften it) from his own cadres that dictated the
jaunty, aggressive tone of his attacks on writers themselves: "As if de-
flecting the listeners' attention from a harsh appraisal of the activities
of the [Leningrad] city committee and demonstrating his own resolve
in the fight against 'sedition,' Zhdanov tooled his speech with a mass of
monstrous accusations and outright invective addressed to Leningrad
writers and their protectors in the journals' editorial boards, borrow-
ing many epithets from Stalin's speech at the Orgbiuro, and for decades
making this speech of his a symbol of the state's criminal attitude toward the intelligentsia."[45]

It is not surprising that Zhdanov's Leningrad speeches—which
Veniamin Kaverin called "invective-overloaded barracks-like drivel"[46]—
pleased Stalin so much that he called them "superlative." Stalin, and
not the writers or the party workers, was their only real addressee.

As opposed to Malenkov, Stalin wanted to give a warning not so
much to the Leningrad party cadres as to writers themselves. Hence he
constantly talked about the "apolitical," "unprincipled," and "vulgar"
faults of the authors criticized in the resolution. Zoshchenko's failings
in the latter two aspects were in particular inscribed into the aesthetics

Stalin proclaimed. An attack on satire was an attack on allegory as such (Zoshchenko's prose was read as allegory, insinuation, and "denigration of Soviet reality"). This was the flip side of the attack on reality itself in Lukov's film.

The battle against Zoshchenko did not begin with the 1946 resolution, nor did it end there. Attacks on him had been incessant since the 1920s, and starting in 1943, they took on the nature of systematic persecution.[47] Stalin's especially hostile attitude toward Zoshchenko can be explained by the fact that, as the author himself suspected, the leader discerned direct attacks on himself in several of Zoshchenko's short stories, as well as derision of his manner of speaking and parody of the Stalinist cult. These suspicions, as Mikhail Vaiskopf has convincingly demonstrated, were by no means unfounded.[48] Zoshchenko deliberately brought these allusions into his texts, not only in one of his stories about Lenin, in which the reader could easily recognize the moustached boor as Stalin,[49] but even earlier in his 1933 story "The Professions I've Had," which was structured entirely on a subtle parody of Stalin's self-glorifications. The abundance and transparency of the allusions in the story unambiguously attest to the fact that this is the writer's strategy, not any sort of coincidental echoes. As a result, Vaiskopf writes, "Stalin, with his pointedly suspicious attention to literature, could easily discern a 'farcical' travesty of his own zeal—and his own biography—in Zoshchenko's language. The persecution organized in 1946 was the cruel victory of parody over the parodist."[50]

It was, however, a Pyrrhic victory. The Central Committee resolutions gave rise to a critical discourse that was supposed to maintain and promote a new "Communist conscientiousness." The key concept introduced into the discourse of literary criticism was the idea of "conscientious/unconscientiousness *(ideinost'/bezydeinost')*," repeated in the resolution's text (in the thirteen paragraphs of its recital) twelve times and the same number of times in Zhdanov's speech. It is telling that Zhdanov mainly mentioned "unconscientiousness"; Zoshchenko was declared a "champion of unconscientiousness" and, in publishing his work, *Zvezda* had engaged in "the propaganda of unconscientiousness," thus becoming a "haven for unconscientiousness." Meanwhile, Zhdanov declared that "there can be no place [in Soviet literature] for putrid, empty, unconscientious" works. After the defeat in the 1905–7 revolution, he said, the Russian intelligentsia had "proclaimed unconscientiousness to be their standard." Russian poets, he continued, had begun to "preach unconscientiousness" and were trying to drag literature down "into the swamp of unconscientiousness." Akhmatova had unquestionably become, he declared, "one of the standard-bearers of empty, unconscientious, aristocratic-salon poetry"; her poetry could only "poison the consciousness of youth with a putrid spirit of unconscientiousness, apolitical attitudes, and despondency," while instead she ought "to teach not in a spirit of nihilism and unconscientiousness but in a spirit of courage and revolutionariness." Akhmatova and Zoshchenko had "railroaded" the "art for art's sake" motto and, "masking themselves with unconscientiousness, [had] imposed ideas on the Soviet people that were alien to them," trying to distract them "from the critical issues of political and social struggle and divert their attention into the direction of banal, unconscientious literature."

The term "conscientiousness" was invoked to replace the concept of "tendentiousness," which had been used in nineteenth-century criticism. The abstract "unconscientiousness" turned out to be anti-Soviet "tendentiousness." The former was ascribed to Akhmatova, who "led the reader away" from the present time. The latter was applied to Zoshchenko, who, on the contrary, wrote "unconscientiously" about the present—that is, in an anti-Soviet manner. This required any of Zoshchenko's texts to be read as necessarily critical, satirical, and subversive. "Unconscientiousness" (that is, anti-Soviet subversiveness) had to be discovered in texts where there was no such tendency at all. This left critics in a potentially comical situation since it demanded a deliberately perverse reading of Zoshchenko's stories.

For example, just after the resolution on the Leningrad journals was published, the Central Committee's Personnel Department prepared a reference document about all of Zoshchenko's works published shortly before the resolution. Among them was a collection of his short stories (essentially a brochure) issued in one of the series published by the journal *Ogonek*. The Central Committee censors criticized every story in it except for "The Adventures of a Monkey," against which the resolution had already fulminated. The criticism went as follows:

> The story "After Thirty Years" tells how the author came to his sister's and "gave every one of her children a present of a hundred rubles for toys. And I gave my own cigarette case, which was engraved 'Be Happy' in gold letters, to her husband. Then I gave her children each a hundred

rubles for wine and candy." The moral of the story is "One ought to love and pity children, at least the good ones." It will be clear to every reader that, in Zoshchenko's opinion, children are not loved in the Soviet Union—not only bad ones, but the good ones as well. And to make everyone happy, you have to give them all gifts. The story "The Poker" relates an amusing incident about how a stoker had only one poker . . . for six ovens. He burned a servant girl with this poker. Then he got the idea to have a poker for every oven. They put in a request, but . . . there were no pokers in the warehouse. This little story could be printed in any foreign newspaper as a model of anti-Soviet propaganda, [showing how] even pokers are scarce in the Soviet Union.[51]

Perhaps only Zoshchenko's own characters could analyze his stories this way. Essentially, that is what happened.

In contrast to the resolutions regarding films and theater, the one about the Leningrad journals created a historical backdrop for discussing the topic of "unconscientiousness." This historicization of the main literary villains was amplified in Zhdanov's speeches, where he had much to say about the "Serapion Brothers," to which Zoshchenko had belonged in his youth, and about the Symbolists and Acmeists, from whose milieu Akhmatova had emerged. Zhdanov even quoted Mandel'shtam (which only a Central Committee secretary could allow himself to do in 1946). The circles widened to include the *Landmarks* figures. Following Zhdanov's lead, critics set about widening them further. They painted a vivid picture of "the terrible atmosphere of spiritual bankruptcy characteristic of decadent literature."[52] Lenin's criticism of "intelligentsia defection" and the "counterrevolutionary" *Landmarks* group came into play, as did Gorky's invectives against bourgeois art and Plekhanov's criticism of the suffocating atmosphere of "literary decay." The history of Soviet literature was also intensively rewritten. Much was said about Mayakovsky's struggle against Futurism and his "polemic with the excesses of 'leftist art.'"[53]

These historical digressions were necessary to intensify the guilt of the accused: Akhmatova and Zoshchenko were not simply "vulgarians," "slanderers," and "hooligans"; they were also representatives of the classes that had been cast down or, as Zhdanov put it, "museum rarities from the world of shadows." Their direct link to bourgeois culture transformed them from mere "harmful authors" into enemies. And Zoshchenko had engaged in hostile activities; slander of the Soviet order was practically a continuation of the White Guards' cause. This was not literary criticism but accusations of criminal offenses. After all, the presence of a link to the "cast-down bourgeois classes" was a circumstance that aggravated guilt. Factors such as these—"slander of the Soviet order," "anti-Soviet sentiments," "attacks"—fit precisely into Stalin's understanding of "unconscientiousness." The following dialogue during the Orgbiuro discussion of the Leningrad journals is noteworthy:

Stalin: He is an advocate of unconscientiousness.
Vishnevskii: He put his most recent things out there without ideas or story lines.
Stalin: Mudslinger tricks.[54]

For Vishnevskii, "unconscientiousness" was the absence of an idea. For Stalin, it was anti-Soviet spitefulness, the antipode of which was "Bolshevik conscientiousness." The example of Zoshchenko showed "the kind of anti-Soviet swamp a writer is led to by a theory of apolitical behavior and of unconscientiousness and by principles of anecdotal and vulgar naturalism."[55] This last incrimination is an ideal description of "unconscientiousness." Some form of the word "vulgar" is applied five times to Zoshchenko in the resolution ("vulgar and slanderous speeches," "vulgar pieces of work," "vulgar libel," "vulgarity," "vulgarian") and thirteen times in Zhdanov's speeches—exactly the same number of times the word "unconscientiousness" appears. Everything that is lacking in a spiritual-romantic dimension—that is, "Communist conscientiousness"—is vulgarity. This is what the second part of *A Great Life* and plays with mundane plots suffered from. Life, when not taken up "in its revolutionary development," according to the Socialist Realist doctrine, turns into a caricature of itself. And in fact, there already were "discernible features of communism" at the threshold, but Zoshchenko "kept fiddling with his invariable, monotonous, monstrously hypertrophied hero, with his grotesquely primitive world and inarticulate speech." The writer simply did not see the "revolutionary transformation of reality": "Fights, scuffles, infinitely filthy love stories, a brutish attitude toward women—this is the only thing Zoshchenko saw in our life."[56] Thus, any kind of "naturalism" turns out to be vulgarity—a heavy-handed naturalism that leads to slander of the Soviet order. This is how Zoshchenko's "vulgarity" differs from that of Akhmatova.

The refusal to take the *skaz* form of narrative into account and the subsequent extrapolation of the characters' positions onto the real-life author were not just in line with the optics of naïve realism typical of the mass reader; they went straight to Stalin's way of reading. And it was not just Zoshchenko that the always suspicious Stalin read this way. During the Orgbiuro discussion of the Leningrad journals, his responses to matters concerning other authors discussed also stand out. For example, when Boris Likharev, editor-in-chief of *Leningrad,* said that the parody of Nekrasov by the "vulgarian Khazin" (as Zhdanov would call him) was merely a parody of a book about Nekrasov, Stalin responded, "It's a trick. The author's putting up a smoke screen." The conversation turns to the poetry of Sel'vinskii, in which some sort of hidden meaning has also been discerned. Again, Stalin pipes up, "It's a trick."[57]

There is yet another, less known and less studied, aspect of the special position that Zoshchenko and Akhmatova occupied in postwar literature, an aspect that did nothing to make Stalin think positively of them: they were the most popular authors in the Soviet occupied territories. Akhmatova's poems and Zoshchenko's satire had been actively propagandized not only in the Whites' emigrant periodicals before the war, but also in the press and textbooks for the occupied territories' schools.[58] Furthermore, "during the war, the satirical works of Mikhail Zoshchenko had been abundantly quoted for propaganda purposes . . . by Goebbels. A year after the Victory . . . someone had not been idle—and translated a collection of the Fascist propaganda minister's speeches into Russian and, with the appropriate parts underlined, had slipped [a copy] to Stalin."[59]

Stalin's attitude toward Akhmatova was rather more complicated. What had been called "unconscientiousness" in relation to her was in fact *privateness.* The unacceptability of any kind of privateness at all (that is, a sphere of personal life inaccessible to monitoring and normalization) led to the virtual disappearance of lyric poetry in the Stalin era (except for its brief spike during the war). It was no coincidence that the 1953 onset of de-Stalinization in literature would begin with discussions about "self-expression in lyric poetry" and "sincerity in literature." Zhdanov explained the disapproval of Akhmatova's work by pointing out that it was "thoroughly individualistic" and that she

herself was a representative of the "landlord-bourgeois trend in literature" that defended the theory of "art for art's sake" (or "beauty for the
sake of beauty itself") and whose proponents "did not wish to know
anything about the people, about their needs and interests, and about
public life" but rather, on the contrary, "strove to take cover from an
unpleasant reality in stratospheric heights and fogs of religious mysticism, in their paltry personal experiences and in digging into their
own petty, shallow hearts." The outcome of all these flaws was individualism—the dangerous illness of non-transparency. The same thing
was said in the resolution regarding *A Great Life:* Pudovkin's too rapt
interest in Nakhimov's personal life had led the director to "slur over"
his role as a historic personality. The sphere of the private was defined
as the haven of unconscientiousness and vulgarity.

A retreat from the world was interpreted as a sign of dangerous
dissidence—as a refusal to understand Soviet reality. At the height of
building socialism, "the sense of the emotional breakdown and depression that permeated all [Akhmatova's] thoughts and feelings become
ever more distinct; the motifs of the fragility of everything on earth, of
disillusionment in life, could now be heard more and more sharply and
nakedly in her work."[60] Hence, it was only a step away from propa-
gating a bizarre spiritual necrophilia: "The theme that embodies the
worst, most putrid aspects of decadence—the theme of death-as-savior,
the death of 'sweetest sleep'—runs throughout her poems like a red
thread."[61] Not only did her verses color her wartime creative work
with motifs of hopelessness and doom ("She attributes some sort of
death-wish attitude to the defenders of Leningrad and portrays their
heroic struggle as a blind and meek movement toward inevitable
death"), but they "sound like a monstrous anachronism in our own
times."[62] The dead/living opposition reaches its apogee in the criticism
of Akhmatova's work meant to prove what Walter Vickery has wittily
called "ruthless optimism."[63]

Ironically, this opposition turned out to be relevant not so much metaphorically as in a concretely historical sense. Beginning in the 1930s,
when after Kirov's death Zhdanov became the "master of Leningrad,"
a joke circulated among intelligentsia circles that he was "sprinkling"
culture with a "Zhdanov liquid" that had been used in the nineteenth
century to "sprinkle" over corpses to mask the odor of decay. In 1946

this joke was revived—and the same Zhdanov liquid was now taken to be fatal and began to be associated with an odor of corpses that it spread. A certain quatrain of Akhmatova's refers directly to this joke:

For such foolishness,
To tell you the truth,
I could get a lead pea
From that secretary.

Be that as it may, Akhmatova herself was sure (and said so more than once when retelling a story told to her by a certain witness of Stalin's "outburst of rage") that the attack on her was provoked by her meeting with Isaiah Berlin: "It turns out that our nun receives visits from foreign spies," Stalin had supposedly said, and then expressed himself with such obscene oaths regarding Akhmatova that she thought it best not to repeat them in conversation with Berlin.[64] Moreover, in Stalin's eyes Berlin was not only a foreigner and an English spy; he was also connected to Churchill's son Randolph, who after the war had served as the Moscow correspondent of the *Daily Telegraph* and the *Morning Post*. And Randolph was directly involved in an incident that sharply intensified Stalin's paranoia and became a starting point for the campaign against the Jewish Anti-Fascist Committee and the resultant murder of its head, Solomon Mikhoels, as well as the downfall of Molotov.

After suffering a stroke in 1945 (which, of course, the Soviet press did not report), Stalin was in recovery in the Crimea when the Western press was actively discussing who his possible successor might be. The author of a number of articles that hazarded guesses as to the state of Stalin's health was, indeed, Randolph Churchill. It was he who approached Molotov during a reception in the Kremlin to suggest an interview, to which the latter unexpectedly agreed. Stalin later took Molotov to task about this, almost accusing him of being recruited by Americans. What worried Stalin most were the discussions about his state of health and about his successors to power. After all, many of the ideological as well as political campaigns of the postwar years (the Jewish Anti-Fascist Committee trial, the Leningrad Affair, the Mingrelian Affair, and the Doctors' Plot) can be explained as a struggle for the redistribution of power in Stalin's inner circle and for influence on Stalin himself. Stalin grew suspicious that someone in his circle was supplying the West with information about his health. Suspicion fell on members of his own family (above all on Svetlana's Jewish husband, Grigorii Morozov), the Jewish Anti-Fascist Committee and Mikhoels, and Molotov's wife, Polina Zhemchuzhina; Morozov and Zhemchuzhina were arrested, and Mikhoels was murdered by a staged car accident. In a sense, Akhmatova was not far from the truth when she told Berlin, "We started the Cold War."

Olga Voronina argues quite convincingly that the ideological volley from all the party's weapons in August 1946 was tied to an American loan on which Stalin was very much counting. Until it became totally clear in July 1946 that the Soviet Union would not receive the hoped-for money (it was given to Great Britain), Stalin held back from provoking the West. But just a few days after the prospects for the loan evaporated, the Agitprop leadership was given orders to speed up the preparation of the resolution regarding the Leningrad journals. From this perspective, the haste with which it was readied—something that all researchers have noted—is understandable, as is something else Voronina notes:

> The resolution targeted culture as the dawning war's new weapon. Just as Soviet readers had to be made aware that their access to "contemporary bourgeois Western culture" was from then on going to be extremely limited, the former Allies had to understand that for them, too, Soviet culture was now placed under a ban. The artists and writers they liked were to be terribly punished; the art they admired or inspired was to be labeled "cosmopolitan" and either destroyed or hidden from public view. Berlin realized this predicament in writing about his visit to Akhmatova in the memorandum for the British Foreign Office. . . . As a courier, Berlin was well chosen. By directing his rage against Akhmatova, Stalin could be certain that his message would be delivered quickly and to the right address.[65]

As usual, however, the political decisions were multifunctional.

"BEAUTY IS OUR LIFE"

Soviet history has few party documents that would produce such a fundamental shift in culture as the 1946 resolution regarding the Leningrad journals. This document can perhaps be placed only alongside the 1932 resolution that created the institutional framework of Stalinist culture and the *Pravda* article "Muddle instead of Music," which marked the new populist platform of Socialist Realism. The three 1946 resolutions sharply veered Soviet aesthetic doctrine in the direction of glorifying the regime, thereby changing the balance between (as Zhdanov defined Socialist Realism) "the truthfulness and historical specificity of the artistic portrayal of reality," on the one hand, and "the greatest heroics and grand prospects," on the other. Since Soviet culture was literature-centered, it was precisely in literary criticism that the new aesthetic doctrine found its perfect implementation.

The problem of the battle between "what must be" and "what must not be" was central to Socialist Realism. Socialist Realist aesthetics operated with a set of oppositions ("realism"/"romanticism," "conflict"/"conflictlessness," "varnishing of reality"/"the truth of life," and so forth). The balancing of these scales was the essential content of Soviet critical discourse. However, much had changed in the late-Stalinist era as compared to the 1930s. Above all, the age of *klassovost'*, the focus on class characteristics, had drawn to a close. With the declaration of building "socialism in one country," and particularly with the definitive end of any question of the regime's legitimacy after the victory in World War II, social reality became quite different. In a 1946 meeting with constituents, Stalin declared that the division between party and non-party was arbitrary. Now, he said, one must speak exclusively in terms of "Soviet society" and "the Soviet people as a single whole." Accordingly, "the battle line between the new and the old, a battle taking place not among social groups as isolated forces but within them, within the people as a single whole, is the most important feature of socialism."[66]

The aesthetic consensus reached in the 1930s boiled down to an understanding of Socialist Realism as a "merging" of realism and romanticism. It was the result of a compromise between the advocates of the "revolutionary romanticism" proclaimed by Gorky and the adherents of the "realism" defended by the Russian Association of Proletarian Writers (RAPP). In that discussion Stalin had supported both sides but had still expressed his preference for "life in its revolutionary development."

In 1947 and 1948, however, during a discussion that unfolded in the journal *Oktiabr'*, this fundamental assumption of Socialist Realist aesthetics was brought into doubt. The discussion itself was a response to the resolution regarding the Leningrad journals and summed up the restructuring of Soviet literature on a new track. In the article that opened the discussion, "The Goals of Literary Criticism" (*Oktiabr'*, 1947, no. 7), Aleksandr Fadeev, Soviet Russia's chief literary bureaucrat at the time and one of the leading theoreticians and practictioners of Socialist Realism, spoke of a "splintering" of the realist and romantic principles in "the old realism" and defined realism that was truly socialist as a method that restored the fragmented link in a qualitatively new synthesis. However, critics who took part in the discussion took this idea to its logical conclusion. Boris Bialik, for example, directly challenged writers to "lift up reality a bit," to make it "poetic" and "lofty" and thereby to "combine" realism and romanticism.[67]

The balance that had been established earlier in Zhdanov's speech at the First Writers' Congress, whereby Socialist Realism combined "the most rigorous, most sober practical work with the greatest heroics and grand prospects," was disturbed.[68] The challenge to "lift up" and "romanticize" reality essentially revealed the gap that existed between reality and what would be "tomorrow" (which literature "reflected" as "setting in today"); if reality had to be "lifted up," then it was not romantic enough in and of itself. This proposition was subjected to a swift corrective, administered by Vladimir Ermilov. He developed his sizable work "For a Militant Theory of Literature!" in one issue after another of *Literaturnaia gazeta,* of which he was the editor-in-chief, in which he diverted the discussion of Socialist Realism into a new channel. He provided a theoretical grounding for the advent of a new modality. The idea of an imminent beautiful life was not in and of itself new in the mid-1940s, but it had originated in a utopian consciousness and was no longer relevant to the postwar consciousness that now dwelt in a time of utopia achieved. The idea of the romanticism of reality itself could be heard in Ermilov's writing, even in his polemic with Bialik. As early as 1947, *Literaturnaia gazeta* had proclaimed in an editorial that "Any most beautiful and bold poetic dream of an artist finds a lively response from millions of Soviet people. Poetry crosses over into life because life itself in our country has become poetic."[69]

But only in the articles that he published in his newspaper in the autumn of 1948 did Ermilov take the logic of his ruminations to the brilliance of the formula "Beauty is our life." Here lay an entire aesthetic program. He explains: "In our Soviet life, poetry and romanticism have become reality itself. We have no conflict between the wondrous and the real, and this is why our artists seek the source of beauty and romance not apart from public life and affairs, but within them."[70] Bialik's concept was incorrect, Ermilov asserted, because from it followed the notion that realism—that is, the artistic study of actual reality—cannot yield anything affirmative and positive, and thus it decidedly rejects the romance of reality, its poetry. On the contrary, "our actual reality [*real'naia deistvitel'nost'*] itself, in its sober, matter-of-fact quotidian existence, is romantic, profoundly poetic to its inner core—and this is one of the foundational principles in defining the essence of Socialist Realism."[71]

Ol'ga Grudtsova had debated Bialik in *Oktiabr'*,[72] but from Ermilov's point of view, she had drawn a faulty conclusion about the need to "reveal the process of becoming a Communist person, the struggle between different principles within it."[73] But Ermilov's concept of "the real romance of our socialist reality itself" removed all the emerging contradictions at a stroke. If "among the leading principles of our aesthetics there should be a principle of the poetry and romance of our actual socialist reality," then "Chernyshevskii's famous thesis, 'Beauty is life,' is in our time decipherable as the principle that beauty is our socialist reality, our triumphant advance toward communism."[74]

The development of Soviet literature continued to be guided by Ermilov's "militant theory of literature" up until 1952. It is not so much the theory of a utopian consciousness as of a post-utopian one. The former was typical of the revolutionary era, particularly in the 1930s. The postwar era was another matter; for it, the notion of the present as the time of utopia *achieved*—that is, a utopia that had ceased to be one, having become reality—was typical. Hence the new essence of specifically postwar Socialist Realism—the era of *Cavalier of the Golden Star* in literature, *Kuban Cossacks* in film, and *The Move to the New Apartment* in painting. Ermilov was in fact the most consistent of its theoreticians at this time. These works would after Stalin's death become the exemplars of "varnishing" and "conflictlessness."

It was precisely the attitude toward the issue of conflict in which the duality of Socialist Realism was most evident, the relatively free existence in it of the apparently contradictory principles that we have discussed. The "theory of conflictlessness" in the form that it was condemned and "revealed" in 1952 can be summarized as follows: the principles of Socialist Realism exclude the possibility of portraying conflicts in contemporary literature, as well as any negative phenomena at all of Soviet life. The Central Committee's postwar resolutions only intensified this tendency. Thus literature engaged in portraying the struggle between "the good and the better" and "the better and the exceptional." Critics wrote in 1951: "Now that the antagonistic classes in our country have been eliminated, a writer should be able to find new, actual collisions and conflicts for his works that reflect the unantagonistic nature of the contradictions existing in socialist society."[75]

Soviet aesthetic theory took this as a point of departure. Let us turn to the works of the leading Soviet aesthetician of the postwar years, German Nedoshivin. The main theme of his work from this period is the problem of beauty, which is always linked to realism since "the concept of beauty always demands its embodiment, being brought to life in a specific, sensate phenomenon. It must become palpable, lest it dissolve in logical abstractions."[76] Doomed to realism, it is described by Chernyshevskii's formula, "Beauty is life." According to Chernyshevskii, art describes life "as it should be, according to our conceptions"; hence, says Nedoshivin, "since we have made life fundamentally the way it should be, have built a socialist society, perceptions about our life merge with the concept of beauty" since "our concepts are the teaching of scientific socialism, the teaching of Marx-Engels-Lenin-Stalin."[77] Beauty is contained within this very teaching, and it is directly linked to Soviet reality: "Nowadays, socialism has become an actual fact. . . . Beauty is born daily and hourly in the life of Soviet society itself. . . . We are not faced with a fatal necessity to choose between truthful portrayal of an ugly reality and disavowal of truth in the name of a quest for a beautiful image. By turning to life itself, striving toward as full and truthful a portrayal of it as is possible, the artist thereby reveals the beauty of socialist reality."[78]

Since typification must be based not on a "statistically average" distribution of a phenomenon or its extent but rather on an accentuation of its "essence," which is supposedly typical, Nedoshivin contended that "in order to reveal reality, an artist must have the opportunity, so to speak, to 'observe' the essence of a phenomenon." Furthermore, "a profound revelation of an essence is impossible without rejecting the indistinct dullness of 'the average.'"[79]

What we see is a programmatic rejection of reality since the "dullness" that Nedoshivin is writing about is in fact the thing that seems (but only seems!) typical since it is widespead. Furthermore, by insisting on reality and refusing to "observe" its pure "essence," the artist risks lapsing into the sin of naturalism, defined as "slavishness to fact." In such a case the artist "goes no further than stating what exists. . . . Passivity with respect to facts masks an unwillingness and inability to go into the heart of things, passed off as an unwillingness to 'fantasize,' as an effort to stick to 'reality.'"[80] According to this desperate logic, Socialist Realism can also be accused of naturalism, as it also goes after a beautiful reality—it does not "fantasize" but merely reflects "the beauty of life."

This *utopian naturalism* is a purely aesthetic phenomenon. It is based on an "aesthetic ideal" that boils down to "an artistic concept of the beautiful and the perfect in life." This last "for us coincides with the common goal of all the historical creative work of the Soviet people—communism."[81] From this perspective, the link between the ideal and the real is attenuated since the former follows directly from the latter: "An ideal image of our time is taken directly from life; the deeper an artist delves into the truth of life, into the truth in which our universal-historical advance toward communism is revealed, the more beautiful it will be."[82]

We should remember that Ermilov was speaking out against a mode of reflection based on metaphor (comparison of an ideal and reality) in defense of the principle of metonymic substitution (an ideal has become reality, beauty has realized an ideal by merging with life and replacing it). In this respect, he was defending "realism." With his new aesthetic formula, he effected a coup. If "Beauty is life" is a metaphorical principle since it refers to reality, then "Beauty is our life" is a metonymic principle that refers to beauty (poetry and life are now one). Predication lies at the heart of metaphor, and substitution at the heart of metonymy. Since they are all based on comparison, poetic tropes in their pure form are rarely present in poetic speech; we regard them here merely as dominant universal expressive mechanisms whose replacement is determined by changing political-ideological aims.

As we have already noted, the aesthetic equivalent of the postwar change in status and legitimacy of the Stalin regime was the representational shift from metaphor to metonymy. This led to structural and functional changes in Soviet art's system of imagery. In the 1930s it had been dominated by allegory; the function of what was portrayed was to shed light on what should be, what was ideologically correct. Hence the hero was an example to imitate, a model for appropriate behavior. What art depicted and reality itself was supposed to be reflected in each other so that the obligatory could be discerned in the reflection. This required a high degree of reference. Postwar culture was based on images that supposedly paralleled reality, that were significantly more symbolic and hence not so much tied to allegory/example and dynamism as to synecdoche/symbol and stasis. Also tied to this is the fact that the "Socialist Realist master-plot" that Katerina Clark describes in *The Soviet Novel* as functioning in 1930s literature became practically irrelevant after the war.

Comparison or metaphor lies at the heart of allegory. Allegory itself is based on a mechanism of metaphorization and, as distinct from synecdoche, is not self-contained. Metonymy is more active than metaphor, and, what is more, by encroaching upon both reality and simulacrum, it removes the boundary between them. The boundary that had existed in prewar Soviet art turned out to be superfluous after the war. If in the 1930s the regime asserted its own legitimacy through reference to the past ("Stalin is Lenin today") or to "Marxist-Leninist theory," then after the war it became self-sufficient; neither the regime nor Stalin himself needed to be "propped up" any longer. We would not err in calling metonymy activated, realized metaphor. If one views Socialist Realism as a link to realization rather than reality, then metonymy can be seen as the basis of replacing reality with an ideological fantasy passed off as "realness." Postwar Socialist Realism differs from the prewar variant in that it was engaged in the active production of this substitute reality. Before the war, "our life" had not yet succeeded in merging with "beauty," becoming "poetry" itself.

Since the dream had become reality, harmonized and perfected, any state of conflict became superfluous: "Naturally, harmony, as the absence of unresolvable conflicts requiring revolutionary interference in art itself, is under our conditions the necessary corollary of the absence of such conflicts in life."[83] As far as problems within Soviet society went, "life, this miracle-working and astute artist, has itself taken care of gathering together the typical traits of the contemporary hero by embodying them in the makeup of our remarkable fellow citizens."[84] When in April 1952 this harmoniously constructed edifice unexpectedly fell apart and received the name "the theory of conflictlessness,"

critics remembered dialectics: "The *dialectical* relationship between reality and romanticism, between life and a dream, are fundamentally
different from the complete coincidence of them that V. Ermilov asserts. When V. Ermilov contents himself with the formula 'Beauty is our
life,' he ends up with a purely mechanical merger of dream and reality,
of romanticism and realism. This identity is futile. By assuming this
point of view, one can easily reach a state of pacified complacency, of
carefree calm. This is not the nature of Bolsheviks. They always want
life tomorrow to flourish even more luxuriantly, even brighter, even
more colorfully than it does today."[85]

This collapse of the theory of conflictlessness happened on the eve
of the "Doctors' Plot," which was to become the precursor of a new
wave of massive purges in Stalin's circle. Life was supposed to flourish even more luxuriantly and brighter, but the unexpected death of
the chief Bolshevik, who was not even remotely in a state of carefree
calm, opened a new chapter in the history of Soviet literature and art,
where the battle against conflictlessness began to fulfill totally unforeseen functions.

In early 1952, Stalin publicly declared (and *Pravda* repeated in an
editorial) that "we need Gogols and Shchedrins." On April 7, 1952,
Pravda included a feature article titled "Overcoming the Lag in Dramaturgy." This directive was finally confirmed in the Central Committee's
report for the Nineteenth Party Congress (in October 1952), wherein
Malenkov declared: "Our writers and artists must castigate the flaws,
limitations, and unhealthy phenomena widespread in our society. . . .
We have no satire. . . . We need Soviet Gogols and Shchedrins, who with
the flames of satire would burn away from life everything negative, rotten, and moribund, everything that slows our forward motion."[86] This
is when criticism launched the broad campaign during which a rejection of "the theory of conflictlessness," "varnishing," and "illustrative-
ness" was proclaimed and the calls for "the truth of life," for portraying
"conflicts," and for a rebirth of satire all resounded. At that time, no
one could determine who had originated the "notorious theory of conflictlessness." Everyone quoted Nikolai Virta's review of the film *Country Doctor,* where this noxious "theory" had supposedly been developed. Nonetheless, Virta had merely expressed what had been written
in any review or critical article between 1946 and 1952. He had not,
of course, devised any sort of "theory" at all. The "theory of conflict-

lessness" was essentially nothing more than the implementation of the principles in the August 1946 Central Committee resolutions. Stalin and Zhdanov were the "authors" of this "theory." But the political aims that dictated the 1946 resolutions had changed by 1952.

Ermilov, who unfailingly managed to get his bearings in the shift of ideological vectors, was the first to sense the beginning of the turnaround. In an article titled "Some Questions on the Theory of Socialist Realism," he honed the formula of the aesthetic ideal of Socialist Realism by introducing the concept of "the struggle for communism" into it as a central element of the "codex of beauty." Ermilov declared that "Beauty is our life, our struggle," thereby attempting to rid his "militant theory" of "passively contemplative elements": "An awareness of beauty as life and of life as beauty, a forceful, active participation in the transformation of reality in the struggle for communism—these are the principles upon which our literature achieves its success."[87] In 1952 it became clear that the issue was not a simple corrective but an abrupt turnaround in the common ideological line. It was necessary to actualize the calls for "ruthless self-criticism," as well as the fragments of Zhdanov's speeches in *Zvezda* and *Leningrad,* such as the following one: "While selecting the best feelings and qualities of the Soviet person and revealing his tomorrow to him, we must also at the same time show our people what they should be like, must scourge the remnants of yesterday, the remnants that hinder the Soviet people from moving forward."

When this "ideological wealth" was reanimated, it became "easy [for critics] to understand what an enormous, truly priceless role our art is called upon to play in the consolidation of a new, socialist order, in the rout and elimination of the enemies of socialism, in the unmasking of everything that is hindering our movement toward communism."[88] In an article with the characteristic title "Negative Images and the Writer's Uncompromising Stand," the critic and literary functionary Boris Riurikov wrote the following: "Soviet literature has glorious traditions of showing the positive hero, the progressive champion of his era, the inspired champion of the victory of the people's cause. But among its most glorious traditions is also the tradition of unmasking the enemy. Without being able to hate, one cannot sincerely love, Gorky taught. A great humanist whose heart burned with a passionate love for the people, he at the same time saw the goal of literature as fostering hatred for everything alien. . . . And if our society, the state, unmasks and severely punishes the enemies of the people, the enemies of our system, then Soviet literature also must create the very same punishment, the very same judgment over the agents of the old world."[89]

The legalistic lexicon of the 1930s precipitously returns to the discourse of literary criticism. The turnaround in ideology that took place in 1952 is directly linked to the impending changes at the highest level of the regime; today, few would doubt that Stalin's death saved the country from a new wave of repressions. All the signs of the brewing storm have been repeatedly pointed out in the literature. The shifting of the ideological vector in 1952 directly reflected this process, and, judging by the sweep, breadth, and intensity of the incipient campaign, it originated directly with Stalin.

The new line was balanced at just this point: the "intensification of class struggle" and the demand for "vigilance" did not disaffirm "the beauty of our life." So at the very height of the fight against conflict-lessness *Literaturnaia gazeta* published an editorial titled "Textbook of Life," in which a line of equilibrium was formulated. But in the *very same* issue of the newspaper was an article by Riurikov that concluded with a threat: "Writers who do not see (or pretend that they do not see) the reality of the influence of the old do not truthfully reflect real-life conflicts, and writers who portray life as sky-blue and idyllic violate the cruel truth of our era—an era of difficult but beautiful and heroic actions."[90]

The campaign against conflictlessness was by no means supposed to conclude with a change in literary policy. It was pursuing specific politico-ideological—mobilizational—goals, bringing public discourse back on the course of confrontational awareness of the prewar and wartime model. Hence, when the "Doctors' Plot," conceived as a prologue to unleashing a new wave of repressions, exploded in January 1953, the 1937 public discourse had already been totally reanimated.

On January 13, 1953, a declaration by TASS and the accompanying text that was the same in all news sources, "Spies and Murderers Unmasked," were published. Referring to *Pravda*'s editorial "Villainous Spies and Murderers Masked as Professors and Doctors," *Literaturnaia gazeta* wrote the following: "No, our success is not leading to an attenuation of the struggle but, on the contrary, to its escalation. The more successfully our country advances along the path toward communism, the more trenchant the struggle of the people's enemies, brought to desperation and doomed to perish, will be. Only rightist opportunists, people standing for an anti-Marxist viewpoint, can think about attenuating the struggle. . . . Love for the Motherland is inseparable from hatred for its enemies, and hatred is action! . . . Vigilance, and vigilance once more!"[91]

The real significance of the ideological campaign aimed at a break with "varnishing reality" and "conflictlessness" lay in this kind of turnaround of public opinion.

The return to 1937-style discourse was a rejection of the lexicon of the 1946 resolutions but not of their essence. This is the "party-mindedness principle" in action: to be politically flexible and capable of reacting operationally to the demands of the current political situation, Stalinist ideology had to be undogmatic and to accommodate opposite principles, one of which, at the appropriate time and in accordance with political expediency, was actualized and became the main one. Thus, immediately after the war, at a time of ideological normalization, these principles demanded "varnishing" and "conflictlessness" in art. In contrast, when Stalin had devised a sweeping new purge in his own circles, the requirement for "Soviet Gogols and Shchedrins" was formulated. Notwithstanding, just as no one in the triumphant era of "conflictlessness" had abrogated the demands for "criticism and self-criticism," the era of "Soviet Gogols and Shchedrins" by no means presupposed an actual criticism of the regime.

The campaign against "conflictlessness" and "varnishing" pursued purely utilitarian political aims and by no means intended for literature to begin portraying authentic real-life conflicts. However, Stalin's unexpected death took this managed process out of control. The criticism of "conflictlessness" and "varnishing," which *within* Stalinist culture had had its own boundaries and limited functions, began to lose them. The battle against "conflictlessness" forged new arguments that were not so easily liquidated as others had been just a few years before. Swift and unexpected changes of the political course after Stalin's death led to it being impossible to neutralize the denial of conflictlessness. The long phase of maneuvering and deliberation that set apart the discussion leading up to the Second Writers' Congress (in December 1954) began. Now even those who were calling for a return to the previous state of affairs could not discount the new circumstances and had to dissociate themselves from "conflictlessness," thereby blatantly contra-dicting their own aspirations.

At this Second Writers' Congress, the discussion already afoot in the press about sincerity and the "conflictless" lie of Stalinist litera-ture erupted. A dynamic participant in it was Margarita Aliger, who declared from the congress podium that writers must stop "hiding be-hind all manner of ramshackle fences like 'the theory of conflictless-ness.'" She said that the theory itself, which "for unknown reasons, and by what means no one can now remember, and, really, there is no point in trying to determine by whom, personally . . . had been elevated somehow into the highest and only correct [theory], and any doubting word about it whatsoever was elevated to the level of almost a political error," was by no means the problem. The problem, she said, was that "a false impression has been created that it is supposedly to blame for all our failures." The theory was not at all to blame, Aliger declared, but rather "the general conditions of literary life, the situation that has developed in recent years in the Writers' Union, where creative discus-sion has been replaced by an often overbearing pounding of a fist on a desk, and any kind of reflectiveness, any attempt to think for oneself and try to resolve this or that issue or any good critical intention has been immediately labeled with various terrible words. Our literature is very tired of terrible words, fists pounding on desks, commands and elaborations [of them], on the one hand, and of made-for-show bal-lyhoo, lowering of quality requirements, self-satisfaction and carefree calm, on the other."[92]

The thaw was only beginning, and it was better meantime not to re-call "by whom, personally" the "notorious theory" had been invented. It had not, of course, been Virta. It had been elaborated in detail in the 1946 Central Committee resolutions. It was precisely these resolutions that had consolidated these "general conditions of literary life" for years to come and had given rise to the highest attainments of Social-ist Realism—the art of "made-for-show ballyhoo, . . . self-satisfaction and carefree calm." In originating quite a number of "terrible words," they became the model for "fists pounding on desks, commands and elaborations."

The 1946 resolutions declared that "Soviet literature is the most conscientious in the world" and demanded "Communist conscientious-ness" from theater and film. The absence of a definition for the desired quality was compensated by a detailed exhibit of various manifestations of "unconscientiousness" that was supposed to explain to artists "in reverse," so to speak, how to create it. The resolutions stated that "unconscientiousness" was the following:

1. "Retreat into the past" or "alienation from the present"; such is the poetry of Akhmatova and those who write about and pine for the past (this poetry is also called "thoughtless"); thus, too, the unconscientiousness of many theaters "carried away with plays about the past";
2. "Finding fault with Soviet reality" (Zoshchenko); the inability to see its achievements and the "visible features of communism in the present" (the second part of A Great Life);
3. Formalism; this is the unconscientiousness of the advocates of "pure art" (Symbolists, Acmeists, the Serapion Brothers); thus, too, of Eisenstein, who bent over backward for form, and of bourgeois playwrights;
4. Focus on entertaining art, any sort of "indulgence of outdated tastes"—this is "vulgarity";
5. Contemporary bourgeois art, to which historical optimism and humanism are alien—the theater of "O'Neills and Maughams," the literature of "all manner of Sartres."

Thus, one by one, the opposite poles are severed: idealization of the past (1) and denigration of the present (2); elitism (3) and egalitarianism (4); the Soviet versus the bourgeois (5), and so forth. This resulted in a dialectically flexible system of categories that bled into each other, the balancing of which would occupy Soviet art in all the time that remained to it. Management of this system assured the power of those whose business was the control and normalization of art. This mechanism could not operate without the "conscientiousness" that was the very essence of cultural policy. Communist conscientiousness is thus a peculiar sort of optics in the approach to reality, a strategy for selecting and evaluating realness, and a means of seeing the world in the Stalinist way. It is a technique for overcoming unconscientiousness and hence for transforming reality with the aim of derealizing life through its representation as realized ideology, a means of producing the Socialist Realist parallel reality of Stalinism.

4 Meta-Stalinism

The Dialectics of Party-Mindedness and the Party-Mindedness of Dialectics

In 1950, the number 2 issue of the journal *Oktiabr'* contained an article by one A. Belik entitled "On Some Mistakes in Literary Studies" (O nekotorykh oshibkakh v literaturovedenii). The article contained the usual demands for Soviet literature, in a Zhdanovist vein, for Communist party-mindedness and ideological restraint. It also repeated well-known statements from a Lenin article required in schools, "Party Organization and Party-Minded Literature" (Partiinaia organizatsiia i partiinaia literatura), that there are no party-less writers, that "freedom of creativity" does not exist, and that literature is always politically engaged and thus always party-minded. But Soviet literature, according to the Socialist Realist doctrine that had been affirmed only in 1946 by Zhdanov, was inherently and openly party-minded.

Then, suddenly, on March 30, *Pravda* allotted a full half page to an extensive editorial entitled "Against the Vulgarization of Literary Criticism" (Protiv oposhleniia literaturnoi kritiki) that stridently attacked Belik's "vulgar sociological distortions." Such ideological attacks were not launched without Stalin's sanction. *Pravda* insisted that Lenin's article must be approached "historically"; if in 1905 Lenin's motto "Down with party-less writers" was politically relevant, then at present, given the "indestructible union of Communists and party-less people," an emphasis on "party-mindedness" could be harmful and even considered "RAPPist recidivism." Belik had set forth the same points that were issued in party resolutions, but he had been more straightforward. His article was written in the best traditions of *Pravda*'s own editorials. Accusing Belik of resurrecting Proletkult and RAPPist sectarianism, *Pravda* called him a doctrinaire, by which it asserted that ideological flexibility was a key element of true party-mindedness. In other words, Belik had understood the principle of party-mindedness too narrowly, while this principle was universal and had nothing to do with a writer's party membership.

The reaction from the Soviet Writers' Union to *Pravda*'s article was totally unexpected: Fadeev and Simonov, the writers closest to Stalin, drafted an editorial for *Literaturnaia gazeta* with the title "Is the Concept of 'Party-Mindedness of Literature' Valid When Applied to Soviet Literature? (A Response to Readers)" (Pravomerno li poniatie 'partiinost' literatury' v primenenii k sovetskoi literature? [Otvet chitateliam]). Since their article could not be "only the opinion expressed by the Writers' Union and *Literaturnaia gazeta*," Fadeev and Simonov asked the Politbiuro for permission to publish it, sending their draft to Stalin for approval.[1]

This editorial, by leaders of the Soviet Writers' Union, suggested no more and no less than a rejection of the concept of party-mindedness and its relegation to the ranks of historical categories (where the concept of "class-orientedness" was already de facto located). The draft sent to Stalin on September 6 indicated that Lenin's article contained "specifically historical content" and thus could not be applied to Soviet literature: "The propositions [in Lenin's article] must not be dogmatically, mechanically carried over into contemporary Soviet literature."[2]

The word "mechanically" is crucial to the understanding of the principle of party-mindedness. Although *Pravda* had criticized propositions in Belik's article that were essentially correct, it was nonetheless right because its own position could not be "mechanical," not to mention "dogmatic" or "scholastic." As the expression of the "party line," *Pravda* was "party-mindedness" incarnate, and its chief characteristic was *dependence on dialectic*. "Mechanicalness" is a synonym of inflexibility, straightforwardness, and, ultimately, adherence to principle (and potentially of opposition). It is impossible to be simultaneously party-minded and principled ("mechanically" applying correct principles). Party-mindedness is a modus operandi, not a position or principles; it is an ability and willingness to change according to an impulse imposed from without. To be party-minded, a position must be flexible since a party-minded position is a political position. Dialectic constitutes the very essence of party-mindedness, if by the latter we understand a mechanism for the functioning of "the lifeblood of the Soviet system—its politics."[3]

Fadeev and Simonov had not understood this. The conclusion they had reached was genuinely revolutionary: "The use of the concept of 'party-mindedness of literature' instead of the concept of the Communist, Bolshevist ideological conscientiousness of Soviet literature cannot be considered correct." Furthermore, as a term used by Lenin under the "specifically historical conditions of a class society," it could not "be carried over to the Soviet literature of our time—of the era of communism being built."[4]

Since Fadeev and Simonov's draft is preserved in the Politbiuro archive, it is clear that this question was prepared for discussion but eventually was halted by Stalin. The leader had rejected Hegel's "law of negation of negation" by not mentioning it in the "philosophical chapter" of his *Short Course,* but he was not about to reject party-mindedness. One might say, however, that the law of negation of negation was not abolished by Stalin but simply "died out" (apparently instead of the state) for lack of necessity; Stalinist ideology has no components that are subject to pure negation as it simultaneously contains thesis, antithesis, and synthesis. The functioning of this ideological *perpetuum mobile* was based on the fact that the negation of negation was situated *within it.* It was impossible to escape this cycle. To understand why Stalin decided to leave the principle of party-mindedness in a politically useful "suspended" state and did not reject it in 1950, when everything seemed ready for this (from *Pravda*'s invective to the article prepared by Writers' Union leaders), one must view party-mindedness not as a *category* but as a *principle of direct political action.* Party-mindedness allowed everything to be "suspended"—even itself.

(THESIS) MARXISM-LENINISM: THE LAW OF UNITY AND OF THE CONFLICT OF OPPOSITES

Under the conditions of the political culture taking shape in Russia, Stalinism became an organic form of the realization of a revolutionary project. A paradoxical ideological constellation came together; revolutionary radicalism was directed here toward the consolidation of the values and ideology whose destruction constituted the very content of the Marxist project. The farther this went, the more it created a profound contradiction between reality and its representation, the latter of which was in addition a key component of legitimization of the regime. If in early Stalinism this pressure was relieved through the aggravation of radical *economic* measures (collectivization and industrialization), in which economic modernization and the creation of state capitalism were positioned as the realization of the Marxist project; if in high Stalinism it was removed in the *political* arena—in the Great Terror, passed off as "intensification of class struggle" and in heroic mythology (Stakhanovites, polar explorers, pilots); if in the war years it became irrelevant since the very survival of the country came into question (although *military* victory was positioned as a "victory of the Soviet regime"), then in late Stalinism, this pressure found a release in straightforwardly *ideological* acts directed toward the creation of cultural, discursive, and conceptual matrices that encompassed every sphere of life—from art and science to economics and politics.

This exposure of the ideological device occurred in all the campaigns of the "Zhdanov era" but found its fullest expression in the 1947 "philosophical discussion." However, before addressing the topics that are directly linked to the postwar realignment of the control mechanism of ideological production, we must understand the problem of discursive anxiety in Stalinism in a broader context and explain why it was philosophy, specifically, that was allotted the leading role in this and why the problem of party-mindedness—for science and art alike—became so acute for philosophy.

As Boris Groys observed, "The Soviet Union understood itself as a state in which all power belongs to philosophy. The legitimacy of the Communist leadership was determined primarily by the fact that it represented a particular philosophical teaching: Marxism-Leninism. The leadership had no other legitimization. Thus philosophizing was always its foremost obligation."[5] Philosophy was not only the domain of Soviet ideological language, but also the political instrument that brought this language into harmony with the regime's urgent tasks. Accordingly, party-mindedness was part of Soviet philosophy as both a practice and an institution.

The political nature of party-mindedness is usually understood only in the sense that it subordinates any principles to the demands of political expediency (that is, it simply relativizes and removes any principles whatsoever), while the real point is that party-mindedness is an ideal instrument of control. The Stalinist system was structured in such a fashion to put everybody under pressure. Everyone was vulnerable because of the fluctuations of the political trends at any particular time, fluctuations that changed the precepts. And since no one could guess these fluctuations, any act was transformed into a sort of Russian roulette; no one could guarantee his or her safety if and when these precepts were declared to have been violated. This game without fixed rules was well matched by undogmatic Soviet doctrine, the fundamental principle of which—that of party-mindedness—suggested subordination to ideological trends, which meant a complete absence of any kind of guarantees whatsoever. This system provided the bureaucratic elite with everything *except* guarantees. In this mobility of precepts ("dogmas"), this rejection of guarantees, lay the fundamental source of terror in which everyone lived. Party-mindedness demanded a lack of dogma, which, in turn, demanded dialectics as the consolidation and obliteration of the boundaries of philosophy—taking it beyond the limits of a scientific discipline into the area of worldview and political ideology.

The nascency of "Marxism-Leninism" itself signified a degeneration of Marxism from a revolutionary theory into a conservative ideology.[6] Since the revolutionary and critical (motivational) potential of Marxism had become dangerous to the regime, the latter's task became to neutralize Marxism through conservation with the help of party apparatchik philosophers—Mark Mitin and Pavel Iudin in the 1930s, Georgii Aleksandrov in the 1940s, and "Aleksandrov's boys" (Petr Fedoseev, Leonid Il'ichev, Mikhail Iovchuk, and Vladimir Kruzhkov) in the 1950s–1980s. But the introduction of the concept of "Marxist-Leninist ideology" was tied to an affirmation of orthodoxy; because the functions of these theories changed from motivation to legitimization with the ascent to power of the adepts of revolutionary theories, "Marxist-Leninist theory" fulfilled not so much a function of motivation as of universal, across-the-board legitimization. Hence any political, social, economic, cultural, or intellectual activity had to be explained in the current redaction of "Marxist-Leninist theory" and grounded in the categories of "Marxism-Leninism." Insofar as the latter, specifically in its ideological function, was the true domain of legitimacy, producing its vocabulary and syntax, these functions determined the role of

"Marxist-Leninist teaching" (that is, "Marxist-Leninist" philosophy proper) in the functioning of the Soviet ideological state.

Merab Mamardashvili observed that "a philosophy took shape in the Soviet Union that in reality was never really a philosophy but merely a part of the ideological apparatus of the state."[7] It would be more accurate to say that philosophy itself was *the product of the ideological apparatus*. The party-mindedness of Soviet philosophy can be understood as the principle of the link between the Marxist philosophical tradition and party institutions, in the same sense that the party-mindedness of Soviet art was the principle of the link between aesthetic practice and the state's ideological institutions. Similar to the way that Socialist Realism was by form an aesthetic practice but in its functions an ideology, Soviet philosophy was also, *functionally,* an ideology. In other words, *it is not the case that ideology was the product of "Marxism-Leninism" but rather the reverse: "Marxism-Leninism" itself, as a construct, was the product of a mutation of Marxist ideology.*

Aleksandr Zinov'ev suggested that Stalinist philosophy was a masterly transformation of Marxist philosophy into an ideology intended for mass consumption. As distinct from Lenin, a thinker who possessed a lively creative intellect, Stalin had an organizational and systematic mind: "In the conditions of a simpler sociopolitical post-revolutionary situation, he [Stalin] created . . . the Vulgate of Marxism that became a world-outlook fare, first in the expanses of the USSR, and then of the entire 'socialist camp.'"[8] However, one must distinguish the nature and function of philosophy from the nature and function of "Marxist-Leninist teaching": the "Vulgate of Marxism" was not so much the product of philosophical reflection as of the workings of the ideological apparatus of a state that was simulating philosophical activity.

In the Stalin era, philosophy was different from all the other sciences in that it was positioned simultaneously as a science, an ideology, and a worldview. By virtue of the fact that philosophy was essentially engaged in the articulation of Soviet ideology in the most abstract and generalized forms and categories, it played a key role in the creation of a parallel axiomatics—that is, a worldview proper that by a number of fundamental parameters was truly different from the axiomatic constants established and accepted beyond the borders of the Soviet Union. And although (beginning in the 1930s) Soviet philosophy was situated within ideology and by official doctrine a part of the superstructure (and accordingly was "ultimately" determined by the economic base), at the same time it was characterized by "relative independence." This latter aspect was brought into doubt by one of the main personalities of the 1940s philosophical squabbles, Zinovii Beletskii, who rejected relative independence in the development of the forms of social consciousness under socialism; this independence, he said, was inherent only in antagonistic formations: "In our society, ideology . . . came into a harmonious relationship with its material base. Now it has no relatively independent aims distinct from the aims of our people, of our state and party. The essence of our ideology is not the preservation of relative independence but exactly the opposite: the ultimate transcendence of relative independence, like a bourgeois relic, owing to a practically revolutionary transformation of society. . . . By its very nature, our ideology cannot be relatively independent."[9] In other words, the very nature and purpose of philosophy as a form of ideological and theoretical reflection of reality underwent a radical change due to the "transforming practice of Marxism," in which philosophy was finally made into an instrument to *change* the world, not to explain it.

This fusion of ideology (philosophy) with the material base and the "permeation" of the material world with ideology became the product of a radical—truly aesthetic—gesture. Essentially, this was a peculiar philosophical version of Vladimir Ermilov's formula, "Beauty is our life," which was based on the "permeation" of Soviet reality itself with poetry. Similarly to how poetry fuses with Soviet reality, ideology dissolves into life, and theory dissolves into practice. Philosophy itself becomes life, which means that it becomes poetry. But Soviet reality becomes an incarnation of ideology, theory (philosophy), and poetry. To the extent that ideology is deprived of independence, reality, too, is deprived of it. Soviet thought did not recognize such a fusion, neither in the 1930s nor after Stalin's death. *It was the pure product of late Stalinism.* In this respect, it was clear to Stalinist philosophers that "Marxist philosophy is qualitatively different from all earlier philosophy in that it does not contain just elements of truth but *entirely* constitutes *objective truth.*"[10] Only religion and poetry could stake such claims. Transformed into both poetry and religion, party-minded philosophy is doubly "true." Since Marxism is truth, a party guided by this teaching has, to all intents and purposes, a monopoly on truth: "Only the philosophy of Marxism, whose champion is the proletariat, constitutes a system of views in which party-mindedness coincides with objective truth."[11]

When words possessing a high degree of terroristic menace become desemanticized in a ritualized literary culture, they not only cease to mean what they had meant, but also lose common elements of meaning, which become unstable and easily replaceable; then all the speakers of this ideological language become extremely vulnerable; the drifting ideological meanings harbor mortal danger.

The harmonization of the ties between language and ideological reality at all levels of reference—semantic, pragmatic, and syntactic —constituted the raison d'être of "Marxist-Leninist teaching" and determined its status. Philosophy was transformed into a sort of ideological machine that not only produced ideological language in an unending stream, but also constantly renewed it. The principle of party-mindedness was necessary for the replacement of politically up-to-date versions of "Marxist-Leninist teaching" to go smoothly and legitimately through any reversals. The peculiar nature of this ideological language lay in its "scientific-ness." Ultimately, it was just this "Marxist-Leninist teaching"—that is, philosophy proper—that supplied its referents. And the function of the domain of Bolshevist language elevated it to the status of a sort of Soviet *scientia scientiarum,* or, rather, a *commissar of the sciences.*

Since Marxism, from which an "elegant philosophical teaching" was created in the 1920s and 1930s in the Soviet Union, was above all a radical political and economic critical theory, not only was it not a philosophy, but it also emanated from an idea of "the end of philosophy." Just when "Marxist orthodoxy" was established in the USSR, Marx and Engels's *Die deutsche Ideologie* was published in 1932 in full in its original language (and in the following year in Russian as well). In this work, it was stated that "Philosophy and the study of the actual world have the same relation to each other as do masturbation and sexual love."[12] Marx's famous eleventh thesis about Feuerbach, which was memorized in Soviet schools, proclaimed that "Philosophers have only interpreted the world in various ways, but the point is to change it."[13] A "remaking of the world" oriented toward scientism and the affirmation of "positivist science" left little room for traditional philosophizing.

The struggle of radical Marxists against the advocates of classical philosophy spilled over in the 1920s into a bitter polemic between "mechanists" and "dialecticians." These discussions determined, in effect, not only the question of the subject matter of Soviet philosophy and the interpretation within it of certain other postulates of Marxism, but also the place, role, and functions of philosophy in the new state. They also resolved, in equal measure, the question of the nature of this state; the process of consolidating Soviet philosophy coincided with the formation of the Soviet ideocracy, in which the new "teaching" was destined to play a quite special role. The question as to what degree philosophy was ideology boiled down to the question of what the status of philosophy in the Soviet "ideological state" was.

The merger of philosophy and ideology lay at the heart of the shaping of the "philosophical front" in the early 1920s. Active participants in this "front" included Leon Trotsky, Lev Kamenev, Nikolai Bukharin, Mikhail Pokrovskii, Vagarshak Ter-Vaganian, Abram Deborin, and the other prominent Bolsheviks who created the main philosophical journal *Pod znamenem marksizma* (Under the Banner of Marxism). The debate about ideology began with an article published in the journal in 1922 by Vladimir Adoratskii, "About Ideology" (Ob ideologii). Following Marxist tradition, the author viewed ideology as "false consciousness." Proclaimed as suspect was anything separated from the material world and hence distorting ideation of it. Adoratskii contended that "in order to decisively free oneself from ideological distortion, one must surmount ideology and replace it with cold-eyed scientific study of the facts of reality, study of the material existence of human society."[14] But since philosophy was regarded as the highest form of ideology, then in full accord with dialectical laws, dialectical materialism in effect signified a replacement of philosophy. According to this view, "scientific ideology" cannot exist; it is a contradiction in terms.

This logically Marxist (and thus negativist) program was first made public by the rector of Petrograd University and prominent Bolshevik Sergei Minin in a 1920 article wherein he stated that "like religion, philosophy is hostile to the proletariat."[15] In the spirit of the times, the article was titled "Philosophy Overboard" (in those same years Proletkult and the Left Front of Arts [LEF]) had thrown Pushkin "and other generals of the classics" off "the ship of contemporaneity"). Two years later, in the same issue of the journal *Pod znamenem marksizma* in which Adoratskii's article was published, Minin would assert that "the term 'philosophy of Marxism' is first, illogical, second, dangerous and harmful, and third, when it is not dangerous, it is superfluous and for this reason alone harmful." Hence the conclusion that the new society "needs science, only science, simply science."[16] But "simply science" would leave no space for party-mindedness. Their incompatibility was explained by the fact that science was understood as "objective" knowledge, but party-mindedness assumed a class-aware "subjectivity."

The "dialecticians" (headed by Deborin), who were confronting the "mechanists" asserted, on the contrary, that only philosophers could defend and develop Marxism. The "mechanists" were called "talmudists"[17] who did not understand what an important place should be allotted to ideology (and, accordingly, to philosophy) in Marxism.[18] The debate quickly mushroomed into political accusations and direct political pressure. "Dialecticians" accused their opponents of rejecting dialectical materialism while bogged down in "mechanistic" materialism and embarking on a path of revisionism (that is, they had essentially become enemies of Marxism). Finally, once they assumed power in the Society of Militant Materialists, the "dialecticians" were able to get their definitive revenge in 1928 on the "mechanists." The decisive factors proved to be "administrative resources" (the party leadership stood with the "dialecticians," and *Pod znamenem marksizma* was in their hands), false political accusations, unprincipled means of debating, intrigues, disrespect for opponents, complete disregard for the ethics of scholarly debate, and political denunciations.

Soviet philosophy as an "ideological discipline" was faced with a serious task: justifying the status of philosophy as the "commissar" of the sciences while being aware that ideology was by no means inscribed in the system of positive Marxist concepts. As far back as 1845, *German ideology* contained an obvious rejection of ideology from the founders of Marxism: "In all ideology, people and their circumstances appear upside-down, as if in a camera obscura."[19] It was from just this viewpoint that Marx criticized his opponents for abstract ideologizing, filiation of ideas, fetishization, and isolation from the real social conditions and connections of material life itself. Furthermore, Marxism kept this attitude toward ideology as "distorted consciousness" until the very end. Thus, in a letter to Franz Mehring on July 14, 1893, Engels would write: "Ideology is a process accomplished by the so-called thinker consciously, indeed, but with a false consciousness. The real motives impelling him remain unknown to him; otherwise it would not be an ideological process at all."[20]

Despite the fact that Marxism was permeated with a rejection of ideology, Soviet philosophy played the same trick with ideology that "scientific communism" did with the Marxist theory of the state: instead of denying it, it set about confirming it. In doing so, the Soviet system demonstrated not so much its "idealism" as a pragmatic "materialism"; at issue were not principles but rather politics. The link between ideology and philosophy grew stronger as Marxism was reborn into "Marxist-Leninist teaching"—that is, into an instrument for legitimizing the regime—until the party-mindedness of philosophy became more important than philosophy itself.

In launching the "discussion on the philosophical front" in 1930, Stalin was pursuing the very same goals as he had on the "literary front": control over the cultural and intellectual elites and subordination of all spheres of cultural and intellectual life to his power. Philosophy, which in his eyes was the central legitimizing force of the regime, could not remain on the sidelines. Just then, three young philosophers, Mark Mitin, Pavel Iudin, and Vasilii Ral'tsevich, all members of the party leadership of the Institute of Red Professors, declared in *Pravda* a "war on two fronts"—against both the "dialecticians" and the "mechanists." In the era of Stalin's war against "deviations" in the party, a "war on two fronts" was in vogue; the "mechanists" were supposedly the "leftist deviation" (liquidationist) and were accused of Trotskyism, while the "dialecticians" were the "rightist" one (the more so as many of them were linked to Bukharin, who had just been cast down from the party's Olympus for his "rightist deviation"). Stalin invented a special name for this deviation: "Menshevizing idealism" (according to exactly the same schema that Stalin would, a year later, invent "Socialist Realism"). The "war on two fronts" was a sort of political incarnation of the law of unity and conflict of opposites. In this perspective, "Menshevizing idealism" became sort of a "negation of the negation," and the "Marxism-Leninism" born on the wreckage of the two "deviations" became a "passage of quantitative changes into qualitative changes." This new quality was the result of purposeful political acts.

The "new philosophy cadres" assigned by Stalin to all the leading posts completely subordinated the "philosophical front" to themselves.

Mitin and Iudin became central figures in Soviet philosophy. The former, once he became a member of the party Central Committee, took up the reins of the Marx-Engels-Lenin Institute and *Pod znamenem marksizma*. The latter became the head of the Institute of Red Professors and then of OGIZ (Union of State Publishers) and finally of the Academy of Sciences' Institute of Philosophy.

The era of "Marxism-Leninism" had arrived, and the main thing that the "new philosophy cadres" had to ratify was the new approach to philosophy, which passed from the sphere of polemics to transform into a rehashing of the sacred texts of the "classics of Marxism-Leninism" (in the Stalinist interpretation) and a battlefield for relentless war against the "enemies of Marxism"; here, too, was the proclamation of the imminent "Leninist stage" in the history of philosophy, when the answers to all the questions in the history of philosophy were already given, and it remained only to "creatively develop Marxism."

When Stalin's essay "On Dialectical and Historical Materialism" was published in 1938 as the renowned "philosophical chapter" of the *Short Course on the History of the Communist Party* (and was declared an "encyclopedia of philosophical knowledge in the area of Marxism-Leninism"),[21] Stalin was proclaimed a "coryphaeus of the sciences" and what he had written, the apex of creative Marxism. Although even then this text was an exemplar of scholastic primitivism and schematic, it became the basis for teaching philosophy and a sort of "catechism of Marxism" that was not subject to interpretation but merely to ecstatic glorification. The party Central Committee had consolidated this mode of "philosophizing" back at the very beginning of the "philosophical discussion" in its January 25, 1931, resolution "On the Journal *Pod znamenem marksizma*," in which it had observed that henceforth the main task of philosophers would be to "work out the Leninist stage of the development of dialectical materialism."[22]

The "Leninist stage" in philosophy was a euphemism. In the first and to this day most complete history of early Soviet philosophy, *The Suppression of Philosophy in the USSR (1920s–1930s)*, examining in detail all the zigzags of the political line in the area of philosophy, Iegoshua Iakhot came to the conclusion that "the official version, that the philosophical discussion of those years allegedly had some sort of other goals than the aggrandizement of Stalin" did not stand up to criticism and that the "Lenin problem" and the "Leninist stage" was nothing more than camouflage, a smoke screen behind which the cult of Stalin was in fact being created.[23] "Lenin was not the issue, nor was the Leninist stage in philosophy," Iakhot wrote. "The reversal on the ideological front signified a radical change of the direction of propaganda, at whose center Stalin had to stand. This is exactly what Deborin's opponents achieved. The uproar over Lenin and the 'Leninist stage'—these were what created the cult of Stalin."[24]

Meanwhile, the main accomplishment of the "Leninist stage" of the history of philosophy was, in the words of the Bolshevik party Central Committee's resolution "On the Organization of Party Propaganda with Respect to the Publication of *A Short Course on the History of the Communist Party*," that thanks to the "philosophy chapter" in the *Short Course*, "the artificially splintered components of unified Marxist-Leninist teaching—dialectical and historical materialism and Leninism—were reunited, and historical materialism . . . was tied to the party's policy."[25] In other words, philosophy was officially proclaimed a political discipline whose party-mindedness became its ineradicable feature.

The transformation of ideology into a key concept of the political lexicon took place in the Great Terror era. It was at just this time that the concepts of "ideological struggle" and "class struggle" merged, and that concepts like "ideological diversion," "the ideological front," "ideological work," and "ideological education (tempering)" became operational categories. The publication of the *Short Course*, which became a sort of conceptualization and synthesis of the Great Terror, was accompanied by a special Central Committee resolution on November 14, 1938, that advanced "ideological tempering of the cadres" as a fundamental task of the party. When after the war the "theory of conflictlessness" triumphed and "class struggle" was translocated into the sphere of international relations, "ideological struggle" was transformed into a sort of internal form of "class struggle." The "intensification of the ideological struggle of two worlds" and the promotion of the thesis that "ideological struggle is a form of class struggle" spurred the famous "Central Committee resolutions on ideological issues" that were adopted beginning in 1946 in reference to theater, cinema, literature, music, and so forth.[26]

The anti-intellectualism that permeated the aggressive attacks on philosophy led to the very subject of philosophy—the domain of ideas—

falling under suspicion: "Anything that was not commentary on current events was unworthy of being called philosophy. It is easy to understand how people were wary of taking up anything that even remotely suggested abstract analysis of abstract categories: it was always vulnerable from the viewpoint of the new directives that were so urgently implemented."[27] Indeed, *Pod znamenem marksizma* asserted that "sidetracking the practice of the socialist construction of scientific thought into the thickets of scholastic abstraction is the enemy's tactic."[28]

This new party-mindedness had of course nothing to do with philosophy. It was really about a stylization of philosophical discourse, purely suggestive in its functions, which boiled down to a "Marxist" formulation of any of the regime's political acts. By articulating Soviet reality in the categories of "Marxism-Leninism," it maximally de-realized it. Here any appeals to non-ideological reality were treated as "objectivism," and any concentration on the conceptual and (methodo)logical foundations of analysis was branded as "apolitical" and a rejection of party-mindedness—that is, as outright politically hostile actions. Suggestive attributes such as "fighting spirit," "passion," "aggressiveness," and "implacability" came to the fore. Accordingly, party-mindedness spilled over into invective, analysis was replaced with rhetoric and blustering, and logic and argumentation gave way to quotations.

Since the events on the "philosophical front" on the cusp of the 1930s were an attack on philosophy as such, attempts to radically restructure philosophy advanced in parallel with the destruction of traditional philosophical practice as a form of activity. Neither Marx nor Engels was a philosopher, and even less so Lenin, not to mention Stalin. They wrote on philosophical themes merely in connection with other political, ideological, and economic subjects that were for them more urgent. It was no accident that Marx called German philosophy "classic." Its embodiment was Hegel, under whose enormous influence Marx found himself.

There has been more than a little written about why Hegel in particular became the target of the aggressive attacks from the "new philosophical leadership," attacks that were intensified even more during and after World War II. Explanations usually boil down to the issue of Hegel's "Prussianness," his political conservatism, idealism, or even racism. As fascism grew, he became a less and less suitable figure on the ideological Olympus. His status, assured by the piety that the "founders of Marxism-Leninism" felt for him, began to diminish at the cusp of the 1920s, and not by chance. Just as it was no accident that this process coincided with the establishment of the "Leninist" (read here "Stalinist") stage in the history of philosophy.

Hegel was too important to Marxism; in fact, he was its philosophical basis (the whole "philosophy of Marxism"—dialectical materialism—laid out in the *Short Course* was merely a retelling of Hegel). Hegel was too powerful as a thinker—so much so that an exposition of the "foundations of Marxism" could not exclude him. Precisely because the "rational core" of the Hegelian system—dialectics—became the foundation of revolutionary theorizing; precisely because Hegel became the embodiment of philosophy as such; and precisely because Hegelian dialectics, curiously perceived as "dialectical logic" or the construction of flexible and erratic concepts, essentially became the Stalinist model of political thinking, the foundation of its opportunism and adogmatism, the original source was subject to receding further from sight.

And, in fact, in the era of party-mindedness philosophy as a discipline changed its nature and discourse so much that a reminder about philosophical culture in the person of Hegel, who embodied "classical philosophy," became inappropriate. In the era when Hegel's legacy was first "carried over" into Marxism and ascribed to Marx and Engels, then to Lenin, and then totally to Stalin, references to Hegel began to be perceived as a challenge. Under these circumstances, a purloined author was discredited in order to justify his further marginalization. In Hegel's case, there was too much that demanded explanation; alongside the "leaders of the proletariat," he was in every sense an unsuitable and too significant figure. Hegel's dialectics were impossible to "abolish," but references to the author began to be replaced by impersonal exposition of "the laws of historical development." When he set forth Hegel's laws of dialectic in the *Short Course* "in his own words" (or, rather, speaking for history itself) and ascribed them to "Marx, Engels, and Lenin," Stalin seemed to be a compiler. The farther it went, the more uncomfortable he became in Lenin's shadow, and it was clear he had no special liking for Engels. The ideological Olympus was becoming too crowded.

The attacks on Hegel can be explained by precisely these "discomforts," which were profoundly political and already correctly sensed by Mitin and Iudin at the cusp of the 1930s. And then they coincided with a convenient excuse to "draw the curtain" on Hegel; it was a good thing that he had praised the Prussian state and Prussian order, was an idealist, and had lacked sufficient piety in his attitude toward Slavs. Divorced from context, however, all of this was merely a *casus belli* in the war declared on Hegel. It was therefore no accident that one of the fundamental accusations leveled by the "new philosophical leadership" against Deborin's people was specifically their "piety" regarding Hegel and their affirmation of his importance to Marxist theory.

The very fact that Marxism did not even try to formulate radically new categories and laws but rather took up the ones formulated by Hegel was sufficient justification to try to marginalize Hegel. The "Hegel problem" had not existed for Marx and Engels, or for Lenin, because they were not trying to solve the representational problems that Stalin was. To solve them, Stalin needing a "teaching" that would leave a suitable honorary niche for himself in it.

Ironically, even as he was being banished by Stalin, Hegel could have explained the logic of this process better than anyone else. If one attempted to show the workings of the laws of Hegel's dialectics, it would be difficult to find a better example than the history of 1920s–1930s Soviet philosophy itself. In it, the law of unity and the conflict of opposites can be demonstrated by the example of the collision of the "dialecticians" and "mechanists" (the 1920s, the Deborin era), the law of the transition of quantitative changes into qualitative changes by the degeneration of "dialecticians" into "Mensheviks idealists," and the law of negation of the negation by the birth of "Marxism-Leninism" (the 1930s, the era of Mitin and Iudin right up to the appearance of the *Short Course,* with its "philosophical chapter"). At the same time, "Menshevist idealism" can be understood as a sort of negation of negation (the Pyrrhic victory of the "dialecticians" over the "mechanists"). In this light, "Marxism-Leninism" became a sort of "synthesis" of the 1920s–1930s battle on the "philosophical front." But it can be viewed simultaneously as a starting point (thesis) for the subsequent expansion of the dialectical triad that was sweeping irrevocably toward a new synthesis/negation.

Thus, the Marxist orthodoxy that took shape in the 1930s should be understood as a thesis (the result of the law of unity and the conflict of opposites), and the 1947 ("Aleksandrov era") philosophical discussion a sort of antithesis; the practical negation of the history of philosophy as such, the decisive discrediting of the philosophical tradition and philosophical discourse, and the transformation of philosophy into ideological journalism on current political themes were the result of a transition of quantity into quality. Hence the ensuing death of philosophy figures simultaneously as a synthesis and a negation of negation. The deadlock that arose (dialectical and historical materialism were essentially closed by the "philosophical chapter" of the *Short Course,* not subject to further development, and after the 1947 attacks on Aleksandrov's book, the history of philosophy was also closed) left a single niche for philosophy: pure party-mindedness that parasitized criticism of foreign scholarship for the needs of "ideological struggle" in the Cold War.

(ANTITHESIS) ZHDANOV, THE PHILOSOPHER: THE LAW OF THE TRANSITION OF QUANTITATIVE CHANGES INTO QUALITATIVE CHANGES

The Aleksandrov era in Soviet philosophy differed from the Mitin and Iudin era, when "Marxist-Leninist philosophy" was dominant, in its revival of the history of philosophy. The latter became a domain where philosophical thought continued to glimmer because, as distinct from dialectical and historical materialism, where truth in the final instance was established and consolidated in Stalin's "philosophical chapter" of the *Short Course* and consequently not subject to any further discussion or interpretation whatsoever, in the domain of the history of philosophy, no fixed canon was established; the "classics of Marxism" had simply failed to express the "fundamental propositions" regarding all the aspects of the history of philosophy. Many themes remained undeveloped, and many problems and names were open to discussion. Furthermore, "dilettantes in philosophy had a harder time getting there, since besides the language one had to know the works of thinkers from the past and the literature polemicizing with them or analyzing their ideas and revealing the sociocultural context of the origin of the philosophical systems of the past."[29]

Aleksandrov was a historian of philosophy. In May 1939 he defended his doctoral dissertation, which was about the philosophy of Aristotle, and immediately left the Komintern to work in the Central

Committee's Agitprop, which had just been created by a decision of the Eighteenth Congress of the Bolshevik party; within a year, he became its head. Aleksandrov's influence on philosophical scholarship in this period was defining, thanks not only to his status, but also because he placed his own protégés (the "Aleksandrov boys") in all the key posts within the ideological apparatus of the Central Committee and the philosophical institutions; some of them retained their posts there even after the fall of their patron in 1947, heading up the "philosophical front" right up to the time of perestroika.

The most ambitious project on the eve of World War II was the multivolume *History of Philosophy,* which was to reevaluate the history of human thought in the light of Stalinist Marxism. Naturally, the parameters of this history were assigned by the overall condition of historico-philosophical scholarship.

The combination of the ideological eclecticism and political volatility of the discipline created the conditions for abrupt shifts. The initiator of these shifts was Zinovii Beletskii, who headed the Moscow State University department of dialectical and historical materialism in the period just preceding the war. He was also the party secretary of the USSR Academy of Sciences' Institute of Philosophy from 1934 to 1943. He was one of the most eccentric characters in Soviet philosophy. Many stories about him circulated. According to one of them, when he was asked what truth was, he flung open the classroom's window (the philosophy department at that time was located on Mokhovaia Street, across from the Kremlin) and, pointing to the Kremlin, exclaimed "That is Truth!"[30] His only scholarly achievement was a doctoral dissertation (not accepted for defense) about German classical philosophy, in which he attempted to find ideas in Fichte and Hegel that became popular in nazism. In early 1944 he wrote Stalin a letter in which he stated that the authors of the third volume of the *History of Philosophy* (which was dedicated to the era in which German classical philosophy flowered) were glorifying Hegel. It was at just this time that the definition (attributed to Stalin) of Hegelian philosophy appeared, one that characterized it as an aristocratic reaction to the French Revolution.

The intensity of the attacks on German classical philosophy during the time of the war was to be fully expected. But breaking away from it, and especially from Hegel, was impossible; the status of Hegelian dialectics was enormous in Marxism, affirmed repeatedly by its "founders" themselves. Lenin had called Hegelian dialectics one of the sources of Marxism, and its revolutionary potential was decisive. Hegel's "idealist system" was now declared reactionary, while his "method" was declared revolutionary. In this light, Hegel was regarded as part of the "humanist legacy" of mankind (and of the Germans as well, along with Goethe, Heine, and Beethoven) that supposedly opposed the misanthropic philosophy of "the Fascist cannibals." Now a reevaluation of this approach was required.

The May 1, 1944, resolution of the Central Committee targeting the "exaltation of Hegel" was provoked by Beletskii's January 27 letter to Stalin the same year. Stalin did not fail to take advantage of Beletskii's attacks on the authors of the third volume of *History of Philosophy* (the title had been awarded the Stalin Prize, First Class) to consolidate nationalist ideology, which was an urgent political objective during wartime. This objective was not of course articulated but rather camouflaged as a struggle against the "serious theoretical and ideological mistakes" that the authors had supposedly let creep in.

Any political solution weaves together the interests of various groups, and thus any such solution has a number of different consequences (including unforeseen ones). Beletskii had pursued his own interests in writing to Stalin; as a personal enemy of Aleksandrov's, he had counted on his attack at that moment being able to harm the all-powerful head of the Central Committee's Agitprop. For his part, Stalin was working at politico-ideological objectives (and only incidentally was he carrying out the usual "renewal of cadres" on the "philosophical front"). But as it turned out, Aleksandrov, whose function was to serve as an instrument in Stalin's hands, was able to brilliantly use the situation for his career goals, not only settling scores with his main opponents, Mitin and Iudin, but also consolidating his own bureaucratic positions.

A debate on the issues of German classical philosophy was held in the Central Committee in February and March 1944, led by Georgii Malenkov. Participating in the three sessions (February 25, March 10, and March 11) were about twenty people, among whom were the Central Committee secretary, Aleksandr Shcherbakov, the authors' collective of the *History of Philosophy*, and the leadership of Agitprop. In this debate, the contrast between the 1930s-type Marxist rhetoric and the new 1940s ideological paradigm was especially perceptible. Shcherbakov, for example, tossing aside the former internationalist schemas, proclaimed with no beating around the bush, "Our enemy is the Germans. Winning such an unprecedented war would be impossible without hating our German enemies with all our being. A certain amount of work in this direction has been done by Tolstoy, Ehrenburg, and Tarle. Is crushing the Germans not the main thing now? But Iudin sits in an ivory tower and preaches a principle of 'scholarship for scholarship's sake' and refuses to see what is happening in real life."[31] The Central Committee functionary Nikolai Shatalin was even more direct in the closing session: "Why have you now found time to defend the Germans? The Germans will be defending themselves when we hang them, but you have found the time to constantly defend the Germans in all three sessions. And this at the time of the Patriotic War!"[32]

The result of this debate was the secret Central Committee resolution from May 1, 1944, "On Shortcomings in Scholarly Work in the Area of Philosophy" (No. 1143/110),[33] which "put an end to the influential Mitin-Iudin alliance and presumably concluded an entire period in the history of Soviet philosophy—from the rout of 'Menshevist idealism' in 1931 up to 1944."[34] Having won a serious bureaucratic battle, Aleksandrov decided to roundly consolidate his position on the philosophical Olympus academically as well by reissuing his 1939 textbook, *History of Western European Philosophy,* in a second edition in 1945 and 1946. This work, essentially a collection of 1930s lectures in the form of essays about European philosophers, was issued in a huge print run (the 1946 printing alone was more than fifty thousand copies) and was recommended by the USSR Ministry of Higher Education as a textbook for institutions of higher education. A campaign of encomia for the book was launched in the press, and Aleksandrov's recent enemies, Mitin and Iudin, nominated the book for the Stalin Prize, which was awarded to it. On November 30, 1946, Aleksandrov was made an academician of the USSR Academy of Sciences. But here Beletskii again denounced Aleksandrov, who was again trying to prove himself correct, and Stalin again heeded Beletskii's arguments. This time, the reasons for the campaign, and its consequences, were completely different.

What was going on behind the façade of the "creative development of Marxism" and of the battle against "deviations" within Soviet philosophy was a constant, relentless, and truly *party-minded* struggle or, more precisely, a "quiet but merciless war";[35] just as Deborin's triumph in the 1920s had signified the fall of radical Marxists and the elevation of Mitin and Iudin on the cusp of the 1930s the fall of Deborin, the elevation of Aleksandrov on the eve of the war signified the fall of Stalin's philosophical Olympians Mitin and Iudin, who found themselves in open opposition to Aleksandrov and his numerous protégés. This interdisciplinary battle (which raged in all the scholarly disciplines) had in this case far more serious consequences since by virtue of the very status of the discipline, philosophers held key ideological positions in the country—from the leadership of Agitprop to that of the Marx-Engels-Lenin-Stalin Institute, the Central Committee Higher Party School, the journal *Bol'shevik* (the party's main theoretical organ), the newspaper *Izvestiia*, OGIZ, and many other key political institutions that were part of the Central Committee *nomenklatura*. This linkage has traditionally explained the events in 1944–47 on the "philosophical front."

Some have suggested that Aleksandrov's dismissal was the result of a multifaceted operation of Malenkov and Beriia to weaken Zhdanov's bureaucracy. This view, shared by many authors, does not account for the fact that in 1947 Aleksandrov was not a "Zhdanov man."[36] From Zhdanov's perspective, he was more of a "Malenkov man," having worked under Malenkov's leadership from 1940 up to the end of the war. Thus it is not at all surprising that it was Zhdanov, who himself had promoted Aleksandrov for the job of Agitprop's head, who now criticized Aleksandrov especially harshly.[37] The assistant head of Agitprop (and Stalin's illegitimate son), Konstantin Kuzakov, said that Zhdanov, the party's key ideologue, had before the war made up the leadership of the Agitprop Central Committee from the people that he trusted. However, since from the beginning of World War II he had spent most of his time in Leningrad and had subsequently been appointed the Soviet deputy to Finland, Agitprop, which had fallen from his oversight, came under Malenkov's control. Thus, when Malenkov fell from grace in 1946, Zhdanov took advantage of the occasion to punish the "unfaithful protégés." Accusations were found for all of them (Kuzakov himself, for example, was accused of overlooking an American spy in his circle).[38]

Aleksandrov's successor in Agitprop, Dmitrii Shepilov, confirmed in his memoirs that Aleksandrov was not a "Zhdanov man"; Zhdanov supposedly told Shepilov that Aleksandrov and his "buddies" had busied themselves with "money-grubbing careerist" activities and that "all those Aleksandrovs, Kruzhkovs, Fedoseevs, and Il'ichevs that had dug themselves in on the ideological front and monopolized everything they got their hands on were not revolutionaries nor Marxists. They were petty bourgeois. They were actually quite remote from the people and were above all preoccupied with arranging their own personal affairs."[39]

Appearing in print more often than permissible for a party functionary of his level, Aleksandrov during the war assembled his articles about war issues from the periodical press and published them as the book *The Enemy Will be Beaten.* Zhdanov reacted to this quite negatively, supposedly saying that Aleksandrov was behaving immodestly in publishing such a book; Comrade Stalin's book *On the Soviet Union's Great Patriotic War* was coming out, and Aleksandrov was all but putting his own book alongside it, which was considered a breach of unwritten rules. Not long after this, Aleksandrov altogether stopped appearing in print.[40]

It was much more significant that Aleksandrov's "immodesty" had supposedly upset Stalin, who had learned from yet another letter of Beletskii's that literally just months after Aleksandrov's book had been awarded the Stalin Prize, its author had been made an academician, and three of his deputies (Petr Fedoseev, Mikhail Iovchuk, and Aleksandr Egolin) had become correspondent members of the USSR Academy of Sciences. Stalin supposedly even demanded that the academy's president, Vavilov, rescind all these appointments, and when he found out that the academy's regulations made this impossible, he promised to "take measures of his own." Iovchuk, from whom Vavilov's instructions to accept the Agitprop bosses into the academy originated, was immediately exiled to Minsk as the Belorussian Central Committee's secretary of propaganda.[41] Here Stalin's hostility to the bureaucrat who had gone too far and to the "Aleksandrov boys" was clear, and the careers of many of them took abrupt downturns after the "philosophical discussion"; Aleksandrov in August 1947 was removed from his job as head of Agitprop (replaced by Suslov) and became director of the Institute of Philosophy; Fedoseev left his job as first deputy of the head of Agitprop (his job going to Shepilov) and soon lost the job of editor-in-chief of *Bol'shevik* as well; and Egolin was transferred to the post of director of the Institute of World Literature.

Much more significant, too, was Aleksandrov's breaking of the hierarchical rules and his "loss of trust" by Stalin. By taking advantage of the Central Committee's resolution for the purposes of consolidating his personal bureaucratic position, Aleksandrov, who by the end of 1946 had been head of Agitprop for six years, was a candidate for Central Committee membership and already a member of its Organizational Bureau, as well as the most influential professional philosopher in the country, had permitted himself to break the unwritten *nomenklatura* rules. With his keen bureaucratic flair, Stalin could not fail to see the bureaucratic end game that Aleksandrov had played in 1944 and could even take this as a personal insult; Aleksandrov not only had dared to think himself an independent political player, but had also allowed himself to do something that no one but Stalin could do: to play his own bureaucratic intrigue to strengthen his personal influence by putting his own people in all the key ideological posts—that is, he had used *Stalin*'s gambit for *his own* purposes. Using Stalin's methods for his own purposes like this could neither go unnoticed nor be done with impunity. Stalin kept a keen eye out lest anyone in his circle should grow too strong or create his own *nomenklatura* group or play his own game. Aleksandrov had given cause to suspect him of such feeble efforts. It seems that this is just why Stalin decided not only to remove Aleksandrov, but also to drag him through all the degrading circles of bureaucratic and academic hell. Thus the idea of the "philosophical discussion" was born.

Beletskii's letter to Stalin that set the anti-Aleksandrov campaign in motion contained insinuations about the Agitprop chief's indiscretions—that he had allowed himself not only to revise the Central Committee's 1944 decision regarding the third volume of the *History of Philosophy* (after using it for his own career goals), but had also organized a laudatory campaign for his own book, giving it "a little push" for the 1946 Stalin Prize. But the main thing was that Aleksandrov had created such a hullabaloo around his own book that many (by virtue of its author's post) began to reckon it "among the classic works"; as E. G. Plimak observed, "Stalin's position as only the 'fourth classic author' of Marxist scholarship was being threatened."[42] Thus, without a doubt, one of the tasks was to confirm that there was only one philosopher in the country. And if Stalin said in 1944 that Hegel was the "aristocratic reaction to the French Revolution," then no one could reconsider this stance without his approval. The simple fact that the Central Committee's (that is, Stalin's) resolution was *perceived* as disavowed by Aleksandrov (never mind that nothing of the kind was the reality) was sufficient grounds for public obstruction. Stalin's desire to reign in the upstart and consolidate his own status as the coryphaeus of all the sciences was so palpable that not once did any of the participants in the discussion state this openly. Ia. A. Mil'ner, for, example, declared: "I find Comrade Aleksandrov a capable philosopher and an even more capable organizer. But he aspired through his official position to stifle any movement whatsoever on the philosophical front. He was too carried away with playing the creator of a school like Aristotle's lyceum. He evidently forgot that the true head of the school has already been working for more than half a century without laying hands on the joy and happiness of all forward-thinking and progressive humanity."[43]

Stalin did not simply initiate the campaign against Aleksandrov; he also orchestrated it down to the smallest details. For example, Zhdanov not only sent his report to Stalin for approval, but also had to ask his permission to redact and exclude three texts of the speeches made during the discussion from the transcript. Furthermore, Stalin took the campaign through to the end, regardless of the fact that the repeated discussion he initiated had no serious motivation whatsoever. When he thought in January 1947 that Aleksandrov had managed to slow down the campaign that he had launched against him, Stalin insisted on having a repeat discussion (that was in all other respects pointless), in the course of which Aleksandrov was nonetheless decisively humiliated.

By making the campaign far-reaching, Stalin was trying to solve another problem other than simply the dismissal of Aleksandrov. What had happened to Aleksandrov was supposed to serve as a warning at all levels of the party bureaucracy. After all, "If a person who had occupied a high party post and was awarded numerous awards and honors can be subjected to a public 'flogging' for not very clear deviations in the area of the history of philosophical problems, then what might be said about other people? . . . No previous accomplishments and honors will be able to shield one from answering for ideological transgressions (imagined or real) if the party Areopagus considers them such."[44] No one was guaranteed against obstruction; this reminder about the absence of guarantees made the intellectual elites particularly receptive to the principle of party-mindedness.

We should also remember that the very appearance of Aleksandrov on the Soviet philosophical Olympus led to a change in the status of

Soviet philosophy as the main ideological discipline, a status that had been established in the 1930s. As we have seen, the formation of philosophy had gone through a number of stages, in the course of which its fundamental principles were shaped. Foremost among them were the domination of dialectical and historical materialism (whereas Aleksandrov had foregrounded the history of philosophy); party-mindedness, which was quite compatible with historical materialism, though less suited to the history of philosophy; and Stalin's status as the absolute authority in the area of philosophy. By authoring a course in the history of philosophy, Aleksandrov had asserted his personal authority in this area (fortified by his bureaucratic status), which was a transgression of the unwritten *nomenklatura* rules. Even these "intra-philosophical" reasons alone were enough to dismiss him.

Thus, when he decided to organize the discussion, Stalin was solving not only a "staff problem" (which he could well have solved without the discussion), but also a purely disciplinary one; ultimately, the basic function of philosophy, as he understood it, boiled down to the ideological legitimization of the regime and by no means to its own history. The dominance of the history of philosophy with Aleksandrov deprived the main ideological discipline of its raison d'être. The most astute participants in the discussion drew attention to this. Teodor Oizerman, for example, an academic who actively participated in these events, asserted that the discussion "was in fact directed against philosophy as such, especially against the history of philosophy, in particular against the study of German classical philosophy, as well as contemporary Western European and American philosophy."[45]

The makeup itself of the participants in the discussion attested to the status of the demarche. At Stalin's insistence, among those invited were the Central Committee secretaries; the Central Committee department leaders; and leaders of the republican, regional, and local party organizations, as well as those of the Moscow and Leningrad party activist groups. In addition to practically all the upper-level party *nomenklatura*, two separate lists enumerated representatives of the USSR Academy of Sciences and its institutes, writers, publishing officials, and others. Judging by its makeup, as Petr Druzhinin so precisely put it, "It was a nationwide ideological forum."[46] The presidium included Central Committee secretaries Zhdanov, Kuznetsov, and Suslov, as well as Matvei Shkiriatov, Aleksandrov, Fedoseev, and Kruzhkov. There were

424 attendees in the hall. Among these were 127 from the Soviet republics and other cities; 161 philosophers from Moscow; 48 scholarly/
scientific workers from other fields; and 88 party workers.[47] The scale
and status of this second debate was supposed to be proportional to
the problems it addressed. These problems were political, focused on
the person of Aleksandrov, and, as usual, ideologically "loaded."

Aleksandrov's book was incriminated above all for its lack of party-
mindedness. Beletskii's 1946 letter to Stalin had already stated that
Aleksandrov's book was "an unpardonable academic précis."[48]

When the "party-mindedness of Soviet science" was mentioned, this
meant above all philosophy. As if through it, the science of sciences,
party-mindedness manifested itself implicitly as well in the specialized
sciences, from biology and physiology to chemistry and physics. Of
course, in the history of philosophy, the principle of party-mindedness
did not manifest itself so openly as in the other areas of "Marxist-
Leninist teaching," such as historical materialism or scientific communism, which were not simply "ideological disciplines" but were essentially formulated in the abstract (philosophical) categories of pure
ideology. Where party-mindedness manifested itself even more obviously was in Soviet art, whose task boiled down to the materialization
of abstract ideological schemas "in artistic images."

This kinship between party-mindedness in philosophy and in art was
reflected in the aestheticization of Soviet philosophical meta-discourse.
The pursuit of philosophy itself began to be described in the same
terms as the work of Soviet writers: "Soviet philosophers are called
upon to creatively elaborate the questions about our society's laws of
development, . . . to generalize the extremely rich material provided by
the practice of socialist construction, to be able to seek out the germs
of the new and to conceptualize their significance . . . and to be in the
first ranks of workers on the ideological front, leading an all-out offensive on the remnants of capitalism in the consciousness of the Soviet
people" (3). Mitin challenged philosophers to "depict in militant journal articles and speeches the life-giving forces of socialism, the might of
our state, the moral strength of our ideology, the greatness of our Soviet
system, and their advantages over decaying bourgeois ideology and the
bourgeois world"; he demanded that they "give our scientific cadres
the task of celebrating, of glorifying, our state, a new type of state, in
serious scientific studies" (129). This discursive link was not accidental;

the principle of party-mindedness was implemented at the same time in Soviet philosophy as it was in art.

In the range of critical observations directed at Aleksandrov, we can see how the philosophical elites understood the principle of party-mindedness. The first to speak, M. V. Emdin, declared that "the fundamental defect in Comrade Aleksandrov's book is that the principle of Leninist-Stalinist party-mindedness in philosophy is violated, and furthermore, this principle is often violated on all points" (7). This was revealed by the fact that, as Emdin calculated, of the sixty-nine philosophers mentioned by Aleksandrov, "there is no specification of the class origins" of forty-eight of them (7).

But there was more than such a quantitative approach that revealed the absence of party-mindedness: "Even Comrade Aleksandrov's language is the useless, empty, liberal language of a bourgeois objectivist, a professor" (10). M. Rozental' expressed this idea even more clearly when he declared that "you cannot sense in the book the seething of the passions that have gripped the warring camps and parties in philosophy, and the fundamental problems of philosophy, around which a violent war has raged over the course of two and a half thousand years and is even now being waged, are not emphasized" (86). But S. V. Morochnik, from Stalinabad, was philosophically paradoxical when he lamented that in criticizing "the reactionary idealist Plato," Aleksandrov himself was not enough of a Plato because he "lacks the passion that distinguishes, for example, the philosophical work of Plato himself" (117). It does not follow from this, of course, that party-mindedness is a style of exposition. Rather, it is a peculiar state of writing, at the heart of which lies an elusive "Bolshevist spirit," whose absence leads to "bourgeois objectivism." With respect to Aleksandrov's book, this is not entirely justified; his exposition of the history of West European philosophy is written in the best traditions of party-minded political writing—full of fact-juggling, demagoguery, and philosophizing. But this definition is exact in another, more general sense: "bookish" books were dangerous not because they expounded a theory in an insufficiently emotional way but because they expounded anything at all and therefore carried the danger of "objectivism."

"Bourgeois objectivism" was branded as "hypocritical" since it engaged in "smoothing over and hushing up class antagonisms, class struggle, and bourgeois classist attitudes that were masked as supra-class, beyond-class, apolitical science, philosophy, and so forth" (16). Given this, it was unclear how to select the material when expounding the philosophical legacy if any quotation had to work as an "objectively true" party-minded concept. Aleksandrov was faulted because he "brings in the jabbering of reactionary philosophers that, by the intention of its authors, is supposed to serve as a fig leaf that conceals the reactionary essence of their views. In this way, Comrade Aleksandrov objectively whitewashes these reactionary idealist thinkers" (11). For example, why should one quote Fichte's "jabbering" if "this can inure our young people to garrulity, to empty talk, to winning over their sympathies with the 'pompous' phraseology of reactionary Fichteanism"? (11).

In other words, what was required was not to expound the material but to express an attitude toward it. This made exposition emotional. The main function of historico-philosophical narrative was declared to be suggestiveness. This meant that one had to speak with "blistering criticism." Aleksandrov's book suffered from being, as V. A. Fomina put it, "insipid and professorial in a bad sense; it has no Bolshevik spark, no authentic passion; there is no aggressive spirit, no lethal sarcasm and irony directed against the enemies of Marxist-Leninist philosophy" (473). It was impossible to write a history of philosophy without sarcasm and vituperation.

Accordingly, one had to reject even the stylistic conventions of historico-philosophical exposition; it was valid to give a characterization of the philosophers being criticized. Thus E. G. Fisher faulted Aleksandrov for his book's having "too many people declared to be 'great,' 'genial,' 'eminent,' 'outstanding,' and 'original.' . . . With this kind of hyperbolic characterization of the past centuries' thinkers, the significance of Marxist-Leninist philosophy is imperceptibly disparaged. . . . The reader begins to muse: Thales already had genial and courageous ideas, Descartes was a great philosopher and his teaching was famous and original, Spinoza and Fourier were geniuses, and so forth. But what did Marx and Engels especially contribute to the worldwide history of philosophy, the reader asks himself" (470).

Scrutiny of a completely different order was demanded, of which David Zaslavskii provided a precise characterization. Stalin's "court" journalist reminded the participants of the discussion that they were above all "writers" and therefore must write in a vivid style. If the history of philosophy is criticism of earlier philosophical systems, then this criticism must be "scathing." Zaslavskii challenged participants to "forge a path in philosophical journalism toward jovial and wicked, sarcastic and scathing derision of the enemy." He insisted that "noble revolutionary-democratic and Marxist traditions stand behind philosophical satire, behind the philosophical pamphlet. Marx and Engels, as well as Lenin and Stalin, not only unmask the enemies of Marxism; they force the reader to laugh at them." He reminded them that "the jovial philosophical pamphlets, feuilletons, and parodies of Engels belong to the classic gold reserve of Marxism." Rhetorically, he asked those assembled, "Is not 'The Holy Family' a series of brilliant philosophical-journalistic feuilletons and pamphlets?" (186). Nor did Zaslavskii forget about the history of his country's thinkers. Recalling the fact that reactionaries and liberals had called the revolutionary democrats "little boys," he concluded his speech with a challenge to Soviet philosophers to become the same kind of "little boys": "I want you, the philosophers of the very youngest social stratum, to be yourselves young, always young, to be the most similar possible to the youngest, most lively, cleverest, and most serious philosopher of our country and of our era—Comrade Stalin" (187).

What we see here is the earlier discourse of party-minded philosophy. Earlier, it was almost wholly focused on the themes of historical materialism and then somewhat awkwardly applied to the history of philosophy. What is new here is that it had to be used for criticism of contemporary philosophy, with which Soviet ideology now found itself in confrontation. This meant absolutely all of contemporary foreign ("bourgeois") philosophy.

In an era of imminent cold war, philosophy had to try and solve the same problems that the Soviet Union was facing in the international arena. It is not surprising that Mitin's last question was, "What is hindering the speeches of our workers on the ideological front from rising to the level of the brilliant speeches of our diplomats?" (129). The ideological discipline had to take on propagandistic and counter-propagandistic functions: "We must write the history of philosophy for the unmasking of contemporary bourgeois philosophy, we must write the history of philosophy for the unmasking of bourgeois culture as a whole," was the challenge of M. P. Baskin (161).

This had at least two serious consequences. First, a retreat from the themes of the history of philosophy. Also in the form of a question, L. O. Reznikov delineated this shift quite well: "Why must the Soviet reader—the Soviet intelligent or student—know about the philosophical views of the Christian theologians Tertullian and St. Augustine but can be ignorant about Bergson's intuitivism or Dewey's pragmatism? Why must he know about the medieval inquisition but can be ignorant of Fascist obscurantism?" (415). Second, a retreat from the methods of the history of philosophy. History is completely replaced by criticism. As the then director of the Marx-Engels-Lenin Institute, Vladimir Kruzhkov, observed, "The history of philosophy must not be regarded as anything other than one of the ideological tools in the struggle against the various ideologies hostile to Marxism-Leninism" (391). The exemplar of such party-minded criticism of philosophical deviations was still Lenin and his "Materialism and Empiriocriticism." This work had not come easily to Lenin, but, as L. Iu. Zvonov said, "Barely overcoming his disgust, he produced a revelation of all the inner reactionary-idealist filth that was camouflaged by the outer pseudo-scientificalness of Machism" (364).

All of this required a radical restructuring of the "philosophical front," which began to be conceived of in purely militaristic categories, adapted to the needs of cold war:

> "We are the warriors of the ideological front," P. E. Vyshinskii said to his colleagues. "We are the soldiers of the Communist army. We are the philosophical artillery of communism. I would compare party-minded criticism to fire control. We fusillade our enemies; we often shoot at closed targets. The party press, as well as the Central Committee, with its criticism of our work, corrects our firing; it shows more visibly where our shells are getting to. And, of course, it is sometimes useful to give foolish gunners a good thrashing. But when we make a mistake, then let our Central Committee criticize us severely better than we ourselves. This is more useful than our remaining with our blunders and, as a result of our poor shooting, leaving our enemies alive." (231)

But these metaphors, as is clear from Zhdanov's contribution to the discussion, were far from reality. The party's chief ideologue explained to the "foolish gunners" that they were not fulfilling their aims and could not yet be counted as warriors:

Is our philosophical front really like an actual front? It is rather more reminiscent of a quiet backwater or a bivouac somewhere far away from the battlefield. The battlefield is still not taken, for the most part there is no engagement with the adversary, reconnaissance is not done, the arms are rusting, the soldiers fight at their own risk and peril while the commanders either gloat over their past victories or quarrel about whether there is strength enough for an attack, whether they perhaps should use help from the outside or on the subject of how much consciousness can stray from reality so as not to seem too backward. (Laughter.) (268)

Laughter, as it turned out, was the only adequate reaction to Zhdanov's "sarcasm."

Essentially, in the course of the philosophical discussion (most of all in Zhdanov's Stalin-approved speech), the most radical approaches to philosophy were legitimized—its subject, discourse, and history. Most of all, this was about rejecting the view of the history of philosophy as a process of the "filiation of ideas." This formulation, which belonged to Beletskii, was intensified by Zhdanov. If the history of philosophy, which (regardless of all the interest in the socio-historical roots of one theory or another) is the history of the filiation of ideas, is not regarded as such any longer, then philosophy itself should accordingly no longer be conceived of as an area of ideas. And, in fact, Beletskii insisted, since ideas reflect only the material interests of classes, one ought to study class struggle and not ideas. Therefore, anyone who (like Aleksandrov) prefers to study ideas is stuck in the framework of bourgeois science, operating with logical categories and analyzing gnoseological concepts. This is where Beletskii found the key to party-mindedness.

All of this forced Z. A. Kamenskii to mount a defense of philosophy as such: "Fear of academicism and abstractness sometimes leads one to forget what the subject of philosophy is—that is, [it leads] to essentially a liquidation of philosophical science, as it happened with historical science in the times when Pokrovskii's school held sway" (381). But the reference to Pokrovskii did not fool anyone; the 1947 campaign was by its very essence "liquidationist" with respect to philosophy. Essentially, Beletskii's definitions were merely an adaptation of Pokrovskii's definitions regarding history to the area of philosophy. Pokrovskii maintained that history was politics cast backward into the past, but Beletskii declared that "what philosophy faced foremost was not so much the interests of knowledge as the political interests of one class or state or another" (317). The idea of merging philosophy with life was no less radical than the Proletkult and LEF ideas of life-creation and the merger of art with life. Beletskii concluded his speech with an expression of confidence that "academicism and scholasticism will in the very near future be decisively eliminated from philosophy. Our philosophy will be completely united with life and will go forward with it" (325).

The reexamination of the subject of philosophy and of the nature of philosophizing led to a most radical anti-historicism. According to Beletskii, the history of philosophy had to be turned upside down: "Marxism cannot be understood from the apex of the history of philosophy; on the contrary, all of past philosophy can be understood and explained only from the viewpoint of Marxism" (319). Mitin translated this challenge into the language of politics: "From the heights of Marxism-Leninism, from the tower of our great Socialist era, from the viewpoint of historical experience accumulated by the Bolshevik Party, we must come to terms with all previous ideational material and put it in its place" (123).

Beletskii quizzed the listeners rhetorically: "Why should we think that for a profound understanding of contemporary problems we should begin with criticism of earlier philosophy? Can a person who stands on Marxist principles seriously think that the contemporary problems of philosophy are connected at all to earlier philosophy? Only a follower of Hegel can think this, not one of Marx" (316). Others expressed similar views as well in the course of the discussion. Mitin asked, "Can the further development of social sciences and philosophy, linked to the geniuses of our era, Lenin and Stalin, be anything but a gigantic step in the development of world culture with which, in its significance, nothing in past history can be compared?" (122). As if replying to this question, V. S. Paukova asserted that since "dialectical materialism was created a long time ago and already has a history of its own development . . . it is long since time that we break free from the umbilical cord that ties us to the prehistory of philosophical thought and enter into its genuine history as exponents of a completely new philosophy that is fundamentally distinct from all preceding philosophical teachings including even the materialist ones" (222). In this perspective, the history of philosophy was dying out from superfluousness.

Since according to Beletskii the philosophy of an exploitative society "gives a distorted representation of reality," then "all the philosophy of past social formations cannot therefore be regarded as science in the strict sense of this word. Idealism never served the interests of science. The philosophy of the ancients cannot be regarded as a science in the sense that we understand philosophy now. The philosophy of the ancients had only scientific guesswork" (318).

Thus, Zhdanov's assertions that "the emergence of Marxism was a real discovery, a revolution in philosophy" and that a completely new period in the history of philosophy began with Marx ("becoming a science for the first time") were only a legitimization of party-minded historicism. At a practical level this led to a definition of the subject of the history of philosophy that essentially swept aside history as such. According to Zhdanov, the scientific history of philosophy "is the history of the origin, emergence, and development of the scientific materialist worldview and its laws. Since materialism arose and developed in a struggle against idealist trends, the history of philosophy is also the history of the struggle of materialism against idealism" (257).

The open-ended teleologism of this definition transformed the teachings of Plato and Aristotle, of the Stoics and St. Augustine, and of Descartes and Bacon into nothing more than material to be compared with "the scientific materialist worldview"—that is, with Marxism, which, as Z. A. Kamenskii observed, "completely deprives us of a historical view of the process of philosophy's development—both in its relationship to a particular theory and on the culturological level."[49] It likewise emerged that since the times of Plato and Aristotle, and of Thomas Aquinas and Spinoza, philosophy had been moving toward a contemplated goal: Marxist materialism.[50] From this perspective, idealism itself could be regarded exclusively as a "negative counter-agent of materialism."[51] Zhdanov's definition also failed to account for the fact that "the history of philosophy simply would not have existed if idealists had not been active in it—Plato and Aristotle, Descartes and Leibniz, Kant and Fichte, Schelling and Hegel. Materialism and idealism are the forms in which humanity tries to fathom the subject of philosophy and are not any sort of antipodes that are distinguished from each other like a master and an apprentice."[52] Finally, this approach practically suppressed the study of non-Marxist philosophy from the second half of the nineteenth and the twentieth centuries, such study being regarded "exclusively as a disintegrating phenomenon, as the result of the breakdown of consciousness, which led to the idea that all of humanity that did not accept Marxism had lost its mind."[53]

Having essentially abolished pre- and non-Marxist philosophy, Zhdanov declared that one must not conclude the study of the history of philosophy with the Marxist stage but rather that one should write about the Leninist (which meant also the Stalinist) stage. In his concluding words, Aleksandrov, manifesting the wonders of restructuring, hastened to develop this idea; since "the history of the truly real science about society, the history of genuinely scientific philosophical knowledge begins with Marxism . . . *the whole* history of philosophy, starting with the most ancient times and ending with the mid-nineteenth century, should comprise one part, and moreover *a not too great one,* of the history of philosophy" (294; my emphasis). Rather the fundamental content should be allotted to the exposition of Marxist-Leninist philosophy and targeted for the "most critical battle against contemporary bourgeois obscurantism" (295).

This is the backdrop against which the relationship to Hegel yet again became the center of the debate. He became the litmus paper on which the party-mindedness of historico-philosophical science was tested, owing to, on the one hand, the significance of this figure in Marxism, and, on the other, the ever-growing unacceptability of it in the new political situation. Such tension created an ideal field of indeterminacy; the more multifaceted this figure became, the more complicated it was to define oneself in relation to it, to find a correct balance of the positive and negative in evaluating Hegel, and the easier it was to come under fire from critics. And this was not because of a wrongly taken step but because of uncertainty whether *any* step in *any* particular direction would later be qualified as correct or mistaken. It would be more accurate to say that there was no correct balance and no reliable direction. The search for and determination of a correct balance or a reliable direction were exceptional instruments of terror in Stalin's hands. Aleksandrov was accused of approaching the history of philosophy (and of Hegel in particular) in a non-party-minded way by not uncovering the "class roots" of Hegel's philosophical system, although as an experienced party propagandist and functionary, Aleksandrov had actually provided responses in his book to all possible accusations preventively. The fact that these responses were ignored was evidence that Hegel was needed only as an instrument of control over the "philosophical front."

In fact, Beletskii had maintained in his letter to Stalin that Aleksandrov's "objectivism" was manifested in the fact that instead of a "class analysis," he regarded the history of philosophy as a "filiation of ideas." But the truth was that on the very third page of Aleksandrov's book (relating specifically to Hegel!) one could read the stridently critical assertion that Hegel "turned the history of philosophy, the history of thought, into an absolutely independent process that begat itself."[54]

Aleksandrov was accused of not appreciating the fact that Hegel was in service to the Prussian crown. However, the section on Hegel in Aleksandrov's book began with the statement that "Hegel defended the autocratic Prussian state that he served" (401) and later noted that "the dogmatic, conservative character of Hegel's views was that the philosopher perceived the reactionary Prussian state regime, along with the monarchy, as a higher manifestation and embodiment of the absolute spirit" (417).

Another accusation was that in his approach to Hegel, Aleksandrov ignored the criticisms in the classics of Marxism; however, his chapter on Hegel began with a quotation from Lenin's *Philosophical Notebooks,* followed by one from the "philosophical chapter" of Stalin's *Short Course.* The Hegel chapter concluded with a veritable cascade of quotations; its final two pages were filled by three huge quotations, one from *Das Kapital* and two from the *Short Course* about the "rational kernel" of Hegel's philosophy and of "Hegel's idealist husk" (422–23).

Aleksandrov was also faulted for not calling enough attention to the contradiction between Hegel's method and his system, although his book emphasized that "Hegel could not draw revolutionary conclusions from his discoveries in the area of dialectics. Hegel's system buried his method. The requirement of Hegel's method to uncover the objective dialectics of development and the requirement of his system to conclude the development with a discovery of 'absolute knowledge' are in most profound contradiction" (415).

Just as unfounded were Beletskii's (and later Stalin's) accusations that Aleksandrov disavowed the Central Committee's 1944 resolution regarding the third volume of *History of Philosophy.* On the contrary, Aleksandrov conscientiously repeated in his own book everything that had been said about nazism's ties to Hegel in the context of the criticism of the *History of Philosophy* volume. He pointedly raised the question, "What did the Fascist obscurantists try to borrow from Hegel?" The answer he supplied was in full accord with the 1944 resolution: "They borrowed Hegel's mysticism and strove to justify the contemporary reaction with the help of his 'philosophy of truth.' Contemporary reactionaries have carried over Hegel's mysticism into a peculiar system of neo-Hegelianism that is a philosophy of militant obscurantism and reaction" (416). In accordance with these same principles, Aleksandrov asserted that "Hegel was a Prussian nationalist," that "Hegel's unrestrained praise of the Prussian monarchy finds its expression in Hegel's deification of the reactionary Prussian state," and that Hegel "attempted in his *Philosophy of Truth* to justify Germany's reactionary attempts to conquer and enslave other countries and peoples. Hegel has a particularly disdainful attitude towards the Slavic peoples, whom he purposely excluded from his outline of world history in view of the fact that the Slavic nation supposedly 'to this day has not expressed itself as a independent phenomenon in manifestations of the Mind in the world'" (418). And his conclusion was entirely in the spirit of wartime propaganda: "Hence, could it be anything but clear that the succeeding reactionaries in Germany, right up to Hitler's band of brigands, would be able to freely use, and in fact have used, Hegel's reactionary blather about necessity to wage predatory wars? Hence, it is no surprise that the German Fascists have relied on Hegel for the 'theoretical' justification of their 'total state' and their brigandish policies" (420).

After all this, to say that Aleksandrov was whitewashing Hegel and revising the rigorous approach to him formulated in 1944 was an obvious lie. This was understood not only by Stalin and Aleksandrov, but also by the participants in the discussion, many of whom were experienced bureaucrats and propagandists; Aleksandrov was being subjected to public opprobrium not for what was being ascribed to him but for something that must not be named. The ease and cynicism with which unsubstantiated ideological transgressions were ascribed to one of the main party hierarchs were supposed to demonstrate the vulnerability of everyone to Stalin's will. Indeed, the flip side of this fear was the sophistication and aggression with which the participants of the discussion reviled Hegel and accused Aleksandrov of whitewashing him.

The 1947 attacks on Hegel were of an unprecedented nature (it is worth noting that, as distinct from the closed 1944 resolution, they were public). It seemed that Soviet philosophers were sizing up the territory, trying to understand how far they would have to go in an actual polemic with the "classics of Marxism." Although, as Aleksandr Makovel'skii proclaimed, "the resolution concerning the liquidation of the Prussian state is a just historical condemnation of the 'Prussian philosophy' of Kant, Fichte, Schelling, and Hegel" (this was now the accepted way of referring to "German classical philosophy"), this did not mean that it had to be completely "written off." Makovel'skii graciously agreed that this condemnation "does not preclude the presence in these systems of individual positive moments noted by the founders of Marxism-Leninism" (210). Other participants in the discussion, meanwhile, doubted even this. L. Iu. Zvonov, for example, rhetorically asked, "When the 'rational kernel' of Hegelian dialectics is a hillock in comparison to the Elbrus of materialist dialectics, is there any need now to also emphasize this 'rational kernel' by praising Hegel to the skies and lapsing into an apologia for him?" (367).

The attacks were directed not only against Hegel's system, but also against the dialectical method itself, the discrediting of which threatened the destruction of the very "foundations of Marxist-Leninist teaching." Nonetheless, Emdin had already proclaimed in the first speech of the discussion that "not only idealism but also the method of German idealist philosophy was reactionary and hostile to the historically great eighteenth-century ideas of materialism" (8). The "class analysis" that Soviet philosophers demonstrated in this boiled down to the fact that, as M. D. Kammari said, "the philosophy of Kant, Fichte, Schelling, and Hegel expresses the ideology of the servility of the German bourgeois to the feudal-cadet Prussian monarchy; unconsciously, in an abstract ideological form, it expressed that tendency of the development of capitalism that Lenin later called the cadet-Prussian way of developing capitalism" (17).

The references to Lenin could not conceal the essence of what was occurring; essentially, a rejection was being suggested of both Marx's and Lenin's appraisal of Hegel as one of the main sources of Marxism. Thus, having declared that "Hegel's conservative philosophical system played the same reactionary role in the history of modern philosophy as Plato's philosophy did in ancient times and theological philosophy in the Middle Ages," V. Svetlov called for an outright revision of the status of German philosophy as one of the three "sources" of Marxism: "We should hardly consider correct Engels's assertion that German idealist philosophy was classical philosophy—that is, the best of the bourgeois philosophical system" (57).

But there was no particular choice; as V. P. Egorshin stated, all of West European philosophy was tied to Christianity, but "the philosophy of Christianity is too meager, obscurantist, even stinky [*sic!*], but it was the inevitable product of its era, and it was before just this stinking source that Schelling, and Kant, and Hegel, and Berkeley, and Mach prostrated themselves" (355). Several speakers reached the point of hysterics. B. A. Chagin, for example, having declared that "from the very beginning, one might say, the bad blood of the German aristocracy, of feudalism and theology, coursed through Hegel's philosophy. This blood poisoned the entire organism of this philosophy," defined this as "bourgeois-cadet philosophy" and stated that "its social roots go back to the emergence and development of the cowardly German bourgeois." Zhdanov even had to make the militant philosopher see reason. The following exchange took place between them:

> Zhdanov: Comrade Chagin, it appears that Hegel is the biggest winner as a result of this debate. (Laughter.)
> Chagin: I think that, from my explanation, he loses. (198–199)

Apparently sensing a boundary that one should not cross, several of the participants began to try to make their colleagues see reason. For example, P. A. Kovchegov (from Kishinev) provoked laughter in the room when he proclaimed that "some comrades have talked themselves into deciding purely and simply to deny anything whatsoever of value in Hegel's philosophy. They have literally discredited Hegel in such a way that Hegel is transformed from the apex of German bourgeois philosophy into not only a wart but a pot-hole" (248).

It was clear to everyone that Hegel was above all guilty of being a German and overvaluing the German spirit and the Prussian state and, accordingly, undervaluing the Slavic peoples. The attacks on Hegel were so intermingled with those on the founders of Marxism themselves that it seemed the Soviet Marxists cursing Hegel and in a nationalist frenzy already openly denying Marx, Engels, and Lenin might even go so far as to start quoting the contemptuous assessments of Russia and Russians from Marx and Engels themselves, alongside which Hegel would seem a Russophile. But it did not come to this since the Hegel question lost its urgency for Stalin after the war and was exaggerated only for the purposes of nationalistic mobilization of the "philosophical front." Stalin did not suggest any radical revision of the "fundamentals of Marxism." Accordingly, Hegel's nationalism was dragged out, but Marx's and Engels's consistently anti-Russian views continued to be left as taboo.

Furthermore, in the course of the scandal that erupted in 1944 around the fourth ("Russian") volume of the *History of Philosophy* (the criticism of which was not part of the Central Committee's resolution), the authors' chief mistake was deemed to be an underestimation of the "independence" of Russian philosophy. Russian "revolutionary-democratic thinkers" had yet to be represented not only as "independent," not simply as direct forerunners of Marxism, but also as having shown the way to West European philosophy: "The most serious flaw in the volume is that it does not regard the views of Herzen, Belinskii, Chernyshevskii, and Dobroliubov as the highest development of pre-Marxist philosophy, and meanwhile these Russian thinkers outstripped Hegel and Feuerbach, were heads above Hegel and Feuerbach, and came closer than anyone else to dialectical materialism."[55] The party-mindedness of Soviet philosophy, as was to be expected, began to produce a new historico-philosophical (sur)reality: the forerunners of Marxism, instead of Hegel and Feuerbach, instead of German classical philosophy, were proclaimed to be Belinskii and Dobroliubov—the "Russian thinkers" of whose existence Marx had not the slightest idea. Judging by what Marx and Engels wrote about Russia, it would be quite difficult to imagine that they would have expected to find any "thinkers" as such in this "slavish," "reactionary," and "Tartarized" country.

Such was the backdrop of the truly fantasy-laden historico-philosophical narrative that had begun to take shape as far back as the late 1930s, a narrative that glorified the "Russian philosophical thought" that was supposedly eclipsing German classical philosophy. Clearly, if Engels's definition of Germany's pre-Marxist philosophy as "classical" was being disavowed, then an even more "classical" philosophy had to replace it. Of course, this philosophy "had to emerge in Russia. It was declared to be the 'revolutionary-democratic philosophy' of Herzen, Belinskii, Chernyshevskii, and Dobroliubov. Need it be said that the Russian 'philosophers' were much more advanced than their German predecessors?"[56] This was justified by the fact, as G. M. Gak professed in the course of the discussions, that "after Leninism took shape, as the apex of philosophic thought and having Russia as its birthplace, the history of philosophy is no longer the history of Western philosophy" (24). Accordingly, the Russian roots of this "apex" had to be found.

The precedence of Russian philosophy (like Russian precedence in general, in all areas of the sciences and arts) becomes a central theme in a new history of philosophy. Aleksandrov had already declared in the introduction to his *History of Western European Philosophy:* "Without carefully studying and using the deep criticism of the philosophical systems of the past provided by the classic writers of Russian philosophy, it is impossible to formulate a scientific conception of the course of development of philosophical thought in the West European countries" (6). Aleksandrov's assistant in Agitprop, Mikhail Iovchuk, specialized in these classic writers. In 1943, the History of Philosophy Department of the Moscow State University was renamed the History of West European Philosophy Department because, on Iovchuk's initiative, the History of Russian Philosophy Department, which he also headed, was created on par with it.

Challenging others in his articles and during the course of the discussion to "ultimately discredit and decisively bury the legend of Russian thought's complete dependence on foreign countries" (217), Iovchuk declared: "The revolutionary Russian thinkers critically surmounted German idealism and other reactionary theories of the West in a pitched battle against the Russian epigones of German idealism and bourgeois sociology who, as we know, fawned on the West, cultivated servility to bourgeois culture and philosophy, belittled the national worth of the Russian people, and regarded Russia as a sort of testing ground for growing the seeds of one or another West European philosophical system" (214). These observations were not only false (Belinskii was a passionate Hegelian),[57] but also duplicitous; the epigones of the sort that saw Russia as a "testing ground" for West European ideas were in fact Russian Marxists. Stalinist national-Bolshevism, which demanded a revision of Marxist internationalism, was a different matter.

After Iovchuk was driven out of the Central Committee in 1947, Ivan Shchipanov assumed leadership of his Moscow State University department (and remained its leader till the end of his life, in 1983). In Shchipanov's speech during the philosophical discussion, he demanded that his listeners "decisively bury nationalist nihilism, the worship of a certain part of our people of bourgeois culture, the underestimation of the creative powers of the Russian people, and the rejection of the independence of Russian culture"; he challenged them to "dispel the manorial and bourgeois legends that Lomonosov was an imitator of Wolff; that Radishchev and the Decembrists were blind followers of the French Enlightenment; that Herzen, Belinskii, Chernyshevskii, and Dobroliubov were humble students of Hegel, Feuerbach, and the like; and that Pisarev was a popularizer of the vulgar materialism of Büchner, Fogt, and Moleschott" (498).

Since the new construct of "Russian philosophy" was created in practically empty space, the material was literally dragged in from all adjacent fields—from the history of science, political and other journalism, and literature.

These patriotic challenges fell on fertile soil. If, as Emdin asserted, "a book on the history of philosophy should set as its goal the fostering in our readers of a feeling of national pride in the Russian people, in its culture and science" (12), then should anyone be surprised that this national pride in the presence of world-class philosophers such as Belinskii and Chernyshevskii demanded disparagement of West European (most of all German) philosophy? Surely enough, B. G. Kuznetsov declared that "Kant's *Metaphysical Foundations of Natural Science* turned out to be a little puddle, while the ideas of Lobachevskii, which never were included in the history of philosophy textbooks, became the beginning of a whole ocean of new ideas in science" (66).

Since the "Russian philosophy" that was being invented before one's very eyes had to be somehow fitted into the history of philosophy narrative, serious historical problems inevitably arose. And here the discussion's participants literally competed for innovative ideas. V. K. Chaloian, for example, disagreed with Iovchuk about to which century to date the beginning of Russian philosophy. He suggested not the fifteenth century but the twelfth: "Russians in the twelfth century were already translating, providing commentary, and creating for themselves, in their own native language, philosophical culture" (144). Besides, since the "countries of the Byzantine civilization not only created a well-developed philosophy, but also saved Hellenic and Hellenistic philosophical literature from perishing" (145), it was they who were the source of the European Renaissance. After all, Western Europe "could not have at its disposal either philosophy or the other branches of the culture of the ancient world, did not have the ancient cultural legacy available. Hence, it is obvious that the source of ideas for the Renaissance of the West could only have been the East, where the German Vandals had not ventured, where the Turkish hordes had still not succeeded in destroying the age-old culture of the advanced peoples of the East" (146). Thus, Chaloian asserted that "we can conclude that the source of Western philosophy is the philosophy created by the peoples of the East. Thus the philosophy and culture of the East penetrates the West through, on the one hand, the Arabs, and on the other, Byzantium. And on these two sources the philosophy and culture of the West are built. All this gives us the right to speak of the Eastern roots of Western civilization" (146).

Then, with reference closer to the present time, T. Aleksanian from Yerevan asserted that if German philosophy was an aristocratic reaction to the French Revolution, then Russian philosophy (in the persons of Belinskii, Herzen, Chernyshevskii, and Dobroliubov), "defending the progressive traditions of earlier philosophy, was in effect a battle against the aristocratic reaction to the French Revolution. This is exactly the same as when, at the end of the nineteenth and the beginning of the twentieth centuries, Russian philosophy in the person of Lenin/ Stalin was a fight against internationalist revisionism" (304). In other words, Hegel and Kant were equated to Bernstein and Kautskii, and Herzen and Chernyshevskii to Lenin and Stalin.

Vladimir Sarab'ianov went even further in the attempt to rationalize a nonexistent connection: if Belinskii, Chernyshevskii, Herzen, and Dobroliubov, who were all part of pre-Marxist philosophy, "are examined not chronologically but as a step in the development of human thought," then a totally new narrative of the history of philosophy is constructed: "If it is quite clear to everyone that the leap from Feuerbach's metaphysical materialism with an idealist understanding of history to Marx/Engels materialism is too steep and sharp, then obviously somewhere between them there must be a unifying link. We seek and find this link in the philosophy of Belinskii, Chernyshevskii, Herzen, and Dobroliubov, who were materialists-dialecticists, admittedly not always consistent, but not arriving at historical materialism" (135).

Let alone the fact that none of these writers was a philosopher (except perhaps Chernyshevskii, who wrote a few works on aesthetics), this schema itself was completely absurd: if one views these writers as a bridge between metaphysics and idealism and Marxism, then Marx turns out to be essentially a successor to . . . Dobroliubov.

The attempts to Russify Leninism as supposedly the "expression of the Russian national character" with the goal of legitimizing the national-Bolshevist interpretation of Marxism, which Iovchuk consistently mustered, ran into serious ideological objections that were voiced during the discussion by M. Z. Selektor. Raising his objections to Iovchuk, Selektor declared that "Leninism is not a purely national and only national, a purely Russian and only Russian phenomenon. Leninism is an international phenomenon having roots in all international development" (428). In polemic with Iovchuk, he accused him of the "slander of Leninism" and of playing along with "ideological opponents."

Essentially accusing Iovchuk of "nationalizing" Marxism in his contributions to the journal *Bol'shevik* in 1945, Selektor declared that "the theoretical falsehood of this construct is that it separates Marxism in Russia from Marx and portrays the issue as if even Marxism (not specifically Leninism, as something new that Lenin contributed to the treasure trove of Marxism, but Marxism specifically) emerged anew in Russia independently of Marx and was the exclusive result of development of the ideas of the revolutionary democrats" (432). But this implied that Lenin's achievements amounted only to the "development of the ideas of the revolutionary democrats," which was a diminution of Lenin's achievements (435).

But the leaders of Agitprop, which held the institutional leverage, did not need to fear ideological arguments. The reality was such that, as L. F. Berdnik observed, "the majority of dissertations in recent years have been written and defended on the subject of the Russian philosophy of the '40s through the '60s of the last century." One had to manifest "political naïveté" to conclude that "the universal infatuation of our young philosophical cadres and of their supervisors with the history of Russian philosophy has gone from a positive trend in our work to an acutely negative one" since "it is essentially a withdrawal, an escape, on the part of our philosophical cadres, from contemporary subject matter into the historical past" (335). On the contrary, this "infatuation" was completely timely and was tied to the overall degradation of philosophical culture.

We are coming back to the source of the 1947 philosophical discussion—namely, to the "cadres" problem, which could not help surfacing in the course of the debate. For some professional philosophers this was a serious problem, as Z. A. Kamenskii and Ia. A. Mil'ner declared during the discussion. Kamenskii pointed out that "our leading comrades who have an advantageous right to appear in print were not and are not at the same time, in the great majority, the most eminent figures in philosophical science. They are actually more administrative types than scholarly people" and "do not have, quite deservedly, scholarly authority." After enumerating all the leading figures of the USSR Academy of Sciences Philosophy Institute, he asked the audience to "name even one of their works that would open a new page in philosophical science, that would constitute an original contribution to it" (366–67). It is significant that a proclamation like this from such a high tribune did not embarrass anyone; none of the leaders of the "philosophical front" felt obligated to "open a new page in philosophical science" or to make "an original contribution to it." Meanwhile, as Mil'ner pointed out, it was just this "comparatively small number of philosophers [who] have essentially monopolized the entire business of publishing philosophy literature in the country, as well as the management of philosophy education and leadership of the philosophical front as a whole" (405).

The problem lay in the incompatibility of philosophy with its status in state ideology. In the conditions of the ideocratic Soviet state, where philosophy was a concentrated form of ideology, posing such questions was Stalin's absolute prerogative. The philosophers' task was specifically to systematize and provide commentary. Judging by the fact that out of all the materials submitted for publication, the only contribution not published was the speech of Khoren Adzhemian, which was rejected initially by B. Kedrov and then by Zhdanov as well (the latter viewed it as "rubbish hostile to Marxism-Leninism"),[58] we can confidently state that Stalin was not aspiring to anything bigger in philosophical science itself. Adzhemian had stated the following:

> We have philosophy workers, popularizers, specialists, historians of philosophy and critics of philosophy. But I can assert that we have no philosophers here in this hall. Why? Because a philosopher means not simply a scholar devoted to philosophical science but a creator of this science.... We should reject with some embarrassment the illusions that we have a lot of philosophers, and see to it that the most creatively gifted

of them have the possibility of manifesting themselves as philosophers—that is, of enriching the nucleus and heart of philosophical science and not just its outer shell [and enriching] the systematization and historical elucidation of this nucleus.[59]

We should provide extensive opportunities for printing any bold, originally conceived work dedicated to the problems of dialectical and historical materialism, logic, ontology, and gnoseology, not from the standpoint of what has hitherto been, but from a completely different one. Hitherto, we have written about philosophy. . . . A creative philosopher should not engage only in criticism of the new reactionary and faddish trends of the bourgeois world, but should [also] himself create new, contemporary, progressive trends, nuances, and genres in the area of philosophy.[60]

Neither an appraisal of the Soviet philosophical works that were essentially popularizing, nor an allegation of the absence of creative philosophers in the USSR, nor even less a call to "provide extensive opportunities for printing any bold, originally conceived work" was in line with Stalin's intentions. The discussion was not meant to provide "criticism of the state of affairs in Soviet philosophy"; it was an attempt to problematize and consolidate the very status of philosophy as commentary on the sacred text that legitimized power. No surprise, then, that Kedrov in his letter to Zhdanov characterized calls to reject commentary and to have "creative philosophers" create text itself as "fundamentally hostile to us" and the very posing of such questions as "slander of our worldview." And, to ensure that Zhdanov would see the necessary parallels, Kedrov declared that Adzhemian had "objectively assumed Zoshchenko's role in philosophy."[61] The irony was that Soviet philosophy, now that it was completely whetted for "denunciatory criticism," could do little more than take lessons from Zoshchenko.

(SYNTHESIS) PURE PARTY-MINDEDNESS: THE LAW OF NEGATION OF NEGATION

The book that appeared as a peculiar response to Aleksandrov's book is, judging by all its external features, an academic publication. Not only was it published by the USSR Academy of Sciences, but it also bore the stamp of the academy's Institute of Philosophy on the binding. Its title, *Against the Philosophizing Henchmen of American-Anglo*

Imperialism, contains not a single neutral, unbiased word. Even the grammatically correct "Anglo-American" is turned around in it to emphasize the dominant evil—the American one. Although the book's subtitle contains a semblance of academicism—*Essays in Criticism of Contemporary American-Anglo Bourgeois Philosophy and Sociology*—this is merely the indication of the field to be subjected to "philosophico-sociological criticism" as this had begun to be understood after 1947; the book would be about neither philosophy nor sociology. Its main subject is a sort of politico-ideological substrate to which philosophy and sociology are reduced. The Soviet principle of approaching philosophy as ideology and as an instrument of political struggle is fully applied here to foreign science.

Among the books about philosophy published in the USSR after the philosophical discussion and before Stalin's death, this one is notable for being the direct response to the turn to criticism of contemporary Western philosophy that was demanded in the course of the discussion.[62] In a situation where dialectical materialism, historical materialism, and now the history of philosophy as well were now closed to discussion, "criticism of bourgeois philosophy" remained the only niche for Soviet philosophy. Here dialectical and historical materialism were, to use Mitin's metaphor, the "tower" from which Soviet philosophers gazed upon contemporary philosophy, and an application was at last found for the history of philosophy, which became simultaneously relevant, topical, and party-minded. We might say that here we see the sought-after synthesis of Soviet philosophy, what it had been striving to become since the early 1920s debates. In this synthesis, Stalinist philosophy finally ceased to feel the burden of the disciplinary frameworks and traditions of European philosophical practice and even to observe any sort of boundary beyond which philosophical science spilled over into ideology. If earlier the demand had been to introduce ideology into philosophy, now nothing remained but pure ideology. There emerged a unique discourse that had not existed before and did not exist afterward; its peculiarity was not the intensity with which the ideological component was manifested, but its abolition of philosophical practice as a type of activity, which now determined everything, from the theme and the approaches to it to style.

This book was exemplary of the restructuring of the Soviet philosophy that had been ultimately consolidated in the new philosophical discourse and set on the course of party-mindedness. But since the basic content of "ideological struggle" in this period was the Cold War, the Cold War defined the parameters of this discourse. Essentially, what had been philosophical discourse now became an alloy of fragments of special (erstwhile philosophical) conceptual constructs, rhetorical propaganda clichés, and suggestive effects. In the new mobilizational philosophical discourse of the Cold War, any other discursive strategies now not only were squeezed out, but it was also as if they had never even existed. When reading the texts of the Soviet philosophers assembled in this book, one cannot believe that just a short time before this they had been able to discuss topics of philosophy that were in any way meaningful.

The book stated that "two camps stand opposed to each other: the camp of black reaction and war headed by the imperialists of the United States and England, and the camp of the fighters for peace, popular democracy, and socialism, at the head of which stands the lamp and standard-bearer of peace in all the world: the Soviet Union" (3).[63] In such a world, philosophy cannot be understood any other way than in the plane of political confrontation. Essentially, philosophers and sociologists as such do not exist in the West. There are merely "ideological menials of the imperialist bourgeoisie—hireling scribblers that call themselves philosophers and sociologists" who "attempt with their idealist, racist, cosmopolitan, and other such inventions to deceive and ensnare the broad masses of the people, to take away their faith in the triumph of progressive ideals of peace, freedom, and genuine democracy" (3). They are all engaged in "fomenting a new world war," serving "the sharks of Wall Street," in order to "prop up and save by any possible means the tumbling-down edifice of imperialism, to provide a basis and justification for the reactionary, aggressive policy of the imperialist bourgeoisie, and to subjugate the people to the interests of [these] trans-oceanic nuclear warmongers." This is precisely the "basic aim of the American-Anglo pseudophilosophers and pseudosociologists." Essentially, "the unmasking of the shameful activities of these diploma-carrying lackeys of the American-Anglo imperialists is the obligation of all representatives of progressive science and philosophy" (3). Hence the task of "criticism" is to show that "bourgeois philosophy and sociology in the United States and England, which have nothing to do with science, are the ideological weaponry of imperialist aggression, the justification and propagation of the fascistization of the capitalist countries" (4). All of this is hurled at the reader in the very first lines of the text.

Paradoxically, by refusing to reexamine philosophy as the filiation of ideas, Soviet philosophy arrived at the filiation of Socialist Realist reality—that is, at the filiation of ideological fictions. The book is permeated with references to reality, but the factual material that it supplies startles anyone who is at all familiar with postwar American history with its inadequacy. For example, it announces that "the military authorities of the United States have established complete control over national education. . . . The biggest capitalist monopolies control the scholarly councils of all universities and colleges, and the presidents of the institutions of higher education are for the most part protégés of the war ministry. . . . Films that might even mention the idea of peace in the slightest are forbidden in America" (11).

The reader is given to understand that "in the entire educational system and in the cultural life of the United States, there is in general engrafted a spirit of chauvinism, of Anglo-American racism, obscurantism, and sacerdotalism; [that] brutal oppression of the people and unleashing a new imperialist war are rationalized"; that "among American youth a tendency toward violence and brigandage is cultivated in every possible way"; that "insistently drummed into the heads of workers is the idea that the most natural condition between peoples and states is a condition of war"; and that in this "propaganda of misanthropic ideas, an especially active role is played by American and English philosophers, sociologists, and journalists, who have reached the very limit of moral decay and cynicism" (11). Accordingly, they are by no means philosophers but rather "the scholarly lackeys of American and English imperialism" and "philosophizing cannibals" (12) and "American cannibals in professors' robes" (15). Since this is so, the only thing one can say about "American-Anglo" philosophy is that "the United States and England have turned into the center of reactionism and obscurantism of the twentieth century," characterized by "incredible cultural backwardness, monstrous ignorance, idealist delirium, and obscurantism" (18).

The first thing that draws our attention is the boorishness of tone. Actually, "polemic" here is nothing more than an excuse for invective. There is not a page in the book where the reader is not faced with an entire deluge of invectives. Some persons are named only once, but they are named with the inevitable epithets that are the only things that remain in the reader's memory since the content of their statements itself has no significance; they are all aimed at the same thing: the "poisoning of the workers' consciousness." For example, the book reports that a certain Professor Davidson "with the fervor of a sly fox of a stockbroker tries to prove the need for further fascistization of America" (115) and that another professor, a certain Johnston, "reveals his own class cretinism" with his sociological conclusions (116–17). The founder of pragmatism, John Dewey, who was over ninety years old when this book was published, had a particularly bad reputation. Here he was called no less than "the fiercest enemy of socialism and the militant apologist of imperialism," a "subjective idealist," and a "despicable menial of the monopolists of the United States." The same page reported that the leader of the American psychological school in sociology, Bernard, "preaches reactionary nonsense" (121), and just a few pages later, we learn that sociologist Walter P. Kennedy "openly calls upon the diploma-carrying lackeys of Wall Street to return to medieval obscurantism" (124).

Certain names and scientific trends enjoyed particular popularity in Stalinist "philosophical criticism." The name of Bertrand Russell, for example, recurs throughout the book in the context of the most unbelievable insults. It is reported that this "philosophizing instigator of war" (16), the "accursed enemy of democracy and progress" (19), the "ideologue of atomic brigandage" (89), the "Fascist-playing philosopher" (252), and "unmitigated reactionary" "viciously propagandizes a 'campaign against the East'—that is, an attack on the USSR and the countries of popular democracy" (12). Furthermore, "this cannibal calls on his Wall Street and City masters to start a war against the Soviet Union without delay and to drop atomic bombs on the Soviet people" (12). The reader is told that "the purpose of Russell's literary-trash history of philosophy is deliberate: he attempts to impose upon the reader the delusional idea (albeit necessary and advantageous to the American-Anglo monopolists) that the apex of all philosophy is the philosophy of American-Anglo imperialism" (20) and that "in the propaganda of war there is no distinction between the Tory Churchill and the 'hereditary Whig' neorealist Bertrand Russell" (62). Therefore it is no surprise that he all but participates in war crimes;

"the various Russells and other English reactionary 'philosophers' now welcome the bloody American aggression in Korea, they rationalize the barbaric bombing by American pilots of peaceful cities and villages, the unheard-of cruelties against the Korean people" (69).

A basic means of discrediting opponents was to link them to Nazis. This imagined connection is created with the aid of a system of substitutions and incredible inferences. For example, it is stated that American scientists occupied with producing poisoning agents and the means of bacteriological war, "following the example of their German and Japanese teachers, test the means of murder they have invented on living people. With the relish of sadists they calculate the quantity of hydrogen bombs necessary to destroy humanity. Science is in the service not of life but of death—such is the extreme extent of the degradation of science in contemporary bourgeois society" (15). Granted, philosophers are not the topic here, but the image of sinister "murderer doctors"—war criminals—is linked to philosophy and/or sociology with the aid of constructs with unintelligible modality: "The contemporary 'atomic' philosophers and sociologists try to 'prove' that the use during wartime of plague and cholera bacteria, the infection of huge populated territories with toxin, and so forth, are 'legitimate' and fully 'ethical' acts" (69).

Another widespread means of discrediting "philosophical opponents" was by pointing out that they were either tied to the American government, or worked for it, or were simply American spies, or by pointing out "the unbreakable bond between American bourgeois sociology and the State Department." For example, it was asserted that "America's war tycoons recruit spies and agents for military-diplomatic surveillance from the milieu of the American figures in science" (16). Science in American universities engages in training "sociologists for diplomatic service—that is, for bureaucratic activities in the State Department. Thus, the training of sociologists in the United States is directly determined, outright, by the political directives of Wall Street. Therefore it is impossible to establish where the bourgeois sociologist occupied with 'theoretical' problems ends and where the bourgeois politician begins, who sits solemnly in the offices of the State Department and organizes conspiracies against freedom-loving states" (104).

The fact that the Western intellectual milieu was predominantly leftist only accentuated its guilt in the eyes of Soviet opponents. Stalin's well-known dislike for Western leftists found additional support here. This discourse is full of moralization enveloped in the form of insults. However, it combines moral rigor with a striking indistinctness of the object of condemnation. In the book's 330 pages there is not a single page of intelligible text that expounds even one hostile philosophical "teaching" whatsoever. Everything is so submerged in suggestiveness that the informational equivalent of what is read is equal to zero. Meanwhile, any attempts on the part of Western scientists to introduce precise methods are also subjected to accusations of "masking": "Statistical-mathematical study techniques give American sociological treatises a pseudo-scientific character, masking their misanthropic, anti-scientific essence" (137).

This discourse was part of the conspiratological macronarrative of the Cold War era. Conspiracy suggested the concealment and masking that Soviet science had to unmask. This was particularly complicated when the exact sciences were concerned. Here, the "draping of idealism in 'realistic' clothes" was detected, which in turn was "accompanied in American bourgeois philosophy by shameless falsification of the facts of contemporary science." Nothing had changed over the past decades: "Just as Mach and Avenarius in their day used the crisis in physics for an attack against materialism and science, contemporary American idealists hitch on to the difficulties emerging in the various areas of the natural sciences in order to have the possibility, by exaggerating these difficulties and distorting the conclusions to which progressive science arrives, to propagandize a 'scientific' sacerdotalism" (272).

All of the philosophical "teachings" examined were bad already because there were too many of them. Only one "teaching" could be true: Marxism-Leninism. All the rest contained different sorts of false ideas and for this reason alone were not worth any serious consideration. Perhaps this is just why the various philosophical trends were spoken of in almost the exact same words.

So the distinctive peculiarity of this critical discourse is the high degree of failure to make distinctions in the material under examination ("criticism"); all theories are harmful, all scientists are not really scientists, all of them are mercenary, and so forth. It is impossible to understand what distinguishes one thing from another. Even English and American philosophy are indistinguishable because "bourgeois English ideologues serve British imperialism, which lets itself be run by U.S.

imperialism," so much so that for Soviet authors "it is even difficult to determine whether one or another contemporary philosopher belongs to the United States or to England" (59). Then it is stated that the main evil comes out of the United States, from which "American imperialists ... export not only arms and detective films, spoiled canned goods and chewing gum, but also the very newest discoveries of their 'philosophers.' These 'philosophers,' who call themselves pragmatists, personalists, neorealists, critical realists, and so on, find imitators among the bourgeois ideologues of the Marshall Plan countries. The German and French existentialists, for example, these despicable ideologues of fascism, find a common language with the American obscurantists playing at philosophy" (38). However, the very next page announces that "the various little idealist schools of bourgeois philosophy that hold sway now in the United States have nothing original in them. They are the decrepit idealist theories of Berkeley, Hume, Kant, Mach, and other reactionary bourgeois philosophers, imported from Europe, freshened up and repainted, and in this fashion passed off as [the United States'] own national product. These theories, expounded with the primitive coarseness characteristic of the American bourgeoisie and stamped as 'made in USA,' appear now under new aliases" (39).

This "philosophical criticism" is located beyond the borders not only of geography, but also of history; all these "eclectic crippled theories that the 'scientist' lackeys of the bourgeoisie are now spreading consist of the odds and ends of the old idealist systems. The toadies of imperialism take theoretical trash that has nothing to do with science, freshen it up, and set it in motion" (177). Hence, Malthus, Mach, and Avenarius are "whipped up" as fully contemporary "henchmen of obscurantism." The lack of distinctions characteristic of this discourse is tied to the unscrupulousness in the choice of what it calls "philosophy" in general. The persons named in the book are completely random. One page, for example, reports the publication of *How to Stop Worrying and Start Living* by "a certain Dale Carnegie," and there the "recipes" of this "American 'philosopher-businessman'" are criticized in detail (76). The following page speaks of the works of the "former student of Russell" (which in and of itself bodes nothing good), the "Austrian emigrant Ludwig Wittgenstein, who was the soul of a clique of mystics and obscurantists organized in Cambridge before the start of World War II." Following the one quotation from Wittgenstein is a condemnation and "class analysis": "In spite of the jabber of such verbiage, his class aim is clear enough: to turn people into meek slaves, the obedient weapon of the instigators of a new world war" (77). There is, however, an apt question: if all these different trends have the same unseemly goals, why are they needed at all? Since explaining it in the categories of conspiracy is difficult, one was left to rationalize an attitude toward it in the traditions of Marxist criticism. One of the articles concludes thus: "The words Marx spoke in his time on the subject of the arch-reactionary customs of the German Junkers are completely applicable to the writings of the menials of imperialism: "They are *beneath the level of history,* they are *beneath any form of criticism,* but they remain the object of criticism, just as the criminal who is beneath the level of humanness remains the object of the hangman"(200).[64]

This purely propagandistic "hangman criticism" is devoid of any analytical potential whatsoever and resorts to the devices of Bolshevist satirical political journalism. In another example, it is said of the prag-matists that they are "full of savage hatred for revolutionary practice. The only sort of practice that has their recognition is the pursuit of profit and the satisfaction of the greedy interests of American imperial-ists. In accordance with this, even truth in their opinion should bring profit, should serve the capitalists; otherwise, what kind of truth *is* it!" (42; emphasis in original).

Fully in keeping with the calls from Zaslavskii, Soviet authors began to produce "philosophical satire." This discourse is characterized by the grotesque flattening of any narrative whatsoever and the introduc-tion of a sort of "class" denominator, which in this case boils down to something like this: "The goal of the pragmatists is to 'theoretically' rationalize the practice of the imperialists. The mumbo-jumbo of the pragmatists about practice is an apologia for the businessman and the capitalist entrepreneur and praise for aggression and imperialist vio-lence" (42). Rationalizing the "true essence" of pragmatism made an incontrovertible *argumentum ad hominem* permissible. William James, the founder of the trend, was an ideologue of "American military ex-pansion," and his entire theory proved that "from its very first steps, pragmatism was nothing more than an ideology of the imperialist ex-pansion of the United States and the pragmatists nothing more than Wall Street lackeys. James, the pragmatist touted by the bourgeoisie of

America and Europe, was a diploma-carrying hireling of the American imperialists" (43).

The rhetorical excesses we have examined here should not be imagined to be merely the result of Soviet philosophical culture. The discourse of suggestiveness itself that fed this culture was the result of the victory of party-mindedness, which simultaneously meant the triumph of a dialectic that operated with polar stances that crossed over into each other and which therefore was always prone to tautological degeneration. There is no escaping into logic from this suggestive discourse. It freezes, as it were, in front of the mirror. From one article to another, the "barefaced distortions" of Western philosophers, who contrasted the "progressive" West to the "barbarian" East, are condemned. This "reactionary contrast-making" reveals "racism, the cosmopolitan propaganda of pan-Americanism and Anglo-Saxon worldwide expansion" (51). And then and there the very same thing is asserted: the contrast of the "progressive" East to the "barbarian" West. This mirroring is emphasized by characterizing the West specifically by its "contemporary barbarity"—the "rapaciousness of monopolies, racial bigotry, Lynch's law, political corruption, Fascist brigandage" and "obscurantism" (152). The mirroring is problematized by the authors, but, what is more, it is emphasized by numerous references to specifically Western examples. For example, the "progressive American political journalist" George Marion is quoted from his *Bases and Empire,* published in translation in the USSR in 1948: "Our foreign policy amounts to the simple assertion that the United States is always right. That is the inevitable conclusion from the high-flown moral teachings. It leaves aside the realm of reality, where the interests of nations and individuals conflict. It creates an imaginary world in which one nation possesses both supreme power and supreme wisdom."[65] This, our text tells us, is Marion "characterizing the openly expansionist nature of the policy of American imperialists in their fight against the democratic forces of peace" (182). The idea that this is precisely what the Soviet authors themselves are asserting with respect to the Soviet Union does not even occur to them. The question of whether it should occur to the reader seems even more irrelevant since the dialectical somersaults demonstrated by the Soviet critics assume a reader whose thinking is subject to the laws of dialectical logic, not formal logic. Only within

the confines of this logic, which retains both poles without disaffirm-
ing either of them and remaining in permanent contradiction, are the
flip-flops of implications—inconceivable within the confines of formal
logic—possible.

This book was in its way the perfected product of late-Stalinist philosophy. Everything in it is remarkable, right up to the last page—but
even beyond it, to the errata sheet tipped in. The errata notes that on
page 70, thirteen lines from the bottom, is printed the word "dogmatic";
this is supposed to read "demagogic." It would appear that in the sarcastic turns born of the humor-satire style that David Zaslavskii called
upon philosophers to use, philosophical irony died. But, it turns out,
it triumphed despite the fact that the boundary between science and
propaganda was crossed in such obvious fashion in these texts—the
material is not discussed but instead demonstratively and grotesquely
distorted, using the most primitive propaganda techniques to do so.

*

Party-mindedness, fully in keeping with the status of the party itself as the "guiding and directing force" of Soviet society, should be
understood as a principle of exercising power that was subject to simultaneous affirmation and defamiliarization. Dialectics was its modus operandi. The laws of dialectics, in the hands of the artist/leader,
become the laws of the thriller. *There are no rules in Stalinism but
party-mindedness (read: dialectics), which itself is merely the principle
of tyranny and, accordingly, the key principle of terror.*

The communicative strategy of Stalinism is based on a textualization
of power, where power is a sacred text and the only source of the text
is Stalin.[66] But he was also the interpreter of the Soviet reality produced
by "Marxism-Leninism." Under these conditions, the task of philosophers and writers amounted to guessing the vector of interpretation—
who at the moment had become the object of the "war of opposites"
(or would be declared an "opposite"), who was subject to the "transition" to a new "quality" and who to that of "negation"? Thus, Stalinist
culture is one of textual anxiety, a culture occupied with measuring
the gap between reality and text, on the one hand, and between the
sacral text produced or approved by Stalin and any individual text,
on the other. Since Stalin exercised the supreme act of writing, engag-

ing in writing itself—from philosophy to literature—became politically dangerous. But at the same time, since the very shaping of the masses was effected through the procedures of correctly reading the texts of power,[67] writing was also the most important activity. Hence not only the high status of Soviet philosophers and writers but also Stalin's attention to text as such.

Thus, as Valerii Podoroga observes, a "correct" reading in Stalinism is impossible in principle, and anyone who attempts to read correctly exposes him- or herself to the danger of being accused of distorting the "letter" or "spirit" of the text: "One emphasized the wrong thing, blurted out too much here, made a slip of the tongue there, now made a linguistic mistake, and so forth; this whole repertoire of 'light' social pathology, all these aphasias, apraxias, and agnosias were not acknowledged in the Stalinist terror machine as something 'accidental' but were interpreted as genuine signs and traces of the political unconscious, as an obvious manifestation of the potential guilt of every person in front of authority."[68] But since what was correct yesterday proved to be mortally dangerous today, the very situation of this "every person," who was faced with the necessity of reading and speaking in a situation where it was unknown how what was spoken and read today would be turned around tomorrow, was a state of terror. Consequently, texts produced under these conditions are texts of terror and must be read as such.

As far as the principle of party-mindedness goes, it not only could not be abolished (as Fadeev and Simonov recommended), but also had to remain in the shimmering zone of semi-rationalized ideological categories—as a reminder, a deterrent, and a "device" of terror "laid bare," for which the 1947 "philosophical discussion" had also served.

5 *Realästhetik*

Populism Instead of Music

The postwar era, so fraught with ideological campaigns, could probably be compared in intensity and breadth only with 1936, when the ideological steamroller threatened theater, cinema, literature, music, ballet, and even book illustration, and the most eminent of Soviet artists were among the condemned, from stage directors Aleksandr Tairov and Vsevolod Meyerhold to film director Sergei Eisenstein and composer Dmitrii Shostakovich.

The Zhdanovist-model campaign bore its own trademark; it usually culminated in a large assembly (of writers, musicians, philosophers, etc.); speeches by Zhdanov himself; and a devastating decree. It is worth noting that after Zhdanov's death, Stalin orchestrated his campaigns somewhat differently; both in linguistics and in economics they were constructed upon a staged "discussion" (letters and articles in the newspapers), after which followed an extensive treatise by the "leading light of all learning" himself that put everything in its place and corrected the "fumblers."[1]

Each of these campaigns was intended to solve broad political, ideological, and aesthetic problems, as well as narrower ones (a struggle among the functionaries closest to Stalin, a struggle for power and privileges in the creative intelligentsia's milieu, Stalin's own tastes and biases). It is usually supposed that the postwar ideological campaigns were aimed at suppressing the intelligentsia that had gotten "out of control" during the war and, in the bigger picture, to bring society back to a prewar model of unanimity; that the very same prewar patriotic purpose ("extirpation of harmful Western influence") was central to them; and that this purpose "was realized by Stalin in his favorite manner: in several directions at once, with unexpected strikes from different sides."[2] However, the strikes were so regular that they lost the element of surprise and became routine (as someone observed at the time, "Before, this had been a lottery, but now it's a line to wait in").[3] Nonetheless, each campaign every time had not only a new object, but also a new ideological focus.

The campaign in music, too, had its own ideological angle; it was here that the battle between "formalism" and "populist spirit" unfolded. Other campaigns had their own "magnetic fields" as well. Many of the categories of the Soviet "fundamental lexicon" that were refined in them were mutually exclusive; Trofim Lysenko's prometheanism in biology was neutralized by pragmatism and the rejection of Nikolai Marr's prometheanism in linguistics,[4] and "cosmopolitanism" in theater criticism was neutralized by the struggle against "bourgeois nationalism" in a number of Ukrainian authors' works and in Kazakh historical studies. And although each campaign had its own ideological and discursive focus, they differed not only in instrumentation, but also in melody and genre.

This chapter will turn to the anti-formalist campaign in music. What makes it so different is that this campaign, apparently so strictly ideological and devoted to a subject so specific as "populist spirit" in music, was to find a continuance not only in music itself, but also in theater, film, and literature. One could of course say that it is in just this fashion that an ideological campaign is effectuated, by "reaching out to the broad masses" of listeners, spectators, and readers, were it not the case that in this instance, a media transformation of "populist spirit" in fact took place; before one's very eyes, *it was transformed from an "aesthestic category" into itself an object of aestheticization.*

The saturation of the media (newspapers, radio, novels, the stage, and the screen) with "populist spirit" not only demonstrates the universality of this category in Soviet aesthetics, but also sheds light on its very nature; the fact that an (apparently) purely professional topic is transformed into a literary (or musical or cinematic or theatrical) work obliges one to suppose that a strictly aesthetic phenomenon is at work here. Corresponding to the "politicization of aesthetics" that Walter Benjamin revealed in revolutionary culture, Stalinism has not only an "aestheticization of politics," but also an *aestheticization of aesthetics*. As we shall see, this pure instance of ideological tautology is the real Stalinist *Gesamtkunstwerk*. Its product is the emptiness that all of these meta-texts, "dear to the people, and accessible to them," were called upon to fill—novels, films, and plays about how properly to create works of art "dear to the people, and accessible to them" (that is, these very novels, films, and plays).

On January 5, 1948, Stalin and a group of Politbiuro members attended a performance of Vano Muradeli's opera *The Great Friendship* at the Bolshoi Theater. The work ignited Stalin's wrath. Work to "correct the mistakes on the musical front" began immediately within the Central Committee apparatus. The initiator here was Zhdanov, who, vying with Georgii Malenkov for influence over Stalin, did not let this opportunity slip by to remind the latter that he was an organizer of large-scale propaganda campaigns.[5] And he began by searching for enemies.

The very next day, January 6, Zhdanov called a meeting in the Bolshoi Theater to discuss Muradeli's opera. Two days later, a memorandum in Zhdanov's name appeared from the Central Committee Propaganda Department's deputy head, Dmitrii Shepilov; Zhdanov distributed it to Stalin, Viacheslav Molotov, Lavrentii Beriia, Anastas Mikoian, Nikolai Voznesenskii, and Malenkov (these apparently had comprised Stalin's retinue at the Bolshoi). Shepilov explained that the former head of the Propaganda Department, Georgii Aleksandrov (who had been removed by Zhdanov the day before), had in the fall of 1947 prepared a memorandum that was intended to justify a ban of the opera and a recall of the published scores, but this memorandum had not been sent "above"; although it recognized that the opera was "faulty," it had interpreted this "fault" in a completely incorrect way: "It did not completely reveal the politically mistaken content of the opera . . . and the fundamental defects of its musical and vocal forms."[6] The memorandum criticized, almost exclusively, the libretto: the first act "creates a distorted impression, as if all of cossackry is rising up as a monolithic reactionary mass against the Soviet government"; the second act, on the other hand, depicts "all mountaineers in idyllic tones as exponents of an inspiring, progressive principle." This created the impression that "the leading revolutionary force is not the Russian people but rather mountaineers" and that People's Commissar Sergei Ordzhonnikidze was acting not so much as the emissary of the Bolshevik Party as "the leader of the mountaineers."[7]

Thus, although the storm clouds had been gathering above Muradeli's opera long before Stalin went to the Bolshoi performance, it was Stalin, Zhdanov, and "along with them, Shepilov" who transformed this particular case into a show trial "on the musical front." Shepilov, Zhdanov's new protégé, turned up front and center in the campaign; he was not only well educated, but also keen on classical music and often cut quite a figure with his vocal talents among a group of friends, among whom was Zhdanov's son Iurii. (The "gilded youth" of that time gravitated to the latter.) This was the first major assignment in the Central Committee to be entrusted to Shepilov, a sort of "trial by fire." Shepilov "assembled a large group of eminent Moscow musicologists and other experts and, with their assistance, prepared a draft of the corresponding Central Committee directive."[8] In a new memorandum, Shepilov launched his attack mainly against Shostakovich and Sergei Prokofiev, accusing the Stalin Prize laureates of formalism, deliberate complexity of musical language, and abandonment of the present time. "When presented to Zhdanov, this material more than anything else lay at the heart of his speech at the assembly of musical figures in the Bolshevik Central Committee and of the committee's resolution, adopted February 10, 1948, 'Concerning V. Muradeli's Opera *The Great Friendship*.'" This resolution was targeted mainly at Shostakovich, Prokofiev, Aram Khachaturian, Vissarion Shebalin, Gavriil Popov, and Nikolai Miaskovskii; these "composers holding to the formalist, anti-popular trend" were mentioned in just this order, apparently according to the degree of their "anti-popular" leanings.[9]

The day after Shepilov's first explanatory memorandum, a three-day conference of figures in Soviet music began in the Central Committee; taking part in it were more than seventy leading Soviet composers, musicologists, and others from the world of music.[10] A debate flared up at the conference among the songwriters who defended the "national traditions" of officially supported "melodic" Russian folk music and the composers accused of formalism and "anti-popular" leanings.[11] The latter occupied prominent positions in the Organizational Committee of the USSR Union of Soviet Composers. The "populist composers" group was given a chance to prove that it was able not only to take leadership away from the country's leading composers, but also to head the union. The group successfully passed this test.

On January 26, 1948, two weeks after the conference ended, the Politbiuro adopted the resolution "Concerning the Change of Leadership of the Committee on Arts Affairs of the Council of Ministers of the USSR and of the Organizational Committee of the USSR Union of Soviet Composers." This resolution effected the removal of the former chairman of the Committee on Arts Affairs, Mikhail Khrapchenko, and dissolved the Organizational Committee of the Composers' Union, creating a new one without any "formalist composers" (installed at its head were Tikhon Khrennikov, as well as the former RAPM (Russian Association of Proletarian Musicians) members Vladimir Zakharov and Mar'ian Koval'). Similar changes were made also in the musical section of the Committee for Stalin Prizes.[12]

Two weeks later, the Politbiuro resolution "Concerning V. Muradeli's Opera *The Great Friendship*" was published in *Pravda,* thus ending the cycle of mocking avant-garde music that had begun in the same newspaper in 1936 with the article "Muddle instead of Music."[13] But this was followed by a meeting, lasting almost a week and a half, of Moscow composers and musicians in the Central Composers House, in the course of which the "formalists" were openly baited. Then the First All-Union Congress of the Composers' Union took place (April 19–25, 1948), which "organizationally consolidated" this latest party victory "on the cultural front." In the period between the February assemblies and the April congress, the campaign had gained momentum. The newspapers had been full of letters from workers and kolkhozniks who supported the resolution and expressed outrage over music that was incomprehensible to the broad masses of workers. The journal *Sovetskaia muzyka* had printed articles in the most stringent tones about the formalists. The journal had published in three consecutive issues, for instance, the three-part article by Mar'ian Koval', "The Creative Path of D. Shostakovich"; the article pinned a political label on literally every one of the composer's works and found "decadent aspects" in all of them. "One is completely justified," Koval' wrote, to call the early works "disgusting"; the opera *The Nose* exhibited "decadence, formalism, and urbanism";[14] and not only the works in "major" genres were thoroughly criticized, but even those in minor forms (for Koval', the "romances" on Pushkin's poems demonstrated that "Shostakovich is a composer with an underdeveloped melodic gift").[15] Accusations of "transrationalism," "poverty of melody," "squalor," and the like were interspersed with remarks expressing outrage that Shostakovich had been bestowed the title of a classic composer of Soviet music. Summing up, Koval' concluded that "Shostakovich has spent many years of his creative life primarily running idle. . . . He has not given his Fatherland what it expected of his great gift."[16]

The chief objection raised by the Propaganda Department against Muradeli's opera in its 1947 memorandum was the problem of the libretto. In the resolution, although this topic is intensified, it is still only touched upon in passing; the "story" of the opera is proclaimed to be "historically spurious and artificial" since it "creates a false impression that Caucasian peoples like the Georgians and the Ossetians were at enmity at the time [i.e., 1918 through the 1920s] with the Russian people," while in fact "the hindrance to establishing friendship among the peoples at that time in the Northern Caucasus was the Ingushes and the Chechens."[17] This assertion, in this form—with direct references to recent repressions—although first made publicly by Zhdanov during the course of the Central Committee assembly, could only have come directly from Stalin.[18]

Meanwhile, the primary emphasis of the resolution was on the musical aspects of the opera:

> The fundamental flaws in the opera stem chiefly from the opera's music. The opera's music is unexpressive, poor. It doesn't have a single memorable melody or aria. It is muddled and disharmonious, constructed out of dissonances throughout, out of combinations of sounds that grate on the ears. Individual lines and scenes that aspire to melodiousness are suddenly interrupted by dissonant noise that is completely alien to normal human hearing and has an oppressive effect on listeners. There is no organic connection between the musical accompaniment and the development of action on the stage. The vocal part of the opera—chorus, solo, and ensemble singing—creates a sordid impression. Due to all of this, the capabilities of the orchestra and singers remain untapped.[19]

The obvious contradiction here was that the resolution concerning formalism and populist spirit was apparently addressed to *The Great Friendship,* despite the fact that the opera itself had no signs of formalism at all and that it was clearly based on popular music, which both Zhdanov and (naturally) the composers themselves understood. Therefore Zhdanov's thesis about "the striking similarity of mistakes" made by Muradeli and by Shostakovich in his opera *Lady Macbeth of the Mtsensk District* (8) in fact brought together two completely different phenomena in order to "pick up" the fundamental themes of the 1936 campaign. What stands out in this are not only the direct references to the 1936 rhetoric (the music is "muddled and disharmonious"), but also the particular strategies for dealing with special musicological terminology; awkwardness in using it is compensated by a deliberate prosaic use of it, a replacement of musicological discourse with one that is populist/industrial. The "poverty" of the music, for example, is defined by the "under-use" of the real "riches" ("the capabilities of the orchestra and singers"), while the music itself is called a "musical accompaniment," as if a circus show or radio program were being discussed, not an opera. In the course of the Central Committee assembly, Zhdanov talked about "riches" in an even more down-to-earth fashion (as if discussing an industrial process): "One must not waste the talents of the Bolshoi Theater singers by keeping them at half an octave, or two-thirds of an octave, when they can produce two octaves. One must not impoverish art" (6). The result of such "mismanagement" was a "serious failure of Soviet musical art" and (just as in a factory) a production "gap" (7).

Yet another source of "riches" that the composers were not utilizing, according to the resolution, was folk music: "The composer is not taking advantage of the riches of folk melodies, songs, and tunes, and the dance tunes with which the creativity of the peoples of the USSR are so rich." And, finally, the last unused resource was classical music: "In chasing after a false 'originality' in music, the composer Muradeli disdained the best traditions and experience of classical opera in general, and Russian classical opera in particular, which is notable for its rich inner content; the wealth of melodies and the breadth of range; its populist spirit; its elegant, beautiful, and clear musical form that has made Russian opera the best opera in the world, a beloved genre of music that is also accessible to the broad masses of the people."[20] As we can see, it was just this Russian classical music that used all the "riches" enumerated here—from singability to clarity to the vocal capabilities of the performers.

The reason for all these misfortunes was declared to be "formalism." Referring back to the assembly of musical figures in the Central Committee, the resolution links the "particular instance" of the "failure" of Muradeli's opera to the "unsatisfactory condition of contemporary Soviet music, the spread of the formalist trend among Soviet composers."[21] To a much greater degree than the 1936 article, the 1948 resolution is a true aesthetic manifesto. It has all the elements of a manifesto's poetics. Completely focused on the character and problems of artistic activity, it is a compositionally perfected text, setting forth an integral system of theoretical propositions and aspiring to establish an aesthetic canon. And although this is a very peculiar manifesto—not simply normative but administrative/normative, meant to ideologically regulate the whole process of composing and performing music—it consistently affirms certain artistic principles and devices, just as any manifesto does. Its only difference from the aesthetic manifestoes of the traditional type is its social paradigm and genre. Manifestoes are usually presented in the form of prefaces, references to books and articles containing criticism, and aphorisms, and they are populated with correspondence between critics and artists. Sometimes they are artistic texts (in verse or in prose), linked in some way or another to theories of creativity, to a particular theme, or to artistic devices. But in this case an institution—more precisely, an administrative/ideological authority—assumes the role of author, and the institutional pronouncement takes shape in the genre of the resolution.

We should note that the resolution concerning Muradeli's opera was not that of the entire Central Committee but rather of the Central Committee's Politbiuro (although phrases like "The Bolshevik Party Central Committee resolves . . . ," "The Bolshevik Party Central Committee states . . . ," and "The Bolshevik Party Central Committee considers . . ." abound in it). What is more, only a few people accompanied Stalin to the preview in the Bolshoi Theater. The mechanism of reduction displaces, step by step, the entity that "speaks": a part (the party) speaks through the "mouth" of its Central Committee (which had more than a hundred members and candidates for membership); in turn, the committee speaks through the "mouth" of the Politbiuro, which in fact is represented by one person, Stalin; Stalin expresses dissatisfaction with the opera behind the scenes (literally!) and delegates another person, Zhdanov, to publicly articulate this dissatisfaction in the name of the

Central Committee and the party. The public nature of this turns the situation around; the opinion of one person, in fact, grows into being the opinion of "the broad masses of laborers"—that is, of "the people." This Soviet mechanism of "manufacturing the people" at the expense of a shift of subjectivity is clearly evident.

What we are also witnessing is the well-honed operational mechanism of Soviet ideological discourse: "Reproductive in its own functions and in its understanding of itself, Soviet bureaucracy cannot speak of itself in any other way than in the form of a conversation about the social whole. The language of social description and of criticism (the people, society, common interests) was the only form accessible to it for universalizing its own interests, knowledge, and symbols."[22] In a wider sense, authority knows no other form of representation than the staged articulation of the opinion of the fictitious entity, "the people." Every time that it constructs "the people," it constructs itself. This discourse gains a particular importance due to the fact that authority in this case is not only expressing its opinion about music, but is actually shaping its own concept of "populist spirit" in art.

The radicalism of the official aesthetic program did not limit itself to consistent anti-modernism. Soviet aesthetics was constructed by a utopian premise that effectively abolished modernism as a historical stage in the development of art. This aesthetics assumed that modernism did not even exist. According to the logic of the historical utopianism of Stalin, Zhdanov, and their adepts, one could and should write music (or poems or plays or paint pictures, etc.) as if the early-twentieth-century aesthetic revolution had not taken place. But this rejection of the revolution in aesthetics did more than just radicalize the conservative rhetoric; in a broader sense, anti-modernism must be understood as a manifestation of a *different, competing* project of "the modern" and of "modernity"—a state-centralized modernization that rested on the "masses" (or "the collective," "the people") that were being constructed. This excluded the "bourgeois" idea of the individual and the philosophy of individualism in anthropology, as well as the "bourgeois" market in economics and "bourgeois" democracy in politics and the "avant-garde" and "formalism" in culture. But this aesthetic gesticulation itself had direct political implications. Quashing the idea, for example, that "composers should not trudge along behind the listener" but instead lead this listener, the authorities in essence undermined a postulate about "the leading role of the party." After all, according to the "axioms of Bolshevism," this role was assured by the fact that the party was bringing a revolutionary consciousness to the masses. Now this elitist and revolutionary theory was being condemned (and, to a lesser degree, it was implicitly abolished); in a state that is "of *all* the people," not only can there be no place for class struggle, but there also can be none for "unconscientious masses." At the same time, the retrograde idea of "learning from the classics" got a powerful new boost. "We are not claiming that the classical legacy is the absolute height of musical culture. If we were saying things like that, this would amount to an avowal that progress ended with the classics. But the classic exemplars remain unsurpassed even now. This means that one must study and study and take all the best that there is from the classical legacy," Zhdanov asserted (142). It was beginning to seem that in this thirtieth year of revolution, it was no longer yesterday's autodidacts that must "learn from the classics" (as in the era of Proletkult, RAPP, and RAPM, when this theory had flourished) but rather the leading composers of the day.

Zhdanov's aesthetic program was constructed *ex contrario*—nothing about contemporary music suited him. His constant references to "normal human hearing" and his naturalism in conveying his understanding of "degraded music" compel us to imagine him as an individual personally offended by his own incomprehension of the "cacophony," afflicted by the "muddle" and desirous of returning music to its premodern "paradise lost"—to "substantial and beautiful ordinary folk music" and to the "richness of melody and breadth of range of classical opera" (142). One need not doubt that Zhdanov was speaking here on behalf of "the broad masses of laborers."

Characteristic here is the Central Committee secretary's willingness and ability to talk about music while casually using musicological terminology ("atonality," "dissonances," "consonances," and so forth) in his speech, not only feeling no embarrassment about this, given his audience (never mind that the leading Soviet composers and conductors, Moscow and Leningrad conservatory professors, and instrumentalists and vocalists from the Bolshoi Theater were all present in the hall), but even accusing others of "ignorance and incompetence in musical matters" (133). Zhdanov insisted that he was talking about ideological, not technical, aspects (he defines music as one of the "areas of ideology"

[132]). Stalin, too, we remember, when he a few years later decided to prove himself in the linguistics field, began his famous work about Marxism in linguistics with a declaration of his own incompetence in linguistics proper. The zeal of Zhdanov's speeches arose from his complete (and fully sincere) conviction in his own rightness and must be explained (no matter how paradoxically) not so much by his status as Central Committee secretary as by his position as a "rank-and-file listener," endowed with the right not only to bring his opinion directly to the musicians, but also to demand that they consider his tastes (which were indeed "those of the masses"). But let us note, too, that this premise of "the masses' taste" was a purely artificial construct; as soon as "the wrong thing"—the singers Vadim Kozin or Izabella Iur'eva, for instance—happened to please the broad masses, it was summarily declared to be a manifestation of philistinism, not of "the people's taste."

This is why we witness the full range of Proletkult- and RAPM-type invectives being hurled at the composers who "cater to the strictly individualistic experiences of a small group of selected aesthetes" (136); hence too the demand for a "natural, beautiful, and human" art instead of one that was "abnormal, deceptive, vulgar, oftentimes purely pathological[,] . . . alien to the masses of the people and meant . . . for 'the elite'" (137). This stance allowed Zhdanov to formulate the principles of populist concerns: "Ignoring the people's demands, their spirit, and their creativity means that the formalist trend in music has a markedly antipopulist nature" (137); "The people don't need music that is incomprehensible to them. The composers ought not to blame the people but rather themselves" (144); "Music that intentionally ignores normal human emotions and that traumatizes a person's psyche and nervous system cannot be popular music, cannot serve society" (145).

The "violence done to art" perpetrated here was the result of the preceding "violence done to life by music." As Zhdanov saw it, in this respect, the real issue was not even the aesthetic problem nor the "deviation from natural, healthy forms of music" (142). Nor was it only about ideology and the "frivolous and savage tendencies to trade off the treasure-house of Soviet musical culture for the sorry rags of contemporary bourgeois art" (147). No, the problem was purely and simply physiological: "Abandonment of the norms of musical art means the destruction of the foundations not only of the normal functioning of musical sound, but also of the foundations of the physiology of normal human hearing. . . . Bad, disharmonic music without a doubt destroys the correct psycho-physiological activity of a person" (146).

This approach to music, which was nothing short of physiological, reveals a curious "realism" on the part of authority as it verbalized the masses' intentions. The "realistic trend in music" that Zhdanov advocated was in this sense not so much stylistically realistic as it was functionally so; it was a matter of extreme pragmatism and realism as an aesthetic strategy of power. By analogy with *Realpolitik* we will call it *Realästhetik*.

The physiology of "beautiful" and "well-rounded" persons requires "beauty" in the world that surrounds them (including the world of sounds). Therefore "The Bolsheviks' Central Committee demands beauty and elegance in music" (143). Hence the description of "innovation" as "a drilling machine or a musical gas chamber" (143) or "a Herostratus-like attempt to destroy the temple of art" (146). In the imagination of party ideologues, the popular consciousness had been moving many years toward the idea that "beautiful and elegant" music was classical music, and Zhdanov, pointing out "the growth of artistic tastes and requirements of the Soviet people," had the right to demand that "we have our own Soviet 'Mighty Handful'" (147–48). In the historical utopianism proclaimed by Zhdanov, modernism and revolutionary art were part of a much more distant past than were the eternally living classics.

The "decline of music," it seemed, was tied to the rejection of patriotic tradition: "This music smacks strongly of the spirit of the contemporary modernist bourgeois music of Europe and America, which reflects the marasmus of bourgeois culture, the complete rejection of the musical art, and the stalemate of this culture." Conversely, "the best traditions of Russian and Western classical music" were being repudiated "as if they were 'obsolete,' 'old-fashioned,' or 'conservative'; the composers who are conscientiously trying to master and develop the devices of classical music are arrogantly slighted as advocates of 'primitive traditionalism' and 'feeble imitation.'"[23]

Conspicuous in the resolution is not only the content, but the very form in which formalism is mentioned. The text itself is permeated with unattributed quotations that refer to a sort of "anti-popular" linguistic reality that is outside public discourse; accordingly, this reality must be carefully reconstructed, ideologically. This is what necessitates the films, plays, and novels in which formalism's adepts articulate these "anti-popular views." It is in just such artistic texts that two linguistic elements come together: alongside the penetration of the negative (but already neutralized) and officially condemned way of thinking into the public sphere, a "positive" discourse consecrated by the resolution is also articulated and grounded in the public sphere.

Since it was an *administrative and institutional* manifesto, the resolution concentrated "on the practical level" on four institutions. These were the conservatory, music criticism, the Organizational Committee of the Composers' Union, and the Committee on Arts Affairs.

Like any experienced party functionary, Zhdanov brushed aside all attempts to "blur the issue" and condemned the effort of "certain comrades to not call things by their own names" and to "play a game partly on the sly": "Of course we are not just talking about repairs, not only about the fact that the conservatory roof is leaking and needs to be fixed. . . . The hole is not only in the conservatory roof. . . . A much larger hole has developed in the foundation of Soviet music" (134–35). Zhdanov accused the foremost composers of seizing power in the Composers' Union to defend the formalist trend. He looked at this in terms of political categories: the "healthy, progressive principle in Soviet music" was being smothered by a formalist trend, alienated from the people, which carried on "all its revisionist activity under a mask of supposed agreement with the basic principles of socialist realism," using "contraband methods" (136). Those already in power knew best the language describing conspiracies aimed at seizing it—and Zhdanov, as a true pupil of Stalin, was a consummate master of this language.

According to this logic, two trends were demarcated, one of which was deemed to be "revisionist," after which the most severe characterizations of them were pronounced (formalism, for example, was equated with "rootless cosmopolitanism" and accused of "disrespecting and disliking one's own people" [138]; "formalist" music was called "anti-popular" [144]), and, finally, the crowning touch of the whole epic was an "organizational" rout. Setting the two trends at sharply opposite poles and thus assigning themselves the necessity of solving an equation with irreconcilable summands, the authorities proceeded to a radical solution of the problem that brought such marginal figures as Vladimir Zakharov and Mar'ian Koval' to the center of attention. A year later, when a similar rout took place in the Soviet Writers' Union after the "unmasking of the cosmopolitan critics," marginal "thugs" such as Anatolii Sofronov, Nikolai Gribachev, and Arkadii Perventsev were promoted to leadership positions. A radical policy in the arts created a maneuvering space. This was a tried-and-true method of management that Stalin had used more than once in the 1930s: "If you don't break it, you don't fix it." The most famous example of this tactic was collectivization and Stalin's article "Dizzy with Successes." Something similar took place as well in the musical arena in 1948: just a year afterward, after a famous telephone conversation between Stalin and Shostakovich, the disgraced composer and his colleagues were forgiven; the composers who had just been subjected to devastating criticism were newly among the Stalin Prize laureates, while the leadership of the Composers' Union was handed over to their opponents.

The resolution challenged Soviet composers "to be inspired by a consciousness of the high requirements that the Soviet people make of musical works and, sweeping aside everything that enfeebles our music and inhibits its development, to guarantee the kind of upturn in creative work that will quickly move Soviet musical culture forward and will lead to the creation of full-fledged high-quality works, worthy of the Soviet people, in all areas of musical creativity."[24] This reveals the resolution's authors to be people who assume that artistic creativity is a consciously driven process of producing "spiritual goods"; one need only "to be inspired by a consciousness" in order to start producing "full-fledged high-quality works," just as one might create articles out of pig iron or steel. Another point in the resolution requires the Central Committee's Directorate of Propaganda and Agitation and the Committee on Arts Affairs to "secure a correction of the situation in Soviet music, a liquidation of the shortcomings indicated in the present Central Committee resolution, and the assurance that Soviet music will develop in a direction of realism."[25] This is indicative of the fact that the authors of this document were in fact the real "formalists," supposing that artistic trends can be managed like the organization of a "battle for the harvest" with merely the assistance of decision-making bodies and organizational measures.

Resolutions, assemblies, plenary sessions, speeches, articles, and "creative discussions" were all lessons to develop an idiom. And the composers did learn how to speak correctly—like Zhdanov, like *Pravda*. But only the greatest of these composers—Shostakovich—could attain the apex of this art.

ANTI-FORMALIST RAYOK

Shostakovich concluded his second speech at the Central Committee assembly, which came right after Zhdanov's devastating remarks, with a portentous statement: "I think that our assembly, after its three days' work, will be of enormous use to us, especially if we make a close study of Comrade Zhdanov's speech. I—like many others, probably—would like to receive the text of Comrade Zhdanov's speech. An acquaintance with this remarkable document can give us a great deal in our work" (163).

And, in fact, the composer began his work with "this remarkable document" immediately after it was published. Thus, toward mid-May 1948, the first version of his *Anti-Formalist Rayok* appeared—with direct quotes from Zhdanov's speech.[26]

A *rayok,* in the definition of Vladimir Dal', is "a box with movable pictures that are viewed through a thick glass." The showing of such a *rayok* (usually operated by a vagrant peasant or a retired soldier) was, as a rule, accompanied by a humorous rhymed commentary. According to historians of Russian folklore, the *rayok* derived from the puppet-show booth, in which a "paradise play" *(raiskoe deistvo)* was performed with painted figures. It was not only the accessible visual series (the brightly colored pictures and the marionettes) that drew the audience ("the people") to the *rayok,* but also, and especially, the verbal commentary, which was satirical and often scabrous, in doggerel verse, and performed to a musical accompaniment.[27] Almost a hundred years before Shostakovich, the Russian composer that he most respected, Modest Mussorgsky, had resorted to just this form when he was creating a musical satire against the aesthetic opponents of the "Mighty Handful" composers. The historical irony is the fact that Mussorgsky's opponents were traditionalists, adherents to the German musical tradition that deprecated Russian "folk" music as unworthy and unfit for use in "high" genres, while Shostakovich was faced with the necessity of defending contemporary music from the zealous followers of the romantic tradition of the populist "Handful" composers themselves (the latter, incidentally, were then being proclaimed "realists"). The genre he chose only emphasized this irony, and the kaleidoscopic quality characteristic of the *rayok* created ideal conditions for montage; like Mussorgsky's work, the *Anti-Formalist Rayok* was full of thinly veiled quotations and allusions.

As to its genre, the *Rayok* is a one-act satirical opera or a dramatic cantata that depicts a party meeting in some sort of Palace of Culture, the meeting being dedicated to the problem of popular spirit versus formalism in music. Delivering speeches in it that parody official rhetoric are the musicologists Edinitsyn, Dvoikin, and Troikin ("Onesie," "Twosie," and "Threesie")—easily recognizable caricatures of Stalin, Zhdanov, and Shepilov. "Musicologist number one," the "dear and beloved great comrade Edinitsyn," launches into expansive discussions of why populist composers write realistic music and the anti-populist ones, formalist music. Then Dvoikin, "musicologist number two, who in addition had a voice and the ability to vocalize," sings that music must be harmonious and aesthetic and that Caucasian operas must have real *lezginkas* (folk dances and melodies) in them. Finally, Troikin-Shepilov appears, issuing the call to write classical music like "Glinka, Tchaikovsky, and Rimsky-Korsakov." His speech transitions to a call for vigilance ("Vigilance, vigilance, 'bout every place and time and thing, / Watch yourself at every turn, extra conversation spurn") and concludes with a virtual cascade of threats: "Block each and every opportunity / For bourgeois ideology / To penetrate our youth. / By this you'll keep our ideas safe. / But if these philistine ideas / Someone is found accepting, / For good we'll put him in the slammer / And house him in a prison camp. / Lock-up, Lock-up!"

The paradox of Shostakovich's personality, in particular, is in the unlikely discord between, on the one hand, the genius of his music, the profundity of his artistic thinking, his strong spirit and personal will, and, on the other, the official image that he maintained by publishing and publicly reading the bureaucratic texts of a loyal Soviet "personality in the arts." Both Soviet and Western admirers of his music have been confused by this incongruity. The simplest way of reconciling it is to think of Shostakovich as a covert dissident who chose this model of survival under the conditions of the Soviet regime; his official image is a mask, and his public statements mean nothing.[28]

A myth of Shostakovich as a hater of The Word as such grew up around him while he was still living. The composer himself did not resist this myth, and more than once, when stating his refusal to write memoirs, maintained that his whole self was in his music. Shostakovich's correspondence with his closest friend, the Leningrad director Isaak Glikman, which was published in the early 1990s, seems also to confirm this thesis; in many of the letters, Shostakovich asks Glikman to write for him either an article or a preface or a speech for an official ceremony that would then be issued under the composer's own signature (and, as Glikman modestly assures us, they were edited by Shostakovich as well; Glikman was not the composer's only speech writer).[29]

This seeming inability to speak "correctly" and this surprising fear of the public word were what created the image of a hater of words. But this image obviously contradicts the personality of Shostakovich, an admirer of Koz'ma Prutkov and Mikhail Zoshchenko, who could quote Gogol's *Dead Souls* from memory.[30] "Could it be that he had the loyal letter that aggrieved so many printed in *Pravda* because he was more or less indifferent to words?" wondered poet Aleksandr Kushner.[31] Could his willingness to use the verses of second-rate poets as cantata texts or his ability to read terrifyingly lifeless clichés from the paper in front of him in a public forum, with absolute lack of feeling, also have come from this indifference? One of the most astute observers of Shostakovich's life, Flora Litvinova, writes, "I think his opinion was that everything [else] would pass, but music would remain."[32] Considering the tense relationship between music and public discourse, one could believe this explanation if it did not lead to an even greater contradiction between Shostakovich's creative work and his "creative behavior."

A most eminent modernist artist, Shostakovich was a master of montage who had perfected the technique of collage and who worked constantly with heterogeneous material—from folk and revolutionary songs to touches reminiscent of the classics; from urban romances to thieves' cant; from Lenin's texts to the poetry of Dem'ian Bednyi, Evgenii Dolmatovskii, and Sasha Chernyi, and even that of Rainer Maria Rilke and Federico García Lorca. His programmatic "quotation" of other verbal texts and musical sources and the heterogeneity of his music makes it consonant not only with modernist aesthetics, but also with post-modernist aesthetics and polystylistics. Shostakovich at the same time had an enormous gift for satire, to which he gave the broadest range of expressiveness—from subtle irony to sardonic grotesqueness.

Parody and biting wit with respect to the official Soviet world permeated Shostakovich's relationship with Glikman. Their correspondence contains crushing irony, and the parody of Soviet style attains to true virtuosity. Shostakovich not only wields the full richness of modulating official Soviet speech to perfection; he masterfully plays on figures of Soviet officialese. Their correspondence, which went on for almost forty years, is full of such parodies; many of Shostakovich's letters consist literally of an ironic interweaving of Soviet verbiage, fully in the spirit of Sots-Art. Glikman himself acknowledged that as far back as the 1930s "Shostakovich was just itching to make a musical parody of Stalin's sayings, slogans, and maxims that he hated, which were endlessly quoted and learned by heart by the country's 'progressive' people. Only many years later did Dmitrii Dmitrievich carry out this intention, when he created his satirical *Rayok*. My conversations with Shostakovich on this highly seditious subject spurred me to think of creating, to the best of my very modest abilities, a cycle of parodic songs. . . . To avoid irreparable harm, these songs were of course concealed as a tight secret and not entrusted to paper, but they were known to a narrow circle of my friends, foremost to Shostakovich, who loved to sing them to a piano accompaniment" (52).

The culture of the milieu to which Shostakovich belonged was generally very ironic. Aleksandr Zholkovskii recalled how his father, after Stalin's death, took his own parody of Stalin's speeches out of its hiding place; it was a "structurally perfect musical miniature with which he often entertained his acquaintances": "International adventurists are called international adventurists because they get into all sorts of adventures of an international nature. Why do they get into international adventures, you ask? They get into international adventures because, being international adventurists by their very nature, they cannot help getting into all sorts of international adventures!"[33] (As an aside, let us note that Stalin's rhetoric of "the fight for peace" was particularly well known to Shostakovich, whom the leader transformed in 1949 into one of the leading "fighters for peace.")[34]

Here is Edinitsyn-as-Stalin's text from the *Anti-Formalist Rayok:* "Comrades! Realist music is written / By populist composers, / But formalist music / Is written by anti-popular composers. / You ask why realistic music is written / By populist composers? / But formalist music is written / By anti-popular composers? / Populist composers write realist / Music because, comrades, being by nature / Realists, they can't help, they can't help writing / Realist music. / But anti-popular composers, being by nature formalists, / Can't help, can't help writing formalist music. / The task, therefore, is this, / That populist composers should develop realist music, / And anti-popular composers should stop / Their more than dubious experimenting / In the area of formalist music." The hackneyed phrases of Stalinist discourse used here, with their obtrusive tautologies, pleonasms, pretentious logic, redundant cyclical constructions, catechism-like rhetoric of question/answer (the questions being asked of oneself), and dual negation all reveal the main characteristic of Stalinist narrative: a gaping emptiness in vacant grammatical constructions.

Edinitsyn's aria, a parody of Stalinist discourse, makes recourse purely to Stalin's favorite grammatical constructions; Dvoikin's speech, on the contrary, is constructed from direct quotes from Zhdanov's speech. Shostakovich selected fragments from it that in different ways adorn the idiom of the party's chief *Kulturträger*, an idiom rich in ideological modulations. It looks as if Zhdanov tries to mollify the shocking demand of the "Bolsheviks' Central Committee" with "beautiful, refined music." The surprised composers might well not believe their ears and take this as some sort of "nuisance"; all of these reactions that Zhdanov suggests should conceal not only the absurdity of the interference of the "Bolsheviks' Central Committee" in the area of "beauty and refinement," but also the shock from such a frank admission; it is not audiences or even "the people" who demand "beauty and refinement"—the same bourgeois virtues that the revolution tried so hard to destroy—from art, but the leaders themselves of the great revolution, the Bolsheviks.[35] The mention of the *lezginka* particularly caught Shostakovich's attention, if we can judge not only according to his statements in *Testimony* (as reported by Solomon Volkov),[36] but also from his correspondence with Glikman, in which he several times refers to this part of Zhdanov's speech.

As is obvious from Zhdanov's own notebooks, these particular themes (refinement and the *lezginka*) made their way into his speech at the instruction of Stalin; that is, they are essentially thinly veiled quotes from Stalin himself. The comparison of contemporary music to drilling machines and mobile gas chambers intensifies the incongruity between the retrograde aesthetic program and contemporary art, and

Zhdanov's pathetic attempts to explain the nuances of using folk music in opera demonstrate his complete helplessness and incompetence. Zhdanov talks about music like an uneducated philistine—like Koz'ma Prutkov, perhaps, or one of Zoshchenko's characters—and Shostakovich insistently accentuates these details in his text.

Having constructed Dvoikin's aria from direct quotes in Zhdanov's speech, Shostakovich continued to quote this same speech in the aria for Troikin-as-Shepilov, thus combining all three "historic speeches" into a single narrative that culminates in an ominous cancan-bacchanale. The first part of Troikin's aria repeats Zhdanov's Central Committee assembly speech but introduces a single detail that refers directly to Shepilov; in his speech at the Second Congress of Soviet Composers, Shepilov involuntarily made his listeners laugh when he mispronounced Rimsky-Korsakov's name (he said "Rimsky-KorSAkov," with the stress on the second syllable of the post-hyphen element, instead of the correctly pronounced and stressed "Rimsky-KORsakov"). Shostakovich plays on this blunder in the *Rayok*.

Troikin's aria is constructed by a successive amplification of allusions from both Soviet music and Soviet penitentiary practice. In the words "Glinka, Dzerzhinka, my Tishinka, my supercrappy *[raskhrenovaia]* poemlet, my suitelette," for example, one can easily discern not only the names of Shostakovich's opponents, the composers Tikhon Khrennikov and Ivan Dzerzhinskii, but also the name of the Dzerzhinskii Square subway station ("Dzerzhinka") at Lubianka, where the KGB building was, and that of Tishinskii Square ("Tishinka"), where there was an enormous flea market. While this built on to the sound patterns of the text from the enormously popular song "Snowberry" *(kalinka, malinka),* it was simultaneously suggestive of the famous "Sailors' Peace" (Matrosskaia Tishina) prison. The exhortations to watchfulness and the concomitant threats ("For good we'll put him in the slammer / And house him in a prison camp. / Lock-up, Lock-up!") that follow this part and are sung by the chorus of "musical activists" reveal the Soviet realities that stand behind these musical allusions and the concern for the "beauty and refinement" of music. This purpose is also served by the transparent hints in the preface (entitled "From the Publisher") to the names of the people participating in this opus; one can easily discern the distorted names of the Central Committee bureaucrats and censors Pavel Apostolov ("Opostylov"), Boris Riurikov ("Sriurikov"), Boris

Iarustovkii ("Iarusrovkii"), and Pavel Riumin ("Sriumin").[37] This last name, in combination with the "Doctor Ubiitsev" (literally "Murderers' Doctor") who is mentioned, alludes also to Mikhail Riumin, the deputy minister for state security who was responsible for the "Doctors' Plot" affair.[38] The fact that Shostakovich devoted so much attention to this preface attests to his regarding the *Rayok* as both a musical *and* a literary work.

The textual material is arranged such that the transition from parody to outright satire is practically removed. This is facilitated by the dual allusions (as noted, for example, when "Dzerzhinka" refers simultaneously to the composer Dzerzhinskii and to Dzerzhinskii Square). The final cascade of threats transforms parody into tragic farce. Thus the emptiness of the populist discourse is first revealed to the listener, followed by exposés of the ideological opportunism and retrograde thinking of the dictated aesthetic program, the unprofessionalism of its adepts, and, finally, the hard-labor "prison camps" that loomed just behind this aesthetic.

Shostakovich-as-author clearly understood what was really at the authorities' center of attention. This was exactly why he focused his satire on the issue of populism. But he had also understood this as a participant at the Central Committee assembly, and for that reason he had mentioned populism more than once in his speeches there.

Populism is the quintessence of Soviet art. Beginning in the early 1930s, art that was "understandable by the people" was the direct concern of the authorities and was above all understood by authority itself because it was a mirror reflection of the elevated image through which authority was projected to its own virtual legitimizing subject. When authority is not legitimate or when the real subject is in a state of total amnesia, it constructs a subject to legitimize itself and simulates the practices of legitimization since it is most of all through them that the exercise of authority takes place. "The people" and populism are the constructs and function of authority. The *Rayok* is a deconstruction of the populist principle, and in this respect it should be understood not only as a parody, but also as an aesthetic manifesto.

The principle of populism that was shaped in such a rigid form in Stalinist culture harks back to the idea of populism that existed in nineteenth-century Russia. The concept of "populism" was the most important part of Sergei Uvarov's famous triplet of "Orthodoxy,

Autocracy, Populism." The other two concepts in it, as Andrei Zorin has shown, functioned more as instrumental categories; the concept of populism was essentially that "the Russian person is the one who believes in his church and his sovereign. Having defined Orthodoxy and autocracy through populism, Uvarov defines populism through Orthodoxy and autocracy."[39] Harking back to the German romantics and the Rousseau-Herder tradition, the idea of populism from the very beginning in Russia was merely a "national redaction of traditionalist values."[40] Therefore it is not surprising that it was entirely oriented to the past, to a tradition that was only able to stand opposed to a Europeanism that was alien to the Russian national spirit.

The young Soviet nation in asserting its identity returned to a traditionalist utopia, to romanticism. It required romantic populism and its own "Mighty Handful," not only because this music was "understandable by the people," but also because it fulfilled the same function that the art of all young nations does—that of producing a national mythology, "roots and soil."[41] The "Mighty Handful" was in this respect a typical national romantic school that, on the one hand, oriented itself to the principles of "popular spirit" (understood as the reflection in music of motifs of national history, psychology, and folklore) and "reality" (a break with obsolete classical norms and the quest for one's own national language in music), and, on the other, essentially repeated the journey of West European music (Berlioz, Liszt, and Schumann). But it can be called "realist" only in the sense that it relied on a specific national mythology. It was romantic music, however, not only in style, but also in content (as the music of a budding national self-awareness, such music is always nationalist). Shostakovich sets up his *Anti-Formalist Rayok* in opposition to this aesthetic program as a peculiar sort of musical counter-manifesto.

Melody itself in the *Rayok* is transformed into a medium of ideological content; the familiar melodic lines are constructed on a logical principle that has an independent ideological significance. The concluding passages of Edinitsyn's speech are set to a motif from Stalin's favorite Georgian song, "Suliko." During Dvoikin's speech another folk melody can be heard, a *lezginka*. Troikin's speech opens with "Kamarinskaia," which Glinka had used as the basis for his famous musical fantasy (as Manashir Yakubov notes, Shostakovich chose from among the numerous different versions of this melody the one that came closest to that of Glinka's work).[42] This shift from folk music to authors' original compositions is accentuated by a transition to contemporary vocal music; following the *lezginka* in Dvoikin's part are musical reminiscences from Shostakovich's own operetta *Moscow, Cheryomushki* (1958), and following "Kamarinskaia" is Tikhon Khrennikov's music from the film *Faithful Friends* (1954). Then—at the end of Troikin's speech— there is a return to "folk sources" (in which another of Stalin's favorite melodies, "Kalinka," is heard) that seems to be there only to afterward emphasize the transition in the finale to the popular French melody from Robert Planquette's operetta *Les Cloches de Corneville*. In both prerevolutionary and Soviet times, the dance and chorus of maids from this operetta were understood to be quintessential kitsch and a true incarnation of "mass culture." It was a cancan, which in Russian had been set to the words "Glance over here, look over there—do you like all of this?" Shostakovich based the music in the final scene of the *Rayok* on the melodies of this cancan, with a mention of the "great leader" (also transforming the skirt-lifting dancers into "musical activists"). He parodied the operetta text: "The great leader taught us all / And never tired of saying, / 'Look here, look there, / Let all our enemies be afraid. // . . . Look thither, look hither / And root out the enemy." What is more, he effectively put a conclusion to the "creative discussion"; the music finally becomes "beautiful," "melodic," and thoroughly "understandable by the people," which is asserted by the transformation of "Kalinka" into a cancan. In the language of contemporary cultural theory, this signifies that "folk" culture is transformed into "mass" culture, into a triumph of kitsch. Anyone could be convinced of this; the film director Ivan Pyr'ev emerged in Stalinist culture as if to specially prove the truth of this rule.

THE FILM: *TALE OF THE SIBERIAN LAND*

The evolution of the portrayal of "formalists" is most clearly evident in the "lower genres." The first reactions to the 1936 campaign were rather abrupt. Caricatures like the one that was published in a March 1936 issue (no. 9) of *Krokodil* depicted "masters of muddle" not only in music, but also in sculpture and painting (fig. 1). Such too was the exaggeratedly caricatured image of the formalist composer in *Anton Ivanovich Gets Angry*. The 1948 campaign, however, differed not only

КАЖДЫЙ САМ СЕБЕ ГЕНИЙ при помощи друзей и знакомых. Новейшее недорогое изобретение для прославления мастеров сумбур
музыке, скульптуре и живописи. Способ употребления ясно указан на рисунке: внизу—маститые мастера демонстрируют способы творческой рабо

Figure 1. Konstantin Rotov, "Geniuses in Their Own Minds" (*Krokodil*, no. 9, 1936). Used by permission.

in genre and performance, but also in its ideological implications and in the scope of people drawn into it. Since a mere year had passed between the 1948 resolution and the famous Stalin-Shostakovich telephone call (with the effective "immediate" rehabilitation of the recently condemned composers), the style of official representation also changed, to which the still published *Krokodil* clearly attested. From the very beginning of the campaign, caricaturists avoided deliberate parody of venerable composers, instead depicting formalists either as allegorical fairytale-like characters ("The Crow and the Nightingale" in *Krokodil* no. 7 [March 10, 1948]; fig. 2) or as some sort of nameless "masters of muddle" from whom the maestros declared formalists themselves suffered. For example, the viewer could easily recognize Shostakovich, Prokofiev, Glier, Miaskovskii, and Kabalevskii in the *Krokodil* caricatures published February 10, 1948 (no. 4), all "bemuddled" (fig. 3).

A year after the anti-formalist campaign, in January 1949, another campaign erupted, this time aimed at "cosmopolitan" theater critics. When this happened, the venerable composers who had by that time been forgiven were not mentioned at all, and the accusations of "cosmopolitanism" that had been heard a year ago were now redirected against certain critics who were armed with "critics' saxophone-bludgeons" that they were "brandishing at the great Russian melodic composers" (*Krokodil,* March 10, 1949 [no. 7]; fig. 4). But another year later, when the 125th anniversary of the opening of the Bolshoi Theater was being celebrated, *Krokodil* (January 20, 1950) published quite respectable portraits of Shostakovich, Kabalevskii, Khachaturian, and Khrennikov, who in the illustration are being urged by the "classical composers" Glinka, Tchaikovsky, Rimsky-Korsakov, and Mussorgsky to come to the Bolshoi. In this caricature, the "guilty" Shostakovich and Khachaturian are depicted as the same kind of legitimate representatives of contemporary Soviet music that the officially recognized Kabalevskii and Khrennikov are (fig. 5).

Let us turn, however, to the cinematographer. Pyr'ev's film *Tale of the Siberian Land,* shot in 1947, hit the screens during the same days in February 1948 when the anti-formalist campaign was in full swing. The film attested to the fact that this campaign was by no means spontaneous but instead prepared step by step within Stalinist culture.

From the boisterous jazz of the *Jolly Fellows* (1934, dir. Grigorii Aleksandrov), who "burst into the Bolshoi Theater," to the majestic

Figure 2. Aminadav Kanevskii, "The Crow and the Nightingale"
(*Krokodil*, no. 7, 1948). Used by permission.

— Что эту музыку критиковать мешает?
— Шумна! Всю критику собою заглушает!

Figure 3. Boris Prorokov, "Not the Right Music" (*Krokodil,* no. 4, 1948). Used by permission.

intonation of "Song of the Volga" in *Volga-Volga* (1938, dir. Grigorii Aleksandrov); from the synthesis of a symphony orchestra and a folk choir to the masses' infatuation with classical music; from the talented performance of classical music in Aleksandr Ivanovskii's prewar films to the creation of one's own "classics"—this path of the "development of populism in Soviet art" that can be read from Soviet musical comedy films was already laid out in the era when the Socialist Realist project was being shaped, especially after 1936, when the anti-formalist campaign broke out.[43] That was precisely the time that the call for creating a "Soviet classic" was first heard; on March 25, 1936, after the premiere of Dzerzhinskii's opera *The Quiet Don,* Stalin, who had attended the premiere, met in the government's box of the Bolshoi Theater with the opera's creators. There he formulated this goal for art: "It is high time we had our own Soviet classic." "Soviet classic" was a formula for tying Socialist Realist culture to a sort of eternity—the Socialist Realist answer to the avant-garde challenge. At the same time, it was also—and perhaps primarily so—an attempt to synthesize highbrow and lowbrow by mutually reducing them.

Pyr'ev's film tells the story of the talented pianist Andrei Balashov, who, wounded during the war, abandons Moscow and the conservatory to go to Siberia, where he plays the accordion in a construction site tearoom; he later becomes a composer and writes the oratorio *Tale of the Siberian Land*. Folk song swells into "classical" music early on, in the opening scene of the lull between the battles for Wrocław. Among the ruins, where the troops are singing a song, first lieutenant Balashov, a former conservatory student, plays "serious" music. The thoughtful

Figure 4. Boris Efimov, "The Pygmies and the Giants" (*Krokodil*, no. 7, 1949). Used by permission.

Figure 5. Mikhail Cheremnykh, "To the 125th Anniversary of the Opening of the Bolshoi Theater" (*Krokodil*, no. 2, 1950). Used by permission.

troops, who have just sung "Our Siberian Land," are transformed before the spectator's very eyes (their faces become more inspired and sterner) and rush into an attack. This is not a contrast but an organic transition of the folk song into symphonic music. They comprise a single exalted space, which is emphasized visually; with the growth of "symphonic" quality, the troops become ever more monumental until they become statue-like, like Evgenii Vuchetich's monument to the soldier-liberator.

The synthesis of melodrama and comedy upon which the film is constructed is based on the conflict between the "classical" (the conservatory) and the "popular" (the tearoom). An opposition like this is the long-past stage of the accession of populism; it is not truly an opposition that Pyr'ev develops but rather a synthesis of spaces. "Studying the classics" has ended, just as the age of *The Jolly Fellows* has, with its "nihilistic attitude toward the classical legacy." If the plots of *The Jolly Fellows* and *Volga-Volga* were constructed by squeezing the popular "creators" out of an "exalted" space (the "sacredness" of which was constantly profaned), then in Pyr'ev's film the central characters unite the conservatory and the tearoom by virtue of their absolutely organic presence in both. According to the Socialist Realist canon, the tearoom is no less "exalted" than the conservatory. It is no accident that the contrast made between them comes from an "alien" character, Olenich, for whom everything that happens in the tearoom is "buffoonery"; to Balashov (the "tavern accordionist") he also contrasts Natasha Malinina, whose voice promises to win her "glory, America, and Europe."

According to the film, there is no substantial difference between the conservatory, in which Soviet grandes dames in white elbow-length gloves, floor-length dresses, and furs strut about, as well as men in frock coats who speak Russian like Malyi Theater actors ("No doubt, dear col-league"), and the smoky tearoom; the conservatory and the tearoom are merely different manifestations of a single—Soviet—cultural space. That the theme of space becomes one of the central themes of the film is no coincidence. The characters are constantly relocating about the country; Balashov goes from the front to Moscow, from Moscow to the Siberian construction site, from thence to the Trans-Arctic zone, and then back to Moscow, only to return to Krasnoyarsk after his Moscow triumph; Malinina (like "a Decembrist's wife," as Olenich says) unfailingly follows after him. Olenich's spaces are "abroad," America, and Europe. The oratorio "brings together," as it were, the "Russian lands"; this hymn to Siberia, the "blessed Russian terrain," is written in the Trans-Arctic zone and then performed in Moscow, only to return to its "native regions." The encounter of the conservatory and the tearoom is an obvious symbol of this mutual expansion, when the conservatory's artists "bequeath their art" to the masses:

> I've widely roamed the country's expanses,
> But now I'm in love with this place.
> Builders, conquerors, we bow to you,
> In token of honor, esteem, and grace.

In turn, the masses give back their own art, spinning into a waltz in a burst of gratitude:

> No, *you* we must thank for your art,
> We're happy whenever you visit.
> Our greetings to Moscow impart,
> And come back as much as you can.

In both a historical sense (the blending of the classical with folk art) and a spatial sense (the unification of Soviet space), *Tale of the Siberian Land* is a demonstration of the vast potential of integration that lies at the heart of Socialist Realism.

The "exaltedness" of the tearoom is one of the film's main themes. The viewer does not yet know anything about the future of the main hero when the cleansing of "real" folk music of the "indecent" content of "vulgar music" occurs. The scene in which Balashov receives the gift of the accordion from the "jolly fellow" who has been belting out something "ugly" on it signifies the sacralization of "real folk music." Just as everyone in the tearoom is delighted with Balashov's art, "everyone" (from Burmak and Nasten'ka to the conservatory professors) will later be enraptured also by his oratorio.

The tearoom is the foundation of Soviet space: "You see only a tearoom here," Andrei tells Natasha, "but I see a people, our simple Russian people." The tearoom embodies a conservatory, but the conservatory is not a "passive object"; it is a sublimated image of this "simple Russian people." Balashov's oratorio is a beautiful, uplifting, "real" image of the masses. In other words, it is an elevated form of populism.

By contrast, Olenich's "performance expertise" is condemned because it presents only the performer himself: "You only flutter along the keys. You live only for yourself, you admire your own playing, and love only yourself," Natasha rebukes him. "Oh, so I am an egotist, a philistine?" Olenich asks, upset. "Yes," she replies. He is merely a very good performer; as Balashov's teacher says, Olenich "brilliantly imitates established models" but is not a "creator" himself. (It is no coincidence that the pianist Balashov becomes a composer—that is, a "creator," and Olenich remains only a pianist.) "Soulless" technique is tantamount to absolute lack of talent. Who needs "expertise" if it does not "elevate" the masses, if it does not express them, if it is not, in other words, populist?

Just as *Volga-Volga* was a film about a song, *Tale of the Siberian Land* is a film about a work called, in full, a "*symphonic* oratorio," the genre of which is deeply fraught with antinomy—a "struggle" between music and words is built into it. This antinomy of genre is the basis of Pyr'ev's work; a film about music is called a "tale." The oxymoronic nature of the situation is resolved by a dramatic expansion of the boundaries of the word. This is a matter not only of expanding words into a musical work (tellingly, Balashov's "creative process" is depicted by the film in such a way that the words come to him first, and the music later arises for them), but also of transforming the characters' speech into a "tale."

As soon as a character's share in a dialogue in the film extends to more than three sentences, his or her speech transitions into declamation. There are several such declamatory fragments in the film; in one instance, the transition is to verse, and in another, to singing. The "symphonic oratorio" itself is a declamation about the expanse and seeming endlessness of Siberia. Balashov's work is the limit of the verbalization of music; its author/performer does not sing to music but rather declaims; the music is nothing more than, as Zhdanov said, a "musical accompaniment." The orientation toward jazz *(The Jolly Fellows),* singing *(Volga-Volga),* opera *(A Musical Story* [1940, dir. Aleksandr Ivanovskii]), and, finally, toward programmatic, thematic, symphonic music (*Anton Ivanovich Gets Angry* [1941, dir. Aleksandr Ivanovskii]) has culminated with the complete triumph of the consecrated declaimed word over the accompaniment of the symphonic orchestra and the chorus.

The "folk" element rises to the level of "the classical." In his film (itself a sort of *Gesamtkunstwerk*) Pyr'ev transforms Balashov's composition into a true *Gesamtkunstwerk*. Nikolai Kriukov's dull, unexpressive music; Il'ia Sel'vinskii's plodding verses; the thunderous orchestra; and the howling chorus—the very texture of this epic oratory—correspond well to the visual texture of the film. With the gaudiness that is uniquely his (and this was one of the first Soviet films to use color), Pyr'ev added, on top of the booming sound, the histrionics, the artificial "pathos," the wildly overdone melodrama, and the psychological inauthenticity (in which the characters do not speak but rather orate), the garish kitsch of the "cinematographic epic poem," to the accompaniment of which Balashov's *Tale of the Siberian Lands* is performed in the Great Hall of the Moscow Conservatory. This visual oratorio incorporated theatrical episodes about the Cossack Ataman Ermak's subjugation of Siberia, executed in the tradition of Russian historical painting. Against a backdrop of landscapes that have a wild combination of fiery heat lightning, garishly red sunsets, and an ultramarine sky, Siberia first rises up as wild, then as the gloomy territory of tsarist punishment or prison, and, finally (with documentary frames), as an immense land transformed by the labor of the Soviet people, with mighty factories and industrial complexes, endless wheat fields, and flourishing cities.

The elevated image of "the people" requires an "absolute epic distance" that allows one to effect the derealization of life in ready-made genre forms. *Tale of the Siberian Land*—this epic created through music, poetry, color film, painting, declamation, and theater—found an adequate genre expression in Pyr'ev's film. It should come as no surprise that in 1948 this film became a "blockbuster," was the most widely shown of all films, and was awarded the Stalin Prize, First Class, the next year.[44] The Stalin Prize, Second Class, went to a play by Sergei Mikhalkov, *Il'ia Golovin.*

THE PLAY: *IL'IA GOLOVIN*

The postwar anti-formalist campaign differed particularly from the prewar campaign in that if in the 1930s the most eminent artists of the revolutionary era were accused of formalism and the corpus of new (Stalinist) classics had still not taken shape (even the most eminent figures, like Meyerhold, were easily removed from it), then toward the end of the 1940s, the pantheon was practically complete. Moreover, it was established in Stalin's own time, and although composers on the level of Shostakovich or Prokofiev or film directors on the level of Eisenstein or Pudovkin were also subjected to public condemnation for their numerous "mistakes," they were at the same time medal winners, Stalin Prize laureates, and recognized masters—the pillars of Stalinist culture—and not to be criticized in the same tones that had been used in the 1930s. Thus, in January 1948, when the events unfolded on the musical front and Stalin needed to get rid of Solomon Mikhoels, he had to stage an assassination (automobile accident) outside Moscow, a subterfuge that would not have been necessary in the 1930s. Thus, the very poetics of the pogrom had changed; although the old "formalists" were still reviled, the judgments were pronounced in a somewhat different tone than that of the 1930s.

Mikhalkov was working on his play at the same time that Shostakovich was writing his *Anti-Formalist Rayok*. He read the newspapers no less attentively than Shostakovich and, of course, was just as familiar with the text of Zhdanov's speech; traces of his work with "this remarkable document" are easily seen in the play, which adapted Zhdanov's "libretto" for an endless ideological recitatif "in the forms of life itself." It has the composer Golovin, of course, who, although talented and honest, has been living too comfortably and too removed from his audiences ("the people"), and his bourgeois wife ("Oh, and by the way, I keep forgetting to ask you what you've heard about our new apartments. They make one promise after another. We're literally suffocating on these seventy meters of ours").[45] There are the children from his first marriage: the artist son, who at first paints only ideologically empty landscapes but is reformed toward the end of the play, and his singer daughter Liza, who understands that her father is writing music "far removed from the people." His tuner brother Stepan tells him the truth straight to his face. There, too, is the tank armies general Roslyi, who reminds Golovin that the people needed his art during the war and still need it; the aesthete critic, who overpraises Golovin's formalist music; and the young composer Mel'nikov, who becomes a bigwig music bureaucrat and helps Golovin "set out upon the wide road of populist art." Even the housemaid, old Lusha, somehow becomes a participant in the clashes "on the musical front."

But what happened to Golovin? How did a composer so beloved of his audiences degenerate into a formalist? Liza attributes this to the influence of Golovin's new wife; after acquiring this bourgeois wife, he stopped transcribing folk songs and turned into a formalist. All of this would have kept going along in the Golovins' dacha, with its quite Chekhovian entourage, had not an "unsigned" article, "Formalist Mannerisms in Music," suddenly appeared in *Pravda*. Everything was immediately turned upside down. All Golovin's fame, as it turns out, had rested on the critics who had previously fawned on him. Golovin's world, too, was now split in half: at one extreme was the critic Zalishaev; at the other was everyone else—his daughter, his brother, General Roslyi, and even the old housemaid.

Old Lusha cannot abide Zalishaev, although she does not understand a thing he says: "I don't like him. He'll come and sit and sit. And he talks such gobbledygook. He talks one way and looks the other" (160). Nonetheless, Golovin finds her to be a rewarding interlocutor:

> Golovin: Look, now they're writing that I'm alien to the people in my work. . . . Lusha, I assure you that I am a Soviet person!
> Lusha: Well, of course! We're all Soviets.
> Golovin: But why do they say that I'm too distant from the thoughts and feelings that my people live by? Why? You don't think my fatherland is not dear to me, do you? They've called me one of the progressive composers of the present time. They've imitated me. . . . And suddenly all these people who praised me, all the ones who valued and understood me, all these people, Lusha, have been declared aesthetes, snobs, and formalists. (160)

Poor Lusha had probably never heard such words.

Then Golovin turns on the radio and stumbles onto, of all channels, "Voice of America": "Suddenly, the loud, unpleasant male voice of an announcer, speaking Russian with a barely discernible foreign accent, fills the whole room." The announcer's voice reveals the following: "This significant work goes beyond the narrow boundaries of national music and sounds like a genuine masterpiece of contemporary musical culture and is clear proof of the great talent of Il'ia Golovin. . . . Unfortunately, the last symphony of this outstanding composer, the Fourth, met a hostile reception in official Soviet Communist circles, who accused the author of formalism and decried the so-called 'anti-popular' character of his music" (160).

Alone among all the characters in the play, only Zalishaev admires Golovin's new symphony. Leafing through the journal *America,* he says, "One would have to be intentionally deaf to appreciating the essence of the Fourth Symphony not to understand those gigantic images that it has within it. What nobility of intellectualism! What a profoundly psychological intonation of the theme! The orchestral palette of Hindemith!" (145). But when he mentions the symphony's success and that "there have been great audiences on all three continents," Golovin's brother objects: "Maybe there have been plenty of audiences, but too few people!" (157). To understand what makes "audiences" different from "people," one must comprehend the significance of the anonymity of the *Pravda* article. When Zalishaev pegs it as "from the higher-ups!," Golovin's brother responds: "From the higher-ups? Might it not be, on the contrary, from below? The ideas it expresses are quite true: 'Music is harmony.' . . . And you could collect so many signatures for this article that the whole newspaper wouldn't be big enough! That's why it's not signed" (157–58).

A return to "the sources" cures Golovin of formalism. General Roslyi, whose staff had been quartered at Golovin's dacha during the war, reappears there. He relates that during the war, his troops had found an old score of Golovin's and had created a regimental song they called "Golovin's Song" based on his music. But the general could not understand the new symphony:

Roslyi: Pardon me for saying so, but I didn't understand a thing about your music. I had a hard time just listening to the whole thing. And that's what I wanted to write you a letter about. I wanted to ask you for whom and why you composed it. But then I read the article in the paper. I'm glad the party explained it!
Golovin: I'm very sorry that I've caused you such suffering.
Rosyli: I wouldn't call it suffering! It was grief! I couldn't sleep all night. I'm lying there thinking, "General, have you lagged behind contemporary musical culture, maybe? You rarely went to the conservatory; you heard too little new music; you're an uncultured person. You don't understand anything about serious music."
Golovin: I'd say that's possible.
Roslyi *(excitedly):* But then I thought and thought and didn't even agree with myself. How could this be, I wondered. I understand Glinka. Tchaikovsky's Sixth Symphony, too. I've listened to Beethoven's Ninth so many times. Do I understand? Yes! I love Russian songs. I sing, myself.

Do they excite me? Sure, they do! But why? Because the soul of the people lives in them, of course. . . . No, Il'ia Petrovich, you haven't composed *our* music. It's not Russian! Not Soviet! (171)

Golovin just cannot grasp this mystical "soul." His aesthete son provides a hint: "Music can be universal, for all peoples." To this, Roslyi replies: "I'd also like for it to be universal, but above all it should be profoundly national, and then, believe me, all humanity will play it and listen to it. But what you wrote, forgive me, is Esperanto. And I don't want to speak Esperanto, nor to sing it, and I won't. I don't understand it, Il'ia Petrovich!" When Golovin responds that Roslyi "could learn Esperanto," the latter angrily answers back, not mincing words, "But why study it? There is no such people. It's . . . they . . . like . . . rootless people made it up" (171–72). This was a reference, as the 1949 viewer understood, to "rootless cosmopolitans"—more simply put, to Jews.

There were, of course, no Jews in the play, and Golovin is treated with profound respect in it. Even the general, after his accusatory tirades, offers him words of support: "Il'ia Petrovich, I'm a Soviet man, and because of that our art is dear to me, and I take it to heart. And I don't want to be tactful, I can't be polite, if this has to make me be quiet or act like a hypocrite. And we love you, we value and look forward to your creations, sometimes patiently—oh, how patiently we wait. . . . So don't be offended by us, your own people, after all, when, with respect and love for you, we sometimes tell you what we think, what we feel, straight to your face" (172).

But how, really, had the great composer become befuddled, and how did his magical healing come to pass? It was not so much the new bourgeois wife who was guilty as it was the fawning critics, who are represented in the play by Zalishaev. The new young head of the Composers' Union, Mel'nikov (easily recognizable as Tikhon Khrennikov), who helps Golovin rid himself of formalism, "unmasks" Zalishaev, talking to him like a prosecutor. When Zalishaev learns that he will be named among other representatives of "a certain group of creative workers in the area of criticism and musicology" (and the play was written after the "unmasking" of the "cosmopolitan" theater critics), he assures Mel'nikov, "My viewpoint on Soviet music and on Soviet art was, is, and will remain our viewpoint on Soviet art." Mel'nikov replies, "Quite true. We know your viewpoint on our art very well. From that viewpoint you have done everything you could to prove that such art does not exist at all, and that if it does exist to some extent, then it should not be spoken of unless condescendingly and with disdain." The downcast "cosmopolitan" defends himself: "I have fought for everything new that could, in my opinion, increase the significance of Soviet art in the broadest sense of the term." Mel'nikov has a ready answer: "And *against* everything new that has increased the significance of this art in our Soviet, party-minded understanding of this term. . . . Yes! I don't deny that you've fought. And in your fight with us you have made all truths into lies, to . . . discredit, humiliate, and even destroy one or another of us who wanted to give, and did give, all of his creative forces back to his people. . . . No, you have never believed in our art! Something else was in your heart. And though you wrote your articles in Russian, they have the same accent that one hears sometimes on overseas radio." The unfortunate "cosmopolitan" says, imploringly, "I love genuine national art and always have," but Mel'nikov is inexorable:

> No! You have not loved it! It wasn't love for it, was it, that made you raise a pandemonium around Golovin's name, who has strayed from the path he was following, from the only path that leads to the heart of the people?! You grabbed him by the hand and started pushing him where our ideological enemies would applaud him. You tried to take him away from us, him, Golovin, who despite all the errors of his way is *ours, not yours!* But we won't let you have him! And he won't come to you on his own, either, because he is a Soviet man, a Soviet artist, because he understands that the seed, in order to become grain, has to grow in soil, not in tooth powders! (181–82)

These angry tirades should not be viewed as merely the playwright's fantasy; this was in fact the style used in those days (and later) by Vladimir Zakharov and Anatolii Sofronov, or Mar'ian Koval' and Nikolai Gribachev, as they "laid down the law" from the tribunes. The "truth of art" comes face to face in them with the "truth of life," revealing the logic of the dominant discourse in culture. On the one hand, the critic is transformed into a political enemy because he "does not believe in our art" and does not "love" it. In other words, at issue is a particular sort of premise for professional activity in the arts; those who do not "believe" and "love" are professionally unfit; Golovin, by contrast, like a prodigal son, returns to the protection of The People. On the other hand, it is constantly emphasized that Golovin (as opposed to the infernal villain Zalishaev) simply lost his way, having earlier written "populist" music. Art is here understood as a path from which one can inadvertently stray. A strong "influence," however, is enough to change everything; "populist" becomes "anti-populist" and then "populist" again. Only thus can one explain the peripeties in arts activity after the war; Stalin Prizes are replaced by public disgrace, after which there are new prizes, the usual honorary titles, awards, and prestigious political assignments.

In fact, like Shostakovich, Pudovkin, or Ehrenburg, Golovin is at the end of the play transformed into a champion for peace. He travels abroad to the peace defense congress with the new head of the Soviet Composers' Union, Mel'nikov (who by a strange confluence of circumstances is thirty-two years old—almost the same age as Khrennikov when he became head of the Composers' Union in 1948). His "Song of the Motherland" now is sung "everywhere." In the final scene, "a brass band strikes up. You can hear the words of his song. The people are singing it":

Choir:
The Soviets stood to the death unrattled,
Holding their lives none the dearer.
Like a banner they raised, when embattled,
The name of their own dear leader. (188)

Thus Golovin, once again, is writing for the people.

STALINIST KÜNSTLERROMAN: *SNEGIN'S OPERA*

Osip Chernyi's novel *Snegin's Opera*—the only novel about Soviet music and musicians to appear since the same author's prewar novel *Musicians*—saw the light during the days of mourning surrounding Stalin's funeral. Thus it was too late to be appreciated for its merit and to receive the Stalin Prize but too early to aspire to realism. Or, rather, it is thoroughly "realist," but since it is a genuine Socialist Realist text, it is a novel of absolute fantasy. On the one hand, it slavishly follows the events that preceded the rout "on the musical front" in the winter of 1948 and is inevitably tied to realia (we easily recognize the Moscow music world since ultimately the distances between the conservatory, the Bolshoi Theater, and the Composers' House are not so great) and full of quite "real" characters (it is not difficult to identify the names of the chairman of the Committee on Arts Affairs, the head of the Composers' Union, or the chairman in the Central Committee assembly). On the other hand, since the author wants to "typify" and "generalize" (that is, to encode the easily recognizable real names), he is just as inevitably obliged to combine the "typical features" of completely different, easily recognizable prototypes. He found himself in the same situation as Gogol's heroine Agaf'ia Tikhonovna, who mused on "sticking Nikanor Ivanovich's lips under Ivan Kuz'mich's nose, and taking some of the swagger that Baltazar Baltazarych has, and maybe adding Ivan Pavlovich's burliness to this, besides." Unlike the heroine of *Marriage*, however, Chernyi knew how to transform an imperfect reality and real historical events in accordance with an ideologically aligned, harmonized scheme.

It is not even a matter of "lying," of which Socialist Realism is traditionally accused, but of the phantasmagorical product of this mimetic writing. In Chernyi's novel, for example, everything would appear to look real. The only thing that disturbs the premise of verisimilitude, paradoxical as this might seem, is the assumption from the beginning that the reader knows about the events that took place in 1948. *Without* this knowledge, the novel is "unrealistic" since it is incomprehensible. But *with* this knowledge the novel is also "unrealistic" since, on the contrary, it can be understood; since the reader's knowledge of 1948 is assumed, the book must be recognized as complete fantasy, although it was in fact called "an accompanying *illustration* of certain well-known situations" and its author was taken to task because he "undertook to illustrate every paragraph of the Bolshevik Central Committee's resolution regarding the opera *The Great Friendship* and A. A. Zhdanov's speech, dogmatically treating each one separately."[46]

The Bolshoi Theater (which in the novel is alternately named outright or obliquely as "the most eminent and glorious opera theater in the country") commissions an opera from four composers. Two of them are "formalists" (who, owing to the Composers' Union, wherein "everyone talks about nothing but 'Giliarevskii and Snegin, or Snegin and Giliarevskii,'" are taken to be "innovators").[47] The reader will already have guessed that this means Shostakovich and Prokofiev (the author attempts somewhat to simultaneously confirm this, by giving Giliarevskii the patronymic Sergeevich and Snegin the first name

Dmitrii, and to conceal it). A split arises from the fact that the author understandably could not in 1953 portray only a confirmed formalist; therefore, he makes one of the composers (Snegin) a musician who has sincerely lost his way and who is searching, striving to overcome formalism in his own creative work, and he makes the other (Giliarevskii) a confirmed formalist, ingrained in his anti-popular sin. The other pair of composers is "populist." One of them, Voloshin, writes "melodically," basing his style on nineteenth-century classics. The other, Aliev, is a young composer from an eastern republic who is writing an opera with a national plot, using national music.

This novel, about the size of *Anna Karenina,* gathered under its covers, as it were, the whole Soviet musical world. It has composers of different schools and generations, as well as representatives of the Composers' Union, starting with its head, Galadzhev (read here: Khachaturian), and ending with the critics, also of the most varying stripe, from formalists to the musicologists who understand their tasks correctly. Here, too, are the functionaries of the Committee on Arts Affairs, including its chairman Kolesaev (read here: Khrapchenko) and the "theater community" in all its variety, from the Bolshoi Theater managing director and the party committee secretary to production directors of varying inclinations, singers of different generations and orchestral musicians (including a beginning concertmaster), and representatives of the conservatory. Populating the novel alongside the "music community" are their listeners. They flood it in great torrents through different "branches" of the plot: a beginner songstress comes to the Bolshoi Theater straight from the factory, bringing various colleagues along, from the factory's director to other workers who constantly express their opinions about music; Aliev brings in both his own professors from the party central committee of his republic and the old *ashugs* (ashiks or singers) who also discuss music; Snegin's wife and father-in-law, both architects, introduce the regional party committee secretary, who as usual "looks at his interlocutors with clear, intelligent eyes" (29) and who, as it turns out, has a stepson who becomes Snegin's favorite pupil. They all know each other, united by a variety of interwoven plot connections, and in the aggregate they represent in the novel the densely populated Soviet world, which is thoroughly tied together, from the most famous of composers to the ordinary worker.

Giliarevskii has written the opera *The Young Guard;* Snegin, *The Partisan Girl* (based on a World War II theme); Voloshin, *Dawn* (about postwar collective farm life); and Aliev, *Patimat* (about revolutionary struggle and the friendship among peoples of the Caucasus). If we combine all of these, we get a combination of Prokofiev's operas *War and Peace* and *Tale of a Real Man,* Shostakovich's *Lady Macbeth of the Mtsensk District,* and Muradeli's *The Great Friendship.* At any rate, the operas are performed in the theater, then for the Committee on Arts Affairs. Giliarevskii's opera evokes horror and is rejected; Voloshin decides to do further work on his; and Aliev's is not quite finished. Only Snegin's opera remains. After his triumphant staging of Tchaikovsky's *Queen of Spades* (the very opera that, by a strange coincidence, Shepilov was said to be able to sing in its entirety, from beginning to end), the director Kalganov undertakes *The Partisan Girl.* Central Committee members are present at the premiere, which turns out to be a total flop. Afterward, an assembly is called at the Central Committee headquarters in Old Square; from it, everyone emerges enlightened, and, finally, the dawn of populism rises on Soviet music.

Snegin's Opera is essentially the first novel about Shostakovich. At its heart is the quite talented leading Soviet composer Snegin, with his quests and strayings. The drama for him is that he ends up "imprisoned" in his own devices. The initially talented and honest composer becomes a victim of modernist "brainwashing," or, more precisely, of a real anti-popular conspiracy. The author explains it thus:

> He grew up in the years when a large and influential group among composers that had joined together as the so-called "Association of Contemporary Music" began to preach that the paths of Soviet and bourgeois music were coinciding. Under the guise of contemporaneity, anti-popular, anti-humanistic, cosmopolitan views were dragged in. . . . People of mediocre talent, or totally ungifted people, became the theoreticians and heralds of the new trend. Enlisting a musician like Snegin was in the interests of this group. . . . They wrote many articles and spoke many words to convince Snegin that eccentric harmonies, pointless tonal leaps, and the cacophony that is so dear to their hearts and minds constitute the musical language of a composer of our times. Snegin surrendered to their praise and appeals. Poison penetrated his talent to the core. (211–12)

So the poisoned composer tries to create works for the people, but the music that results is "cold" and "anti-realist," "excites no one," and is ultimately "anti-popular." To write in a realist way means following in the vein of folk songs (as we have seen, the *lezginka* had to be "populist," "substantial," "beautiful," and "real"), but instead of doing that, Snegin not only himself chases after some kind of "generalizations" that only he understands, but also tries to force the young composer Aliev (read here: Muradeli) to follow this false path. (Nevertheless, Aliev does not heed the advice of the venerable Snegin because he is striving for "populism" in his own opera.)

Snegin's wife Natasha tries harder than anyone else to explain his mistakes to him. She approaches him cautiously: "Dima, do you think about your audience?" (15). No, floundering in his doubts, Snegin does not think about his audience. Meanwhile, everyone, even the housemaid (it is worth noting that in these plays and novels, wherein everyone talks of nothing but serving the people, the characters live extremely comfortably, invariably surrounded by housemaids and chauffeured cars waiting at the entrances) talks only about the fact that this music is incomprehensible. "Of course, Vadim Klement'evich wrote for those who understand," the old housemaid says. "But I wonder if there are many of them? . . . But we are like everyone else! Singing and music, these we understand. But it's totally impossible to understand Vadim Klement'evich!" (187). Everyone tries to explain to Snegin that his music is incomprehensible because it is not national, that he is possessed by "a pernicious idea that musical thought is identical among different countries. But nowadays everyone understands definitively that it cannot be anything but Russian, that is, Soviet" (418). The party regional committee secretary with the "intelligent eyes" has a conversation with Snegin about the fact that Snegin must not simply isolate himself in the world of his own experiences (which has a certain air of the tragedy of existence and a fear of the future that is alien to the people):

> "Threats don't scare us, because we, the whole nation, are creators. And we despise the imperialists because they have only one passion left—destruction. But are you—" he stopped, facing Snegin—"a creator?"
>
> "I think so, yes," Snegin answered in a dull voice.
>
> "But always? A simple man, when he has rolled up his sleeves, would start working, but you pile up complications in your own consciousness and you yourself stand in fear of them. Who needs that? . . . And another thing. . . . You have complicated your language to the limit. There is almost no melody—it looks like you have turned off the big highway onto a footpath. You think that others will follow you, but the footpath is only for individualists." (32)

Snegin cannot understand what others want of him. He tells his wife:

> What you're pushing me to do is write in pat perfect phrases. You would probably like it if *The Partisan Girl* had the traditional equilibrium among all the parts or if I made perfect little numbers instead of constantly developing symphonic action. But just think: to paint the era of struggle and battles in a clearly harmonic and simply melodic way?! . . . I admit that clarity in art has its attractions. But then I'd have to reject the idea of becoming a contemporary artist. A boyar's costume and a peasant's bast shoes are equally impossible for a Soviet hero to wear. So can you force him to sing in classical style, give him various cavatinas and arioso passages? Of course not. Let there be less singability, let the music be even awkward, then it will reflect the novelty of our times—that's what I need." (16–17)[48]

"I still think an opera without singability is bad, Dima!" Natasha objects. Snegin: "But a 'kolkhoznik quartet'? A 'partisan's aria'? Doesn't the very combination of these words seem artificial?" (17).

Snegin endlessly expresses such sentiments as "Distinctive laws of musical development exist. We cannot now speak the language of Tchaikovsky and Glinka—we would all become epigones. . . . Can I make a leap, cast aside my quest, start writing music that anybody would recognize as accessible? Why, it would be primitive!" (23–24). Kalganov, the director, also understands this. But although he is not ecstatic about Snegin's new opera, he is convinced that he should support the composer in his quest. He explains to Snegin's importunate wife that "you cannot repeat nor make variations on the melodic turns of the classics and meanwhile pretend that you are creating something new." This evokes her stormy reply, "What good is something new if it deprives me of the most essential thing—joy, spiritual delight?!" (179–80). Her father becomes genuinely upset over his son-in-law's music: "Why would a gifted person waste his talent?! Why do they accept this thunder of frantic voices and harsh chords, these noises that sound like a saw or an auger, as progressive Soviet art?" (180). In this list, Snegin's father-in-law forgot to mention, apparently, only the famous drilling machine.

Snegin-as-Shostakovich reacts painfully to the rejection of his family and friends. In moments of desperation, he begins to reason exactly like Shostakovich's persecutor, Zakharov: "When the war was already over, he never once asked himself whether the trend he was following was true or not. Indeed, it was in these years that he discovered, to his surprise, that the Soviet song that had long ago won the people's recognition had managed to cross the borders, conquering all obstacles that were put in its path. . . . Could Snegin really put even one of his own orchestral works alongside it? This idea troubled him and gave him no peace" (220).

Snegin is hindered from becoming a "great social artist" by his isolation, as the author explains:

> The detachment and isolation of a man immersed in himself prevented him from turning back onto the road of great art. Ultimately, the power of the devices he had mastered was too great, and the makeup of the feelings that had dominated his soul were taking root instead of disappearing. . . . He kept up with the life of the country more through newspapers and books, and when he encountered people from other professions, he often experienced a weariness of spirit. He was isolated by his own nature, didn't know how to make friends, and his creative work, without receiving enough nourishment from without, separated him from life rather than bringing him closer to it. His compositional ideas took the place of a lively interest in people, squeezed this out into the background. (213)

Hence the direct path toward anti-popular formalism. Thus Snegin, without wishing to, begins to resemble Giliarevskii, about whom we know, for example, that his ballet had had a run in Leningrad, but "several years ago his opera was staged; true, it didn't run for long and is now forgotten" (226). The image of Snegin-as-Shostakovich begins to split in two, becoming transformed into that of Giliarevskii-as-Prokofiev. At this point, the author falls into a new trap. Mark Shcheglov, who sharply criticized the novel in *Novyi mir* (but without any other rhetorical possibilities available at the time to defend Prokofiev and Shostakovich), observed: "The presence in the novel of the image of the formalist composer Giliarevskii profoundly distorts the real situation in Soviet music in those years. . . . One cannot by any means agree that one of the Soviet Union's most influential and famous composers could in 1948 be such an 'Arnold Schoenberg.'" There was no such anti-popular, anti-Soviet figure at the fore back then. The idea of any sort of prototype alone in this case is insulting. The author of the novel, hoping at whatever cost to create a vivid impression, laid down the black ink too thickly."[49] Thus Chernyi, for his portrayal of the "denigrator of Soviet reality," was himself accused of "denigration."

We know that Giliarevskii is writing the opera *Young Guard,* which much aggrieves Snegin, as he himself would have liked to have written an opera about this organization (16). The very choice of Fadeev's novel for Giliarevskii naturally refers to Shostakovich, one of whose first signs of "reform" after the February 1948 resolution was the music for the film *Young Guard.* In fact, Shostakovich wrote in 1950, "I set about writing the music for *Young Guard* with particular excitement, which was made even greater by the fact that I had been getting ready to write an opera about the members of the Young Guard. . . . My entire creative passion was spent on the picture instead of the opera. I have absolutely no regret about this, and I still have not rejected the idea of using what I have already written for a symphonic work about the Young Guard."[50]

The symphonic work never did materialize (and the 1947 opera *Young Guard* had already been written, by Iulii Meitus, before the 1948 resolution was published). However, certain statements made by Giliarevskii are almost word-for-word quotes from the speech Shostakovich made at the Central Committee assembly. For example, about Giliarevskii we learn that "the technology of art interested him more than anything else, and he tried to keep what had to do with the area of feeling outside the bounds of conversation. Characterizations such as 'twenty measures of sheer melody,' 'a beefed-up brass section,' or 'muted voices' avoided the necessity of mentioning just *what* was included in these twenty measures and muted voices" (89). Shostakovich had said in his speech that "it is not enough to create two, three, or ten or more measures of good music" and that in order to create a melody, "you must have, along with talent, great skill as well." Shostakovich's speech revealed that Muradeli's opera failed not because the composer had incorrectly understood his mission but rather because "he did not have enough skill" (161).

Giliarevskii is yet another hypostasis of Shostakovich, his "dark side," as it were—the "devil incarnate" of anti-popular formalism. His music evokes horror in everyone who hears it. Here is the reaction of the shocked Voloshin:

> The events of the novel arose in Voloshin's imagination; behind them were daring feats, the passion of youth, selflessness, sacrifices, and blood. He could see, distinctly and in sharp relief, the real-life prototypes of the characters—Ulia Gromova, Zemnukhov, Tiulenin. . . . What Giliarevskii was performing at first surprised him with its coldness, its complete lack

of passion, and then offended him to the bottom of his heart. Could this man sitting in front of him really be the one who served as an example for so many to imitate? He could feel such disrespect for the listener emanating from his music, such disrespect for Soviet life, that he wanted to shout at him to stop. Neither the inventiveness nor the sparkles of feeling that flared up now and again changed anything. On the contrary, the music seemed even more hostile, and the abrupt collisions with tonality, as if the chords had torn into the body of melody, seemed even more offensive. (92)

Voloshin's ire is predictable:

> To write about people who performed immortal feats, who sacrificed their lives, with such indifference! It's horrible! . . . I myself had a brother, a young man of just twenty years old, killed in the war, and do you think I can calmly listen to how the images of Gromova and Zemnukhov are disfigured? Can the people who paid with the blood of their loved ones and their own for today's celebration listen to this without getting upset? . . . Do you understand, Evgenii Sergeevich, what has happened to you? Shutting yourself off from life with your expertise. . . . You are proud of your technique, but it has led you to the verge of catastrophe: it has left nothing alive in you, it has completely suffocated you. What kind of *artiste* or artist *are* you? (93–96; emphasis in original)[51]

This is what Voloshin says out loud, but he is also thinking to himself: "Why, this is deceit! The party shows such faith in composers, but they don't justify it! They value a worker, an engineer, or a scientist for the good that they do, but what about a composer? What if his labor is worthless, even harmful, and gives the people nothing? Truth be told, Giliarevskii ought to be forced to do some other kind of work. And I mean forced. But could you really crush the stubbornness, the formalist narrow-mindedness of a person who has set himself above all the rest?" (101). And, in fact, it is but a small step between the "bewilderment" about talented people who "do not want to" write melodious music and the perceived necessity of forcing them to "want to."

The novel describes Giliarevskii's music as "a skeleton chosen over a living person, bared teeth instead of a natural and charming smile" (399). But on the other hand, when Kalganov heard Voloshin's opera *Dawn,* which is about kolkhoz workers, "he was gripped by a sensation of freshness, as if he were drinking cool water. Everything was melodic, elegant, and balanced, and the spirit of poetry made the music warm" (231). Elsewhere "the colors that Voloshin had applied" are described as "clear, sometimes muted and sometimes, on the contrary, very bright"; they create "optimistic scenes, full of movement and life"; and "the smoothly developing action, the symphonic breadth of the orchestral pictures made you remember the operas of the past" (401). This "elegant" music is the product of the composer's serious deliberation. Voloshin is above all worried by the Socialist Realist problem of making the heroes poetic: "To endow them with extraordinary features would not be right—heroes on opera stilts would not convince anyone. But neither did he wish to resign himself to making them ordinary and commonplace. What he had to do was find the heroic in the everyday and do this in such a way that the truth of our times would be preserved" (84).

The other populist composer, Aliev, has an even more complicated task: he must make his own people's music "accessible" to the Russian audience. His opera, which is about a popular uprising against feudal lords, has as a central figure the leader of the uprising and a central theme of the shepherd Kamil's love for the girl Patimat. It is Muradeli's *The Great Friendship,* still in the making. But in it, all the problems have correct solutions. The audience is won over by its "simple flow of melodies": "The slow and peaceful melodiousness awakened the memory of the expanses of mountain valleys. In the unusual intonations of the music one could detect the folk origin, made deeper and richer by the author's imagination. You got the feeling that you were drinking crystal-clear water that is both sweet and at the same time quenches the thirst" (403). But though "Aliev discovered bright melodic figures and a fullness of sound in his choral arrangements and orchestral compositions," some things remained unclear for him: "He had yet to resolve a great many issues: how to combine classical orchestral style with the usual playing of a national ensemble; how, while preserving the uniqueness of folk melodies, to make them equally accessible to a Russian, a Ukrainian, or a Lezgin. When the melodies of his people finally were heard with the same fullness that Russian choirs produce, his own experience made him understand that this path was the only true path. Harmony made these melodies richer, brighter, and deeper" (40). Merely by becoming like "Russian" music, this music becomes "harmonious" and "true."

Chernyi's "realist novel" progresses, as it were, in two dimensions of fantasy. In one of them, the heroes are placed symmetrically, like chess

pieces; they say preposterous things to each other, act in a psychologically unbelievable fashion, orate, philosophize, and in general are more
like some sort of functions than "realistic" characters. In the other dimension, which arises inevitably by reason of the "realistic authenticity" of the plot that follows certain events and their participants, the
novel is similar to a strange collage; the easily recognizable features of
the Central Committee assembly's participants are interwoven, as it
were, as in the daydreams of Gogol's Agaf'ia Tikhonovna: Zakharov's
nose has been affixed above Shostakovich's lips, and Khachaturian's
burliness has been added to Muradeli's swagger.

The only thing that makes this whole surrealistic picture homoge-
neous is, in fact, language. The author is so absorbed in the elements of
party invectives that he himself begins to produce a strange hybrid of
Zhdanov's musicology and Stalin's oratorical art:

> The intricate combinations of the xylophone and the bassoon, the kettle-
> drums and the twelve trumpets, the tubas and the piccolos—all these
> flabbergasting combinations—did not achieve the main thing: they did
> not excite anyone. The orchestra thundered, and the volume became
> staggeringly loud, but it nonetheless remained deformed. It was not able
> to conceal the empty coldness of the music. The listener asked, ever
> more insistently, "Who needs such compositions? Whom are they help-
> ing to live? Whom have they spiritually enriched?" Sometimes, in reply,
> words about the brave innovations of the composers would be thrown
> about. "What's the innovation?" he would ask, irritated. "In the garish-
> ness of the content? In the ugly, deafening loudness? Who is indulging
> the pointless exercises of this handful of persons that have lost touch
> with the people? (237)

The beginning of this passage—from the enumeration of the musical
instruments to the "staggeringly loud" volume—sounds quite Zhda-
novian. On the other hand, the second part—with the cascading questions, the familiar turns of asking and answering, the sarcastic phrases
such as "such compositions" and "brave innovations," and, finally, the
typical Stalinist interest in who is secretly "indulging" the "handful" of
renegades—betrays the author as a painstaking copyist.

The composer's connection to the listener is not only the guarantee of success, but also the key to creative working itself. Generally
speaking, the author conceives of the audience's influence in a quite
literal way; when Aliev and Voloshin want to verify how the listener

will interpret their new operas, they go to a workers' club, perform fragments of their future productions there, and watch the reactions of the working-class listeners: "Collective taste, like a hard chisel, cut out everything unsuccessful or immature, ground off what was superfluous, and imbued the successes with luster and strength. The authors would try to see concentration, and sympathy, and, as might be the case, distraction, on [the listeners'] faces. Thus, little by little it would become clear what had slipped past them and what had succeeded in leaving a lasting impression in their memory" (732).

The requisite that followed after "accessibility" was "realism," which was evidenced in "images." The novel speaks endlessly about such images: Giliarevskii and Snegin are constantly accused of creating "distorted images," "cold images," or "false images." The singers contend that Snegin's opera can be sung only in a "mechanical" fashion since, as one of the female singers says, "I can't feel or see the image" (576); only by capitulating to the director did the singers, as the author informs us, "temporarily cease perceiving the falseness of the images that they had to sculpt" (627). In other words, the images come across as "false," still unmaterialized.

This elusive "image" is the foundation of "realism," a subject about which the theater's party secretary, Ipatov, talks constantly:

The opera has Soviet people in it—Marina, Sushchev, partisans, kolkhozniks. . . . But to tell you the truth, I can't see any Soviet features in them. You must not depict our person *[nash chelovek]* this way; this is falsity and hypocrisy. . . . You have some kind of Hamlets singing; everybody has so many complexities in his soul, you want to scream bloody murder. What kind of "heroism" is this? It's boring soul-searching. It has nothing whatsoever to do with our understanding of heroism. And I won't even start on the musical language. . . . Do you really think this is how the party raised the question of the Soviet person's image in art? If you would just look at the resolution concerning the drama theaters' repertoire. . . . (208)

But one could just as easily have "looked at" the resolution concerning the cinema, in which Eisenstein was accused of "Hamletism."

Ipatov never tires of talking about realism. "Even before the war, the party warned several composers, including Snegin, but you're citing his authority," he tells the theater director. "The heartrending voices keep saying that he's known all over the world. But just who makes up this so-called world abroad—that's what I'd like to know. . . . These ideological questions are not just an experiment. You're not asking yourself the simple question of whether his music is realistic, is it truthful" (583). Ipatov asks the director Kalganov about *The Partisan Girl:* "But is it truthful in tone? Can you say, after verifying it against the tuning fork that should resonate in your conscience as a Communist, that it is truthful?" (235). The embarrassed Kalganov is dumbstruck. And even when Voloshin asks Ipatov, "Aren't you exaggerating the faults of Snegin's opera, Pavel Artem'evich? It has good parts in it, outright outstanding ones," the only thing the party organizer can say is, "But it's too removed from realism!" (621). What this "realism" is becomes clear from the musicological analysis of the opera that Ipatov himself provides: "Is Marina—a Soviet girl, and a heroine besides—really a partisan? Twenty measures in a row—what is *that?* You have her singing on the high notes, in the most annoying register, challenging the people to a rebuff, expressing feelings of indignation. . . . Why, this is hysterics, not a challenge!" (410).

But try as he might, Ipatov (a former trumpet player!) cannot convince his colleagues that he is right. It is not surprising that the idea of party leadership takes on intricate forms for him. When he is stepping into the entrance of the Composers' House, for instance, he has a sudden epiphany: "Ipatov was amazed by how much music was coming from all the floors. He thought, irritatedly, that there was too little order in it. They were doing *so* much composing! Could they really not do it in such a way that the music of the composers living there would start flowing like water flows over a field, guided by solicitous hands?" Voloshin, who was one of the composers living there, remarked, "They ought to force Giliarevskii to work some other way. And I mean that— force him to" (101).

But the main concern of the party leaders, of course, was the listener, whom the formalist composers had forgotten. Accessibility was the main thing the party demanded of music. Thus, if the author takes his hero to the factory, then it is not only so that the latter can meet with the workers who are interested in how "music is born from labor and from life" (242), but also so that the director can correct him and, at the same time, can explain to Snegin that music cannot be "naturalistic" and the composer cannot be "a slave of the rhythms surrounding him" (243). In this way he anticipates, as it were, what a certain person "acting as chairman" (that is, Zhdanov) will say at an assembly in the Central Committee after the flop of Snegin's opera, that in this case the music will "recall the noise on a construction site when excavators, stone crushers, and cement mixers are all working" (455). Indeed, some of the characters simply orate as if from the transcript of this assembly. This is especially true of Snegin's father-in-law: "Do you think I'm the only one who's so backward? Ask anyone you like: the listener has had enough of this cacophony and confusion; it makes him sick. Get together any audience and put one of the ultramodern composers face to face with them—what do you think they'll tell him?" (455).

The novel advances inevitably toward the flop of Snegin's opera: "The production that was intended to show images of Soviet people in opera never reached Soviet people—the false, distorted images evoked disappointment, irritation, and bitterness" (648). The flop in turn leads to the Central Committee assembly, which is presented as a sort of act of redemption and a reach for something higher. In this sanctuary, people are completely changed: "Everyone was filled with a special, new feeling; an hour before that, they had heard a speech that went down in the history of the people's spiritual culture" (693). (The reference is, of course, to Zhdanov's speech.) Snegin is shaken by the weightiness of the event:

> Suddenly, he caught himself staring intently at the Central Committee members sitting behind the table. . . . The realization that he was in the presence of Stalin's closest assistants, that they were the ones now interested in music's problems, took hold of him, forced him to forget everything else. Perhaps the day before they had taken part in deciding an issue with a new, grandiose building project, or new energy resources, or problems in natural science. Now they had invited musicians to the Central Committee; but perhaps that evening they would meet with philosophers or forestry specialists. The more Snegin thought about this, the more the feeling of amazement grew at the scale of their energy and the endlessness of their labor. . . . The measure by which the value of creative work was measured here was different; it was completely different from that by which the artist measures himself. With a keenness that he had never felt before, Snegin understood the abyss that lay between creative works that left the listeners indifferent and cold and those that went to serve the people without holding anything back. (700)

Thus, as the assembly went on, even "attempts to defend his work only irritiated him, and they seemed inappropriate and dishonest" (701–2).

Snegin would not have been an artist if he had not felt the sweetness of torment, the beauty of the chairman-executioner's speech: "The speech of the assembly chair rose above everything else that he heard and that was incised into his memory. The force of its generalizations was irrefutable, and, having submitted to it, Snegin understood that it was referring to much more than himself alone: the whole group of composers had acted in unity; by diverting art away from the great road, they had done enormous damage to it. Sensitive to form, he took in the whole speech, completely, because it was perfect in form" (702). Snegin had heard, literally, the ready-made text on the basis of which his new "populist" work would soon be written. That is apparently why "he walked and walked, nowhere in particular, feeling a spiritual fullness he had never felt before" (703).

After the assembly, as after a cleansing storm that has passed over the world, the vault of heaven was finally high and clear: "The ideas of populism and realism ultimately won out; formalism was routed, and no more does anything hinder the development of art; the mishmash, confusion, and muddle all came to an end" (694–95). But it was not only the musicians that matured before one's very eyes; it was also the audiences: "After the Central Committee resolution about music, the listener—everyone could feel this—rose up with greater responsibility and had a great feeling of expectation regarding art. The whole atmosphere of artistic life was, as it were, ozonized by the resolution" (722).

Giliarevskii had nothing to say at the assembly; Snegin, on the other hand, made "a short but honest and sincere speech, in which he acknowledged both his former path and the opera that he had created to be fallacious" (696). Here the image of Snegin again begins to split: first Shostakovich becomes Muradeli, and then he agrees with Koval'. Be that as it may, after the assembly the hero turns up at the factory to meet the same workers who had regarded him with admiration before the flop at the Bolshoi Theater. He makes them a solemn promise: "If I had managed to write a quartet or a symphony, that still wouldn't have been the answer. The answer might be the opera that I'm thinking I'll write" (736). Here the author steps away from his hero and looks around the hall with him: "Good, dear faces, trusting eyes. . . . At that moment he suddenly felt that he could actually compose something good, something very good, that would come from the bottom of his heart" (736). This meant an opera that was truly populist.

Most likely, this is how the *Anti-Formalist Rayok* came to be.

*

So why is the opposite of "populism" not "ideological unconscientiousness" (which is the enemy of "ideological conscientiousness" and "party spirit"), nor "rootless cosmopolitanism" (to which "Soviet patriotism" stands opposed), nor "anti-historicism" (the opposite of "historicism" and "a solicitous attitude toward the past") but rather "formalism" (which existed only as a trend in aesthetic theory)? Ultimately, formalism is not a style, nor a "method," nor an ideology, nor a corpus of artistic texts. It is *only* a methodology. On the contrary, populism is a style *and* a trend *and* an ideology. In brief, whatever it might be, it is *anything but* a methodology. What was called "formalism" in Stalinist culture was modernism, which was truly the opposite of populism according to a great range of parameters (anti-traditionalism, "innovation"/tradition, professionalism/spirituality, device/content, rationalism/emotionalism, internationalism/nationalism, and so forth); besides which, "ideological conscientiousness," "party spirit," "historicism," patriotism, and "a solicitous attitude toward the past" are, after all, merely different aspects of populism. However, it was by no means accidental that out of all this spectrum, what was chosen to stand opposed to populism was "form."

Populism (as a *category* for describing art) is not simply anti-modernism but, more precisely, anti-formalism; this is because, as distinct from the other key definitions in Stalinist aesthetics—party spirit or class consciousness, even realism and "typicalness"—populism is itself devoid of form. It is a category that could never be distinctly articulated. To ultimately define it (that is, to give it a form) would have meant defining Soviet art as anti-modernist nationalist kitsch, as a conservative aesthetic utopia, or as party-oriented ideological primitivism. It is worth noting that in this context, the discussion goes far beyond the boundaries of music, strictly speaking (and of art in general); at issue is the Soviet variant of modernization as the alternative to the European (bourgeois) project of the modern and modernization, the latter being defined by some scholars as "conservative modernization." Soviet socialism was by no means the product of "historical progress" but rather a reaction to liberalism, modernization, and individualism—this "fruits of the Enlightenment" reaction to the bourgeois-individualistic political and economic project.

Populism (as a *characteristic* inherent in art) likewise rejects, above all, form: "the people" (or nation), as the product of an ideological construct, knows no form since, if given one, it loses its defining characteristic, the magic of simulative logic of virtual ideological constructs (such as spirituality or irrational "love for the Fatherland") and ceases to fulfill its most basic function in de-realizing life. Historically, the principle of populism was always affirmed through an idea of wholeness and organicity. Even before Uvarov and Aleksandr Shishkov, Friedrich von Schlegel understood "the people" as an organic whole. For obvious reasons, any German legacy in the roots of populism was not even mentioned in the Zhdanov era. On the contrary, the idea of populism was linked to an organicity that was alien to any "form" whatsoever. Russian art was "organic," and there was a reflection of its spirituality in its "formlessness," while "form" was, on the contrary, the very thing alien to Russian spiritual liberty, something Western, European, and above all rationalist in a German way. Paradoxically, the originally German "populism" returned as an alien (and specifically German) rationalism and "formalism." Viktor Shklovskii quipped that according to an old custom, Russian flax returns to Russia as Dutch linen; we might add that this is only so that it can again turn into flax.

"Formalism" is the key to populism in Stalinist culture; it was used in an oblique sense and, as one can see, was a metaphor that—in a reverse reading—allows one to understand the content of populism itself. *Populism is the image of the masses as the authorities wanted to see them.* Since they were a completely ideal quantity, a "sublime object" of power, "*the* people" needed a referent. But since real people could not be such a referent, art busied itself with the mass-media production of "The People"—its own consumer and the fundamental generator of populism. In this respect, populism is a functional rather than a qualitative definition; it is not a characteristic but an industry that is busy fulfilling an urgent political task. After all, "The [virtual] People" expressing themselves in the product of this art—in songs about the forests, cantatas in defense of peace, tales about the Siberian land, in the new operas of the Snegins and symphonies of the Golovins—do not simply replace real people. In the process of de-realizing life, they lose any kind of paths and means of articulation whatsoever. This "side effect" of Soviet artistic production was, essentially, the fundamental "effect." There, a new aesthetic law was established: "Art serves the people" to the extent that the people serve art. As a result, to the extent that real people were transformed into the audience of the heroic and "elegant" cantatas and oratorios, Soviet art created the medium in which authority no longer needed the extraordinary terroristic measures that it had required in the 1930s for the legitimization of its own power. The state thereby compensated the replacement of the real with the sublime. Having already happened in life, this replacement continued also in art so that it finally became the real "reflection of life." In other words, it became "ultimately populist."

6 *Gesamtwissenschaftswerk*

Romantic Naturalism and Life in Its Revolutionary Development

STATE ROMANTICISM

> Said he: Polyphony is over—
> Your love of Mozart was in vain,
> Now comes arachnid stone deafness,
> The rift here is stronger than our strength.[1]

Poets rarely deal with themes from the natural sciences, but the poem "Lamarck," written by Osip Mandel'shtam in May 1932 at the height of the Stalinist revolution, is utterly full of "the noise of time" that was heard by contemporaries. Thus Nadezhda Mandel'shtam wrote that "it is no longer apostasy and isolation from real life but the horrible collapse of living creatures who have forgotten Mozart and rejected everything (the brain, vision, hearing) in this realm of arachnid deafness. Everything is horrible, like a biological process in reverse."[2] But in this there is yet another face that is turned not so much toward sociopolitical history as toward the intellectual and cultural history of the late 1920s and early 1930s, when a heated debate flared up between Darwinists and the proponents of neo-Lamarckism, which had emerged in the early twentieth century on a wave of anti-positivism in philosophy, science, and aesthetics. As Boris Gasparov so pointedly observed, "The utopian ideas of this time about the 'transformation of nature'—especially the early experiments of T. D. Lysenko—were in one way or another tied to neo-Lamarckism. In this context a dynamic idea of evolution that foregrounded 'transformation' of an organism was considered a revolutionary, dialectical approach. On the other hand, genetics, which asserted the impossibility of inheriting acquired characteristics, was equated to a form of the mechanistic 'objectivism' characteristic of capitalist-era science."[3]

Despite the fact that neo-Lamarckism and Bergsonism were condemned for "idealism," genetics remained hostile to "Marxist biology." Neo-Lamarckism was not eradicated in Soviet science. To Lamarck's "idealism" was contrasted Leibniz's "metaphysics," which influenced the shaping of Darwin's ideas, his "trite evolutionism." Darwin could not be forgiven for repeating, more than once, Leibniz's formula "Nature does not make leaps." This was newly remembered in 1950, when a debacle in linguistics broke out and Stalin spoke out against the Marrist ideas of "leaps in development." It emerged that leaps in the development of language were impossible, but in the development of living matter—inevitable; the "Mendelist-Morganists" were criticized for asserting the immutability of the substance of heredity; not recognizing the inheritance of acquired characteristics; and suggesting that heredity is changed by mutation, by chance, and does not depend upon the organism's living conditions. In other words, geneticists asserted the same thing as did Marr's opponents, with whom Stalin had joined. Two years after supporting Lysenko in 1948, Stalin took up a directly opposite role; the Lysenkovian romanticist turned into the anti-Marr realist. Darwin was charged with "trite evolutionism and denial of leaps."[4] In the Marxist schema of German classical philosophy, Lamarck assumed the place of Hegel (a dialectician but an idealist) and Darwin that of Feuerbach (a materialist but a metaphysician). Thus a niche was created for synthesis—the "Marxist" Lysenko. Lysenko's dialectical idea was similar to Marr's idea, for whom any languages could be compared with any others. In the same way for Lysenko, the grains of rye could be discerned in the ears of wheat, the grains of wild oats in the panicle of domestic oats, and the seeds of the turnip families in the spermatophyte of cabbage. According to Lysenko's "agrobiology," this indicated that "the process of gradual qualitative change leads to a leap and the formation of a new species."[5]

A revolution always contains a strong romantic charge within itself, and the Russian Revolution was no exception. In this light, Lysenko's theory, just like Marr's theory, with its vehement criticism of the positivism that preceded it (whether it was comparative linguistics or genetics), "functioned as one of the manifestations of the romantic-revolutionary spirit that opposed positivist science 'in the Victorian spirit.'"[6] A comparison of the two most influential ideological campaigns of the late-Stalinist era—in biology and linguistics—that Stalin initiated and in which he then took a most direct and fervent part, indicates that revolutionary romanticism remained an important part of the late-Stalinist politico-aesthetic project. Transformed, this romanticism became one of the main elements of the entire politico-ideological construct of Stalinism, a construct based on dialectical counterweights necessary for the political instrumentalization of the ideological campaigns in the various sciences.

The use of romantic, class-oriented discourse at some points and realistic-scientific discourse at others was politically instrumental, and hence one never really abrogated the other. There is nothing "earth-shaking," of course, about Stalin's 1950 rejection of romantic Prometheanism, class-oriented science, and 1948-style party-mindedness, nor anything that radically changed, as some have suggested, the whole paradigm of Soviet discourse. David Joravsky, Alexei Yurchak, and Ethan Pollock, for example, are inclined to think that Stalin's turn-around toward "objective scientific value" in 1950 supposedly signified a rejection of "party-mindedness" in favor of the "objective laws of science" and became a precursor (if not the beginning) of the Thaw era.[7] But the reality is that Stalin defended romanticism and voluntarism in 1948 just as easily as he did realism and scientific rigor in 1950 and then successfully synthesized them in 1952 in the course of the economic discussion. Political expediency was the dominant factor in each case.

The politico-aesthetic dimension of the natural science themes—or rather the themes tied to the science of life, biology, that occupied such an important place in the Soviet intellectual and cultural history of the late-Stalinist era, which we will address—is tied to the trend in art that would seem to be the remotest from science: romanticism. Nor was it any coincidence that revolutionary romanticism, precisely, turned out to be the precursor of Socialist Realism. Ultimately, the idea of creativity and created life lies at the heart of romanticism—an idea central to both biology and Socialist Realism. It is the creative principle that unites such different (if not to say opposite) spheres as art and science. Romanticism can be thought of as their point of intersection—the moment of the creative act, of the rebellion against long-held notions, of the confrontation of stagnation and established norms and canons. It is the domain of dissidence (suffice it to recall Zamiatin's idea that art is always the destiny of heretics, which is also true for science). At this juncture the contrasts from which the relations between art/science and life are cut out reveal themselves. Thus the striving of science for clarity and precision contradicts the freedom it needs as a condition for its existence. And science is thereby alien to the romantic disposition since after all romantics "loved nebulae and indistinctness. Where everything is brought to clarity, there is no freedom."[8]

Although realism should be more akin to science, "competition with reality" itself is a "romantic utopia," the use of which Naum Berkovskii saw in that art, in its striving to "rise to the level of reality . . . acquired new mysterious powers that did not serve romanticism as much as it did the artistic realism that was replacing it and did replace it."[9] The era of romanticism in natural science and its culmination in "creative Darwinism," which we will discuss here, also turned out to be historically justified by the fact that its chief adepts, such as Trofim Lysenko or Ol'ga Lepeshinskaia, essentially committed an act of self-destruction by opening a path to realism (genetics).

In yet another aspect Socialist Realism turned out to be akin to romanticism—in the orientation toward a heroic creative personality. In Socialist Realism, just as in romanticism, these were the great scientists, artists, fighters against routine, and revolutionaries who with their creative energy transform reality. The genius of these creators does not submit to rules but rather creates them. Just as in romanticism, the birth of which accompanied the growth of nationalism, such heroes in Socialist Realism often were a part of politically instrumentalized "useful history." The birth of national heroes in Stalinism is an echo of the romantic genesis of Socialist Realism, which could be called *state romanticism*. As we know, Socialist Realism emerged simultaneously as a political instrument and an aesthetic program. As distinct from its political curators (Stalin, Zhdanov, Shcherbakov), its chief adepts (Gorky, Lunacharskii) saw it from the beginning as a synonym of revolutionary

romanticism. Gorky declared outright that "revolutionary romanticism is essentially a pseudonym of socialist realism,"[10] and Lunacharskii spoke of "socialist romanticism."[11]

The relations between Socialist Realism and revolutionary romanticism always remained complicated and muddled since from RAPP
times the latter was closely associated with reactionary idealism, subjectivism, agnosticism, and mysticism. Realism, on the contrary, was
associated with progressivism and materialism. Nonetheless, the logic
of the deformation of reality in Socialist Realism, at the heart of which
lies "life in its revolutionary development," cannot be understood without a "romantic" component. Socialist Realism drank in revolutionary
romanticism (a bright and fruitful trend in early Soviet art), instrumen-
talizing and transforming it into *state romanticism,* which definitively
came together in the late-Stalinist era.

If in the first years after the introduction of Socialist Realism the
discussions about its combination of realism and revolutionary romanticism (since this was the platform Gorky advanced) were tolerated,[12]
then from the late 1930s (with the death of Gorky, the return of former
RAPPists to leading roles in the literary hierarchy, and the strengthening of the positions of the journal *Literaturnyi kritik* and the group of
György Lukács and Mikhail Lifshits in it) mentions of "red romanticism" disappeared. In the postwar era (after the discussion of Socialist
Realism in the journal *Oktiabr'*, the ascension of Vladimir Ermilov's
"militant theory of literature," and later the struggle against "conflictlessness") revolutionary romanticism became a negative concept and
politically rather dangerous (it was suggested that the people fighting
for "revolutionary romanticism" found Soviet reality insufficiently romantic).[13] The irony was that in the late-Stalinist era of the triumph of
"revolutionary romanticism" in "Michurinist biology" and the "visible features of communism," in the "great Stalinist structures" and the
"conflictless" heroes filling the pages of Soviet journals, its very mention became impossible.

In fact, there were profound differences between romanticism and
Socialist Realist *state romanticism:* if the former asserted the sharp
conflict (even up to the point of explosion) between dreaming and reality, then the latter arose from their merger; if the former spoke of the
death of an ideal, then the latter asserted its victory; if the former asserted tragedy, romantic irony, pessimism, and despair, then the latter,

on the contrary, proclaimed heroicism and historical optimism; if the former cultivated solitude and individualism, the latter embraced collectivism; if the former suffered from passivity, then the latter affirmed activism and the remaking of reality; if the former saw its ideal in the past, then the latter looked to the future (which was most strikingly manifested in the assertion of variability and the denial of heredity and genetics in Soviet biology).

Many elements of romantic aesthetics, too, were variously transformed in Socialist Realism. Thus, if in accordance with romantic irony, a dead romantic hero is the ideal, then the Socialist Realist hero himself embodies this ideal (here, by the way, there are also features of similarity: the titanism of the romantic hero in his struggle against the hostile forces of nature and the elements is akin to that of his Socialist Realist protagonist). The conflict between dreaming and reality (the prose of life and the poetry of the dream) is conditioned by the romantic concept of both the dream (the beautiful, the perfect and the unattainable, inscrutable by reason) and of reality itself (which is base, soulless, and ridden with philistinism). Hence the rejection of the latter as humdrum and prosaically limiting. Hence, too, the resort to the irrational, the pretersensual, and the tendency toward the grotesque and toward fantasy. All of this was contraindicated by Socialist Realism. No less alien to it was romanticism's characteristic conflict between the individual and society and its solitary hero, who embodies the idea of the fight against tyranny. A powerful individual who rises up against society's laws was in Socialist Realism an image that belonged exclusively to the past. Hence it exhausts also its interest in the fantastic, which here should figure in "the forms of life itself," even if speaking about the heroes of national folklore or fantasy/fairytale characters; Lysenko himself (the "people's academician") and the agronomic miracles produced by his "magical" science are just such phenomena.

Nonetheless, the marriage of Socialist Realism and romanticism was far more lasting than it might seem. Socialist Realism is the aesthetic of a regime that had long ago lost any ties whatsoever to its beginnings in Marxist "enlightenment" roots. This populist politico-aesthetic project proved to be consonant with the romantic anti-Enlightenment spirit, the romantic reaction to Enlightenment rationalism. The only difference was that Socialist Realism, as a politically instrumentalized project, did not abolish but rather synthesized opposing principles, with the aim of ideologically manipulating them. Thus, if romanticism contrasted the cult of nature to the Enlightenment cult of reason, and the idea of *returning* to roots to the Enlightenment idea of *progress,* Socialist Realist revolutionary romanticism combined the one with the other, dialectically asserting an idea of "historical *progress*" through a "Great *Retreat.*" If the romantics spoke out against materialism and mechanistic empiricism and to replace the rationality of classicist conflicts introduced the free personality and a rebellious subjectivism that repudiated social and moral laws, then the volitional principle dominant in Socialist Realist "revolutionary romanticism," which called for going beyond the boundaries of reason and the limits of physical possibilities, was fully concordant with romantic intuition and fantasy. If instead of the Enlightenment's Higher Reason, romanticism consolidated the ideas of pantheism and a Living God, then Socialist Realism confirmed an atheistic religion with a cult at the heart of which stood an eternally living Stalin. The central aesthetic category of both romanticism and Socialist Realist *state romanticism* is that of the sublime. What is formless, irrational, eternal, and evocative of amazement is all typical of both romanticism and Socialist Realism. Finally, Socialist Realist romanticism shares with romanticism the idea of a synthesis of the arts, which is the apex in the aesthetic of romanticism.

Few could combine all these antinomies in theory and embody them in practice better than Trofim Lysenko.

AGROBIOLOGY: NATURAL-SCIENCE ROMANTICISM IN ACTION

The "people's academician" Trofim Denisovich Lysenko was in every sense a Socialist Realist character. An iconic figure in Stalinist culture, today he is regarded as nothing more than a "charlatan of science." However, Lysenko's ideas were rooted in revolutionary culture, and the "author" of these ideas was a skilled manipulator of revolutionary fantasies.[14] The Lysenko phenomenon, which was most vividly exposed in the postwar years, is interesting as the culmination of revolutionary romanticism in the Stalin era, as the radical realization of the Socialist Realist politico-aesthetic project.[15] The political instrumentalization of romantic fantasy-making allowed Lysenko to gain unprecedented influence in biology, all the more striking as his entire "path in science" was based on falsification, and his ascent was accompanied by the complete unverifiability of his "achievements," an ascent that caused tremendous damage to the country's economy.

At the heart of Lysenko's state romanticism, where the environment triumphed over heredity, lay no knowledge of nature and its laws but rather a justification of biology as the science of seizure and submission. The triumph of this ideology cloaked in biological metaphors and the creation of the army of its enemies in the form of "Weismanist-Mendelist-Morganist" bogeymen signaled a decisive instrumentalization of science for the purposes of political mobilization.

In Lysenko's numerous speeches and writings we encounter ideological metaphors; Lysenko is interesting as a politically astute ideologue, a persistent doctrinaire, a flexible orator, and—by no means least of all—an experienced philologist who knew and used as arguments in scientific, political, economic, and, ultimately, personal debates certain "facts" from the science of agrobiology that he invented.[16] As the creator of "advanced biological science," Lysenko of course rejected Darwinism, which had traditionally been a cornerstone of the "materialistic worldview." For him, the chief interest in Darwin was as a teleologist and philosopher of expediency: "By his theory of selection, Darwin gave a rational explanation of expediency in living nature."[17] The requirement for *expediency* was to become central in Lysenko's understanding not only of nature, but also of the tasks of science. However, there was no love affair with Darwin. The obstacles for Lysenko (as they were later for Ol'ga Lepeshinskaia) were positivism and "evolutionism": Darwin recognized only "quantitative changes"; there was "no origin of the new in the nuclei of the old," no "transition of one quality into another." Failing to find in Darwinism Hegel's "laws of dialectic" as they were interpreted in the philosophical chapter of Stalin's *Short Course,* Lysenko pinned a political label on Darwinism ("a theory of sheer gradualism *[postepenovshchina]*" [316]) and introduced the idea of progress into evolutionary science by defining species as "stages" or "steps of the gradual historical development of the organic world" (321).

Lysenko saw his task as interbreeding Darwinism with "Marxism." However, the latter was present for him in the form of two pre-Marx components: the dialectics of Hegel and the materialism of Feuerbach. Only Marx's revolutionarism remains—namely, the requirement for "transformation and change of the world." This requirement, as Lysenko thought, was satisfied only by one theory, that of Ivan Michurin. Michurin was proclaimed the "dead father" of the new science of life (such "dead fathers" had to exist in every sphere; in Socialist Realism, for instance, Gorky and Mayakovsky were proclaimed to be such figures, as they bore the light, as it were, of the ever-living Father). Michurin's theory, Lysenko declared, "elevated Darwinism to a fundamentally new level, changed it from a theory explaining the origin of various organic forms into a theory that gives agricultural practice the possibility of transforming the organic world" (417).

All spheres of biological existence underwent a profound transformation in this light. What occurred here, right before one's eyes, was not so much an extrapolation of Marxist theory onto the world of "living nature" (which had already been done by Engels) as *a transformation of biology into total metaphor*. The arena of knowledge modeling is transformed into a sort of conceptual cell of "Marxist laws." This process can be observed not only in formulas such as "the transformation of one species into another occurs in leap-wise fashion" (60), but also in broad generalizing constructions. We will pause on one of these that is tied to a key concept in biology: interspecific struggle, which constitutes a direct parallel to the key concept in Marxism, class struggle.

"The property of self-thinning [*samoizrezhivanie*], inherent in wild vegetation, especially forest sorts," Lysenko asserted, "is essentially that dense shoots of a particular species by their mass oppose other species in a struggle and at the same time regulate their own numbers such that they do not interfere with each other, do not compete with each other" (407). This picture is undoubtedly an allegory; nature is wisely set up (it has no [capitalist] "competition") in exactly the same way socialism is. So that this might be even clearer, Lysenko in another work (entering into open polemic against Darwin) leads the reader to a conclusion about the absence of "intraspecific competition"; there is only interspecific (read: class) struggle: "It would be incorrect to assume that rabbits, for instance, suffer, although indirectly, more adversities from each other because they are more similar in their needs than animals of other species, for instance, wolves or foxes, not to mention all kinds of infectious diseases caused in rabbits by organisms very distant from them in terms of species and genera" (371). Total allegorism finally leads Lysenko "to a rejection of intraspecific struggle and the cooperation of individuals within the species [class?] and recognition of interspecific struggle and competition, and likewise to cooperation among different species [class struggle?]" (61). Marxism is transformed into an actual reservoir of metaphors, into a totally aesthetic phenomenon.

Explaining the theory of the hated "Mendelism-Morganism" in a popular style, Lysenko stated that every chicken comes from an egg, but not a single egg develops from a chicken; eggs develop directly from eggs, and thus the "body of the chicken" cannot exert any influence at all on heredity. Hence, what develops does not enter into heredity; the "embryonic plasma" is everywhere active. Instead of an "egg-egg" scheme, Lysenko advocates an "egg-organism-egg" scheme (goods-money-goods?), while the "living body" of the chicken, which must be influenced to change heredity, is central.

Before we go on to Lysenko's fundamental idea ("influence on heredity"), let us turn our attention to the living/dead opposition. "Dead elements of nature," Lysenko wrote, "in assimilating to a living body, cease to be what they had been, not only in appearance, but in a strictly chemical way as well" (203). Stylistics is important here; the awkward constructions of "what it actually is" or "what they had been" are a sort of shock-absorber, to take away the brunt, since the apparent meaning of this statement leads to the dead becoming alive: "Dead nature is the origin of the living" (238). Faced with this, the boldest fantasies about the management of heredity faded.

"The nature of the living body," Lysenko continues, "is fundamentally different from the nature of the dead body. The more a dead body is isolated from the influence of or interaction with conditions of the external environment, the longer it will remain what it is. But the living body obligatorily requires certain conditions of the external environment in order to be alive. If a living body is isolated from the external conditions necessary to it, it will cease to be what it is. This constitutes the fundamental difference between the nature of the living and the dead body" (160).

This definition, which conceals behind stylistic correctness a complete absurdity, is in and of itself important; the characteristics of "living" versus "dead" are given not by definition of the internal state of the "body" but via certain external characteristics. Meanwhile, some sort of situation is imagined in which some "body" (whether "living" or "dead" is unimportant) can exist outside of "external conditions."

It might be supposed that this has something to do with a kind of "un-shaped" substance that Ol'ga Lepeshinskaia discovered since in principle any "body" has to be located in "conditions" that are "external" in relation to it; otherwise, it loses any identity and "corporality"; it "ceases to be what it is"—that is, a "body." As a result, this whole construct turns out to be irrelevant to the definition of "living" or "dead." One might suppose that this is a stylistic figure, an ordinary sophism based on a number of repetitions from which something completely incongruous "follows." In this regard, the cited text recalls the constructs of Stalinist narratives. But in fact the connection here is much more profound. It is not only a matter of stylistics, but indeed of constructs of thought.

Lysenko's constructs are completely invented shams, which makes them definitively akin to Stalinist logic. In fact, Lysenko allows no rebuttals at all: "In our understanding, the whole organism consists only of the ordinary body well known to all. There is no special substance at all in the organism that is distinct from the ordinary body" (193). Meanwhile, inconceivable things occur with this "living body":

> External conditions, once excluded and assimilated by the living body, are no longer external conditions but internal—that is, they become particles of the living body and for their own growth and development now require the food and the conditions of the external environment that they themselves had been in the past. The living body, as it were, consists of individual elements of the external environment that have been transformed into elements of a living body. . . . Thus, by management of the conditions of life, it is possible to include in a living body new conditions of the external environment or to exclude one or another element from the living body. (166)

So the "living body" appears, as it were, not to have anything external to itself—everything "external" turns out to be not simply internal but rather a component of the "living body." Perhaps what is being suggested is not simply a "living body" that is "anima-ted" but rather, concretely, an "anima" or consciousness—that is, the same formless "essence" that Lepeshinskaia discovered. Thus all the operations Lysenko described working on this "body"—management, control, change directed into the direction necessary to "mankind," and so forth—acquire a quite definite attribution. This is not about biology but precisely about power over the body and about the techniques of its functioning—that is, *about politics*. In this context, Lysenko's explanations become understandable: "By external we understand every-thing that is being assimilated, and by internal, that which assimilates" (174). The whole world of the "living body" ends up in the field of power and subjugation since the processes of assimilation are the func-tions of power.

As Lysenko sees it, this creates enormous practical perspectives. For example, in horticulture and in animal husbandry, by raising new va-rieties one can "not only preserve, but indeed reinforce the needed he-reditary characteristics and the qualities of the original parent forms" (13). Hence the intensification of the criticism of Darwinism, which "assumes recognition of only quantitative changes—changes simpli-fied only to increase or decrease—and overlooks, or rather does not know, the necessity and regularity of transformations, transitions from one qualitative condition to another" (14–15). But in Lysenko's hands, "from being a science that primarily explains the past history of the organic world, Darwinism becomes a creative, effective means for sys-tematic mastery, from the practical perspective, of living nature" (59).

"Soviet creative Darwinism" is a purely political phenomenon, and thus it is totally dialectical; it rejects both the "one-sided, flat evolution-ism" (315) ("flat evolution without leaps" that exposes "metaphysical thinking" [60]) of Darwin and the "idealism" of Lamarck but takes "materialism" from Darwinism and the idea of "active development" ("dialectic") from Lamarckism. But since the center of study becomes "natural-historical laws," Lysenko provides the reader with not only dialectical materialism, but also historical materialism. He owes all of this to "Michurin's theory—creative Darwinism" (15), but "the Stalin-ist theory of gradual, hidden, and unnoticeable quantitative changes that lead to rapid qualitative radical changes, helped Soviet biologists to observe in plants the facts of realization of qualitative transitions, of transformation of one species into another" (16).

The basis of Lysenko's theory is a peculiar understanding of the *tasks* of "scientific knowledge." He shapes these tasks in accordance with the "transformative activity of the Party," and thus the categories of "regularity" and "coincidence" become central; "formalist bourgeois genetics" (332) is bad (and "formalist" and "bourgeois") because it is constructed on coincidence.

Science, according to Lysenko, must "foresee," "be active," must provide "planning" and "perspective," and "be practical." In other words, it must control—that is, exercise—the functions of power. In biology this means "controlling and purposefully changing the nature (heredity) of organisms" (254). Hence from the understanding of the functions of scientific knowledge arises the polemic with August Weissmann, according to whom "hereditary substance" is independent of the "living body"—that is, essentially uncontrollable and not subject to any kind of influence. We are dealing with transformed ideology; if we put man in the place of the "living body," then the very idea of education and reeducation—and more broadly, of social "controllability"— becomes ineffectual; if in the place of "scientific foresight" we put the well-known subject of this foresight, "Marxist-Leninist theory," and in place of "agricultural practice," the "socially transformative activity" of power, then both turn out to be completely meaningless.

Hence Lysenko characterizes Thomas Morgan's "'science' about the nature of living bodies" as "powerless," while "our Michurinist agrobiological science" is "effective." "Hereditary" in Lysenko's interpretation turns out to be the dead counterbalanced to the living—the "living body" or "living substance" (as if by irony, one of the sections of his report at the infamous session of the Lenin All-Union Academy of Agricultural Sciences in August 1948 was titled "The *Fruitlessness* of Morganism-Mendelism" [emphasis added]). Lysenko's formula, on the contrary, is a call for action and control: "Heredity is the effect of the concentration of influences and conditions of the external environment assimilated by organisms in a number of preceding generations" (53). Thus heredity is a completely controllable phenomenon and can even become a product of such control. Lysenko indicates the path to this control: the famous "vernalization," or "deliberate control of the development of field plants" (84). This was tied to the idea of "development in stages" in which, according to Lysenko, the same laws of dialectic applied: "The varieties of wheat existing in nature, and similarly of rye and barley, are not limited to sharply isolated groups, one winter and the other spring. They are tied by transitional series from more winter to less winter, i.e., to spring. The winter forms, being represented by a correspondingly selected array of varieties, gradually transition to spring forms, and vice versa, the spring forms to winter forms" (93).

Let us investigate the metamorphoses of this reforging of the "living body." The task is primarily to "slacken heredity" since "organisms with slackened heredity are more pliable, more plastic in the sense of acquiring new properties and characteristics needed by the experimenter. By raising the progeny of such pliable, plastic organisms in defined conditions from generation to generation, we get coordination of organs, functions, and processes; we get the new, relatively stable and reinforced—i.e., relatively conservative—heredity of the organism that we need" (451). If we remember that this is about the "living body," of which man is a sort, the Machiavellian nature of these biological fantasies becomes apparent.

But in the world of agrobiology—this sort of model of the Soviet socium—all the laws of a disciplinary society are at work. In general, everything is transparent in the allusive "Lysenko theory" (in this sense, the level of metaphor fully corresponded to the level of mature Socialist Realist writing). For example, the metamorphoses described there are particularly likely when (in the "environment") the "external conditions" are least appropriate (in the "weak link of imperialism"?), which requires a "tempering of varieties"—namely, "in regions with unfavorable overwintering conditions, and especially in localities with unfavorable development conditions, winter wheat can turn into rye" (16). The fact that the new "living body" was the product of "tireless concern" should likewise raise no doubts since, after all, the varieties of the new plants were also "created by means of strictly determined selection, including systematic breeding" (40). In the center of this whole breeding-disciplinary process stands the "mentor," a projection onto Michurin's "method of the mentor—the breeder and improver" (194) of the variety, so esteemed by Lysenko.

Lysenko describes this whole process in great detail, beginning with "slackened heredity" (that is, it is not only the new that is important, but also the path of struggle against the old). The plants ("living bodies") to which slackened heredity is ascribed are those "in which their conservatism is liquidated, and their selectivity to conditions of the external environment is weakened" (212). This is an important stage, after which work on "directed heredity" begins. But how does one "slacken" heredity? Lysenko indicates three ways: (1) by means of grafting (splicing plants of different species); (2) by means of influencing, at particular moments, through external environmental conditions, the course of one or another developmental process; and (3) by means of hybridization (particularly of sharply contrasting forms) (212). In the GULAG, for instance. . . .

The changes being spoken of are doubtlessly profound and organic. So "a changed branch or bud in a fruit tree, or an eye (bud) of a potato tuber, as a rule, cannot influence a change of heredity of the progeny of the said tree or tuber, which takes its direct beginning from the changed parts of the parent organism. But if one cuts off this changed part and grows it separately as an independent plant, then the latter, as a rule, will possess the already changed heredity" (49). What we see is a description of a process of socialization directed at the "progeny of the organism," a "cutting" (say, the socialization of a child by alienating him from his family through a pioneer organization, Komsomol, school, and other institutions, does in fact basically lead to the creation of an organism with "changed heredity").

Later the process will take off on its own since for the "new generation" all of the artificiality of the reforging will no longer be familiar and will become a natural "dwelling place": "The conditions that were inappropriate, unsuitable to one process or another of the preceding forms, will become normal to and necessary for the new generation" (219).

The whole thrust of Lysenko's theory is the passion for control of the "living body." For this reason, Michurin's favorite idea, which Lysenko called "the most important law" of Michurin's theory, was so essential: "With the interference of man, it is possible to force any form of animal or plant to change more quickly, and moreover in a direction desirable to mankind" (45).

It only remains to name this "man" and to learn that knowledge of the requirements of the "living body" provides the possibility of controlling its life and development. Control allows one to "establish the methods of changing" the nature of the organism "in a direction needed by mankind," which in turn permits "purposefully changing the heredity of organisms" (46–47).

Lysenko created a completely Machiavellian theory, not in the form of outright statements about ways of seizing and maintaining power, but in the guise of biological metaphors. This is why the nature of Lyskenko's scientific discourse is important. Its language is amazingly reminiscent of the hybrid, familiar in Stalinist texts, of bureaucratic and colloquial styles, and accessibility (all those "chickens and eggs," "rabbits and wolves," and the like). The language Lysenko wrote in was understandable to authority. Many of his passages are a sort of stylization of Stalinist discourse, so saturated are they with tautological ellipses and pleonasms.

Lysenko was a Socialist Realism–era revolutionary romantic. In a practical way, he translated Gorky's romantic anxieties into the discursive plane of late Stalinism. He could be called the new Gorky. What is Lysenko's formula—"The development of Darwinism in agroscience is primarily assimilation of Michurin's theory" (464), the basis of which is not to wait for "favors from nature" but to take them from it—if not a reformulation of Gorky's calls to "bridle nature"? What distinguishes Lysenko's zeal for agronomic "domestication" of the plants and animals created by foolish nature ("All varieties of domesticated plants are created on a good, cultivated agronomic foundation. In other words, good cultivated agrotechnology is the basis for the domestication of varieties of plants" [491]) from Gorky's "hymn to culture"? Even Gorky's inherent biologism in aesthetics is turned inside out in Lysenko's "mirror of science," which is turned upside down by aestheticism in biology. For example, Lysenko is incredibly enraged by the fact that Mendelians, "by their operations on a plant with the most powerful poison—colchicine—and by various other torturous influences on plants, *disfigure* these plants."[18] These "mutilated" plants cannot interbreed; they "suffer." "And the Mendelian geneticists of our Union call such *disfigurement* directed change of the nature of the organism!" Lysenko exclaims (335). Meanwhile, Michurin selected "*beautiful* varieties" and provided a "*beautiful* theory" (336; emphasis added). Lysenko repeated everything—right up to the passionate battle against the flies hated by Gorky—after the "founder of Socialist Realism."

We are witnesses of the process described by Michel Foucault as "expansion of the political field," to the extent that a scientist (Foucault primarily distinguishes biologists, evolutionists beginning with Darwin) turns into a politician, squeezing out the "universal intellectual" (who had come to replace the "great writer"). Characterizing this "new personality," Foucault writes, "He is no longer the rhapsodist of the eternal, but the strategist of life and death. Meanwhile we are at present experiencing the disappearance of the figure of the 'great writer.'"[19] How is one to know whether these are disappearances or births of the "new type of writer"? Merab Mamardashvili astutely noted that this kind of genetics "could be in [Andrei] Platonov's characters" and that Lysenko himself was "a purely literary phenomenon."[20]

AGROBIOLOGY: *ARGUMENTUM AD BACULUM*

The Lysenko phenomenon went far beyond the boundaries of science. Lysenkoism could not function outside the public sphere, and thus it was served by an extensive half-fantasy paraliterature (by Vadim Safonov, Vladimir Elagin, Gennadii Fish, Viacheslav Lebedev, Aleksandr Mikhalevich, Aleksandr Popovskii, and many other writers). The titles of the books about Lysenko are themselves telling: *The Art of Creation* (Popovskii; Moscow: Profizdat, 1948); *The Science of Abundance* (Fish; Moscow: Sovetskii pisatel', 1948); *A True Soviet Story* (Fish; Moscow: Molodaia gvardiia, 1949); *The Earth in Bloom* (Safonov; Moscow: Molodaia gvardiia, 1949). These books created an integral picture of reality as it was reflected in the fictive world of "Michurinist biology" and translated "creative Darwinism" from the language of science to that of the mass reader. Without them, many things in the new science would have remained incomprehensible to these readers. An army of journalists, science fiction writers, and poets served to produce them. However, the role of playwrights in all this is particularly interesting since theater personalized the events and brought them maximally close to the mass spectator, providing viewers with the "arguments and facts" of Michurinist science "in the forms of life itself."

The play *Sibiriachka* (1950), co-written by Evgenii Zagorianskii and science fiction writer Aleksandr Kazantsev, one of many works about events on the "biological front," gives us some idea of how this happened. The action takes place in a Siberian provincial city in 1946–48, in the period leading up to the infamous session of the Lenin All-Union Academy of Agricultural Sciences in August 1948, where Lysenko, supported by Stalin, finally destroyed Soviet genetics and established his monopoly in biology. The young biologist Aleksei Novikov, just returned from the front to his hometown laboratory and his former professor, Skrypnev, has completely "changed the landmarks" in science. As a student, he has, like everyone else, done experiments with fruit flies, which he has irradiated and then studied the genetic changes in the resulting mutants. But at the front, Aleksei met "a guy from Rostov" who bred branchy-eared wheat of a new, super-high-yield variety as a hobby. Now he wants to introduce a new variety himself, in the Lysenko way: the environment changes the plant, and then these changes are transmitted through heredity. Skrypnev and another of his pupils, the careerist Granovskii, are also trying to produce a new variety of Siberian wheat, but they are going about this through irradiation of the seeds.

Aleksei's fiancée, Natasha, is also Skrypnev's student and, coincidentally, the daughter of the regional party committee's secretary. Aleksei explains to her that they must not work "the old-fashioned way." A professional debate arises between these biologists in love. Natasha states that "acquired characteristics are not transmitted by inheritance. Genes are the substance of heredity. It [the substance] is unchanged, and cannot be influenced through the body! Think about fox terriers. For two hundred years their tales have been docked, but have you seen even one puppy born tailless?" Aleksei, who has read every issue of the *Vernalization* journal that Natasha had been regularly sending him on the front [*sic!*], declares in response that "it is not tail docking that is needed, but developing characteristics in organisms without which they cannot live." The absurdity of these arguments (one must suppose that if a dog was no longer fed meat, it would give birth to vegetarian puppies) is concealed behind the urgency of the goal: Aleksei is against "playing blind man's bluff" with nature. "That is not science! That is roulette!" he angrily exclaims. What is needed is "to raise branchy-eared wheat, train it, and transform it into a stable variety."[21]

The basic representational problem of these texts is glaring: the necessity of recreating allegedly professional communication in such a way that it is comprehensible to a viewer. The explanation, for example, of what "Soviet creative Darwinism" is ("Darwin's theory of evolution is itself subjected to evolution," Aleksei informs his beloved) and what is good about Lamarck is provided during a conversation with the student Suren Petrosian (although, given its degree of simplicity, this could have been spoken in a kindergarten); Aleksei explains that "a giraffe has a long neck because trees are tall—in order to survive, it must stretch its neck—'either die out, or hold out,' and the mole's vision has atrophied—'what the heck does it need eyes for, if it lives underground?'" According to Aleksei, this is exactly what Lamarck supposedly said, and Darwin merely added the idea of natural selection to Lamarckism: "These 'Darwinists' finish Darwin's words for him! [They say] what he didn't even say! That it's only a matter of natural selection! No one knows why Lamarck was anathematized.... Nothing but natural selection!" The exclamation marks throughout are supposed to convey how confused the ill-starred "Darwinists" feel.

The play depicts Darwinists as doctrinaire fanatics. The regional party committee's secretary, Burov (who is also a professor of philosophy), having passed a sleepless night reading several dozen thick books on genetics, has come to the conclusion that the enemies of "forward-looking methods in biology" are dangerous because of their intolerance of their opponents: "The fury with which the authors of these fat works try to eradicate dissenters is amazing." The day before, he knew nothing about genetics but has over a single night easily come to understand everything. He tells his troubled daughter, who cannot come to terms with her Communist fiancé criticizing Darwin, that Engels had also criticized Darwin, although he also "defended [him] from Dühring's assaults."

Burov possesses not only amazing cognitive abilities, but also heuristic pedagogical ones. The play shows vividly how "creative Darwinism" and "Michurinist biology" arise *directly* from Marxist-Leninist philosophy. Aleksei's experiment fails; the ear of wheat he raised yields forty-eight kernels instead of the two hundred typical of the branchy-eared variety. And although everyone tells him that he wants too much, that a one-and-a-half-times increase of the yield is "already a lot," he is adamant in his striving to reach the goal. He is wracked with doubts as to what exactly he did wrong. They all try to reassure him, but they cannot suggest anything. Only Burov, as a philosophy professor and regional committee secretary in one, gives him a master class in applied Marxism and creative Darwinism. This scene is worth reproducing:

> Burov: The one who thinks materialistically is right.... Super-yielding wheat should grow in Siberia.
> Aleksei: But how? How am I supposed to do that?
> Burov: I don't know. I'm not a biologist. Let's think this over together. You resurrected Lamarck's theory.... You reapplied Lamarck's theory to plants. That's very interesting. Nature changes organisms over thousands of generations. You wanted to accomplish this over tens of generations.... You went the route of crossing and hybridization and used the example of Timiriazev's followers.... That's all correct. But why is your branchy-eared [wheat] so puny?

Aleksei: The summer is short, with too little time for development. . . .

Burov: Right. Let's think. Engels said that the struggle for existence is manifested not only in devouring each other, but also in the form of struggling for space and light. . . . Trees, you see, stretch toward the light. . . . Maybe it's also possible to acclimate branchy-eared wheat to a short summer . . . only we'd have to waste too many generations on this, and we don't have time. So it turns out that a branchy-eared wheat that could better grab hold of everything it needed to live would survive in our conditions.

Aleksei: Sergei Gavrilovich. . . . I. . . . Wait. . . . Let me think. . . . Grab hold? How can it grab hold of more sun?

Burov: You have taken up Lamarck's old idea. But an idea is not a can of preserves that can sit there as long as you want. Even if the idea is true, it is 140 years old. Over these years it is bound to have developed, changed its appearance, demanded new forms. That is dialectics, Aleksei, and you can't do anything about it. Search!

Aleksei: More sun! More time to grow! How can this be done? (*Runs around the greenhouse.*) I took what existed already. . . . I exercised old characteristics. . . . I exercised old characteristics. Wait, Sergei Gavrilovich, don't go! I wanted branchy-eared wheat to learn to be satisfied with too little. . . .

Burov: But it's greedy. . . .

Aleksei: I crossed it with early-ripening [wheat], infused new blood. . . . It started to mature, but badly. . . . It took revenge on me. . . .

Burov: In adapting to conditions, it was itself changed. That's logical.

Aleksei: Wait, Sergei Gavrilovich. Now I'll. . . . But if. . . . Yes. But if the conditions themselves were improved?

Burov: It will repay the kindness. . . .

Aleksei: Turns out I only did it halfway . . . half the job. . . . (*He runs to the desk, takes out a book, writes something quickly. Burov quietly leaves. Aleksei writes something, crosses it out, writes something else. . . .*)

Thus, before our very eyes, a discovery is made—creative Marxism gives rise to creative Darwinism, which in turn yields branchy-eared wheat. Similarly to how a solution itself grows out of a problem ("Super-yielding wheat should grow in Siberia"), just as unfailingly a miracle occurs before the wheat has appeared. The wheat gives rise to . . . communism. Here is a conversation between two kolkhoz chairmen:

Galkin: How the branchy-eared [wheat] will spread to all the kolkhozes, through the whole Union! . . . What will this be?

Askarov: It will be a sea of bread. An ocean.
Galkin: And then they will proclaim—free bread!
Askarov: Free bread?
Galkin: For all citizens of the Soviet Union. Understand? Abroad, people are dying from hunger, but we have free bread. Then let them wonder what's happening.
Askarov: That, Galkin, will already be communism.

Socialist Realist romanticism literally inundates the scene, such that the line between reality and dreaming rapidly disappears. This is where the demonstration of "achievements" is brought in. Aleksei has not yet had time for his discovery to be made before he submits his dissertation for defense, which ends up a failure; it is categorized as "anti-scientific." But he does not lose heart: "I've become twice as strong! Now I'll crush them! They are rejecting facts! It *is* wheat! I'll crush them with the harvest! They can't beat Michurinist science! Hundreds of kolkhozes are already sowing the stubble-fields." How a super-yielding wheat could appear over the course of a few months, even with Michurinist methods, is not clear. Even less clear is what harvest he is talking about and how hundreds(!) of kolkhozes could be sowing it when a stock of seed could not have been created over the time passed since the "discovery."

The viewer is supposed to believe that the wheat has been produced, but the university's academic council has refused to admit the obvious. But then the institutional catharsis sets in—the last stage of introducing forward-looking science. Burov returns from Moscow. He is outraged by the failed defense. He summons Skrypnev and simply suspends him from working. When Skrypnev calls for allowing different trends in science to coexist, Burov does not beat around the bush: "Life shows that Lysenko and his followers—Novikov and others—are genuine Darwinists. Creative ones! And you are their enemies, which is the essence of Comrade Lysenko's report, approved by the Central Committee of our party. Any trend is good when it moves forward. Your trend, Professor Skrypnev, takes us backward. On the path to communism we must build and create. Everything that hinders us from doing this is reactionary and should be swept aside." No arguments could help the orthodox Darwinist Skrypnev: "I am a professor. I've been a professor thirty years. I have graduated thousands of specialists. My research has been translated into dozens of languages! I have taught. . . . I am an honorary member of two universities. I have an *honoris causa* doctorate from the Sorbonne! I am a member of the British Royal Society! ... I will go to Moscow! I will go complain about you to the Academy of Sciences!" Burov's answer: "They would understand you better at the British Royal Society."

The purifying romantic storm of "personnel adjustments" passes over the scene, but it does not leave Aleksei to rest on his laurels. Now, after creating the "Sibiriachka" variety of wheat, he wants to study perennial wheat—"sow it once, but have a harvest every year." Burov exhorts his mentee: "Come on, if you dream big, you will create a huge breeding station. To the glory of Michurinist science. Prepare an estimate, and aim higher; don't be shy. The regional party committee will support it." The committee supports everything that Aleksei asks for, so much so that he is simply stunned: "It's just like in a fairy tale." But this is not a fairy tale, but romantic reality, and Burov rises and responds: "You and I will have no rest. But we don't need rest! For us, there is no old age. There's no solitude. Yes, there's not even death, maybe. . . . (*Goes to the window.*) Look into Tomorrow, Alesha. . . . It's here . . . close. . . . We are breathing the air of communism. And there is real happiness in that." In this poetically zealous world of the Bolshevist will, scientific arguments, rational conclusions, and appeals to reality are powerless because they fail to take into account the basis of the Socialist Realist vision—"life in its revolutionary development."

PROTO-LYSENKO: THE MICHURINIST MYTHOLOGY

At the Politbiuro session on May 31, 1948, Stalin declared that "Lysenko is today's Michurin."[22] This statement is remarkable for the fact that, consciously or not, Stalin in referring to Lysenko used the construction that applied to a single person in the country—to himself: Stalin was "today's Lenin." The very application of this formula signified the supreme political esteem of whoever it might be and was practically a coronation of the country's main agrobiologist. It also signified that the same devices for creating a cult that were used for Stalin himself were applied (although in limited form) to the public legitimization of Lysenko. And in turn this suggested that *the transformation of Lysenko into Michurin is impossible without the transformation of Michurin into Lysenko*. In exactly the same way, Lenin had been Stalinized in order to correspond to his "best pupil." In Aleksandr Dovzhenko's film *Michurin*, Michurin himself put his special status into words at the end (and the whole second half of the film is constructed as a series of triumphs and the apotheosis of "the great Michurin") when, after being borne aloft to a podium, he declared: "Blessed is the labor of the people, and blessed are the names that have brought me to the podium: Lenin and Stalin. O great people, I act with you in a great time, and I have taken a small part of your immortality upon myself. The people's dreams are coming true. My dream is coming true. I see the future of the Motherland in bloom and I say, 'I am happy.' Onward, my contemporaries! May our Soviet land be transformed into a garden." Michurin personally puts himself on a par with Lenin and Stalin and even declares that he has taken a small part of their immortality upon himself. In and of itself, such a self-confident admission takes him beyond the boundaries of the role of the usual "father" (which every science had).

"There is no limit to the bold greatness of human reason, and among us this reason is growing with unbelievable speed both qualitatively and quantitatively. The wonders created by the inexhaustible energy of I. V. Michurin are not unique; wonders are being created in all areas of a science masterable only by liberated reason," Maxim Gorky tirelessly exulted, and he insistently advised writers to know three realities—the past, present, and future.[23] He demanded that they know how to see the future not only in the future, but also in the present, in the phenomena of the present time. "We must somehow include this third reality now in our everyday life; we must depict it," Gorky wrote. "Without it, we will not understand what the method of Socialist Realism is."[24] And, in fact, outside the boundaries of this Socialist Realist optics it would have been impossible to portray Michurin—an almost folkloric figure, just this kind of miracle worker that emerged from Gorky's pen.

Dovzhenko was partly forced to undertake the making of *Michurin*. He returned to the screenplay of the picture *Life in Bloom*, conceived before the war, in January 1944, just after the catastrophe that had befallen his *Ukraine in Flames* screenplay. The accusations of nationalism and insufficient "Soviet patriotism" that Stalin had hurled at him (at the height of the Great Patriotic War!) in a Politbiuro session remained profoundly traumatic for him. And although work did not keep him from having the subsequent heart attack, it saved him from a decisive disgrace and oblivion. The screenplay was already finished by March

1946 and was immediately published in the journals *Iskusstvo kino* and *Novyi mir;* in 1947 it came out as a separate book. The shooting of the film also began in 1947. But in early 1948, demands for reworking parts of the already filmed picture trickled in. An entire year of remakes was required before the new version of the film finally hit movie screens on January 1, 1949. Dovzhenko and his assistant and wife, Iuliia Solntseva, were awarded the Stalin Prize for the film, although it was the Second Class prize. But this signaled forgiveness.

Michurin solved several problems at once for the disgraced director. First, the hero of the film was Russian, which immediately obviated any possible accusations of nationalism (about which Dovzhenko wrote straightforwardly in his diary); second, the picture ideally fit in to the making of biographical films that was being encouraged at the time; third, it became part of the urgent campaign for Russian preeminence in science; finally, it glorified the father of "Michurinist science," which after the infamous session in the Lenin All-Union Academy of Agricultural Sciences made the film's premiere one of the testimonies to Lysenko's triumph and part of the campaign to legitimize him as Michurin's successor. This last context played a cruel joke on Dovzhenko's film.

Dovzhenko recalled how Beriia had reprimanded him for grudging a few meters of "little film" to glorify Stalin. Dovzhenko had shown a bit of generosity at the ending of *Michurin:* "Michurin's victory in the battle for materialist science was crowned by a telegram from I. V. Stalin."[25] But this did not help. As Grigorii Mar'iamov recalled, "Stalin had watched the [initial version of the] film through the eyes of Lysenko. There followed a long list of modifications that were not consistent with either the internal concept of the film or its style. The fundamental demand amounted to showing Michurin's active rejection of the theoretical ideas of the Weismanists/Morganists, the broad extent of Michurin's experience in biological science and in practice, and the support of Michurin's undertakings on the part of Soviet scientists and officials in power. . . . Dovzhenko had resisted with all his might."[26]

Pressure was exerted through Iurii Zhdanov himself, who with his precipitate actions against Lysenko had caused the avalanche that buried Soviet genetics.[27] In keeping with the ritual, the director thanked the censors who had forced him to set about deliberately changing the film for the worse. "I am immeasurably grateful to the party," Dovzhenko wrote. "The meeting with Comrade Zhdanov, his advice and guidance, the whole style of the discussion, and his goodwill and sensitivity have all been permanently imprinted in my memory. After this meeting I saw that I and our creative collective were faced with the issue of fleshing out the image of Michurin, of portraying his historic role and the struggle and triumph of materialism over idealism."[28]

As opposed to the majority of Soviet directors who had acquired the subjects of their biographical films from Stalin's own orders, Dovzhenko had arrived at his choice of hero himself. And the alignment was complete: the chief romantic of Soviet cinema created a picture about the great romantic in science that became a masterpiece of Socialist Realist romanticism. Dovzhenko had hoped to create *Michurin* as a Russian version of his Ukrainian-themed *Earth*. How else could the disgraced director prove his "Soviet patriotism"? The tie of *Michurin* to the pantheism and natural philosophy of *Earth* was emphasized by Dovzhenko's similar system of characters, in the same kind of ecstatic iconoclasm, and in the demonstratively similar imagery. But Dovzhenko was a too politically convinced and independently thinking person, too profoundly feeling and creative an individual to carry out his political orders without injecting his own vision, emotionality, and faith into them, traits that frequently led him far astray. This made his breakings on the ideological rack even harder, a situation in which he found himself more than once—after *Earth*, after *Shchors*, and especially after *Ukraine in Flames*. Similarly to how *Earth* fell outside the usual kolkhoz propaganda in whose service it had been ordered, the film about Michurin "did not stay within the confines of the schema of the historico-biographical screenplay that was being shaped at the time. The dramatic quality of the Michurin figure, who was perceived as a solitary, suffering martyr, was shocking. People wanted to see the great man not experiencing doubts [but] as a happy conqueror of the forces hostile to him. And [they wanted to see] these forces as straightforwardly clear and absolute in their universally recognized negativity."[29]

So Dovzhenko began, as forced to, to ruin the film by turning Michurin into a champion against Weismanism/Morganism, a forerunner of Lysenko, and even making him foretell "the great Stalinist transformation of nature." After releasing the disfigured film in January 1949 with the title *Michurin*, Dovzhenko said that after all the remakes, the film became absolutely foreign to him, turned into something entirely not his. The inner tragedy of the romantic was diminished to the level of topical scientific debates; crisis and the subsequent collapse of romantic impatience, vanquished by inexorable time and death, were replaced by the hero's frustration and irritability.

Contemporaries insisted that the remakes only went to the benefit of the film. But cinema historians are unanimous in the opinion that they ruined the film and that the finished version is but a poor copy of the powerful original. Rostislav Iurenev responded to the film immediately after its release by declaring that the screenplay *Life in Bloom* and the first version of the film were built on two parallel themes—the joyous theme of life and creation and the tragic theme of solitude, old age, and death. It was just in this second vein that the "solitary, prickly, and impatient Michurin was suspicious and abrupt with the people around him. He did not ask for love but for compassion. Fighting for a method to change nature, the scientist grew old; nature conquered him. And perhaps without its maker wanting it to, the film said man is mortal."[30] To Iurenev's relief, only hints of this conflict remained in the second version. Now the plot skimmed along familiar rails; gone was the hero's "halo of victimhood and solitude. The theme of national spirit, and the theme of the party spirit of Michurin's creative work, resounding in full force, rid the film of the elements of pessimism. Michurin found immortality in the affairs of a people led by the party of Bolsheviks."[31]

Nonetheless, Dovzhenko's powerful concept could not be completely obliterated. As Evgenii Margolit so astutely observes, this comes across through a "canonical church fresco from underneath which a second image can be discerned—a fierce one, apocryphal to the point of heresy."[32] Margolit justifiably saw *Life in Bloom* as "essentially, a confessional work—a meditation on [Dovzhenko's] own artistic method," at the center of which was "the drama of a man striving to find a common language with nature, in his frantic quest hastening his own time, chasing it, and hence inevitably coming into conflict with the world around him."[33] Dovzhenko understood the conflict between a genius and his milieu not from a class viewpoint but existentially (and also, of course, autobiographically). "Timiriazev, Michurin, Ushakov. . . . The peculiarity of great people is apparently that while carrying out the historical task of their state system, they outgrew the task and, at the moment of outgrowth, thereby came into conflict with the system,"

Dovzhenko noted in his diary in 1945, at the height of his work on *Life in Bloom*.[34]

Such a collision not only did not fit into the applied concept of cinema as a propaganda instrument (be it for "Michurinist biology" or "Russian preeminence in science"), but was also profoundly alien to the Stalinist interpretation of science, art, creativity, and the role of historical persons. In remaking the film, Dovzhenko was essentially painting over his heretic scientist, transforming the rebel and romantic into a character of the dreary Stalinist pantheon, rewriting revolutionary romanticism into Socialist Realism. The artist-romantic Dovzhenko fully understood what he had to do: "I must reject what I have created, hate what I exulted in, that which is assembled from many subtle components, and recreate a hybrid work—an old epic poem about creativity and a new story about hybridization," he bitterly noted during the remaking of the film.[35]

This purely romantic collision was alive and well in the 1920s and had not quite died out in the 1930s but had become completely impossible in late Stalinism. The screenplay and the history of the production of Dovhenko's film, the transition from *Life in Bloom* to *Michurin,* is the best illustration of the fate of revolutionary romanticism in the Stalin era, a vivid demonstration of what "life in its revolutionary development" was. It is all about how impulse, creativity, thought, and will stop, ossify, and turn to stone. Dovzhenko emerged from this skirmish physically and morally broken.

Without doubt, Dovzhenko's Michurin is an autobiographical character. This quality of autobiography breaks out in the screenplay at times in expansive lyrical digressions, at others in choppy sentences that sound like sighs: "Years passed. Strength was exhausted. The path was hard." Michurin is the worn-out romantic Dovzhenko, exhausted by the struggle with life. Like Dovzhenko himself, he is misunderstood by the narrow-minded, impoverished society of the provincial town, Kozlov, made up of priests, police officers, and local landowners and their wives, who characterize him as "a difficult man and, of course, dangerous." The only thing Father Khristofor can see in this dreamer is "a terrifying degree of arrogance."

Dovzhenko emphasizes in every way possible the otherworldliness of his hero. In a conversation with scientists, Michurin confesses, embarrassed, "I have been raising plants since I was four. All my life I have been sitting in a little garden bed and looking down." About the ensuing reply, "Many people look down," the academician Pashkevich, an admirer of Michurin, observes: "They do. Only some of them see a puddle, and others see stars. [Michurin] sees stars." Michurin responds by saying, "I see my dreams." Arising before the viewer's eyes is the image of a romantic misunderstood by everyone, immersed in his dream.

A watchmaker—it would be hard to find anything more opposite a romantic hero. The opposition of watchmaker:romantic is so meaningful for Dovzhenko that he reconceptualizes a standing classic cinematic metaphor—a broken clock and the scene of the father's death in Pudovkin's *Mother*. The death of Michurin's wife is given thus in the screenplay: "Candles were burning at the head of the deceased woman's bed. The clocks on the wall were ticking. There were many clocks—different sizes, with different pendulums. The pendulums interfered with each other by the difference of their rhythms, and time stumbled anxiously, unsteady from the stubborn disagreement between the pendulums." Dovzhenko depicts Michurin himself as a tragically misunderstood urban eccentric: "'Here, I'll fix the clocks, the clocks. I'll fix the old clocks! I'll repair the little machines!' Michurin cried in a tinkling voice as he walked through the city, imitating the knife-grinders."

"You are depressing your neighbors," Father Khristofor challenges him. To which Michurin answers, "I'm serving people far away." To serve those far away—humanity, future generations—is part of a breeder's profession. After all, the results of his experiments will be known across the years; his work is not confined within a single human life. For the romantic Michurin, this is the source of real tragedy. His whole life is hard daily labor, the fruits of which emerge very slowly, if at all. Michurin himself lives a long life, but his wife passes away prematurely, having lived out her days alongside a difficult man obsessed with his trees and embittered by failures. Only in saying farewell with her does Michurin fall to his knees before her, realizing the full tragedy of the situation: "I'm here; forgive me, Sasha. Forgive me for belonging to the trees my whole life."

Michurin's helper, the garden's watchman Terentii, having spent his long life's journey alongside him, passes away peacefully and sublimely: "I forgive you everything, and forgive me, too. You never let me speak, but I was happy with you my whole life. So many saplings and fruits of the earth. Goodbye. . . . I am earth, and I go back to the earth." Michurin himself dies the same way, as Dovzhenko says in the screenplay: "He was so old and had done so much that no one wept for him, and his death brought to the hearts of his descendants only a quiet contemplation of gratitude and reverence for the high adventure of human life."

The passing of Michurin's wife is tragic. But the passing of the horticulturist and his faithful Terentii are presented just as the passing of the grandfather in *Earth*—as a natural process, a part of the cycle of nature. Their calmness is tied to the fact that Michurin's passing takes place in Soviet times. Before the revolution, Michurin had felt like he was at a dead end: "The way out came for me and for the people at the same time. The great proletarian revolution brought it," he says. For Michurin, like for Dovzhenko himself, the revolution was a great cleansing storm that brought freedom. It opened up conditions for the realization of the most daring dream. Hence its very leaders are interpreted as romantics in the film. In one of the most dramatic scenes in the film, Michurin walks through a snowstorm and a blizzard to his dying trees, bringing news of the death of Lenin. A profound old man, he is wracked with grief: "The great dreamer will not come to our garden. In the name and honor of the immortal man who brought our country to first place in history, who showed us who we are, let us continue his work. May he abide with us in bloom, forever living, as the earth is alive and the people who gave birth to him in an endless rise to higher things."

The "great dreamer" who had left life behind is represented in the film by the "all-Russian elder" Mikhail Kalinin (chairman of the All-Russian Central Executive Committee), who visits Michurin in Kozlov (then already renamed Michurinsk). Dovzhenko devotes the most poetic passages of his screenplay to Kalinin's visit. Their meeting is described as parallel to the condition of nature itself, full of harmony. And they talk about "high aesthetics"—about the millions of trees raised throughout the country. "I envision how the best qualities of our people will flourish under our nurture, how customs will grow milder, characters ennobled," Kalinin says. Captivated, Michurin echoes the sentiment: "A most grandiose picture!" The two spend the night in conversation on the bank of a river that seems asleep. Dovzhenko, drunk with this future beauty, paints a picture of the realized Michurinist dream. Nature is a beautiful canvas, always open to the human artist who is constantly "mastering it." Michurin's garden, along whose paths the two righteous men dreamers walk as through a bucolic paradise, is the realized idyll of the happiness to come, which was called "conflict-less" and which was the fulfilled age of late Stalinism. Nature knows no conflicts; even struggle in it is predetermined and rational. Nature is beautiful and doomed to beauty, and man's encroachment makes it indeed quite perfect, fills it with reason. Michurin explains to his guest that "nature, just like society, is unfortunately still in a very rough draft." But if this draft is so beautiful, what will the finished product look like? The viewer is left no doubt that it is beautiful. Through their incredible beauty, the bewitching panoramas of Michurin's garden are designed to throw a bridge up between nature and the man who is transforming it.

Michurin's garden is transformed, finally, into a complete meta-phor for the Soviet country, in which the "creator-human" created by the Bolsheviks transforms nature. Kalinin agrees with the gardener: "You're right, Ivan Vladimirovich; you're completely right. Our Moth-erland should turn into a socialist garden. . . . Vladimir Il'ich said: in the socialist garden the full cycle of human life will be closed—both the precious labor education of the child and the comforting existence of old age." And Michurin, like an echo, responds, "Yes, the circle will be closed." As Liudmila Belova observed, "Always true to the affirma-tion of beauty, Dovzhenko makes his hero produce beauty from nature itself, hastening Nature and improving it."[36]

The remaking of nature constitutes the foundation of the whole aes-thetic of Dovzhenko's *Michurin*. It is no coincidence that at the end of the film Michurin writes a letter to the "country's chief gardener," Stalin; for the first time, Dovzhenko finally mentions Stalin as the chief dreamer (although he is missing from the frame).

Nonetheless, Michurin held the place of honor in this cohort of dreamers—right after Gorky. The film is literally stitched together with his statements about the remaking of nature. They are precisely the ones that Lysenko constantly leaned on. The majority of these statements, of course, were not actual quotations but rather invented by Dovzhenko as a development of Michurin's well-known challenge to "not wait for favors from nature" but to "take them from it." Dovzhenko's film greatly intensified the radicalism of Michurin's views and expanded the range of his quotations that Lysenko needed to refer to the gardener he had chosen as his forerunner. Hence *Michurin quoted Lysenko in the film so that Lysenko could quote Michurin.* Michurin acts as an ideological double of Lysenko in the film and says the same things as "the people's academician," only more expressively.

Although forced to do so, Dovzhenko makes his hero go deeper and deeper into the debates about genetics, Darwinism, and Mendelism that were obviously unknown to Michurin. On the cusp of the new year of 1900, at the academician Pashkevich's, Michurin breaks out into a truly Promethean monologue: "I would like to encroach on the world order in this year! For nineteen centuries of our era man has observed a mysterious changeableness in nature under the influence of changeable environmental conditions. But what if I rebel and create changeableness in nature as I wish? What I'm talking about is creating planned hereditary changes. . . . What then will dare to compare with the might of the people, when labor on earth will become creativity, art? And everything, everything will become something else."

Michurin begins debating with Mendel in the very first frames of the film as he explains the uniqueness of his approach to the hybridization of plants, informing his American guests that "Mendel does not explain the development of fruiting plants, but I have begun to work on modeling a new plant. Taking advantage of the instability and malleability of young plants, I am directing its movement, shaping its essence." On hearing this, the Americans glance at each other, and Father Khristofor crosses himself.

Michurin in the film is charged with formulating the principles of Lysenko's "Michurinist biology." He formulates his "laws" over his dying wife: "We live in one of the stages of a time of nature's ceaseless creation of new forms of living organisms, but due to nearsightedness we do not notice it. . . . The characteristics of breeds do not pass from generation to generation in unchanged form. They are shaped anew in each generation with development, from the emergence of sprouts to the adult state." Since Michurin embodied "the people's science," he shared his conclusions with those around him in "the people's language" as he himself defined it. This language is full of imagery and zeal: "Now we are getting opportunities to discover new plants with unheard-of characteristics. Now, from the depths, so to speak, of future centuries, we are summoning to life trees that would have had to wait through millennia of slow evolution before coming to light. And not only trees." This was precisely the kind of language Lysenko spoke. Many of Michurin's statements repeat those of "the people's academician" almost to the letter.

Playing the role of the Mendelian, a formalist scientist detached from reality and therefore the object of Michurin's endless attacks, is Professor Kartashov, whom even the new varieties of plants created by Michurin do not convince that heredity can change. Such disbelief of the obvious was a mark of not only a lack of scientific conscientiousness, but also a political dissident. Kartashov calls Michurin an "empiricist-deductivist," and Michurin calls Kartashov a "bureaucrat."

The assertion of Soviet exceptionalism plays an important role in *Michurin*. And, in fact, "Michurinist science" had no prospects at all beyond the Stalin regime. Its inconvertibility was interpreted as uniqueness. No one was able to dream the way the Russian gardener did, nor did anyone manage to achieve the successes that he had. Hence the film begins with the arrival of Americans who intone blatantly exaggerated praise to Michurin. The scientist Meyer declares: "What I have seen is genius. You, Mr. Michurin, are an amazing person, and I will never forget you. I say it was worth coming from America to shake your hand. I'm happy. . . . This is immense for the power and depth of its conception. I have sensed here, for the first time, what man is capable of. This is almost supernatural. . . . It's extraordinary! I have traveled the whole planet. I have seen the world of plants, but here I have understood the most important thing about it. It's almost supernatural." These dithyrambs are only necessary so that reviewers can remark on how Michurin is visited by "Americans, businesslike to the point of impudence, who offered to buy both 'Mr.' Michurin himself and his garden, and even the surrounding Russian landscape, and received a proud rebuff in return."[37]

It is well known, however, that Michurin told the story more than once about the Americans who constantly came to lure him away to America for the purposes of self-advertisement and to mobilize support from the Soviet government to expand his garden and receive state subsidies. This story was, on the whole, the product of his fantasy. Although Frank Meyer of the U.S. Department of Agriculture actually did come twice to Kozlov, he did not make any attempt to persuade Michurin to leave his native land. He merely wanted to buy several varieties of plants from Michurin, but when the price Michurin came up with was too high, the deal fell through.[38]

Since Lysenko's "agrobiology" was chiefly constructed on political and ideological arguments and had a very flexible evidentiary basis and a complex relationship to the facts, the assertion of "Michurinist biology" as a science, which was a central goal of Lysenko's, was constructed on proof of its "realness" and "connection to life." Dovzhenko's film takes on compensatory functions. Dovzhenko's Michurin is often like a magician who impresses his guests and opponents not so much with argument as with miraculous facts, constantly showing them either a new plant variety or a new fruit he has raised or else a new method and new characteristics, taking them now from his pocket, then from a desk drawer, or else plucking them from a garden bed, then from a tree. They can try them, examine them, feel them, sniff them. The proof becomes palpable and in obvious fashion prevails over any theoretical argumentation whatsoever. Thus Michurin fleshes out Lysenko; for proof of the latter's positions, one must look in the fictional film about the former.

A reviewer of the film who remarked that "Michurinist theory is inseparable from kolkhoz and sovkhoz practice," that "it is the best proof of the unity of theory and practice in agricultural science," and that "widespread development of the Michurinist movement is impossible without kolkhozes and sovkhozes" had no idea how right he was.[39] Without collectivization and "kolkhoz practice" there would be no "Michurinist theory" either; the kolkhoz system that led the country into agricultural catastrophe generated the demand for a Lysenkoist "creative Darwinism." This system was the "production base" of this "theory" and the only consumer of the "third reality" that it created.

SOCIALIST REALIST VITALISM

The old Bolshevik Ol'ga Lepeshinskaia was a figure of the same mold as Lysenko—not only because they both went down into the history of science as charlatans, but also because the radicalism and fantasy of her ideas could compete with Lysenko's most audacious fantasies. In all other respects they were very different people. As opposed to the peasant's son Lysenko, Ol'ga Borisovna Lepeshinskaia was born in 1871 in Perm to a very rich family and then left home. In her memoirs, *The Path to Revolution: Recollections of an Old Bolshevik,* published in 1963 (while she was still alive!), Lepeshinskaia tells how she grew up in a family of factory owners, awoke to the oppression of the proletariat, left to study in the capital, began to take part in revolutionary activity after becoming friendly with the "Union for the Struggle to Free the Working Class" in Petersburg and with Lenin (she joined the party in 1898), met her future husband Panteleimon Lepeshinskii there, and later followed him to Siberia. In Siberia, she became an intimate of Lenin and Nadezhda Krupskaia, and the greater part of her memoirs is devoted to descriptions of their encounters there.

The natural sciences, however, remained Lepeshinskaia's chief passion. Petersburg and an acquaintance with Darwinism became catalysts for an internal upheaval. Thus Lepeshinskaia recalls, "After reading Darwin's *Origin of Species,* I came to the correct conclusion that the god in whom I had believed before that does not exist and that all the church ritual that I had more or less observed was nothing more than barbarianism and stupidity."[40] The future Bolshevik had already followed this "glorious path of many" together with her husband. Lepeshinskii was a professional revolutionary, an agent of the newspaper *Iskra,* and likewise one of the oldest party members, who was for some reason not particularly successful after the revolution; he had been a member of the board of the People's Commissariat of Education and one of the organizers of the Department of Party History (Istpart), had held the honorary post of director of the Historical Museum, and was until his death in 1944 (at age seventy-six) the director of the Museum of Revolution. Who knows; maybe this passion for museums preserved the life of this old Bolshevik? All her life, Ol'ga was a much more active person. Her glory days were the late 1940s and early 1950s. Her pursuit was science.

Lepeshinskaia's memoirs provide much more for an understanding of her personality than do her biological works. In the memoirs, she plays the role of a true Soviet writer. Her writing is literally saturated with Socialist Realist literary flavor. For example, the still young future "old Bolsheviks" evidently did have the sort of relationship that Lepeshinskaia herself describes; after endless exiles and escapes, while living in a semilegal situation with her husband, she goes to Switzerland to continue the education interrupted by Siberia. "On the eve of my departure, Lepeshinskii gave me his final advice and orders and said, 'Remember your political work as well while you are studying the natural sciences.'"[41]

So this was what Lepeshinskii told his young wife, with an infant daughter, when he was seeing her off to Lausanne for who knows how long. What we are seeing here, without doubt, is literary characters; this is how secretaries of party committees usually talk to their wives in Socialist Realist novels. Evidently the boundaries between science and "political work" in the activities of the future "outstanding Soviet biologist" Lepeshinskaia were erased from the very beginning, and hence what followed from "political work"—a peculiar ideological aesthetic multiplied by revolutionary fantasies—spilled over into her scientific "discoveries" with the same energy that captivates us even now.

Lepeshinskaia made the journey from medical assistant to academic in medicine; she finished the assistant's courses and then, with enormous gaps, seemingly not finishing her studies anywhere and mixing natural sciences with "political work," spent years in St. Petersburg and Lausanne. One of Lepeshinskaia's official biographers, Vadim Safonov, observed quite astutely (and somewhat unexpectedly) that "it was the life and work of a Bolshevik that truly gave her her main, priceless, *scientific* education; the institute was merely a professional extension, a technical elaboration of this education."[42] She actually dealt in "generalizations," directly extrapolating Marxism onto biology—and skipping the proof. As a person with a difficult temperament, she had a hard time getting along with people. Her last duties were as chief of the Cytological Laboratory and afterward as director of the Morphological Institute of the USSR Academy of Medical Sciences.

Lepeshinskaia spent long years in her laboratory of fantasies. What brought her fame were the truly fantasy-laden ideas about the origin of life and the existence of some sort of "living substance." The theme of the origin of life had long engaged Soviet researchers. The influential Soviet academic Aleksandr Oparin was made famous for his study of it, advancing a theory as early as the mid-1920s of the origin of life on Earth from a primitive broth of organic substances. Oparin was one of those influential functionaries in science who supported Lysenko and Lepeshinskaia after the war. However, Lepeshinskaia's ideas were not taken seriously in the 1930s and evoked supercilious jokes until they came into demand after the war—during Lysenko's attack on the "biological front." Lysenko started to pay particular attention to them.

Lepeshinskaia was given high awards and honors (including the title of academician), was a Stalin Prize laureate and a deputy of the USSR Supreme Soviet, and was awarded the Order of Lenin. The triumphal procession of the theory of "living substance" began.

Lepeshinskaia's ideas are primarily interesting as an important cultural phenomenon: how did the degradation of "revolutionary romanticism" into a truly medieval scholasticism occur in the late-Stalinist era? Telling in this respect is the remark made by one of Lysenko's opponents, biologist Iakov Rapoport, who had visited Lepeshinskaia's laboratory: "I left it with the impression that I had visited the Middle Ages. And only after a certain time did I learn from official communications that I had been at the summit of the scientific Olympus."[43]

Looking into Lepeshinskaia's work, we are dealing with an aesthetic phenomenon. It had all really started with literature; Lepeshinskaia had begun her later-famous book, *The Origin of Cells from Living Substance and the Role of Living Substance in the Organism*,[44] published with a foreword by Lysenko (where one great hoaxer had gone into ecstasies over the "brilliant, subtle experiments" of another master of the genre), with a reference to none other than Dmitrii Pisarev, whom (she did not forget to mention) Lenin highly regarded and whose card Lenin even kept in his album along with the cards of Aleksandr Hertzen and Chernyshevskii. Pisarev had warmly accepted Darwin's ideas and materialistic ideas in biology in general. Thus, Lepeshinskaia suggested, a connection with the "advanced revolutionary thinking of Russia" was reestablished, and the glorious tradition was thus continued.

The references to Darwin here, however, are only homage to this "glorious tradition"; the trend in biology to which Lepeshinskaia belonged, and which Lysenko championed, was more Lamarckian than Darwinian. Lamarckism was being actively revived in the 1920s, and there were lively discussions about it in such journals as *Pod znamenem marksizma* (Under the Banner of Marxism) and *Vestnik Kommunisticheskoi akademii* (Communist Academy Herald), which were more politico-ideological than scientific in nature. Nonetheless, the appeal to Lamarckism was still considered to be "in bad taste" in the 1920s; it smacked of a return to the "prescientific" stage in the history of biology, to the "science" of the era of Paracelsus, who had suggested procedures like the following to extract "living substance": "Take a certain human liquid and leave it to putrefy, first in a sealed-up pumpkin, then in a horse's stomach for forty days, until it starts to move, live, and stir about there, [a movement that] is easy to observe. That which is left is still unlike a human at all but is transparent and amorphous. But afterward, if one daily, carefully, and prudently feeds it with human blood and keeps it for a period of forty weeks in the constant, even warmth of the horse's stomach, then a real living child, albeit small, will result." Jean Baptist van Helmont had also suggested something similar for making mice out of grain moistened with liquid from a dirty shirt.

Lepeshinskaia began to be openly accused of charlatanism. She defended herself by saying, "Ridiculous ideas about autogenesis of complex animals from putrefied water and all sorts of rubbish have had nothing at all to do with science" (10–11). Lepeshinskaia's "general hypothesis" is as follows: "If there is living protoplasm that is not a cell but that has the capability of metabolism, and the metabolism in a squirrel is a sign of life, then this is living protoplasm, and it cannot remain unchanged; it must develop and produce new forms of a higher order—for example, moners [monery]—and afterward, cells as well." Hence, "the closest source from which a cell can arise can only be living substance, i.e., as we understand it, protoplasm with nuclear substance dispersed in it in the form of chromatin, nucleic acids or of chromatic substance; thus the study of the origin of cells must begin with the study of this living substance" (71).

The first thing that draws attention is the mention of something "dispersed" and vague as to "form." The definition Lepeshinskaia gives dispels any doubts: "Living substance is a protoplasmic mass, not having the form of a cell, containing within itself in one form or another nuclear substance, but not having the form of a nucleus, rather being present in the protoplasm or in a diffused or atomized state" (85). Thus the basic characteristic of "living substance" is its absolute *formlessness:* a mass that has no conceivable form at all, present in a diffused or atomized state.

This strange consistency of the "substance" evoked a number of questions in the professional milieu. Lepeshinskaia was accused of having a definition that suffered from indistinctness. She responded by giving a "new definition"—namely, that "living substance is something unformed, consisting of a mass that possesses vital activity" (190). Foremost in these definitions are life and the absence of form. In fact, we are presented with life itself, a sort of elusive medium, an unformed "essence" (let us remember that Paracelsus had mentioned exactly something that "begins to stir about," something "transparent and without a body"—probably the soul itself).

It turns out, however, that this very "essence," since it is something that is undefined by its nature, is furthermore situated in some sort of state between life and death, and one cannot definitely say whether it is alive or dead. So when discussing viruses, Lepeshinskaia writes that they are biomolecules capable of growth and reproduction. By their origin, she states, they are "the simplest form capable of exchanging substances and of vital activity, and [they] *stand at the borderline between living and dead. . . .* They are both a 'living creature' and a 'non-living substance'" (87–88; emphasis added). This collision of life versus form obliges one to assume that "life" is something organically hostile to form. It is no surprise that the old revolutionary Lepeshinskaia was the person destined to discover this kind of "life." Her revolutionary romanticism helped her to envision rather than actually see that very formless "living substance" that was supposed to warm the heart of the romantic. After all, life stripped of its form is absolutely free, not limited by any laws and institutions, canons, and norms—the embodiment of the romantic ideal.

Debating with Lepeshinskaia in scientific language was useless—she understood only ideological arguments. Lysenko deftly employed ideology for transparent metaphors, but this was the only language Lepeshinskaia spoke. Accusations were made that her work on the origin of cells from living substance "is no more than a return to pre-scientific fantasies about the origin of fish and frogs from stagnant water and mud," that her "scientific experiments" were like "fantastic descriptions," and that "with her discovery, she refutes all evolution and all contemporary embryology, but this does not concern her, since she desires to realize a 'revolutionary approach' to the problem." Furthermore, accusers charged, her ideas belonged to a long ago bygone, infantile stage in the development of science and stood outside its (science's) limits. In short, "there is nothing to debate here, and one must have a great sense of humor in order to seriously refute the strange ideas expressed in abundance recently by O. B. Lepeshinskaia." To all this Lepeshinskaia responded, "We believe that raising the question of spontaneous generation . . . is in keeping with revolutionary teaching and materialist ideology" (25).

Nonetheless, the comparison of her work to "prescientific natural-philosophy fantasies" about the origin of living creatures from lifeless matter was especially insulting to Lepeshinskaia. She insisted that her theory differed from these "fantasies" in the "scientific, methodologically consistent statement of the problem of the origin of cells not only by means of division, but also by means of neoplasm from living substance" (184), and she asserted that her detractors were "following the path of pure metaphysics, and by doing so, slowing the progress of Soviet science" (186). She usually responded to her numerous detractors in the following manner: "Academician Zavarzin, do you agree with this idea? If you agree, then you must retract your rebuke of me for the absence of definitiveness in characterizing 'living substance.' But if you disagree with this idea, then you must stand opposed to Engels, from whom I literally quoted this idea" (190).

One may judge the level of the old Bolshevik's argumentation according to passages like the following, with which her book is abundantly sprinkled: "Experimental biology and Darwinian evolutionary teaching have smashed Vitalist nonsense to smithereens" (74). Clearly, however, this is an ideological debate. The fact that its arena is biology, not completely accustomed to such debates, should not surprise us; this was a continuation of the debate about humankind during the era wherein, as Raymond Bauer so precisely puts it, "psychology *per se* was literally rooted out and replaced by physiology and biology."[45] Lepeshinskaia accepts Darwin's materialism but rejects his evolutionism as not leaving a place for revolutionary leaps. "The mechanistic trend in science that recognizes a slow and gradual development of nature that does not allow new revolutionary leaps in development, of new forms with new qualities," she suggested, "is a harmful anti-Marxist trend, against which the most fierce battle must be waged" (75). The closest enemy turned out to be the great Rudolf Virchow, who maintained that the cell is the smallest morphological unit capable of vital activity. Lepeshinskaia allotted him the role of one of Lysenko's "Mendelist-Morganists."

In criticizing Louis Pasteur and Darwin for the fact that "they did not recognize development in nature and on the question of the origin of life, they relied on a viewpoint of the preexistence of the very simplest forms of life, eternally repeating [it] from generation to generation, inherited from their ancestors" (20), Lepeshinskaia came closer than anyone to the ideas of Lysenko. It goes without saying that at its very heart, Lepeshinskaia's "science" was aimed most of all against genetics, which did not acknowledge her revolutionary zeal. In attempting to prove "the possibility of cell increase not only by means of division of preexistent cells, but also by means of the transformation of living substance toward the formation of cells" (187), Lepeshinskaia maintained that her detractors "are completely unable to digest new revolutionary ideas that are contrary to all the old assumptions in the area of genetics that they have accepted as truth" (187); that "the reason for transmission of inherited characteristics must be sought not in the chromosomes but in the structure of the whole cell and in the vital activity of the living substance in it" (188); and that only if this could be accepted, "geneticists [would] take the proper path of studying the phenomena of inheritance and [would] not rely on the metaphysical viewpoint of the immutability of chromosomes created once and for all. Inherited characteristics are transmitted not only by chromosomes, but by the whole cell and by the whole organism depending on the environment" (188). Even more definitively, she writes, "Inherited characteristics are transmitted not by chromosomes. . . . The transmission of inherited characteristics is a more complex process and depends . . . on the external environment and on social conditions" (207). These last statements repeat Lysenko's basic assumptions almost verbatim.

Paradoxically, Lepeshinskaia embodied the metaphor of the Lysenkoists, who accused Mendelian geneticists of believing in some sort of "inscrutable genes," in some sort of nonexistent "inheritance substance." Accused of idealism, geneticists responded that although the inheritance substance was in fact still undiscovered at the time, there was no cause to doubt its existence since genes were quite real. But then Lepeshinskaia showed with her "discovery" what the geneticists' "idealism" looked like when she replaced their "inheritance substance" with "living substance." For all intents and purposes, her discovery was, one might say, the embodiment of the "idealism" that the Lysenkoists ascribed to geneticists.

Neither Lepeshinskaia's "theory" nor its triumph would have been possible without the support of the chief Soviet biologist; the rise of the old Bolshevik's career was linked to the fact that Lysenko needed an expansion of scientific support after his elevation in August 1948; he needed "discoveries" that would support his "theory." And their impact was assured by the media attention they received.

The Tur brothers, who specialized in topical political themes, wrote a play titled *Third Youth,* whose main characters are hard not to identify as the heroes of "advanced Soviet science": Elena Nikolaevna Snezhinskaia, the doctor of biological sciences and an "old Bolshevik, a person with an excellent biography," as Lepeshinskaia, and Martyn Petrovich Trofimenko, the agrobiologist academician, as Trofim Lysenko. Not only did the authors make no attempt to conceal the prototypes of their play; it was as if they made it their aim to flaunt them. It was well known, for instance, that Lepeshinskaia brought up Dolores Ibárruri's son Ruben among her own adopted children and grandchildren in the periods when his mother could not be with him. Ruben died near Stalingrad during the war. All of this is reproduced in the play. Even Snezhinskaia's theory miraculously turns out to be one about a living structureless substance and non-cellular forms of life.

The problem, however, was that Lepeshinskaia's "discoveries," just as those of Lysenko, were not backed up by facts; they had no evidentiary basis. In addition, official biographers of both Lysenko and Lepeshinskaia could not sidestep the laser focus of these figures' studies on predetermined (as if "anticipated" by the classics of Marxism) results, a strange thing for science. Safonov wrote that her "fearlessness" in science lay in the "clarity of the awareness of her goal, an absolute theoretical readiness for what suddenly turned up under the microscope."[46] Translated from zealous Soviet officialese, this meant that theory had to justify the goal, and practice had to subordinate what was observed to this expediency. But "what suddenly turned up under the microscope" convinced very few. As Rapoport writes, everyone even then knew the worth of Lepeshinskaia's experiments: "Examination of her histologic specimens convincingly showed that [her results were] all the result of crude defects in histologic technique."[47] It is no surprise that the materialization of these discoveries could come to fruition only on the stage and screen, in fiction and the popular press.

In his book *Trailblazers* (wherein the long biography of Lepeshinskaia is entitled "Fearlessness"), Safonov devoted entire pages to breathtaking descriptions of exactly *what* "Lepeshinskaia saw with her own eyes" and *what* revealed itself to her "researcher's eye." She saw how life arises from emptiness and/or lifeless matter. She saw what no one else had ever seen—not because this did not exist in nature but because "no one had yet observed this amazing sight. . . . And how could they have observed it? People who were not searching for what Lepeshinskaia sought (and found) . . . only began their observations where Lepeshinskaia was already almost finishing hers."[48] These descriptions are real science fiction that nonetheless had pretensions not only of absolute realism, but also of scientific validity. Direct appeals to reality and pretensions of scientificalness are declared on behalf of Lepeshinskaia in the play, where Snezhinskaia repeats that "verification is the mother of research" and constantly argues precisely about the validity of her discoveries.[49] It is interesting that she finds this validity in the ability of these discoveries to be "anticipated" (or rather, made imperative) by Marxist teachings: "My deductions are taken from the facts, not pulled out of thin air! They were already anticipated by Engels," says Snezhinskaia, "quoting" Lepeshinskaia.

The word "anticipated" occurs constantly in the play. Refuting Virchow, Snezhinskaia declares, "Engels with genius anticipated that life exists also in a pre-cellular stage, that there are the simplest beings lying even lower than the cell level. This means life in its original form was created not by a deity but arose on its own from lifeless matter, in the process of its perpetual development. As proof of this materialization we are attempting to artificially create a cell from a substance that has no cellular structure."

When serving merely for the affirmation of the "anticipations" of a great teaching, science itself brings forth no ideas. Curiously, here at issue is not foretelling but *anticipating*. Such an important role for *guessing* in science diminishes the importance of research and inquiry in it, as well as the level of the verifiability of its results, and a teleological imperative transforms natural science into an arena for proofs of the correctness of the political "anticipations" in the classics of Marxism. When it is tightly connected to them, science is doomed to perennial topicality. Snezhinskaia's discovery "has significance for practice. For medicine, for agriculture. Take, for example, a curse of mankind that is so terrible, cancer. Hitherto medical students have studied cancer cells. But what if we could block the progress of this disease in its still pre-cellular development? Perhaps this is where the center of research should be redirected." This idea would subsequently become the basis for Nikolai Dashkiev's science fiction novel *The Triumph of Life* (1950).

Snezhinskaia's daughter, who figures in the play, has as her prototype Lepeshinskaia's daughter, Ol'ga Panteleimonovna. The latter (who by the way was a party member beginning in 1918) was not only her mother's assistant in scientific work, but also a writer. After a visit to their "family laboratory" (Lepeshinskaia's laboratory was set up in her apartment, and her daughter and son-in-law worked there as well— a "real family scientific cooperative"), Iakov Rapoport recalled how Ol'ga Panteleimonovna let him in on the research that she was doing: "I will quote this astonishing information literally: 'We take the dirt from underneath mama's nails and examine it for living substance.' That is, this experiment apparently served as one of the experimental proofs for the origin of living organisms from nonliving matter. I [at first] took this information of Ol'ga Panteleimonovna's as a joke but later understood that it was not a joke but real information about a scientific experiment."[50]

Rapoport's reaction was quite typical of Snezhinskaia's detractors, about whom the venerable academician Trofimenko declares in the play, "The science workers who have still not rid their own scientific thinking of the metaphysical approach tend to reject the theoretical conclusions of Professor Snezhinskaia."

These "progressive Soviet scientists" are surrounded in the play by both ecstatic, young, devoted student-worshippers and antagonists in the person of academicians Klenov and Kvashnin, as well as the un-principled politico Loshkarev, editor-in-chief of the journal *Voprosy biologii,* who, since he is cheek by jowl with the geneticists, tries to be "both ours and yours." Although the latter are all against Snezhinksaia-as-Lepeshinskaia, Kvashnin, as a real scientist, is at the end obliged to believe in the correctness of his scientific opponent. Klenov, however, a malicious careerist, perseveres to the end in his battle against "creative Darwinism." As director of the Institute of Biological Problems, where Snezhinskaia works, he does not allow her to carry on her research and during an evacuation of the institute destroys the results of her years of experiments.

The traditional plot—the conspiracy of the slaves to routine against a scientist-innovator—continues to unfold. Klenov and Kvashnin want to "bring a coordinated response to Snezhinskaia and once and for all put an end to these anti-scientific pretensions, these risky experiments," and they publish their own collective letter. This is about a real "letter of thirteen"—an unsuccessful attempt to stop Lepeshinskaia's advance toward the scientific Olympus. And, indeed, what did the opponents of Lepeshinskaia's unstoppable rise have left? In the words of the ecstatic biographer of the triumphant Lepeshinskaia, they "did not refute Lepeshinskaia, did not try to contradict the facts she brought forth with any other facts, or her hundreds of experiments with those of others, or her precise photographic documents. . . . After all, there was nothing to contradict there; these photographic documents existed. But the reviewers . . . anathematized [her] dissent. They agreed on an accusation of forgery." These were "battle methods infinitely remote from genuine quests for scientific truth and so familiar from the Morganists' defamation of the Michurinists."[51]

To Kvashnin's declaration that Snezhinskaia's laboratory was "interfering with science," one of her students, Polynsteva, replies with a challenge: "Out of date, yes. And if we have to, we'll tear it down completely." The chief argument in favor of Snezhinskaia's discoveries was their revolutionary nature. Despite this, everyone around her compared Lepeshinskaia's work to medieval quackery. The idea of the "living substance" itself, the rejection of the cellular nature of living organisms and of the understanding (linked to Virchow) of pathology as pathology of the cell was a rejection of scientific medicine, a retreat into the age of the "blasteme" and the debates about the organism's "juices," and almost back to Hippocrates. It was totally romantic biology. Just as Gothic ruins attracted the romantics, Paracelsus drew Lepeshinskaia. Klenov accuses Snezhinskaia of "dragging science backward, into the Middle Ages." He finds no historical optimism or romance in the work of the old revolutionary Snezhinskaia, but she sincerely believes that it is her opponents who are "dragging science backward" and that only she is moving it forward.

While the old people are accusing each other of obscurantism, Snezhinskaia's daughter conspiratorially reports that the attacks on the old Bolshevik are "an extremely well thought-out tactic. The tactic of Professor Klenov's scientific battle." She explains that their opposition to Snezhinskaia is "a self-preservation instinct. They're afraid of us. After all, if it turns out we're right, it means that their life, work, and books will become meaningless. And their fame, titles, even their dachas, will be undeserved." The notion of science as a path to fame, and of scientific discussion as a fight for dachas, reflects precisely the cultural and ethical profile of the "talented scientific youth" who are attacking the old academicians. But it also reflects the nature of the viewer's perception of what is taking place in the play. When all was said and done, the battle over dachas was much more understandable to mass viewers and readers than the one over the unfathomable "living substance." They came out on the side of the authors and heroes of these plays, which rid science of its romantic aura.

The conflict reaches its culmination during the war, when in the course of the evacuation Snezhinskaia's laboratory is destroyed and she supposedly has no way of proving the correctness of her conclusions. She demands that the laboratory be rebuilt. And when Klenov explains to her that "demanding now that a laboratory be rebuilt for your experiments . . . in a time when our loved ones, our sons, are dying, when the Fascists are on the Volga—not a hand is being raised," Snezhinskaia ups the degree of urgency of her discovery: "Precisely because it is a matter of the fate of our country, war is not taking our quarrel away; it is making it worse. Virchow's dogmas, you see, are with the ones who are breaking through to Stalingrad today!" Kvashnin responds that this is "nonsense! We are not racists! What of the fact that Virchow is a German? We cannot discount his great work." Snezhinskaia sweeps this aside, employing a completely racist argument: "You are cramming Russian biology into a Prussian uniform, and you want to button it up to the throat with all the buttons. Soviet science will strangle in this uniform!" Ironically, Klenov replies, "It's better to go around in someone else's clothing than to show yourself among people, forgive me, in Adam's getup."

Like Moses with tablets describing the origin of life in his hands, Snezhinskaia brandishes *The Origin of Cells from Living Substance and the Role of Living Substance in the Organism* in the air. In the ending of the play we witness a scientific debate where everyone now supports Snezhinskaia. This is about a real event, the Conference on the Issue of Living Substance and Development of Cells, which took place May 22–24, 1950, giving Lepeshinskaia her crown.[52] What went on behind the scenes of the published transcript of this conference is narrated in detail by Iakov Rapoport in his own memoirs. He relates how this "most shameful spectacle was played out"; the conference was behind closed doors, with admission only by special invitation to a strictly selected list of participants, and "since [Lepeshinskaia's] own specimens, upon which she had based her stunning conclusions, could not be shown, in view of their lack of even infinitesimal signs of professional competence," they were made for her by others. Rapoport did not bother to expound upon the contents of the presentations: "It was systematized gibberish that any contact with elementary scientific exactingness would have made go up in smoke."[53]

The film shown in the hall about Snezhinskaia's experiments trying to show how life is generated horrifies her scientific opponents: "I saw it, I saw it! . . . I wanted to close my eyes. . . . It's a verdict, after all. . . . And her book . . . truly spoken, 'Weightier than a great many tomes.' . . ." But what did the detractors of Snezhinskaia-as-Lepeshinskaia see on the screen? What Lepeshinskaia herself saw, "a cell, the chief form of life, did not preexist but came together before one's very eyes. It came together from the very beginning"—out of a proto-cell, out of diffused living substance. Now, in the words of her biographer, "thousands of people can see what the researcher had seen: the films have been shot, [and they] show how a yellowish ball turns into a genuine little cell, and the cell divides, as a cell is supposed to, a chromosome with complex figures appearing in the young nucleus, the chromosome that formed before our very eyes!"[54] As Rapoport said, they were observing "the result of crude defects in histologic technique."

Only Klenov is unconvinced. After writing to the Council of Ministers, he waits for support to come from them. The parcel that arrives from the council plunges him into a stupor; it is a resolution granting Snezhinskaia a Stalin Prize, First Class. (It is telling that the decision was made before the discussion of the discovery had ended; the scientists had still not grasped the particulars, but the Stalin Prize had already been awarded to Snezhinskaia—just as it was with Lepeshinskaia, ignoring the usual procedure.) The Tur brothers' play not only conceded nothing of its zeal to its prototype, but also became itself a part of Lepeshinskaia's "discovery," as well as an exemplar of *state romanticism,* and the play's main character is "life in its revolutionary development" itself.

Lysenko also spoke at the May 1950 conference. Indeed, it was thanks to him that Lepeshinskaia was "discovered." As Rapoport observed, "These two 'coryphaei' found each other."[55] Lysenko found a "biological" justification for his own theories in Lepeshinskaia's "theory." To him it was obvious that "rye can arise from wheat, just as different species of wheat can give rise to rye. Those same species of wheat can give rise to barley. Rye can also give rise to wheat. Oats can give rise to wild oats, and so forth."[56] Lysenko also found the explanation for these unheard-of metamorphoses in Lepeshinskaia's work; her theory that "cells can form also not from [other] cells, and they help us to construct a theory of the transformation of certain species into others."[57]

However, it is worth seeing Lysenko and Lepeshinskaia not only as two "maniacal ignoramuses propping each other up," but also as two emblematic cultural phenomena.[58] Their biological fantasies—unverifiable, demanding constant politico-ideological feeding and repressive institutional efforts, zeal, and exaltation and materializing exclusively on the discursive and aesthetic level—are an exemplar of *state romanticism.* There were romantic creator-geniuses (although in a Soviet orchestration) at work in it, but behind the pictures of a vehement struggle in science one can already discern a fantasy-laden Socialist Realist world: "How can you see anything abroad you could compare to, for example, the people's Soviet agricultural science? The Americans are trying in vain to fathom its 'secrets' (which have provided the kinds of harvests from our fields such as there never were in all the eight or ten thousand years that man has tilled the earth). They don't understand that these 'secrets' are tied to the Soviet spirit in which our science grows."[59]

The Socialist Realist production of hyperreality here reaches the limits of "depicting life in the forms of life itself," transitioning into a "realistic grotesque" and, finally, into the pure fantasy with which Socialist Realism had a hard time, and here it was helped by "revolutionary romanticism," which mended the cracks in the picture of reality. This fantasy is filled with the "romance of communism," which spills out onto Soviet reality. Not by chance did Lepeshinskaia's biographer dedicate the final pages of her biography to the subject of Western science fiction:

> What the structure of capitalism was powerless to realize, it entrusted to its fantasy writers; they wrote about a dream while still calling it fantasy. Fantasy is not constrained by anything—readers know in advance that there is no bridge from it to reality. "In a hundred, maybe a thousand years." And yet in not a single fantasy novel from the past (or from

the capitalist world at present)—from all of Jules Verne, Wells—could we read about things even remotely similar in scope to what is being realized in our country. Even their dream, the best in their dream (and we mean the better things, not the vile cannibalistic actions that are flourishing in the literature of today's capitalism in the most overblown way)—is so much more niggardly and petty, inferior to our reality![60]

Essentially, the Lysenko-Lepeshinskaia science also burned the bridges to reality, leaving the reader *beyond* reality, face to face with a Soviet ideological phantasm. Mandel'shtam concluded the poem "Lamarck" with words suggesting that nature had retreated from people: "And it [nature] forgot the folding bridge, / Too late to lower it" for them, leaving them in "arachnid stone deafness." The characters figuring in this conditionally plausible world are complete grotesques.

THE ROMANTIC GROTESQUE

So Lysenko claimed that he had discovered a "law" according to which "new species originate in the nuclei of old species." The problem was that no one had ever seen this "law" in action; no one had had a chance to observe rye or barley giving rise to various species of wheat, or, on the contrary, rye itself giving rise to wheat, or oats to wild oats, and so forth; no one had observed in nature the changes in intracellular structure described by Lysenko. These assertions remained unproven until "evidence" was physically presented to scientific society and not just theoretically based on some sort of mystical, murky phenomena and processes. Lepeshinskaia's "discovery" possessed just such magical properties—a sort of cell-less "supposedly living" substance from which living cells could emerge.

This allowed Lysenko to assert that through a stage of this "living substance" one species could turn into another. In other words, one mystical foundation gave the groundwork for the next. The decisive support that Lepeshinskaia received from Lysenko was personal in the sense that he required her conclusions to bolster his "theory." What the organizers of the campaign could not foresee was the uncontrollability of the consequences of legitimizing this fantasy-laden "science." The affirmation of Lysenko's theories and the subsequent recognition of Lepeshinskaia opened the floodgates for a real flood of the most absurd "discoveries," when the most incredible things became reality. Basically thanks to provincial actors, a theater of the biological absurd arose before one's very eyes:

- Leningrad University associate K. M. Zavadskii reported that juvenile dividing plant cells (meristematic cells) began to emerge from a "living substance" invisible to the author, during which several of them in the early phases had no nuclei;
- A professor in Riazan, L. S. Sutulov, observed the transformation of an invisible "living substance" into lymphatic cells, from which connective tissue was formed;
- An "honored worker of RSFSR science," Odessa professor V. V. Avergurg, described the strange behavior of tuberculosis bacteria: they supposedly enabled the transformation of non-pathogenic cells into pathogenic ones in the presence of the same invisible "living substance";
- A professor in the Dnepropetrovsk medical institute and corresponding member of the USSR Academy of Medical Sciences, N. I. Zazybin, announced the neoplasm of nerve fibers from living substance;
- N. N. Kuznetsov, a docent in the Kishinev Medical Institute, reported that he had sewn pieces of peritoneum into the abdominal cavities of dogs and cats taken from the region of a cattle blind gut (cecum) after treating them with formalin and 70 percent alcohol and sterilizing them in an autoclave, but since "living substance" cannot be killed, the procedures lethal to living tissues had no effect whatsoever on the living substance of the tissues of the killed peritoneum, which not only became alive again, but also acquired full vitality, and new vessels emerged in it, and so forth;
- The department chair of histology at Rostov University, Docent F. N. Kucherova, described how she pulverized mother-of-pearl buttons and injected the powder into animal bodies. "Living substance" emerged from the powder. As mother-of-pearl is obtained from shells that earlier were living, they have accordingly retained the characteristic of the living;
- Professor G. A. Melkonian from Erevan announced that in a glass bottle containing formalin, which is poisonous to all living cells, where a tapeworm specimen extracted from a human tibia bone after many years had been kept, in accordance with Lepeshinskaia's law of the transition of nonliving into living, new living and growing bones appeared. Melkonian and his colleagues supposedly could not believe their own eyes and took out the bones, but more and more new bones began to form in that same liquid.[61]

The last report listed here appeared in the academic journal *Uspekhi sovremennoi biologii* (Successes of Contemporary Biology). Rapoport saw this last story as merely "gibberish [that] the respectable journal published with a call for readers to send the journal material containing similar observations, in view of their great scientific interest," adding an account of how the editor of the journal himself, Aleksandr Studitskii, became famous for a sensational experiment: "He removed an animal's rectus femoris muscle from its tuberosity and transformed it into a pulpy mass. He filled the tuberosity, which was subsequently removed, with this mass. After some time had passed, a normally shaped and functioning muscle formed in the place of this mass. For this work, Studitskii and his associate Aleksandra Striganova were awarded a Stalin Prize."[62]

It was not so much the fact that a Stalin Prize was awarded that was surprising, but that it was awarded for scientific achievements and not for achievements in the area of literature and art. Aleksandr Studitskii was actually not just a scientist—with a doctorate in biological sciences, a professor, a department head at Moscow State University, a laboratory director at the USSR Academy of Sciences, and editor of an academic journal. In addition, he was also a propagandist, author of the lively feuilleton "Fly Lovers Are Human Haters" in the journal *Ogonek,* illustrated with the much reproduced caricatures by Boris Efimov, which depicted geneticists as Ku Klux Klansmen, Fascists, and war criminals.[63] But most important, he was a successful fantasy writer, an author of science fiction novels. He wrote his first science fiction story in 1948, so his science and writing careers took off at the same time.

The themes in which Stalinist science immerses us allow us to rethink the view established in literary history that science fiction was in decline in the Stalin era. One might as well talk about the flowering of science fiction in the era of late Stalinism. Not only were the "scientific" fabrications of Stalinist biologists fantasy, but their fortunes were too. Undoubtedly, the most striking was the story of Gevorg Bosh'ian, practically the most undisguised charlatan, although ill-starred as well, who published the book *On the Nature of Viruses and Microbes,* in which he wrote about the transformation of submicroscopic viruses into bacteria, into "a microbial form visible under the microscope," and about the reverse transition of bacteria into viruses.[64] These "discoveries" were of a most radical nature. Bosh'ian claimed, for example, that a microbial cell consisted of thousands of virus particles, each of which could give rise to a new microbial cell, and that if viruses were gradually "domesticated" to a particular nutrient medium, one could achieve their transformation into microorganisms; further, that viruses could develop in artificial nutrient media, and not only in the presence of living cells; that antibiotics were living substances; that sterile immunity did not exist, and any immunity was infectious; that microbial cells could be obtained from cancer cells; that Louis Pasteur's experiments were erroneous; and many other such claims.[65] These unheard-of "conclusions," of course, were not in any way corroborated, and such assertions themselves "repudiated ideas that had been considered fundamental in virology, in microbiology, in immunology, and in the theory of cancer, and, in consequence, in veterinary science, medicine, and many other disciplines."[66]

Bosh'ian's "discovery" made a stunning impression. Rapoport recalled how "Once, a famous figure in medicine, holding Bosh'ian's wretched book in his hands and brandishing it about in a huge forum, proclaimed, 'The old microbiology is finished. This is your new microbiology.' That is, Bosh'ian's microbiology had come to replace that of Pasteur, Koch, Ehrlich, and others."[67]

Among the leading Soviet publicists, writers, poets, playwrights, and theater and film directors recruited to popularize Soviet scientific accomplishments, there was also a modest beginner Russian-speaking writer from Kharkov, Nikolai Dashkiev, who (as we noted above) wrote one of Ukraine's first science fiction novels in 1950, *The Triumph of Life*. As it was becoming clear that the mounting "achievements of Soviet medicine" were turning out to be unsound, the author reworked his novel until almost the end of his life. The book came out in four editions (1950 and 1952, and revised editions in 1966 and 1973) and enjoyed enormous success. From all the printings, there were 165,000 copies in all. On the heels of the success of this novel, Dashkiev wrote (also in Russian) a biographical story about Ol'ga Lepeshinskaia, "By the Untrodden Path," which did not sink into oblivion with its main character but was translated by the author and his younger son Nikolai into Ukrainian in 1973–74. Lepeshinskaia's exploits continued to live on even after her scientific unsoundness was unmasked.

The Triumph of Life tells the story of what science can achieve when it aligns with the course of Lysenko's "Michurinist biology" and, aided by Lepeshinskaia's "living substance," probes the mysteries of the microbes discovered by Bosh'ian. (In the foreword to the novel, the author warmly thanks a number of scientists, the first of which is Bosh'ian, and lets the reader know that "the book has little fiction in it. Much of what was merely likely five years ago has already been accomplished.")[68] This exemplary Socialist Realist work is interesting in that it employs various genre conventions—those of adventure narrative, children's literature, the war story, and the science fiction novel.

In an underground city where Nazis have in secret laboratories produced a terrifying bacteriological weapon and tested it on Soviet prisoners, Professor Braun, unbeknownst to the SS, creates from a lethal virus a miraculous concoction that can kill all microbes. Like a mad Dr. Mabuse, the professor is portrayed with jittery hands and a droopy lip, muttering something to himself under his breath; he is slovenly but has a menacingly intense stare. First we hear his monologues, which he usually utters with a "frightful, disheveled [look], with glittering eyes," periodically losing consciousness and throwing sheets of formula-littered paper about the room; then we see how "the professor's enormous misshapen shadow was cast upon the laboratory's walls."

These caricatured cliches of German expressionism give place to a Soviet children's tale about war. A fourteen-year-old Soviet partisan-scout, Stepan Rogov, appears in Braun's laboratory; the professor had rescued him after an unsuccessful escape from a concentration camp. As is usual in Socialist Realist novels, the most fantasy-laden thing is not what it should be but what should seem plausible. We learn, for example, that after the boy repaired a radio and started to listen to news from Moscow (in a deep bunker full of Nazi officers!), he "categorically refused to speak German with the professor, trying to prove that Max Braun ought to take up the study of Russian seriously." Their conversations made an indelible impression on the old professor, and although they did not save the professor from madness, they helped him create a medicine against all illnesses—a universal anti-virus, thanks to which no bacteria at all will frighten mankind; "a single solitary drop of it can annihilate half of all microbes on the globe! What then of bacteriological warfare? A myth! Nonsense! A man will become almost immortal—he will live two hundred and three hundred years."

With the usual mad glitter in his eyes, Braun tells Stepan the terrifying secret: "Soon—very soon!—I will create in this laboratory, from inorganic substances, from nonliving matter, a living molecule! I will create life!" Braun is a big admirer of Darwin, but he doesn't believe in the immutability of living substances, supposing that "microbes are eternal. They are just as nature created them at the beginning of its creative journey, when chemical elements combined by chance into a particular combination that from the very first moment proved to be viable." Stepan reads his *Introduction to Microbiology* in hopes of understanding the secret of creating artificial microbes, "but he didn't even suspect that no one cared any more about everything written by the professor, [writing that] was long ago cast aside by advanced Soviet science, and that Professor Braun—a student of Louis Pasteur and Robert Koch—along with valuable knowledge had adopted all his teachers' mistakes, had advanced these mistakes, and was taking a road that leads into a dead end." Nonetheless, he creates a vaccine, and Stepan rescues the precious ampule of Braun's anti-virus when he flees from the underground city, from the allies to whom the Germans had given over a factory to conduct further experiments, only now under Anglo-American supervision.

When he gets back to the motherland, Stepan initially tries to test Braun's vaccine. But as Petrenko, the party organizer of the Microbiological Institute (and later Stepan's research supervisor), explained to him, Braun "had consistently skidded toward mechanistic positions, trampling on the basic principles of materialism. . . . Iron logic suggested to the docent Petrenko that a person who didn't understand the Marxist laws of the development of nature couldn't create anything significant. Professor Braun's drug, as far as Petrenko was concerned, was doomed in advance to failure." And failure overtook it. The vaccine fell into the hands of the villain Velikopol'skii (who would later turn out to be a saboteur), who wanted to claim it for himself, but it turned out to be useless since it only slowed the progress of diseases and could not cure them. Nonetheless, the main goal of Braun's vaccine was achieved—it kindled a dream in the boy-partisan of creating a wonder-working medicine.

Then Stepan goes to study in evening school, to which his local kolkhoz sends him, after which he enrolls in the biology department of a university where the student Communists mold out of the former partisan a Soviet biologist who will be destined to create a vaccine and save mankind from diseases and, right along with it, from the chief enemies—imperialists. Stepan knows that "not only the German Fascists but also the Japanese ones had made tons of lethal bacteria to use against the Soviet Union, swarms of plague-infested rats. The American imperialists are threatening war. . . . And the underground city fell into the Americans' hands." The creation of an anti-virus becomes an important political act.

The party organizer-virologist tells the students that "the Soviet scientist, Professor Lepeshinskaia, proved that pre-cellular forms of life are possible. In certain cases more-or-less complex proteins become viable, and hence, by artificially creating a protein, we will thereby create life. . . . Will we be able to create complex, viable proteins artificially? It seems we will." And then a new magnificent discovery of the present time is made (they follow one after another in the Soviet Union). Stepan's friend tells his classmates about it: a book by a certain G. M. Zar'ian, *On the Nature of Viruses,* has appeared, which "Stepan and Tania [Stepan's girlfriend] feverishly leaf through, and the more they penetrate its meaning, the more they are filled with a feeling of respect for the author. Surely such discoveries are made once in a hundred years." Pasteur is desecrated; "a hundred years ago the Paris Academy awarded a prize to the eminent microbiologist Pasteur for proving the impossibility of spontaneous generation of life on earth in our times. . . . But now a Soviet scientist has proven that, after all, Pasteur was awarded the prize undeservedly. Professor Zar'ian's experiments. . . ."

Several students are worked into a nihilist frenzy: "'Ah, Pasteur, Pasteur!' Karpov said disdainfully, waving his hand. 'He held up the development of microbiology for a hundred years! . . . Right, Stepan?'" But Stepan, as a self-possessed Soviet student, explains the danger of such nihilism: "Does the fact that Zar'ian proved the existence of living microorganisms in penicillin, which was considered sterile, really force us to reject this drug? This is not the point, my friends! The point is that Zar'ian's theory is a new step in cognition. Professor Zar'ian has for the first time provided a real materialist explanation of observed facts."

Zar'ian's discovery demonstrated that microbes transform into viruses, and various viruses turn out to be merely a stage through which various microorganisms pass. Hence endless transformations of one into another occur. These transformations, as Lysenko demonstrated, can be controlled since according to Lepeshinskaia, life exists on the pre-cellular level. This incredible biology is what brings the heroes of this novel to their discovery, a real "triumph of life."

They work on creating a cancer vaccine, but they have to fight the dangerous enemy Velikopol'skii, who claims that cancer is a hereditary illness. Our heroes, of course, cannot reconcile themselves to this theory. So the student Rogov throws the gauntlet to the professor by publicly announcing that his theory is erroneous because "a cancer virus preserved in gametes and transmitted by heredity is the same gene the Weismannists, formalist geneticists, have. . . . You think an organism is a passive environment. That contradicts Pavlov's theory and Michurinist microbiology." Velikopol'skii's declaration that all his statements are supported by facts is parried by another student—the secretary of the institute's Komsomol organization and Stalin stipend-holder—who has his own scientific research: "Facts can be interpreted different ways, but your theory is incorrect and, moreover, harmful!" This discussion goes on for page after page in the novel, but the argumentation used in it is seemingly copied out of Lysenko and Lepeshinskaia. The opponent's conclusions are not false because they contradict facts, which "can be interpreted different ways," but because they "contradict Pavlov's theory and Michurinist microbiology." And finally, a much more horrible thing for a scientific theory than being "incorrect" is being "harmful."

Our heroes, on the contrary, create a useful theory. To enable this, the novel introduces an old professor who, way back before the revolution, observed "Ivanov's disease," which made its victims unsusceptible to practically any other disease; its virus destroyed other species of viruses in the living organism. From it, a vaccine against cancer can be created. Now Stepan searches for the Ivanov's disease virus and finds it in the boatswain of an English schooner that he meets by chance in Leningrad. For all the money Stepan has on him, as well as his watch and his clothes, the boatswain agrees to provide some blood, and Stepan and his friends manage to create a cancer vaccine from this blood. Fully in accordance with the miracles described in the scientific journals in those years, the heroes carry out the same operations as real professors in provincial institutes of higher learning. Just as the Erevan professor Melkonian had seen living, growing bones appear in his long-kept glass bottle of lethal formalin with the tapeworm specimen extracted from a human tibia bone, the heroes of Dashkiev's novel raise living organisms in jars. So the reader is present for the battle happening, for the first time in history in a human-controlled thermostat, between the Ivanov's virus and the cancer virus.

Meanwhile, on his return to England the boatswain catches the eye of an English spy, and a saboteur is sent to Stepan's lab to blackmail Velikopol'skii into being an accomplice in destroying the vaccine. The destruction is effected by raising the temperature of the thermostats where the vaccine is kept and adding special physiological solutions that completely annihilate the Ivanov's virus. The English had the Ivanov's-infected blood of the boatswain at their disposal but nonetheless failed to make a vaccine. This was because they did not have the correct theory. They did not know something that "creative Darwinism" could tell them: "By influencing a virus with a change of external conditions it is possible to reorganize its structure, forcing it to accumulate the hereditary changes acquired by each generation."

Zar'ian's "materialist theory" saves the day; the discovery of "stadiality" in the development of viruses and "the possibility of the existence of invisible forms of the infectious principle" in them makes it possible to resurrect the Ivanov's virus destroyed by the saboteurs; after all, as Lepeshinskaia and Bosh'ian had demonstrated, life is ineradicable. Then the long battle to change the viruses' properties began. "This was a lengthy, wearisome process that lasted a year and a half. Generation after generation, the viruses were cultured in unusual conditions, acquiring and accumulating those very characteristics that were needed. ... Slowly—day by day, step by step, experiment after experiment—the viruses changed their characteristics. Gradually, the Ivanov's virus lost its impregnability; it was now easily injected not only into masses of 'living tissues,' but into living organisms as well." As a result, the heroes not only received the Stalin Prize, First Class, but also learned how to "restructure viruses" to create "good viruses."

But never mind the viruses! Stepan goes home to his old kolkhoz, which over the intervening several years has been miraculously transfigured:

Self-driven combines, electric plows, forest-protection zones, electrified stables and swine farms, clever and complex machines for cleaning and vernalizing grain—all that Stepan saw that day and the next one no longer excited his imagination. Stepan looked only at the people.

What of the machines? Tomorrow they will be created even more perfect, even cleverer. But what will create them, control them, is people. ... Stepan sensed that a new generation was growing up. This generation perceived communism as a real, realized Tomorrow.

Although it allowed for living in this "Tomorrow" today, Socialist Realism would be politically nonfunctional if it did not, at the same time it demanded transformation of life "in its revolutionary development" also assume a "truthful, historically concrete portrayal of reality." Socialist Realism cannot function in unbridled, nonpolarized space. Its effect begins in the moment of mutual neutralization of opposing poles/modes. This space of threats, repression, and striving for mutual destruction transforms the aesthetic strategies of Socialist Realism into political ones. And, of course, vice versa.

7 The Power of Grammar and the Grammar of Power

Linguistic Realism

CONJUGATING MARXISM: WORD-FORMATION THROUGH IDEOLOGICAL HYBRIDIZATION

In Fedor Abramov's novel *Paths and Crossroads,* which tells a story about postwar life in a northern village, after a couple of drinks certain peasants are talking with the kolkhoz chairman, who is having a consciousness-raising session with them:

> "Ivan Dmitrievich, what's this they're saying about our having saboteurs again?"
>
> "What saboteurs?"
>
> "Some kind of academicians. They say they wanted to wipe out the Russian language, it seems. . . ."
>
> "The language?" Arkadii Iakovlev asked, terribly surprised. "What do you mean, the language?"
>
> "Yes, yes," Ignatii Baev eagerly concurred. "I heard it, too. Joseph Vissarionovich himself, they say, set them straight. In the newspaper, *Pravda.* . . ."
>
> "Well, there you go," the old watchman sighed. "This is a fine thing! Last year some kind of cosmopolitans sold out to the foreign capitalists; this year it was academics. . . . I don't know what the authorities are doing about it. Why can't they get rid of these bastards?"[1]

After a lively exchange on the subject of consciousness ("Shut up with the consciousness thing! Consciousness. . . . Can I feed the cows in wintertime with your consciousness?"), the conversation turned to, of all things, linguistics. The kolkhoz chairman could not keep up with the conversation since Stalin's "works on language" had appeared right at haymaking time, and he was not prepared for such a momentous subject. However, the district party committee undertook the discussion in earnest, convening a regional meeting on the issue. The chairman covered thirty-one miles on horseback without a respite, changing horses twice, to get to the regional clubhouse on time, but even the party leadership could say little about the heart of the matter: "Podrezov [the regional committee secretary] did not mince words. And to the question of what conclusions practitioners—say, kolkhoz chairmen—should draw from Comrade Stalin's works on language, he answered forthrightly, 'Work hard.' And, not sparing himself at all, he added, self-critically, 'And as far as all these subtleties with language are concerned, I don't really understand them very well myself, either.'"

The only person who was an expert, as it turned out, was the regional committee's instructor, the party propagandist Ganichev. It was he who explained the essence of the issue:

> Yes, Joseph Vissarionovich has given us a quite a task. At first, when all these so-called academicians started publishing in *Pravda,* I was a little bit afraid. That's it, I thought; I'm finished—I should step down. I didn't understand a damn thing. But when Joseph Vissarionovich published his articles, everything became clear! You can't understand anything from these so-called academicians. You see, all this scribbling of theirs is bogus scholarship, just trying to addle your brains. . . . The scum are multiplying among us, and they're throwing a wrench in the works left and right. . . . They've even started in against the natural sciences and attacked Lysenko himself.[2]

The era of "addling brains" (literally: the "so-called academicians" were accused of separating language from thought) reached its apex in the summer of 1950, when Stalin personally participated in the *Pravda* discussion about linguistic problems that he himself had inspired. He destroyed academician Nikolai Iakovlevich Marr's "new theory of language," which had dominated Soviet linguistics in the 1930s and 1940s, heralding the advent of the "Stalinist theory of language."

The collisions involved in the linguistic debate, the epicenter of which was formed by Marr's theory and "Comrade Stalin's works on linguistic issues," have called forth significant scholarly interest. Above all, Marr himself, as a radical and paradoxical thinker, a temperamental polemicist, and a clearly unique personality, played such a decisive role in the development of Soviet linguistics that without him, its history would simply be impossible, just as the history of Soviet literature, for example, would be impossible without Gorky. The scale of the influence of this charismatic figure on the development of linguistics was enormous. It is no surprise, then, that Marr landed in the center of linguistic historians' interest,[3] but only rarely in that of the historians of culture.[4] But even in these rare latter instances, aside from the problems of purely historical linguistics, it is the peculiarity of Marr's theory itself and of his personality in the context of early Soviet cultural mythology that have been central to the treatments of Marr and Marrism and not their later far-reaching politico-ideological implications. The rout of Marrism has been examined outside the context of Soviet political culture, Soviet cultural history, and the evolution of the Soviet politico-ideological project. Notwithstanding, the cultural/ideological aspect of the events in Soviet linguistics in the early 1950s was no less peculiar and historically significant than Marr's theory itself. "Stalin's teaching about language," which was worse than Marr's in terms of its paradoxicality and radicalism, undoubtedly surpassed it in politico-ideological significance; had Stalin's "works on linguistic issues" not appeared, Marr's concepts would have continued to be a completely marginal doctrine (and, what is more, an intensely fading one) of a completely marginal scholarly discipline. Stalin imbued it with political urgency, ideological weight, and social resonance.

Marr is interesting not so much as a destroyer as a tragic figure in a tragic era. He differed from other authors of megatheories in postrevolutionary Russia such as Trofim Lysenko and Ol'ga Lepeshinskaia not only in that he was an educated and honest person, but also in that he constructed a linguistic theory that became a reflection of, and a therapy for, his own very personal traumas. In the revolutionary culture, the ideas that Marr defended were socially resonant for many people; in the 1920s and early 1930s, many were suffering from the same traumas. In 1950, when Stalin unleashed his wrath on Marrism (sixteen years after Marr's death), the Soviet Union was already a different country. The 1920s traumas no longer interested it, as it was suffering from completely different complexes.

Katerina Clark called Marrism "Promethean linguistics" and wrote about its irrationality.[5] Although Marr's theory, in conflict as it was with logic and linguistic history, had no rational underpinnings, like Lysenko's "agrobiology" it was based on a rationale of its own peculiar sort—romantic and voluntarist. The basis of this rationale was the will. The ideological underpinning came from Marx's famous thesis that the task of philosophy is not to explain the world but rather to remake it. The means and the arena for Marr's realization of this task were the fantasies that sublimated desires and traumas into an ideologically saturated literary text.

The link between Marr's linguistic theory and biology is quite easy to trace. It is obvious not only in his use of "paleontology" as a key term, but also in his constant and aggressive use of such terms as "hybridization," "crossbreeding," "relict types," "propagation of languages," "strains of languages," "mutations," and, of course, "hybridization of languages" as he understood it: "a structurally simple language, i.e., one not 'hybridized,' like a weak creature in the struggle for life, would be doomed to perish."[6] These were no longer analogies, no longer metaphors. Marr thought in the same categories as did the ideologues of "Michurinist biology." But many others at the time also thought in terms of this aggressive romantic biology. In his linguistic treatise Stalin would provide a broad definition of Marxism as a revolutionary science—a science of political transformations, and a science not of explaining the world but of changing it. As Georgii Aleksandrov explained, it was a science about "how to change the laws of life," which proclaimed that it was "necessary to discard the decrepit old world of capitalism and build a new one—a young and healthy, strong and growing world of socialism, of communism."[7] Accordingly, Marxism can be understood as a social science of life, a sort of social biology.

Since for Lysenko the development of a plant was the product of interaction with the environment, of mutation and adaptation to the environment, and not of the inheritance and action of a genotype, "the scientist's task," as Konstantin Bogdanov observes, was "to direct this mutation into the necessary channel, to create the conditions in which the plant itself will improve its own nature. . . . In the world of plants, if one understands this world as a whole, development is all-out and endless. In it, as in language as well, 'everything is contained in everything,' and therefore 'everything' can be turned into 'everything': the languages of Georgia into the languages of North America, apple trees into plum trees."[8]

Boris Gasparov situated Marr's theory in an even broader philosophical context: "Marr's theory, with its vehement criticism of comparative

philology, not totally lacking in insight, emerged as one of the manifestations of the romantic-revolutionary spirit that were opposed to the
positivist science of the 'Victorian age.'"[9]

Marr's criticism of positivist linguistics was linked to Lysenko's
neo-Lamarckian biology through, as Gasparov notes, the "Bergsonian
structure of thinking" common to both. The advocates of this structure
"attempted in the first third of the century (in biology as well as in philology and aesthetics) to work out an alternative to what they regarded
as a new (avant-garde) version of the positivist 'mechanical' approach
upon which Bergson's critical zeal had been originally focused."[10]

The method of philosophical interpretation of these scientific concepts helps to elucidate the ties among them, but it does not allow
us to answer the question of why, two years after Lysenko's Stalin-
sanctioned ultimate victory, Stalin personally participated in the rout of
Marr's scientific empire. We must seek the answers, it seems, not only
on the aesthetic (literary) and philosophical levels, but also on the level
of political ideology, a part of which Marr's teachings were.

The debates surrounding Marr both in the early 1930s and in the
early 1950s revolved around his "Marxism." His "new theory of language," proclaimed a true incarnation of Marxism in linguistics at the
cusp of the 1930s, was in 1950 cast down from its Marxist pedestal by
the principle judge of ideology. Stalin declared that "Marr shouted a lot
about Marxism, but he was not a Marxist" and called him a "vulgar-
izer." This was what Marxists were usually called in the post-class era of
the Stalin regime. And although the adjective "Marxist" itself in Soviet
Russia had a completely different import in the 1920s than it did in the
second half of the 1930s and up through the 1950s, if one views Marxism as a particular kind of conceptual and categorical framework and
compares similar applications in philosophy, history, literary studies, art
criticism/history, jurisprudence, and many other disciplines in the 1920s
and early 1930s; if one situates the linguistic discussions that took place
during the shaping of the "new theory about language" in the context
of the discussions on other cultural and scientific "fronts" (the broader
context of the ideological debates in those years), then one can definitively state that Marr was indeed a spokesman for a specifically "Marxist" linguistics (like the "Marxism" of Mikhail Pokrovskii in history, of
Nikolai Krylenko and Evgenii Pashukanis in jurisprudence, Valer'ian
Pereverzev and Vladimir Friche in literary studies, and the like). The

fact that Marr's teaching was fantasy-laden, illogical, or scientifically unproductive and that its adepts accused each other of "social-Fascist contraband," of course, does not make it "anti-Marxist."

Marr believed that "a national language, of an entire nation, does not exist; rather, there is a class language, and the languages of one and the same class in different countries, given the identical nature of the social structure, manifest more typological affinity to each other than the languages of the different classes within one and the same country, within one and the same nation."[11] The national language was declared a fiction, and class languages became the only genuine reality. This was logically an internationalist (far from reality as it was) concept of language.

This was, to be sure, "Marxism in linguistics," a truly "Marxist approach to language." Stalinism, however, was based on the traditional national model. By referencing national language and ridding it of any class halo, Stalin reconstructed the concept of a "people" and a nation, in the definition of which language played a key role (we should remember that in Stalin's definition of a nation, language assumes first place as the most significant identifying characteristic). Accordingly, Stalin wrote about the "pan-national position" of language, that language serves not classes but the nation as a whole. The collision between Marr's and Stalin's ideas was only a matter of time.

Marr's orientation toward class became a convenient target in the post-class era. Arousing Stalin's particular indignation was Marr's detection of class differentiation as early as the Paleolithic period and his assertion that classes existed in primitive society. According to Marr, it seemed, a classless society had never existed, language was born as an act of magic, and the magicians themselves were the first exploitative class. With the separation of the human collective from the animal world, class language emerged (as a source of supremacy): "We must not be silent, nor even hesitate to say that a supra-class language has not hitherto existed; language was class-conscious from the moment of its first appearance, from the moment that spoken language appeared; it was the language of the class that took control of all the implements of production of those eras, including magic–production."[12]

According to Marr, then, a class society had existed in the era of the late Paleolithic and did not originate in the era of the decay of the tribal system (and here Marr had engaged in open polemic against Engels). If

Stalin rose in defense of Engels (whom he did not like and had himself openly criticized), it was only because important political implications ensued from this; according to official Soviet doctrine, communism was a sort of return to a primitive order—to the social justice of "primitive communism." But now it seemed that there had not been any primitive communism at all, and even primitive society had been structured by class. In other words, Marr's pronouncements implied that a society cannot exist at all without class (at least that, historically, class structure and sociality had arisen simultaneously) and that class (and accordingly "man's exploitation of man") was inherent in human nature itself. Marxism's most important argument—that classless society is natural, while an exploitative society is the product of the perversion of human nature—was crumbling. Now it appeared that one should not speak of the perversion of human nature but rather of its realization. In this case, Marxist criticism was misdirected; claims needed to be filed against human nature itself, not against an "exploitative society." Thus consistent Marxism was coming into contradiction with political expediency and, in doing so, was becoming an ideological burden. So the real issue was not whether Marrism was "Marxism in linguistics" (it was, undoubtedly) but rather that in post-revolutionary cultures, baseline principles yielded to purely political priorities. And in this respect, Marrism must be understood as a phenomenon of political ideology.

It was in just this capacity that the negative content in Marrism predominated over its positive program. Marr had first and foremost taken a stand against Indo-Europeanist thinking, against the traditional concepts of the nature of language and language development. The majority of Marr's own statements, and in particular those of his ideological defenders, consisted of criticism of "pseudoscience." The Marrists' constructs of "science" and "pseudoscience" were built by a mirrored principle. That their "positive program" was a negative reflection of the postulates of the repudiated "pseudoscience" was remarkable enough; moreover, in building up their new reality, they were obliged to again build up connections between reality and the new linguistic picture of the world they had created, and the further their criticism of the "pseudoscience" advanced, the more Marr had to concoct absurd explanations for linguistic reality. For example, if according to traditional notions language was tied to national culture, then according to Marr it was an ideological superstructure and had a class-oriented nature. Or if traditional Indo-European linguistics examined the history of language in the context of internal linguistic evolution, then Marr advocated the idea of stadial development of languages and maintained that with a society's transition from one socioeconomic formation to another there was a transition of language into some new capacity (through linguistic revolutions, "leaps," and other such violent processes). In yet another case, when established views maintained that a single protolanguage gradually disintegrated into separate but genetically related languages, Marr asserted that language development proceeded in the opposite direction, from multiplicity to unity.

These assertions entailed the necessity of reexamining a whole series of derivative assumptions. Among them, for example, was the need to explain the origin of the various languages. Marr maintained that they arose independently of each other; thus languages considered undoubtedly related (even dialects of one and the same language) were not related in reality; they were not related at all and in fact originally arose independently of each other. The obvious similarities among languages were declared the product of hybridization (two different languages formed a new language, a successor to both ancestors, as the result of interaction between them). Having cast aside the protolanguage theory, Marr found himself obliged to fill the gaping hole thus formed. Hence arose the idea that all the world's languages arose from the four elements, and the language researcher's task was reduced to "linguistic paleontology"—that is, the search for these elements in all languages in the mists of history.

Since these types of theories were built up not as the result of analyzing material and were not the products of positive knowledge but rather were created as counter-theories, they crumbled in collision with real linguistic material, which constantly required them to be tied somehow to reality. However, the negativism of the Marrist scheme (like that of Lysenko's agrobiology or Ol'ga Lepeshinskaia's theory of "living substance") had Marxist doctrine itself as an exemplar; in it, the weakness of its positive program was compensated for by the intensity of its criticism of capitalism.

Thus we can posit the complete irrelevance of the positive content in these theories since their function boiled down to replacing reality and producing ideological constructs (which filled the vacuum in the "scientific Marxist-Leninist worldview") instead of producing positive knowledge or being of practical use. "With every new historic victory of the working class, the organizing, mobilizing, and transforming power of its scientific worldview—of Marxism-Leninism—grows ever stronger."[13] The reason for this growth is the special character of Soviet science; if the "advantages of capitalism" are observed in economics (science is important here to the extent that it stimulates industrial growth and production efficiency, which in turn leads to a rise in the living standard and to further growth of production), then the "advantages of socialism" are more than anything else argued theoretically, "scientifically," via "the only true Marxist-Leninist teaching," which is itself the foundation for any science—from linguistics to chemistry.

Thus the status of Stalin's statements about linguistics is certainly superior to any positive knowledge and to any conceivable effectiveness. In the case of linguistics, Stalin speaks out against the absurd Marrist scheme and attempts to show the rightness of traditional linguistics; but in Lysenko's case he, on the contrary, sanctions the rout of science and the propagation of absurd Lysenkoist agrobiology. In both cases he turns out to be right, which suggests the irrelevance itself of the content of Stalin's position. Therefore, it would not be a mistake to assert that *as a whole, Soviet science was not "under the heel of ideology" and did not "suffer from an ideological dictate" but was rather itself a political ideology, a special form of ideological discourse.*

In this capacity, Soviet science was purely a *politically instrumental* phenomenon. What was politically expedient in it was convincing and effective. As it was an ideology, Soviet science was *expansive.* As mechanisms for creating a parallel reality, ideologies always strive to destroy the reality that threatens the picture of the world they have created; hence, expansion is a natural form of their existence. The larger the area of reality that is ideologically transformed, the higher the chances are that this ideology will survive. Directly related to this is the fact that "Stalin's teaching about language" spread, over the course of three years, into all the social sciences and humanities, in every one of which something was found that needed restructuring "in the light of Comrade Stalin's works."

MARXISM AND LINGUISTICS ISSUES:
THE IDEOLOGICAL SYNTAX OF STALINISM

"Comrade Stalin's work" entitled *Marxism and Linguistics Issues* is a fifty-page brochure. It contains an article that occupied one page in

Pravda in the course of the discussion (on June 20, 1950) and four short responses to readers in the form of letters (one from July 4 and three from August 2). In the three years following its release, Stalin's text was endlessly cited and commented upon. Nonetheless, as Vladimir Alpatov observed, "We have devoted little serious analysis . . . to Stalin's work itself."[14] When the text has been examined, it has been primarily by historians of linguistics. Notwithstanding, as early as 1950 linguists were forced to transform themselves into philosophers when they undertook a commentary on Stalin's arguments about general themes. Stalin's theorizing itself obliged them to discuss not so much linguistics as topics like the base, the superstructure, and class awareness.

Stalin's text was at first extolled as an example of his scientific genius; then it was substantially forgotten. A fair amount has been written about Stalin's reasons for writing it but nothing about the reasons for its being forgotten. The fact that it lacks a single original thought (or, if there is just one—that the Russian language developed from some sort of "Kursk-Orlovsk dialect"—it is incorrect) can scarcely justify the oblivion to which it was consigned. Stalin never strove for novelty in his thinking but rather aimed at political expediency. In every case, the forcefulness of his thought is in its efficacy, not its originality. The reason his "work" has been forgotten is not so much that after his death his name was preferably left undisturbed unless there was a particular need or that when the Soviet Union came to an end, there were a great many more important reasons for referring to Stalin than his relatively inoffensive (in the light of their consequences) linguistic disquisitions. Nor is it the fact that for historians, the brochure is "about linguistics," while for linguists it is merely a page in history. The main thing is that Stalin's text is not about language at all. In other words, its relation to linguistics is quite peripheral. Above all it is a meta-text and a striking example of Stalin's theorizing about "Marxism" with examples taken from linguistics; that is, the real issue is "Marxism," and "linguistic issues" are merely mentioned in passing. It is a text about Stalin, not about language.

Stalin's "work" is constructed by its author's typical principle of question-and-answer, in which he formulates the questions himself and provides the answers. This allows Stalin to completely control the course of the discussion. The basic text, then, consists of four questions that he asks himself (on behalf of some "group of young comrades").

The first question is about the base and the superstructure, and the second, about the relationship to class. The third asks what language is (if not a superstructure and not a class phenomenon). Here, Stalin's discourse about assimilation/subordination, the victory of one language over another, sudden disruptions in language, and the revolution in a language as a condition for transitioning from an old nature to a new one is more from the arena of politics than linguistics. The fourth and final question is about the role of the current discussions in overcoming the crisis in Soviet linguistics; that is, it is more about the workings of scholarly institutions than about language.

Stalin's "answers" are also only marginally connected to language, and they focus on general propositions that are merely applied to language. The four "answers to colleagues" are supposed to compensate for this deficiency, so it seems. And, in fact, these "comrades" are specifically interested in questions about language, but from Stalin's answers it again becomes clear that his main concern is not linguistic but political. The first letter, for example, to "Comrade Krasheninnikova," is constructed in the form of answers to an interviewer who tries to balance an already declared stance: if Stalin speaks against Marr, his interlocutor wonders whether there is something positive about Marr; if Stalin says that semantics is harmful, Comrade Krasheninnikova wonders whether semasiology, at least, has even some sort of rational principle; if Stalin says that language is not a class phenomenon, his correspondent asks whether one should at least consider "the essence of the ideas expressed" as class-related, and so forth. Every time, Stalin "backtracks," so to speak: yes, of course, there is much that is "valuable and instructive" in Marr; yes, he has "works written with talent"; yes, semantics is useful if not taken to absolutes; and so on and so forth. The three other letters are dedicated to a definition of Marxism and a criticism of dogmatism ("Reply to Comrade A. Kholopov"), the curious question of how deaf mutes think if they have no mastery of language ("Reply to Comrades D. Belkin and S. Furer"), and, finally, issues of class again—how to interpret the concept of "class jargon" ("Reply to Comrade Sanzheev").

In brief, Stalin examines linguistic topics, properly speaking, only in passing. For him, linguistics is one of the "social sciences," in which he is an undisputed specialist; he starts out by saying, "I am not a linguist, and, of course, I cannot completely satisfy the comrades. As far as Marxism in linguistics goes, just as in the other social sciences, I do have a direct relationship to this."

Striking here is the almost complete anonymity of the objects of criticism; only at the end, when the matter of personal accusations arises, does Stalin name a few names. Usually, however, they are indistinctly referenced "comrades" (my emphasis throughout in the following): *"Certain of our comrades* have concluded that . . ."; *"These comrades* forget that . . ."; "Do *these comrades* think that. . . ?"; "The mistake that *these comrades* make is that . . ."; "It appears that *the esteemed comrades* have distorted Lenin's views"; *"Certain of our comrades* have dragged themselves along in the footsteps of the Bundovites"; and so forth. The absurd anonymity of these invectives reaches an apogee when Stalin, in yet another rhetorical passage, poses the question, "Do *the aforementioned comrades* acknowledge this tenet of Marxism?" The "comrades" were in fact not "mentioned" by name, and the word "comrades" is used more than forty times in the text.

This is not simply a matter of a stylistic feature. Anonymity is a defining strategy of Stalin's text, which is replete with impersonal constructions such as the following, wherein the third-person "they" is not identified (my emphasis throughout): *"They reference* Marx; *they quote* one place in his article . . ."; *"They reference* Engels; *they quote* Engels' words . . ."; *"They reference* Lafargue . . ."; "Finally, *they reference* Stalin. *They include* a quote from Stalin about . . ."; *"They say* that. . . ."* This anonymity, which is on the whole characteristic of Stalin's public discourse, is the expression of the narrative tension between academicism and the status of the text; on the one hand, a political text is passed off as an academic one; on the other, the status itself of the text does not permit its author ("the coryphaeus of the sciences") to get bogged down in details, much less to name names (he dwells only on Marr and mentions his successor Ivan Meshchaninov only in passing, as well as his correspondents and the participants of the discussion to whom he makes reference). It is not that Stalin wants to emphasize the prevalence of the mistakes made by these "comrades" who are referencing, quoting, or just "saying." His own status does not give him the right to make specific references by name; ultimately, he as leader is engaged not in correcting linguists but in giving voice to certain truths that are far more important than any specific individuals, not to mention all of linguistics put together.

The peculiarity of Stalin's text is not its content but rather its form of presentation. On the one hand, it manifests as an example of comradely criticism in an atmosphere of scholarly discussion and party-spirited democracy and accordingly is presented in an "ordinary" way; this text, longer than any of Stalin's over the preceding ten years, is printed with a modest signature as "one of" those received by the editors. On the other hand, the status of a statement made by Stalin himself was such that even a short welcoming telegram without real content, or two sentences in response to some correspondent's question, were printed on the front pages of all the country's newspapers in huge letters with an enormous portrait of him. But in this case, Stalin is speaking simultaneously as a private individual (just another citizen who has gotten interested in linguistics and who decides to take part in a newspaper discussion), as a scholar, and as the leader.

As a "private individual," he publishes his text in exactly the same format as the other participants of the discussion. As a scholar, he demonstrates his mastery of the material and shows off his knowledge of the details and the special terms. Thus, like Zhdanov discussing atonality in music, he talks about semasiology and pointedly observes that Marr has "particular works that are good and written with talent" wherein he "conscientiously and, I must say, expertly examines particular languages." The reader is of course unaware that the basic source of Stalin's linguistic wisdom are the *Great Soviet Encyclopedia* and D. N. Kudriavskii's introductory textbook on linguistics, published in 1912 in Tartu; that Stalin read these works only a few months before writing this new "work of genius"; and that the person discussing Marr's abilities as a language researcher is one who does not know a single foreign language. Finally, as a leader, Stalin declares, "If I were not convinced of the honesty of Comrade Meshchaninov and the other people in linguistics, I would say that such behavior is tantamount to sabotage"; such a declaration could not be made by either a private individual or a scholar. This is almost the only place in the text where Stalin lifts his mask.

The goal of this text boils down to positioning a scholar as a leader, and the goal is achieved by positioning a leader as a scholar. Scholarliness is a most significant legitimizing underpinning for power, and Stalin displays it mainly in using the appropriate jargon. For example, one of his favorite usages in this treatise is the word "formula," which he employs forty times(!); it holds second place, perhaps, only to the word "comrade(s)." Here are examples (my emphasis throughout): "Can our comrades really not be familiar with the Marxists' famous *formula* about. . . . Do they agree with this Marxist *formula?*"; "The *formula* regarding the 'class nature' of language is a mistaken, non-Marxist *formula*"; "Russian Marxists have concluded that Engels's *formula* envisions the victory of socialism in all countries. . . . As one can see, we are dealing with two different *formulas*. . . . Dogmatists and talmudists might say . . . that it is necessary to discard one of the *formulas*. . . . But Marxists cannot help saying that the dogmatists and talmudists are mistaken, for both these *formulas* are correct, but not absolutely, and each is correct for its own time: the *formula* of Soviet Marxists for the period of the victory of socialism in one or a few countries, and Engels's *formula* for the period . . . in which the necessary conditions will be created for applying Engels' *formula*"; "In its development, Marxism cannot but be enriched by new experience. . . . Certain of its *formulas* and conclusions cannot but change with the passage of time; they cannot but be replaced by new *formulas* and conclusions. . . . Marxism does not acknowledge unchangeable conclusions and *formulas*."

Can there be anything "more scientific" than "formulas"? They transform Stalin's text into perfect "science." However, it is not simply a question of Stalin's creating science through his choice of words. The legitimacy of his power is projected specifically through science. In a short, three-page speech he gave for a reception for high school workers on May 17, 1938, the word "science" and its derivatives occur forty-three times (my emphasis throughout):

> In its development, *science* knows quite a few courageous people who knew how to tear down the old and create the new, despite any obstacles whatsoever. *Men of science* like Galileo, Darwin, and many others are known to all. I would like to concentrate on one of such *coryphaei of science* who is, in addition to that, the greatest man of our times. I have in mind Lenin, our teacher, our educator. Remember the year 1917. Based on *scientific* analysis of the social development of Russia, based on *scientific* analysis of the international situation, Lenin concluded that the only way out of the situation was the victory of socialism in Russia. This was a more-than-unexpected conclusion for many *people of science* at the time. Plekhanov, one of the outstanding *people of science*, spoke disdainfully at the time about Lenin, stating that Lenin was "delirious." Other *people of science*, no less famous, stated that "Lenin has lost his

mind," that he ought to be locked up somewhere far away. At that time, all and sundry *people of science* were against Lenin as a person who was destroying *science*. But Lenin had no fear of going against the grain, against stagnation. And Lenin was victorious.

There you have an example of a *man of science* who boldly waged war on obsolete *science* and paved the way for new *science*.[15]

The opposition between "people of science" and "men of science" (who were also "coryphaei of science") allows us to see Stalin constructing—as always, via Lenin—his own image. In an era when science and progress inspired a cult, the terms "leader" and "coryphaeus of science" were practically synonyms. Science needs power for its advancement; power (a leader) needs science for its (his) legitimacy. The consolidation of the status of science becomes a most significant state task (after the war, "scientists became one of the most significant elite groups of Soviet society, ranking just below party/political, economic, and military elites").[16] As distinct from capricious market capitalism, socialism develops according to the scientifically established laws of Marxism-Leninism or, in Georgii Aleksandrov's oxymoronic definition, "the scientific ideology of the proletariat."[17] The spirit of science becomes a synonym for the legitimacy of the political system. For Stalin, science is a special ideological arena in which he expresses himself in the specific style of debates/directives. His thinking is always politically refined and efficacious; one might say that, as it is directed toward a definite practical goal, it is exemplary of "the connection between theory and practice." His thinking always moves between polar opposites and operates with unambiguous categories. (This by no means makes Stalin's thinking itself unambiguous; on the contrary, as we shall see, his rigor only compensates for the absolute relativism of his debates.)[18] His text is replete with such unambiguousness:

QUESTION: Is it true that language is a superstructure on the base?
ANSWER: No, it is untrue.

QUESTION: Is it true that language always was, and will remain, class-oriented. . . ?
ANSWER: No, it is untrue.

QUESTION: Did *Pravda* act rightly when it opened up a free discussion on the issues in linguistics?
ANSWER: Yes, it did.

Pairs of opposites like "correct/incorrect," "right(ly)/wrong(ly)," and so forth are hyperabundant in Stalin's text (my emphasis throughout the following examples): "It is absolutely *correct* that . . ."; "It would be absolutely *incorrect* to think that . . ."; "Lenin is absolutely *right* about this"; "Lafargue was not *right*"; "Was Marr *right* to ascribe language to the category of implements of production? No, undoubtedly, he was *incorrect*"; "You no doubt are *correctly* interpreting my stance on the issue of dialects"; and so forth. Another favorite pairing is "true/untrue": "Of course, it is *untrue* that . . ."; "All of this is *true*"; "This, of course, is *untrue*." Hence there is the constant reminder of someone's "mistakes" (the word and its derivatives crop up more than twenty times in the text): "Confusing language with superstructure means making a serious *mistake*"; "I think there is nothing more *mistaken* than such a conclusion"; "Our comrades are making at least two *mistakes* about this"; "Our comrades' *mistake* here is that . . ."; "However, it would be deeply *mistaken* to think that . . ."; "Of course, Marr's works are not made up completely of *mistakes*"; "Marr made some egregious *mistakes*."

Practically speaking, those who wrote that Stalin created the greatest "work" in the history of linguistics were correct; it is truly a scientific text of extreme truth and extreme effectiveness. Each time (no matter in which context) that Stalin pairs "right/wrong" or "true/untrue," he confirms his absolute power. His absolute truth is assured by absolute power. This power is consolidated by truth, and truth, by power. The demonstration of both is a twofold act, and they are realized in it. Any statement Stalin makes is an act of demonstrating power. Ultimately, these statements are acts of exercising power.

As Boris Groys observes, "A Communist revolution is a transfer of society from the medium of money to the medium of language. It implements a true linguistic turn on the level of social practice. . . . Communism is a project, the goal of which is to subordinate economics to politics, in order to provide the latter with sovereign freedom of action. The medium of economics is money. Economics operates with numbers. The medium of politics is language. Politics operates with words—arguments, programs, and resolutions, as well as orders, prohibitions, instructions, and regulations."[19]

Stalin's wide-ranging statements about the base and the superstructure are striking for the rather surprising anthropomorphism in them (my emphasis throughout):

The superstructure is born from the base, but this by no means indicates that it only reflects the base, that it is passive, neutral, or *has an indifferent attitude toward the fate of its base,* to the fate of classes, to the nature of the [social] order. On the contrary, once it has made its appearance, it becomes a supreme active force, it *actively assists* its base to take shape and consolidate itself; it *takes all the necessary steps* to help the new order to finish off and liquidate the old base and the old classes.

Indeed, it cannot be otherwise. The superstructure is created from the base in order to *serve* it, to *actively help* it to take shape and consolidate itself, to *actively fight* for the liquidation of the old base that has outlived its time and its old superstructure. It need only *reject this service role it has;* the superstructure need only to *move from a position of active defense of its base to a position of indifference toward it,* to a position of an identical attitude toward [all] the classes, and it will lose its essence and cease being a superstructure.[20]

These personifications are supposed to substitute for an answer to the question of what place language has in the system of relations between the base and the superstructure if it does not belong to either one. According to Stalin, language is so all-encompassing that it is not even described in ordinary Marxist categories: "Language must not be ascribed to either the category of bases or the category of superstructures. Neither should it be ascribed to the category of 'intermediate' phenomena between the base and the superstructure since such 'intermediate' phenomena do not exist. . . . Does this fact give grounds to ascribing language to the category of implements of production? No, it does not." The operational sphere of language is unlimited. Language is ultra-historical and eternal, like a people or a nation itself since the bases and the superstructures are replaced, but language is not.

Stalin's text leaves far more questions than it provides answers. For example, if language is not a superstructure, then what exactly is it in the system of Marxist coordinates? Or how can the superstructure "reject" the defense of its own base, and if it can (even theoretically!) "lose its essence and cease being a superstructure," then what does it become?

Money in capitalism—this is what language in socialism can be compared to. From Stalin's treatise it is clear that when he talks about language, he conceives of it in terms of a medium, in terms of political economics: "There is a fundamental difference between language and the means of production. The difference is that the means of production produce material goods, while language produces nothing or else 'produces' nothing but words. To put it more precisely, people who possess the means of production can produce material goods, but the same people, if they have language but do not have the means of production, cannot produce material goods. It is not hard to understand that if language could produce material goods, chatterboxes would be the wealthiest people in the world."

This is exactly what demonstrates communism: he who is master of language becomes all-powerful. In another passage, when the topic shifts to the connection between language and thinking, the metonymic construction becomes completely transparent: "Being directly connected to thinking, language registers and fixes in words and in the union of words in sentences the results of the working of thought, the success of man's cognitive work, and thus makes the exchange of thoughts in human society possible." In this capacity language plays the role of a medium, a universal means of exchange, and a general equivalent (that is, money).

Stalin's work about language is first and foremost a meta-text. As a matter of fact, it reveals Stalin's mechanism of presentation and his mode of thinking. By speaking out against Marrist semantics, Stalin insisted on the priority of grammar, which the Marrists snubbed as "formalism." An expert at political games, Stalin had no difficulty discerning the nature of this snub: "'Formalism' was invented by the authors of the 'new teaching' to make the battle against their opponents in linguistics easier."

If there was anything in grammar that attracted Stalin, it was the fact that it deals with "laws." He talks endlessly about these "laws" (my emphasis throughout): "When hybridization occurs, one of the languages usually emerges as the victor . . . and continues to develop according to *the internal laws* of its own development"; "Hybridization does not produce a new, third language but rather preserves one of the languages . . . and gives it the possibility of developing according to *the internal laws* of its own development"; "The Russian language continued to advance and to become perfected according to *the internal laws* of its own development"; and so on.

In their universality, these magical "laws" originate in the "laws" of history and logic, and Western scholars are criticized for rejecting them. The chief commentator of Stalin's texts, Georgii Aleksandrov, former head of the Central Committee's Agitprop, wrote: "One of the most characteristic examples of the displays of the most profound idiocy in contemporary bourgeois science is its rejection of both the general and the specific laws governing social development. The bourgeois 'scientists' literally take up arms against the very notion of a 'law.'"[21]

Stalin's real subject is not even language but logic, although in his "work" it is not mentioned even once. Actually, what he describes as grammar is in fact logic. For Stalin, logic was indeed the universal language. For him it replaced history and no doubt was the basis for his interest in language. This is why we should refine what we say about Stalin's work not really being about language; even in the places where Stalin touches directly on the topic of language, strictly speaking, he is in fact talking about logic. The universality of logical laws has come together here with the totality of language.

It was the affirmation of this totality that led Stalin to reject the characterization of language as a superstructure. He specifies four characteristics that distinguish language from a superstructure, and each of them is one of the facets of totality:

- First, bases and superstructures change, but language practically does not. In other words, one should not exaggerate novelty in language. It is total in its stability, in its immutability against the backdrop of social changes.
- Second, bases and superstructures are class-related, but language is not. In other words, one should not exaggerate the significance of differentiation. Here language plays the role of an underpinning for de-differentiation, social homogeneity, and unification. In its social totality and its use by "all the people," it is reminiscent of a party that also becomes the only one of "all the people" in a totalitarian state. Like a party, language, as Stalin says, "identically serves all of society, all classes of society . . . independently of social standing." The Bolshevik party, after the adoption of Stalin's constitution in 1936, was just such a party.
- Third, superstructures, just like bases, live through a certain era, a certain segment of time, while language is the product of a great many eras. This longevity reveals its transhistorical totality. That which is not subject to history and change, is steeped in tradition and socially stable, is the important thing. Superstructures, on the contrary, are short-lived.
- Fourth, language is unique. As opposed to the superstructure, which according to Stalin has a "narrow and limited" sphere of influence, "language reflects changes in production immediately and directly,

without waiting for changes in the base. Therefore the sphere of influence of language, which encompasses all the domains of human activity, is much broader and more varied than the sphere of influence of the superstructure. More than that, it is almost unlimited." Thus language is total in its uniqueness and unique in its totality. (Arnol'd Chikobava, Stalin's main linguistic adviser, subsequently emphasized in particular this uniqueness: "Before, it was considered unthinkable that in the sphere of social phenomena, elements could exist without being part of the base or the superstructure. Comrade Stalin has proven that such a social phenomenon can exist, that language must be recognized as such a phenomenon.")[22] Furthermore, the superstructure reflects changes in production indirectly—through economics and the base, while language does so directly (and needs no institutional formulation). This unique universality and directness constitute yet another facet of totality.

Thus Stalin develops (in reverse) a corpus of *total linguistics* that—through logic—essentially describes the laws of total sociology and politics. In actuality, he talks about social phenomena. He declares, for example, that "the vocabulary of a language acquires a very great significance when it acts by the command of the language's grammar." This "acting by command" is reminiscent of the "leading role" of the party in society. (This formulation also reveals Stalin's purely bureaucratic vision of reality.) Thus it was easy for interpreters of Stalin's text to discuss "the organizing role of grammar in language."[23] Grammar has the same relationship to language as logic has to thought and the party and its leader to society. Grammar, logic, and party/leader—these are the higher powers that produce laws.

The universality and historical primacy of logic are what determined Stalin's rejection of the theories about the prelogical thought of primitive man that had been suggested to Marr by Lévy-Bruhl and Cassirer.[24] As a matter of fact, Stalin was returning Soviet linguistics to the logical school in grammar from the seventeenth and eighteenth centuries that had to a significant extent developed under the influence of Cartesian rationalism (the laws of language are a reflection of the laws of logic since a word is a sign of a concept and a sentence an expression of judgment). For Stalin, before there was logic, language was not language (thought for him was a synonym of logic and hence of language). Spoken language was primary for him ("Spoken language, or the language of words, was always the only language of human society," he declared), but he had no more arguments to support such an assertion than Marr did when he invented his primitive sign language.

The unique nature of language that Stalin pointed out lay in its "grammatical structure": "Thanks to grammar, language acquires the ability to clothe human thoughts in a material envelope of language." One might say that for Stalin language was public thought, thinking out loud. Language was the logical framework of thought: "The grammatical structure of a language, as it is common to all classes of a particular nation . . . substantially differs from the grammatical structure of the language of a different nation, while the true logical structure of thought is common to all classes and nations that inhabit the globe."[25] One might paraphrase Stalin's famous definition of Soviet culture to say that, for him, thought is logical in content and national in form (i.e., in language). In other words, language (and grammar, more than anything else) was for him a national form of the universal laws of logic upon which thought was based.

Like language, thought does not belong to the superstructure; in just the same way, logic, like grammar, does not have the features of a superstructure or of class. It followed from Stalin's "teaching" that "in the life of a society, logic fulfills a function of the same order as that of language, to which it is directly tied, without intermediary. Language is the material envelope of human thoughts. If language is a tool for communication among people, without which society cannot exist, then the service role of logic is that it provides forms and laws for correct thinking."[26]

Many commentators on Stalin's "teaching about language" have noticed that it was in fact about logic: "In Stalin's understanding of it, grammar is a scientific discipline similar to logic. But as distinct from formal logic as a science about the laws of correct thinking, grammar studies the laws of constructing the speech that realizes thought."[27] For Stalin, grammar is logic as it manifests itself in language, and language is materialized logic; his "formula . . . helps to reveal the connection between the grammatical structure of language and the logical structure of thought and makes it possible to correctly evaluate the significance of elementary logic as the grammar of language. . . . Logic is the grammar of thought, and grammar is the logic of language."[28] Thus logic governs thought like grammar governs speech.

Having rehabilitated one discipline, Stalin had to rehabilitate another. The rehabilitation of grammar was the natural result of the rehabilitation of logic and its return to the school that had immediately preceded it. Stalin had intended to rehabilitate logic in 1941, but this was realized only in 1946 with the adoption of the Central Committee's resolution to have logic and psychology taught in middle school. During the sway of Marrism, "grammar as a school subject in fact disappeared from the middle school and was replaced by the notorious 'observations of language,'" while language and literature took up more than 40 percent of instructional time.[29]

Very shortly before this it had been held that formal logic was a vestige of the past, an example of scholasticism, formalism, idealism, and metaphysical thinking. The *Brief Dictionary of Philosophy* published in 1940 stated that "the laws of formal logic are contrary to the laws of dialectical logic" and that "formal logic is vapid, impoverished, and abstract, for the laws it establishes and its categories do not correspond to objective reality."[30] But now the logic that had been persecuted from all sides returned in triumph. Its advocate was the country's chief thinker, who had personally demanded that logic be taught in the middle and upper schools.

It did not take long for commentators of Stalin's text to discover an "inseparable connection" between grammar and logic and between language and thought: "Just as the vocabulary of a language in and of itself, outside the connection to the grammatical structure, still does not constitute language itself but is merely raw material for it, the conceptual component of thought, considered outside the connection to the logical structure, serves merely as the raw material for thought."[31] The works of Stalin himself served as proof that "truth" could be born only from logic: "The classic examples of concrete truth are Stalin's definitions of concepts."[32]

For Stalin, logic was a basic instrument for rationalizing politics and interpreting the "laws of history." As it turned out, however, Marxism did not recognize any laws; according to Stalin, it "does not recognize immutable conclusions and formulas that are invariable for all times and periods." This very important theme is developed in Stalin's reply to Comrade Kholopov, whom he accuses of being dogmatic and doctrinaire because he observed a contradiction between what Stalin had said earlier and what he was now saying. A consummate casuist and politician, Stalin treated quotations, declarations, and principles opportunistically. His ideological flexibility (the same thing that he branded as political opportunism) gave rise to a contradiction; on the one hand, he was a pragmatist, and on the other, he constantly insisted on his faithfulness to the principles of the "Marxism-Leninism" that he himself had invented and modified when politically expedient. In this he could not do without dialectical logic, which allowed him to combine contradictory strategies with respect to the texts of the "classic authors"—to simultaneously dogmatize them and bring them to naught. Stalin wrote mockingly about "doctrinaires" and "talmudists" who saw "dogmas" in the "formulas" of Marxism, that they "do not try to understand the essence of a thing, that they quote formally, isolated from historical circumstances." As a result, they end up "in a hopeless situation." He condemned them because they "learn the texts of summaries and old formulas of Marxism but do not understand their content."

Stalin's creative work and absolute privilege lay in legitimizing and ideologically justifying a political stance—that is, in essentially rewriting these "old formulas." However, he refrained from accusing the "talmudists" and "dogmatists" outright of bad intentions. Other commentators would do this for him. Aleksandrov, himself one of the main Marxist "talmudists," explained that the danger of these activities lay in the fact that their perpetrators "castrated the living spirit of Marxism" and "were essentially intent on liquidating linguistics as a science."[33] Having been himself accused a few years prior of perversions in philosophy, Aleksandrov declared that "vulgarizers in philosophy denied the active role of progressive theory and of social consciousness, thinking that consciousness only haphazardly 'follows' after existence or coincides with it and merging the superstructure with the base, dissolving it in the base and even in production."[34]

Furthermore, it came to light that the doctrinaires "substituted a forced scholasticism for dialectic," that "the talmudists and dogmatists drove the revolutionary spirit out of dialectic, turned it into a baby's pacifier, into an artificial scheme and a lock pick," and in so doing essentially "acted as liquidators of dialectical and historical materialism." These crimes on the philosophical front were leading to monstrous consequences: "The vulgarization of Marxism, dogmatism, and talmudism leads to a lack of perspective, to a transformation of people into wheeler-dealers and nitpickers; it leads to the subordination of the Soviet people to bourgeois ideology, and ultimately is intended to liquidate Marxism." Thus, when all was said and done, the "political significance" of the activities of these talmudists, doctrinaires, and dog-matists lay in the "attempts to sow doubt about the prospects of the development of our country in its path to communism";[35] that is, these activities were leading to legally punishable offenses.

Stalin's attempt to find historical roots for his anti-dogmatism (fully in keeping with dialectical logic) led to a criminalization of dogmatism:

> Pedants and dogmatists, the hidden and masked enemies of Marxism and of the working class, continued to cling to the old formula of Marx-ism about the impossibility of socialism being victorious in one country. They held up and slowed down the development of the revolutionary movement of the working class, the fight for socialism. Trotsky, Zinov'ev, and Kamenev—the enemies of Leninism, the enemy's paid agents—were among the ranks of those who, in committing the foul crime of betrayal and deceit of the working class, clung to Engels's obsolete formula in order to delay the development of the socialist revolution, to wreck the possibility of socialism's triumph in Russia.[36]

It was only a step from this to a condemnation of "Tito-Rankovich's despicable Fascist-Trotskyite gang" and of "Truman- and Churchill-type people" who were like "a predator run amok, who rushes about, rages and raves, and jumps from one gamble to another; the ground under his feet is on fire."[37] Even the Proletkultists who were mentioned only in passing, to whom Stalin relegated the Marrists, were not sim-ply a historical reference. Their activities were now being characterized as "a betrayal of the proletarian revolution, a betrayal of socialism. Counterrevolution lurked beneath the ultrarevolutionary phrases of these 'Proletkultists.'"[38] Stalin had no need of going this far.

As an instrument of threat, his logic was first and foremost dialecti-cal. As Mikhail Vaiskopf put it, "Dialectic as a basic feature of the en-tire individual and behavioral system of Stalin's personality cannot be doubted."[39] And, as Groys noted, "Stalin's texts about linguistics in fact proclaim a contradiction by the supreme rule of logic." Groys explains that "language can be total only when it includes both all possible as-sertions and denials, as well as all the possible combinations of these; that is, it not only allows but indeed demands logical contradiction of its own statements." A political program based on such logic, Groys concludes, "provides access to the totality of political space and allows one to operate not through exclusion, but through integration."[40]

In this light it becomes clear why the Marrists shared the fate of other ardent revolutionaries, from the RAPPists and Proletkultists mentioned by Stalin to the leading Marxist historian and party functionary Mikhail Pokrovskii, who had contributed greatly to Marr's rise in the late 1920s: "The only ones who survived were those . . . who understood that if a particular assertion is considered true, it does not follow thereupon that a different, contradictory assertion is not true. As opposed to formal logic or the dialectical logic of the Hegelian type, the logic of dialectical materialism is total."[41] This is why such logic easily accommodates both support of Lysenko and the rout of Marr. Total logic as the logic of coercion and threats "affirms paradox as a life principle that also includes death in it, as an icon of totality. Total logic is like that because it allows totality to reveal itself in all its radiant brilliance, because it conceives of and affirms the totality of all possible statements simultaneously. Total logic is genuinely political logic—in equal measure both paradoxical and orthodox."[42]

Formal logic excludes paradox, and Hegelian dialectical logic assumes a historical transcendence or removal of paradox. But "total logic is an open logic that recognizes both thesis and antithesis and excludes no one. Dialectical materialism functioned as an exception of exception. It recognized any oppositions. It strove for absolute openness and accordingly excluded anything that did not want to be just as open."[43]

The 1950 discussion was a triumph of this totality, and it demonstrated the full ideological reversibility of Stalinism; two diametrically opposed schools—Marrism and Indo-Europeanism—were in the first and second halves of one and the same year interpreted in absolutely opposite ways. Literally the same things for which in April 1950 Marrism was officially extolled (scientific rigor, Marxism, patriotism) and Indo-Europeanism was discredited (scientific laxity, idealism, cosmopolitanism) changed places in July, when Marrism was indicted for scientific laxity, idealism, and cosmopolitanism. In such circumstances, it becomes irrelevant to speak of the ideological *content* of one or another school in science since any school can acquire the opposite characteristics, depending on the state of political affairs. Stalin's supradialectical logic signaled the end of any kind of "dogmatism" and the arrival of a post-doctrinal era that made either the triumph of revolutionary-romantic, leftist Hegelianism (Lysenko) or its defeat (Marrism) irrelevant. Essentially, the very fact of Lysenko's ascent with the almost simultaneous rout of Marr was a convincing demonstration of Stalin's non-dogmatic thinking and of the political potential of his dialectical logic.

For Stalin the anti-Marrist campaign, as well as his support of Lysenko two years before that, were (like the majority of his decisions) purely political acts. Ideological arguments had long been purely instrumental, legitimizing underpinnings for one kind of political step or another. Accordingly, his "views" had no relationship at all to the particular line he was supporting at a given moment. The marginal notes he made in the summer of 1948 in the report Lysenko had prepared for the biological discussion were published only in the 1990s. Next to Lysenko's assertion in the report that any science is class-related, Stalin inserted several question marks and the taunting question "Even mathematics?"[44] Nonetheless he lent his support to Lysenko's class-related biology, which he would "win back" two years later in linguistics; key Marrists Georgii Serdiuchenko and Fedot Filin would give him an excellent opportunity to speak out on this score.

Had they known about Stalin's remark, would they have removed their thesis about the class-awareness of science and language? (After all, mathematics and physics formulas are the same kind of language.) A full year after Stalin's foray, Filin publicly renounced Marrism and his former views, as did the majority of Marrists. Nonetheless, they were by no means any greater opportunists than Stalin or Marr himself. If for his own self-affirmation Marr had required not a class-oriented but a nationalist-oriented theory, he would not have written about classes, as he had not done before 1923. Had Stalin's political interests in the summer of 1950 come together differently, he would have tried to prove the class nature of linguistics (as he had done in philosophy in 1947 and in biology in 1948). As a rule, Stalin could argue for (and prove) whatever he wanted to if it was politically expedient. Similar to the way in which Marr, when inventing prehistory and some sort of linguistic world, was actually engaged in therapy for his own complexes and traumas, Stalin, by means of supporting certain schools/trends in science and culture and condemning others, was solving purely political problems. Politics had long ago become a sublimation of his trauma and need for projecting his own greatness. And the ideological arguments were only the rationalization of these needs—simultaneously the means and the arena for realizing them.

Thus Marr fell victim to politics but not by any means to ideology. And if "revolutionary science" was sanctioned in the Lysenko case but routed in linguistics, it was not least of all because Stalin quite often elevated those whom he destroyed and then destroyed those whom he had elevated (examples of which were the restoration of the status of Shostakovich and Prokofiev after the 1948 events or, on the contrary, the public humiliation of Sofronov during the 1949 campaign). A cold political logic always stood behind Stalin's apparent inconsistency. Some have noted the influence that the Lysenko affair had on the linguistics situation. But we must also see the reverse of this: Lysenko could easily have seen his possible fate in the rout of Marrism. This veiled threat (so that the "winners" would not go too far) was a typical political move of Stalin's; frightened "winners" are always easily managed. In the Stalinist world, no one was supposed to feel like an absolute winner or feel completely secure. Victory, as well as security, was relative, and this was the most significant source of terror.

No doubt, Stalin's participation in the linguistics discussion allowed him to consolidate his reputation as a theoretician and his status of coryphaeus of the sciences. After the *Short Course* had come out in 1938, he had not published any theoretical works. After the war, the *Short Course* was officially attributed to him; now all quotations from the book—and scarcely any other work could avoid citing it— appeared only in the form of direct attribution to him, such as, "As Comrade Stalin pointed out in the *Short Course*. . . ." Among his formally listed published works after the war were merely two public speeches and a few decrees of the Defense Ministry, welcoming letters and telegrams, and maybe ten short replies to questions from foreign correspondents. Even before the war, Stalin's public appearances (that is, in newspapers) were extremely rare, and after the war they almost altogether ceased. Sometimes half a year could pass without a single public statement attributed to him. Against this backdrop, the fifty-page brochure seemed like a real ideological eruption, and it provided fodder for many years to come.

This carefully calculated revelation of the leader to the masses was so effective that it removed obvious questions. For example, why had Stalin taken up arms against Marr and Meshchaninov, whom he himself had previously honored with two Stalin Prizes? It is worth remembering that for his attacks, Stalin only wanted "stars." All of his ideological acts were directed at figures who were emblematic in their own domains—Akhmatova or Zoshchenko, Eisenstein or Pudovkin, Prokofiev or Shostakovich. The peculiarity of the linguistics affair was that in all the previous campaigns such figures were available either at one extreme (like Akhmatova, Eisenstein, or Shostakovich) or at the opposite extreme (like Lysenko). There were no real leaders in linguistics at either extreme; neither the frightened Meshchaninov and Viktor Vinogradov, who had stepped down as dean of Moscow State University's comparative-historical linguistics department (because of their caution), nor the storming and raging Serdiuchenko and Filin (owing to their lack of status) could aspire to this role. It was just this chasm that created the niche for Stalin's personal intervention (which would be repeated two years afterward in the course of the economics discussion).

Stalin possessed the keen sensitivity of an actor and always accurately calculated the effect of his public intervention into public life; among such effects one should include the demonstration of accessibility (he answers letters from "comrades," readers whom no one knows); systematicness (prizes and honors exist in and of themselves, and his opinion, in and of itself); and objectivity (no one is above criticism). In the overwhelming majority of cases, Stalin preferred to solve problems behind the scenes, not only avoiding the abuse of his public appearances, but also making them rarer and rarer, shorter, and more enigmatic as the years passed.

Stalin's discourse, his total logic, was the flip side of the totality of his power. At the heart of it was secrecy; total power is indeed secret power. Stalin's logic is only at first glance transparent; in actuality, it is full of mysticism and ambiguity. Accordingly, the full energy of a text from him is aimed at demonstrating the transparency of its arguments.

The main thing that Stalin demonstrated by his public intervention was that he was the one who determined the content of any area of science. In other words, the demonstration of power becomes the meaning and the basic function of power. "Language as a means of communication between people in a society serves all the classes of society equally, and in this respect, it manifests a sort of indifference to the classes," Stalin wrote. "But people, individual social groups, and classes are by no means indifferent to language. They try to use language to their own interests." Stalin was definitely not indifferent. In Russian history one could scarcely find any another politician who succeeded in using language to his own interests with greater success.

STALIN, THE LINGUIST: THE FUNDAMENTAL LEXICON

One of Stalin's basic politico-ideological goals was, undoubtedly, the replacement of the class paradigm with a nationalistic one. He systematically went about achieving this from at least the mid-1930s. Victory in World War II consolidated this shift. Stalin's interest in national problems was the stimulus for his interest in language. It is obvious that his arguments for "the great stability and colossal resistance of language to forced assimilation" did not originate simply from his rejection of Marr's concept of language hybridization; in them, language was a metaphor for a nation. Similarly, others of his assertions were not so much linguistic arguments as political and nationalistic ones in which "the Russian language" was merely a metaphor for the Russian people themselves: "The Russian language, with which the languages of a number of other peoples crossed in the course of its historical development, always emerged the victor"; "The vocabulary of the Russian language was enlarged at the expense of the vocabularies of other languages, but this not only did not weaken the Russian language, but, on the contrary, enriched it"; finally, "The national identity of the Russian language did not suffer the slightest detriment" as a result of these hybridizations.

Marrism was, on the contrary, specifically cosmopolitan in its explanation of linguistic history. This is true not only of Marr himself, but also of his successors, especially Meshchaninov, with his concept of the universality of grammatical conceptual categories, and Solomon Katsnel'son, with his theory of "latent syntactic morphology." Marr's successors promoted his idea of a single "glottogonic" (language-creating) process, which assumed that the same creative principle that is generally natural in mankind is also characteristic of language, and insisted on a universalization of grammar in the approach to different languages. Stalin, on the contrary, talked about national peculiarities of the grammatical structure of languages.

Thus the theories developed by the Marrists were condemned as cosmopolitan. Linguistics again began to operate with supralinguistic categories. "The basic reality that a linguist-historian deals with is a *people,*" Vasilii Abaev wrote. "He starts out with them and returns to them."[45] The erstwhile universalism was replaced by a curious linguistic nationalism. In this romantic variety of linguistics, language was described in the categories of "love" and "faith." It was asserted, for example, that "the contemporary linguistic obscurantists of the bourgeois . . . deliberately and knowingly complicate the issue of the nature and essence of a language . . . in order to undermine the love of nations toward their own language[s], the faith in language as a tool for communication among people."[46] Marr's internationalist-utopian romanticism was decisively replaced with a traditionalist-nationalist variant. Quite late, Soviet linguistics returned to the nineteenth-century Indo-European approach. The strong nationalistic component that characterized this "reactionary-romantic" type of linguistics, and that was a necessary stage of the formation of bourgeois nations, turned out to be necessary in the era of the formation of the first socialist nation, which had already passed through the stage of a class-oriented prehistory.

It was just this historic shift that was fixed in Stalin's text. Nonetheless, Stalin's interest here, as always, was not so much the past as the future. He insisted that "the development of a language took place not by the destruction of an existing language and the building of a new one, but by the expansion and completion of the basic elements of an existing language." Furthermore, "the transition from one sort of language to another sort took place not by means of an explosion, not by means of a one-time destruction of the old and construction of the new, but by means of a gradual and lengthy accumulation of elements of the new sort, of the new structure of the language, by means of the gradual dying out of the elements of the old sort." Stalin decisively rejected Marr's stadial "explosion" theory: "If the theory of stadiality really recognizes sudden explosions in the developmental history of language, then so much the worse for it." He wrote ironically about those who were still blinded by empty revolutionary fantasies: "We must by all means inform our comrades who are enthralled by explosions that the law of transition from the old sort to the new by means of an explosion is inapplicable not only to the history of the development of language; it is not always applicable, either, to other social phenomena at the level of the base or the superstructure."

Without hesitating, Stalin took his evolutionary approach beyond the bounds of the linguistic field, extending it to history and politics. The anti-revolutionary zeal of Stalin's irony directed at the "comrades who are enthralled by explosions" was understood to be a new view of the nature and prospects of the development of Soviet society. An explosion, it was now explained, is characteristic only of a class society in which there is an ongoing struggle between hostile classes, but, for example, in the transition from socialism to communism there can be no question of any kinds of explosions at all; here "the transition from an old qualitative condition to a new one takes place without an explosion." Furthermore, "the base of a socialist society develops gradually, without an explosion of the existing order," and, also without any explosions, "the state, too, will die out after the victory of communism in the whole world, [and] the nations and national languages will merge."[47] Thus, as a result of Stalin's intervention in linguistics, Marxism was enriched with a "theory about the three forms of qualitative changes": by way of an explosion, by way of a leap without an explosion, and by way of a gradual transition from one sort to another (without an explosion).

One of the leading philosophers of the Stalin era, Bonifatii Kedrov, set about to provide a foundation for this theory and wrote about "Stalin's new interpretation of the law of transition from the old sort to the new."[48] If evolution had earlier been thought to be connected to quantitative changes and revolution with qualitative ones, now the very form of changes by which revolution was easily transformed into evolution was subjected to scrutiny. The concept of a "leap" became the chief object of the debate. The leap, it seemed, was no longer connected to revolution, and although it was connected to the transition of quantity to quality (with the transition from an old "quality" to a new one), it was "independent of how much time this transition takes, whether it is completely in an instant, without any intermediate stages whatsoever, or is lengthy, sequentially passing through a series of intermediate steps, [or whether it is] violent or comparatively peaceful."[49]

It also came to light that "leaps can play out in different ways— quickly or slowly, violently or peacefully, instantaneously or gradually."[50] Leaps were now possible through an explosion but also through "a gradual transition."[51] The leap could be broken down, as it were, into two different forms: an explosion or some sort of lengthy, gradual action. The first form was what Stalin in his linguistic treatise called "a single act of a decisive blow," "a sudden transition from an old quality to a new quality," or a "one-time destruction of the old and construction of the new"—that is, something characterized by suddenness, a single action, and single occurrence. The second form was a leap that was realized, as Stalin wrote, "by means of the gradual and lengthy accumulation of elements of the new sort, . . . by means of the gradual dying out of the elements of the old sort." In other words, it involved an evolutionary process that previously could not by any means have been called a leap.

This "explosion" was now defined as "a special form of leap" that arises "when a decisive obstacle created by the old stands in the way of the inception and development of the new"; this obstacle fights with the new "to its last breath." Then "the new . . . , because it is invincible, sooner or later tears down the barrier and . . . in an expansive wave like a hurricane, explodes into life, asserts itself in it, thus consolidating its victory over the old."[52] It is not difficult to recognize revolution in these metaphors. Those who were professionally engaged in deciphering Stalin's cryptograms could make out his subtext without difficulty: after the victory of "the new," the era of the "explosion" ended once and for all.

Metaphor is replaced by a new trope, the oxymoron. The "gradual leap" is an example. The fact that a gradual transition started being called a "leap" not only eliminated the boundary between revolution and evolution, but in fact also replaced the former with the latter while still preserving the notion of a leap. Now it was claimed that the gradual leap was connected to contradictions that were not antagonistic, while the explosion was connected to antagonistic ones. But since antagonistic, unresolvable contradictions do not exist under socialism, then an explosion (i.e., revolution) also cannot exist; hence the transition to communism will also take place in the form of a gradual leap (which meant, in particular, that the onset of communism was completely unverifiable).

Taking an example from the natural sciences, Kedrov explained Stalin's discovery thus: "If before Stalin's work appeared . . . , when people talked about gradualness, they usually had in mind the gradualness of only certain quantitative changes, now they envision the gradualness of the course of the leap itself—i.e., the gradualness of the *qualitative* change. The ordinary vaporization of liquid water is just such a case of the gradual transition from an old state to a new one."[53] One must suppose that before 1950, this phenomenon had lacked the necessary explanation.

Of course, the real issue is not these anecdotal sophisms but the fact that the definition of the boundaries of change in the political arena was being decisively transformed into a purely interpretational operation. Trying to explain this change, Kedrov wrote that a summary leap is completed "not at one particular moment as a sudden, single-act and quick transition; rather it encompasses a whole area of changes without sharp boundaries. Therefore one cannot determine the point at which the leap has finished, just as one cannot determine at which specific count of hairs lost a man becomes bald, or the specific numerical point at which things being removed from a pile of things makes a pile cease to be a pile."[54] Thus, the issue is *a purely philological procedure.*

The definition of the leap becomes relative not only in time, but also in terms of substance; what in one context is defined as a leap turns out in another to be merely something of lesser scale, something less profound, less major, and, ultimately, less "qualitative"—that is, a non-leap. As Kedrov noted while summing up, "More minor leaps act as transitions between the various *phases* of the development of the given object."[55] Clearly, this applies also to the "phases of socioeconomic formations." The total transformation of the political field by metaphor is accompanied by the total relativization of the categories with which it had traditionally been described. We should note that what happened here was not only a renaming of evolution as revolution, but also that the very "explosion" (i.e., revolution) about which Stalin had so disdainfully spoken now logically fit into the negative semantic field.

Even the very notion of "development" received a new semantic attribute. Thus it was revealed that language developed not only without explosions, but also without any leaps at all. "Language develops this way because, since it is not class-oriented, it is free of antagonistic social contradictions.... Language develops in such a way that no radical breakdowns and no revolutions at all happen in it; rather a very slow and gradual transition of it from one state to another takes place; its *development,* which encompasses many centuries, takes place."[56] It was now no longer possible to say for sure how qualitative changes take place. For example, how, as a result of uninterrupted "development," do the territorial dialects noted by Stalin get transformed into national languages, and how do the latter, in turn, merge as a result of the victory of communism in the entire world into one common language? One must suppose that this question belongs in the category of questions about baldness, involving a purely philological operation of nomination. One must simply approach such things *historically.* As Stalin had previously observed, "Everything depends on the circumstances, the place, and the time"—in other words, on political expediency.

Gradual improvement was now declared to be Soviet society's only form of development. The *Short Course* had already asserted that "the USSR had entered a new period of development, a period of completing the construction of socialist society and of the gradual transition to a Communist society."[57] Now "Stalin's famous statement" acquired a "philosophical" shape: "The gradual transition from the old state to the new one is a peculiar, special form of resolving the contradictions of a non-antagonistic nature that operate in our society."[58] Socialism had to transition into communism by means of vaporization, like water transitioning into steam.

This is why, even as the country was undergoing "a gradual transition to communism," the notion of communism itself had to be as unspecific as possible so that it would be impossible to either precisely define its boundaries or verify its beginning. Thus criticism arose of "the attempts to depict the future Communist system in every detail and to define the norms of the objects of consumption that would completely satisfy the needs of socially developed people"; also targeted was "the construction of specific plans for transitioning to the principle of no money charged to satisfy the personal needs of laborers" since "such a narrowly distributional approach is fundamentally incorrect and contradicts the methodology of Marxism-Leninism."[59]

Really, if state capitalism and the ever-strengthening state could be passed off as socialism, then why could it not be passed off as communism as soon as it became a matter of simply rewriting the "obsolete formulas" of the classics of Marxism? For Stalin's total logic was indeed an instrument for rewriting "formulas": "The victory of communism on a worldwide scale leads to the dying out of the state and *the political superstructure in general. . . .* To build communism in the USSR and assure the victory of communism on a worldwide scale, to prepare the conditions for the aforementioned changes in the socialist superstructure, we must in our time *strengthen* and develop the existing superstructure since only *strengthening* the socialist state prepares its dying out in the future when the capitalist surroundings are liquidated."[60] This logic reproduces Stalin's sophisms at the Sixteenth Party Congress, when he explained that socialism and the state simultaneously do and do not contradict each other: "The higher development of state power with a view to preparing the conditions for the dying out of state power—that is the Marxist formula."[61] Now Stalin was affirming that the state would be preserved even under communism if the danger from without was not eliminated when communism arrived.

The late-Stalinist era was the peak of Socialist Realism's "conflictlessness." Social contradictions were disappearing along with the end of class struggle. They were now marginalized: "Under these historical conditions, all the acridity of class struggle in our country, including the class struggle in the area of ideology, has shifted to the international arena."[62] Philosophers had to examine anew the law of unity and struggle between opposites. This law, it was announced,

> is realized under socialism in opposition to an antagonistic society in such a way that what is advancing in it is not the hostility and the collision of the various classes but rather the constantly growing convergence between them, their constantly growing harmony and unity. . . . Socialism has changed *the nature of the contradictions* of social progress. . . . The intense peculiarity of the manifestation of the law of unity and struggle between opposites under the conditions of socialism is that the unity of social forces is not only the basis for resolving the contradictions between the new and the old, but also the basis of *a completely different type* of struggle between the old and the new.[63]

Quite a short time before this, in 1947, and fully in keeping with orthodox Marxism, Mark Rozental' had written that "the struggle between opposing tendencies and aspirations at a certain phase of its development inevitably has an explosion as its result. . . . At the beginning of this process, the unity between opposites is still more or less solid. But the struggle between opposites undermines this unity and makes it less solid until at a certain phase the contradictions explode it and destroy it."[64] However, it was now clarified that "notions like the 'destruction' or 'overthrow' of an old form cannot at all be regarded as a description of the dialectic of content and form, for such notions merely reveal the particular instance of dialectic inherent only in an antagonistic society."[65]

Studies of unity, not contradictions, became the fashion in Soviet philosophy (only "capitalist contradictions" were possible). The word "explosion," which in revolutionary culture had had strictly positive political connotations (as in the "revolutionary explosion"), now apparently acquired a distinctly negative meaning. The concept of "peace," on the contrary, was growing in popularity—surely an unexpected about-face for the "philosophy of the revolutionary masses." Such were the unanticipated political fruits of Stalin's linguistic anti-dogmatism.

"IN LIGHT OF STALIN'S WORKS . . .": LESSONS IN THE DEVELOPMENT OF SPEECH

The conquest of linguistics by Marr and a huge number of his influential followers took years; "Stalin's teaching about language," however, became an independent discipline overnight. All the newspapers reprinted Stalin's article, and, like the orders of the Supreme Commander in Chief during the war, Iurii Levitan read it over the radio.[66] In just a few days, millions of copies of it were printed. Starting in the autumn of 1950, all the linguistics programs in the colleges and universities were abolished, and a new course in "Stalin's Teaching about Language" was introduced (without any materials or textbooks for it). The course began to be taught in all humanities departments and was made a compulsory discipline in the degree requirements for philology.

A wave of "All-Union discussion" swept through the country, from rural district committees to the academic institutes in the capitals. Scholarly sessions and conferences devoted to "the realization of the guidelines and the creative mastery of the theoretical propositions contained in the new works of the great coryphaeus of science" started to be held annually to mark the anniversary of the publication date of Stalin's "works."[67] The "grubbing of the linguistic soil, the eradication of the weeds of the 'new teaching' about language in linguistics theory and practice" resulted in the production of a huge number of books and articles criticizing Marrism.[68] Among these were the Academy of Sciences' two-volume (eighty printer's sheets) *Against Vulgarization and Perversion of Marxism in Linguistics,* which was a particularly distinct reminder about the very same kind of work, the two-volume *Against the Historical Concept of M. N. Pokrovskii* (1939–40), in which the equally "vulgarizing" school of one of Marr's patrons had been routed earlier, and its *Fundamental Issues of Soviet Linguistics in Light of the Works of J. V. Stalin.* The Academy of Sciences' Institute of Philosophy issued two editions of *Issues of Dialectical and Historical Materialism in J. V. Stalin's Work "Marxism and Linguistic Issues."* Moscow State University published *Linguistics Issues in Light of the Works of J. V. Stalin.* Uchpedgiz (the state publishing house for pedagogical literature) issued handbooks and methodological materials for the "Stalin's Teaching about Language" course. Materials were published from joint sessions of various departments of the USSR Academy of Sciences—social sciences, history and philosophy, economics and law, literature and language—and from an enlarged session of the Learned Councils of the Linguistics Institute, the Philosophy Institute, the History Institute, and the Eastern Studies Institute. A joint session of the Academy of Sciences' Literature and Language Department and the USSR Academy of Pedagogical Sciences issued materials, as did another joint session of the Academy of Sciences' Linguistic Institute, Ethnography Institute, History Institute, and its Institute for the History of Material Culture. A great number of such conferences were also held in the academic establishments of the national republics and regions.[69]

This massive wave of conferences and publications was a reflection of the truly tectonic ideological shift produced by Stalin's articles, a shift that was not so much conceptual as discursive and representational. Stalin had revealed himself to the masses in a way that was in all respects unexpected and original. The originality lay not only in the genre (participation in a scholarly discussion), but also in the sphere in which "Stalin's genius" was applied—simultaneously exotic and elite/prestigious, specialist and generalist.

Stalin's text is like a discursive black hole that sucks in entire scholarly/scientific disciplines; they disintegrate at ever-increasing speed and produce more and more textual fragments. Put another way, one might compare this ever-expanding discourse originating from Stalin's text to a progressive tumor that continually metastasizes to new organs and tissues. As a sacred object that gives birth to text and procreates discourse, this short text truly engenders oceans of literature. But what was the real function of this discourse, when a dictator's word was subject not so much to interpretation or even commentary as to tautological "recycling"? The only operations allowed were dissection and systematization.

The basic characteristics of Stalin's work are its comprehensiveness and depth, as well as its foundation-setting nature—Stalin laid down principles, went into depth and specifics, offered proof, and "illuminated things in a new way." This last is similar to what might happen if a new work by Marx or Lenin had turned up, shedding new light on the entire edifice of "Marxism-Leninism," or to some kind archaeological discovery or find that would turn the former notions upside down, before the revelation of which some significant part of reality had lain hidden.

The luster of truth radiated by Stalin's text was so intense that it should have blinded not only rank-and-file readers, but even the most authoritative scholars. Viktor Vinogradov declares that "the history of language science knows no other example wherein the great work of a thinker so quickly and so decisively sent the development of linguistics onto new paths in all the progressive countries of the world. The history of language science cannot name any other works that could have exerted such a powerful and salubrious influence on the progress of linguistic thought."[70] Stalin's brochure had already entered the pantheon of the "Marxist-Leninist scientific legacy": "Rich in the content of great ideas and with a huge number of theoretical generalizations, Stalin's work . . . will serve, like *Anti-Dühring, Materialism and Empiriocriticism,* and other immortal creations of Marxist-Leninist thought, as an inexhaustible spring that feeds science with great ideas and will arm it with the creative spirit of Marxism."[71]

The range of themes encompassed is sometimes narrowed to specific scholarly subjects ("In Stalin's works we find most significant guidelines for solving problems in the area of orthography")[72] and sometimes expanded to global dimensions: "In his work, Stalin shed light on a whole range of the most complex problems of Marxist philosophy and the history of society, the theory of knowledge, dialectics and logic, ethnography and the history of folklore, linguistics and literary studies, political economy and other social sciences, which are [all] drawing and will draw from Stalin's genial works on linguistics new creative ideas, new conclusions and formulas of Marxism, and new stimuli for scientific discoveries."[73] These new conclusions and formulas of Marxism now had to be deciphered, as if they were some sort of sacred symbols.

The basic reason for the occultness of the knowledge in Stalin's work and the difficulty in understanding it was that his arguments were elevated to the status of scientific laws and formulas of the very same purely discursive force that Marr's fantasies, in his time, had been declared to possess. With the sophisms that he had managed to fit into a single newspaper article, Stalin "revealed" an enormous number of scientific "laws." He discovered general laws of the development of language, among which were "the law of gradual change in language" (that is, language develops slowly), "the law of the inequality of the tempos of change in the structural elements of language" (some grammatical categories change faster than others), and "the law of relative stability of the structural elements of language" (grammatical structures remain stable despite changes in vocabulary). Now these were not simply truisms—they were "laws."[74] When Stalin said something about the hybridization of languages, this meant that he (as Vinogradov asserted) "discovered the laws of hybridization and merger of languages at various stages of the development of society";[75] when he said that the internal laws of language changed at different times with a different dynamic, this was called "the law of unequal development of the different aspects of language."[76]

But it was not only "laws of language" that Stalin revealed to the world. Likewise, he

> revealed the laws of the development and change of the base and super-structure, the regularity of the fact that class struggle does not mean the rupture of society [*sic!!*], the regularity of the disintegration and destruction of temporary and unstable empires[, and] the laws of the development of nations and their languages under the conditions of capitalism and after the victory of socialism on a worldwide scale, and the laws of the development of capitalism . . . and, in connection with this, the laws of the development of proletarian revolution and the regularities of development of the socialist state when surrounded by capitalist states, the possibility of building a higher phase of communism under these historical conditions.[77]

Stalin needed only to say that "everyone knows that no science can develop without discussions" in order for this truism to be called "Comrade Stalin's discovery of the law of development of advanced science"[78] (though he had "discovered" this "law" with the words "everyone knows"). Thus, a few scattered phrases here and there, or the simple mention of an obvious fact, could be called when translated to the language of scientific explanations "a true historical and theoretical-sociological foundation."

Another reason for the difficulty in understanding Stalin's discoveries lay in the contradiction between the extent of a statement he made and the discursive eruption to which it gave rise. Therefore it was necessary to somehow explain the cryptic quality of his "laws" and "theories" (my emphasis throughout): "Stalin's articles on the issues of linguistics are not simply a collection of separate and scattered statements on separate linguistics issues but rather constitute an integral, profoundly well-thought-out system of views, a Marxist teaching about language knowledge *in an extremely concise exposition*";[79] Stalin had revealed the laws of language "with irresistible persuasiveness and *laconic simplicity*";[80] his works had "in *an unusually clear, precise, and laconic form* explained the essence of language."[81]

This "laconism" of Stalin's works was in sharp contrast to not only the supposedly extensive grasp of the various domains of science and life intrinsic in them, but also the interest shown in them. In other words, the exotic topic of Stalin's exploration itself demanded justification; it was not easy to position linguistics as an object of mass interest. Meanwhile, the status of this text could not be limited to the observation that "Stalin's genial work ... is being studied by the broad strata of the Soviet intelligentsia."[82] A much broader range of devotees of language studies was required: "Interest in the issues of language studies provoked by Stalin's works has become nationwide."[83] Furthermore, "the broad strata of the Soviet intelligentsia, of workers, and of kolkhoz residents are studying this work; they are pondering its most profound meaning and significance and are drawing inspiration from it for their own activities in the building of communism."[84]

The urgent political potential of linguistics was similarly not at all obvious. Thus it was constantly emphasized that "Stalin has given us a remarkable, classic response to *the most complex issues that life poses*," that "this work responds to *the burning issues* of building communism and is *a programmatic document* for our party,"[85] and that "Comrade Stalin's works on the issues of linguistics are profoundly connected to *the contemporary period* of the development of our Soviet society."[86]

All of this required a reproduction of Stalin's discourse itself that was based on a multiplication and magnification of every statement. Thus any phrase from "the founders of Marxism-Leninism" was transformed into a "regulation" of Stalin's; a "regulation" would in turn become a "teaching" or "generalization" of the entire universal experience of development. These techniques of hyper-interpretation led to dizzying conclusions:

> Stalin's work on the issues of linguistics calls on people everywhere to escape from imperialist oppression and exploitation, and it foreshadows the imminent revolution of the downtrodden masses and the prospects of the victory of socialism in all countries. This attracts and captivates hundreds of millions of people, for it reveals a path for them to a free and happy life. . . . Stalin's work on the issues of linguistics reveals to all peoples the prospect of the national, independent existence of their countries and the liquidation of national-colonial oppression. . . . This inspires hundreds of millions of people languishing under imperialist oppression to fight imperialism. . . . Comrade Stalin's work . . . arms the contemporary camp of peace, democracy, and socialism with a most powerful means of fighting for peace. . . . Stalin's work on the issues of linguistics powerfully promotes the victory of a policy of peace among nations, unmasks the ideological stances of the instigators of the new war, and justifies a policy of peace.[87]

At the other extreme, this foregrounding of linguistics led to the inclusion of "contemporary obscurantist semanticists," "American obscurantists playing at philosophy," and other "ideological lackeys of the bourgeoisie" in the circle of those discredited along with Marr.[88]

Since post-Marxist Western philosophy was everywhere regarded negatively, criticism of "ideological opponents" in connection with Stalin's work was characterized by references to thinkers that had apparently been long forgotten. Thomas Malthus, for example, was particularly popular. This eighteenth-century cleric, as it turned out, was a current opponent of Soviet philosophers. In the epic world of Soviet politico-ideological criticism, citations were made of 1938 party resolutions and Stalin speeches from the 1910s and 1930s as if nothing had changed over the past decades and seven-year-old Central Committee resolutions were as relevant as those made days before.

A dense obscurantism hovered above all this. Aleksandrov, for example, writes that cybernetic ideas are "utter nonsense" and that "only an outright swindler" could claim that language could be systematized with the aid of "counting machines"; such developments "are a pseudo-scientific fabrication that shows the powerlessness and disintegration of bourgeois linguistics and the laughable nature of the attempt by foreign linguists to throw off the creation and development of real science, to replace it with 'counting machines' that have no relation whatsoever to the subject. One hardly need say what harm these nonsensical 'ideas' do to science."[89] Another philosopher maintains that "the monstrosity of this pseudo-science [i.e., cybernetics] is that it wants to replace a person with a counting machine. Cybernetics is one of the links in the misanthropic aspirations of the Wall Street operators."[90] It is no surprise that Malthus turns out to be a worthy opponent of Soviet medieval philosophical thought.

The reference here to the Middle Ages is completely justified. Pondering today the questions formulated by Aron Gurevich with regard to the Middle Ages, one will realize just how much a traditional society that was far from modernized turned out to be the "weak link of imperialism." Gurevich writes:

> Is it really not surprising from the contemporary point of view that, for example, a word or idea in the system of medieval consciousness had just the same degree of realness as the world of objects, as the things to which common notions correspond, and that the concrete and the abstract were not distinguished, or in any case the borders between them were blurry? That in the Middle Ages, repetition of the thoughts of ancient authorities was considered prowess and the expression of new ideas was condemned? That a plagiarist was not subjected to prosecution while originality could be considered heresy? That in a society in which a lie was regarded as a great sin, the fabrication of a forged document for the justification of legal and other rights could be considered a means to establish the truth and a pious act?[91]

All these questions could as easily have been addressed to Soviet society as well. The answer to them should be not so much "astonishment" as a clear understanding of the rightness of the logic of *historical realism* articulated by Stalin; if "the transition from an old qualitative condition to a new one" did in fact take place with the help of an "explosion" in the case of 1917 Russia, then, first of all, this could not lead to anything "qualitatively new" (the product of explosions is ruins, and Stalin was a restorer). This "new state" (or "new quality") itself was suspect; Russia remained a country with a political culture that completely corresponded to the Soviet historical experience, which Stalin also understood perfectly. Second, neither the society nor its political elites (the Soviet bureaucracy) were ready for profound social modernization (even the limited industrial modernization was extremely superficial). Finally, a real "transition to a new state" is possible only by the paths of "gradual and lengthy accumulation of elements of the new sort, . . . by means of the gradual dying out of the elements of the old sort"—that is, by evolution, and hence necessarily (as post-Soviet experience also attests) within the limits of history. This political and historical realism is manifested in Stalin's linguistics studies.

"History does nothing at all substantial without a special necessity for it," Stalin pointedly remarked in his linguistics treatise. In this respect, he was acting as history itself.

8 Socialist Surrealism

Representing Life in the Forms of Life Itself

"HAMMER AWAY AND DRUM IT IN"

On May 13, 1947, Stalin summoned the country's three highest-placed literary functionaries to the Kremlin: Soviet Writers' Union general secretary Aleksandr Fadeev, his deputy, Konstantin Simonov, and the party secretary of the union's Executive Board, Boris Gorbatov. He had commissioned them to come up with a broad campaign for the propaganda of Soviet patriotism. As Simonov recalled, Stalin told them the following:

> "This is the kind of topic that is very important and that writers need to get interested in. This is the topic of our Soviet patriotism. If you take our average intelligentsia, the scholarly intelligentsia, professors, doctors," Stalin said, constructing phrases with that special intonation characteristic of him, which I have memorized so exactly that I think I could literally reproduce it, "they don't have a sufficiently ingrained feeling of Soviet patriotism. They have an unjustified worship of foreign culture. They all feel immature, not 100 percent, and have gotten used to considering themselves in the situation of perpetual students. This is an obsolete tradition; it goes back to Peter [the Great]. Peter had good ideas, but soon too many Germans crept in; it was a period of worshipping Germans. Look how hard it was, for example, for Lomonosov to breathe, how hard it was for him to work. First it was the Germans, then the French; it was the worship of foreigners," Stalin said.[1]

Stalin had brought up this topic earlier as well—in particular, during the discussion of Leningrad journals at the Central Committee Organizational Bureau on August 9, 1946, and during a meeting on February 26, 1947, with Eisenstein and the other creators of *Ivan the Terrible*. And now, having heard from Fadeev and the other two Writers' Union leaders about the topics that prominent writers were working on, Stalin declared, "That is all good. Nonetheless, it is not the main thing. The main task for writers, the general task, is fighting against kowtowing to foreigners."[2] A good half hour of the conversation, which lasted an hour and ten minutes in total, was devoted to the development of this idea.

Patriotic mobilization and the cultivation of nationalist feelings were understandable in war conditions. After the victory, Stalin's declared concern about the people's patriotism and the greatness of Russia could seem politically incomprehensible, but psychologically it made complete sense; the brief encounter with the West had undermined the parallel reality constructed by Stalinism and created cognitive dissonance. The country had to conform to its new status of superpower, which it did not economically, culturally, or politically. Most of all it had to conform to the *greatness of its conqueror-leader*. As the "liberator of humanity from the Fascist plague" and the "father of the people," Stalin could not be the leader of a country whose elites perceived themselves (as he saw it) as students of the West, which he, "the greatest military commander of all times and nations," haughtily challenged. Stalin's zealous attitude to the country's greatness was merely a projection of his concern for his own greatness, image, and status. This explains Stalin's growing attention, as Simonov noted, to the theme of Russian preeminence, kowtowing to foreigners, and—later—cosmopolitanism: "Stalin had an attitude that was severe, and also oversensitive, toward everything that he embedded in the concept of 'kowtowing to foreigners.' After the war's being won, in the devastated and hungry victor-country this was his sore spot."[3]

This is why Stalin saw putting an end to deference to foreigners as a fundamental task: "Why are we worse? What is the matter? We must hammer away at this point for many years, must drum this subject into people's heads for maybe ten years." Then Stalin gave Fadeev a four-page document to read aloud about the "KR" affair—a scandal surrounding the handover to the West of Nina Kliueva and Grigorii

Roskin's manuscript containing a description of the anti-cancer medicine they had created. What Fadeev read aloud was the text, written by
Zhdanov and edited by Stalin himself, of an indictment for a "court of
honor" that was to begin the following day. The writers found themselves unwilling participants in the dress rehearsal Stalin had arranged
for the trial. During the reading, Stalin paced up and down around
his desk, listening attentively and scrutinizing their reactions. All said
and done, this was an attack on the intelligentsia, and Stalin wanted
to see the victims' reactions: "He was doing a test, trying it out on us,"
Simonov quite astutely observed, understanding that Stalin "was testing what kind of impression this letter that he had dictated was making
on us, intelligentsia folk—Communists, but intelligentsia nonetheless—
about Kliueva and Roskin, also two intelligentsia people. Perhaps he
had dictated it, or quite possibly he had written it himself. In any case,
this letter was dictated by his will and no one else's."[4]

Since the experience of war and freedom, of independence in decision making, of the temporary departure from the Soviet ideological
parallel reality, brief but profound in its intensity and influence, and
the Soviet occupational forces' experience of encountering different
realia and standards of living during their brief stay in the West all
presented a substantial threat to the regime, the regime was subject
to transformation and change. This was a complex and multistage
process. At each stage there was a modification of experience through
squeezing it out and replacing it without verification, and it had to be
compensated through a preservation of verisimilitude. Just as Socialist
Realism asserted *"the representation of life in the forms of life itself"*
as a fundamental stylistic mode, the postwar politico-ideological construct that ultimately yielded something directly contradictory to lived
experience was based on *"realistic verisimilitude."* Accomplishing this
required realism, about which Barthes observed that "no mode of writing was more artificial" since "the writing of Realism is far from being
neutral, it is on the contrary loaded with the most spectacular signs
of fabrication."[5]

To understand how collective and individual experience were refashioned, how the view of the world in postwar Soviet society was structured during the very period when the final tuning of the Soviet nation's coming together after the war—with its complexes and traumas,
anxieties and phobias, illusions and notions about its own greatness

and messianic role—was occurring, we must see these signs, follow the modes of this transformation, and discern the figures and tropes that were used in this process of massive *politico-aesthetic immunization.*

At first the experience of contact with the West is transformed into an *inferiority complex* ("kowtowing"). This is imposed as a patently false diagnosis since the Soviet intelligentsia, who had experienced a widespread patriotic uplift as a result of the victory, suffered least of all from it. Obviously, the only person for whom the greatness already available was too little was Stalin himself, as he no longer wished to be "Lenin's faithful student" or to remain in the shadow of the "classics of Marxism." Widespread infection had the goal of developing ideological antibodies—more specifically the shaping of Soviet national narcissism through the construction of a *superiority complex* (expressed in the "feeling of Soviet pride," the struggles for "the preeminence of Russian science," and so forth). The complex process began with the organism's assimilation of the weakened "microorganisms" to develop immunity against the virulent strains that extreme forms of political disloyalty were, such as (the next false diagnosis) "rootless cosmopolitanism," which was nothing more than a projection and figure of repulsion (the "cosmopolitan equals anti-patriot" formula was asserted with transparent anti-Semitic connotations) and completed the process of narcissism's rebirth as paranoia, the last stage of transforming the experience of the encounter with the West—its alienation.

Thus we may identify the following modes of transformation: inferiority complex → superiority complex (delusions of grandeur) → paranoia. They are realized through the corresponding political tropes: "kowtowing" → "national pride" → "cosmopolitanism." Finally, their realization takes place through the following genres: patriotic play → biographical film → anti-Semitic pamphlet. The only thing that unites them is a principle of fabrication; dangerous social symptoms are falsified since "kowtowing" and "cosmopolitanism" were symptoms not of a social trauma but of Stalin's own trauma. Extrapolation of this false symptomatology onto the whole of society required a profound deformation of both current political events and history, with the goal of simulating illness. Plausibility, precisely, was a criterion for simulation and the result of falsification. And the Socialist Realist "representation of life in the forms of life itself" turned out to be exactly the appropriate stylistic formulation for this strategy, which was executed in different ways in the various genres. And if the result of these representational efforts looked improbable, then by no means was it because it employed some sort of fantasy means or forms of conventionality; it was because Stalinism, as one of the most conspiratological regimes, was based on conspiracy theories in which any reflection of reality came out completely distorted without the admixture of any fantasy. It was completely fantastic, just as the world of paranoia is fantastic.

But thus far we are merely at the beginning of this journey. "And pleased with the effect he had produced, strolling along the endless table, Stalin repeated what he had started with: 'We have to destroy the spirit of self-effacement.' Then he added, 'There has to be something written on this subject. A novel.' I said it was more a subject for a play."[6] Without even suspecting it, Simonov had invented a new genre in Stalin's office—the "patriotic play."

THE SCENOGRAPHY OF PARANOIA

Creating the new genre was up to the country's main dramatists—Stalin and Zhdanov. Their "artistic collaboration" was to result in the creation of the "KR affair" and the "courts of honor." This undertaking was unique in that, on the one hand, it was essentially the first ideological campaign, which became the first indicator of an abrupt transition to Cold War ideology, an atmosphere of paranoid secrecy, aggressive nationalism, and self-isolation that gripped the country, and a rhetoric of bombastic self-aggrandizement. This campaign provided the fundamental ideological vector of late Stalinism: an affirmation of patriotism and of the superiority of Russian science and a fight against kowtowing, both of which mushroomed into anti-cosmopolitan hysteria. On the other hand, it was the only action of such a scale that was kept secret and had a public expression exclusively in literature, theater, and film.

The factual outline of the story goes as follows: biologist Grigorii Roskin proved in 1931 that the single-celled microorganism *Trypanosoma cruzi* (and an extract of its cells) inhibits the growth of cancerous tumors in animals. Furthermore, people who had had trypanosomiasis turned out to be immune to cancer. At the time Roskin published a series of articles in both Soviet and foreign journals about using trypanosome infection as biotherapy against cancerous tumors. When in 1939 he met the experienced infections specialist (and energetic organizer), microbiologist Nina Kliueva, he passed the baton to her to work on the vaccine so that she could bring the drug derived from the trypanosomes (which, using the first letters of their surnames, they called KR) to clinical trials and production. The work continued during the war, and toward the end of 1945 they had obtained experimental variants of the drug with serious positive results and in sufficient quantities.

The work had progressed to the level where an expansion of laboratory studies and a start of experimental production were needed. The funds for this were not forthcoming; moreover, scientific bureaucrats had tried to get in on this successful discovery, which promised glory, forcing the discoverers to turn to the government for financing and to prove their priority through publishing the results of their experiments. They understood that they needed to assert their priority through championing the preeminence of the country since due to the absence of financing and the necessary equipment in the USSR, the medicine would ultimately be created in the United States. Their letters to party leaders (including Zhdanov) about how the important discovery was not being financed by the medical and academic higher-ups brought them to the attention of the highest leadership. As a result, Kliueva and Roskin found themselves embroiled in high-level politics in 1946.

Zhdanov personally took charge of the laboratory and informed Stalin about the discovery. This was followed by a story of the unprecedented elevation, and then just as precipitous a downfall, of scientists. First there was Stalin's personal support of the project; allocation of resources; and, at the same time, successful reports in the Academy of Medical Sciences about the new method of cancer biotherapy, articles in the central newspapers, journals, and magazines (including mass-oriented ones like *Ogonek*), and radio interviews. This produced a sensational effect—enormous public interest, a frenzy. Through the channels of the All-Union Society for Cultural Relations with Foreign Countries (VOKS), the information was widely propagated into the United States. As a result, the American Embassy in Moscow was flooded with letters and telegrams about the drug, which forced the new U.S. ambassador to the USSR, Walter Bedell Smith, a professional spy who had replaced Averell Harriman in March 1946, to take a lively interest in the discovery.[7] Smith even insisted on a personal meeting with the drug's creators. This meeting, with the agreement of "the appropriate agencies" (the minister of health and the leaders of the Academy of Medical Sciences) and in the presence of officials, took place on June 20, 1946, in the Institute of Epidemiology. In response to Smith's offer of collaboration and technical assistance, the Ministry of Health prepared a special project. In October, a delegation of Soviet medical personnel (including oncologists), headed by academic and secretary of the Academy of Medical Sciences Vasilii Parin, set out for the United States. Since their visit coincided with a special U.N. session dedicated to international collaboration at which Molotov was slated to speak, Parin requested permission from Moscow to take the American-Soviet medical society the manuscript of Roskin and Kliueva's book that described the discovery, which had already been accepted for publication in the USSR, and a sample (which was past its expiration date at the time) of the medicine they had created. Parin did not, however, hand over the actual production technology for the drug. Meanwhile, the beginning of the Cold War was changing priorities. Stalin and Zhdanov decided to take advantage of everything that was happening for the start of a new ideological campaign. Parin's actions were interpreted as a handing over of a state secret. Upon his return he was arrested and accused of espionage, Health Minister Georgii Miterev was dismissed from his post, and a "court of honor" was organized to try Roskin and Kliueva.

Stalin very much liked the idea of resorting to courts of honor, a practice that had been used in prerevolutionary Russia, and Zhdanov immediately set about developing and readying the first such court for Kliueva and Roskin, with the goal of teaching the people the "spirit of Soviet patriotism" and the fight against "kowtowing" and "cosmopolitanism." The biologists' trial was conducted in every detail like a special operation, and it was closely supervised by Stalin and Zhdanov. What is more, the two of them were the actual players of all the basic roles in this production, not only setting up the screenplay of the process and changing it on the fly, but also casting all the roles, editing the basic documents, the participants' speeches, and the conclusions, and directing all the participants like puppets. Stalin's personal role as director was at all stages of the "KR affair" all-encompassing; evidently remembering the show trials in 1936–38, he not only redacted all the documents on behalf of the various juridical instances (the "statement of the public," "bill of indictment," "court's decision," the transcripts, and so on), playing all the parts in the judicial orchestra and simultaneously conducting them, but he also got involved in all the details, down to reading the transcripts from the wiretapped conversations from Kliueva and Roskin's apartment.

A truly surrealist scene played out with the newly appointed minister of health, Efim Smirnov, when Stalin invited him to a meeting in the Bolshoi Theater, where the opera *Prince Igor* was being performed that evening. When Stalin asked him how he intended to organize the "court of honor," Smirnov tried to expound his idea of how he thought it should proceed. But Stalin interrupted him to explain the "main peculiarity" of the scenario he had conceived: there was no need of attorneys or the accused's final statement after the speech of the public prosecutor.[8] This completely Kafkaesque trial, in which the accused could not defend themselves and thus were completely without rights in the face of an outright malicious slander, allowed the prosecutor not only to interpret certain actions without any basis of evidence, but also to simply make up events that had never taken place.

Stalin and Zhdanov proved themselves true masters of the mystery-suspense genre. Zhdanov revealed the scenario of the upcoming spectacle in an almost finished form in his remarks in the project for the Ministry of Health concerning the "court of honor":

> Point out the role of the Americans more forcefully and stridently. They didn't simply "take an interest" in the business but "wormed their way" into it; they surrounded the laboratory and, with the help of our fools and scoundrels, stole the invention. Along with that it should be pointed out that the Americans do not let us in anywhere and do not decrypt their discoveries. . . . Should we not take Waksman, with his streptomycin, and find out whether he gave us the technology for the medicine? . . . Show the story of true betrayal, the anti-state and anti-patriotic behavior of Kliueva and Roskin. . . . Lack of faith in the strength and possibilities of our country. . . . Bowing and scraping and kowtowing to foreigners. . . . A contemptuous, nihilist-lordly attitude toward their own people, going back to prerevolutionary times, typical of that part of the old intelligentsia that was out of touch with the people and looked at them through the eyes of their masters—lords, noblemen, capitalists. . . . Portray genuine humanism. Humanism is not cosmopolitanism, which betrays the interests of its own country, the interests of its own social order. . . . Foreigners have harped on [our] inferiority. They will not respect those who don't respect themselves. They mock the weak.[9]

As if lit by a magic lantern, everything began to look new. For example, according to Zhdanov, Kliueva and Roskin's crime was that they had "declassified the drug." But the inventors maintained that they did not even know that it was classified! What is more, Roskin declared that the drug could not be classified: "I reported on this work every year to the Scientific Counsel of the Ministry of Health, a number of whose members are judges here, and no one told me that the work was classified. . . . If even one person had told me I had to keep it secret, the minister's viewpoint, on the contrary, was to publicize the undertaking widely, to organize work in Kiev, Kharkov, and Leningrad, to get a great number of people involved."[10] (The minister had hoped that the Americans, having offered help to bring the drug into production, would provide the technology and equipment to carry out experiments, but now he was also a "defendant," and the American help was declared to be a "bribe.")

By this logic, many of the actions of the "defendants" took on a surprisingly sinister tinge. Thus Zhdanov rebuked Kliueva and Roskin because they "undertook to broadly publicize their work," which "drew the attention of foreign spies, [and] they strove for their own popularity (as if the end result of scientific work is not alerting the scientific community of the results achieved in the experiments and that scientific discussions are not what advances science), [and] they received a gift— a bribe" (a Parker pen).[11]

During the trial, a truly surrealist dialogue took place between a member of the "court of honor," a certain Kovrigina, and the "defendant" Roskin in the scholarly audience:

> "The fact that you have taken your work abroad and even before that published separate chapters of it. . . . By doing this, have you or have you not caused harm to the government, to our state—that is, by doing it, have you [not] brought the preeminence of the Soviet Union under threat?"
>
> "By printing and publishing the work, I asserted its preeminence. There are no other means of asserting preeminence."[12]

Whatever did not fit into this absurd picture was simply written off as espionage, which had become the universal plot twist. Academic Parin's trip to America, for example, as well as the arrival of the American scientist Robert Leslie in the Soviet Union, had been sanctioned by the Politbiuro. Now Parin was being declared an American spy, and Leslie, an American secret service agent. Only within their paranoid logic could Stalin and Zhdanov create motives that seemed totally "realistic." The result was that the most natural activities in science were distorted and, translated into party-legalistic newspeak, changed to the point of unrecognizability; the ambassador turned into a "hardened secret service agent" and his interest in the drug into a "maneuver" and a "demarche of American intelligence"; the American offer of technical assistance and invitation to collaborate became "bribes," as did the souvenir from the publisher; the publication of the results of the scientific experiments was proclaimed "declassification," and the handover of the book's manuscript (which was already in production in the USSR—without a chapter about the technique of producing the drug, no less) to American scientists was denounced as "kowtowing to foreigners," "divulgence of a state secret," and an "anti-governmental act seriously damaging state interests."

The text of the bill of indictment, supposedly sent to the Central Committee by the party committee of the Ministry of Health, was redacted by Zhdanov, then corrected by Stalin and sent to Petr Kupriianov, an academic of the Academy of Medical Sciences, for public reading in the "court of honor." This "complaint to the Central Committee" created by Zhdanov also included the names of several "authors" in the suit. Zhdanov was troubled by a lack of "incisiveness" in the original variant. His notebooks included ideas for reworking and transforming the text into a "militant document": "Spread Parin's guilt around more. . . . Hammer the point home that in exchange for the people's money, they [scholars] have to give everything back to the people. . . . Peck the exaggerated prestige of America and England to pieces. . . . We will publicize widely concerning espionage."[13]

Only when he had decided that the genre had matured for "artistic embodiment," a mere day before the trial, did Stalin hold a general rehearsal in his office, inviting the leaders of the Writers' Union to it and forcing Fadeev to read the document aloud so that he could relish its effect.

The "court of honor" trying Kliueva and Roskin, which ran June 5–7, 1947, in the conference hall of the Counsel of Ministers in the presence of more than fifteen hundred people (the entire leadership of the Ministry of Health and the Academy of Medical Sciences, all the leaders of Soviet medicine—directors of colleges and research institutes), was not even mentioned in the press. The 1946 ideological resolutions were too targeted, concentrated on specific examples, and did not provide

a unified vector. Now the vector had an unambiguous designation—
"Soviet patriotism" and "the fight against kowtowing"—and the con-
tours of the subsequent anti-Semitic "fight against cosmopolitanism"
were already hinted at.

This whole propaganda move was kept secret until July 16, 1947,
when the "Secret Letter of the Communist Party Central Committee
about the Trial of Professors Kliueva and Roskin" appeared; it laid out
the whole story, finally, in Stalin's own interpretation. We can assume
that the entire enterprise had in fact been launched for the sake of this
letter. This document could not be located for almost half a century in
the archives, although 9,500 copies had been distributed throughout
the country at the various levels of the hierarchy of state power, with
the demand for it to be read and discussed at closed party meetings
and to provide detailed replies to the Central Committee. After the
discussion, all copies of the letter were supposed to be destroyed, and
mention of the "KR affair" in the open press was forbidden. Only by a
miracle was the full text of this document preserved in some chink of
the party's bureaucratic machine.

We should regard this "Secret Letter," written on the heels of the
trial, as that very *statement of the prosecutor and of the defendant
without an attorney or final statement* that Stalin so heartily wished
to pronounce on the subject that was agitating him. The reality in the
letter invented by the leaders, even if somewhat corrected in the defendants' testimony, was subjected to ultimate deformation, and all the
accusations and suspicions, both conceivable and inconceivable, were
declared proven. Everything was covered over by a web of secret service logic and conspiratorial justifications, forming an absurd world
of motifs turned inside out, circumstances upended, words distorted,
documents falsified, actions invented, and explanations adapted. The
subject of the patriotic play was finally ready.

THE PATRIOTIC THEATER OF THE ABSURD

The specially commissioned plays and films created on the heels
of the "KR affair" in 1947 and 1948 (Konstantin Simonov's *Alien's
Shadow*, Aleksandr Shtein's *The Law of Honor*, and Abram Room's
Court of Honor), refashioned to take account of new political exigencies (Fridrikh Ermler and Boris Romashov's *Great Strength*), or sim-

ply written at the time by a ready-made pattern (Anatolii Mariengof's *Court of Life,* Oizer Gol'des's *Other People*) differed, of course, from each other—in the casts of characters, in the circumstances in which they took place, in the problems they attempted to solve—but as a whole they are *a single text* since they all referred to a single prototext (the Central Committee's "Secret Letter") and its author, Stalin, who, in staging the "theatrical-cinematic 'KR drama,'"[14] was in essence the true creator of the genre of the "patriotic play."

However, as Nikolai Krementsov observed, "Although the 'orchestration' and players were different, the 'conductor' and the 'leitmotif' were the same in all three performances [Simonov's and Shtein's plays and the Room film]; both the two plays and the film were merely dramatized illustrations to the 'Secret Letter' that the Central Committee distributed to party organizations in the summer of 1947."[15] This is both true and not quite true; the aestheticization of certain political moves is capable of producing not only a direct (propagandistic) effect, but also an opposite, often explosive, one. It can, for example, rise to the absurd and reveal the manipulations and fabrications that lie at the heart of these moves. This is by no means to suggest that these texts are subversive. It is simply that the arbitrariness that in politics is easily curbed by repression turns into the absurd in an art that aspires to verisimilitude, when, as in this case, Socialist Realism turns into *socialist surrealism.*

Simonov was commissioned to write *Alien's Shadow* immediately after the Kliueva-Roskin court of honor had concluded. When the commission was fulfilled and the play turned over to the Central Committee, Stalin telephoned Simonov personally with directives about how the text should be revised,[16] after which the play ran at the Moscow Art Theater and was awarded a Stalin Prize. The prize was also awarded to Shtein's play, *The Law of Honor* (both plays were performed more than a thousand times in Moscow's leading theaters and in dozens of theaters throughout the country).[17] Even before the trial, the idea had arisen of a film about "the patriotism of Soviet scientists" based on the plot Stalin had created. Dramatist Shtein and director Room were put in charge of producing it. They had been given passes to the hearings at the court of honor and provided with all the necessary materials. Thus the original screenplay was ready in draft already toward August 1947. *Court of Honor* had a wide run in the country's cinemas (in just a year it was seen by 15.2 million viewers) and was awarded the Stalin Prize, First Class.

The original screenplay, however, so closely followed the Stalin-Zhdanov plot that some in the Central Committee were dissatisfied with it, declaring that it "uses almost all the material from the court of honor in the Roskin and Kliueva affair, keeping even individual particulars," which did not permit the authors to bring the viewer to "the necessary artistic conclusions and generalizations." The Central Committee asked that a veil be drawn over the link to the "KR affair"—specifically, to change the cancer studies to "some other scientific problem; otherwise the critical aspect of the film will seem to be addressed only to Roskin and Kliueva, which is least of all needed, and not to the ranks of people who are manifesting to one degree or another kowtowing to the West."[18]

Although, even after the reworking, Shtein's play and screenplay and Room's film were literally full of details from the *real* "KR affair," these productions struck both audiences and historians as being absolutely *unrealistic*. "The majority of viewers did not recognize the production as a 'dramatization' of actual events. Even the American ambassador, Walter Smith, who had seen all three works and described one of the plays in his memoirs, recognized neither the KR affair (which he had also described in the memoirs) nor even himself."[19] If the experienced secret service agent Smith could not recognize himself, what could we expect from the Soviet audiences who, judging by their responses to such works, considered them "totally unbelievable" and "absolutely unrealistic"?[20] Everything seemed improbable: the naïveté of scientific directors and great scientists (who did not understand how their discoveries could be used by "the enemies of peace" when this was the *only* thing that all the newspapers were writing about), their complete lack of unaccountability to various kinds of collective bodies (above all, the party committees), their high-handedness (when they decide for themselves whether to hand over the manuscript to an American publisher, as if every Soviet organization did not have its own "secret department" that would have intervened),[21] and finally, their impunity. The accumulation of these inconsistencies transformed these plays/films that strove for almost a documentary quality into completely absurd performances.

The plots of all these works began at the threshold of a discovery of enormous significance; Trubnikov, the hero of *Alien's Shadow*, is the director of a bacteriological institute in a provincial city who is on the verge of creating a vaccine against the most serious infectious diseases (typhus, tularemia, the plague); the characters in *Law of Honor* and *Court of Honor*, microbiologists Losev and Dobrotvorskii, have created a pain medicine that Dobrotvorskii is convinced all mankind needs since everyone suffers from pain; scientist Virigin from *Court of Life* has developed a poison to exterminate locusts; and in Oizer Gol'des's *Other People* a compound will any moment now be created to fight tuberculosis.

Future conflict was already inherent in the very nature of the discoveries; they were such that they could be used both to save and to harm people. In *Court of Life*, for example, it emerged during experiments that the poison killed not only locusts, but also, when it emitted a sort of unknown gas, everything living, and only by chance had it not killed a person. In *Alien's Shadow*, the truly magical effect of the vaccine was based on the discovery of a method whereby it was possible to almost infinitely change—weakening and intensifying—the infective force of the microbes. After many years of experiments, Trubnikov had managed to achieve a dramatic increase in the infectiousness of the most varied sorts of microbes, and now, in order to obtain the vaccine, he had to achieve just as strong a debilitation of their infectiousness.

This duality of the discoveries plays an important role in the conflict since it is precisely the *harmful* discoveries that the American spies attempt to steal. But the heroes in these plays fail to understand this: "You'd have to be really crazy for the possibility of such a monstrous use of science to occur to you!" says Trubnikov. Such naïveté in a great scientist infuriates the party protagonist Makeev: "You'd have to be really crazy for this *not* to occur to you!" The same applies to Virigin's discovery; it is not the locusts that interest the Americans but the element that he discovers as a byproduct: the gas that kills everything live.

These plays, like a lot in Cold War–era Soviet art, betray something significant about Soviet phobias. From them one could assume that Americans were exclusively occupied with producing biological weapons. This passion of the enemies for toxic microbes and poisons that could kill masses of people was doubtless part of Stalinist paranoia, the last gasp of which would in five years be the "Doctors' Plot," where Stalin's phobias materialized. But in the meantime the microbiologists engaged in searching for medicines and saving humankind are the exclusive actors here.

Corresponding to the duality of the discoveries is the pairing of the characters. In *Court of Honor/Law of Honor,* it is Dobrotvorskii and Losev; in *Alien's Shadow,* Trubnikov and Okunev; and in *Court of Life,* Kandaurov and Virigin. The first in the pair is either a politically naïve person (Dobrotvorskii), a purely positive character (Kandaurov), or else has features in his nature that do not permit him to see the true face of his antagonist (Trubnikov). The antagonist is either a dishonorable egoist (Losev), an infernal villain and spy (Okunev), or a spiteful, envious person (Virigin). Meanwhile, the first in the pair is an actual scientist, while the second, as the villain, merely uses science for his own purposes (espionage, self-affirmation, vanity).

The scientists supposedly making discoveries of worldwide importance are people who had been involved in the war, have lost people close to them, and have shown true heroism and self-sacrifice in science (Trubnikov, for example, for sixteen years has infected himself with the most terrible diseases in doing experiments upon himself). In order to find a point of contact between the scientists and the villains paired with them, the authors depict the former as childishly naïve. They fail to understand the simplest things. As Trubnikov's sister tells him, "You have fallen behind yourself. . . . As a person, you have not kept pace with yourself as a scientist."

The spy-novel intrigue of these plays and films boils down to this: the Americans who, either using spies *(Alien's Shadow, Court of Life)* or a dishonest partner of the main protagonist *(Court of Honor, Law of Honor)* try to get their hands on the discovery, but at the last minute, due to the vigilance of a relative *(Alien's Shadow),* the collective *(Court of Honor, Law of Honor),* or an honest American *(Court of Honor),* the enemy's intention is foiled. This collision is in fact what distinguishes these works from each other.

All the main characters in these works are to some extent beset by vanity. Some, like Losev or Virigin, are pathologically ambitious, while others, like Dobrotvorskii or Trubnikov, are only inclined to be vain, but enough so as to be caught up in the spies' nets. The spies (Okunev, Landmure, Wilby, Craig) take full advantage of such vanity. The fame that the individualist scientists seek is the only thing they are not supposed to have. Fame and/or glory, like their scientific achievements, belongs to the people, the country, the state, and, ultimately, to "the government"—that is, to Stalin. Fame is an attribute of the sovereign and the buttress of his legitimacy. Hence, any claims to fame are cut short. It it precisely the yearning for personal glory that manifests the "bourgeois individualism" brought in from the West, and therefore vanity and "kowtowing to the West" are interlinked.

The question of to whom the discoveries belong is uppermost in these plays. Although Losev, who sees science as a source of fame, honors, and rewards, is vain, it is unclear what drives him to hand over the manuscript to the Americans—surely not the Parker pen. During the court of honor the following curious detail is uncovered: the Bureau of Inventions refuses to patent the drug, which drives Losev mad. He informs the assistant minister that he will "find a way to preserve his own priority and Dobrotvorsksii's." Vereiskii, the prosecutor, asks Losev to explain how he had planned to "preserve this so-called priority." Abashed, Losev replies, "I regard the refusal [of a patent] as an infringement of my rights and those of Professor Dobrotvorskii . . . the rights to a discovery made by us, Comrade Public Prosecutor!" The presiding judge says, "Nobody is going to litigate those rights away from you." Thus, priority is supremely important when it is a question of the country (this is *Soviet* priority!), but when it is a question of individuals, it is turned into "so-called priority." In fact, there is nothing here but preeminence; the discovery is not a military secret, nor does it have a military dimension. Preeminence is self-sufficient. Its preservation is *an act of state ambition*.

These plays promoted a Stalinist understanding of science, a purely applied one that essentially boiled down to a single function: the development of arms production. Hence it is by definition nationalistic and secret, and it belongs to the state. This is why all these plays feature endless discussions of "world science." Indeed, it is the illusion of apoliticalness that is the ideological basis of the "carelessness" and "slackening of vigilance" on the part of the honest, as a whole, Soviet scientists. The fight against "world science" is one of the main themes of these plays. Central here is the greatness of Russian science, supposedly stolen from it by foreigners, and all the plays feature arguments about this.

These works were mainly addressed to members of the scientific intelligentsia, who were on the whole significantly more advanced than the average audience member as far as reading ideological codes and understanding Soviet political rituals were concerned. But the majority of the plot absurdities from which these plays were literally stitched together nonetheless paled in comparison with the most obvious: the glaring discrepancy between the material state of Soviet science depicted in them and reality. The action in them flowed through shining new laboratories, broad corridors, pompous foyers, luxurious academics' office-libraries, huge halls, and new buildings equipped with the latest in technology. But when U.S. ambassador Smith met with Kliueva and Roskin, it was no accident that their meeting was in the office of the director of the Institute of Epidemiology; as journalist E. Finn noted, it was "apparently the only room where one could somehow receive a foreign guest" since "the whole institute produces an extremely poverty-stricken impression, and Kliueva and Roskin's laboratory even more so."[22] Kliueva had no offices, nor assistants, nor equipment. "We haven't had and still don't have (and don't know when we will have) minimal equipment, the simplest instruments (microscopes, thermostats, refrigerators, centrifuges, and so on), the necessary reagents, and reliable heat," she complained in a letter.[23]

The splendid new institutes, the super-contemporary interiors of which spectators saw on the stage and screen, had nothing in common with the poverty that prevailed in reality. Not to mention that the USSR, in which the discoveries saving humanity were supposedly being made, was suffering from shortages in the simplest medicines: "The country's medical profession, which had heroically performed in the war years, was put into a most difficult position, and the country's population, given the deepening rift with other countries that produced medical supplies, suffered monstrous difficulties in the search for the medicines they needed."[24]

In reality, the fundamental discoveries in medicine and microbiology in the postwar years were in fact being made in the West, most of all in laboratories in the United States. The hot pursuit in the USSR at this time was genetics, and against a backdrop of patriotic hullabaloo, obvious charlatans of science were winning state support. In addition to the odious Lysenko, we might mention Ol'ga Lepeshinskaia, who had recommended treatment of gastric ulcers, arthritis, and cancer with chicken albumen and who had tried to argue that a soda bath made according to her recipe would cure hypertension and sclerosis and would stop the onset of old age. Fully in the spirit of Lysenko (as noted in chapter 6 above), veterinarian Gevorg Bosh'ian stated in 1949 that viruses could transition into microbes as the result of the "domestication of viruses" in a new nutrient medium. This typical opportunist unexpectedly received the supreme support: he was awarded the degree of Doctor of Medical Sciences and the title of professor, and he became head of the secret laboratory of the N. F. Gamaleia Research Institute of Epidemiology and Microbiology. Assistant veterinarian Dorokhov dissolved cattle horns in nitric acid and offered this poison to cancer patients. Technician Anatolii Kachugin preached healing with heavy metal salts. Aleksandra Troitskaia, a veterinary doctor from Kaluga, gave her patients an extract from cancer cells as a vaccine. In the atmosphere of insanity that gripped the country, patients dragged themselves to these hoaxers in droves.[25] Apparently to make this picture ultimately surrealistic, Soviet art depicted the creation of the most advanced medicines (those that were at the time being created in the United States) in the USSR, with American spies (headed by the ambassador) supposedly chasing after them.

The cognitive dissonance was too great for these plays to convince anyone of anything (would the supposed discoveries really be handed over to Americans?) or to cure "kowtowing to the West." But still, they were "representation of life in the forms of life itself"—life as it seemed to Stalin's paranoid consciousness, which gave rise to the patriotic play as the most fitting genre for this.

This type of play was just as unusual as the court of honor itself—a new species of show trial. If in the 1930s such trials were constructed around staged sessions (though disguised NKVD operatives were sitting in the auditorium), and if transcripts and documentary evidence (though falsified) were shown to the public, and if such trials followed a sort of trial logic (though subjugated to the scenario written in the Kremlin), then the new show trial was completely performance-adapted and aestheticized, turning into an *actual* theatrical performance. The real (that is, fabricated from the outset) "KR affair" and trial were classified, but their public representation was presented in the forms of spectacles and films. This is not theatricalized performance, with the real participants in the roles of actors (as in the 1930s), but real theater, with professional actors in the roles of the participants.

Obviously, such an unusual form of representation was influenced by the functions of the punitive act itself and hence by the nature of the fabricated "crime." The aims of the Great Terror–era show trials were the public discrediting and physical destruction of real and imagined political opponents, as merited by the crimes attributed to them (treason, espionage, sabotage). But in the case of the "KR affair," the aim was ideological: a condemnation of "kowtowing to the West" and the cultivation of "Soviet patriotism." Promotion of the latter most of all required propaganda, and plays and films fulfilled this "educational" function. But since Stalinist education is always repressive, kowtowing and the lack of patriotism were depicted here as *bordering on* crime. In deciding between a trial-spectacle and a spectacle-trial, Stalin this time chose the latter; this allowed for rising above the phenomenon and concentrating on the politico-ideological impact with an indispensable element of threat (as distinct from the persons in the 1930s show trials, typical representatives of the Soviet intelligentsia, which was completely loyal, Soviet-thinking, and sincerely dedicated to the regime, Kliueva and Roskin had simply "turned up" in the wrong place at the wrong time, and not only were they unlikely candidates for destruction, but they were also the creators of work recognized as useful).

The opportunity specifically to pronounce the prosecutor's indictment, which would be the final word, was what attracted Stalin to the idea of the court of honor; indeed, the role of prosecutor suited him best of all. This is precisely why the main ideological message of the "Secret Letter" was put into his closing speech. Although this message was twofold, it was based on singularly fantastic premises at both extremes; the letter made accusations of kowtowing and simultaneously spoke of greatness. Both these principles are included in the text of the closing arguments that the public prosecutor, the lieutenant-general of the medical services, Academic Vereiskii, presents in *Law of Honor/ Court of Honor*. His passionate speech consists of two parts, the first of which is concerned with nonexistent kowtowing:

> To whom would you want to give away the treasures of our science, its noble discoveries, its beautiful aspirations? To those who are striving to cast humanity into the infernal hell-fire of a new war? To those who brandish the atom bomb over the globe? For the sake of humanity's happiness—we will not allow it! . . . Are we, Soviet scientists, to be "passportless" vagabonds among humanity? Are we to be rootless cosmopolitans? Are we to be Ivans that don't remember our motherland?

After a pause, Vereiskii steps out to the proscenium and delivers the second part of the speech, which refers to just as unprecedented a greatness of pan-Russian science:

> In the name of Lomonosov and Lobachevskii, Sechenov and Mendeleev, Pirogov and Pavlov, who preserved, like a sacred banner, the primacy of Russian science! In the name of Popov, Ladygin, and other inventors whose discoveries are brazenly appropriated by foreigners! In the name of the Soviet Army soldier who liberated a desecrated and dishonored Europe! In the name of Professor Dobrotvorskii's son, who heroically died for the Fatherland, I ACCUSE YOU!

The bitter irony of the ending of *Law of Honor/Court of Honor* is that it referred in an obvious fashion to Émile Zola's famous article "J'accuse...!" This reference to a text that had become one of the most brilliant statements of the struggle against anti-Semitism a half-century before only emphasized the situation of the most unbridled Judophobia and nationalist hysteria that these plays and films promoted. By a coincidence, Room's film *Court of Honor* came into distribution on January 25, 1949, three days before *Pravda*'s editorial about "cosmopolitan" theater critics was published, an article that served as the start of a new, blatantly anti-Semitic stage of the patriotic campaign. The film passed the baton, as it were, of mass paranoia and indoctrination further, taking them to a new level. The wartime experience of the encounter with the West was at first marked in the "KR affair" as an inferiority complex (kowtowing), then displaced by a superiority complex (Russian preeminence), and, finally, defined in a nationalistic way—through the stigmatization of certain "'passportless' vagabonds among humanity" (almost all of whom happened to be Jews or at least have Jewish surnames), highlighting the specific carriers of infernal evil (rootless cosmopolitanism). The stereotypes shaped at this time were imprinted forever in the masses' consciousness and became rooted in the corresponding political culture. Reaching the next step, the physical destruction of internal enemies—the "murderers in white coats" from the "Doctors' Plot"—was hindered by the death of Stalin.

VISUALIZATION OF THE DELIRIUM OF GREATNESS

In the era of the postwar shortage of films, the only flourishing genre was the biographical film. It held a solid place in the thematic plans and dominated all the other genres. After the fiasco with *Ivan the Terrible,* films were made about Admirals Nakhimov and Ushakov; about the scientists Ivan Pavlov, Aleksandr Popov, Ivan Michurin, Nikolai Zhukovskii, Nikolai Pirogov, Nikolai Miklukho-Maklai, and Nikolai Przheval'skii; about the composers Mikhail Glinka (two films), Modest Mussorgsky, and Nikolai Rimsky-Korsakoff; and about the writers Vissarion Belinskii, Taras Shevchenko, Jānis Rainis, and Abai Kunanbaev. Many of these films were awarded Stalin Prizes. All the leading Soviet directors took part in the work on them—Vsevolod Pudovkin, Aleksandr Dovzhenko, Grigorii Kozintsev, Mikhail Romm, Sergei Iutkevich, Grigorii Roshal', Leo Arnshtam, Aleksandr Razumnyi, Gerbert Rappoport, Grigorii Aleksandrov, and others. New biographical films were in the thematic plan for 1953–54—*Lomonosov, Pushkin, Ivan Franko, Surikov, Repin, Kramskoi, Tchaikovsky, Spendiarov, Bazhenov the Architect, Mendeleev,* and others. Only one of them, *Lomonosov,* was made, coming out in 1955.

With rare exceptions, the postwar "historico-biographical" films were the result of neither the creative intentions of their creators (Stalin personally approved the lists of themes and subjects, and the writers/directors and performers were chosen by the Ministry of Cinematography) nor the declared commemorative aims (the different anniversaries to which these films were timed) or educational ones ("the popularization of science and propagation of scientific knowledge"). The political propaganda function of these films, which differed only in the means of packaging their ideological content, was part of the total reexamination of the history of science in the light of "Russian preeminence," and they can be understood only in this light.

Like a contrast shower, Soviet patriotic propaganda varied two opposite ideological messages; on the one hand, it reiterated an inferiority complex ("kowtowing to the West"), and, on the other, it instilled a superiority complex ("Russian preeminence"). The delirium of one's own greatness was the response to "kowtowing," and the more absurd the accusations of anti-patriotism and cosmopolitanism, the more radical the forms of boosting patriotic immunity were. The latter will be discussed here.

In producing a world of historical phantasms, Soviet art remained true to its basic stylistic device by attempting to present the product of traumatic fantasizing as credibly as possible. This "realism" emerged as the result of the mid-1930s populist shift and was the response to popular demand; as they were being introduced to culture, the peasant masses demanded "realistic credibility." Grigorii Kozintsev, who did a great deal to consolidate the biographical genre in Soviet cinema, described this transition in his diary:

> The hyperbole and caricatured exaggeration in the art of the early revolutionary years did not conceal its fantastic nature; it did not occur to young artists to consider such imagery a depiction of reality. Then the poster began to be passed off as the real thing; cartoonish roles were played in serious fashion, "for real," and caricature crept into historical scenes. Then representational means changed, it would seem, to the point of being unrecognizable; an external verisimilitude appeared, but the concept of the object—with schematism, unilinearity, and exaggeration—remained, to all intents and purposes, poster-like.[26]

Thus stylistic verisimilitude began to shape the most radical ideological fantasies. Its arsenal contained the most varied devices—from conjectures to outright falsifications.

The chief aim of these films was the glorification of Russia's scientific accomplishments through personification, which was supposed to lend concreteness and authenticity. Since the filmmakers had to affirm non-obvious "superiorities" (either unrecorded or "stolen by foreigners") and to operate with dubious facts (either unconfirmed or outright fabricated), these films are constructed such that their main characters looked as vintage as possible, submerged in the "classical past," the era from which they appear to the viewer, usually taking life from busts or stiffened into them. The "history" thus quickly cobbled together was naturalized by being covered by an artificial patina, which intensified the effect of authenticity. For example, according to the screenplays, *Zhukovskii* began with a bronze bust and *Przheval'skii* and *Pavlov* ended with busts of bronze or marble, and in the endings of the films, the characters "broke out of" their bronze or marble shells, as it were, and, alive, looked into the future. This gaze remained that of a monument brought to life. What is more, these were not different monuments but one; the gazes of the various heroes were completely identical—Zhukovskii, as the screenplay stipulated, watched "with a gaze fixed on the future"; Miklukho-Maklai looked into the distance "with eyes full of faith"; the film about Popov ends just the same, with his gaze "fixed forward, into the future"; and at the end of his film, "Przheval'skii gazes into the distance" with the very same expression.

The conviction that the aim of the biographical genre amounted to extolling the main character was shared by all the creators of these films (perhaps only Eisenstein was the exception, but what had happened with his *Ivan the Terrible* became a lesson to all the rest). Grigorii Roshal', who created the films about Abai, Pavlov, Mussorgsky, and Rimsky-Korsakoff, asserted that only Soviet cinema embodied the correct approach to the hero, while "the biographical filmmakers in bourgeois art extremely often simply slander the characters in their films. They distort their acts and scrape together from statements made by them whatever abominable and disgusting concept of Fascist-leaning capitalism suits them."[27]

In the context of reassessing the history of science, one cannot disregard the distortions of biographies made by Soviet cinema, nor its "piecing together" of the most outrageous concepts from the heroes' statements; these techniques functioned by simulation of "the forms of life itself" and created the effect of historical verisimilitude. These techniques arose from a goal that justified stressing biography, one that was "one-hundred-percent positive" in depicting the main characters, who were the embodiment of "the glory of Russia"—its forward-looking sciences, its progressive art, its humanism and internationalism. History came into conflict with ideology, which is really what constitutes the fundamental genre-internal collision of artistic biography; to be biographical, a novel (or film) must be based on all the known biography of a historical person, which means that it corresponds to the facts; to be a novel (or film), it must be interesting, which means plot-driven— that is, fiction. This nerve of the biographical genre in Socialist Realism was anesthetized by ideology.

The biographies of the characters in these films were subjected to monstrous deformations. The creators of the film *Ivan Pavlov*, for example, were endlessly congratulated on the similarity of the actor to the prototype; Pavlov's chauffeur followed the made-up Aleksandr Borisov around, unable to believe he was not Pavlov,[28] and one of Pavlov's students was enraptured over how successfully the filmmakers had managed to incorporate the documentary newsreel of the Moscow congress of physiologists containing Pavlov's speech, although the film did not in fact use the newsreel at all—so convincing was the actor playing

Pavlov.[29] But the more externally similar the actor was to Pavlov, the less similar his character was to that of the real Pavlov. One could say that the proportions of similarity and differences here were compensatorily intertwined; the further the created character diverged from the real Pavlov, the more similar in appearance he had to be.

The fundamental problems with the Soviet appropriation of Pavlov began after the revolution, which Pavlov did not accept, despite the golden rain showered upon him by the Soviet government, vested in keeping him in Soviet Russia. According to the film, after the revolution (to which Pavlov's attitude is not specified), he remained a patriot. A certain foreign emissary suggests that he leave the country: "We people of the West consider it our duty to rescue the immortal treasures of Russia from the Bolsheviks. We will be happy to rescue you for humanity." Pavlov's response is full of sarcasm: "What, are you buying up Russian goods dirt cheap? And Russian scientists as well? Or haven't they offered you Saint Isaac's Cathedral? You're not interested in Peter's monument? For a song." Having been told that he "can work in any institute in the world" and that "for humanity, it doesn't matter where you will work," Pavlov bursts into a patriotic monologue in the spirit of Academic Vereiskii in *Court of Honor* ("Science has a fatherland, and a scientist is bound to have it! I, sir, am Russian, and my fatherland is here, no matter what happens to it. You should know I am not a rat. And the ship is *not* going down!") and drives away the "benefactors."

Such scenes were extremely popular in biographical films; attempts by foreigners to "buy" Russian scientists met with irate rebuffs of the "foreign benefactors." Popov did this in the film devoted to him, and *Michurin* begins with a similar scene. All of this patriotic mythology that ran from one film to another was, of course, fiction, and in Pavlov's case, outright falsification. Pavlov, desperately struggling to survive in hungry Petrograd in 1920 and with a deeply negative opinion of the situation and prospects of Soviet Russia, had in fact had it suggested to him that he leave for Sweden after the revolution, and he was not only ready to do so, but had even asked the authorities to release him, along with his colleagues, to go abroad. This explained the inclusion in the film of the material about the "passionate concern of the Soviet authorities" for Pavlov's work, the decree of support for him signed by Lenin, the privileged position of both him and his school, and the attention of the authorities, who were ready to do anything to win Pavlov over and convince him to remain in Russia for considerations of prestige.[30]

Appearing in the film as a hint of this is the visit of Gorky, whom Lenin supposedly sent to find out what Pavlov needed. Gorky tells Pavlov, "[Lenin] considers you his ally, a Bolshevik in science." This apparently is supposed to justify Lenin's concern about Pavlov. The filmmakers, as well as film critics afterward, had a hard time choosing their words to describe Pavlov's "evolution." He supposedly "did not immediately grasp the events of the revolution, did not immediately understand and accept the Bolsheviks' policy, but loyalty to the Russian people helped the scientist make the right choice."[31] The proof of this was the film itself, which revealed "the nature of Pavlov's patriotism, by virtue of which the great scientist could not but accept the revolution, despite all his efforts to stay out of politics."[32] The onscreen Pavlov struggles with himself, and at the end "discover[s] anew, as it were, his motherland, [and] furthermore, the concepts of motherland and government are now for him one, as indeed for all Soviet people. And he is hastening to do as much as possible for his country,"[33] and he was then supposedly manifesting "a most sincere desire to comprehend the great teaching by which the Bolsheviks are guided."[34] What is more, toward the end of the film he supposedly "becomes an ardent Soviet patriot. He is proud of his great people, the wisest and most democratic government in the world, the bright ideas that lead the people along a path of progress, showing the way for all the world's peoples."[35]

All of this had nothing to do with the real Pavlov. When his correspondence with Soviet leaders was published in the post-Soviet era—his letters to Viacheslav Molotov, Nikolai Bukharin, and Grigorii Kaminskii—the abyss that lay between him and the regime became clear. In a letter dated October 10, 1934, to Kaminskii (then the people's commissar of health)—a letter that was a response to the commissar's birthday congratulations to Pavlov on the occasion of his eighty-fifth birthday—Pavlov wrote about his attitude toward the October Revolution, which was "almost directly opposite" Kaminskii's, for whom the revolution "imbues the motherland's wonderful movement forward with courage." On the contrary, Pavlov saw "its enormous truly negative aspects" in the "long-standing terror and unchecked willfulness of power," which transformed "our nature, which was besides rather Asiatic, into a shameful-slavish one. . . . And can you do much good with slaves?" Pavlov answered his own question thus: "[For] pyramids, yes; but not [for] common genuine human happiness."[36]

Distortion of the real political positions of their characters is typical of all these films. Such piling on of outright falsifications, obvious misrepresentations, and baldest lies is difficult to find in any other genre of Soviet cinema since biographical films, as distinct from ordinary artistic ones, made use of the lives of *real* historical people. But it was precisely biographies that the heroes of these films were lacking. The Soviet biographical film told essentially one and the same story, creating with various names the biography of the champion of Russian preeminence in the sciences. It created roll calls that transformed the various films about different characters into one endless film and that produced a densely populated world of Russian science and art where one and the same roles were often played by the same actors. The same motifs transferred from one film to another (Zhukovskii and Miklukho-Maklai, Przeval'skii and Pavlov, and Michurin and Popov all came up against a shortage of resources and indifference from tsarist bureaucrats); similar interiors—scientists' offices and aristocrats' apartments, ceremonial halls and laboratories; the main characters talk endlessly about their discoveries, asking each other leading questions (these dialogues fulfill a purely informational function so that viewers could understand what the research was about). But characters born of the plot functions created the entourage of these films. Among them is the inevitable throng of enraptured students that always surrounded Pavlov and Zhukovskii, Popov and Pirogov. They delivered the revolutionary speeches in the films and, with sparkling eyes, talked about the accomplishments of their teachers. The biographical films and plays included an inevitable spectrum of conservative opponents of the progressive scientists, and they were to be found not only in the highest levels of the bureaucracy, but also in the scientific milieu itself. We find such scenes in films about Zhukovskii, Pirogov, Przheval'skii, Michurin, and Pavlov.

Viewers knew in advance that they were to become witnesses to Pirogov's creation of Russian field surgery, Popov's invention of the wireless telegraph, Pavlov's discovery of conditioned reflexes, Przheval'skii's reaching Central Asia and his refinement of the question of mountain ridges, Michurin's conquest of selective breeding, the proof of Miklukho-Maklai's correctness, and Zhukovskii's unraveling of the mysteries of winged flight. But in the hero's path, as in a fairy tale, a saboteur appears. The main collisions in the films are tied to plotlines concerning "villains." In *Miklukho-Maklai* it is the scientist's venal servant and a plot of Germans and Englishmen. Przheval'skii is tailed by an English agent, the "botanist-scientist" Simon, and the situation with the venal servant is also repeated here, in this case with Przheval'skii's guide. This secondary plot becomes the fundamental pivot on which Przheval'skii's entire journey to Tibet via China hinges. In *Pirogov,* the plot against "the father of Russian surgery" took on particularly sinister forms. Certain papers of a revolutionary nature (including a transcription of Belinskii's letter to Gogol') are stolen from Pirogov's assistant, Skulachenko, who is arrested. During an operation in which Pirogov is demonstrating the effect of anesthesia, he is slipped some poisoned ether, as a result of which the patient almost dies. In fact, in the first biographical film about scientists, Kozintsev, who was Jewish himself, was the first to create the image of poisoner-doctors, who would materialize over the years into the "murderers in white robes" of the "Doctors' Plot."

These biographies were derivatives of plot functions. Such was *Zhukovskii,* in which the aim of asserting "Russian preeminence" in aviation was central. In addition, the motif of "Russia—motherland of aviation" was linked not only to the main character, but also to secondary characters. The pronouncement of the Soviet Air Force's Political Department on a screenplay by Anatolii Granberg attested to an atmosphere in which the affirmation of "Russian preeminence" in aviation was ongoing. The screenplay *mentioned* various pilots whose contributions to the development of world aviation were universally recognized. But even mentioning their names provoked the wrath of the Political Department, which declared that the author had not manifested sufficient patriotism: "There is no need for the scenario to talk about the flights of Truchon, Santos Dumont, the Wright brothers, Blériot, and others abroad in the later years after the invention and first flight of an airplane by A. F. Mozhaiskii in 1882, for this unintentionally makes one think of an attempt to advertise the efforts of foreigners."[37]

This is why it was so important to Pudovkin to tie Zhukovskii's work on the mathematical calculation of a flying machine to the "successful flight" of Mozhaiskii's machine on July 20, 1882, since Mozhaiskii himself was proclaimed the first successful flier in the history of aviation. As opposed to Zhukovskii, whose role was (and indeed remained

so after the film) not so comprehensible to the viewer (theory, the physics of flight, mathematical calculations), Mozhaiskii, with his apparatus
that supposedly had risen into the air, was the living embodiment of
"Russian supremacy." During a discussion in the Artistic Council of the
USSR Ministry of Cinematography on December 1, 1949, Pudovkin
said that it was so important for him to "tie Zhukovskii and his work
also to the events that were in the area of aviation, which was created
by the hands of Russian individuals," that he resorted to "an altera-
tion of historical documentation" and included a scene of Zhukovskii
meeting Mozhaiskii in person that, however, "was an extreme surprise
. . . to all the specialists in the Arts Council," and it was then that the
idea arose to include the episode with Mozhaiskii in Zhukovskii's conversation with Mendeleev as an "illustration of the recollections" of
the latter.[38]

However, the way in which Pudovkin introduces this scene shows
how awkward the director felt in bringing in knowingly unproved
"events" and trying meanwhile to avoid accusations of deliberate "al-
teration of historical documentation." In the film, Mendeleev, who supposedly saw Mozhaiskii's flying apparatus himself, tells Zhukovskii
about the "facts" of the airplane experiment. Yet he does not tell him
about what he saw, which would be natural, but instead reads Zhukovskii a letter from a certain officer containing an account of "the
story of a simple soldier" who himself saw Mozhaiskii's airplane rise
into the air at Krasnoe Selo. This is how Mendeleev relates the story
to Zhukovskii: Mozhaiskii "built a big apparatus and, *supposedly,* it
rose into the air. . . . This sounds like a legend. And, in fact, *it just
remained a legend.*" This scene is shown as a flashback. The stipula-
tions emphasized in the text and the triple "wrapping" of the historical
fabrications betray Pudovkin's uncertainty and explain the specialists'
"extreme surprise."

The concealment of the "facts" is also served by Mendeleev's irate
monologue, which is supposed to explain to the viewer that since the
military department was engaged in all of this, the experiment was
classified: "Mozhaiskii's calculations and theoretical considerations
were buried in the bowels of the War Ministry for inscrutable but malicious reasons, for the [ministry] did not give Mozhaiskii any money
and thereby ruined him and his work only because the work was begun by a Russian person and not by any foreign authority, which the

[ministry people] blindly believe and, like monkeys, senselessly and blindly repeat what they are told," Mendeleev tells Zhukovskii, and then exclaims, in a rage, "These bureaucratic autocrats did not lift a finger to support Mozhaiskii's work. . . . We don't have Mozhaiskii's plans, nor his model, nor his apparatus, and now we must carry on his work without using what he discovered." It is not a stretch to flesh out this series: since there is neither a model nor plans, neither apparatus nor documents, there is also no proof of the very event passed along as historical fact.

To the same degree that Pudovkin embellished Mozhaiskii's accomplishments, he smeared those of Dmitrii Riabushinskii. The latter was presented as an embodiment of the cosmopolitan bourgeoisie and a counterweight to the patriotic accomplishments of Mozhaiskii and Zhukovskii. From one of the richest families of Russian industrialists and bankers, Riabushinskii was a brilliantly educated specialist in the area of hydro-aerodynamics and the founder of the Aerodynamics Institute in Kuchino; after emigrating to France, he became president of the Russian Philosophical Society and the Association for the Preservation of Russian Cultural Values Abroad. He had in April 1918 insisted on nationalizing the Aerodynamics Institute, then lived as an emigrant for many decades without French citizenship, which he had refused to accept as he continued to consider himself Russian; he kept his Russian emigrant's Nansen certificate up until the day he died. His scientific accomplishments are attested by his election as a corresponding member to the French Academy of Sciences (1935), his doctorate of sciences at the Sorbonne (1920), and his election to professor in the Russian Higher Technical School in France. Pudovkin portrayed him as an ambitious, half-educated person, a cold-blooded profit-seeker, and a spiteful anti-patriot.

The film shows a businessman who demands that all the work of Zhukovskii and his students be published under his name. Riabushinskii looks for an advantage in the fact that the Wright brothers set up a motor in the glider and remained aloft a few minutes; he was thus "a greedy plunderer interested in only one thing: how he could more advantageously use the foreign 'novelty.'"[39] Meanwhile, when Zhukovskii learns about this, he merely remarks, "But Captain Mozhaiskii achieved this twenty-one years earlier and a lot more successfully." Pudovkin's Riabushinskii does not believe in Russian science and industry: "All of our Russian attempts to build and invent planes are utter rubbish. . . . It is much more expedient to buy what is invented there, in the West—that is, to buy foreign designs and exploit them here, in Russia. This is profitable and sound."

During the war Zhukovskii tries to explain to the grand duke that "we have the strongest group in the world of aerodynamics scientists. . . . Thanks to them we can count on planes from the lightest to the heaviest, multi-engine ships. In America they can not even imagine this. Nor in Europe," but the latter merely asks him, "Tell me what you are after, I would say, for yourself—for yourself personally?" Perplexed, Zhukovskii says, "I'm talking about Russia, Your Highness. I personally don't need anything." He explains to the most august duke that "it is not worth it for our Russian manufacturers to build our designs because it is more profitable to collect foreign-branded airplanes," for which the duke finds a convincing (in his opinion) explanation: "Logically! Foreign orders strengthen our ties to allies, and that at the moment is our salvation." "Russian manufacturers" meant above all Riabushinskii. It is he who buys up the parts of the "Newport" planes abroad, assembles them in his own plants, and then presents the planes to the War Ministry—a monopolist buyer. Zhukovskii is crushed: "All our achievements are being sold. Russian science, thought, honor, and pride—everything is being sold." The Riabushinskii slandered in the film was an ideal target, allowing for ties among "monopolistic capital," corruption, and anti-patriotism.

Zhukovskii constantly talks about Russian "firsts" in the film. Here the first plane capable of taking twenty people up into the air is created. "They don't want to believe abroad that we are building the 'Il'ia Muromets,' but it's already flying." When someone suggests that it would not be bad to learn a little from others, he answers: "There's no one to learn from. . . . We can teach *them!*" All of the accomplishments in aviation in America, England, Germany, and France have led only to a rise in the rate of flight accidents and to a crisis attested to in the film by the episode with Nesterov. The loop-the-loop that he performed on August 27, 1913, thanks to Zhukovskii's calculations, was supposed to demonstrate that the future of aviation was not in "the art of the pilot" (as the "French school" asserted) but in precise calculations and engineering. And these are what Zhukovskii produces. The main idea of the film boils down to the notion that Russian science develops *in parallel to* world science and is radically different from it. It does not fit into it; it surpasses it. Western science develops thanks to the capitalist relations built into it. Russian science is spiritual and does not want to become part of the buy-and-sell; but by falling into the hands of anti-patriots who sell it "wholesale and retail," it is doomed.

The story of Zhukovskii's life depicted by Pudovkin is the endless journey of ascent to the heights of scientific glory accompanied by dith-yrambs pronounced from all sides to the scientist, who is constantly surrounded in the film by a dense throng of ecstatic pupils—*raznochi-nets* students. He is praised not only by Mendeleev, but also by physi-cist Aleksandr Stoletov and mathematician Sergei Chaplygin. "The groundwork of a new science—aerodynamics—has been laid," the scientific council of Moscow University proclaims. The "law of aero-dynamic lift" discovered by Zhukovskii "has no less significance for science than Newton's law of universal gravity," Chaplygin declares. "The whole world flies now on 'Zhukovskii's wings' and uses 'Zhukov-skii's propeller,'" his new pupils, the "red pilots," are convinced. Finally, Lenin proclaims him "the father of Russian aviation" and creates by a special decree the Central Aerodynamics Institute (TsAGI), into which Riabushinskii's institute in Kuchino is incorporated.

The apotheosis is prepared by all the events in the film. "The fate of science is now in strong hands," Zhukovskii declares at the end. And the viewer sees entire squadrons of supermodern airplanes. Zhukov-skii's final glance is turned toward the "not-too-distant bright future"; an airplane has appeared on screen, carrying a banner with Stalin's pic-ture on it, and the leader's words appear: "We had no aviation industry. Now we have it." The question of superiority becomes crystal clear in the Cold War conditions—it is a matter of Soviet strength:

The closing frames of the film show this strength. The flight-ready ma-chines stand in symmetrical ranks at the airport. Now they are on the runway. Now they rise into the air. Heavy multi-engine bombers move through the sky; the newest jet-propelled planes hurtle with fantastic speed—one, three, five, a host of them. . . . And in the hearts of mil-lions of toilers, honest people of all the world, arises a calm assurance that these indestructible air armadas will wreck the bloody plans of all the world's enemies and frustrate the open acts of aggression to which the American-English imperialist instigators of war are now transition-ing. This demonstration of our aerial might is a triumphant apotheosis that worthily concludes the story of the life and work of the great son of our Motherland, the father of Russian aviation, Nikolai Egorovich Zhukhovskii.[40]

But there is more to these films than outright falsifications. The Soviet biographical film was *programmatically* anti-historical, inundating the "Soviet patriotism" shaped by this genre with anti-historicism.

First of all, such a film's interpretation of the nature of scientific knowledge in the nineteenth century was exceptionally anti-historical. Typical in this respect are the films about Przheval'skii and Miklukho-Maklai. In these, it is not so much "Russian preeminence" that is foregrounded but rather the moral superiority of Russian science over Western science. This shift was supposed to conceal the real goals of the nineteenth-century traveler-scientists. Portrayed in these films as humanist scientists and enthusiastic travelers, Miklukho-Maklai and particularly Przheval'skii, who was a military geographer and a major general in the Russian Army, engaged in science to the degree that it was part of routine colonialist practice. Like the majority of geographic expeditions in those years, their excursions were by no means (as the films depicted) a contribution to pure science and philanthropy but rather were for the study of remote colonized areas or still uncolonized territories, the manners and customs of the tribes that inhabited them, and useful fossils and mineral resources therein; they also helped fill in geographical details of these regions. Of course, it was these imperial goals that engendered anthropology and ethnography in the nineteenth century, as well as other scientific disciplines later regarded as fully respectable.

All such goals are completely disregarded in these films. On the contrary, Russian naturalists and travelers in them are humanist scientists, and the natives are their friends and brothers, while *all* Western travelers are colonizers and are *without exception* scoundrels, spies, racists, and murderers. Although the British Royal Geographic Society had called Przheval'skii "the world's most outstanding traveler" and had awarded him its Founder's Gold Medal in 1879 for his work, it was precisely Englishmen who turned out to be his main enemies. The film depicts Disraeli as a sinister, "cold, spiteful Jesuit" who issues orders, if not to have Przheval'skii ruined then to do everything to disrupt his expeditions.[41] "The Russian traveler Przheval'skii is going to

Tibet, but the English traveler Marcherry has been killed in China. . . . I would have preferred the reverse," Disraeli says, and sends the English spy/botanist, adventurer, and murderer Harold Simon, "a person without prejudices," after Przheval'skii. Simon organizes a disruption of Przheval'skii's expedition and spins intrigues against Przheval'skii both in Russia (as a result of which the Russian government recalls Przheval'skii right before he is set to enter Tibet) and in China (by bribing bureaucrats who then refuse provisions and horses for his expedition). The Englishmen's hostile actions are depicted in such a straightforward manner that during the discussion of the film in the Ministry of Cinematography's Artistic Council Pudovkin declared "the Englishmen were presented schematically."[42]

Przheval'skii was transformed into an almost exemplary Soviet scientist, while he was in fact merely a typical nineteenth-century amateur scientist. His books about Central Asia are full of the wildest stereotypes, racist prejudices, and aversion to everything "Eastern" that were widespread in the nineteenth century. He considered the peoples of Asia culturally inferior, and he called the Chinese lazy, treacherous, cowardly, and dirty. His definition of a Chinese person as "a cross between a Jew and a Moscow swindler" became famous. All of this was combined with his calls for imperialist takeovers in Asia. For example, he challenged the Russian government outright to unleash war in China by provoking a rebellion of the local Buddhist and Islamic inhabitants against the Chinese authorities and to annex the northern Chinese provinces of Xinjiang and Inner Mongolia, pointing out the weakness of Chinese authority in these territories. Przheval'skii took no pains to conceal the aims of such takeovers: "To fully take advantage of the benefits offered by the Amur basin, we must also control its important tributary, the Songhua, which irrigates the better part of this basin, and in addition, at its upper reaches, the area bordering the northern provinces of China. Once we occupy all of Manchuria, we will make ourselves the nearest neighbor of this state and, not to mention our trade relations, can firmly consolidate our political influence here."[43] Przheval'skii's calls to "study" Asia "with a rifle in one hand and a lash in the other" are well known. Like the English, he was an active participant in the "Great Game" and received vast sums of money from the Russian government for his expeditions, as well as bribes from khans, satraps, and emirs. And he was rushing to Lhasa in order to win the Dalai Lama over to the side of Russia.

Nonetheless, the critique of racism in the film is directed exclusively against the West, as if Russia were not an empire and Russian tsarism were not engaged in colonialism and the extirpation of the native peoples. In 1950, China occupied Tibet. According to the film, the Russians had welcomed this "act of justice" (since Tibet had not fallen to the English) for more than a century. The following conversation takes place between the Russian ambassador in Peking and his interlocutor:

> "Tibet is the Dalai Lama's seat. It is the key to influence over 250 million Buddhists living in Asia."
> "The English premier, it seems, would not mind putting this key in his own vest pocket."
> "Meanwhile, the key is locked up tight in a Chinese box."

By redirecting Russian imperialist pretensions to England, the film's authors ascribe Przheval'skii's intentions to the English. The English scientist-spy states to the British ambassador: "I intend to study archeology. A stone pillar stands at the entrance to Lhasa. On it is carved a treaty about the merger of Tibet with China. The hell with the pillar! We will prove that Tibet historically is not an indivisible part of China. Besides, we need a reasonably good map of possible British domains."

Przheval'skii, on the contrary, is an ardent internationalist and humanist, a pure scientist. "I am a naturalist," he says, and informs the grand duke that he is prepared to give up his uniform if military duty hinders his service to science. His harsh, often racist statements about the peoples of Central Asia and China are in the film reduced to a half-hint in a verbose monologue after the Tibetan expedition: "Even plants and animals have adapted to the harsh conditions of nature. In the most horrible places in the Gobi Desert I saw life. But man does not simply adapt. He can change a harsh environment. After all, there are oases in the desert, created by persistent human labor. Would it not be possible to shift the boundaries of the oases, to completely conquer the desert in the future? But first, the peoples of inner Asia must free themselves from Buddhist passivity, from feudal slavery."

One is left to wonder what sort of liberation the People's Liberation Army of China has brought to Tibet. Przheval'skii is depicted as a friend

of the Mongolian people; he studies the daily life of the Mongolian no-
mads, sitting with them in their yurts and recording their folklore. He is
shown as the friend of the Korean people; he rescues a wounded Korean
man and comes without weapons to the Koreans, who are waging war
on the Japanese and Americans (the film came out at the very height of
the Korean War). He is presented as the friend of the Chinese people;
while traveling through China, he distributes rice to poor Chinese and
declares, "I believe the future will link the fate of our Fatherland with
the Chinese people! And this is where we should see the meaning of our
labor." And when he reaches the ocean in the Far East, he says, "The labor of the Russian man will transform these shores," as if the Maritime
Territory had not been seized from the Chinese just on the eve of his
expedition, in 1858—and as if these expeditions themselves were not
the usual colonial undertakings with the basic goals of prospecting, description, and mapping of the new territorial acquisitions. According to
the film, only the English used science for imperialist/colonial purposes.
The film mentions the imperial theme in general (Maritime Territory,
Tibet, Central Asia, the Great Game) as having absolutely nothing to
do with Russia and as being relevant only to England (which is playing
the Great Game—but with whom?). Obliged to retreat from continu-
ing his journey to Tibet, the onscreen Przheval'skii exclaims, "We will
not cede the honor of discovery to England! For me, Tibet is a matter
of science. For them, it is a second India."

Another distinctive feature of these films is that they asserted an extremely primitive view of scientific discovery as such. The makers of
the Popov film, for example, not only resorted to outright falsifications,
but also created a knowingly deceptive picture thanks to their intentional distortion of the nature of a scientific discovery of such a scale
as that of the wireless telegraph, upholding a childishly naïve notion
about it as some sort of enlightenment that comes to a single (Russian)
person. The discovery of the radio was not, nor could it be, a single
act. "Radio" is a huge complex of physical phenomena understood in
their interdependency and a whole host of physical adaptations whose
perfection has not been achieved to this day. They were neither "discovered" nor "created" at a single moment by one scientist.

Popov continued the experiments of Heinrich Hertz, but according
to the film, he surpassed him, having already in 1889 expressed the
idea of using electromagnetic waves to transmit messages distantly, an

idea no one believed, including Hertz himself. However, progress in science occurs due to each successive scientist, who perfects the methods and he experimental bases of the studies, surpassing the work of predecessors. Discoveries are links in a whole chain of discoveries. In reality, Popov perfected already complete devices—Hertz's vibrator, Branly-Lodge's coherer (a glass tube with metallic filings), the antenna invented by Nikola Tesla (the film attributes even this to Popov, who supposedly created "the first antenna in the world"), and so forth. In parallel, Marconi also perfected these devices. Thereafter came a host of other improvements. The fixation on one person supposedly "making *the* discovery" is artificial. To state that someone "invented the radio" is just like saying that someone invented travel on wheeled transport or sailing. Moreover, the film ascribes not only the invention of the radio to Popov, but also in passing the 1897 discovery of the phenomenon on the basis of which radiolocation was later developed, while in fact the effect of radio wave reflection from solid bodies was first observed by Hertz as far back as 1886.

Aleksandr Popov is film evidence in the endless suit about Russian priority in the "invention of radio." In the very first frames, two textual splash screens inform the viewer that "radio was born in Russia" and that "it was created by our great fellow countryman, the remarkable scientist and patriot Aleksandr Popov." So the film is, in the words of one reviewer, "the story of the invention of radio by our genius fellow countryman Aleksandr Stepanovich Popov and of the theft of this invention by the opportunist of science, the Italian Marconi. There are many known instances when a Russian invention has been shamelessly appropriated by foreign moneymakers and put forth as their own. But the story of the theft of the invention of radio largely exceeds all the rest by its insolence and shamelessness."[44] It is unsurprising that this is not so much a story of the "discovery of radio" as one of precisely its "theft," which is paradigmatic for the whole campaign of struggle for Russian "firsts," one filled with national phobias, historical lamentations, and victimhood alternating with self-aggrandizement and glorifications.

This story is rendered in the film in the genre of the classic conspiracy. On May 7, 1895 (old calendar: April 25, 1895), at a meeting of the Physics Division of the Russian Physics and Chemistry Society, Popov delivers a lecture and demonstrates his "wireless telegraph."

Immediately after the lecture, he is approached by the engineer Lemke, who in Russia represents a certain "prominent British electrical company." The following dialogue ensues:

> Lemke: Your discovery should be put on a solid commercial footing. If you grant the right to a monopoly. . . .
> Popov: Commercial footing. Right to a monopoly. . . . You think that's what I work for? My labor belongs to my country.
> Lemke: You should hurry, Mr. Popov. Another inventor still hasn't turned up, but he could, Mr. Popov.
> Popov: Is that a threat?
> Lemke: Advice.

Alongside the familiar contraposition in this dialogue of spiritually patriotic service to bourgeois-cosmopolitan mercantilism lies what makes it truly interesting: essentially, Popov rejects the recognition, patenting, and widespread introduction of his discovery by declaring that it belongs to his country. Need one be surprised that it did continue to belong to the country after the inventor himself refused international recognition? Need one be surprised, moreover, that the Russian Admiralty did not want to buy up Popov's devices but only those the English and French produced (since they had "excellently placed production") if Popov himself rejected the production opportunity offered to him? The reason for the refusal is, though totally devoid of logic, highly moral. This was supposed to conceal the real reason, which is left unspoken: Popov's experiments were classified since he was to all intents and purposes in service to the military. Popov was developing a means of transmitting signals at a distance while working in the Naval Ministry as a teacher of military courses in Kronstadt. The film mentions this, but his experiments are depicted as the free, creative quest of a scientist. It is clear, however, that precisely due to secrecy Popov's glory was much less widespread than that of Marconi, which of course is not communicated to the viewer since any hints at classified science (and science, even if it had nothing to do with defense, especially after the "KR affair," became absolutely classified in the USSR) were not permitted. It is impossible to simultaneously maintain the secrecy of a discovery and to have it recognized worldwide. Allowing this contradiction helped the unfailing plot instrument: conspiracy.

The film takes the viewer from St. Petersburg to gloomy and smoky London, where Lemke arrives from Russia and Marconi from Bologna. Their meeting takes place in the office of the banker Isaacs, whose name and overall appearance emphasize his Jewish heritage. He offers to create a joint stock company whose goal is to make Marconi's discovery "the property of all mankind." Haggling flares up between Marconi and Isaacs about who will receive what portion of the profits. Here Marconi is presented as an unprincipled tradesman far removed from any science whatsoever. Since the wireless telegraph will lead to losses for telegraph companies, he, as owner of the patent, is ready to sell them his invention: "Let them lock it up behind ten locks." Only Lemke's response that "you can find everything in London. You can even find another Marconi" brings the Italian back to reality and makes him more compliant. The German Lemke, the Italian Marconi, and the Jewish Isaacs, in charge of an English bank, round out the assembly of stereotypes for an "international conspiracy."

By the end of the first third of the film, the story of the "discovery of radio" has been fully explored. Two-thirds of the picture has practically nothing to do with the scientific theme. Here there is merely a pictorial illustration of the invention's results, and the story explores how persistently foreigners tried to "buy" Popov; how Marconi stole Popov's diagram; and how Popov, with the support of Mendeleev and Makarov, defended his precedence and, along with it, the preeminence of Russian science. After Popov reads in a newspaper about Marconi's invention of the wireless telegraph, the last fifty of the eighty-seven minutes of the film are dedicated to the "unmasking" of the Italian. The culmination comes in the scene where Popov meets Marconi.

Popov is sent to this meeting by the Naval Department; he is to evaluate the apparatus for purchase. Marconi humbly asks Popov to come help with his work: "I need you, Mr. Popov, your knowledge, your experience. . . . Believe me, I will not remain in debt. I will create amazing work conditions for you. You see, in our times you can't do anything without money. And with me you will have everything. . . . I don't begrudge anything for science." Popov responds by breaking out into an angry tirade: "Don't you dare talk about science. You see it only as a means of profit. You shamelessly appropriated someone else's invention for yourself and are trading in it. Well, it's quite obvious that that *is* your calling. But science is not a screen for business dealings." Accordingly, Popov's discovery saves people from a ship foundered on rocks and fishermen stuck in an ice floe, while Marconi engages in business and trades with just the kind of impostors that he himself is.

Also peculiar to these films is the exaggeratedly simplified image that they promote of the functioning of science as perpetual conflict. In the scientific milieu depicted in them (even when "theft" is not the topic), everything is based on aggressive ideological or nationalistic confrontation, which excludes the very foundations of science—knowledge exchange, open dialogue, productive discussions. In *Academic Ivan Pavlov*, no one encroaches on the discoveries of the main character. On the contrary, he is a scientist widely recognized in the world, and his status is constantly confirmed by foreigners (a Nobel Prize, honorary titles awarded abroad, and so on). However, since action in these films is impossible without a struggle against scientific opponents, struggle is built in them by an emphasis on opposites: the naturalist-materialist Pavlov versus the foreign mystic-idealists.

Along with this, Pavlov's status is deliberately exaggerated. When he is about to be presented an honorary degree in Cambridge, he is told, "These walls have seen Newton and Darwin. Now this honor will come to you." In comparing Pavlov to scientists that achieved a revolution in science and created whole new disciplines and paradigms of scientific thought, the filmmakers depicted the English scientists as disgusting medieval old men with hostile attitudes toward Pavlov; the only unclear point is why, with such an attitude toward him, they award him an honorary degree. The only conclusion the film seems to suggest is that Pavlov is doing Cambridge an honor by accepting the degree. After all, even his trips abroad are accompanied by blatant advertising: "All the world's academics want to hear Pavlov!"

The filmmakers were seconded by the critics. For example, about Cambridge University's award of the honorary doctorate to Pavlov, a reviewer wrote that the English "are again honoring Pavlov for his previous work; only now has European science grasped its greatness and profundity. . . . Not only in time is he impossibly far ahead of the English scientists. He has made a qualitative leap in science that is impossible for their class-limited thinking to grasp."[45] The reviewer praised the filmmakers for the scenes with foreign colleagues in which everything worked toward proving "superiority": "In these collisions [and these are always precisely and only "collisions"; other forms of interaction between Russian and foreign science are impossible], the actor lets you feel, with his precise intonations, his bearing full of dignity and simplicity, and his restrained but also evocative facial expressions, how great the superiority of the Russian scientist over his West European opponents [but never "colleagues"!] is, how high he carries the banner of our advanced science."[46] This mix of provincial conceit and imperial messianism reaches its height in the film *Mikhailo Lomonosov,* in which "the first Russian scientist" constantly argues with the Germans surrounding him, who do not want to let Russian science emerge.

THE SOCIALIST REALISM OF FOOLS: THE DISCREET CHARM OF ANTI-SEMITISM

A victory has conquerors; a defeat has the guilty. Conspiracy theories always amount to a search for the guilty. Conspiratology is the lot of the losers. Its flowering is an indicator of historic defeat, which is unconsciously compensated by projection of guilt onto external forces. Historic successes and prosperity simply do not presume the presence of the guilty. If we look at the late-1940s and early-1950s anti-cosmopolitan campaign from this perspective, then we must recognize that it was something bigger than a simple surge of Stalin's anti-Semitism buttressed by widespread everyday anti-Semitism. The existence of such a widespread development of conspiratological theories and anti-Semitism in the country that had defeated fascism speaks more to the fact that behind the thunder of victorious communiqués and bombast about Soviet superiority, the achievements of the advanced Soviet system, the success of the economy, and Russian historical preeminence in science, there remained a profoundly wounded mass consciousness that continued to deny reality and to fill in the cognitive dissonance with the conspiracy theories that permeated the official Soviet discourse tied to both the external world (imperialist conspiracy) and the internal one (the fifth column as represented by cosmopolitan Jews).

The idea of a Jewish conspiracy that totally engrossed Stalin in the postwar years, although not encouraged by Soviet propaganda either before or during the war, was easily assimilated by the populace because in the fantasy-laden world of conspiracy theories, the object of hate is in principle indestructible. But here the object was amplified due to the encounter between the prerevolutionary Judophobia still preserved in the half-peasant consciousness of the Soviet man and the Bolshevik conspiratology actively inculcated into mass consciousness in the Great Terror era. The result was an ill-defined picture of reality that showed through in both "workingmen's letters" and in a great many ordinary anti-Semitic incidents that took place during the war and after it.[47] This stratum of mass consciousness would be exploited by Stalin in his originally nationalistic, then xenophobic, and afterward frankly anti-Semitic rhetoric.

Conspiracy requires, like no other narrative does, a "representation of life in the forms of life itself" simply because improbability detects it and contradicts the very idea of conspiracy as a secret. Thus the verisimilitude that conceals conspiracy is an indispensable factor of its representation. The probability of someone else's conspiracy is tied to the fact that the authors of these theories *themselves,* as a rule, were participants in conspiracies of a sort; usually they belonged to certain groups that either sought recognition, or were dissatisfied with their status, or felt threatened, or the like. Of this sort in the late 1940s was, for example, a group of writers who aspired to power; they constituted the so-called Russian party that was born at the time at the junction of the party apparatus and the writers from the bureaucratic elites. Its members included the most active initiators of the "struggle against cosmopolitanism," such as the playwrights Anatolii Sofronov and Anatolii Surov, the prose writer Mikhail Bubennov, and the poet Sergei Vasil'ev, the author of the much-talked-of anti-Semitic poem "Without Whom One Is Happy to Live in Rus'."[48] Another such group was the semi-official "realist artists" to whom Ivan Shevtsov, the author of the scandalous novel *The Aphid,* was close. This milieu, sensitive to its complete dependence on the regime and its vulnerability to free criticism, constantly coordinated its activities. The groups' own phobias, reactions, and tactics—since this was the only experience they knew—were extrapolated onto their opponents. Hence, their writings are primarily *self-description.* The appearance of Jews as the chief agents of conspiracy was a product of a shift that occurred after the war, when anti-Semitism was essential at the state level and became systemic. This was a purely postwar phenomenon.[49]

The extensive literature about Stalinist anti-Semitism mainly examines political acts (campaigns, repressions, and the like). However, these acts were always bashfully half-hidden. Their rationales and motives not only were not documented, but they also were not articulated. Therefore, what has been retained in texts—from newspaper satires telling about ubiquitous thieving Jews who were rogues and troublemakers to literary works where a Jewish conspiracy would sometimes take on a universal scope—is the only thing that has preserved for us the character of Stalinist anti-Semitism, not so much as a political instrument as a sort of integral imaginary phenomenon meant for mass consumption.

To designate the Jewish enemy, late-Stalinist propaganda used definitions that were formally neutral but that evoked the necessary associations. This created a constant ambiguity in Soviet anti-Semitic discourse (bureaucratic folklore example: "So they won't think you an anti-Semite, call a kike a cosmopolitan"). For example, the title of the article "Crushing Blow Dealt to Judas's Gang" in the journal *Krokodil* referred to the image of the betraying Judas but hinted at the nationality of the "enemies."[50] The term "Zionist" (noun or adjective), widely used in the press, produced the same effect. This is precisely the term that Shevtsov used in *The Aphid*. The conspiracy rhetoric that permeates his novel was almost a reflex reaction to the social tension that the regime artificially produced by uncovering one "conspiracy" after another—be it that of "kowtowing," "cosmopolitans," or "murderer doctors."

The heyday of conspiracy theories had been the reaction to the French Revolution. Like a virus, they would come to life every time that society was led into a state of anxiety and fears. But in the Modern Era they turned into a true secular religion. The surge of these theories in the Modern Era reflected the need to explain the collapse of a seemingly unshakeable *ancien régime*. This collapse was so unexpected, the break with medieval civilization so inevitable, and the upheaval so profound and so fraught with far-reaching economic, social, and political consequences that it needed an explanation. But the level of a patriarchal society's political culture changed too little, and the earlier one remained the explanatory matrix. Hence Divine Providence did not disappear, but a new fetish came to replace God: humans' will and reason. In this respect, conspiracy is a sort of replacement of Revelation for an ill-defined, immature patriarchal consciousness disintegrating under the pressure of the Enlightenment, already having lost the integrity of faith but not yet having gained a basis in reason. Conspiracy gives the masses who have been cast out of the traditional matrices of thought explanations of the world missing outside of religion. Hence it contains elements of both religion (a parallel reality fitted to a ready-made picture of the world, teleologism) and rationalism (total logicalization, the search for cause-and-effect links and the hidden reasons for phenomena lying within the interests of agents, and fitting the world into a logically interconnected system). This drama that burst onto Europe after the French Revolution finally arrived in Russia, with a century's delay.

Twentieth-century mass societies had their own trajectories of development and immanent logic that determined the agitational and mobilizing functions of conspiracy theories; nothing mobilizes better than a threat, and a conspiracy is always an inevitable threat. It is no accident that the twentieth century—the century of mass societies—also became the century in which conspiratology triumphed; Lenin and Stalin, Hitler and Mao Zedong, Khomeini and Gaddafi, a multitude of dictators and mass movements of all possible stripes—from extreme-right and Islamist to radical-left and anti-globalist—produced an enormous number of conspiracy theories and fed off them. In Russia's case, it was long ago noted that the Bolshevik ideology of conspiracy and counter-conspiracy lay on well-prepared soil; prerevolutionary Russian society was permeated with belief in conspiracy and ideas of victimhood at all levels—from the uneducated masses who believed that almost every tsar who died was the victim of conspiracy or, on the contrary, had remained alive when he stopped ruling, to intellectual Slavophiles who suspected the West of insidious conspiracies and machinations against Russia (in today's slang, "Russophobia"). All of Russian political culture was shaped by a paranoid belief (actively supported by tsarism) in hostile surroundings and by a conviction that politics is always the product of violence and that it is made "behind the scenes" in a sort of parallel reality. It was no accident that *The Protocols of the Elders of Zion,* a true apologia of conspiracy that was widely distributed and exerted a great influence on many generations of people in various corners of the globe, became one of the most original intellectual monuments of Russian political culture. Bolsheviks with the Leninist idea of a "new type of party," which in Stalinist interpretation was transformed into an "order of sword-bearers," were the natural product of this culture.

Late-Stalinist conspiratology was an organic product of Bolshevik ideology. But in its realization it collided with the national specifics of a peasant country and was therefore doomed to anti-Semitism, all the more so as conspiratology was permeated with anti-Semitism from the moment of its inception. Ideas of liberalization, democratization, and modernization—social, economic, political, and cultural—were interpreted as a direct challenge to the traditional legitimacy of absolutism based on the total integrity of the social body tied together by Christian dogmas, a union of absolute power with both the church that legitimized it and the subjugated masses. In this whole, by definition, there could be no place for emancipation and civil society. Secular populism (both right- and left-leaning) continued the counterrevolutionary tradition, masked in forms of anti-liberalism and anti-bourgeois sentiment. Hostility to liberalism and progress united such dissimilar strata of society as the petit bourgeoisie and the peasantry, radical socialists and conservative bureaucratic and army circles, Orthodox clerics and nationalist-bent secularists.

All of this created the niche for conspiracy; it transformed this construct into a working mechanism, provided grounds for the ties among its agents, and, finally, filled in the politico-ideological content. Hence, a direct line leads to the *Protocols of the Elders of Zion* and the Black Hundreds pogroms, to *Mein Kampf* and the Holocaust, and to the fight against cosmopolitanism and the Doctors' Plot. In late Stalinism we are confronted by a hybrid of the densest archaic-religious fears and populist Judophobia of a Fascist recension, of anti-capitalist rhetoric and chauvinist propaganda.

Soviet Jews in the 1940s found themselves between the hammer of Nazism and the anvil of Stalinism. It is telling that the conspiratological delirium in which Stalin dwelt after the war led him to the very same opening idea that Hitler had formulated, calling Jews conspirators and "universal poisoners"; in its final chord—the conspiracy of the Doctors' Plot—Stalinism arrived at a concrete materialization of this Nazi invective. In this respect late Stalinism, in which anti-Semitism was institutionalized, instrumentalized, and transformed into a systemic phenomenon, there was neither a peculiar nor a mild form of anti-Semitism, as some researchers assert. Its "mildness" as compared to the Holocaust lay only in the fact that it was cut short by Stalin's sudden death before the stage that could be fully compared to the consequences of Nazi genocide could materialize, with the majority of Soviet Jewry ending up in exile, an outcome that in all likelihood the Doctors' Plot was supposed to bring about. The "peculiarity" of Stalinist anti-Semitism is defined by its being tabooed, which was the result of politico-ideological restrictions that weakened before one's very eyes. But the culture is where it can be seen. Similar to how in Nazism "Jewish Bolshevism" turned out to be the flip side of a "Jewish plutocracy," in late Stalinism Jews were subjected to defamation as both radical rightists (counter-revolutionaries) and radical leftists (modernists).

This historical excurse in the era of the emergence of conspiratology was required because late-Stalinist culture addressed this theme directly in Vladimir Solov'ev's now utterly forgotten play *The Golden Plague (Betrayal of a Nation)*. Solov'ev belonged to the category of Soviet playwrights who, ready for any politically commissioned work, would execute this work with passion. He wrote the majority of his play in verse, a master of this craft. A factory electrician who became a Komsomol poet, Solov'ev was a typical shock-worker writer of the Russian Association of Proletarian Writers, "called into literature." All of his work bespeaks his political flair. During the short thaw of the early 1930s, he wrote the play *A Personal Life* (1934), and in 1938, a play about industrial saboteurs, *Alien*. In 1939, riding the wave of the patriotic turning point, his play *Field Marshal Kutuzov* appeared, which was awarded the Stalin Prize in 1941. (At the start of the war, Kutuzov was especially in demand; Stalin promoted the idea that the retreat of the Red Army and the Germans reaching Moscow was part of a strategic plan to destroy the enemy, and Kutuzov was the closest historical parallel.) Solov'ev's dramatic poem *The Crossing* appeared in 1943, and a play about the underground, *Victory Road*, in 1948. Solov'ev's most successful project turned out to be his two-part dramatic work in verse, *The Great Sovereign*, which emerged in 1945. This was created within the context of the campaign to rehabilitate Ivan the Terrible. In 1946, the same year that the second part of Eisenstein's film was suppressed, Solov'ev's play was awarded a Stalin Prize. The play was a justification of a wise and farsighted leader who was forced to use violence "for the sake of the great Russian tsardom." Ten years later, in 1955, Solov'ev would rewrite the play, forcing the tsar to repent of killing innocent people. Solov'ev wrote *The Golden Plague (Betrayal of a Nation)* at the height of the anti-cosmopolitan campaign, in 1952. He would rewrite it also, in 1960. At the height of Khrushchev's anti-religion campaign in 1963, he would write an anti-religious screenplay for *The Little Caster of History*. But before that, on the heels of the Twentieth Party Congress, he wrote the play *Chameleons*. All of Solov'ev's work would seem to suggest that a play with such a title might be autobiographical, but it was in fact, fully in the spirit of the times, satirical.

The Golden Plague was about the Paris Commune, one of the favorite subjects of Soviet art—from the great number of novels, poems, paintings, and monuments to such films as Grigorii Kozintsev and Leonid Trauberg's *New Babylon* and Grigorii Roshal's *Paris Dawns,* as well as Boris Asaf'ev's ballet, *Paris Flame.* This subject contained a whole collection of Socialist Realist effects—"the triumph of a people in revolt," "the tragedy of the proletariat's liberating struggle" (who did not envision "a new type of party"), treachery, and the boundless cruelty of the "doomed classes." But Solov'ev's play was radically distinguished in this torrent of works. Essentially, the Paris Commune in it was merely a backdrop. At its heart lay the idea of conspiracy and its dramatization. All of its action took place in the offices of bankers who "trafficked France," and the Rothschilds were at the center of the conspiracy. All the other characters—communards, the inhabitants of Versailles, Bismarck—are depicted as mere puppets in the Rothschilds' hands. The Rothschilds' ability to maintain good relations with hostile regimes, and their enormous wealth and influence, made them the "archetype" of secret Jewish might and supranational power.[51] The classic accusation was that they unleashed wars; provoking them, they traded arms and issued loans, profiteering from others' misfortunes. Instead of "class struggle," the explanatory factor for historical events became banking operations and schemes.

Solov'ev continued the tradition of leftist anti-Semitism, that of the "socialism of fools," born in Vienna in the late nineteenth century, when certain leftist populist leaders began to preach a struggle against Jewish bankers and "world Jewish capital" as (instead of) "class struggle." Many Social Democrats made fun of this variety of socialism. But when fascism came to replace the European socialist movement and National Socialism combined rightist anti-Semitism and racial theory with the "class" struggle of leftist radicals and Jews, the result was the Holocaust. After the war, the "socialism of fools" disappeared from European politics for a while, returning to it only in the late 1960s, along with support for the "national liberation movement," and later with anti-globalism. It was in just this interval of the first postwar years that the Stalinist regime took up the baton of leftist anti-Semitism, declaring war on "rootless cosmopolitans" and "world Zionism." Since accusing Jews of warmongering after the Nazi atrocities was complicated, Stalin used euphemisms along the lines of a Zionist conspiracy. This duplicity helped him position himself as a Marxist internationalist.

Solov'ev's play broke so dramatically with the Soviet tradition of representing the Paris Commune that it required historical clarifications. The author of its foreword, the eminent Soviet historian of modern France Aleksandr Molok, perfectly matched to the play's author, was a specialist in topical, politically expedient historical themes. When in the early 1920s the theme of the Paris Commune became politically expedient, he wrote the book *Sketches of the Daily Life of the Paris Commune in 1871* (1924). When Stalin's "Marxism-Leninism" appeared in the 1930s, Molok published *Marx and the June 1848 Uprising in Paris* (1934). In the late 1930s (before the Molotov-Ribbentrop Pact), the hot topic was German militarism, and Molok's *German Intervention against the 1871 Paris Commune* was accordingly issued in 1939. During the war, the anti-German theme again became relevant, and yet a new book of Molok's appeared, *German Military Brigandage in Europe (from the Tenth to the Twentieth Century)* (1945).

This ability to make history relevant in the light of urgent political aims helped Molok to explain to the reader why Solov'ev's play was so important to "today's reader." Thus, he writes, "As a result of the treachery of the ruling elite, France is now again occupied, again transformed into a colony of foreign imperialism. It is occupied by the troops of the American imperialists who are preparing to unleash a new world war against the camp of peace, democracy, and socialism."[52] Molok decoded the historical allusions, stating that Solov'ev "with great incriminating force" had portrayed "the agents of the counterrevolution camps." Thus, he assured the viewer that although Thiers, the "ringleader of the Versailles government, the chief oppressor of the Commune," is not in the play, Baron Rothschild and the vice-director of the French Bank, the Marquis de Sec, were the "real masters of the fate of France at the time" and that Solov'ev had succeeded in "revealing the secret springs that the darkest reactionary forces in all countries had set into motion, also including Thiers in France. Therefore the figure of Thiers in this treatment of the theme is secondary for the author."[53]

Since interpreting history through a Jewish conspiracy was something new for Soviet readers and viewers, Molok tried to legitimize

Solov'ev's approach to history with a reference to Marx. He claimed that "in describing the sordid secret arrangement that representatives of French banking capital made (to the detriment of the French people) with the representative of Germany's banking capital (who was close to Bismarck), the author relies on the revelations made by Marx in his work *The Civil War in France* and in his letters of the time."[54] Although Marx felt no sympathy for Jewish bankers, he was not inclined to view history from the office windows of a Rothschild bank. It goes without saying that from this perspective Thiers was a secondary figure. Furthermore, politics itself, when confronted with Jewish money, receded into the background. Thus the main historical figures retreated into the shadows and Jewish bankers emerged from them. Accordingly, racist conspiratology replaced class struggle. Therefore, lest readers get distracted from the present time, Molok reminded them that the "incriminatory zeal of the play, focused not only against the 1871 French bankers, but also against today's Wall Street magnates, against all of today's imperialism, achieves its greatest power in the images of Rothschild and de Sec";[55] that is, he pointed out that a conspiracy of Jewish bankers was by no means history but the underlying cause of the Cold War.

From the very first scene, the play draws the reader/viewer into a world of conspiracy. The revolutionary leader of the Paris communards, Rigaud, has begun to see it clearly. This conspiracy is linked to Jewish bankers: "France and Prussia are at war, but secretly / A debate rages on the bourse: Who will win for sure, / The Rothschild house in Frankfurt-am-Main / Or the Rothschild house in Paris? That's the question! . . . But who *are* the Rothschilds? They're hardly / A credit to France and Prussia!" Here the reader/viewer is initiated into the secret of cosmopolitanism: "A banker can live in any world capital, / In his own homeland or settled in someone else's, / You wonder where the banker's homeland is? / I'll tell you: where he has put his safe! . . . No! France has not yet risen. / The Rothschilds are not a base for France! / But wait till the people take the power, / Then it will be a Nation in the great sense of the word!" In accordance with this logic, France and Prussia are the victims of a real, *secret* war unleashed by the Rothschilds and the Bleichröders to get rich. From this perspective, a union of France and Prussia against the cosmopolitan Rothschilds would be a manifestation of internationalism. The cosmopolitanism of Jewish capital is contrasted to a peculiar international union of anti-Semites. This anti-cosmopolitan international is quite remote from traditional nationalism and has a decidedly internationalist aspect; different countries have different enemies, but they all have one enemy in common: international Jewish capital.

So as not to confuse "bourgeois cosmopolitanism" with "proletarian internationalism," Solov'ev introduces the character of a doubting communard, Clément, who erupts in questions: "Well, are the cosmopolitans only bourgeois? / And do they gather gold only from someone else's country? / And what of Dąbrowski, our famous friend? / After all, he's not rich. But he's a cosmopolitan? / Leaving his homeland, he went to find freedom / And found a new country, one out of the many." Dąbrowski himself immediately appears in the scene and delivers a long monologue, in which he confesses, "I carry my Fatherland in my heart / And the country that sometimes gives me refuge / I do not call my Motherland. / Every people has its Motherland. / And whoever serves the people / Wherever he might be—amid a distant march / Or in exile—is, in his heart, where his own people are." Thus the idea of internationalism is alien to the Dąbrowski portrayed in the play; his heart is wholly devoted to the "Motherland." It is another story with the Jewish bourgeoisie: "The voice of the Motherland is unknown to gold. . . . / It is rootless. It's here, now there. / And he who serves gold is hot / On the heels of this gold. / All who serve gold have its nature. / They have no home, nor motherland, / They, like gold, are rootless, / And roam about the world together. . . . No. / I see no resemblance between them and us. / We dream of different things, both asleep and awake. / Your Rothschild is not a Frenchman, though he lives in France, / But I am a Pole, though I don't live in Poland!" With the stigma "rootless," the portrait of the Jew is complete. And although the Polish nationalist and leftist adventurer Dąbrowski has nothing to do with "proletarian internationalism," the main thing is that Rothschild is defined as his chief enemy.

After this preliminary ideological bombardment at the barricades, readers find themselves in the bankers' elegant offices—most frequently in that of the head of the Bank of France, the Marquis de Sec, where Rothschild and the international adventurist and German spy Rosa Blum shortly appear. Here we finally learn in detail how "France is being sold" and what the Jewish conspiracy is. The Soviet reader/viewer, unfamiliar with the principle of how banks function, had to be shown everything from A to Z. De Sec provides this demonstration in the play:

> De Sec (to Rothschild):
> Allow me, now, as frankly as possible,
> To touch on several of your secrets:
> Your younger brother Anselm, he has a bank in Vienna,
> But the middle one—in London?
>
> Rothschild:
> Nathan.
>
> De Sec:
> Just so. They are the ones that three years ago
> At Bismarck's behest set up together
> [For] his government for a certain campaign
> A loan through Bleichröder you know about.
> The Rothschild house, it seems, was not slighted,
> Prussia has paid the interest up till now.
> And thus the Germans besieged Paris,
> And we are having this conversation.
> But we must pay five billion francs
> By agreement of the warring sides.
> Let Bismarck deposit them in the banks
> Of your two brothers, Sir Baron!
> But who will lend France this sum?
> Our gold reserves, alas, are not so rich. . . .
> Who will give us gold? Tell me (confidentially). . . .
>
> Rothschild:
> Well . . . I don't know.
>
> De Sec *(bowing to Rothschild):*
> The third brother!
> Prussia pays interest on the loan to the two brothers,
> But the third will get it in full from France.
> But what's the main finance secret here?
> That there's two countries here but just one bank!
> Though you will give your money to France.
> But this, really, is only what it looks like,
> Since it will end up—in the end—
> In your London and Vienna banks.
> There's no more France, sad though this be!
> There's no more Prussia. There's the house of Rothschild!

The banker de Sec differs little in his argument from the revolutionary Rigaud; both are convinced that France and Prussia are puppets in the Rothschilds' hands. Rothschild does not remain in debt and tells de Sec that he knows he has huge sums of money at his disposal, stolen by him when he was manager of the Bank of Turkey. But de Sec, as opposed to Rothschild, about whose wealth everyone knows, conceals the fact that he is rich. Due to the fact that this money is illegal, it cannot be released into circulation, having become "dead capital." And since de Sec has an interest in their making a profit, Rothschild proposes that he provide a quarter of the credit sum that France needs. The suggestion pleases de Sec, but as an official person, he prefers not to make a show of his own money and instead prefers to lend it to Rothschild so it will bring him profit through Rothschild. In exchange, he is prepared to share a percentage of the income.

Only once they have insured their own interests do the bankers proceed to the topic of a peace treaty. It is they who decide the fate of the war. What bothers de Sec the most is not the huge contribution that France will have to pay but the fact that France "will lose Lorraine and Alsace. / And there are mines there, you know. . . . / I'm afraid the stockholders—/ The owners of the mines—will make a big fuss. / Then, you know, Paris will also get madder than hell." Rosa Blum intervenes in the conversation, as Bleichröder's representative. He is now the *third* Jew in the play, who, as everyone knew, was Bismarck's right hand and who played a prominent role in the unification of Germany and its economic ascent in the nineteenth century. Blum reproaches de Sec because he could even imagine "that Bleichröder / Has suddenly betrayed our interests. / The mine owners cannot take offense: / We assure you, in writing if you want, / That their interests—of course, in the big deals, / That is, in the range of six-figure sums—/ Will not suffer, but the minor stockholders / We will not be able to protect." The peace treaty issue is resolved.

Now each party rushes to take care of his or her own business. Blum goes to notify her boss about France's agreement to the conditions of the peace treaty: "Bleichröder wants to know about it right away, before / The exchange knows, so the day after / He can gamble on your stocks, no risk." De Sec still has to "buy" the minister Favre and General Trochu, both of whom are for sale. One of them tries to hike his price: "A minister's portfolio, for example, / Can you calculate it as a promissory note? / A thing like that, Baron, is worth plenty everywhere. / Think about it!" The other threatens: "Soon, perhaps, the time will come / When you will find the Paris communards / At your safes and at your banks." But Rothschild will not negotiate: "I'll be waiting for you at the bank, tomorrow at 10. / And you, dear Favre, I will be happy to see. / The war is lost already, when all is said and done. / So, Mr. Trochu, I hope you'll come."

The question of the place of politicians and politics in history is key. The conspiratological approach to history shifts the responsibility from the puppet politicians to the puppeteer bankers. This view, according to the play, is shared by Rothschild himself. His response in one of the conversations with de Sec is remarkable:

Rothschild:
Marquis, you can tell me, exactly.
How much has "the honor of France" cost us?

De Sec:
Trochu and Favre? About . . . two million.

Rothschild:
How expensive good-for-nothing power is!

And, in fact, given this approach to history, public power is not worth anything—not only in the past, but also as projected onto the present. The lack of publicity of Jewish conspirators in the past had to be explained by the omnipotence of Jews in the Soviet present, when they had become practically invisible; Jewish theaters, schools, and press agencies were closed; Jews were removed from all government posts that were at all important; there were no Jews among the widely publicized war heroes, shock workers, or cultural figures. On the contrary, their participation in the war was diminished in every way possible; their enormous contribution to science and to the creation of the Soviet military potential were classified; and Jewish surnames in the popular consciousness were almost exclusively associated with anti-patriotism, speculation, and theft, associations that were facilitated by the campaign in the press. In the early 1950s, when in connection with the Jewish Anti-Fascist Committee (JAC) and the Doctors' Plot the anti-Semitic campaign reached a culmination, there was a need to explain how such a marginalized part of the population could be so socially harmful.

The play provided an answer to this question; the issue was conspiracy (Zionist spies in the JAC, cosmopolitan critics, murderous doctors).

However, the conspirators' plans were foiled in the play by the people, who rose against them. Paris is in the hands of the communards. And Rothschild and de Sec organize a new conspiracy—no longer with a profit motive but with the goal of destroying the danger threatening them. To save themselves from the communards, they need troops, but there are no capable troops in routed France, and any troops that could be had are unreliable. Rothschild's idea is simple: appeal to Bismarck. De Sec is amazed: "You think he has French troops?" "What about our prisoners?" Rothschild reminds him: "Bismarck, you know, cannot / Release them. Lightly armed. / But he has the whole army of the Sedan captive. / First, it has enough bayonets, / And second, some facts suggest, / It has not heard the mutineers' speeches." Rothschild has no doubt that for the sake of "choking the Commune" Bismarck would resort to such a move. "But without money—no!" The last remark evokes only de Sec's ironic retort: "Yes, Sir Baron, the path to interest isn't easy / For the money that you did not lend."

Deceiving the "betrayer national" Belieu, de Sec forwards the cash to Versailles. Using it, Thiers manages to assemble troops and squash the Commune. Bismarck in turn agrees to release the French prisoners. In exchange, he demands that the billion-francs contribution be paid significantly earlier. Asked where they should get the money, he replies, "Take out a loan" . . . from Rothschild, no less, although at a grossly higher interest rate. This whole plotline is a sort of Freudian slip; Bismarck behaves exactly as the Germans had in the spring of 1917, bringing the Bolsheviks through to Russia in a sealed train, only with the opposite goal—not to squash a revolution but to kindle it.

Then Rothschild assures de Sec that his role in the rout of the Commune was much greater that that of Thiers. After all, without the 100 million francs brought to Versailles, Paris would not have been taken: "For the Commune's being gone, and for peace in the country / We're no less obliged to you than to Thiers / And Bismarck." Such praise sickens de Sec: "Sir Baron, I beg you, please / To stop saying I did so much / To bring it off. Let this be a secret. / Thiers did it all, only him! / Otherwise the people will rise up again. / And they could remember these days. / Let the politicians quarrel with the people, / Why with us? We're fine in the shadows. / Better let another story / Make the rounds.

I would appreciate it if you, Baron, / Would tell everyone the story about the old communard / Whom I rescued!"

De Sec himself suspects that Rothschild was the one who gave Bismarck the idea to shorten the time for paying the contribution: "You almost made France, you know / Pay you the interest on a future loan. / So Bismarck shortened the time of the deal / Of all our payments, so France must / Rush to take out loans, even at high interest. . . . And compared to the prior one, this is a horrible / Contract—its terms. And I fear / This wasn't pulled off without your little hand, / And they call little hand Bleichröder right?" Now it is Rothschild's turn to ask de Sec not to mention him in connection with the sudden toughening of the agreement's conditions and to remind him that the advantage here is mutual: "Bleichröder helped us. Yes, for this moment / We waited a long time, but it finally came. / I guaranteed the interest, / And you saved the capital. / In sum, France needs a loan, / And I will happily give it the necessary sum. . . . But I'll ask you to forget, to not even think about / All of what I've told you now, Marquis. / Only Bismarck hastened payments for the French!" To which, grinning, de Sec replies, "Like only Thiers squashed the Commune!"

The mix of cynicism and histrionics that permeates the play reaches its apex in the ending. On the eve of the trial of the communard Genton, the newspapers are breathless in their gratitude to Rothschild: "The French can sleep in peace: / Rothschild's bank is giving the government a loan! / How noble this is! / The world has never seen such kindness! / Rothschild is the father and savior of the people! / *Petit moniteur* extra! / Long live the baron! / Savior! Bravo! Bravo! / It's nice to live, when such people exist!" Rothschild's modest response? "Good lord! I'm really ashamed! / I thank you for the honor!"

But the play's ending is histrionic, in Genton's last statement at the trial: "But there are orphans, mothers, and widows / To whom I want to confess at my hour of death / That we are guilty before them / *(to the spectators present at the trial)* / For not shooting you!" The reason for everything is the kindness of the communards "drunk with freedom": "Well, obviously we were as unsuspecting as children / Since we saw even you as people. / We spared you, not driving you out of your burrows. / We even spared you from the shackles. / But we should have wiped you out, like tigers. / Throttled you like snakes, trampled you like spiders!" The very existence of the Commune, according to

Genton, is a lesson to their descendants—that enemies deserve destruction: "But even our blood, flowing in torrents, / Let it not wipe away all our guilt, / So they can see it! So our descendants / Will not have to pay with it the next time, too!"

It is telling that the enemies, as they are portrayed here, are not so much class enemies as national ones. They are the enemies of the people, who here are by no means understood in a class sense. All the old anti-Semitic stereotypes are used here in depicting them: greed, "blood money," their unleashing of wars and the destructive forces of "rootless capital." Calling for the destruction of "you who buy the cheap sweat of the people, / Who pay for blood in gold, / Who see as mere profit items / Honor, conscience, and love," Genton constantly returns to the theme of national betrayal: "Not only France have you shamefully sold / For your gold. Out of your greed / You'd gnaw through the throats of your own parents / And would sell your own children!" These people are destroying the future: "The flowering gardens you'll turn to ash, / The houses to ashes, and everything that lives to dust." But they have no past, as well: "Your every step on earth is celebrated / By the bloody feast of the Golden Plague!"

Having completely dehumanized the enemies, deprived them of a past and future, and called them the enemies of the human race and beasts, Solov'ev concludes the play with Genton's monologue, which threatens the enemies with complete annihilation: "And those whom you, helped by iron, / Having shown your beastly faces plainly, / Drove into the earth of Père Lachaise, / Have lain down as the foundation of the World Commune. / You haven't ripped their lives from life. / Not as spectres, not in midnight gloom / Will they appear to you, but the spectre of Communism / Will remind you of their faces on earth. / Today you'll take the interest from France / For your 'helping' your own country! / But your turn will come! when all is said and done / We'll get it back in triplicate with your blood!"

These invectives, curses, and bloodthirsty calls for carnage thundered against the conspirators (all of them Jews) from the pages of books and the boards of theaters at the end of 1952 and the beginning of 1953, when the anti-Semitic hysteria reached its limit and new Jewish conspirators, this time "murderer doctors," replaced the house of Rothschild in the black art of tireless Zionist conspiracies. But even this did not satisfy the author. The play, it seemed to Solov'ev, did not provoke enough interest, a situation that forced him on March 13, 1952, to appeal to Suslov with a letter in which he complained about the delay in publishing such a topical work: "I have written a play about a cosmopolitan conspiracy of the international bourgeoisie with the active participation of the Rothschild houses in London, Vienna, and Paris, a conspiracy against revolutionary Paris in 1870 and 1871,"[56] but the risk-averse people in the repertoire-publishing division of the Committee for Arts Affairs had already held it up for five months. All of this was happening

> in these days of the Atlantic bloc, which is the cosmopolitan alliance of the bourgeoisie, knocking together in their brutal hatred for the Soviet Union, rejecting even their national affiliation—what could be more relevant, effective, and militant than an unmasking of this cosmopolitan alliance from the standpoint of proletarian internationalism? . . . The five months' delay of such a play by the repertoire-publishing division, that is, the postponement of its production for the whole theater season in these days of the so-called cold war, when our ideological struggle against the capitalist world has reached its culmination, seems not only overly cautious but even mushrooms into political short-sightedness, if not something worse.[57]

Thus the conspiracy theory–obsessed author concluded, angrily hinting at cosmopolitans remaining among the workers of the Committee for Arts Affairs.

The complaint worked: the play immediately appeared in print. But even this could not pacify Solov'ev. After the play was published in the journal *Teatr* (and afterward as a separate book), he began writing to Stalin's personal secretary, Aleksandr Poskrebyshev, now with complaints that there were no reviews and that production of the play was being readied only in the Pushkin Leningrad Drama Theater and the Lesya Ukrainka Kiev Theater, while the "theaters with all-union status" (MKhAT, the Malyi, and the Vakhtangov) were "stubbornly declining" it, preferring instead to stage *The Living Corpse, Two Gentlemen of Verona, The Fruits of Enlightenment,* and other such "repertoire of a more placid nature." And although the preference the leading theaters gave to Shakespeare and Tolstoy sorely distressed the author of *The Golden Plague,* the reply given by Nikolai Bespalov, the chairman of the Committee for Arts Affairs, to the Central Committee's inquiry noted that he did not consider it "advisable to oblige the directors of MKhAT, the Malyi, and the Vakhtangov to put on Solov'ev's play."[58] But obliging them was not necessary after all; a few months after its premiere, the play was removed from the repertoire. With Stalin's death, the usual "Zionist conspiracy" went bankrupt, as it turned out to be merely the imaginary projection of the usual Stalinist conspiracy.

9 *Gesamtkriegswerk*

Cold War Hall of Mirrors
in the Ministry of Truth

The term "cold war" was coined and first used by George Orwell a few weeks after the end of World War II in his article "You and the Atomic Bomb," published October 19, 1945, in the London *Tribune*. Working on the novel *1984* at the time and understanding better than some the nature and mechanics of totalitarianism, Orwell was not only a paradoxologist, but also a real master of the oxymoron. Suffice it to recall his ministries of Peace and Plenty and those of Truth and Love; his equation "two and two makes five"; his slogans ("War is peace," "Freedom is slavery"); and, finally, the keyword of Newspeak, "blackwhite." These oxymorons are true pearls of dialectic logic. They combined two mutually exclusive concepts, allowing for "impudently claiming that black is white, in contradiction of the plain facts." "Cold war" was indeed such an oxymoron.

Over seven decades we have managed to forget that this very concept was part of the geopolitics of Orwell's dystopia. In his *Tribune* article, the writer explained that it was the atomic bomb that had led to the division of the world into Oceania, Eurasia, and Eastasia, enormous superpowers that were forced to maintain an unspoken agreement to never use nuclear weapons against each other (nuclear parity, the doctrine of guaranteed mutual destruction). But the development of weapons of mass destruction itself, which made them invincible, obliged them to remain in a state of constant "cold war"—in a state of peace that was not really peace and war that was not war. In 1945, this all sounded like complete fantasy.

When the concept invented by Orwell became a political and historical term, it lost, apparently, all connection whatsoever to Newspeak. This can be explained by the fact that its original content was completely lost. Political experts have studied "cold war" (and their studies themselves largely became part of it), but very few cultural historians did.[1] Nonetheless, if one understands "cold war" aesthetically, as part of Orwell's reality, as an oxymoron, its uniqueness becomes clear, and not because it was a primarily ideological war that used no weapons, nor even because it was an imaginary war *par excellence*. These are all derivatives from the nature of war, which, as in an oxymoron, is similar to the nature of the magnet: the effect of attraction is conditioned by the effect of repulsion, and the magnet itself is as much repulsion as it is attraction. As in a real oxymoronic bond, the superpowers remained in the state of "cold war" because they did not want war and at the same time worked on it; they "fought for peace" by being at war. Peace is no more than tranquility, the preservation of the status quo; war is dynamism and disruption of the status quo. The uniqueness of cold war is its oxymoronic nature; if traditional war is a system of actions aimed at the violent destruction of the status quo (even if one of the sides struggles to preserve it, the other side [or sides] fight[s] to change it), then a cold war is one in which *both* sides fight for the same thing—for the preservation of the status quo. In other words, *the goal of cold war is the preservation of peace*. Accordingly, if the goal of a war is the preservation of the status quo, then a "fight for peace" is essentially a form of the propaganda of war. This is the nature of Orwell's "cold war," a concept that best encapsulated the nature of postwar peace.

Orwell's oxymoron took root not least of all because it most adequately reflected the internal paradox of the phenomenon it signified; the ideology and art produced by the Cold War, as the product of wartime propaganda, were patently false in one sense and just as strikingly truthful in another. False at the informational level, as any propaganda is false, they were truthful in that they reflected better than anything else the Soviet traumas, complexes, anxieties, and phobias, the real political aspirations of the regime and their reworking of ideological directives. Similarly to how Soviet art was a reflection and extrapolation of ideological fantasies onto everyday Soviet life, the Cold War culture created the Other, who was actually the most adequate image of the Self; it was essentially a projection and displacement of the creator's image. In this respect, Soviet art was thoroughly mimetic, and in it we are dealing with Socialist Realist mimesis.

In the history of the formation of the Soviet nation, the postwar years occupy an exclusive place, thanks largely to the status change of the Soviet Union after World War II; it was transformed from a pariah state into not only a superpower, but also one of the poles of the bipolar world that was taking shape. As in any nation-state project, one of the key roles here was played by the image of the enemy, which shaped identity through the image of its own Other. Before 1945, the enemies of the USSR were Germany, Japan, Finland, and Poland. Meanwhile, America occupied a completely peripheral place in the well-developed Soviet political demonology. After the war, when the former enemies were overthrown, the United States became the main enemy. This change of enemy proved crucial to the new nation. As A. A. Danilov and A. V. Pyzhikov observed in *Birth of a Superpower,* "It was in the period from 1945 to 1953 that the course of Soviet foreign policy that existed right up to the end of the '80s was shaped."[2] But as history has shown, this course and this image of the enemy proved so strong that it survived the breakup of the Soviet Union itself and, due to popular demand, was easily revived in post-Soviet Russia, where anti-Americanism—by no means a product of the 1930s but precisely of the late-Stalinist era— has become practically state policy. This is all the more reason to understand its sources and the strategies of its consolidation.

THE STALINIST "URBI" ET "ORBI": *REALIDEOLOGIE*

The Stalinist postwar policy, whether with respect to former allies or the defeated Germany and Japan, West European countries or Soviet-bloc satellites, Greece or Yugoslavia, Iran or Turkey, Korea or China, was one of arm twisting, manipulations and barefaced blackmail, political murders, intimidation and terror, provocation and adventurism.[3] In the new world that developed after the war, in which the Soviet Union became a superpower, Stalin easily rejected agreements with his former allies and used the country's might and authority to attain one-sided geopolitical advantages and advancement of the Soviet imperial project, in which war was allotted by no means the last role (Stalin, as is well known, assumed its inevitability and did little to conceal this). The fact that his recent allies had also often resorted to such methods is no doubt important to an understanding of the sources and the course of the confrontation between the East and the West that developed after the war. But simple mirroring could hardly help to explain the specifics of the Soviet position, which (as distinct to that of the West) required a totally different ideological packaging.

In one of his first public statements in the Cold War era, which was published just two weeks after Churchill's "Sinews of Peace" address, on March 22, 1946, in response to the questions of Associated Press correspondent Eddie Gilmore, Stalin, without a word about Churchill's speech, proclaimed that apprehensions of war were groundless since "neither nations nor their armies seek a new war. They want peace and seek to secure the peace." He linked "the present war scare" to the actions of "certain political groups that are engaged in propaganda for a new war and are thus sowing the seeds of dissension and uncertainty." In other words, the incipient confrontation was an imaginary war, the fruit of propaganda. Responding to a question of what should be done to avert this, Stalin formulated his understanding of the Cold War as a purely propagandistic enterprise: "It is necessary that the public and the ruling circles of the states organize widespread counter-propaganda against the propagandists of a new war, as well as for the maintenance of peace; that not a single utterance of the propagandists of a new war gets away without the rebuff it deserves on the part of public opinion and the press; that in this way the war-mongers be promptly exposed and given no opportunity to misuse freedom of speech against the interests of peace."[4] In short, just changing propaganda from both sides would be enough to cause the "war scare" to fade away like a phantom.

Among Stalin's numerous postwar interviews about the issues of international politics, a curious sort of *meta-interview* stands out particularly: Stalin's conversation on April 9, 1947, with Harold Stassen, who had been Minnesota's governor from 1939 to 1943 and who would subsequently (1948–53) serve as the president of the University of Pennsylvania; the topic was the principle of peaceful coexistence. Stalin had developed a thesis that wars by no means arose only between nations that represented different systems. Thus, "the economic systems in Germany and the United States are the same, but war nonetheless arose between them." This chain of logic was unorthodox for a Marxist: "The economic systems of the United States and the USSR are different, but they did not fight each other, but rather cooperated with each other during the war. If two different systems could cooperate during the war, then why can they not cooperate in peacetime? This means, of course, that if there is a desire to cooperate, then cooperation is quite possible despite the different economic systems. But if there is no desire to cooperate, then even despite the same economic systems, states and peoples can come to blows."[5]

So, it turned out, everything was determined not by "historical laws" of the development of society and of class struggle but by "the desire to cooperate." The Soviet Union even "cooperated" with the just vanquished Nazis, forgetting about irreconcilable class and ideological contradictions and "historical laws," and if the result of such cooperation became war, it would turn out that the absence of a "desire" to cooperate on Hitler's part was to blame. All of this was a preamble to a disavowal of earlier ideologically irreconcilable pronouncements. And this triumph of Realpolitik evoked Stassen's puzzled question about how the USSR could cooperate with capitalist countries. After all, this would contradict all of Stalin's previous statements. Stalin replied that he "could by no means say that two different systems could not cooperate. . . . He, J. V. Stalin, stands on Lenin's view of the possibility and desirability of cooperation between two economic systems. Equally as regards the desire of the people and the Communist Party in the USSR to cooperate; they have such a desire. Unquestionably, such cooperation would only be useful to both countries."[6]

Stassen could only respond to such disarming revisionism by saying that "the statements he had referred to were made by J. V. Stalin at the Eighteenth Party Congress and at the plenary session in 1937. The topic[s] of these statements were 'capitalist encirclement' and 'monopolistic imperialist development.' From J. V. Stalin's statement made today, he, Stassen, concludes that now, after the defeat of Japan and Germany, the situation has changed." In revising Marxist doctrine (based on the idea of class struggle) and history (by rewriting Lenin and transforming him into a "champion of peace"), Stalin reflexively rejects ideology in favor of Realpolitik. Without beating around the bush, he told his American interlocutor that the mutual accusations of monopolist capitalism (United States) and totalitarianism (USSR) were nothing more than propaganda: "As far as the enthusiasm for criticisms against monopolies and totalitarianism go, this is propaganda, and he, J. V. Stalin, is not a propagandist but a businesslike man. We should not be sectarians, J. V. Stalin says. When the people wish to change the system, they will do so. When he, J. V. Stalin, met with Roosevelt and discussed the questions of war, he and Roosevelt did not impugn each other as monopolists or totalitarians. This significantly helped him and Roosevelt to establish mutual cooperation and achieve victory over the enemy."[7]

Stassen said things to Stalin that were unacceptable from an ideological viewpoint. For example: "The United States has managed to stave off the development of the monopolist and imperialist tendencies of capitalism, and meanwhile, workers in the United States have taken advantage of the right to vote to a much greater extent than Marx or Engels could have imagined." But Stalin did not contradict Stassen. What is more, he stated that Marx and Engels "could not of course have foreseen what would happen forty years after their deaths."[8]

This, of course, was a "message to the West." But what could have been the reason for such a publication in the USSR? Stalin was the only "businesslike man" in the country who could practice "creative Marxism." Departing from orthodoxy and reexamining the "obsolete propositions of Marxism" were his prerogative alone. Stalin was ultimately a fanatic of power, not of an idea. Politics was not subordinated to his ideology, but, on the contrary, ideology was called upon to legitimize politics. This is clear in his speeches.

Stalin's first public reaction to the Churchill speech were his responses to the *Pravda* correspondent, published on February 14, 1946. In his favorite genre (answers to questions he asked himself), Stalin gave a real master class in cold war. Here he appeared in the role of propagandist while simultaneously acting as a mediator (a re-translator of Churchill's speech, bringing its content to Soviet readers) and commentator. The extent of the deformation to which Churchill's speech was subjected shows how far Stalin was prepared to go in propaganda— namely, the degree to which he allowed distortion of reality. The goal of propaganda was simple: to dress the new enemy in the former enemy's clothing. Churchill's cause was supposedly the furthering of Hitler's cause: "Hitler began to set war loose by announcing his racial theory, declaring that only people speaking the German language represent a full-fledged nation. Mr. Churchill begins to set war loose, also by a racial theory, maintaining that only nations speaking the English language are full-fledged nations, called upon to control the destinies of the entire world."[9]

Churchill of course said nothing of the kind, although Stalin seems not to notice, replacing the absence of an actual statement with logic (as if what Stalin said were actually Churchill's words and merely needed further interpretation); if "German racial theory brought Hitler and his friends to the conclusion that the Germans, as the only full-fledged nation, must rule over other nations," then "English racial theory brings Mr. Churchill and his friends to the conclusion that nations speaking English, being the only full-fledged nations, should rule over the other nations of the world."[10] Logic fulfills a dual function here: it shifts the issue of the actual fact of the statement toward its logicality and simultaneously creates a foundation for the further development of the theme—the pure product of Stalin's invention—which begins to live an independent life. It is logical to suppose that domination will please no one since "nations had shed blood over the five years of a cruel war for the sake of the freedom and independence of their countries, and not to exchange Hitler's domination for the domination of Churchill. It is hence quite likely that the nations not speaking English and in addition comprising the vast majority of the world's population will not consent to enter into a new enslavement."[11] The Soviet reader will joyfully detect Stalin's sarcasm in this "likelihood," thus experiencing a feeling of unity with him.

Stalin not only distorts Churchill, but also speaks a different speech for him, and if he twists the meaning of his statements, even changing them into their opposites, then it is merely in order to tear away the covers, as it were, of respectability from what is said; this is his discursive alibi, should it occur to anyone to expose his deceit. The process of "co-creation" assumes a high degree of imagination. The further it takes Stalin from the original text, the freer his relationship to reality becomes. He actively creates a new reality. It is in this very speech that Stalin informs the nameless "*Pravda* correspondent" that the Soviet Union lost seven million people in the war—"several times more than England and the United States of America combined";[12] that is, he divulges a figure four times less than the actual losses. This bald-faced lie reflects approximately the proportions of truth and lies in Stalinist propaganda as a whole: 1:4.

But even this is still merely the "artillery preparation"; in both cases, Stalin's statements are unverifiable since the Soviet readers do not know exactly what Churchill said and are unaware of the real number of victims in the war. What they do well know is that for centuries, right up to 1939, Poland had been the strategic opponent and enemy of Russia, a country that Russia had "divided" with Germany no fewer than five times, consistently and mercilessly destroying its statehood. And now Stalin is defending Poland from England. This complicated task requires the listeners' complicity, and Stalin achieves this by means of several logical somersaults.

First, Stalin resorts to the logic and phraseology of Realpolitik: "One wonders what can be surprising about the fact that the Soviet Union, wanting to secure itself for the future, attempts to get to the point that governments loyal to the Soviet Union exist in these countries. How could anyone, without losing his mind, categorize these peaceful aspirations of the Soviet Union as the expansionist tendencies of our state?"[13] But people need not "lose their mind" to understand that to secure "loyal" governments in sovereign states means advancing an expansionist policy that can perhaps only be "peaceful" in the sense that it secures peace for the Soviet Union—but not for these countries. While openly admitting that the USSR interferes in the internal affairs of these countries, Stalin immediately tries to prove something directly contradictory: that "Mr. Churchill has no justification to insist that the leaders of contemporary Poland can allow 'domination' in their country by the representatives of any foreign states whatsoever." Accusing Churchill of slander of not only "Russians" but also of Poles, Stalin concludes that "Mr. Churchill is displeased that Poland has made a turnaround in its policy toward the side of friendship and unity with the USSR."[14] "There was a time" (a telling lack of specificity) in which "elements of conflicts and contradictions predominated" (a telling understatement) in the relations between Poland and the USSR, which allowed "statesmen like Mr. Churchill to play upon these contradictions, to get his hands on Poland under the guise of defending it from the Russians, and to intimidate Russia with the specter of war between it and Poland." Thus it was not Russia/USSR that divided Poland with

Germany for a century and a half, and it was not England that declared war on Germany after its collusion with the Soviet Union and its incursion into Poland, but rather that both Poland and the USSR were the victims of England. This drawing of the reader into the process of distortion, making him/her an accomplice in the propagandistic act, was an important element in Stalin's suggestive strategy. The intimate contact established between the reader and the leader was based on a concealed mutual understanding: the reader knows that something is not quite right in these arguments, and Stalin is counting on this knowledge, teaching the Soviet reader a lesson in rewriting the past that has not yet even become history. Essentially, the lie itself is based on the fact that it is deliberately reworked into "truth" by the reader.

But this discourse was just a prelude to Stalin's main goal—the justification and legitimization of the USSR's actions in the countries of Eastern Europe. Churchill had asserted that "the Communist parties that were very insignificant in all these eastern states of Europe have gained extraordinary strength that far outweighs their numbers, and everywhere they are striving to establish totalitarian control; police states prevail in almost all these countries even now, with the exception of Czechoslovakia, and no genuine democracy exists in them." Stalin not only refutes this argument, but also derides it in the most primitive fashion: "A single party presently holds dominion in England, the Labor Party, whereby the opposition parties are deprived of the right to participate in the leadership of England. This is what Mr. Churchill calls genuine democracy." This is not the case in Poland, Romania, Yugoslavia, Bulgaria, and Hungary, where "a bloc of several parties—from four to six parties—governs and the opposition, if it is more or less loyal, is assured the right to participate in leadership. Mr. Churchill calls this totalitarianism, tyranny, and a police state. Why, on what basis—don't expect an answer from Mr. Churchill. Mr. Churchill does not understand what a ludicrous position he puts himself in with his clamorous speeches about totalitarianism, tyranny, and police states."[15] In this familiar territory—the "unmasking" and ridicule of "infamous bourgeois freedoms"—Stalin feels quite assured.

But in order to neutralize the absence of factual bases and not to become mired in the essence of the contradiction (and most of all, not to go into the details that would threaten to destroy the whole ideological edifice), Stalin goes further, justifying "the growth of the Communists' influence" by claiming that it is "historical law": "The influence of the Communists grew because in the difficult years of the domination of fascism in Europe, the Communists proved to be reliable, brave, and self-sacrificing champions against the Fascist regime and for the freedom of the peoples."[16] This is why "millions of 'simple people,' having tested the Communists in the fire of battle and resistance to fascism, decided that Communists fully deserve the trust of the people. This is how the influence of the Communists in Europe grew. Such is the law of historical development."[17]

History is thus transformed into logic. In the course of a single speech one can observe how current policy (the chain of falsification and deliberate lies) merges with the ideology justifying this policy and defines with itself the suggestive strategies of Stalinist propaganda. Stalin's device is every time simple: consistently ignoring the disjunctions of the discourses of Realpolitik and ideology, he introduces a mammoth dose of ideology as a logical base for political arguments. The "two Stalins" (politician and ideologue) that are revealed are designed to conceal the real Stalin who is orchestrating the plots, the state coups, the political murders, and terror.

The question of how to understand the phenomenon that in Sovietology acquired the name "dual policy" was always the main problem in interpreting the Soviet line in international relations. Ideologically, this was the dichotomy between "socialism in one country" and "world revolution"; this collision was institutionally embodied in the positions taken by the Commissariat of Foreign Affairs and later the Ministry of Foreign Affairs (state, Realpolitik) and the Comintern/Central Committee (the party, ideology). The fact that both these lines were carried out by the same people with identical assumptions as to worldview, operating with the same arguments, doomed this policy to systemic contradictions. The discourse that shaped the policy was based on the constant merger of Realpolitik logic with the plane of ideological manipulation by suggestion. The discursive overlap became explicit when it attained a personal dimension. This drama culminated in Stalin, as the highest incarnation and personification of both the Soviet state and Communist ideology.

Stalin knew a faultless recipe to remove this tension. Possessing absolute freedom to combine politics and ideology, he usually used a device that one might call an "indirect lie"—that is, he said something patently false from a factual standpoint but made the ideological fog so dense that separating the factual from the ideological became impossible. Stalin's excessive philosophizing gave way to a zeal just as excessive. This device can be called an *ideological pleonasm.*

Thus it stood before 1949, while the Soviet Union had not yet become a nuclear power. The emergence of the atomic bomb in the USSR was a breakthrough moment in the self-consciousness of the Soviet leadership. Since one was not supposed to contradict the other, the buildup of Soviet military might led to intensification of the rhetoric of peace. The Soviet atomic bomb was supposed to serve peace since it fortified the "bastion of peace"—the Soviet Union. The technological breakthrough that made the emergence of the bomb possible was couched as something completely natural and ordinary and was announced in a markedly tranquil tone. The reaction of the West to this event, on the contrary, was portrayed as a panicked one. The event of the successful test of the bomb was shrouded in secrecy.

When the obligatory "*Pravda* correspondent" posed the question, "What do you think about the clamor of late in the foreign press about the testing of an atomic bomb in the Soviet Union?," Stalin's reply was deliberately low key: "Actually, we did have a test recently of one of the types of the atomic bomb. The testing of atomic bombs of various sizes will be carried out in future as well, according to the plan for defending our country from attack by the Anglo-American aggressive bloc."[18] Another question followed about how "various U.S. agents are raising the alarm and shouting about a threat to U.S. security": "Is there any justification for such an alarm?" In the same spirit, Stalin replied that there were "no justifications whatsoever for such alarm," since "these U.S. agents cannot but know that the Soviet Union is not only against the use of atomic weapons, but is also for their prohibition, for a cessation of their production." However, since "in the event of a U.S. attack on our country, the ruling circles of the United States will use an atomic bomb," the Soviet Union was "forced" to have atomic weapons "to meet the aggressors fully armed."

The fact that the Soviet Union, which accused the West of "atomic diplomacy" and an "arms race," had developed an atomic bomb was an obvious contradiction to the rhetoric of peace. In such instances, Stalin resorted to philosophizing, purposely repeating his argumentation, as if it was unclear to someone: "Of course the aggressors want the Soviet

Union to be disarmed in the event of their attack on it. But the Soviet Union disagrees with this and believes that the aggressor must be met fully armed. Consequently, if the United States is not thinking about attacking the Soviet Union, the U.S. agents' alarm must be considered pointless and spurious, for the Soviet Union is not contemplating an attack at any time on the United States or on any other country."[19]

Stalin and his readers of course know perfectly well that the United States is "considering" an attack and is now "unhappy with the fact that the secret to atomic weaponry is now held not only by the United States, but by other countries as well, and worst of all, by the Soviet Union. It would like the United States to be a monopolist in producing the atomic bomb so that the United States would have the unlimited possibility of frightening and blackmailing other countries." This logic seems incomprehensible to Stalin. Rhetorically, he asks "What justification, really, do they have for thinking this way? What gives them the right?" He answers to the effect that "the interests of preserving peace" demand "most of all, liquidation of such a monopoly and unconditional prohibition of atomic weaponry right afterward." The fact that the USSR has a bomb, in Stalin's logic, will only bring this moment closer: "The advocates of the atomic bomb can set about an embargo of atomic weaponry only in the instance that they see that they are no longer monopolists."[20]

Stalin's remarks had a number of intended listeners; he was informing Western leaders about a change in the balance of power and, as a "businesslike man," was suggesting a zero-sum game; he was attempting to convince "peace-loving humanity" that the Soviet mastery of the atomic bomb was making peace more solid since the USSR was the "bastion of peace"; and the most intimate communication was addressed to his fellow countrymen: by manipulating emotions, Stalin was inspiring confidence in his own powers, and by fortifying his superiority complex, was hinting at something bigger, provoking bravado and impishly "winking" (the West is terrorized and panicking, but we are emphatically at ease). This emotion management was based on intimate contact with the reader, who fully embraced Stalin's view of peace and saw Stalin's excessive philosophizing as intentional mockery of the enemies, downcast and ridiculous in their panic.

Soviet literature, which engaged in this same manipulation of emotions, followed Stalin in laying bare the device. Characteristic in this respect is Sergei Mikhalkov's poem "On the Soviet Atom," written hot on the heels of Stalin's remarks, in which Stalin's techniques are literally disassembled into an emotional-semantic series, and the message is translated into a much more accessible register, that of the *chastushka*. As opposed to Stalin's interview, Mikhalkov's poem is addressed exclusively to an internal consumer. Thus, the logic games are replaced in it by outright mockery, which had merely been hinted at by Stalin. First, there is the joyous news, shrouded in mystery but conveyed in a modest tone:

Мы недавно проводили
Испытанья нашей силе,
Мы довольны от души
Достиженья хороши!
Все на славу удалось,
Там, где нужно, взорвалось!
Мы довольны результатом
Недурен советский атом!

Not long ago we made a test
To see whose power is the best;
We're quite pleased, you'll understand
Our accomplishments are grand!
It all splendidly succeeded—
It exploded right where needed!
The outcome's made us very happy:
The Soviet atom's not too shabby![21]

Then follows mockery of the panicked and stupefied West and its leaders. What is more, "Soviet pride" is asserted here exclusively by means of sarcasm intended to conceal the real object of pride—the bomb:

Как услышала про это
Иностранная газета,
Зашумела на весь свет:
"Рассекречен наш секрет!
И у русских есть сейчас
То, что было лишь у нас!
Как же русские посмели?
Трумэн с Эттли проглядели!"
Неужели,
В самом деле,

Проглядели?
Ха-ха-ха! . . .
Ачесоны,
Моррисоны
Доведут вас до греха!

The foreign press, with ears alert
To headlines did the news convert
The whole world heard it shout:
"Now our precious secret's out!
And now the Russians have for sure,
What was only ours before!
But why were the Russians all so daring
When Attlee and Truman both were staring?!"
Did they really,
Look so silly,
Actually?
Ha, ha, mind!
The Achesons
And Morrisons
Will get you in a bind!

Following the exposition of Stalin's narrative, Mikhalkov seemingly speaks above the heads of the Soviets to "peace-loving society," but since the addressee is only the Soviet reader, he drowns out the love of peace with sabre rattling:

Подтвердил товарищ Сталин,
Что мы бомбу испытали
И что впредь еще не раз
Будут опыты у нас.
Бомбы будут! Бомбы есть!
Это надо вам учесть!
Но не входит в наши планы
Покорять другие страны,
Ни британцев,
Ни германцев,
Ни голландцев
Да-да-да!
Вы не бойтесь,
Успокойтесь,
Не волнуйтесь, господа!

Comrade Stalin's words made known
The bomb was tested here at home
And that in future, going hence
We'll do some more experiments.
We got some bombs, and we'll have more!
So you'd better know the score!
But we don't have it in our plans
To try and conquer foreign lands,
Not the Britons,
Nor the Germans,
Nor the Dutchmen
Hee, hee, hee!
Don't look worried with a frown,
Calm yourself and settle down,
Don't be scared, now, no siree!

The call for a ban on atomic weapons at the end of Stalin's interview is absolutely incompatible with the poem's joy that "We got some bombs, and we'll have more!" and the threats in it ("So you'd better know the score!"), but the aim of texts like Mikhalkov's is to say outright what Stalin, for political reasons and because of his status, did not want to (and could not) articulate. If Stalin concluded his epistle with peace-loving passages, Mikhalkov on the contrary ends with aggressive anti-American rhetoric, which was supposed to distract attention from the incompatibility of statements so stridently conveyed and so contradictory:

Мы хотим, чтоб запретили
Жить на свете смертной силе,
Чтобы с атомным ядром
Приходило счастье в дом.
Вы ж хотите запретить
Всем его производить,
Чтоб служил на свете атом
Только вашим хищным Штатам,
Вашим Штатам,
Синдикатам
Да магнатам.
Эге-гей!
Ваши планы
Все обманы,
Их не скроешь от людей!

We want to see the world refuse
The atom's strength for death to use
The atom's core not used for fright
But in the home, for warmth and light.
But you'd forbid, had you your druthers
Its production by all others,
The atom's service you would own—
Your predatory States alone
All your States,
Syndicates
And magnates.
Hey hey hey!
All your plans
Shenanigans,
People see them plain as day!

Stalinist discourse is always located in a shadowy zone of dual meanings: of Realpolitik and ideology, of diplomacy and "giving the wink" to the Soviet audience, of logical games and concealed passion. Through its various aspects it is addressed *separately* to "the city" and "the world," specially adapted to varying registers. The basic function of a translation of a Stalinist text into a *raeshnik* is the removal of this duality and an explication of the message that Stalin read for the ideal Soviet reader as a demand. The text of the court poet is a Stalinist text adapted (down to the *raeshnik* level) for the mass reader. Stalin and the writer did not shape the reader's demands but simply followed what the reader wanted to hear. This assured discursive recognition and accessibility, a unity of empathy and mutual understanding of a worldview that ultimately cemented the "moral and political unity of the Soviet people" with their leader.

This unity was assured, of course, not only by propaganda, but also by the entire evolution of Stalin's political philosophy, the culmination of which figured in his last public appearance—the enigmatic concluding speech at the Nineteenth Congress of the Soviet Communist Party, on October 14, 1952. This philosophy was a hybrid of a pragmatic and strict Realpolitik and the most radical revolutionariness. This combination, which presented a serious challenge on the representational plane, was inevitable in the situation in which the Soviet Union ended up at the beginning of the Cold War, having saddled itself with the burden of resisting the surrounding world while being significantly weaker than it economically and less integrated into worldwide political structures, which, as time has shown, led ultimately to the collapse of the Soviet postwar geopolitical project. To compensate for these weaknesses, Stalin was forced to bluff, to constantly demonstrate strength and pragmatism, and to justify these with an ideology that was completely unadaptable to this role. Instead of the usual report given at the congress, he made a short speech in which he talked exclusively about foreign policy and, like a patriarch, addressed himself exclusively to the representatives of the "brotherly parties." In this speech, which was interpreted as a sort of "political testament," Stalin practically declared that Communists would have to occupy the place of a national bourgeoisie since the latter had "thrown the banner of bourgeois-democratic freedoms overboard" along with the banner of "national independence and national sovereignty." Now the "representatives of the Communist and democratic parties" would have to take up these banners and "take them forward" if they wanted to "rally the majority of the people around themselves" and "become the leading force of the nation."[22] A challenge for Communists to fight for bourgeois freedoms and national interests, the overcoming of which had been the historical mission of communism, looks like a caricature of Marxism. But the mixing of utopian ideology with political realia and national interests led to precisely this result; we will call this mixture *Realideologie*.

THE VULGATE OF STALINISM: THE "FIGHT FOR PEACE" AND THE IMPERIAL IMAGINARY

In Stalinist *Realideologie,* Marxist class orthodoxy was so densely colored with nationalism that even from a distance it ceased to remind one of its internationalist past, which official discourse continued to reference. It had finally been transformed into the ideological legitimizing instrument of Soviet imperial policy. It became impossible to understand (the more so on the level of the masses' perception) where one thing ended and another began.

Marxism, at the heart of which lies the internationalist-class idea, degenerated into a statist, nationalist doctrine asserting that "the Communist parties in all countries are now parties of patriots of their countries, and they are waging war against antipatriotic reactionary forces that are against the people."[23] Consequently, the idea of a "worldwide proletarian revolution" was transformed into support of "the national-liberation movement in all the world." The place of the proletariat and the bourgeoisie was now occupied by "national-patriotic" and "cosmopolitan" forces in conflict. Although the old set of concepts was still used, they all took on dual meanings. For example, it was asserted that "proletarian internationalism finds its highest manifestation in Soviet patriotism. . . . Outside Soviet patriotism there is no proletarian socialist internationalism."[24] But since "Soviet patriotism" was merely the ideological equivalent of Russo-Soviet national exceptionalism, it was impossible to understand how it could be distinguished from nationalism, as it remained in the shadowy zone of Stalinist *Realideologie*.

Moreover, the forking Stalinist discourse did not allow for keeping a balance between ideological orthodoxy and current policy because the mass consumer, who, beginning in the mid-1930s had been consistently brought up in the spirit of "Soviet patriotism" and during the war had been subjected to the influence of aggressive nationalist propaganda, displayed a natural unreceptiveness to orthodox Marxist rhetoric. Against the backdrop of intensifying international opposition and autarkic tendencies in internal policies (the fight against cosmopolitanism, Russo-Soviet nationalism, anti-Westernism, state-level anti-Semitism, and so forth), earlier orthodox Marxist doctrine was subjected to almost complete disintegration.

The task of political journalism under such conditions boiled down to a domestication and instrumentalization of Stalin's signals sent to the external world and, consequently, a translation of official political doublespeak (which, as suggested in Orwell, was wholeheartedly dominant in the public culture of cold war) into the language of the Soviet mass consumer.[25] This language was not fixed but rather was constantly changing under the influence of multidirectional political factors. Soviet writers faced the task of working out a public discourse that would harmonize political realism, ideology, and the masses' expectations; Stalin's revisionism, ideologemes, and political justifications would be brought into at least relative unambiguousness, creating a somewhat coherent discourse in which the authorities' intentions, the masses' beliefs, and political expediency would be correctly interwoven.

Two extremes can be clearly discerned in Cold War Soviet political journalism: aggressively nationalist, in which the internationalist component was completely leveled out, and "Westernist," in which the nationalist component, although dominant, was positioned such that it would be at least comprehensible beyond the borders of the Soviet Union. The first of these was addressed exclusively to the Soviet audience and was purely populist, appealing to the masses' tastes; the second was closer to the more advanced part of Soviet society, addressed to listeners beyond its borders, and harked back not only to the national cultural tradition and values, but also to orthodox internationalist class-conscious doctrine.

The emergence of the first extreme was linked to the goals of social mobilization and the necessity of providing a simplified populist version of Stalin's doctrine. One of the most striking representatives of the nationalist trend was Leonid Leonov. He had rarely engaged in journalism before the war. During the war, however, he played an active part in the anti-German propaganda, and with the postwar swerve of Soviet ideology toward nationalism, isolationism, and anti-Semitism, he began to publish voluminous articles that laid the foundations of Soviet nationalist political journalism.

Leonov-as-journalist was bitingly sarcastic, but his bombastic histrionics and the awkwardness and grandiloquence of his images, as well as their depressing sameness, betray his lack of a sense of humor. The basic features of his contributions—spite and aggression—were indicators of weakness and an aggrieved ego, not of strength. The spiteful derision with which he wrote about a "star-spangled demon" that was seducing Europe and, like a vampire, sucking the last drops of blood from its practically exsanguinated body, borders on hysteria: "Destitute Europe will not satiate its hungry little children for a good while yet. It has no other small change other than its soul for buying the transoceanic ration, and it is paying, paying, and paying for cigarettes and canned pork stew with the bloody scraps of its so-called freedoms. The many-starred demon stands over Europe in all its magnitude, and the European children fearfully look first at its hands with the bowl of lentil soup, then into its cold indifferent eyes."[26]

America, drinking "the blood of Christian infants," appears elsewhere in the guise of "a well-fed foreign merchant, weighing about ninety kilograms, bursting with health" who "barters away from little Italian and French boys—orphans, maybe!—their last hope for happiness for a piece of cake. 'You oughtn't, brothers!' the Russian *muzhiks* would disgustedly say about this hellish business! As they say, may

God ease your sinful soul on your dying day, unknown transoceanic master!"[27] Leonov's writing style is easily seen in this scene, obviously modeled closely on Dostoyevsky. This is the style of the author of *A Writer's Diary*—an embittered, gloomy nationalist who hates the too successful West and is mired in endless "reckoning" with it. These accounts he wants to settle are almost always dishonest and amoral. But the confidence with which this distorted moral feeling was asserted proves how vulnerable to manipulation a society that found itself in the world of wishy-washy *Realideologie* was.

Having declared that "the transoceanic prosperity is to a certain extent paid for with our children's blood," Leonov paints the scene of an invitation to a Christmas celebration "in a transoceanic capital" of a Russian boy in a Russian shirt who "with his little child's voice related horrifying things about the German invasion, which made the blood long curdle in the veins of the transoceanic lady-patronesses." He told how once "the Fascists wanted to buy Alesha's Christmas tree from him, and when he refused, they took it by force. Of course, such a move of German fascism deserves all sorts of censure, but it seems to us that Alesha's information was obviously lacking. It would have been smarter to commission his sensible correspondent to get an interview with the piles of children's ashes in the great ovens of Majdanek and Babi Yar."[28] Without mentioning that the blood taken in Babi Yar and Majdanek was Jewish, and not that of little boys in Russian shirts who have inexplicably ended up in "transoceanic capitals," Leonov demonstrated more than simply moral unscrupulousness. Such techniques stridently demonstrate the ties between the anti-Westernism, nationalism, and anti-Semitism that lay at the heart of Cold War Soviet propaganda. Cold War propaganda was above all *military propaganda,* the basic content of which was nationalism.

Leonov proclaimed patriotism as an uber-value. The world he created was devoid of a personal dimension. It was a world of irrational-poetic collective bodies: "We love the fatherland; we are ourselves physically woven together from particles of its skies, fields, and rivers." The person has nothing individual at his disposal, neither life nor talent: "The motherland gave you life and talent." Talent is neither a coincidence ("it is not a lottery ticket by which the lucky person is given, out of turn, leather boots or a motorcycle with a trailer") nor the property of its owner; it is "a treasure recompensed by the historical experience and torture of previous generations; it is handed out with a moral receipt, like a Stradivarius violin, to a young talent, and the motherland has a right to demand a return with interest, so that the national treasury does not grow scanty." This is why any product of creativity is the nation's: "On any universal treasure lies the ineradicable stamp of the nation where it was born. And if you have managed to sing something worthwhile in life that has tugged at the hearts of simple people, then it is merely because your weak voice has sounded alongside the ancient chorus of your Great Motherland."[29]

But Soviet patriotism, monstrously combining within itself an imperialism passed off as internationalism and nationalism, is unique. Leonov proclaims this patriotism as an object of pride. Meanwhile, the stress is laid on the national, which becomes the source of universal greatness. According to Leonov, "Soviet patriotism is the patriotism of the Soviet person who has proclaimed his fatherland the moral refuge of all progressive humanity. Yes, we love our own, *what is ours,* because upon it lie the stamps of the dreams and golden hands of our geniuses; yes, we hold dear this home, *our* home, created by the deeds of our forebears and fully armed by the achievements of the five-year plans, but not only because it has the graves of our forefathers, the priceless implements of civilization and unbroken trunks of goods. Our fatherland is better than others because it is the salutary prototype of human society."[30]

The point of departure for Leonov's arguments is the historical primacy of Russia. He hardly talks about the Soviet Union. The country he writes about restored the history that fell apart in 1917. It is the earlier Russia-as-trailblazer. And the one who "goes before the century, like a guide blazing a trail into the country where there are not yet any sailing directions and Cook's routes, taking upon himself all the difficulties and the contingencies of the unknown, he is the elder brother. To such people has always belonged seniority in a family, as well. Such people answer to history for the preservation of the whole human spiritual patrimony." But "we cannot be otherwise, we are more clear-sighted, we are older in the human race."[31] Leonov calls such patriotism "the highest degree of patriotism that as yet exists in only our country, but it shines far across its borders. This is patriotism not only for oneself, but also for others . . . and, ultimately, more for others than for oneself. It is the patriotism of wisdom and seniority; we live here, but our kinfolk are scattered everywhere—along the horizontals of space and the verticals of time. 'We are humanity.' "[32] While combining nationalistic universalism and Russian messianism and exceptionalism with Soviet internationalist virtues, Leonov hastens to emphasize that his "pan-humanness" has nothing in common with cosmopolitanism. The patriotism he describes "is not the ecumenical cosmopolitanism of some of our distinguished contemporaries who are ready to include in the concept of the motherland any point of the galaxy where there are candies and cafés, department stores, and hotels with service."[33]

The condescending mention of "department stores, and hotels with service" refers to the West. And this is where Leonov gives free reign to his sarcasm and arrogance. In the tradition of the Russian discourse about the West, this is a clear symptom of wounded national pride, which is the psychological source of this narrative. Leonov's historical constructs—and in them, precisely, he finds justifications for his insults and traumas—are a form of rationalization of these chronic complexes. Arrogance is symptomatic of them, and the more profound and painful these complexes are, the haughtier and more disdainful the attitude toward the object of envy becomes, an envy easily read in the deliberate falsification of history and in the hubris that cloys Leonov's historiosophical constructs. He writes disdainfully about the West in general (and about America in particular), insisting that "we have the right to regard West European culture through the eyes of the heirs, a culture we defended in two most terrible battles and from which, incidentally, its other branches came, including the transoceanic one." The two battles to which Leonov refers are the Mongol Invasion and Nazism. Regarding the former, here Rus' did not simply save Europe but indeed created the very conditions for its development:

> For three whole centuries we resisted to the death, unwavering, while young Europe laid the foundations of its universities. Our children lived miserably then, without pampering, without books, without gingerbread. A land covered with blood had no need of Shakespeares and Ronsards, but rather of Peresvets and Oslyabyas. It is not the lover's lute nor the majestic tragedy of Moorish jealousy or feckless vanity that is heard in the Song of Igor's Campaign but something more serious. With them Hamlet was already doubting the joys of existing, but we alone fought for their very right to take breath. Nevertheless, we do not grumble at our fate; after every trial something was added in our body

and soul; this is where the titan's muscles and the intrepid astuteness of the wise man come from.[34]

It is not only the outright falsification of history that grabs the attention here; Rus' chose the vector of anti-Western development, seeing a much lesser evil in the Tatars than in the West—and from that time forward devoutly believed in the rightness of this choice, canonizing Aleksandr Nevskii. The very designation of "young Europe" in the words of the Russian writer is characteristic here; it is suggested that it is not Rus',' which arose on the outskirts of Europe's outskirts and embraced European civilization later than all others (while constantly questioning this choice), but Europe, which already had thousands of years of history by the time—Greek, Roman, and Christian—that is "young." This fantasy-laden juxtaposition of "young Europe" and "ancient" Russia-the-wise was supposed to justify "the patriotism of seniority." And, in fact, the wise man thought about life and death, while pampered, frivolous Europe, doubting the joys of existence, was occupied with such trifles as jealousy and feckless vanity.

This mythology of denial creates a parallel world in which history is suspended in a peculiar dimension. The basis for verifying it is not reality but its correspondence to the author's traumatic logic. Leonov violates common axioms, making it both impossible to consider his constructs in correlation to real history and useless to look for the countries he talks about in this overturned globe. With regard to anything whatsoever, Russia was the wisest, the oldest, the most forward-looking. Everything that happened in Russia from the outside was "unrecognizably ennobled simply from its presence in the Russian heart—to the same degree that our Rublev is superior to Byzantine models and Italian primitives."[35]

Leonov rebukes the Westernizer Peter the Great because "impatience deafened in Peter the voice of wise prescience—as this will resound through the ages—by completing great things, he inured the great Russian people to copying the foreign and despising our own." The "German-Dutchmen" brought by Peter into Russia were organically incapable of becoming part of Russian culture, Leonov was convinced: "It would be ridiculous to consider them nurturers of a renewed Russian culture. They were never fit to become cells of the state intellect of Russia, which had its own cruel fate, inconceivable to the West, but only an instrument in the hands of the raging tsar." However, when Peter died, "these 'fledglings of Peter's nest' quickly degenerated into a mediocre Holsteinian moth, into Biron and Benckendorff, Dubelt and Stürmer, who was simply the tsarina's flea in a velvet camisole. Very few of them fruitfully took root in Russian science and blended into their new motherland. The majority lived like a little island, becoming the upper crust of society, friends and even kinfolk of the tsar. But even as they prospered and multiplied, filled themselves with arrogance and fat, they were afraid of the so-called 'Slavic soul,' which to a foreigner had always seemed a sort of suspect thing with a fuse, and they strove to protect their descendants from the vicissitudes of the future."[36]

This is where Leonov finds the sources of "the formula of the age-old primacy of the West in our spiritual life": "Over the course of a century this imported microbe pretty well sapped the faith of the great Russian people in their national strengths. The grand folk of the capital ultimately tried, by their language and customs, to set themselves apart from their black kinfolk huddled in their lowly huts. They strutted around in their imported feathers and rags, squandering Peter's capital. Having no support in their own fatherland, they looked for it outside it." The grandees are not bad, it turns out, for their essence as a class but precisely because of anti-patriotism, if not their direct participation in an anti-Russian conspiracy, the goals of which were completely clear to Leonov: "They had to simultaneously strip naked, spiritually disarm our country, and then, under the local anesthetic of national doubt, prepare from it a nutritious and safe dish for the centuries to come. It is interesting how quickly and parasitically this myth of Russia's thousand-year apprenticeship to Europe was injected into our perpetual modesty, even shame, when it came to evaluating our contributions to all mankind. . . . Having already taken our blood or ideas, they always pushed aside our brother—whether a soldier or a scholar!—from the cake at the concluding feast."[37]

Casting aside "modesty, even shame," Leonov discusses Russian historical grievances and accounts to settle with the West, but we must not think that all of this is merely the creation of a historical soil upon which the discourse of cold war will sprout. It is exactly the reverse: Leonov's historiosophical fantasies are primarily designed to fund a nationalistic mythology that will grow into a cold war discourse. It is the Cold War that creates the political demand for this discourse and makes it relevant. In Leonov's speech at the First All-Union Conference of Peace Advocates, this process of fusing nationalism with Cold War discourse is particularly apparent.

An American "large-scale capitalist faction" was pouring "evil gold on the fresh wounds of Western Europe. The future gladiators are noisily fortifying themselves with the lentil soup for which the governments have sold their national independence and the sovereign primogenitures of their nations."[38] The "American faction" was buying a peculiar commodity—"the levy is expressed in the most valuable currency, which is stronger than any gold standard"—soldiers' blood.[39] An ominous cloud of worldwide conspiracy hangs over these pictures. Addressing himself to "the simple people of the workshops and fields," Leonov declares that although "they have no time to investigate the particulars of the crafty and complicated beyond-disgusting procedures of the hyperbolic Marshall business, with which the transoceanic money whales are preparing to squeeze out more tons of gold or the inherent equivalents of blood even from this lowly, flattened-out, destroyed Western Europe that is scattered somewhere in the detritus," they know perfectly well "who is running things on the American continent, who is sitting at the desk of hatred for the Soviet Union."[40] It was the American capitalists, well-known from Soviet caricatures, with the characteristic Semitic look. This discourse is ever more reminiscent of the Nazi denunciation of the "plutocratic regimes" bought out by the worldwide Jewry that was sending the nations into battle.

Leonov does not spare his sarcastic arrows to ridicule the West as a whole and the malignant American demon in particular. The pent-up emotion of his invective was purely propagandist. The populism of Leonov's sarcasm allowed readers to associate themselves with this narrative. Here Leonov used the very same technique as Stalin did when, having told a deliberate lie, he immediately began philosophizing, as if it were a matter of something already proven and only requiring some interpretation. In exactly the same way, Leonov hurries through even his invectives, taking the sarcasm to the level of the grotesque. As a traumatic reaction to the dissonance between a heroic ideal and an actual situation, sarcasm always suggests an opposite, heroic-pathetic extreme. Such an extreme is "my people," appearing in a pose of epic tranquility. This is just as they figured with Stalin when he was ironically speaking with the "*Pravda* correspondent" about the panic and the "racket" that had seized the West on the news of the Soviet Union's newly acquired atomic bomb. Stalin's "Soviet people" also looked tranquilly at this "fuss." But where Stalin only hints at this, Leonov paints the full picture: "[The people] know about all the enemy airbases that are targeting our cities. They hear the blatant, blunt calls from the transoceanic yellow journalists to hack to pieces, bludgeon, and burn our women, old men, and children. They know a lot more, and they smile and keep quiet, just as the very same giants of the working class of the near and distant West, whom the Atlantic Pact wants to inspire to a campaign against the Soviet motherland of all workers, keep quiet for the time being."[41]

These "giants" are described with such sympathy because Leonov wants to see himself as one of them. He, like all the Soviet people, is disturbed by the American demon. This is why Leonov's spiteful tirades are so convincing for the mass Soviet consumer, who has experience similar to his and a similar mental profile. However, all these invectives are too nationally grounded and traumatic and accordingly completely unconvertible. This is why the obverse of nationalistic propaganda was "Westernist," translating these traumas into a language understandable to the West, and therefore less suitable for the internal consumer. The main agent of this type was Ilya Ehrenburg.

A most brilliant wartime journalist, Ehrenburg immediately after the war undertook the journalism of "the fight for peace," transforming himself into one of the main propagandists of the Cold War era. His journalistic writing demonstrates the direct link between the discourses of war and peace in Soviet culture. The new enemy, who was intensively shaped in postwar culture, had not changed typologically from the war times and thus remained Fascist: "Our opponents say we call everyone we don't like Fascists. This is untrue; what is true is that all Fascists don't like us. Not only do they not like us, they call for war against us. If they behaved otherwise, they would not be Fascists. . . . Before Fulton and before Washington there was the balcony in Piazza Venezia and the stadium in Berlin."[42] Re-dressing the recent allies in Nazi clothing required more than a little work on "transforming reality," but since there was no time for creating the new image of the enemy, the abundant ideological and propaganda resources that had been invested in the creation of such an image during the war (at which Ehrenburg had also surpassed others) had to be utilized.

If Leonov's rhetoric was addressed to a Soviet audience to teach it the language of imperial arrogance and haughty sarcasm, then Ehrenburg resorted to orthodox class rhetoric, which allowed him to go beyond the boundaries of narrow nationalism and to position the Soviet imperial project as internationalist. Nor is this surprising: Ehrenburg was the only one saved from among the main "Stalinist Westernizers" of the 1930s, and he had become the main Soviet emissary in the worldwide antiwar movement.[43] His task was to attract Western leftists to the Soviet side; therefore his rhetoric had to be understandable to them. "We are not alone," he wrote. "All the peoples of the world are with us. Against us are those Americans who are against the American people. Against us are those English who are against the English people. Against us are those French who are against the French people."[44]

Even in the description of what peace meant to the Soviet people, Ehrenburg referenced not so much the greatness of the state as everyday life, painting almost an idyll of tranquility and "constructive labor." He engaged in the same kind of emotion management as Leonov, but he appealed to somewhat higher, cultured emotions. It is for just this reason that his depictions are less emotional and more picturesque. There is less in them of the sarcasm and hysteria that permeate Leonov's writings. In Ehrenburg, "tranquility and restraint" are a demonstration of "our strength." This is not so much a physical strength as it is spiritual. It was with just this spirituality that the Soviet people stood against the spiritually impoverished world of the West. Nonetheless, the West is rendered differentially; Europe is proclaimed to be almost an ally of the USSR in its opposition to America, and the Soviet Union becomes the heir and successor to European civilization, which is falling apart under the pressure of American barbarism: "We know that the Atlantic Ocean, which separates Europe from America, exists. But what is 'Atlantic culture'? The architecture of old Spain is much more similar to the architecture of old Georgia or Armenia than to the architecture of the Aztecs. The biography of Paris is more reminiscent of the biography of Prague than the biography of Atlanta or Philadelphia. Amsterdam or Stockholm is much more akin to Leningrad than to Chicago. Only to a person who has galloped three hundred yards on his head could it occur to combine the Propylaea with the Chicago abattoirs, or Hugo with the segregation law, and to compare all of this to Turgenev or Tchaikovsky."[45]

Ehrenburg, the chief official "Westernizer" of Stalinism, translates the argument with the West into a language comprehensible not so much to an internal as an external consumer. A French or Italian leftist intellectual would be comforted by the contrast of the concept of "Atlantic" and "Western" culture, uniting Europe with the United States, and the concept of a "European" culture uniting Europe with the Soviet Union: "No 'Truman doctrines' will separate our culture from the European one, even if Marshall writes a hundred thousand checks."[46] Ehrenburg transfers the dispute into the arena of culture, which makes his argumentation more accessible to the West European addressee than to the Soviet consumer, for whom the disdainful-insulting tone of Leonov's reproaches addressed to "the West" (including Europe) were much more familiar.

If for the nationalist Leonov there was Russia (and the USSR as its historical incarnation) and the West, then for Ehrenburg there was culture (Europe and Russia/USSR) and barbarianism (America). The dispute about Europe was an important component of the new doctrine: America was written off as not cultured enough. The space of European culture was precisely where the Soviet Union had to demonstrate its "seniority." In this aspiration to prove not its revolutionariness but rather its cultural traditionalism, the idea of worldwide revolution was definitively done away with. For Ehrenburg, who had always been closely tied to revolutionary art, such conservatism was not an aesthetic program that he consciously defended. His ties to Russian art were devoid of the hysterical traumatic psychology that erupted in the real traditionalist, Leonov. Ehrenburg's attitude toward the West and toward Western culture was permeated with respect. It had not a trace of the disdain and the fulminating hybrid of inferiority complex and superiority complex that transformed Leonov's journalism into a cascade of sarcasm and hatred. For Ehrenburg, the revolutionary tradition was not empty rhetoric and homage to the Soviet regime as it was for Leonov. He tried to build it into a new traditionalism: "Precisely because we are innovators; precisely because our Soviet culture is closely linked to revolution and is forward-looking, we value the great past of mankind—both our own and others.' The sacred stones of Europe are not only in Rome, in Paris, in London, and in Prague; they are also in Kiev, in Novgorod, and in Moscow. From the vandals plotting a third world war we are protecting a new, more perfect form of society and the centuries-old relics of humanity."[47]

For Ehrenburg, the Soviet Union remained the only defender of and heir to European civilization: "We are now the most steadfast, the most unselfish defenders of European culture" since the bourgeoisie was no longer capable of creating anything.[48] And this was the last refuge of the bygone class awareness, internationalism, and aesthetic revolutionism. Ehrenburg poignantly tried to fit Soviet patriotism into the bygone revolutionary frame. He exerted no less effort in this than Leonov did in trying to fit orthodox Marxist values into nationalistic Russocentric discourse. But Leonov did not seek help from culture. He called upon pure trauma. They came together in Soviet messianism. Ehrenburg's "Europeanism," his European patriotism, was looking for its own soil. Everything that was nationally grounded became a counterweight to everything cosmopolitan ("rootless") accumulated in the image of America: "We defend the great and multifaceted beehive of Europe: the cities dear to all, the museums, the schools."[49] Europe is the natural Soviet ally by virtue of its antiquity and historical "rootedness." The United States is contrasted to it as a world of barbarity and lack of culture—that is, a world of "rootlessness." And only the Soviet Union gives the world an exemplar of patriotism that allows the ancient peoples "not to barter their birthright for a bowl of American lentils."[50] As the "hotbed of worldwide revolution," the Soviet Union is transformed into a hotbed of worldwide patriotism and defense of cultural traditions. The fact that the classical paradigm of wartime consciousness transitions into the Soviet mystery play of the Cold War–era peace with practically no changes is tied to the absolute and mirror-image nature of this turnover; the defenders remain the same (the Soviet Union), the enemy remains "Fascist" (with only a geographical displacement to the other side of an ocean), and the victim is Europe ("The shadow of death lies upon Europe, upon its stone nests, upon its gardens and museums, upon its factories and libraries").[51]

THE WARTIME POETRY OF PEACE: THEMATIZATION OF IDEOLOGICAL IDIOMS

The "political poetry" of Socialist Realism dedicated to the celebration of leaders, the glorification of joyous Soviet life and the "peaceful labor of the Soviet people," or else to the "struggle for peace," has persistently been considered a sort of rhymed graphomania. All its shortcomings, critics seem to have thought, arose from the attenuation of "creative individuality" in "general assertions." In this both official/ Soviet and dissident/Sovietological criticisms completely concurred. And in fact, if we approach it with the traditional understanding of the nature of poetry as the sphere of expression of the subject of poetic creativity, an impersonal or subjectless poem is an oxymoron and is considered a simulation of poetry. Actually, the poet as the subject of creativity is absent here. In this sense, what we are dealing with is not poetry, and its authors are not poets. This is definitely not social poetry, nor even less the political poetry that ended in the USSR back in the 1920s, since the social (political) authorial "I" is absent from it.

But the subjectlessness of this poetry is a sham. The author in it is a medium of collective bodies, a molder of their will, intentions, phobias, and traumas. The collective bodies, however, do not possess language. This language must be created. The ideological machines of mass societies are the factories for this language. And Socialist Realist poetry is a true academy of the language of collective bodies. The authorial "I" in it is a modeled ideological construct that has managed not only to internalize official discourse, but also to produce its most refined— idiomatic—forms. At the same time, this poetry models an ideal Soviet subject that is more potential than reality. Therefore the function of this poetry is to breathe life into this subject—conviction, faith, zeal, passion. Hence the philosophizing, acting, pathos, and declamation that are so characteristic of it. The function of this poetry is tripartite: conversion of ideological assertions into an idiom; thematization; and making the worked-out ideological idioms suggestive. Without this discursive fuel, ideology could not function, and the Cold War, which was *par excellence* ideological, could not have continued.

Ideological constructs are by definition polysynthetic. It is the *relationship* among the elements of these constructs that conceals the ideological distortion. Thus any attempt to uncover these relationships turns into an act of ideological deconstruction. In the idiom—a phraseological fusion not subject to further analysis—the link among its component parts does not come into question. Thus these non-analyzable constructs, the most successfully worked out and delivered in poetry, are the most lasting and effective form of the functioning of ideologemes. In the guise of established constructs, they are best assimilated by the masses' consciousness. Therefore, in order to be politically instrumentalized, ideological constructs must first be converted to an idiom. Soviet poetry was the instrument of this conversion.

Idioms by their very nature require historical inculcation. Accordingly, the development of the idiomatics of the Cold War could not be anything else but the reworking of the earlier wartime mythology actively worked out in the 1930s[52] (and in the war years particularly)[53] in what the Soviets called "defense literature." At its heart lies a Manichaean picture of a world torn into two parts. The naturalization of this rift was one of the fundamental tasks of the postwar "fight for peace" poetry. The split of the world is stable, like the position of the continents. In Sergei Smirnov's poem "Two Flags," geography itself becomes the symbol of the naturalness of this split:

Над Чукоткой,
В полярном тумане пролива,
Флаг Советов
Стоит на скале горделиво.

Над Аляской,
На острове серого цвета,
Флаг чужой, полосатый,—
Америка это.

Здесь рождается утро
И с первого шага
Направляется в сторону
Красного флага!

День шагает к Москве
С пограничной Чукотки,
Тает тьма
От его молодецкой походки!

А под небом Америки
Все еще длится
День вчерашний,—
По штатам бредет от столицы. . . .

Оба флага—
Как два пограничных солдата
Флаг восхода
Горит против флага заката.

И на красном—
Рассвета багряные краски.
И на пестром—
Вчерашние тени Аляски. . . .

Over Chukotka,
In the polar mist of the strait,
The flag of the Soviets
Stands proudly on a cliff.

Over Alaska
On a gray-colored island
Is the other's flag, striped—
This is America.

Here the morning is born
And with its first step
Sets out in the direction
Of the red flag!

The day moves on to Moscow
From distant Chukotka,
The darkness thaws
From its valiant step!

But under the American sky
The day from yesterday
Still lingers on—
It wanders the states from the capital. . . .

Both flags are
Like two frontier soldiers.
The flag of dawn
Gleams against the sunset flag.

And on the red one
Are the crimson sunrise colors.
And on the striped one
Yesterday's shades of Alaska. . . .

Sunrise/sunset is an ideologically charged idiomatic construct of both prerevolutionary and early Soviet poetry. But if it earlier was a metaphor of the civilizational opposition of East and West and had no localization (America), now it is not only naturalized and localized, but also domesticated. Soviet poetry achieved its greatest successes in this domestication of ideological idioms. The success of its other mission—historicization—was much less obvious since historicization of the Cold War relied on two opposite principles—a doctrinal/class principle and a Soviet/imperial principle.

The first appealed to class solidarity and, in the spirit of the Bolshevik rhetoric of the World War I era, contrasted imperialist war to civil war. In this poetry, war was naturalized through history. One of the most famous poems of the "fight for peace," Konstantin Simonov's "Red and White," concluded with the imperialists, racists, and obscurantists of contemporary America all being the same "whites": "Мир неделим на черных, смуглых, желтых. / А лишь на красных—нас—/ И белых—их" (The world is not divided into black, swarthy, and yellow people / But only into reds—us / And whites—them). Simonov explained to the reader that these "whites" were the legendary characters of the Soviet revolutionary era: "На белых—тех, что, если приглядеться. / Их вид на всех материках знаком, / На белых—тех, как мы их помним с детства. / В том самом смысле. Больше ни в каком. / На белых—тех, что в Африке ль, в Европе, / Их красные—в пороховом дыму, / Как мы—своих, прорвут на Перекопе / И сбросят в море, с берега, в Крыму!" (Into whites, the ones that if you look, / Their kind is familiar on all continents, / Into whites, the ones we remember from childhood, / In the very same sense. No more, no less. / Into whites, those who in Africa, or Europe / We reds, in the gunpowder's smoke, / Breaking through the last time at Perekop, / Will cast from the shore into the sea, in Crimea!)

But the victories in this "war for peace" were regarded not so much in an internationalist perspective as in a specifically imperial one. Addressing his daughter, Ukrainian poet Aleksandr Pidsukha spoke on behalf of a generation in "To My Daughter": "За тридцать лет, / Что с той поры минули, / Мы полпланеты к солнцу повернули. / Когда ты будешь в возрасте моем, / Мы всю планету к солнцу повернем!" ("In the thirty years, / That from that time their course have run, / We turned half the planet toward the sun. / When the time comes that you reach my age, / We'll have turned the whole planet to that stage!") The generalized Soviet "we" obliges us to think that the "sun" here is the same one that with its "valiant step" "moves on to Moscow / From distant Chukotka."

Nonetheless, the main line of historicization in this poetry was tied to the war that had just ended. Even in this, the references to earlier, revolutionary history were becoming less and less relevant. *The poetry of the "fight for peace" was by all parameters still the same wartime poetry.* Most of all, it was so in the things linked to the image of the enemy. The recent allies in the anti-Hitler coalition were proclaimed

Fascists: "Всем людям к счастью дверь открыта. / Свет нашей правды—всем свети! / И только лишь из Уолл-стрита / Ведут на Нюренберг пути" (The door to happiness for all lies open. / May the light of our truth shine on all! / And only from Wall Street / Do the paths to Nuremberg lead) (Iurii Borev, "History's Roads"). Politicians of the West were proclaimed Fascists in all their incarnations: "Пусть он теперь зовется Маршаллом. / Кенноном или Гарриманом,—/ Какой бы он костюм ни нашивал, / Нас трудно провести обманом. / Фашист не скроется под маскою" (Let him call himself Marshall now, / Or Kennon or Harriman—/ No matter what costume he sews on, / We're not easily fooled. / A mask will not conceal a Fascist) (Viktor Bershadskii, "Encounter in Novorossiisk").

Nowhere was the *militarist* nature of Cold War–era Soviet propaganda manifested more stridently than in the "fight for peace" poetry, which exploited mainly the idioms of Soviet wartime propaganda from 1941 to 1945. Having been proclaimed Fascist, the enemy was accused of inhumane crimes and suspected of felonious plots against the Soviet Union: "В Афинах, Вьетнаме, Корее, Китае / Залившие кровью холмы и долины, / Они нашу родину ныне мечтают / Сломить, превратить в пустыри и руины; / Сжигать города и разбойничать люто, / Бомбить, убивать в колыбелях малюток" (In Korea, China, Athens, or Vietnam / Drenching hills and valleys in blood, / They dream now of crushing our motherland / And turning it into wastelands and ruins; / Of burning the cities and ferociously looting, / Of bombing and killing babies in cradles) (Anastas Ventslova, "Ranks Closer!").

This is exemplary war poetry, which in the years of the war (especially the first part, up to mid-1943) consisted entirely of pictures of inexpressible violence, monstrous atrocities, and unbelievable suffering. The central figure here was almost always a child—an ideal victim that mobilized people and cried out for retribution. Just a few years after the victory, the motif of anxiety about the future again arises in Soviet poetry, personified in a frail child. Threats to the lives of children became almost palpable. Emilian Bukov in the poem "Sun of Peace" declares that the American "brigands" are worse than Huns: "Но есть на свете худший сорт бандита. / Кто не щадит и материнских слез, / Кто золотую бритву Уолл-стрита / Над детским горлом высоко занес" (But there is a sort of bandit, the world's worst / Who has no mercy even for a mother's tears, / Who Wall Street's golden razor / Has poised high above the throat of a child). The Gestapo was portrayed this way in 1942 in Soviet poetry, and concentration camp doctors thus: "Ученый, дипломированный варвар! / Его тревожит мирный сон ребят: / Во тьме лелея замысел коварный, / Он копит свой бесчеловечный яд" (A learned barbarian, with a diplomat's veneer! / He is troubled by children's peaceful sleep: / In darkness coddling his perfidious scheme / He amasses his inhuman poison). The poem ends with a rhetorical question: "Что, что дороже для людей и мира, / За что народов грянут голоса: / За ядовитый, тусклый взгляд банкира / Иль за ребенка чистые глаза?" (What, oh what is dearer to the people and the world? / What do the voices of the peoples thunder for? / For the banker's toxic, lackluster stare / Or for the pure eyes of a child?). Enemies turn up left and right, not only soldiers, but also the diplomats and politicians that this poetry reckons to be the same as soldiers but in civilian clothes; there are no peaceful people among them: ". . . после войны ушли в дипломаты / Начальники их штабов. / И возлюбили их генералы / В посольских дворцах уют" (. . . After the war their chiefs of staff / Retired as diplomats. / And their generals came to love / The comforts of embassy palaces) (Aleksei Surkov, "Raise Your Voice, Honest People!").

The culmination of the transformation of this "peace poetry" into war propaganda came in the calls for the physical annihilation of "the enemies of peace": "Презренному Черчиллю, Даллесу, Баруху / Сумеем / Поганые глотки заткнуть!" (Despised Churchill, Dulles, and Baruch / We will / Choke their vile throats) (Aleksandr Zharov, "Full Force!"). The guarantee of peace thus understood can only be force: "Быть войне или не быть—зависит / От того, как будем мы сильны. / Армия советского народа, / В нерушимой крепости твоей / Будущего солнечные своды / И судьба счастливая детей" (Whether or not there'll be war depends / On how strong we will be. / O Soviet People's Army, / In your indestructible strength / Are the sunlit arches of the future / And the happy fate of the children) (Evgenii Dolmatovskii, "Will There Be War?"). The "peace army" demands mobilization, readiness for a true *war for peace*: "«Мир!»—на стройках стропила шепчут, / «Мир!»— деревья шумят в саду, / «Мир!»—я слышу на всех наречьях. / За такую мечту человечью, / Если надо, я в бой пойду" ('Peace!' the trusses whisper at the building sites, / 'Peace!' the trees are sounding in the garden, / 'Peace!' I hear it in every dialect. / For such a human daydream / I will join, if need be, in the battle") (Ivan Baukov, "I Need Peace for This").

"Peace army" and "war for peace" are not so much poetic tropes as they are the products of the oxymoronic nature of the Cold War itself, in which *the "fight for peace" was actually a form of militant action, an act of war.*

Like any war poetry, the Soviet "fight for peace" poetry was not subject to conversion; it produced an exclusively internal Soviet discourse, and the internal audience was its only consumer. The idioms developed in it allowed mass readers to find their bearings in the postwar world, in which the country found a new situation appropriate to its new imperial role and its new status as a superpower, which had unexpectedly befallen it as a result of the victory. The masses' consciousness needed the usual ideological restructuring and the geographical realignment in which Soviet poetry was engaged.

Paradoxically, the seeming subjectlessness of this poetry made it a transparent and direct translation of collective experience. The collective complexes and traumas projected in it are based on the unconscious transfer of earlier-experienced relationships with one person to another person (and in this case, from one collective body to another). Here, pressing political needs and the experience of violence merged in a single act of creating an ideological idiom. One example was typified in the scenes of humiliation, the descriptions of which fill this literature and that bear the stamp of the lived experience of collective bodies—an undoubtedly traumatic experience and simultaneously the only one intimately known. The behavior of the strong humiliating the dignity of the weak, censored on the ideological level, is subconsciously projected as psychologically desirable since the only acceptable position here is considered to be that of strength.

Such was the humiliation, for example, of exploited peoples by colonizers. In Aleksei Surkov's poem "At a Teheran Bazaar," from his book of poems *Peace to the World,* the English are presented in the guise of almost theatrical colonizers modeled from those at the beginning of the century: "Их обуви тяжелый стук тупой / Не первый год привычен слуху здесь. / Они, как броненосцы, над толпой / Несут колонизаторскую спесь. // И если вдруг посмеет человек / Хоть слово им сказать наперекор, / Украшенный насечкой гибкий стек / Взметнется в воздух и погасит спор. // Своей холодной наглостью храним. / Уйдет обидчик цел и невредим. / А полицейский, лютый к бедняку, / Приложит льстиво руку к козырьку" (The dull heavy clatter of their boots is / A familiar sound here, for more than a year. / Like battle-ships, over the crowd / They lord their colonizer's arrogance. // And if out of nowhere someone should dare / To utter one word of defiance to them, / The riding crop, flexible, decorated with notches / Flung up in the air, soon squelches the argument. // Saved by his cold insolence alone / The aggressor escapes without a scratch. / But the policeman, cruel to the pauper, / Unctuously puts his hand to his cap.). This scene of individual humiliations is replaced by a generalizing picture of national humiliations in the poem that concludes the book, "Road to the South," where "psychologism" is replaced by caricature: "Лев Ирана, бедняжка, / Не изрыгает гром. / Здесь он юлит, как дворняжка, / Перед британским львом. // Нефти пьянящий запах / Мил британскому льву. / Мнет он в хозяйских лапах / Пальмы, людей, траву. / Каждый князек в округе / Служит ему, как раб. / Все здесь—рабы и слуги: / Фарс, индус и араб" (The lion of Iran, poor little thing, / Won't dare to spew forth his thunder. / Here he is cringing, like a little cur / In front of the British lion. // The intoxicating scent of oil / Is sweet to the British lion. / In his proprietor's paws he / Squeezes palms, and people, and grass. / Every princeling around him / Serves him like a slave. / Everyone here is a slave or a servant: / The Parsee, Hindu, and Arab). Everything serves the process of "national enslavement" (on the ideological level) and of humiliation (on the psychological level): "Пусть под пятою зверя / Участь страны горька—/ Славят продажные перья / Иго нефтяника. / Пусть у раба рубаха / Съедена потом дотла—/ Благословенье аллаха / Шлет британцу мулла" (Even if the country's lot / Is bitter under the heel of the beast—/ The venal journalists' pens / Glorify the oilman's yoke. / Even if the slave's shirt / Is eaten up with sweat—/ The blessing of Allah / The mullah will send to the Briton). The poem (and the whole collection) concludes with a depiction of complete humiliation: "...Там, где хозяева слабы, / Гости наглы, сильны / В водах Шат-эль-Араба / Крейсеры отражены" (Where the hosts are weak, / The guests are insolent, strong. / The waters of Shatt al-Arab / Reveal the reflections of cruisers). The colonizer-exploiters' impunity and their insolence cry out for revenge. Thus an endless chain of revenge-humiliation is portrayed here. The Americans humiliate the Europeans (and a huge majority of Soviet caricatures are about this).

The experience of the collective bodies is permeated with violence. In these scenes one can easily read the projection of intrinsic arrogance.

This is how the strong are supposed to behave—and how they did behave at this time in Iran, Indochina, or Eastern Europe. The reader sees much experience in these Soviet texts that is *specifically* Soviet; the qualities attributed to the English and Americans were above all a displaced mirror projection of the Soviets' *own* political culture, the product of the Soviet subjects' newfound self-confidence due to the "greatness of the state" being attributed to them. As a result, the image of the Other became much more mimetically valid than the image of Self (of the heroes of *Cavalier of the Golden Star* or *Kuban Cossacks*). The more archaic the aesthetic of these mimetic practices and mechanisms was, the stronger the ideological effect of this transfer became. These practices and mechanisms intensified the deeply rooted conventions due to a strengthening of the link between the real and the symbolic. Since this kind of mimetic literature was exactly what was in demand, the poetry that today is viewed as propaganda was at the time understood by the mass reader to really be poetry—that is, highly integrated text bound by conventions (vocabulary, rhythm, genre, and so forth).

The statements of the "simple Soviet people" made "in defense of peace," as part of a political ritual, belonged to a strictly conventional ideological discourse devoid of any spontaneity. This discourse (as well as the visual representations of the "fight for peace" theme) was internalized and desemanticized. The rituals, writing, and discursive conventions of the "fight for peace" that were finally set in stone in the 1960s–1980s were actually shaped at the end of the 1940s and the beginning of the 1950s. Like the majority of the basic Soviet ideological rituals of the post-Stalinist era, they are the products of late-Stalinist culture, where the "simple Soviet person" began to speak in the voice inculcated in him/her by the "fight for peace" poetry. Acquiring a language from this poetry, the collective bodies mastered it to such a degree that they became capable not only of speaking it, but also writing in it. The ideal Soviet subject that was produced in these texts materialized in creative work. The writing of readers transformed into poets was such a widespread phenomenon that in the early 1950s several publishers even issued anthologies of poetry about peace whose authors were milkmaids and weavers, librarians and truck drivers, schoolchildren and teachers, technicians and soldiers, electricians and railroad conductors, and managers of warehouses and pig farms, all of whom reproduced almost all the stylistic conventions, narrative forms, and techniques of the canonized narratives.[54] The amateurs' "fight for peace" poetry reveals one of the most important functions of professional Soviet poetry: it was a political logopedia occupied with the formation and inculcation of ideological constructs—tropes and idioms that in the aggregate assembled the vocabularies and conventions of Cold War speech practices and codified them. Keeping in mind that this was above all a war of ideologies and political gestures, it would be hard to overestimate the role of these constructs in the postwar standoff.

Thus, the "fight for peace" poetry is really the wartime poetry of the years preceding it (1941–45) but now in "new clothes"—thematized in the new reality of the Cold War. The wartime poetry—with its descriptions of Fascist atrocities, calls for revenge, authorized tragic excess and cherished heroism, pervasive lyricism and mournful nostalgia—though losing its *thematic* relevance when the war ended, preserved the mobilizing potential that was needed, it turned out, in the conditions of the Cold War. Accordingly, it received a second life in a different thematic orchestration. Cold War idioms camouflage the carcass of the earlier wartime literature and simultaneously reveal it explicitly, intensifying this mobilizing potential. But since this poetry is devoid of the real-life feeling that permeated wartime poetry during actual danger, it is frankly derivative, dominated by artificial pathos and forced suggestiveness. It is the poetry of transference: the reflected image of the very collective body whose voice and reflection it is is displaced into the world of the enemy. The oxymoronic nature of wartime propaganda narratives is such that it neutralizes, relativizes, and desemanticizes any long-standing statement. Even in simulating peace and the fight for it, Stalinism, as a form of war, produced the discourse of war. But designing this ideological communication was not enough. It still had to be brought to the people in a form accessible to them.

ENTERTAINING COLD WAR: AN EQUATION WITHOUT AN UNKNOWN

"Weak argument: talk loudly." Winston Churchill's famous marginal note is a classic example of a meta-equation. More precisely, it is a reminder of the basic principle of the equation—tautologies. We will call this the principle of total valency; both halves of any equation strive toward self-repetition. In this respect, an equation is the ideal image of any reflection. Mimesis is tautological, and tautology as a universal phenomenon has its equivalent not only in mathematics but also in art; if in mathematics it takes form in an equation, then its ideal genre equivalent in art is detective fiction. Between detective fiction and the equation lies the riddle (the equation is the rationalization of a riddle, and detective fiction is its dramatization). As it grows into "higher" genres, the riddle preserves its principle: two equal sides with unknowns, in which the sides demonstrate their dissimilarity, while the recipient knows in advance that they are identical. A riddle is a game. The process of solving it essentially boils down to proving the obvious; one knows from the start that the meanings of the two functions given are equal. This transforms the whole process into a sort of intellectual ostensibility.

On Soviet soil, the vicissitudes of the genre memory of detective fiction had their own anamnesis; classic detective fiction had been expelled from the sphere of reading, and a Soviet version had failed to take shape. The 1920s and 1930s battles against "the Pinkerton stuff" and "Mess-Mend trash" led to the death of the genre. Since the problematic aspects of private life (the "juicy parts" of detective fiction) were squeezed out of the sphere of "artistic presentation," the only escape was the arena of pure politics; in the 1930s, the children's "adventure story" genres were under pressure from the "ideological confrontation of two systems," and the detective-fiction plots in "artistic products for adults" featured the figures of saboteurs, spies, and the like. However, this did not contradict the nature of detective fiction, which is an overtly social genre. One of its functions (on one side of the equation) is constant: law. The other function is variable. No matter how the variable changed, it was easy to model the first part of the equation, for detective fiction is, after all, a socially moralizing genre that requires the triumph of the social order (embodied in the law). Deprived of private themes, the detective story turns into a reflection of the drama of the state. In this respect, the history of the Soviet detective story is the embodiment of the political trauma of the Cold War era. There are two circumstances that we should keep in mind here.

The first is that the authors were practically all the same figures (playwrights, prose writers, and poets were also screenwriters), which frees us from the necessity of examining all the different genre manifestations of the political detective story in postwar art and to focus on cinema, which due to its synthetic nature combined "fight for peace" poetry, the "patriotic play," and the "political detective-story novel." We will discuss the following films: Aleksandr Dovzhenko's *Farewell, America* (*Proshchai, Amerika,* 1951; unfinished); Grigorii Aleksandrov's *The Meeting on the Elbe* (*Vstrecha na El'be,* 1949; screenplay by the brothers Leonid and Petr Tur and Lev Sheinin); Mikhail Romm's films *The Russian Question* (*Russkii vopros,* 1948; based on Konstantin Simonov's play) and *The Secret Mission* (*Sekretnaia missiia,* 1950); Abram Room's *Silvery Dust* (*Serebristaia pyl',* 1953; from August Jakobson's script); and Mikhail Kalatozov's *The Conspiracy of the Doomed* (*Zagovor obrechennykh;* from a screenplay by Nikolai Virta). A comparison of the screenplays with the filmed material shows a surprising level of discipline on the part of the directors. The ideological status of the scripts required very precise adherence to the text (in fact, *The Russian Question* and *The Conspiracy of the Doomed* were adaptations of very popular plays, which were at the time being performed in theaters all over the country). At the same time, during the period of the *malokartin'e* (few pictures), directors had no great choice of scripts.[55]

The second circumstance is the dramatic weakening of the purely detective-story plot, under ideological pressure. Vsevolod Vishnevskii called Dovzhenko's script "great literature" and "a great action movie" that "absolutely must be printed in a thick journal."[56] Regarding the "entertainment potential of these 'crime' films," Maiia Turovskaia wrote that "the genre structure of these films is very attenuated: the spy intrigue does less to move the plot than it does to arrange it."[57] The true proof of this "weakening" is the fact that the theme of each of these films can be described in one sentence without regard to the plot or the specific events:

> *Farewell, America* is about how an honest young American woman cannot live in the espionage den that is the American embassy in Moscow, and she severs ties to America to become a Soviet citizen;
> *The Meeting on the Elbe* is about how Americans collaborated with former Nazis in occupied Germany while plundering it;
> *The Russian Question* is about how an honest American journalist refuses to carry out his bosses' orders to write a book about how the Russians want war and loses his job when he writes the truth about the Soviets' love of peace;

Silvery Dust is about radioactive weapons developed in secret U.S. laboratories by American scientists working with former Nazis, preparations for war, experiments done on black Americans, and the "fight for peace" in America;

The Conspiracy of the Doomed is about how Americans organize a conspiracy against Communists within the coalition government in an unspecified East European country, and how the Soviet Union comes to the rescue;

The Secret Mission is about how the American allies conducted separate negotiations with Germany during the war in an attempt to turn back the advance of the Soviet Army into Europe.

But it is just this "plot weakness" that is almost the most interesting thing in these films; it allows us to understand exactly which factors influenced "genre memory" and why the Soviet political detective story turned out one way and not another. Although analyzing the anti-American cinematic products from the late-Stalinist era from a content standpoint yields little—their "content" cannot be read without crossing over into the "artist/regime" relationship—the themes of "traumas" and "unconscious reflection" nonetheless do not allow one to avoid the theme of the "artist/regime" relationship. Turovskaia characterized these anti-American films as "the worst, the most untrue, and the most false thing that there was in ["Zhdanovist" culture], when artists could hardly plead 'misunderstanding' or appeal to 'faith.'"[58] Even in the context of "social-Freudian" analysis, this is debatable. First, these films were no "worse" or more "false" than, let's say, *Kuban Cossacks* or *Cavalier of the Golden Star;* second, they were no more cynical than, for example, *The Fall of Berlin.* The "artistic products" of Socialist Realism cannot be described in such categories, as Turovskaia herself convinces us when she demonstrates the unconscious nature of the displacement in these films of the "image of the enemy" into an "invented America."

Much more convincing is what Vladimir Antropov wrote about Dovzhenko's *Farewell, America:* "One need only accept the director's rules of the game" to wonder whether "this is such an unrecognizable and strange Dovzhenko."[59] Or Sergei Trimbach's words:

Was it only opportunistic considerations that motivated the director? Was that why he made this propaganda piece about nefarious American diplomats from the embassy that fiercely hated the Soviets' country, a flat satire about the representatives of what many now imagine to be the "promised land"? But that is now. In Comrade Stalin's times the Soviet man, even if he was an outstanding director, piously believed that America was a country of social and other horrors, where Negroes were lynched and women raped, where fat-bottomed and fat-lipped millionaires with cigars in their teeth mercilessly ordered poor people around. "A corrupt land. America." This is what Dovzhenko wrote in his own hand.[60]

The entire evolution of Dovzhenko's creative work speaks to how organic this anti-American film, released after half a century, was for him.

It is not only the stylistics of the scripts, but also the global scope of the ideas that unite Dovzhenko's postwar projects. "Global problems are solved in the script, and they can be conveyed only with the temperament of political journalism. Everything will work out for us if we free ourselves from everyday trifles and rise above them," Dovzhenko wrote in his diary about *Farewell, America,*[61] and his working notes on the film indicate that "it will be a broad panorama of our planet's public life circa 1950. . . . Everything must be significant, incidental, and like a testament, all at the same time."[62] But this could be applied to any of Dovzhenko's ideas with the very same logic, most of all to his film *Poem of the Sea.* Again, the director expresses these same assumptions: "I want to call [*Farewell, America*] a film-poem. I took a journalistic theme to express in the language of art. . . . The director absolutely must be drawn into the script. He can stay silent but still express himself through a voiceover text. Elevate the whole of nature to its level and embody everything in the poetry of the age. . . . For a proper portrayal, several techniques of generalization are needed. Where there is no accuracy, there is a line of synthetic generalization."[63] With Dovzhenko, as is well known, everything came out best with "synthetic generalizations." Hence the opposition that later passed directly into *Poem of the Sea.* There is the eternal: the Old Petrovites are the "broad Ukrainian high road," "the ancient Chernigov lands, as far as the human eye can see," "Princess Olga's knoll," the "solitary primordial tree that has rustled through many centuries," the "epic Old Petrovite field," the "race of time and sublime peace," "Sviatoslav's horses," "giant battles among the clouds," and so forth.[64] But the present is transferred to America: when the main character, Anna, returns to her native Pennsylvania, there she finds "nothing that is close to her heart, that made her cross the ocean. She didn't see the farm, or her brother, or her mother's grave. The wind was blowing. The sky grew dark from the dust. The breeze was carried along the plains, lifting up the soil and carrying it from the fields in gray stripes that looked like smoke." Her mother's grave had been destroyed: "The devils leveled everything yesterday," a neighbor says, referring to the machines that were clearing a military airport on the site of the American "Petrovtsy," preparing America for war.

These very same expressions, literally, would be used in *Poem of the Sea* to describe both the old Ukrainian village with its Scythian graves and the threat of turning the land into "dust," not because of America, but due to hot, dry winds. The image of the enemy is replaced: instead of America, the enemy is nature. Dovzhenko still found an object to depict his bursting apocalyptic vision; in *Poem of the Sea,* this was the desert advancing on Ukraine, which justified the flooding of hundreds of Old Petrovtsy. Whole scenes from the unfinished "American project" will make their way into the "sea" project: the child and the monument to his hero father (where the father is a living general, and the monument will pass into the scene with the mother mad with grief), even the child's poem—pure Dovzhenko poetry ("don't let the enemy's curses, flames, and cries for mercy weaken you," "in the threat and rumble and grinding of iron," "I died in a moment of ecstasy"):

> Я наступал тогда, и враг бежал,
> Бежал мой враг передо мною!
> Я счастлив был, хоть и прожил немного,
> И в бронзе я стою. . . .
> На страже поколений.[65]

> I attacked then, and the enemy fled,
> My enemy fled before me!
> I was happy, though I lived but briefly,
> And in bronze I stand. . . .
> Standing guard over the generations.

This doggerel of Dovzhenko's, like a bad translation (and a typical exemplar of Dovzhenko's writing) will go into *Poem of the Sea* word for word. But the main thing is the paranoia that colors all of Dovzhenko's late work, an expression of his "deathly fatigue," if not of a sickness. The scenes of "the meeting of the association of progressive figures of American culture, attended by thousands" and of the May

Day parade in Moscow in *Farewell, America* are full of Dovzhenko's typical hysteria. "Fighters for peace" pontificate from platforms in all anti-American films. But only in Dovzhenko is this so "beautiful" and effusive: "America has turned into a moral torture chamber!"; "We are carried to catastrophe with a speed that America has yet to know!"; "We are participants in the greatest madness that has ever infected humanity"; "We are moving into the history of the mid-twentieth century in spiritual tatters. With police banners over an America that has lost its freedom!"; "The shadow of the atomic bomb has cut off the light! Everyone is under Wall Street's lock and key! Science is stolen! The nation's entire intellect is surrounded by bullets!"; "I'm sitting in prison. . . . Down with the Thomas Commission! Long live freedom! Long live Peace! The hell with war! We want Peace! Peace! Peace!"; "We have sunk into deep mental depression!"[66] The result of this "deep mental depression" was the film *Farewell, America*.

"Improvise, add some phrases to the role. Play me a newspaper, texts. The material now is just like that," Dovzhenko says to the actor who plays the American diplomat-spy Marrow. He goes on to note that "Movement is essential. This is a great thing in film. Movement should not be self-sufficient, movement limited by words."[67] Thus the introduction of motion into a newspaper's words. Dovzhenko as a writer had had enough words, including his own, too many words. Only "movement"—a plot—was lacking for him. And this was created by the masters of intrigue—the Tur brothers and Lev Sheinin, Vyshinskii's assistant, whose writing desk was accommodated squarely in the USSR State Prosecutor's quarters.

The Meeting on the Elbe, which was the number one film in distribution in 1949, is the only one (except for Dovzhenko's unfinished film) where Russians and Americans meet in direct confrontation. Equating Americans with Nazis is not "the only secret of the batch of Cold War films."[68] There are many secrets here, and they are of a special nature; we are in a world of games where, trying to solve a riddle, we are immediately told the solution. The film could have ended after the first frames—a scene of the flight of "barely alive Nazis" from the German city of Altenstadt, occupied by the Soviet Army, to the American zone, aboard the ship *Adolf Hitler*—but then we would not find out why they are fleeing. The spectators know, of course, just as in a bad detective story they know not only who has been killed, but also who the murderer is—only the detective cannot figure this out. But as if that were not enough, here the detective too knows everything. The main intrigue hovers somewhere on the periphery of the action; the mission of the American female journalist/spy and of the Nazi criminal Schrank, who are supposed to steal patents for military optical devices from the Soviet zone, it turns out, was from the very beginning "under close surveillance" by the intellectual Soviet city commandant, Kuz'min. It is utterly unclear why the convoluted plot was necessary—with the journalist, the decoy Nazi claiming to be a resistance fighter, the concealment of the patents in some ruins, or the commandant's "affair" with the journalist and the rose to commemorate this—when the secret flight of the city's mayor and his return to the Soviet zone along with a whole group of progressive engineers required no special efforts and when virtually anybody could enter the American zone rather easily.

These self-evident anecdotal "pinholes" and this negligence suggest that the "espionage intrigue" does not so much "arrange the plot" as it reveals the basic—descriptive—layer of the "internal subject." The detective story *becomes* descriptive. It is so much of an anti-detective situation that the film's actual—ideological—plot bleeds through from beneath the fragments of the reduced plot construction. Nevertheless, the detective plot cannot be detached; we are presented with the classic solved "equation." The Elbe, into which the shreds of the "Allied obligations" fly from the hands of the American general, is a sort of "equals sign" between functions.

One of these functions is Soviet, and the other is American. The Russian attack is a monumental picture of struggle, while the American one shows soldiers with bottles of alcohol. The meeting of the two currents is "the heaviest consequence of war," according to the American general. This general is totally occupied in buying up shares in German industry ("What the hell, we're the winners!"), creating a Social Democratic government tasked with undermining the influence of the Communists, and spying and working with the Nazi secret service, while the Soviet commandant frees the political prisoners first thing. The Americans plunder Germany, whereas the Soviet general proclaims, "Now we need the key to the soul of the German people." In keeping with this, the Soviet commandant reads Heine's verse and restores a monument to him, while the still broken monument to Kaiser Wilhelm in the American zone serves as a visual refrain and reminder.

The film shows a world already separated. In the Soviet zone, people are engaged in the education of children, as "this is Germany's future." In the American zone, they are busy plundering the country. The mayor is "an honest German" who by the end of the film has evolved from "partylessness" to a realization of the Russians' rectitude; here, handing over the briefcase containing the ill-gotten patents to the Soviet commandant, he tells the latter: "Two worlds have met on the Elbe, on the two banks. Germany must make a choice. I remain on the bank where a new, democratic, and united Germany is being born." As to the American zone, he sees it in a stunned apocalyptic vision, with night clubs, brothels, prostitutes, and lines for bread where the unfortunate Germans "exchange German culture for stewed pork, beans, and cigarettes." The theme of cultural opposition is central. Of course, the American general and, later, a senator speak about the beginning of a new war against communism; of course, the problem of producing a new weapon is actively discussed; of course, the spectator is told that the Marshall Plan is a plan to prepare for aggression against Russia. But the main thing is the cultural incompatibility of the two countries.

The United States and the USSR are discussed. "We love America," the Soviet commandant declares, "a country of brave and honest people. The country of Jack London, Mark Twain, Whitman, Edison, and Roosevelt. We love and respect the people of America." But this passage should not be viewed in the traditional comparison of "the two Americas" but from the perspective of Europe. Cold War films are not anti-bourgeois but specifically anti-American. The national paradigm developed during wartime for portraying an enemy operates infallibly in postwar culture. References to class here are actually only an arrangement for the base plot. Europe is simply not taken into account by Commandant Kuz'min. He reads Heine aloud but immediately declares to the German mayor that in comparison with the centuries-old Russian culture, all of Germany is worth nothing. "If we took all of your Germany away, down to the last lantern, that wouldn't avenge even a tenth of the damage that Germany has wreaked on my motherland." Nonetheless, the Soviet mayor has no thought of actually taking anything out of Germany, while the Americans are busy doing nothing but this.

The plot of *The Meeting on the Elbe* is thus the non-meeting of two worlds. This equation with a not-equals sign ($\neq$) is a "mathematical record" of the condition of the postwar world. The end of the film has a close-up of the drawbridges over the Elbe, and over this the final words of the Soviet commandant are heard: "Farewell. We met you as allies, lived as neighbors, and we are parting as friends. Do everything to prevent us meeting as enemies in the future. . . . Remember, the friendship of the peoples of America and Russia is the most important issue facing humanity now."

Here, however, we are in the grip of mathematics, on which it is difficult to impose our own logic. The main figure to express this logic is the journalist, who is like a frontier guard, standing on the border between the two parts of the equation. Convertibility makes the journalist almost a symbolic figure; the American journalists in *The Meeting on the Elbe* and *The Conspiracy of the Doomed* are spies, but the one in *The Russian Question,* on the contrary, is the main positive hero. The journalist is also a self-image; Soviet directors and writers, of course, did not know a real America. The majority of them (primarily the writers, of course) had recently been war correspondents, and therefore they depicted (like Simonov, for example) the world they knew. But the journalist's job there was to possess real information and to distill it into propagandistic newspaper slop, the true domain of cynicism. This cynicism makes journalists more akin to politicians, and their place is alongside politicians. The journalist is a politician and, if necessary, a scout and/or spy, and this is why these films have so many of them. Thus it is that the "batch" of Soviet anti-American films begins (chronologically) with *The Russian Question,* a film based on a play about a journalist.

Here we should return to the structure of the equation; no matter what sign stands between the two functions (equals or, as in this case, not-equals), the functions are equivalent. Therefore the idea that in Cold War films the image of the enemy was shifted to America, since Soviet reality (with plots, political murders, provocations, terror, demagogy, and deceit) could not be described in Soviet "forms of life itself," is just as correct as its opposite: everything shown in these films is just as false as it is true. Of course, when an American newspaper prints a report that Russian aircraft have appeared over Eritrea in 1948, this provokes, to put it mildly, mistrust. Journalists themselves know that it is a cheat. But it is not a bigger lie, after all, than the statement that the only thing Soviet commandants in the occupied zone were doing was teaching German children in schools and reading Heine aloud.

The world of Soviet anti-American films depicts the American reality of the McCarthy era so exaggeratedly that the critical mass of the fantasy substantially outweighs this reality. American anti-Soviet films such as *The Iron Curtain, My Son John, I Was a Communist for the FBI,* and others portrayed Soviet reality the same way. However, it is true that this was one of the most gloomy periods in twentieth-century American history. There was no change in American reality just because Soviet authors "displaced their own 'moral climate' into an invented America."[69] In discussing a "social-Freudian complex of native [Soviet] film" and a "degree of terrifying authenticity," and in reading the anti-American as the Soviet inverted,[70] one must remember that the exposure of displaced Soviet complexes in these films changes little; the American press did in fact lie, American intelligence agencies organized conspiracies, the United States developed weapons of mass destruction, and democratic freedoms were curtailed in America at the time. However, on the *Soviet* screen all of these essentially true facts turned into lies because the Soviet Union did all of these things on a significantly greater scale. Although the values of both functions were equal, a corrective to the focus is required. The spectator is always shown only half of the equation, but the propagandist text nevertheless can be deciphered, since the other half is easy to construct according to the principle of mirror reflection. Consideration of the "mirror surface" reveals the goals, structure, and functions of propagandistic discourse and turns the process of reading into the process of detecting meaning where a tautological emptiness seems to gape.

Let us look from this viewpoint at *The Russian Question,* in which, as the newspaper magnate Macpherson says, "There can be no middle." This "middle"—journalist Smith's naïve attempts to "go along the edge," to get away with "half-truths," and to avoid a direct answer to the question of whether the Russians want war—was, in fact, an attempt to eliminate the mirror since the truth is much more complex than an unequivocal "yes" or "no." However, this is not clear to anybody in the film's perspective. Most important, it should also not be clear to the spectator, who has been driven by a binary logic into the impasse of "the truth/falsehood about Soviet Russia." Moreover, the issue of how truthful the picture of America is should not arise. This, we repeat, is irrelevant within the framework of the equation.

At the center of film is the editorial "kitchen" (or laundry!) in one of the largest New York newspapers. This picture is drawn "densely"; we are presented an anthill-like space in which "the whole world's dirty laundry is shaken up" and the informational slops for the American philistine are "cooked up" as required by "the masters of Wall Street." Everything, from the police chronicle ("the corpse of a girl on a road-way, guts wound around a column, and brains on the window of a drug-store") to international information (Russian journalists have brought money for striking coal miners; Russians share everything, from bikes to wives), is permeated by sensationalism and falsehood.

But the main thing is the cynicism with which the play itself was writ-ten. When John Steinbeck visited Moscow in August 1947, he made special mention of *The Russian Question,* declaring that "Simonov has manifested the most complete ignorance and nonsense in his inferences about what the life of the press is like, its techniques, and its people. He in fact knows nothing about it and has literally accused writers and journalists of selling their souls for money. The play is so laugh-able that in the United States they have started talking about staging it as a comedy on the theme of how Simonov has slandered America."[71] As if anticipating the problem, the characters talk about truth and ly-ing more than anything else. The journalists themselves talk. Nobody believes in what he or she does, and everyone knows everyone else is lying ("Half of the Americans think the complete opposite of what we write anyway"); everyone is ashamed ("What, these Russians are still good guys? . . . That's rotten of them! If they were worse, it wouldn't be so shameful"); everyone talks about his or her own painful conscience and tries to find it in each other. Some drink their misery away ("The bank of good hopes has burned down"); others give in, and yet others just work for the money. Smith's words hover above all this hopeless-ness: "It is impossible to be honest and happy at the same time."

The argument about truth and falsehood had its source in twentieth-century Russian literature, in the play by Gorky, the founder of Social-ist Realism, *The Lower Depths (Na dne).* If we subtract the character Luka and the appeal to Christianity from this play, we get *The Russian Question.* Among the inhabitants of the "fleabag" on Fifth Avenue are the same hopeless drunks (almost a third of the film is set in the Press

Bar, where the characters have their "Russian conversations" while getting drunk on whisky), the same cynics, the same exploiters, and the
same self-deceivers. The same angry monologues in defense of man are
heard here. The lesson of the classics is taken into account, however;
here these monologues are pronounced not by the drunken Satin but by
Smith, who rises in esteem before our very eyes. He grows from an apolitical but honest journalist, who had spent the war with "Russian guys
in trenches near Gzhatsk" and had written a book about the battle at
Stalingrad, into a fighter. By the end of the film he repeats things like, "I
have written the truth," "I shall not become a rascal," and "I've become
ashamed for us all. I have remembered that I am a human being." And
however much he is told that resistance is useless ("We need war, and
a bad Russia is necessary for war"), the hero will not relent. We might
think that we have a romantic hero, but it appears that truth is the
only way out, the only means of self-preservation (the fate of Smith's
journalist friend Murphy, who commits suicide after declaring on a live
broadcast, "I'm leaving your gang!," is the alternative).

As always, the rhetoric accrues toward the end of the film. On behalf
of "all the honest people of America," journalist Smith makes an angry
speech at a meeting of peace supporters:

> I have written an honest book about Russia. For the forty-seventh time
> I'm telling you its content because in our country, the country of free-
> dom of the press, there is no publishing house that would dare to print
> it. For having written this book I was fired and thrown out on the street.
> For traveling around the country and telling its content, in our coun-
> try, the country of free speech, I am summoned for questioning by the
> Commission for the Investigation of Anti-American Activity. But this
> too will not silence me! For a long time I naïvely thought that there
> was one America. But there are two. And if there is no place for me in
> the America of Macpherson and Hearst, then I will find myself a place
> in the America of Lincoln and Roosevelt. America is not Wall Street,
> not a hundred billionaires, two hundred newspaper kings, and a thou-
> sand venal journalists. America is the people; it's us! They tell us that
> America's enemies are beyond the ocean, in the Soviet Union. It's a lie!
> The enemies of America are here. Four blocks from here, on Wall Street.
> They are here, four hundred kilometers from here, in Washington, in the
> war ministry. The enemies of America are those who say that Russia is
> threatening us with war. Nobody is threatening us with war. It's a lie!
> It's them, the enemies of America, who are pushing us to war. They say

that we Americans are a strong nation. Yes, we Americans are a strong nation. Strong enough to wring the necks of our own warmongers.

The key words in this text are "[non-]freedom," "lie[s]," "enemies." What we witness, of course, is a Soviet character, which is given away by more than simply the habit of measuring the distance from New York to Washington in kilometers instead of miles. The schism of America is the basic message that encircles Romm's film. It begins with a montage of documentary footage in the following order: the Statue of Liberty, Manhattan from above, street-level views of Harlem, the distribution of soup to the unemployed, a luxurious banquet, grain dumped into the water, milk pouring into a river, the breakup of a demonstration, the work of printing presses, the packing of newspapers, the countrywide dispatch of trains carrying newspapers, people reading newspapers, black women washing linen, the preparation of food in Harlem right out on a roadway, the Empire State Building from bottom to top, a cancan in a cabaret, a manicure salon for dogs, and the text "America, 1946."

This is an example of a false equation; Romm's image of "New York, city of contrasts" creates a situation where an equation is within one of the functions (still with the not-equals sign, $\neq$), whereas the Soviet side is presented not only through Smith's manifestos, but also by his very brief (and hence specially emphasized) mentions of what he saw in the USSR. When our hero dares to write the truth about whether the Russians want a war, these images come to him, in the following order: Red Square, the Moscow underground, the turbines of the Dniepr Hydroelectric Station, a machine-building factory, collective-farm fields, and children sitting at school desks. This documentary footage of peaceful labor is contrasted to the montage of American reality. It is essential to make the right move in order to solve this rebus; we place the two different Americas in brackets and obtain one function; the Soviet pictures are another function. Between them lies full convertibility; we need only tag together the pictures of everyday postwar life in the USSR (poverty in communal apartments, famine in villages, bread lines with ration cards, and so forth) for the mirrored quality to appear. In this case, the second picture (function) is "equal" to itself. What Simonov/Romm show differs very little from the "untruths" of Macpherson and Hearst. It is neither the truth nor a lie but rather full valency.

Another example of this political "chemistry" is presented in *Silvery Dust*. An invention of Professor Samuel Steel, a radioactive poison that breaks down several days after being sprayed and destroys all life, allows for a "quiet occupation" of the requisite territory: no destruction, no protests, no disinfection, no decontamination, a minimum of expense—and a real detective-story plot.

The Pentagon wants to buy Steel's discovery. The representative of the army, General Mac Kennedy, associated with a certain Eastern Trust, is interested in having the order transferred to his bosses on Wall Street, whereas the project had been financed by the Southern Trust, headed by Anthony Bruce. The process of tender begins. Trying to delay the deal, the general insists on conducting "control experiments" on human subjects. But there is no "human material" at hand, and the delivery of "a shipment of Korean or Chinese prisoners of war" takes a long time. Bruce decides to use black people on death row for his experiments, but none are available at the moment. Then, along with the sheriff, a judge, and the state governor, he concocts a plot against six black people arrested during a peace activists' meeting; they are charged with the attempted rape of a white woman. A former Nazi colonel working for Steel gets involved in the plot when General Kennedy orders him to steal the production formula for the poison, a silvery-gray dust. This conspirator incites Steel's son to steal his father's keys, but the attempted robbery ends pitiably; Steel's son is exposed to radiation and dies. Steel himself, it turns out, had been a poisoner; he had poisoned his teacher and married his daughter, thus inheriting the laboratory. Blackmail is ineffective, however, and Steel dies when the general and the gangsters helping him try to force the secrets out of him. At the end, organized fighters for peace first stop the Ku Klux Klansmen who wanted to lynch the unfortunate prisoners, and then they rescue the prisoners themselves, who were already shut up in Steel's chambers of horror.

This is the terrifying story, which is matched by appropriate settings: catacombs, bunkers, lab gowns, flickering lamps, and so forth. It is first of all a detective story; the ideological debate that develops during the course of the action serves only as a setting for the intrigue. This arrangement is crucial; the endless monologues provide the detective story with meaning. The monologues are, of course, delivered by fighters for peace—Steel's adopted son and daughter, a doctor, a simple worker, and the blacks who collect signatures for protests and declarations supporting peace. In a dinner-table conversation with his parents, Steel's son bursts out in tirades such as this: "My motherland has a hundred forty million Americans. And this America I love. But you . . . we'll wring your necks before you start your predatory war . . . and put straitjackets on you and your friends!"

The plot is advanced by family conflict (in *The Meeting on the Elbe, The Conspiracy of the Doomed,* and *Silvery Dust,* young people rebel against their parents in surface conflicts that suggest the future is in good hands) and by the inevitable epiphany of an honest but apolitical scientist. "Talking loud" near the ending of these films is typical; the theme of confrontation is endless. The rhetoric, which is the result of the inability to resort to the traditional means of an actual war (in the context, one might say "hot war"), is inflamed only by "incendiaries of war" and (especially) by "peace advocates." The final scene of *Silvery Dust* is in the Steel house, turned upside down with a corpse in an armchair, with the sordid figures (as in a Kukryniksy caricature) of the ex-Nazi, the American general, and the millionaire Bruce retreating before the powerful advance of the fighters for peace. "Look at the faces of these two-legged jackals," the main protagonist, O'Connell, says to his companions-in-arms, the fighters for peace, and then, to the "defendants," "One day you'll end up on the gallows by the people's tribunal!"

Scenes like the finale in *Silvery Dust* are, of course, no longer cinematic but theatrical; the sensation of a game never abates, and words are stifling (let us recall that Dovzhenko said, "Movement is limited by words"). This explains the choice of stage actors for the roles in these films. One can of course conjecture that *Silvery Dust* was an expression of the "possibility of speaking in plain terms about experiments on humans, of provoking disorder and arrests, of blackmailing each other" to depict "totalitarian regimes."[72] But it was hardly an expression of "secret freedom," and, what is more, these things actually happened (although without caricatured displacement); blacks in America were in fact lynched, weapons were developed, patents were stolen, and conglomerates fought over military contracts.

It is a different matter that a detective story without a secret does not amount to much. But the secret in a political detective story is a conspiracy, even if it is *The Conspiracy of the Doomed.* The answer to the "riddle" is embedded in the very title of Kalatozov's film: any "conspiracy" is doomed since the pure tautology of the events arises from the words that mark the same political realities in different ways. This film, which, according to Turovskaia's on-point definition, is "a huge film-slip-of-the-tongue, Freudian style" really uncovers the internal mechanics of state coups from coalition governments to one-party systems, a number of which took place in the countries of Eastern Europe at the end of the 1940s.[73] The script of revolutions remained the same in the Soviet bloc countries and later (Hungary in 1956, Czechoslovakia in 1968, and so forth). For the "masses of the people" to be reconciled to the Communists, there had to be conspiracies, and dissolutions of parliaments, and manufactured famine, and instigation, and intimidation, and dictatorships, and the propaganda activities of the Soviet intelligence agencies, and "betrayal of national interests." And although it does not follow from this that the countries of Western Europe, especially those where the Communists' influence was strong, accepted the Marshall Plan without serious political turmoil, nor that the American embassies in these countries were engaged exclusively in "cultural links among the nations," the actions of the Soviet occupation powers were exponentially more violent.

Virta's play, upon which Kalatozov's film was based, was not coincidentally called *In One Country* when it left the main thing unsaid: where is the main character in this spectacle—that is, the occupation troops? From the events that unfold right after the war in some sort of Romano-Hungaro-Czechoslovakia (other variants might be suggested) it is quite impossible to understand in whose "occupation zone" this imaginary country is located. Judging by the fact that the Americans operate covertly in it, through diplomat-spies, it is not their zone. But Moscow, too, turns out to be somewhere far away (only at the end of the film do the Communists finally manage to send a delegation to Stalin). It follows that there were no occupation troops in postwar Europe and that the countries of Europe developed in conditions of complete independence. In a film about a state coup (!) there is not a single soldier (if we discount the peripheral local conspirator-general).

Let us assume that the people themselves in fact decide their destiny. In this scenario, the people are shown as crowds walking between the governmental cars with slogans such as "Long live Stalin!," "The Marshall Plan is our death!," and "We do not want to wear an American collar!" and amicably displaying their solidarity with the Communists. Then another unknown function appears: why, with such obvious support from the electorate, do the Communists have a minority in parliament, and why is the representative power in the hands of some sort of "espionage rabble"? (All the political leaders of the country, except the Communists, of course, find themselves hired and rehired by the Nazis, the Americans, and the Vatican so that it is quite impossible to decide who is whose agent.) The impression is created that this surprising country exists, as it were, in two "zones" simultaneously.

On the one hand are the conspirators, whose center is the American Embassy. The ambassador himself, "the boss of this whole gang of murderers and provocateurs,"[74] promises power to each of the rival parties. Meanwhile, the thing most desired by all the representatives of this "gang of traitors" (for some reason comprising two-thirds of the parliament) is American intervention. American weapons, which had arrived in the "peace trains" instead of bread, are stored right in the church for conspirators (the trains are of course festooned with American cigarette advertisements and the Stars and Stripes, while a jazz band travels on the roof). Clearly, from now on no protection of national interests can be expected. The conspirators are selling "our freedom and blood for lentil soup," to quote the words of the main heroine, Communist Hanna Lichta.

On the other hand, Communists, who everywhere are surrounded by portraits of Stalin, advocate calling on the Soviet Union for help (the Americans organized the export—to Yugoslavia, of course—of all bread on the eve of the parliamentary vote on the Marshall Plan), arguing that "Stalin is the friend of the peasant. He is the friend of the people. More than once he has helped us, and he will help us again." They quote Lenin and Stalin, exclusively, from a podium in parliament. The debates go something like this: "We must accept the Marshall Plan. The Americans are giving us dollars! Dollars!" Hanna Lichta, the "people's conscience," replies: "Lenin said, 'In every dollar is a clod of mud, in every dollar are traces of blood,'" or "Look for your happiness in the atomic bomb!" or "The Social Democrats are a party of traitors! . . . Munich is your business; Hitler, your business; and the new war is also your business!" or "We are for peace, whose bringer is the Soviet Union" or "Wall Street is panicked by crisis and revolution. . . . The Marshall Plan is a death plan!" The Communists (along with the people, of course) swear loyalty to the Soviet Union (the film opens with an oath at a monument to Soviet soldiers—"The flame of friendship between our peoples will never go out!"—and ends in a national oath: "Teacher and friend! . . . We swear to Stalin and the Soviet people to protect the freedom and independence of our country! We swear to fight for peace and to protect our friendship with the great Soviet Union and the countries of people's democracy!"). Why does the leader of another state need to swear to "protect the freedom and independence of our country"? This is also from the realm of Freudian slips.

But when the elements in a valence equation are cut off (along with the heads of the opposition), the equation is reduced to its denominator: the oath to Stalin. It turns out that the whole "intrigue" has no meaning; the conspiracy was inspired, the conspirators are "hit," the masks are torn away, and the people have been taught a lesson. The situation is not the usual one in a detective story; it is as if the detective himself has committed the crime and then investigates it himself. After all these genre perversions, *The Secret Mission* comes across as almost a pure detective story—an espionage film—with real secret agents, secrets, chases, murders around the corner, recruitment, betrayals, snooping, stolen secret-service lists, hidden microphones and microfilms, horrible criminals, and good Soviet mamas named Masha who take their "secret mission" into "the beast's den." In brief, there are all the cherished props of the detective genre, which only thinly disguise the cumbersome propagandistic design of the film. It was no accident that *The Secret Mission* and *The Conspiracy of the Doomed* were the leading films distributed in 1950.

"From the viewpoint of the unwritten laws of the 'detective story' genre, the absence of an extraordinary and singular specific feat of the heroine-spy would seem to bespeak the weakness of the plot"—but this, Soviet critics argued, was a superficial view of the matter. But the "matter" is that the film essentially lacks any invention, any fiction: "The main story that the film tells is not a fantasy. The story of the unprecedented treachery of the diplomats of Anglo-American imperialism, who during the war conspired with Hitler's headquarters behind the backs of their ally, is actual history, well known today throughout the world."[75]

Romm achieves this "actual history" by introducing documentary footage into the film that shows the "victorious Soviet offensive." To the three tasks of the "secret missionaries" (the American senator and the representative of the American intelligence)—(1) to persuade the Germans to make a "completely confidential capitulation to the West," (2) to buy up the patents owned by German industry, and (3) to gain possession of the Nazi intelligence in the Balkans—Romm opposes his own tasks to convince the spectator that (1) Anglo-Americans played virtually no part in the war, (2) Americans are tradespeople who were worried only about profit and wanting to plunder the enemy, and (3) the Americans are the direct successors of the Nazis.

Since the plot construction of a detective story boils down to the task of "tearing off the mask," the figure of the spy is not only completely organic, but also functionally irreplaceable.

All the films discussed here have a lot to say about the participation of the Americans in the war. In *The Meeting on the Elbe* the American soldiers meet the Soviet Army with the slogan "Americans will not forget the feats of the Russians," as though they were meeting not allies but rather the liberators of the United States. Romm unfurls a metaphor: the Germans in fact capitulated in the West, and this explains the progress of the Anglo-American armies. "The garrisons will surrender," Himmler promises the senator, "even if three bicyclists ride into the city, and it makes no difference if they're drunk or unarmed." Immediately, scenes picture the Germans surrendering cities to the Anglo-Americans, welcoming them with bread and salt (a confused German general reports that a white flag had flown in one of the garrisons for two days, whereas the Americans had not even shown any sign of advancing on it). And right afterward the eastern front is shown, with panoramic views of the "real battles."

The pervasive argument made by all these Cold War films—that America equals imperialism—is also developed by Romm. The first thing the American senator says to his German partners in the negotiations is, "I am a merchant, a businessman." Then he immediately discloses to them the completely confidential date of the Soviet attack, communicated by Stalin to Churchill in a personal message. The authors force the aged senator to make his way through the front line to London after getting a call from "the bosses from Wall Street," to meet with German industrial magnates in Krupp's house, and, finally, to agree that the Americans will bomb the eastern part of Germany (which will become the Soviet zone) whenever possible and protect industrial installations in the western zone (never mind that the West was where industry was concentrated and that these regions had already suffered from the monstrous bombings of the Allied air forces).

No doubts should remain, either, about the Americans inheriting everything from the Nazis, even the intelligence agencies, which, as Bormann tells his American visitor, "you will soon need for the fight against democracy and the Bolsheviks." But need we say that everything discussed at the top-secret meeting at Krupp's house was immediately leaked in Moscow? Lists of Nazi agents in the Balkans were copied and transferred to Moscow the same evening. All of this was thanks to the chauffeur, Martha (who was also the Soviet spy, Masha, as well as Romm's wife, actress Elena Kuz'mina).

Still, one cannot but agree with the critic who, writing about *The Secret Mission* in 1950, stated that the Soviet spectator finds it "oppressive to find oneself so close, for so long, to the representatives of a world of evil, to be a witness to the conflicts, intrigues, and vile acts committed by Hitler's people and the Americans."[76]

A favorite device of the detective story is the introductory "Meanwhile. . . ." And there it is: on that very day in April 1945 when the Soviet spy died after fulfilling her "secret mission," the Soviet and American forces closed in from both sides to a city called Altenstadt. They met on the River Elbe. But we have seen this already, and the circle is complete. Thus is the postwar world divided.

But having made a correction to the mechanism of the mirror reflection of the functions in the equation, we will understand that Cold War films do paradoxically restore the equality of the divided parts of the world. This dramatized ideology did not become the past but rather formatted the Soviet worldview for the decades ahead. All these "meetings," "farewells," "missions," "plots," and "questions" have not ceased to cause pain. They have simply lost their verbality; the action contained in them has turned into a "verbal adjective," into "silvery dust." But the dust will not settle after a few days, as in the laboratory of Professor Steel; the geopolitical model of the world contained in these films not only did not recede into the past, but seven decades later still dominates the minds of millions of people in post-Soviet Russia.[77] The reasons for the success of this "batch of Cold War films" lay in that they bore "a feeling of profound satisfaction"—they alleviated the trauma of a new world order. It was precisely these earliest postwar years that saw the formation of the new picture of the world that was to be the defining one for the decades to come; in these years, the new Soviet identity took shape—the image of a superpower that till this very day, when neither that world nor that country exists any more, still suffers its former pain.

*

Thus, the flicker of the *logos* of Stalinist *Realideologie* was caused by the status limitations of its founder and the gap between ideology and politics. These limitations were overcome with the help of Soviet literature and art. We have seen how this disintegrating discourse found integrity in Soviet war journalism, the task of which was to reduce an image of the world that was split between ideology and politics to a single denominator for the purposes of social mobilization. However, this image was merely a populist version of official ideology, and it distorted the real picture of confrontation even more. The duality was assimilated by the mass consumer, a duality that molded the ideological and political dual world, when the main ideological postulates were recoded (nationalism, for example, was called internationalism) and changed the perception of political realia. Nonetheless, both images— the ideological and the topical-political—were officially sanctioned. Their interaction at the level of the masses' perception constituted the basic drama of propagandistic Cold War journalism. The task of art in this situation boiled down to the amplification and adaptation of official discourse but even more so to its thematization. This thematization was invoked to conceal the profoundly traumatic nature of Cold War discourse. This last is distinctly visible in postwar Soviet poetry. Finally, in film a synthesis of the split images—of the self and the Other—takes place.

Cold War art—propagandistic and based on crude lies—turned out to be the most adequate reflection of the duality of political aspirations and ideological imperatives, an exact copy of mass traumas. The falseness of this art by no means contradicts its veracity. Similar to how *Kuban Cossacks* was a reflection of the ideological fantasies of everyday Soviet existence, the late-Stalinist culture of the Cold War reflected the Other, which was in fact the most adequate image of the Self. In this sense, this culture was entirely mimetic. The constant process of modeling the Self through the image of the Other that was realized in it allowed not only the "materialization" (verbally, visually, musically, and so forth) of the fantasies of one's own phantom greatness and peaceableness, but also the mixing of the trauma of the constant war that raged in Russia for essentially half a century, from 1905 to 1956—three revolutions, World War I and the civil war, widespread famine, collectivization, industrialization, cultural revolution, the Great Terror, World War II, the postwar "eight years of gloom." Ending in its acute phase, this war shaped whole generations of people who were, as Mandel'shtam said, cast out of their biographies like billiard balls thrown out of the pockets. Soviet society, which consisted for the most part of semi-urbanized peasants; the Soviet economy, which never adapted to modernization; and the Soviet state, which did not simply reproduce but indeed magnified the basic flaws of the Russian Middle Ages—all of this could not disappear in the course of the incidental, short-term, and superficial perestroika. This is why, after a short pause, Russia returned with such irrevocable readiness to the same old fantasies of imperial grandeur and phantom pains, reproducing with such inevitability the same old political culture and familiar rhetoric. The country created by Stalin did not escape this past, which has remained as its present. Putin's Russia returned (with some modifications, of course) in a natural fashion to late—but still not bygone—Stalinism.

Notes

INTRODUCTION

1. Lifshits, *Chto takoe klassika?*, 33; emphasis in original.

2. D. Samoilov, *Pamiatnye zapiski*, 161.

3. From Iurii Trifonov's documentary novel, *Otblesk kostra* (The campfire glow, 1965).

4. The title of one of the first books about Soviet literature to be published after Stalin's death, *Rays of Light*, is telling (see Zhabinskii, *Prosvety*).

5. D. Samoilov, *Pamiatnye zapiski*, 164.

6. Turovskaia, "30–40-e," 73.

7. See Silina, *Vneshnepoliticheskaia propaganda v SSSR v 1945–1985 gg.*; Fateev, *Obraz vraga v sovetskoi propagande 1945–1954 gg.*

8. Stalinism (and late Stalinism in particular) should be seen as a point of departure for the new (post-Stalin) era. It is treated as such in Lovell, *The Shadow of War*; Jones, *Myth, Memory, Trauma*; Cohn, *The High Title of Communist*; and other works.

9. Danilov and Pyzhikov, *Rozhdenie sverkhderzhavy*, 120–21.

10. See Clark, *Moscow, the Fourth Rome*; David-Fox, *Showcasing the Great Experiment*.

11. Ryklin, *Prostranstva likovaniia*, 98.

12. Danilov and Pyzhikov, *Rozhdenie sverkhderzhavy*, 185.

13. Popov, *Rossiiskaia derevnia posle voiny*; Zubkova et al., *Sovetskaia zhizn', 1945–1953*.

14. Zima, *Golod v SSSR 1946–1947 godov*; Kostyrchenko, *Stalin protiv "kosmopolitov"*; Brent and Naumov, *Stalin's Last Crime*.

15. Danilov and Pyzhikov, *Rozhdenie sverkhderzhavy*; Gorlizki and Khlevniuk, *Cold Peace*.

16. Adibekov, *Kominform i poslevoennaia Evropa, 1947–1956 gg.*; Narinskii et al., *Kholodnaia voina*; Nezhinskii, *Sovetskaia vneshniaia politika v gody*

"kholodnoi voiny" 1945–1985; Lel'chuk and Pivovar, *SSSR i kholodnaia voina;* Gaiduk, *Stalin i kholodnaia voina;* Gaiduk and Egorova, *Stalinskoe desiatiletie kholodnoi voiny;* Danilov and Pyzhikov, *Rozhdenie sverkhderzhavy;* Gorlizki and Khlevniuk, *Cold Peace;* Zubok, *Inside the Kremlin's Cold War;* Fitzpatrick, *On Stalin's Team.*

17. Afanas'ev, *Sovetskoe obshchestvo,* vol. 2; N. S. Simonov, *Voenno-promyshlennyi kompleks SSSR v 1920–1950-e gody;* Zubkova, *Poslevoennoe sovetskoe obshchestvo;* Filtzer, *Soviet Workers and Late Stalinism;* Fürst, *Late Stalinist Russia;* Leibovich, *V gorode M;* Volynchik, *Sovetskoe gosudarstvo i obshchestvo v period pozdnego stalinizma, 1945–1953 gg.*

18. For an analysis of this crisis, see David-Fox, *Crossing Borders,* 1–47.

19. Lahusen, *How Life Writes the Book;* Gromova, *Raspad.*

20. Vlasova, *1948 god v sovetskoi muzyke;* Ilizarov, *Pochetnyi akademik Stalin i akademik Marr;* Krementsov, *V poiskakh lekarstva protiv raka.*

21. Tomoff, *Creative Union;* Frolova-Walker, *Stalin's Music Prize.*

22. Dunham, *In Stalin's Time;* Iankovskaia, *Iskusstvo, den'gi i politika;* Pollock, *Stalin and the Soviet Science Wars;* Tikhonov, *Ideologicheskie kampanii "pozdnego stalinizma" i sovetskaia istoricheskaia nauka.*

23. D. Samoilov, *Pamiatnye zapiski,* 165.

24. See Burke, *What Is Cultural History?,* 120–43.

25. Bauman, *Liquid Modernity.*

26. See Eagleton, *The Ideology of the Aesthetic.*

27. Ryklin, *Iskusstvo kak prepiatstvie,* 71.

28. See, for example, Schnapp's *Staging Fascism.*

29. See Mosse, *The Nationalization of the Masses;* Michaud, *The Cult of Art in Nazi Germany;* Gentile, *The Sacralization of Politics in Fascist Italy;* Falasca-Zamponi, *Fascist Spectacle;* Ben-Ghiat, *Fascist Modernities.*

30. Jameson, *The Political Unconscious,* 35.

31. Eagleton, *Ideology,* 5–6. Emphasis in original.

32. Brandenberger, *Propaganda State in Crisis,* 6.

33. Ankersmit, *Aesthetic Politics.* Citations of this work in the following discussion are indicated by page numbers in parentheses. All emphases are in the original.

34. *Pervyi vsesoiuznyi s"ezd sovetskikh pisatelei,* 4, 5.

35. Gudkov and Dubin, "Ideologiia besstrukturnosti," 219.

36. Stalin, *Sochineniia,* 3 [XVI: 1946–1953]:139–40.

CHAPTER I. VICTORY OVER THE REVOLUTION

1. See Corney, *Telling October.*

2. See Brandenberger, *National Bolshevism.*

3. Overy, *Russia's War,* 298.

4. Stalin, *Sochineniia,* 16:7.

5. Ibid.

6. Ibid., 16:11, 12.

7. See Tumarkin, *The Living and the Dead;* Palmer, "How Memory Was Made"; Brunstedt, "Bureaucratizing the Glorious Past."

8. See Vizulis, *The Molotov-Ribbentrop Pact of 1939;* Paul, *Katyn;* Maresch, *Katyn 1940;* Etkind et al., *Remembering Katyn.*

9. See Jones, *Myth, Memory, Trauma.*

10. Unless otherwise noted, all translations are by Jesse Savage.

11. *Nazdar* is Czech for "hello" or "hi."

12. Quoted in *Literaturnaia gazeta,* March 8, 1947.

13. Tiupa, *Khudozhestvennost' literaturnogo proizvedeniia,* 101. Emphasis in original.

14. Bakhtin, *Problemy poetiki Dostoevskogo,* 79. Emphasis in original.

15. Tiupa, *Khudozhestvennost' literaturnogo proizvedeniia,* 125.

16. Borev, *O tragicheskom,* 287.

17. Ibid., 291.

18. Ibid., 387.

19. See Dobrenko, "Grammatika boia—iazyk batarei," in Dobrenko, *Metafora vlasti,* 290–317.

20. Kukulin, "Regulirovanie boli," 621–22.

21. Ibid., 625.

22. See Barskova, *Besieged Leningrad;* Kirschenbaum, *The Legacy of the Siege of Leningrad.*

23. Vishnevskii, *Sobranie sochinenii,* 4:185.

24. Kukulin, "Regulirovanie boli," 629.

25. Paperno, *Stories of the Soviet Experience,* 23.

26. See Hodgson, *Voicing the Soviet Experience.*

27. Ginzburg, *Prokhodiashchie kharaktery,* 105.

28. The Radio Committee broadcasted for blockaded Leningrad; it received an enormous amount of mail, about which it would comment on air. These broadcasts were hugely popular among the residents of the besieged city.

29. Ryklin, *Prostranstva likovaniia,* 44.

30. Poliak, "O 'liricheskom epose' Velikoi Otechestvennoi voiny," 292–99.

31. Subotskii, "Oruzhie pobedy," 166.

32. Surkov, "Tvorcheskii otchet na zasedanii voennoi komissii SSP 12 iiulia 1943 g." 331–42.

33. Knipovich, "'Krasivaia' nepravda o voine," 212.

34. *Oktiabr',* nos. 1–2 (1944).

35. *Zvezda,* no. 4 (1944): 119.

36. Brainina, "Khrustal'naia bukhta."

37. Matskin, "Ob ukrashatel'stve i ukrashateliakh," 287.

38. Gel'fand, "Literaturnye igry L'va Kassilia."

39. *Leningrad,* nos. 7–8 (1945): 26–27.

40. Urry, "How Societies Remember the Past," 52.

41. Bennett, *The Birth of the Museum,* 76.

42. Ibid., 146. Emphasis in original.

43. Margolit, *Zhivye i mertvoe,* 353.

44. See Brandenberger, *National Bolshevism.*

45. Margolit, *Zhivye i mertvoe,* 360.

46. A. Solov'ev, "Puti razvitiia novogo zhanra," 17.

47. Zhdan, "Obraz velikoi bitvy," 24.

48. Marin, *Portrait of the King,* 71.

49. Ibid.

50. Ibid., 72.

51. Ibid., 73.

52. Bennett, *The Birth of the Museum,* 34.

53. Margolit, *Zhivye i mertvoe,* 362.

54. Manevich, *Narodnyi artist SSSR Mikhail Chiaureli,* 119.

55. Ibid.

56. Romm, *Besedy o kino,* 40–41

57. Mar'iamov, *Kremlevskii tsenzor,* 104.

58. Ibid.

59. Vesnik, *Zapiski artista.*

60. Margolit, *Zhivye i mertvoe,* 362.

61. See Anderson et al., *Kremlevskii kinoteatr,* 834, 842–43.

62. See Bagrov, "Zhitie partiinogo khudozhnika."

63. Ermler, *Dokumenty,* 62.

64. Ibid.

65. Ibid.

66. Belova, *Skvoz' vremia,* 224.

67. Sutyrin, "Velikii perelom," 21.

68. Kovarskii, "Istoriia pobedy," 26.

69. Ermler, *Dokumenty,* 153.

70. Bazen, "Mif Stalina v sovetskom kino," 159.

71. Ibid., 161.

72. *Iosif Vissarionovich Stalin,* 203.

73. Iurenev, *Sovetskii biograficheskii fil'm,* 227.

74. Petrov, "Fil'm o geroicheskom srazhenii," 22.

75. Sutyrin, "Velikii perelom," 22.

76. Ibid.

77. Zhdan, "Obraz velikoi bitvy," 27.

78. See Ryklin, *Prostranstva likovaniia.*

79. Margolit, *Zhivye i mertvoe,* 365–66.

80. Bazen, "Mif Stalina v sovetskom kino," 162.

81. Quoted in Mar'iamov, *Kremlevskii tsenzor,* 67.

82. Gabovich, *Pamiat' o voine 60 let spustia,* 40.

83. Gudkov, "Pobeda v voine," 38.

CHAPTER 2. FROM METAPHOR TO METONYMY

1. Quoted in Mar'iamov, *Kremlevskii tsenzor,* 83.

2. Among the most notable works on *Ivan the Terrible* are Thompson, *Eisenstein's* Ivan the Terrible; Tsivian, *Ivan the Terrible;* Neuberger, *Ivan the Terrible;* Bordwell, *The Cinema of Eisenstein;* Goodwin, *Eisenstein, Cinema, and History;* Kozlov, "Ten' Groznogo i khudozhnik"; Kleiman, "Formula finala"; Uhlenbruch, "The Annexation of History."

3. Uhlenbruch, "The Annexation of History," 723.

4. For the full text of Aleksandrov's letter to Stalin, see Artizov and Naumov, *Vlast' i khudozhestvennaia intelligentsiia*, 546–48.

5. Tsukerman, "Dvoinaia 'myshelovka,' ili samoubiistvo fil'mom," 93.

6. See Dobrenko, *Stalinist Cinema and the Production of History*, 54–59.

7. Levin, "Istoricheskaia tragediia kak zhanr i kak sud'ba," 91.

8. Russian State Archive of Socio-Political History (RGASPI), F. 17, Op. 125, Ed. khr. 378, L. 80, "Stenogramma soveshchaniia v TsK po voprosam kino 26 aprelia 1946 g."

9. Aleksandrova, *Sovetskii istoricheskii roman i voprosy istorizma*, 23.

10. Ibid., 84.

11. Markov, *Problemy teorii sotsialisticheskogo realizma*, 236.

12. Pudovkin, "Sovetskii istoricheskii fil'm," 235.

13. Ibid., 236.

14. Quoted in "Vsesoiuznoe soveshchanie rabotnikov khudozhestvennoi kinematografii," 322.

15. K. Simonov, *Glazami cheloveka moego pokoleniia*, 189–90.

16. K. Simonov, *Soldatami ne rozhdaiutsia*, 681.

17. Quoted in Gromov, *Kinooperator Anatolii Golovnia*, 137.

18. Iurenev, *Sovetskii biograficheskii fil'm*, 131.

19. Ibid., 133–34.

20. Pudovkin, *Sobranie sochinenii*, 3:63.

21. Quoted in Russian State Archive of Socio-Political History (RGASPI), F. 17, Op. 125, Ed. khr. 282, L. 20, "Stenogramma Plenuma SP 5–8 fevralia 1944 g."

22. Quoted ibid., F. 17, Op. 125, Ed. khr. 468, L. 10–11,. "Obsuzhdenie na khudozhestvennom sovete pri Komitete po delam kinematografii kinofil'ma *Admiral Nakhimov* (stenogramma 13 fevralia 1946 goda)."

23. Pyr'ev and Galaktionov quoted ibid., L. 12, 13.

24. Quoted ibid., L. 14–15.

25. Quoted ibid., F. 17, Op. 125, Ed. khr. 291, L. 19.

26. Quoted ibid., L. 12.

27. Anderson et al., *Kremlevskii kinoteatr*, 730–31.

28. Quoted ibid., 724.

29. Uhlenbruch, "The Annexation of History," 278.

30. Perrie, *The Cult of Ivan the Terrible in Stalin's Russia*, 105.

31. Quoted in "Zasedanie khudozhestvennogo soveta pri komitete po delam kinematografii," 293.

32. Iuzovskii, "Eizenshtein!," 42.

33. Vishnevskii, "Fil'm 'Ivan Groznyi.'" The Vishnevskii quotes that follow are from this article.

34. See Allilueva, *Dvadtsat' pisem k drugu*, 82.

35. Quoted in Iuzovskii, "Eizenshtein!," 62.

36. Quoted in Vishnevskii, "Iz dnevnikov 1944–1948 gg.," 67.

37. Uhlenbruch, "The Annexation of History," 283.

38. Quoted in Russian State Archive of Socio-Political History (RGASPI), F. 17, Op. 125, Ed. khr. 468, L. 29, "Obsuzhdenie II serii *Ivana Groznogo* na Khudsovete Komiteta po delam kinematografii, 20 fevralia 1946 goda."

39. Iurenev, *Sovetskii biograficheskii fil'm*, 150.

40. For a detailed analysis of this campaign, see Platt, *Terror and Greatness;* Perrie, *The Cult of Ivan the Terrible in Stalin's Russia.*

41. Vishnevetskii, *Sergei Prokof'ev,* 567.

42. Levin, "Istoricheskaia tragediia kak zhanr i kak sud'ba," 92.

43. Quoted in "Zasedanie khudozhestvennogo soveta pri komitete po delam kinematografii," 293–94.

44. Quoted ibid., 285.

45. Quoted in Russian State Archive of Socio-Political History (RGASPI), F. 17, Op. 125, Ed. khr. 468, L. 29, "Obsuzhdenie II serii *Ivana Groznogo* na Khudsovete Komiteta po delam kinematografii, 20 fevralia 1946 goda."

46. Quoted in "Zasedanie khudozhestvennogo soveta pri komitete po delam kinematografii," 291.

47. Quoted ibid., 295.

48. Quoted ibid., 284–85. Ironically, two years later, in 1948, the actor who had played Vladimir in *Ivan the Terrible,* Pavel Kadochnikov, played the main role of the "real Soviet man," Aleksei Meres'ev, in the film *The Story of a Real Man.*

49. Quoted ibid.

50. Quoted in Iuzovskii, "Eizenshtein!," 46.

51. Quoted in "Zasedanie khudozhestvennogo soveta pri komitete po delam kinematografii," 284.

52. Quoted ibid., 293–94.

53. Goodwin, *Eisenstein, Cinema, and History,* 180.

54. For an overview of this discussion see Frolova-Walker, *Stalin's Music Prize,* esp. ch. 9, "The Trouble with Musorgsky."

55. Deutscher, *Stalin,* 562–63.

56. Uhlenbruch, "The Annexation of History," 283–85.

57. See Kozlov, "Ten' groznogo i khudozhnik"; Kleiman, "Formula finala."

58. Quoted in Vishnevetskii, *Sergei Prokof'ev,* 569.

59. Stalin, *Sochineniia,* 18:422.

60. Dobrenko, *Stalinist Cinema and the Production of History,* 37–43.

61. Gerasimov, "Iskusstvo peredovykh idei," 170.

62. Manevich, *Narodnyi artist SSSR Mikhail Chiaureli,* 144.

63. Ibid.

64. Vaisfel'd, *Epicheskie zhanry v kino,* 27.

65. Ibid., 79.

66. See Iustus, "Vtoraia smert' Lenina."

67. Bazen, "Mif Stalina v sovetskom kino," 162. Further page references to this text in the discussion that follows are given in parentheses.

68. Russian State Archive of Socio-Political History (RGASPI), F. 17, Op. 125, Ed. khr. 468, L. 139.

69. Ibid., L. 140.

70. Ibid.

71. Ibid., L. 141.

72. Ibid., L. 139–40.

73. Chiaureli, "K vershinam masterstva," 46.

74. Iurenev, *Sovetskii biograficheskii fil'm*, 211.

75. Belova, *Skvoz' vremia*, 227.

76. Manevich, *Narodnyi artist SSSR Mikhail Chiaureli*, 69.

77. Quoted ibid., 100–101.

78. Quoted ibid., 101.

79. Quoted in Smirnova, *Aleksei Denisovich Dikii*, 30, 31.

80. Chiaureli, "Voploshchenie obraza velikogo vozhdia."

81. Ibid.

82. Anderson et al., *Kremlevskii kinoteatr*, 734.

83. Mar'iamov, *Kremlevskii tsenzor*, 94–97. See Margolit and Shmyrov, *(Iz"iatoe kino)*, 99–102.

84. Margolit and Shmyrov, *(Iz"iatoe kino)*, 101–2.

85. See Brandenberger, *National Bolshevism*.

CHAPTER 3. THREE RESOLUTIONS ABOUT BEAUTY

1. Margolit, *Zhivye i mertvoe*, 365.

2. Stalin, *Sochineniia*, 18:422.

3. Russian State Archive of Socio-Political History (RGASPI), F. 17, Op. 116, D. 262, L. 73–74.

4. A headframe is a structure above a mineshaft that accommodates the mine hoist.

5. Quoted in Anderson et al., *Kremlevskii kinoteatr*, 754–55, 761.

6. Ibid., 761.

7. Quoted in "Vsesoiuznoe soveshchanie rabotnikov khudozhestvennoi kinematografii," 339.

8. Ibid., 340–41.

9. Rodionov, "Obrazy fil'ma," 23.

10. Groshev, "Obraz nashego sovremennika v kinoiskusstve," 15.

11. Lukov, "Liubimaia i blizkaia tema," 20. Quotes in the following two paragraphs are also from this source.

12. "Zakliuchenie Khudozhestvennogo soveta Ministerstva kinematografii SSSR po fil'mu 'Donetskie shakhtery.'"

13. Iurenev, "Trudnaia zhizn' 'Bol'shoi zhizni,'" 17.

14. Iurenev, *Sovetskii biograficheskii fil'm*, 225.

15. Quoted in Levin, "Sovet da liubov'," 84.

16. Burov, "Poniatie khudozhestvennogo metoda," 77.

17. See Pudovkin, "Rabota aktera v kino i sistema Stanislavskogo," 128–29.

18. Burov, "Poniatie khudozhestvennogo metoda," 79.

19. Margolit, *Zhivye i mertvoe*, 366.

20. Russian State Archive of Socio-Political History (RGASPI), F. 17, Op. 125, D. 465. References to this document in the following discussion are indicated by the number of the manuscript sheet in parentheses.

21. The memorandum is in Russian State Archive of Socio-Political History (RGASPI), F. 17, Op. 125, D. 465.

22. Shtain, "Samoe glavnoe," 36.

23. Ibid., 37.

24. Ibid.

25. Russian State Archive of Socio-Political History (RGASPI), F. 17, Op. 133, Ed. khr. 306 (Otd. Khudozh. lit-ry i iskusstva TsK), L. 1. Further references to this document in the text are indicated by the sheet number in parentheses.

26. Artizov and Naumov, *Vlast' i khudozhestvennaia intelligentsiia*, 594.

27. *Pravda*, April 7, 1952, 2.

28. See Kalashnikov et al., *Ocherki istorii russkogo sovetskogo dramaticheskogo teatra*, 49.

29. Lomidze, "Za pravdivoe otrazhenie zhiznennykh konfliktov v literature," 155.

30. See Dobrenko, *Political Economy of Socialist Realism*.

31. Kholodov, "Deistvuiushchie litsa v poiskakh avtora," 79.

32. Surov, "Nashi zadachi," 311–12.

33. These materials were published for the first time by Denis Babichenko in *"Literaturnyi front."*

34. Levonevskii, "Istoriia 'bol'shogo bloknota.'"

35. Kapitsa, "Eto bylo tak."

36. The voluminous reports of the statements made by figures in literature, film, and theater in relation to the Central Committee resolutions and Zhdanov's speeches, prepared on the basis of secret service information and distributed to the party leadership, show a complete absence of any sort of dissident "attitudes among the creative intelligentsia" that these resolutions were supposedly designed to "suppress." See Babichenko, *"Literaturnyi front,"* 240–52.

37. Pavlenko, *Sobranie sochinenii v shesti tomakh*, 532.

38. Berlin, "The Arts in Russia under Stalin," 62–63.

39. See Timenchik, *Anna Akhmatova v 1960-e gody;* Sarnov, *Stalin i pisateli,* 2:611–828.

40. See Blium, "'Beregite Zoshchenko. . . .'"

41. See Yarmolinsky, *Literature under Communism,* 16–43; Swayze, *Soviet Literary Politics, 1946–1956;* Hankin, "Postwar Soviet Ideology and Literary Scholarship"; Vickery, "Zhdanovism (1946–53)." This story is examined in greater detail and substantiated by new archival materials in Babichenko, *Pisateli i tsenzory,* 111–48, and Babichenko, "I. Stalin," 139–88.

42. Babichenko, "I. Stalin," 163.

43. See V. Volkov, "Za kulisami," 42–51.

44. Demidov and Kutuzov, "Poslednii udar," 51.

45. Babichenko, "I. Stalin," 178.

46. Kaverin, *Epilog,* 46.

47. See Domar, "The Tragedy of a Soviet Satirist, or the Case of Zoshchenko"; Blium, "Khudozhnik i vlast'," 81–91; Sarnov, *Sluchai Zoshchenko.*

48. See Vaiskopf, "Stalin glazami Zoshchenko," 51–54.

49. Concerning this episode, see Chukovskaia, *Zapiski ob Anne Akhmatovoi, 1952–1962,* 2:157.

50. Vaiskopf, "Stalin glazami Zoshchenko," 54.

51. Russian State Archive of Socio-Political History (RGASPI), F. 17, Op. 125, D. 460, L. 35.

52. Plotkin, "Sila sovetskoi literatury," 39.

53. Maslin, "Poet i narod," 61.

54. Quoted in Babichenko, *"Literaturnyi front,"* 206.

55. Plotkin, "Propovednik bezideinosti—M. Zoshchenko," 104.

56. Ibid., 101.

57. Quoted in Babichenko, *"Literaturnyi front,"* 199, 200.

58. See Ravdin, "Blokada Leningrada v russkoi podnemetskoi pechati 1941–1945 godov," 274–314.

59. Demidov and Kutuzov, "Poslednii udar," 52.

60. Sergievskii, "Ob antinarodnoi poezii A. Akhmatovoi," 85.

61. Ibid.

62. Ibid., 87.

63. Vickery, "Zhdanovism (1946–53)," 104.

64. See Timenchik, *Anna Akhmatova v 1960-e gody,* 32, 253.

65. Voronina, "'We Started the Cold War,'" 71.

66. Chertkov, "Nekotorye voprosy dialektiki v svete truda I. V. Stalina po iazykoznaniiu," 330.

67. Bialik: "Nado mechtat'!" and "Geroicheskoe delo trebuet geroicheskogo slova."

68. Zhdanov, *Sovetskaia literatura—samaia ideinaia, samaia peredovaia literatura v mire,* 13.

69. "Vysokaia otvetstvennost' sovetskogo literatora."

70. Ermilov, "Za boevuiu teoriiu literatury!"

71. Ibid.

72. Grudtsova: "O romantizme i realizme" and "V plenu skhemy."

73. Ermilov, "Za boevuiu teoriiu literatury! Protiv otryva ot sovremennosti!"

74. Ermilov, "Za boevuiu teoriiu literatury! Protiv 'romanticheskoi' putanitsy!"

75. Vasil'ev, "Zametki o khudozhestvennom masterstve S. Babaevskogo," 180.

76. Nedoshivin, "O probleme prekrasnogo v sovetskom iskusstve," 82.

77. Ibid., 84.

78. Ibid., 89.

79. Nedoshivin, *Ocherki teorii iskusstva,* 220.

80. Ibid., 226.

81. Ibid., 334.

82. Ibid., 333.

83. Nedoshivin, "O probleme prekrasnogo v sovetskom iskusstve," 97.

84. Kholodov, "Dramaticheskii konflikt," 6.

85. Tarasenkov, *O sovetskoi literature,* 114.

86. The speech was published in Pravda, October 6, 1952.

87. Ermilov, "Nekotorye voprosy teorii sotsialisticheskogo realizma."

88. Plotkin, "O pravde zhizni," 139.

89. Riurikov, "Otritsatel'nye obrazy i neprimirimost' pisatelia."

90. Riurikov, "'V zhizni tak ne byvaet.'"

91. "Bditel'nost'!"

92. Quoted in *Vtoroi Vsesoiuznyi s"ezd sovetskikh pisatelei,* 282.

CHAPTER 4. META-STALINISM

1. Russian State Archive of Recent History (RGANI), F. 3 (Archive of the Politbiuro), Op. 34, Ed. khr. 189, L. 33.

2. Ibid., L. 39.

3. Ibid., L. 41.

4. Ibid., LL. 44–45.

5. Groys, *Kommunisticheskii postskriptum,* 42.

6. On the correlation between Soviet philosophy and ideology, see Zweerde, *Soviet Philosophy, the Ideology and the Handmaid,* especially part 3, "Philosophy and Ideology: The Soviet Case" (201–305).

7. Mamardashvili, "Mysl' pod zapretom."

8. Quoted in V. V. Sokolov, "Nekotorye epizody predvoennoi i poslevoennoi filosofskoi zhizni," 71.

9. Quoted in Batygin and Deviatko, "Delo professora Z. Ia. Beletskogo," 227.

10. M. A. Leonov, "Mesto i rol' filosofii v obshchestvennoi zhizni," 31; emphasis in original.

11. Ibid.

12. Marx and Engels, *Sochineniia,* 3:225.

13. Marx and Engels, *Sochineniia,* 3:4.

14. Adoratskii, "Ob ideologii," 207.

15. Quoted in *Armiia i revoliutsiia,* no. 5 (1922): 16–26.

16. Minin, "Kommunizm i filosofiia," 194, 195.

17. Rumii, "Otvet odnomu iz talmudistov."

18. See Iakhot, "Podavlenie filosofii v SSSR (20–30-e gody)" (part 7, "Chrezvychainoe usilenie roli ideologii").

19. Marx and Engels, *Sochineniia,* 3:25.

20. Marx and Engels, *Izbrannye pis'ma,* 462.

21. *Kommunisticheskaia Partiia Sovetskogo Soiuza v rezoliutsiiakh i resheniiakh s"ezdov, konferentsii i plenumov TsK,* 3:316.

22. *Pravda,* January 26, 1931.

23. See Iakhot, "Podavlenie filosofii v SSSR (20–30-e gody)" (part 6, "Problema leninskogo etapa v filosofii: Imia Lenina kak prikrytie stalinskogo kul'ta"), 73.

24. Ibid., 81.

25. *Kommunisticheskaia Partiia Sovetskogo Soiuza v rezoliutsiiakh i resheniiakh s"ezdov, konferentsii i plenumov TsK,* 3:316.

26. See Glovin'skii, "'Ne puskat' proshlogo na samotek'"; Dobrenko, *Stalinist Cinema and the Production of History,* 183–96.

27. Iakhot, "Podavlenie filosofii v SSSR (20–30-e gody)," 114.

28. Konstantinov, "Eshche raz o politike i filosofii," 64–65.

29. Ogurtsov, "Podavlenie filosofii," 111.

30. Quoted in Batygin and Deviatko, "Delo professora Z. Ia. Beletskogo," 226.

31. Quoted in Kostyrchenko, *Tainaia politika Stalina,* 255.

32. Ibid.

33. The resolution was not printed but was described in Fedoseev, "O nedostatkakh i oshibkakh v osveshchenii nemetskoi filosofii kontsa XVIII i nachala XIX

vekov." See also Esakov, *Akademiia nauk v resheniiakh Politbiuro TsK RKP(b) i VKP(b), 1922–1952*.

34. Batygin and Deviatko, "Sovetskoe filosofskoe soobshchestvo v sorokovye gody," 633.

35. Batygin and Deviatko, "Delo akademika G. F. Aleksandrova," 211.

36. See Fitzpatrick, *On Stalin's Team;* Sadovskii, "Bonifatii Mikhailovich Kedrov," 33.

37. A. Ia. Zis' (who participated in the discussion) recalled that "the discussion of the book, and especially the critical remarks made about it, gave Zhdanov obvious satisfaction, which he did not conceal" ("U istokov zhurnala 'Voprosy filosofii,'" 47).

38. See Zhirnov, "Naznacheny vinovnymi."

39. Shepilov, *Neprimknuvshii*, 125–33. Nothing supports the conclusion made by Ethan Pollock that "when Aleksandrov lost his position in Agitprop, Zhdanov lost a key ally in the ideological wing of the Party" (*Stalin and the Soviet Science Wars*, 40).

40. Zis,' "U istokov zhurnala 'Voprosy filosofii,'" 47.

41. Sokolov, "Nekotorye epizody predvoennoi i poslevoennoi filosofskoi zhizni," 80.

42. Plimak, "'Nado osnovatel'no prochistit' mozgi,'" 11.

43. *Voprosy filosofii*, no. 1 (1947): 404. Transcripts of the discussions of Aleksandrov's book *History of Western European Philosophy* were published in this issue of the journal. All further references to these transcripts in the text below will be indicated by page numbers in parentheses.

44. Krivonosov, "Srazhenie na filosofskom fronte," 66.

45. Quoted in "K 50-letiiu zhurnala 'Voprosy filosofii,'" 23–24.

46. Druzhinin, *Ideologiia i filologiia: Leningrad, 1940-e gody*, 1:126.

47. There were eight sessions; ninety-eight people signed up for the debates, and forty-six gave speeches (Russian State Archive of Socio-Political History [RGASPI], F. 77, Op. 3, Ed. khr. 32).

48. Quoted in Novikov, "Trebuetsia utverdit' odin avtoritet vo vsekh oblastiakh," 64.

49. Kamenskii, *Istoriia filosofii kak nauka v Rossii XIX–XX vv.*, 60.

50. See Plimak, "'Nado osnovatel'no prochistit' mozgi,'" 15.

51. Kamenskii, *Istoriia filosofii kak nauka v Rossii XIX–XX vv.*, 61.

52. Ibid.

53. Ibid.

54. Aleksandrov, *Istoriia zapadnoevropeiskoi filosofii*, 7. Further references to this book in the text below will be indicated by page numbers in parentheses.

55. Ibid.

56. Batygin and Deviatko, "Sovetskoe filosofskoe soobshchestvo v sorokovye gody," 631.

57. Shkolnikov, "The Philosophical Cap of Yegor Fjodorovič or Becoming Belinskij," 175–87.

58. Russian State Archive of Socio-Political History (RGASPI), F. 17, Op. 125, D. 492, L. 41.

59. Ibid., D. 490, L. 61., Transcript, vol. 3: Texts of those who did not speak in the discussion.

60. Ibid., LL. 80–81.

61. Ibid., D. 492, LL. 35–37.

62. Stalin insisted on this in his last public speech at the session of the Bureau of the Presidium of the Communist Party's Central Committee on October 27, 1952: "The propaganda of political economy and philosophy must be seriously organized. Only [one must] not get distracted by the unity of opposites; this is Hegelian terminology. The Americans refute Marxism, slander us, and try to discredit us. We must unmask them. We must acquaint the people with the ideology of the enemies, criticize this ideology, and this will arm our cadres" (*Sochineniia*, 18:589).

63. From here page references to this volume will be provided in the text in parentheses.

64. Marx and Engels, *Sochineniia*, 1:401; emphasis in original.

65. Marion, *Bazy i imperiia*, 17.

66. Podoroga, "Golos pis'ma i pis'mo vlasti," 110.

67. Ibid.

68. Ibid.

CHAPTER 5. *REALÄSTHETIK*

1. Kozhevnikov, "Igry stalinskoi demokratii i ideologicheskie diskussii v sovetskoi nauke."

2. S. Volkov, *Shostakovich i Stalin*, 484.

3. Quoted ibid., 491.

4. See Clark, *Petersburg, Crucible of Cultural Revolution*, 201–23.

5. Kostyrchenko, "Malenkov protiv Zhdanova," 88.

6. Artizov and Naumov, *Vlast' i khudozhestvennaia intelligentsiia*, 626.

7. Ibid., 627–28.

8. Kostyrchenko, "Malenkov protiv Zhdanova," 88.

9. Ibid.

10. For more details, see Maksimenkov, "'Partiia—nash rulevoi.'"

11. This was an old debate that went as far back as the 1920s, when the basic polemic was between, on the one hand, the Association of Contemporary Music (ACM), the leading modernist group of musicians that promoted the avant-garde in music (among whose members were Shostakovich, Nikolai Roslavets, and the aforementioned Miaskovskii, Shebalin, and Popov) and, on the other, the Russian Association of Proletarian Musicians (RAPM). RAPM was close to the Russian Association of Proletarian Writers (RAPP), and its aesthetic program was similarly retrograde, based on "learning from the classics" and venerating the "classical heritage." Among the voluminous Western literature on this subject, see Krebs, *Soviet Composers and the Development of Soviet Music*; Haas, *Leningrad's Modernists 1917–1932*; Edmunds, *The Soviet Proletarian Music Movement* and *Soviet Music and Society under Lenin and Stalin*; and Nelson, *Music for the Revolution*.

12. Artizov and Naumov, *Vlast' i khudozhestvennaia intelligentsiia*, 628–29. An exhaustive analysis of the history of the preparation of the 1948 resolution

and its consequences, based on archival materials, can be found in Vlasova, *1948 v sovetskoi muzyke*. The institutional aspects of the campaign and its role in the transformation of the USSR Union of Soviet Composers are examined in great detail in Tomoff, *Creative Union*.

13. See Maksimenkov, *Sumbur vmesto muzyki*.

14. Koval', "Tvorcheskii put' D. Shostakovicha," Part 1, 54.

15. Ibid., Part 2, 37.

16. Ibid., Part 3, 19. Not long afterward, Koval' would vigorously attack Prokofiev's opera *Story of a Real Man* (see, for example, his devastating speech during the discussion of opera in Leningrad's Malyi Opera Theater on December 4, 1948, quoted in Rakhmanova, *Sergei Prokof'ev*, 129).

17. Artizov and Naumov, *Vlast' i khudozhestvennaia intelligentsiia*, 630.

18. *Soveshchanie deiatelei sovetskoi muzyki v TsK VKP(b)*, 7. Further references to this work in the text are indicated by page numbers in parentheses.

19. Artizov and Naumov, *Vlast' i khudozhestvennaia intelligentsiia*, 630.

20. Ibid.

21. Ibid., 630–31.

22. Gudkov and Dubin, "Ideologiia besstrukturnosti," 219.

23. Artizov and Naumov, *Vlast' i khudozhestvennaia intelligentsiia*, 631.

24. Ibid., 634.

25. Ibid.

26. For a detailed analysis of the composition history and the fundamental musical and literary sources of the *Anti-Formalist Rayok*, see Yakubov, "Shostakovich's Anti-Formalist Rayok."

27. See Kelly, "Territories of the Eye"; B. M. Sokolov, *Khudozhestvennyi iazyk russkogo lubka*; Nekrylova, *Russkie narodnye gorodskie prazdniki, uveseleniia i zrelishcha*.

28. See S. Volkov, *Shostakovich i Stalin*; MacDonald, *The New Shostakovich*.

29. On Shostakovich's friendship with Glikman, see Wilson, *Shostakovich*.

30. See Emerson, "Shostakovich and the Russian Literary Tradition."

31. Quoted in Mokrousov, "Tainaia zhizn' D. D. Shostakovicha."

32. Quoted ibid.

33. Zholkovskii, "Novye vin'etki," 112.

34. On Shostakovich's participation in Stalin's "fight for peace," see Fay, *Shostakovich*, 172, 180–81.

35. It is worth noting that the word "refined" had an unambiguously satirical and parodic meaning in the 1920s; in Vladimir Mayakovsky's comedy *The Bedbug* (1929), the character Prisypkin longs for a "class-conscious, sublime, refined, and ravishing triumph"; a 1929 comedy of Mark Donskoi's, now lost, was titled *You Will Provide a Refined Life!* (it was also titled *Fop*); and Mikhail Zoshchenko's short stories often played upon this word.

36. Shostakovich, *Testimony*, 145.

37. These clusters of "sr" are meant to suggest the Russian verb *srat'*—"shit."

38. For more on the decryption of these allusions, see Yakubov, "Shostakovich's Anti-Formalist Rayok," 151–57.

39. Zorin, *Kormia dvuglavogo orla*, 366.

40. Ibid., 363.

41. Although operas and classical symphony concerts were attended somewhat better than performances of Soviet composers' music, classical music was never "popular" to any extent; in both cases, numerically quite modest audiences are involved.

42. Yakubov, "Shostakovich's *Anti-Formalist Rayok,*" 144.

43. On the corresponding tendencies in Soviet musicology, see Ryzhkin and Safarova, "Sovetskaia muzykal'naia estetika v 30-e gody."

44. We should note that the image of the scolded and later repentant composer appeared again in Soviet film in 1956, in Leonid Lukov's *Different Fates.*

45. Mikhalkov, *Il'ia Golovin,* 146. Further references to this play in the text are indicated by page numbers in parentheses.

46. Shcheglov, "Bez muzykal'nogo soprovozhdeniia . . . ," 242.

47. Chernyi, *Opera Snegina,* 409. Further references to this novel in the text are indicated by page numbers in parentheses.

48. This last tirade repeats almost literally the accusations of awkwardness, "songlessness" (due to too many recitatifs), and naturalism that were leveled against Shostakovich's *Lady Macbeth of the Mtsensk District,* and, twelve years later, against Prokofiev's *Story of a Real Man.*

49. Shcheglov, "Bez muzykal'nogo soprovozhdeniia . . . ," 248. We should note, however, that there was a student of, if not Schoenberg, his associates Berg and Webern, who figured (admittedly, somewhat marginally) in the musical life of the time. This was the composer and musical theorist Filipp Gershkovich, whose home was frequented by all of unofficial musical Moscow in the 1950s; his works have now been partly published.

50. Shostakovich, *D. Shostakovich o vremeni i o sebe,* 143.

51. This applies equally to Prokofiev; with reference to his *Story of a Real Man* (which was performed also in 1948), he was accused of "sacrilege against the heroic deeds of the Soviet people." See Lobacheva, *"Povest' o nastoiashchem cheloveke" S. S. Prokof'eva.*

CHAPTER 6. *GESAMTWISSENSCHAFTSWERK*

1. Epigraph: Osip Mandel'shtam, "Lamarck," translated by Gregory Freidin.

2. Quoted in Mandel'shtam, *Sobranie sochinenii,* 1:520–21.

3. Gasparov, "Lamarck, Schelling, Marr," 189–90.

4. Troshin, "Znachenie truda I. V. Stalina 'Marksizm i voprosy iazykoznaniia' dlia estestvennykh nauk," 387.

5. Ibid., 390.

6. Gasparov, "Lamarck, Schelling, Marr," 196.

7. Joravsky stated that "in 1930 he [Stalin] had subjected scientists to a strict new rule of *partiinost'* [party-mindedness]; in 1950 he turned about and opened the door to demands for release from *partiinost'*" (*The Lysenko Affair,* 150), although these were all rhetorical exercises and, of course, no one freed scientists from the obligation of party-mindedness. Yurchak put it this way: "Earlier, in the 1930s, the *nauchnost'* [scientific value] of a theory was closely associated with the

partiinost' (consistency of one's thinking with the party worldview) of a scientist; but now *nauchnost'* was associated with 'objective scientific laws'" (*Everything Was Forever until It Was No More*, 45–46). Pollock suggests that "beginning in 1950, the pressure to subordinate scientific authority to party authority diminished throughout the bureaucracy. Lysenko's prolonged influence on Soviet agriculture and biology was a striking anomaly" ("From *Partiinost'* to *Nauchnost'* and Not Quite Back Again," 115).

8. Berkovskii, *Romantizm v Germanii*, 23.

9. Ibid., 454.

10. Gorky, *Sobranie sochinenii*, 27:159.

11. See Lunacharskii, "Sotsialisticheskii realizm."

12. See, for example, Rozhkov, *Nuzhna li nam romantika.*

13. Only with the weakening of the Socialist Realist doctrine after Stalin's death and the emergence of the theory of Socialist Realism as a historically open system was the interest in the role of revolutionary romanticism revived. See Markov, *Genezis sotsialisticheskogo realizma;* Zalesskaia, *O romanticheskom techenii v sovetskoi literature.*

14. See Gasparov, "Razvitie ili restrukturirovanie."

15. On Lysenkoism as a politico-aesthetic phenomenon, see Dobrenko, *Political Economy of Socialist Realism*, 90–99.

16. See Stanchevici, *Stalinist Genetics.*

17. Lysenko, *Izbrannye sochineniia*, 22. Further references to this work in the text are indicated by page numbers in parentheses.

18. Railing against the "last-born children of genetics," Mitin asserted that they were encouraging "disgusting monstrosities that are causing a legitimate feeling of indignation among the Soviet people" (*Za materialisticheskuiu biologicheskuiu nauku*, 68).

19. Foucault, "Truth and Power," 129.

20. Mamardashvili, *Neobkhodimost' sebia*, 200.

21. All quotes in the text below are from Zagorianskii, *Sibiriachka.*

22. Medvedev, "Stalin i Lysenko," 231.

23. Gorky, *Sobranie sochinenii*, 30:216.

24. Gorky, *O literature*, 409.

25. Iurenev, "Tvorets," 26.

26. Mar'iamov, *Kremlevskii tsenzor*, 98–99.

27. See Pollock, *Stalin and the Soviet Science Wars*, 41–71. In a wider political, historical, and ideological context, see Krementsov, *Stalinist Science*, 129–83.

28. Quoted in Grachev, *O kinofil'me "Michurin,"* 4.

29. Belova, *Skvoz' vremia*, 245–46.

30. Iurenev, "Tvorets," 26.

31. Ibid.

32. Margolit, *Zhivye i mertvoe*, 375.

33. Ibid., 380.

34. Quoted ibid., 380.

35. Dovzhenko, *Sobranie sochinenii*, 3:565.

36. Belova, *Skvoz' vremia*, 245.

37. Iurenev, "Tvorets," 26.

38. See Kepley, *In the Service of the State*, 138.

39. Grachev, *O kinofil'me "Michurin,"* 11.

40. Lepeshinskaia, *Put' v revoliutsiiu*, 27.

41. Ibid., 105.

42. Safonov, *Pervootkryvateli*, 355; emphasis in original.

43. Rapoport, "Zhivoe veshchestvo i ego konets," 261.

44. Lepeshinskaia, *Proiskhozhdenie kletok iz zhivogo veshchestva i rol' zhivogo veshchestva v organizme*. References to this text in the following discussion are indicated by page numbers in parentheses.

45. Bauer, *The New Man in Soviet Psychology*, 51.

46. Safonov, *Pervootkryvateli*, 362.

47. Rapoport, "Zhivoe veshchestvo i ego konets," 265.

48. Safonov, *Pervootkryvateli*, 373–74.

49. Quotes from the play are translated from the 1953 edition of the play *(Tret'ia molodost')* published by Iskusstvo.

50. Rapoport, "Zhivoe veshchestvo i ego konets," 260.

51. Safonov, *Pervootkryvateli*, 376.

52. See *Soveshchanie po probleme zhivogo veshchestva i razvitiia kletok*.

53. Rapoport, "Zhivoe veshchestvo i ego konets," 266–67.

54. Safonov, *Pervootkryvateli*, 367.

55. Rapoport, "Zhivoe veshchestvo i ego konets," 268–69.

56. Lysenko, *Novoe v nauke o biologicheskom vide*, 28.

57. Rapoport, "Zhivoe veshchestvo i ego konets," 268–69.

58. Ibid., 267.

59. Safonov, *Pervootkryvateli*, 382.

60. Ibid., 379.

61. All of these aspects of the "discoveries," along with a detailed analysis, are presented in Soifer, *Stalin i moshenniki v nauke*, 390–99.

62. Rapoport, "Zhivoe veshchestvo i ego konets," 276.

63. Studitskii, "Mukholiuby—chelovekonenavistniki."

64. Bosh'ian, *O prirode virusov i mikrobov*.

65. Soifer, *Stalin i moshenniki v nauke*, 388–89.

66. Ibid., 389.

67. Rapoport, "Zhivoe veshchestvo i ego konets," 260–61.

68. Quotes from the novel are translated from the first (1950) edition (Dashkiev, *Torzhestvo zhizni*).

CHAPTER 7. THE POWER OF GRAMMAR AND THE GRAMMAR OF POWER

1. Abramov, *Puti-pereput'ia*, 14–15.

2. Ibid., 56–57.

3. See Thomas, *The Linguistic Theories of N. Ja. Marr*; L'Hermitte, *Marr, marrisme, marristes*; Alpatov, *Istoriia odnogo mifa*; Gorbanevskii, *V nachale bylo slovo . . .*; Ilizarov, *Pochetnyi akademik Stalin i akademik Marr*.

4. See Vasil'kov, "Tragediia akademika Marra"; Gasparov, "Lamarck, Schelling, Marr"; Clark, "Promethean Linguistics," in *Petersburg, Crucible of Cultural Revolution;* Murashov, "Pis'mo i ustnaia rech' v diskursakh o iazyke 1930-kh godov."

5. Clark, *Petersburg, Crucible of Cultural Revolution,* 207–8.

6. Marr, *Izbrannye raboty,* 1:175.

7. Aleksandrov, "Trud I. V. Stalina 'Marksizm i voprosy iazykoznaniia'—velikii obrazets tvorcheskogo marksizma," 28.

8. Bogdanov, "Ot pervoelementov N. Ia. Marra k michurinskim iablokam," 341–42.

9. Gasparov, "Lamarck, Schelling, Marr," 196.

10. Gasparov, "Razvitie ili restrukturirovanie," 25.

11. Marr, *Izbrannye raboty,* 2:415.

12. Marr, *K bakinskoi diskussii o iafetidologii i marksizme,* 10.

13. Azizian, "Tvorcheskii kharakter marksizma-leninizma," 37.

14. Alpatov, *Istoriia odnogo mifa,* 184. There are perhaps only three previous works centered on the analysis of Stalin's text as a phenomenon of Soviet cultural history: Groys, "Net nichego vne iazyka"; Sandomirskaja, "Iazyk-Stalin"; and Ilizarov, *Pochetnyi akademik Stalin i akademik Marr.*

15. Stalin, *Sochineniia,* 1 [1934–1940], 276–77. In discussion below Stalin quotes are from this volume.

16. Kozhevnikov, "Igry stalinskoi demokratii i ideologicheskie diskussii v sovetskoi nauke," 52.

17. Aleksandrov, *Trudy I. V. Stalina o iazykoznanii i voprosy istoricheskogo materializma,* 5.

18. As Mikhail Vaiskopf observes, this semblance of definiteness is generally characteristic of Stalin's style, in which "everything is evasive, everything bifurcates—the only stable thing is the illusion of the unbending solidity and clarity of the definitions" (*Pisatel' Stalin,* 59).

19. Groys, "Net nichego vne iazyka."

20. Aleksandrov went farther than anyone else in animating the superstructure: "The imperialists' vehement political and ideological battle against communism bespeaks the fact that the superstructure of a bourgeois society, like a faithful dog, serves its master" (*Trudy I. V. Stalina o iazykoznanii i voprosy istoricheskogo materializma,* 260).

21. Ibid., 136.

22. Chikobava, "Uchenie I. V. Stalina o iazyke kak obshchestvennom iavlenii," 70.

23. Iartseva, "Smeshenie leksiki i grammatiki v 'teorii' N. Ia. Marra," 352–53.

24. Desnitskaia, "Ob antimarksistskoi teorii proiskhozhdeniia iazyka v obshchei sisteme vzgliadov N. Ia. Marra," 56–57.

25. Andreev, "Nekotorye voprosy teorii poznaniia v trude I. V. Stalina 'Marksizm i voprosy iazykoznaniia,'" 170.

26. M. A. Leonov, "Mesto i rol' filosofii v obshchestvennoi zhizni v svete truda I. V. Stalina 'Marksizm i voprosy iazykoznaniia,'" 258–59.

27. Pospelov, "Uchenie I. V. Stalina o grammaticheskom stroe iazyka," 108.

28. Andreev, "Nekotorye voprosy teorii poznaniia v trude I. V. Stalina 'Marksizm i voprosy iazykoznaniia,'" 177.

29. Barkhudarov, "Osnovy prepodavaniia russkogo iazyka v shkole," 84.

30. *Kratkii filosofskii slovar'*, 296, 297.

31. Andreev, "Nekotorye voprosy teorii poznaniia v trude I. V. Stalina 'Marksizm i voprosy iazykoznaniia,'" 179.

32. Ibid., 182.

33. Aleksandrov, "Trud I. V. Stalina 'Marksizm i voprosy iazykoznaniia'—velikii obrazets tvorcheskogo marksizma," 33–34.

34. Ibid., 34. We should note that it was Stalin's extrapolation of language beyond the bounds of the Marxist categories (as neither base, superstructure, nor intermediate phenomenon), precisely, that led to the "dissolution" we have indicated. After Stalin's "work" was published, it was asserted that literature (as a product of language) is also not part of the superstructure. See the materials of this discussion in "Voprosy literaturovedeniia v svete trudov tovarishcha Stalina po iazykoznaniiu, 15–19 maia 1951 g.," 310–11.

35. Aleksandrov, "Trud I. V. Stalina 'Marksizm i voprosy iazykoznaniia'—velikii obrazets tvorcheskogo marksizma," 36.

36. Konstantinov, "Protiv dogmatizma i nachetnichestva," 420.

37. Ibid., 424, 453.

38. Troshin, "Znachenie truda I. V. Stalina 'Marksizm i voprosy iazykoznaniia' dlia estestvennykh nauk," 392.

39. Vaiskopf, *Pisatel' Stalin*, 103.

40. Groys, "Net nichego vne iazyka."

41. Ibid.

42. Ibid.

43. Ibid.

44. See Rossiianov, "Stalin kak redaktor Lysenko."

45. Abaev, "Istoriia iazyka i istoriia naroda," 44.

46. Aleksandrov, "Trud I. V. Stalina 'Marksizm i voprosy iazykoznaniia' i ego vydaiushchaiasia rol' v razvitii obshchestvennykh nauk," 24.

47. Kommari, "I. V. Stalin o marksizme v iazykoznanii," 52.

48. Kedrov, "O razlichnykh putiakh perekhoda ot starogo kachestva k novomu," 70.

49. Ibid., 73.

50. Ibid.

51. Ibid., 74.

52. Ibid., 75.

53. Ibid., 83.

54. Ibid., 84–85.

55. Ibid., 87; emphasis in original.

56. Ibid., 107–8; emphasis in original.

57. *Istoriia VKP(b). Kratkii kurs*, 331

58. Kedrov, "O razlichnykh putiakh perekhoda ot starogo kachestva k novomu," 135.

59. Ostrovitianinov, "Znachenie truda I. V. Stalina 'Marksizm i voprosy iazy-koznaniia' dlia razvitiia ekonomicheskoi i pravovoi nauki," 145.

60. Chesnokov, "Marksizm-leninizm o bazise i nadstroike," 177; emphasis in original.

61. Stalin, *Sochineniia*, 12:369–70.

62. Aleksandrov, *Trudy I. V. Stalina o iazykoznanii i voprosy istoricheskogo materializma*, 50–51.

63. Chertkov, "Nekotorye voprosy dialektiki v svete truda I. V. Stalina po iazy-koznaniiu," 321, 328; emphasis in original.

64. Rozental', *Marksistskii dialekticheskii metod*, 261, 265–66.

65. Chertkov, "Nekotorye voprosy dialektiki v svete truda I. V. Stalina po iazy-koznaniiu," 346.

66. Medvedev and Medvedev, *Neizvestnyi Stalin*, 259.

67. "Ot redaktsii" (From the editors), in *Sessiia Otdelenii obshchestvennykh nauk Akademii nauk SSSR*, 6.

68. Vinogradov, "Razvitie sovetskogo iazykoznaniia v svete ucheniia I. V. Stalina o iazyke," 81.

69. See the accounts of work in the USSR republics recorded in the joint session of the Academy of Sciences' social sciences departments; in this anniversary session, presidents from all the republican Academy of Sciences branches reported the restructuring work done in connection with Stalin's works (*Sessiia Otdelenii obshchestvennykh nauk Akademii nauk SSSR*, 161–221).

70. Vinogradov, "Razvitie sovetskogo iazykoznaniia v svete ucheniia I. V. Stalina o iazyke," 74.

71. M. A. Leonov, "Mesto i rol' filosofii v obshchestvennoi zhizni v svete truda I. V. Stalina 'Marksizm i voprosy iazykoznaniia,'" 286.

72. Gvozdev, "Voprosy sovremennoi orfografii i metodika ee prepodava-niia," 117.

73. Vinogradov, "Nauchnye zadachi sovetskogo literaturovedeniia," 5.

74. Zvegintsev, "Poniatie vnutrennikh zakonov razvitiia iazyka v svete rabot I. V. Stalina po iazykoznaniiu," 199.

75. Vinogradov, "Razvitie sovetskogo iazykoznaniia v svete ucheniia I. V. Stalina o iazyke," 48.

76. Vinogradov, "Znachenie rabot I. V. Stalina dlia razvitiia sovetskogo iazy-koznaniia," 15.

77. Aleksandrov, *Trudy I. V. Stalina o iazykoznanii i voprosy istoricheskogo materializma*, 140.

78. Ibid., 121.

79. Chernykh, "I. V. Stalin ob osnovnom slovarnom fonde iazyka," 126.

80. "Predislovie" (foreword), in *Voprosy teorii i istorii iazyka v svete trudov I. V. Stalina po iazykoznaniiu*, 3.

81. Vinogradov, "Razvitie sovetskogo iazykoznaniia v svete ucheniia I. V. Stalina o iazyke," 17.

82. "Predislovie" (foreword) in *Voprosy dialekticheskogo i istoricheskogo materializma v trude I. V. Stalina "Marksizm i voprosy iazykoznaniia,"* 1:3.

83. Vinogradov, "Razvitie sovetskogo iazykoznaniia v svete ucheniia I. V. Stalina o iazyke," 20.

84. Aleksandrov, *Trudy I. V. Stalina o iazykoznanii i voprosy istoricheskogo materializma,* 6.

85. Aleksandrov, "Trud I. V. Stalina 'Marksizm i voprosy iazykoznaniia'—velikii obrazets tvorcheskogo marksizma," 22–23.

86. Aleksandrov, "Trud I. V. Stalina 'Marksizm i voprosy iazykoznaniia' i ego vydaiushchaiasia rol' v razvitii obshchestvennykh nauk," 19.

87. Aleksandrov, "Velikaia sila stalinskikh idei," 18–20.

88. Aleksandrov, "Trud I. V. Stalina 'Marksizm i voprosy iazykoznaniia'—velikii obrazets tvorcheskogo marksizma," 10–11.

89. Aleksandrov, *Trudy I. V. Stalina o iazykoznanii i voprosy istoricheskogo materializma,* 261–62.

90. Troshin, "Marksizm-leninizm ob ob"ektivnom kharaktere zakonov nauki," 226.

91. Gurevich, *Izbrannye trudy,* 2:28–29.

CHAPTER 8. SOCIALIST SURREALISM

1. K. Simonov, *Glazami cheloveka moego pokoleniia,* 124.

2. Ibid.

3. Ibid.

4. Ibid.

5. Barthes, *Writing Degree Zero,* 67–68.

6. K. Simonov, *Glazami cheloveka moego pokoleniia,* 125.

7. Smith had been Eisenhower's secret service chief of staff during the war and headed the CIA after his return from the Soviet Union.

8. Esakov and Levina, *Stalinskie "sudy chesti,"* 194.

9. Quoted ibid., 135–36.

10. Quoted ibid., 172.

11. Quoted ibid., 137, 160.

12. Quoted ibid., 173.

13. Quoted ibid., 136.

14. Krementsov, *V poiskakh lekarstva protiv raka,* 199.

15. Ibid., 193.

16. K. Simonov, *Glazami cheloveka moego pokoleniia,* 155.

17. An account of the creation and staging of Simonov's *Alien's Shadow* and Room's film *Court of Honor* can be found in Krementsov, *V poiskakh lekarstva protiv raka,* 173–99.

18. Quoted in Krementsov, *V poiskakh lekarstva protiv raka,* 187.

19. Ibid., 193–94.

20. Ibid., 194.

21. The "first department" was essentially a branch of the secret police that controlled access to documents and secret information, any contacts with foreigners (including publication), and even the use of typewriters and any printing and/or copying devices. In the plays, the spies reprinted the manuscripts without any problems at all.

22. Quoted in Krementsov, *V poiskakh lekarstva protiv raka,* 204.

23. Quoted ibid., 205.

24. Esakov and Levina, *Stalinskie "sudy chesti,"* 115.

25. See Mlechin, *Kreml'—1953,* 194–95.

26. Kozintsev, *"Chernoe, likhoe vremia . . . ,"* 116–17.

27. Roshal', "Istoriko-biograficheskii fil'm," 17.

28. Roshal', "Obraz velikogo uchenogo," 39.

29. Borisov, "Rabota nad istoricheskim obrazom," 60.

30. Materials having to do with this period in Pavlov's life were published in the perestroika period. See Esakov, ". . . I akademik Pavlov ostalsia v Rossii," 78–85.

31. Iurenev, *Sovetskii biograficheskii fil'm,* 115.

32. Krasina and Sosnovskii, *Narodnyi artist SSSR Aleksandr Fedorovich Borisov,* 20.

33. Ibid., 22.

34. Ibid., 26.

35. Lukin, "Zhizn', posviashchennaia narodu," 15.

36. Quoted in V. O. Samoilov and Vinogradov, "Ivan Pavlov i Nikolai Bukharin," 101, 112.

37. Russian State Archive of Socio-Political History (RGASPI), F. 17, Op. 132 (Arkhiv Agitpropa TSK KPSS, 1948–1953), D. 251, 73.

38. Pudovkin, *Sobranie sochinenii,* 3:76–77.

39. Nedobrovo, *Zhukovskii,* 23.

40. Ibid., 36–37.

41. Petrov, "O fil'me 'Przheval'skii,'" 78.

42. Pudovkin, *Sobranie sochinenii,* 3:141.

43. Quoted from the original (in Arkhiv RGO, F. 13, Op. 1, D. 14, L. 246), in Zakharenko, "Istoriia geograficheskogo izucheniia i kartografirovaniia Dal'nevostochnogo prostranstva Rossii i Kitaia."

44. Okhotnikov, "Fil'm o velikom izobretatele," 27.

45. Lukin, "Zhizn', posviashchennaia narodu," 14.

46. Ibid.

47. Quite a few of these are recounted in Kosheleva et al., *Sovetskaia natsional'naia politika.*

48. Vaksberg, *Neraskrytye tainy,* 261–65.

49. See Kostyrchenko, *Stalin protiv "kosmopolitov."*

50. *Krokodil,* no. 3 (January 30, 1953): 2.

51. Pipes, *Conspiracy,* 88.

52. Molok, foreword to V. Solov'ev, *Zolotaia chuma,* 5. The quotes in the text are taken from this volume.

53. Ibid., 9.

54. Ibid.

55. Ibid.

56. Russian State Archive of Socio-Political History (RGASPI), F. 17, Op. 133, Ed. khr. 363, L. 44.

57. Ibid., L. 54.

58. Russian State Archive of Recent History (RGANI), F. 3 (Arkhiv Politbiuro TsK KPSS), Op. 34, Ed. khr. 225, L. 74–75.

CHAPTER 9. *GESAMTKRIEGSWERK*

1. There are a number of excellent works on the cultural history of the Cold War based on American material, among them Caute, *The Dancer Defects,* and Saunders, *Who Paid the Piper?* However, such a history from the Soviet perspective has yet to be written.

2. Danilov and Pyzhikov, *Rozhdenie sverkhderzhavy,* 287.

3. See chapter 1 ("Sovetskii soiuz v poslevoennom mire") ibid. and Applebaum, *Iron Curtain.*

4. Stalin, *Sochineniia,* 16:32.

5. Ibid., 57.

6. Ibid.

7. Ibid., 59.

8. Ibid.

9. Ibid.

10. Ibid., 25.

11. Ibid., 26.

12. Ibid.

13. Ibid.

14. Ibid., 27.

15. Ibid., 27–28.

16. Ibid., 28.

17. Ibid., 29.

18. Ibid., 183.

19. Ibid., 184.

20. Ibid.

21. Quoted in Mikhalkov, *Satira i iumor.*

22. Ibid., 228.

23. Vyshinskii, "Sovetskii patriotizm—dvizhushchaia sila razvitiia sovetskogo obshchestva," 425.

24. Vyshinskii, "Kommunizm i otechestvo," 56.

25. See Brooks, *Thank You, Comrade Stalin!*

26. L. Leonov, "Beseda s demonom."

27. Ibid.

28. Ibid.

29. L. Leonov, "Rassuzhdenie o velikanakh."

30. Ibid.; emphasis in original.

31. Ibid.

32. Ibid.

33. Ibid.

34. Ibid.

35. Ibid.

36. Ibid.

37. Ibid.

38. State Archive of the Russian Federation (GARF), Fond 9539, Op. 1, Ch. 1, D. 3 (Leonid Leonov's speech at the First All-Union Conference of Peace Advocates, August 25, 1949), L. 1.

39. Ibid., L. 11–12.

40. Ibid., L. 7.

41. Ibid., L. 13.

42. Ehrenburg, *Za mir,* 14.

43. See David-Fox, *Showcasing the Great Experiment.*

44. Ehrenburg, *Za mir,* 18.

45. Ibid., 23–24.

46. Ibid., 25.

47. Ibid., 37.

48. Ibid., 38.

49. Ibid., 196.

50. Ibid., 144.

51. Ibid., 130.

52. See Dobrenko, *Metafora vlasti,* ch. 4.

53. See ibid., ch. 5.

54. See, for example, the collections: Pokrovskaia, *Za mir,* and *Stikhi o mire.*

55. In the *"malokartin'e"* period, annual film production dropped from around a hundred in the 1930s to under fifty from the mid-1940s until after Stalin's death. See Belodubrovskaya, *Not According to Plan.*

56. Dovzhenko, "Operatsiia bez narkoza," 75.

57. Turovskaia, "Fil'my 'kholodnoi voiny,'" 101.

58. Ibid., 99.

59. Antropov, "Chuzhoi Dovzhenko?," 89.

60. Trimbach, "Vyzhzhenaia zemlia Aleksandra Dovzhenko," 82.

61. Dovzhenko, "Operatsiia bez narkoza," 74.

62. Dovzhenko, "'Nado igrat' ne klinicheskii sluchai, a dramu,'" 77.

63. Dovzhenko, "Operatsiia bez narkoza," 74–75.

64. Dovzhenko, "Proshchai, Amerika (Fragmenty stsenariia)," 730.

65. Ibid., 732–33.

66. Ibid., 733–34.

67. Dovzhenko, "'Nado igrat' ne klinicheskii sluchai, a dramu,'" 78–79.

68. Turovskaia, "Fil'my 'kholodnoi voiny,'" 100.

69. Ibid., 106.

70. Ibid.

71. Quoted in Russian State Archive of Socio-Political History (RGASPI), F. 17, Op. 128, D. 259, 17.

72. Turovskaia, "Fil'my 'kholodnoi voiny,'" 106.

73. Ibid.

74. Galanov, "Ekran izoblichaet podzhigatelei voiny," 25.

75. Pogozheva, "Missiia, perestavshaia byt' sekretnoi," 12, 15.

76. Ibid., 15.

77. See Borenstein, *Plots against Russia.*

Works Cited

Abaev, Vasilii. "Istoriia iazyka i istoriia naroda." In *Voprosy teorii i istorii iazyka v svete trudov I. V. Stalina po iazykoznaniiu.*

Abramov, Fedor. *Puti-pereput'ia.* In *Sobranie sochinenii.* Vol. 2. Leningrad: Khudozhestvennaia literatura, 1981.

Adibekov, G. M. *Kominform i poslevoennaia Evropa, 1947–1956 gg.* Moscow: Rossiia molodaia; AIRO-XX, 1994.

Adoratskii, Vladimir. "Ob ideologii." *Pod znamenem marksizma,* nos. 11–12 (1922).

Afanas'ev, Iu. N., ed. *Sovetskoe obshchestvo: Vozniknovenie, razvitie, istoricheskii final.* Vol. 2: *Apogei i krakh stalinizma.* Moscow: RGGU, 1997.

Aleksandrov, Georgii. *Istoriia zapadnoevropeiskoi filosofii,* 2nd ed., expanded. Moscow and Leningrad: Izd-vo AN SSSR, 1946.

———. "Trud I. V. Stalina 'Marksizm i voprosy iazykoznaniia' i ego vydaiushchaiasia rol' v razvitii obshchestvennykh nauk." In *Materialy ob"edinennoi nauchnoi sessii Otdeleniia literatury i iazyka Akademii nauk SSSR i Akademii pedagogicheskikh nauk RSFSR.*

———. "Trud I. V. Stalina 'Marksizm i voprosy iazykoznaniia'—velikii obrazets tvorcheskogo marksizma." In *Voprosy dialekticheskogo i istoricheskogo materializma,* vol. 1.

———. *Trudy I. V. Stalina o iazykoznanii i voprosy istoricheskogo materializma.* Moscow: Gospolitizdat, 1952.

———. "Velikaia sila stalinskikh idei." In *Voprosy teorii i istorii iazyka v svete trudov I. V. Stalina po iazykoznaniiu.*

Aleksandrova, L. P. *Sovetskii istoricheskii roman i voprosy istorizma.* Kiev: Izd-vo Kievskogo un-ta, 1971.

Allilueva, Svetlana. *Dvadtsat' pisem k drugu.* Moscow: Kniga, 1989.

Alpatov, Vladimir. *Istoriia odnogo mifa: Marr i marrizm.* Moscow: Nauka, 1991.

Anderson, K. M., L. V. Maksimenkov, L. P. Kosheleva, and L. A. Rogovaia, comps. *Kremlevskii kinoteatr, 1928–1953: Dokumenty.* Moscow: ROSSPEN, 2005.

Andreev, I. D. "Nekotorye voprosy teorii poznaniia v trude I. V. Stalina 'Marksizm i voprosy iazykoznaniia.'" In *Voprosy dialekticheskogo i istoricheskogo materializma,* vol. 2.

Anisimov, I. I., et al., eds. *Sovetskie pisateli na frontakh Velikoi Otechestvennoi voiny,* vol. 1. Moscow: Nauka, 1966.

Ankersmit, F. R. *Aesthetic Politics: Political Philosophy beyond Fact and Value.* Stanford, CA: Stanford University Press, 1996.

Antropov, Vladimir. "Chuzhoi Dovzhenko?" *Iskusstvo kino,* no. 9 (1996)

Applebaum, Anne. *Iron Curtain: The Crushing of Eastern Europe 1944–1956.* New York : Doubleday, 2012.

Artizov, Andrei, and Oleg Naumov, eds. *Vlast' i khudozhestvennaia intelligentsiia: Dokumenty TsK RKP(b)—VKP(b), VChK—OGPU—NKVD o kul'turnoi politike, 1917–1953.* Moscow: Mezhdunarodnyi fond "Demokratiia," 1999.

Azizian, A. K. "Tvorcheskii kharakter marksizma-leninizma." In *Voprosy dialekticheskogo i istoricheskogo materializma,* vol. 2.

Babichenko, Denis. "I. Stalin: 'Doberemsia do vsekh' (Kak gotovili poslevoennuiu ideologicheskuiu kampaniiu. 1943–1946 gg.)." In *Iskliuchit' vsiakie upominaniia . . . : Ocherki istorii sovetskoi tsenzury.* Minsk: Staryi svet-print, 1995.

———, comp. *"Literaturnyi front": Istoriia politicheskoi tsenzury 1932–1946 gg.; Sbornik dokumentov.* Moscow: Entsiklopediia rossiiskikh dereven', 1994.

———. *Pisateli i tsenzory: Sovetskaia literatura 1940-kh godov pod politicheskim kontrolem TsK.* Moscow: Rossiia molodaia, 1994.

Bagrov, Petr. "Zhitie partiinogo khudozhnika." *Seans,* June 15, 2018.

Bakhtin, Mikhail. *Problemy poetiki Dostoevskogo.* Moscow: Sovetskii pisatel', 1963.

Barkhudarov, S. G. "Osnovy prepodavaniia russkogo iazyka v shkole." In *Materialy ob"edinennoi nauchnoi sessii Otdeleniia literatury i iazyka Akademii nauk SSSR i Akademii pedagogicheskikh nauk RSFSR.*

Barskova, Polina. *Besieged Leningrad: Aesthetic Responses to Urban Disaster.* DeKalb, IL: Northern Illinois University Press, 2017.

Barthes, Roland. *Writing Degree Zero.* New York: Noonday Press, 1991.

Batygin, G. S., and I. F. Deviatko. "Delo akademika G. F. Aleksandrova: Epizody 40-kh godov." *Chelovek,* nos. 1, 2, 3 (1993).

———. "Delo professora Z. Ia. Beletskogo." In *Filosofiia ne konchaetsia*.

———. "Sovetskoe filosofskoe soobshchestvo v sorokovye gody: Pochemu byl zapreshchen tretii tom 'Istorii filosofii'?" *Vestnik Rossiiskoi Akademii Nauk* 63, no. 7 (1993).

Bauer, Raymond A. *The New Man in Soviet Psychology.* Cambridge, MA: Harvard University Press, 1959.

Bauman, Zygmunt. *Liquid Modernity.* Cambridge: Polity, 2000.

Bazen, Andre [André Bazin]. "Mif Stalina v sovetskom kino." *Kinovedcheskie zapiski,* no. 1 (1988).

"Bditel'nost'!" [editorial]. *Literaturnaia gazeta,* January 17, 1953.

Belodubrovskaya, Maria. *Not According to Plan: Filmmaking under Stalin.* Ithaca, NY: Cornell University Press, 2017.

Belova, Liudmila. *Skvoz' vremia: Ocherki istorii sovetskoi kinodramaturgii.* Moscow: Iskusstvo, 1978.

Ben-Ghiat, Ruth. *Fascist Modernities: Italy, 1922–1945.* Los Angeles: University of California Press, 2001.

Bennett, Tony. *The Birth of the Museum: History, Theory, Politics.* London: Routledge, 1995.

Berkovskii, Naum. *Romantizm v Germanii.* St. Petersburg: Azbuka-klassika, 2001.

Berlin, Isaiah. "The Arts in Russia under Stalin." *New York Review,* October 19, 2000.

Bialik, Boris. "Geroicheskoe delo trebuet geroicheskogo slova." *Oktiabr',* no. 2 (1948).

———. "Nado mechtat'!" *Oktiabr',* no. 11 (1947).

Blium, Arlen. "'Beregite Zoshchenko . . .': Podtsenzurnaia sud'ba pisatelia posle avgusta 1946-go." *Zvezda,* no. 8 (2004).

———. "Khudozhnik i vlast': 12 tsenzurnykh istorii (K 100-letiiu M. M. Zoshchenko)." *Zvezda,* no. 8 (1994).

Bogdanov, Konstantin. "Ot pervoelementov N. Ia. Marra k michurinskim iablokam: Ratsional'nost' i absurd v sovetskoi nauke 1920–1950-kh gg." In *Absurd i vokrug: Sbornik statei,* edited by O. Burenina. Moscow: Iazyki slavianskoi kul'tury, 2004.

Bordwell, David. *The Cinema of Eisenstein.* Cambridge, MA: Harvard University Press, 1993.

Borenstein, Eliot. *Plots against Russia: Conspiracy and Fantasy after Socialism.* Ithaca, NY: Cornell University Press, 2019.

Borev, Iurii. *O tragicheskom.* Moscow: Sovetskii pisatel', 1961.

Borisov, Aleksandr. "Rabota nad istoricheskim obrazom." *Iskusstvo kino,* no. 3 (1950).

Bosh'ian, Gevorg. *O prirode virusov i mikrobov.* Moscow: Medgiz, 1949.

Brainina, Bella. "Khrustal'naia bukhta." *Znamia,* no. 4 (1944).

Brandenberger, David. *National Bolshevism: Stalinist Mass Culture and the Formation of Modern Russian National Identity, 1931–1956.* Cambridge, MA: Harvard University Press, 2002.

———. *Propaganda State in Crisis: Soviet Ideology, Indoctrination, and Terror under Stalin, 1927–1941.* New Haven: Yale University Press, 2011.

Brent, Jonathan, and Vladimir Naumov. *Stalin's Last Crime: The Plot against the Jewish Doctors, 1948–1953.* New York: HarperCollins, 2003.

Brooks, Jeffrey. *Thank You, Comrade Stalin!: Soviet Public Culture from Revolution to Cold War.* Princeton, NJ: Princeton University Press, 2001.

Brunstedt, Jonathan. "Bureaucratizing the Glorious Past: Moscow's Victory Memorial Project during Late Socialism." In *Excavating Memory: Sites of Remembering and Forgetting,* edited by Maria Theresia Starzmann and John R. Roby, 25–41. Gainesville: University Press of Florida, 2016.

Burke, Peter. *What Is Cultural History?* Cambridge: Polity, 2008.

Burov, Aleksandr. "Poniatie khudozhestvennogo metoda." *Iskusstvo kino,* no. 9 (1952).

Caute, David. *The Dancer Defects: The Struggle for Cultural Supremacy during the Cold War.* Oxford: Oxford University Press, 2003.

Chernyi, Osip. *Opera Snegina.* Moscow: Sovetskii pisatel', 1953.

Chernykh, P. Ia. "I. V. Stalin ob osnovnom slovarnom fonde iazyka." In *Voprosy iazykoznaniia v svete trudov I. V. Stalina.*

Chertkov, V. P. "Nekotorye voprosy dialektiki v svete truda I. V. Stalina po iazykoznaniiu." In *Voprosy dialekticheskogo i istoricheskogo materializma,* vol. 1.

Chesnokov, D. I. "Marksizm-leninizm o bazise i nadstroike." In *Voprosy dialekticheskogo i istoricheskogo materializma,* vol. 1.

Chiaureli, Mikhail. "K vershinam masterstva." In *Dvadtsat' let sovetskoi kinematografii: Sbornik statei.* Moscow: Goskinoizdat, 1940.

———. "Voploshchenie obraza velikogo vozhdia." *Iskusstvo kino,* no. 1 (1947).

Chikobava, Arnol'd. "Uchenie I. V. Stalina o iazyke kak obshchestvennom iavlenii." In *Voprosy iazykoznaniia v svete trudov I. V. Stalina.*

Chukovskaia, Lidiia. *Zapiski ob Anne Akhmatovoi, 1952–1962,* vol. 2. Moscow: Soglasie, 1997.

Clark, Katerina. *Moscow, the Fourth Rome: Stalinism, Cosmopolitanism, and the Evolution of Soviet Culture, 1931–1941.* Cambridge, MA: Harvard University Press, 2011.

———. *Petersburg, Crucible of Cultural Revolution.* Cambridge, MA: Harvard University Press, 1995.

————. *The Soviet Novel: History as Ritual.* Chicago: University of Chicago Press, 1981.

Cohn, Edward. *The High Title of Communist: Postwar Party Discipline and the Values of the Soviet Regime.* DeKalb, IL: Northern Illinois University Press, 2015.

Corney, Frederick. *Telling October: Memory and the Making of the Bolshevik Revolution.* Ithaca, NY: Cornell University Press, 2004.

Danilov, A. A., and A. V. Pyzhikov. *Rozhdenie sverkhderzhavy: SSSR v pervye poslevoennye gody.* Moscow: ROSSPEN, 2001.

Dashkiev, Nikolai. *Torzhestvo zhizni: Nauchno-fantasticheskii roman.* Khar'kov: Khar'kovskoe knizhno-gazetnoe izd-vo, 1950.

David-Fox, Michael. *Crossing Borders: Modernity, Ideology, and Culture in Russia and the Soviet Union.* Pittsburgh: University of Pittsburgh Press, 2015.

————. *Showcasing the Great Experiment: Cultural Diplomacy and Western Visitors to the Soviet Union, 1921–1941.* New York: Oxford University Press, 2011.

Demidov, V. I., and V. A. Kutuzov. "Poslednii udar: Povest'." In *Leningradskoe delo: Sbornik statei,* ed. V. I. Demidov and V. A. Kutuzov. Leningrad: Lenizdat, 1990.

Desnitskaia, A. V. "Ob antimarksistskoi teorii proiskhozhdeniia iazyka v obshchei sisteme vzgliadov N. Ia. Marra." In *Protiv vul'garizatsii i izvrashcheniia marksizma v iazykoznanii,* vol. 1.

Deutscher, Isaac. *Stalin: A Political Biography.* 2nd ed. New York: Oxford University Press, 1966.

Dobrenko, Evgeny. *Metafora vlasti: Literatura stalinskoi epokhi v istoricheskom osveshchenie.* Munich: Otto Sagner, 1993.

————. *Political Economy of Socialist Realism.* New Haven: Yale University Press, 2007.

————. *Stalinist Cinema and the Production of History: Museum of the Revolution.* New Haven: Yale University Press, 2008.

Domar, Rebecca A. "The Tragedy of a Soviet Satirist, or the Case of Zoshchenko." In Simmons, *Through the Glass of Soviet Literature.*

Dovzhenko, Aleksandr. "'Nado igrat' ne klinicheskii sluchai, a dramu': Rabochie zapisi k fil'mu 'Proshchai, Amerika.'" *Iskusstvo kino,* no. 9 (1996).

————. "Operatsiia bez narkoza: Dnevnikovye zapisi." *Iskusstvo kino,* no. 9 (1996).

————. "Proshchai, Amerika (Fragmenty stsenariia)." In *Sobranie sochinenii.* Vol. 4.

————. *Sobranie sochinenii.* Moscow: Iskusstvo, 1966–69.

Druzhinin, Petr. *Ideologiia i filologiia: Leningrad, 1940-e gody; Dokumental'noe issledovanie,* 2 vols. Moscow: Novoe literaturnoe obozrenie, 2012.

Dunham, Vera. *In Stalin's Time: Middleclass Values in Soviet Fiction*. Durham, NC: Duke University Press, 1990.

Eagleton, Terry. *Ideology*. New York: Verso, 1990.

———. *The Ideology of the Aesthetic*. Malden, MA: Blackwell, 1990.

Edmunds, Neil, ed. *Soviet Music and Society under Lenin and Stalin*. London: Routledge, 2004.

———. *The Soviet Proletarian Music Movement*. Oxford: Peter Lang, 2000.

Egolin, A. M., S. M. Petrov, and I. V. Sergievskii, eds. *Voprosy literaturovedeniia v svete trudov I. V. Stalina po iazykoznaniiu*. Moscow: Izd-vo AN SSSR, 1951.

Ehrenburg, Ilya. *Za mir*. Moscow: Sovetskii pisatel', 1952.

Emerson, Caryl. "Shostakovich and the Russian Literary Tradition." In *Shostakovich and His World,* edited by Laurel E. Fay. Princeton, NJ: Princeton University Press, 2004.

Ermilov, Vladimir. "Nekotorye voprosy teorii sotsialisticheskogo realizma." In Egolin, Petrov, and Sergievskii, *Voprosy literaturovedeniia v svete trudov I. V. Stalina po iazykoznaniiu.*

———. "Za boevuiu teoriiu literatury!" *Literaturnaia gazeta,* November 13, 1948.

———. "Za boevuiu teoriiu literatury! Protiv otryva ot sovremennosti!" *Literaturnaia gazeta,* September 11, 1948.

———. "Za boevuiu teoriiu literatury! Protiv 'romanticheskoi' putanitsy!" *Literaturnaia gazeta,* September 15, 1948.

Ermler, Fridrikh. *Dokumenty: Stat'i, vospominaniia*. Leningrad: Iskusstvo, 1974.

Esakov, V. D. comp., *Akademiia nauk v resheniiakh Politbiuro TsK RKP(b) i VKP(b), 1922–1952*. Moscow: ROSSPEN, 2000.

———. ". . . I akademik Pavlov ostalsia v Rossii." *Nauka i zhizn',* no. 9 (1989).

Esakov, V. D., and E. S. Levina, *Stalinskie "sudy chesti": Delo "KR."* Moscow: Nauka, 2005.

Etkind, Alexander, Rory Finnin, Uilleam Blacker, Julie Fedor, Simon Lewis, Maria Mälksoo, and Matilda Mroz. *Remembering Katyn*. Cambridge: Polity, 2012.

Falasca-Zamponi, Simonetta. *Fascist Spectacle: The Aesthetics of Power in Mussolini's Italy*. Los Angeles: University of California Press, 1997.

Fateev, A. V. *Obraz vraga v sovetskoi propagande 1945–1954 gg*. Moscow: IRI RAN, 1999.

Fay, Laurel. *Shostakovich: A Life*. New York: Oxford University Press, 2005.

Fedoseev, Petr. "O nedostatkakh i oshibkakh v osveshchenii nemetskoi filosofii kontsa XVIII i nachala XIX vekov." *Bol'shevik,* nos. 7–8 (1944).

Filosofiia ne konchaetsia. . . . Iz istorii otechestvennoi filosofii. XX vek. 1920–50-e gody. Moscow: ROSSPEN, 1998.

Filtzer, Donald. *Soviet Workers and Late Stalinism: Labour and the Restoration of the Stalinist System after World War II.* Cambridge: Cambridge University Press, 2002.

Fitzpatrick, Sheila. *On Stalin's Team: The Years of Living Dangerously in Soviet Politics.* Princeton, NJ: Princeton University Press, 2015.

Foucault, Michel. "Truth and Power." In *Power/Knowledge: Selected Interviews and Other Writings 1972–1977,* ed. Colin Gordon. New York: Pantheon Books, 1977.

Frolova-Walker, Marina. *Stalin's Music Prize: Soviet Culture and Politics.* New Haven: Yale University Press, 2016.

Fürst, Juliane, ed. *Late Stalinist Russia: Society between Reconstruction and Reinvention.* London: Routledge, 2006.

Gabovich, Mikhail, ed., comp. *Pamiat' o voine 60 let spustia: Rossiia, Germaniia, Evropa.* 2nd ed., corrected and expanded. Moscow: Novoe literaturnoe obozrenie, 2005.

Gaiduk, I. V., ed. *Stalin i kholodnaia voina.* Moscow: Institut vseobshchei istorii RAN, 1998.

Gaiduk, I. V., and N. I. Egorova, eds. *Stalinskoe desiatiletie kholodnoi voiny Fakty i gipotezy.* Moscow: Nauka, 1999.

Galanov, B. "Ekran izoblichaet podzhigatelei voiny." *Iskusstvo kino,* no. 3 (1950).

Gasparov, Boris. "Lamarck, Schelling, Marr." In *Literaturnye leitmotivy: Ocherki russkoi literatury XX veka.* Moscow: Nauka, 1994.

———. "Razvitie ili restrukturirovanie: Vzgliady akademika T. D. Lysenko v kontekste pozdnego avangarda (konets 1920–1930-e gody)." *Logos* 21, nos. 11–12 (1999).

Gel'fand, M. "Literaturnye igry L'va Kassilia." *Oktiabr',* nos. 11–12 (1943).

Gentile, Emilio. *The Sacralization of Politics in Fascist Italy.* Cambridge, MA: Harvard University Press, 1996.

Gerasimov, Sergei. "Iskusstvo peredovykh idei." In *30 let sovetskoi kinematografii: Sbornik statei,* edited by D. Eremin. Moscow: Goskinoizdat, 1950.

Ginzburg, Lidiia. *Prokhodiashchie kharaktery: Proza voennykh let. Zapiski blokadnogo cheloveka.* Moscow: Novoe izd-vo, 2011.

Glovin'skii, M. "'Ne puskat' proshlogo na samotek': 'Kratkii kurs VKP(b)' kak mificheskoe skazanie." *Novoe literaturnoe obozrenie,* no. 22 (1996).

Goodwin, James. *Eisenstein, Cinema, and History.* Urbana: University of Illinois Press, 1993.

Gorbanevskii, M. V. *V nachale bylo slovo . . . : Maloizvestnye stranitsy istorii sovetskoi lingvistiki.* Moscow: Izd-vo Universiteta druzhby narodov, 1991.

Gorky, Maxim. *O literature*. 3rd ed. Moscow: Sovetskii pisatel', 1937.

———. *Sobranie sochinenii*. Moscow: Khudozhestvennaia literatura, 1949–53.

Gorlizki, Yoram, and Oleg Khlevniuk. *Cold Peace: Stalin and the Soviet Ruling Circle, 1945–1953*. Oxford: Oxford University Press, 2005.

Grachev, V. *O kinofil'me "Michurin."* Moscow: Goskinoizdat, 1949.

Gromov, E. *Kinooperator Anatolii Golovnia: Fil'my, svidetel'stva, razmyshleniia*. Moscow: Iskusstvo, 1980.

Gromova, Natal'ia. *Raspad: Sud'ba sovetskogo kritika, 40–50-e gody*. Moscow: Ellis Lak, 2009.

Groshev, A. "Obraz nashego sovremennika v kinoiskusstve." *Iskusstvo kino*, no. 4 (1951).

Groys, Boris. *Kommunisticheskii postskriptum*. Moscow: Ad Marginem, 2001.

———. "Net nichego vne iazyka: Stalinskie zametki o iazykoznanii." Paper presented at the conference on Soviet history and culture in Melbourne, Australia, July 2006.

Grudtsova, Ol'ga. "O romantizme i realizme." *Oktiabr'*, no. 8 (1947).

———. "V plenu skhemy." *Oktiabr'*, no. 2 (1948).

Gudkov, Lev. "Pobeda v voine: K sotsiologii odnogo natsional'nogo simvola." In Lev Gudkov, *Negativnaia identichnost': Stat'i 1997–2002 godov*. Moscow: Novoe literaturnoe obozrenie, 2004.

Gudkov, Lev, and Boris Dubin, "Ideologiia besstrukturnosti: Intelligentsiia i konets sovetskoi epokhi." *Znamia*, no. 11 (1994).

Günther, Hans, and Evgeny Dobrenko, eds. *Sotsrealisticheskii kanon*. St. Petersburg: Akademicheskii proekt, 2000.

Gurevich, Aron. *Izbrannye trudy*. Vol. 2: *Srednevekovyi mir*. Moscow: Universitetskaia kniga, 1999.

Gvozdev, A. N. "Voprosy sovremennoi orfografii i metodika ee prepodavaniia." In *Materialy ob"edinennoi nauchnoi sessii Otdeleniia literatury i iazyka Akademii nauk SSSR i Akademii pedagogicheskikh nauk RSFSR.*

Haas, David. *Leningrad's Modernists 1917–1932*. New York: Peter Lang, 1998.

Hankin, Robert. "Postwar Soviet Ideology and Literary Scholarship." In Simmons, *Through the Glass of Soviet Literature*.

Hodgson, Katherine. *Voicing the Soviet Experience: The Poetry of Ol'ga Berggol'ts*. Oxford: Oxford University Press, 2003.

Iakhot, Iegoshua. "Podavlenie filosofii v SSSR (20–30-e gody)." *Voprosy filosofii*, no. 11 (1991).

Iankovskaia, G. A. *Iskusstvo, den'gi i politika: Khudozhnik v gody pozdnego stalinizma*. Perm': PGU, 2007.

Iartseva, V. N. "Smeshenie leksiki i grammatiki v 'teorii' N. Ia. Marra." In *Protiv vul'garizatsii i izvrashcheniia marksizma v iazykoznanii,* vol. 2.

Ilizarov, B. S. *Pochetnyi akademik Stalin i akademik Marr: O iazykoved-cheskoi diskussii 1950 goda i problemakh s neiu sviazannykh.* Moscow: Veche, 2012.

Iosif Vissarionovich Stalin: Kratkaia biografiia. Moscow: OGIZ, 1947.

Istoriia VKP(b): Kratkii kurs. Moscow: Politizdat, 1938.

Iurenev, Rostislav. *Sovetskii biograficheskii fil'm.* Moscow: Goskinoizdat, 1949.

———. "Trudnaia zhizn' 'Bol'shoi zhizni. '" *Sovetskii ekran,* no. 4 (1989).

———. "Tvorets." *Iskusstvo kino,* no. 1 (1949).

Iustus, Ursula. "Vtoraia smert' Lenina: Funktsii placha v period perekhoda ot kul'ta Lenina k kul'tu Stalina." In Günther and Dobrenko, *Sotsrealisticheskii kanon.*

Iuzovskii, Iosif. "Eizenshtein!" *Kinovedcheskie zapiski,* no. 38 (1998).

Jameson, Fredric. *The Political Unconscious: Narrative as a Socially Symbolic Act.* Ithaca, NY: Cornell University Press, 1981.

Jones, Polly. *Myth, Memory, Trauma: Rethinking the Stalinist Past in the Soviet Union, 1953–70.* New Haven: Yale University Press, 2013.

Joravsky, David. *The Lysenko Affair.* Chicago: University of Chicago Press, 1970.

"K 50-letiiu zhurnala 'Voprosy filosofii': Zhurnal vchera i segodnia (Vstrecha v redaktsii)." *Voprosy filosofii,* no. 8 (1997).

Kalashnikov, Iu. S., et al., eds. *Ocherki istorii russkogo sovetskogo dramaticheskogo teatra.* Vol. 3: *1945–1959.* Moscow: AN SSSR, 1961.

Kamenskii, Z. A. *Istoriia filosofii kak nauka v Rossii XIX–XX vv.* Moscow: Esalan, 2001.

Kapitsa, Petr. "Eto bylo tak." *Neva,* no. 5 (1988).

Kaverin, V. *Epilog.* Moscow: Vagrius, 2006.

Kedrov, Bonifatii. "O razlichnykh putiakh perekhoda ot starogo kachestva k novomu." In *Voprosy dialekticheskogo i istoricheskogo materializma,* vol. 2.

Kelly, Catriona. "Territories of the Eye: The Russian Peep Show *(Raek)* and Pre-Revolutionary Visual Culture." *Journal of Popular Culture* 31, no. 4 (Spring 1998).

Kepley, Vance. *In the Service of the State: The Cinema of Alexander Dovzhenko.* Madison: University of Wisconsin Press, 1986.

Kholodov, Efim. "Deistvuiushchie litsa v poiskakh avtora." *Teatr,* no. 5 (1952).

———. "Dramaticheskii konflikt." *Teatr,* no. 8 (1947).

Kirschenbaum, Lisa. *The Legacy of the Siege of Leningrad, 1941–1995: Myth, Memories, and Monuments.* New York: Cambridge University Press, 2009.

Kleiman, Naum. "Formula finala." *Kinovedcheskie zapiski,* no. 38 (1998).

Knipovich, Evgeniia. "'Krasivaia' nepravda o voine." *Znamia,* nos. 9–10 (1944).

Kommari, M. D. "I. V. Stalin o marksizme v iazykoznanii." In *Voprosy dialekticheskogo i istoricheskogo materializma,* vol. 1.

Kommunisticheskaia Partiia Sovetskogo Soiuza v rezoliutsiiakh i resheniiakh s"ezdov, konferentsii i plenumov TsK. 7th ed. 4 vols. Moscow: Politizdat, 1954–60.

Konstantinov, F. V. "Eshche raz o politike i filosofii." *Pod znamenem marksizma,* no. 10 (1936).

———. "Protiv dogmatizma i nachetnichestva." In *Voprosy dialekticheskogo i istoricheskogo materializma,* vol. 1.

Kosheleva, L. P., et al., comps. *Sovetskaia natsional'naia politika: Ideologiia i praktiki, 1945–1953.* Moscow: ROSSPEN, 2013.

Kostyrchenko, Gennadii. "Malenkov protiv Zhdanova: Igry stalinskikh favoritov." *Rodina,* no. 9 (2000).

———. *Stalin protiv "kosmopolitov": Vlast' i evreiskaia intelligentsiia v SSSR.* Moscow: ROSSPEN, 2009.

———. *Tainaia politika Stalina: Vlast' i antisemitizm.* Moscow: Mezhdunarodnye otnosheniia, 2001.

Koval', Mar'ian. "Tvorcheskii put' D. Shostakovicha." Parts 1–3. *Sovetskaia muzyka,* nos. 2, 3, 4 (1948).

Kovarskii, N. "Istoriia pobedy." *Iskusstvo kino,* no. 1 (1946).

Kozhevnikov, A. B. "Igry stalinskoi demokratii i ideologicheskie diskussii v sovetskoi nauke: 1947–1952 gg." *Voprosy istorii estetstvoznaniia i tekhniki,* no. 4 (1997).

Kozintsev, Grigorii. *"Chernoe, likhoe vremia . . .": Iz rabochikh tetradei.* Moscow: Artist, Rezhisser, Teatr, 1994.

Kozlov, Leonid. "Ten' Groznogo i Khudozhnik." *Kinovedcheskie zapiski,* no. 14 (1992).

Krasina, T., and I. Sosnovskii. *Narodnyi artist SSSR Aleksandr Fedorovich Borisov.* Moscow: Goskinoizdat, 1952.

Kratkii filosofskii slovar'. Moscow: Politizdat, 1940.

Krebs, Stanley Dale. *Soviet Composers and the Development of Soviet Music.* London: Allen and Unwin, 1970.

Krementsov, Nikolai. *Stalinist Science.* Princeton, NJ: Princeton University Press, 1996.

———. *V poiskakh lekarstva protiv raka: Delo "KR."* St. Petersburg: Izd-vo RKhGA, 2004.

Krivonosov, Iu. I. "Srazhenie na filosofskom fronte: Filosofskaia diskussiia 1947 goda—prolog ideologicheskogo pogroma nauki." *Voprosy istorii estestvoznaniia i tekhniki,* no. 3 (1997).

Kukulin, Il'ia. "Regulirovanie boli: Predvaritel'nye zametki o transformatsii travmaticheskogo opyta Velikoi Otechestvennoi/Vtoroi mirovoi voiny v russkoi literature 1940-kh—1970-kh godov)." In Gabovich, *Pamiat' o voine 60 let spustia.*

Lahusen, Thomas. *How Life Writes the Book: Real Socialism and Socialist Realism in Stalin's Russia.* Ithaca, NY: Cornell University Press, 1997.

Leibovich, Oleg. *V gorode M: Ocherki sotsial'noi povsednevnosti sovetskoi provintsii v 40–50-kh gg.* Moscow: ROSSPEN, 2008.

Lel'chuk, V. S., and E. I. Pivovar, eds. *SSSR i kholodnaia voina.* Moscow: Mosgorarkhiv, 1995.

Leonov, Leonid. "Beseda s demonom." *Literaturnaia gazeta,* December 31, 1947.

———. "Rassuzhdenie o velikanakh." *Literaturnaia gazeta,* September 27, 1947.

Leonov, M. A. "Mesto i rol' filosofii v obshchestvennoi zhizni." *Voprosy filosofii,* no. 1 (1952).

———. "Mesto i rol' filosofii v obshchestvennoi zhizni v svete truda I. V. Stalina 'Marksizm i voprosy iazykoznaniia.'" In *Voprosy dialekticheskogo i istoricheskogo materializma,* vol. 2.

Lepeshinskaia, Ol'ga. *Proiskhozhdenie kletok iz zhivogo veshchestva i rol' zhivogo veshchestva v organizme.* Moscow: Izd-vo Akademii nauk SSSR, 1945.

———. *Put' v revoliutsiiu: Vospominaniia staroi bol'shevichki.* Perm: Permskoe knizhnoe izd-vo, 1963.

Levin, E. "Istoricheskaia tragediia kak zhanr i kak sud'ba: Po stranitsam dvukh stenogramm 1944 i 1946 godov." *Iskusstvo kino,* no. 1 (1991).

———. "Sovet da liubov'." *Iskusstvo kino,* no. 11 (1991).

Levonevskii, Dmitrii. "Istoriia 'bol'shogo bloknota.'" *Zvezda,* no. 7 (1988).

L'Hermitte, René. *Marr, marrisme, marristes: Une page de l'histoire de la linguistique soviétique.* Paris: Institut d'études slaves, 1987.

Lifshits, Mikhail. *Chto takoe klassika?* Moscow: Iskusstvo XXI vek, 2004.

Lobacheva, N. A. *"Povest' o nastoiashchem cheloveke" S. S. Prokof'eva: 60 let spustia.* Moscow: Kompozitor, 2008.

Lomidze, G. "Za pravdivoe otrazhenie zhiznennykh konfliktov v literature." *Voprosy filosofii,* no. 5 (1952).

Lovell, Stephen. *The Shadow of War: Russia and the USSR, 1941 to the Present.* Chichester: Blackwell, 2010.

Lukin, Iu. "Zhizn', posviashchennaia narodu." *Iskusstvo kino,* no. 2 (1949).

Lukov, Leonid. "Liubimaia i blizkaia tema." *Iskusstvo kino,* no. 3 (1951).

Lunacharskii, Anatolii. "Sotsialisticheskii realizm." *Sovetskii teatr,* nos. 2–3 (February–March 1933).

Lysenko, Trofim. *Izbrannye sochineniia.* Moscow: Moskovskii rabochii, 1953.

————. *Novoe v nauke o biologicheskom vide*. Moscow: Sel'khozgiz, 1952.

MacDonald, Ian. *The New Shostakovich*. London: Fourth Estate, 1990.

Maksimenkov, Leonid. "'Partiia—nash rulevoi': Postanovlenie TsK VKP(b) ot 10 fevralia 1948 goda ob opere Vano Muradeli 'Velikaia druzhba' v svete novykh arkhivnykh dokumentov." Parts 1–2. *Muzykal'naia zhizn'*, nos. 13–14 (1993) and 15–16 (1993).

————. *Sumbur vmesto muzyki: Stalinskaia kul'turnaia revoliutsiia, 1936–1938*. Moscow: Iuridicheskaia kniga, 1997.

Mamardashvili, Merab. "Mysl' pod zapretom: Mesto filosofii v sovetskoi sisteme" [interview by Annie Epelboin]. https://www.mamardashvili .com/ru/merab-mamardashvili/avtobiograficheskoe/mysl-pod-zapretom .-mesto-filosofii-v-sovetskoj-sisteme1.

————. *Neobkhodimost' sebia*. Moscow: Labyrint, 1996.

Mandel'shtam, Osip. *Sobranie sochinenii*. Moscow: Khudozhestvennaia literatura, 1990.

Manevich, Iosif. *Narodnyi artist SSSR Mikhail Chiaureli*. Moscow: Goskinoizdat, 1953.

Maresch, Eugenia. *Katyn 1940: The Documentary Evidence of the West's Betrayal*. Stroud: History Press, 2010.

Margolit, Evgenii. *Zhivye i mertvoe: Zametki k istorii sovetskogo kino 1920–1960-kh godov*. St. Petersburg: Seans, 2012.

Margolit, Evgenii, and Viacheslav Shmyrov. *(Iz"iatoe kino)*. Moscow: Kinotsentr, 1995.

Mar'iamov, G. *Kremlevskii tsenzor: Stalin smotrit kino*. Moscow: Kinotsentr, 1992.

Marin, Louis. *Portrait of the King*. London: Macmillan, 1988.

Marion, Dzhordzh [George]. *Bazy i imperiia*. Moscow: Gos. izd-vo inostrannoi lit-ry, 1948.

Markov, Dmitrii. *Genezis sotsialisticheskogo realizma: Iz opyta iuzhnoslavianskikh i zapadnoslavianskikh literatur*. Moscow: Nauka, 1970.

————. *Problemy teorii sotsialisticheskogo realizma*. Moscow: Khudozhestvennaia literatura, 1978.

Marr, Nikolai. *Izbrannye raboty*. 5 vols. Leningrad, 1933–37.

————. *K bakinskoi diskussii o iafetidologii i marksizme*. Baku: Izd-vo AzGNII, 1932.

Marx, Karl, and Friedrich Engels. *Izbrannye pis'ma*. Moscow: Gos. izd-vo polit. lit-ry, 1947.

————. *Sochineniia*. Vol. 1, 2nd ed. Moscow: Gos. izd-vo polit. lit-ry, 1955.

————. *Sochineniia*. Vol. 3, 2nd ed. Moscow: Gos. izd-vo polit. lit-ry, 1955.

Maslin, N. "Poet i narod." In *Protiv bezideinosti v literature*.

Materialy ob"edinennoi nauchnoi sessii Otdeleniia literatury i iazyka Akademii nauk SSSR i Akademii pedagogicheskikh nauk RSFSR, po-sviashchennoi trudam I. V. Stalina po iazykoznaniiu i voprosam prepo-davaniia iazykov v sovetskoi shkole (27–29 noiabria 1950 g.). Moscow: Akademiia pedagogicheskikh nauk RSFSR, 1951.

Matskin, A. "Ob ukrashatel'stve i ukrashateliakh." *Znamia*, nos. 11–12 (1943).

Medvedev, Zhores. "Stalin i Lysenko." In Medvedev and Medvedev, *Ne-izvestnyi Stalin.*

Medvedev, Zhores, and Roi Medvedev, *Neizvestnyi Stalin.* Moscow: Prava cheloveka, 2001.

Michaud, Eric. *The Cult of Art in Nazi Germany.* Stanford, CA: Stanford University Press, 2004.

Mikhalkov, Sergei. *Il'ia Golovin.* In *Sovetskaia dramaturgiia 1949: P"esy.* Moscow: Iskusstvo, 1950.

———. *Satira i iumor.* Moscow: Goslitizdat, 1953.

Minin, Sergei. "Kommunizm i filosofiia." *Pod znamenem marksizma,* no. 11–12 (1922).

Mitin, Mark. *Za materialisticheskuiu biologicheskuiu nauku.* Moscow: Izd-vo Akademii nauk SSSR, 1949.

Mlechin, Leonid. *Kreml'—1953: Bor'ba za vlast' so smertel'nym iskho-dom.* Moscow: Tsentrpoligraf, 2016.

Mokrousov, Aleksei. "Tainaia zhizn' D. D. Shostakovicha." *Domovoi,* no. 4 (2005).

Mosse, George. *The Nationalization of the Masses: Political Symbolism and Mass Movements in Germany, from the Napoleonic Wars through the Third Reich.* New York: Howard Fertig, 1975.

Murashov, Iurii. "Pis'mo i ustnaia rech' v diskursakh o iazyke 1930-kh godov: N. Marr." In Günther and Dobrenko, *Sotsrealisticheskii kanon.*

Narinskii, M. M., et al., comps. *Kholodnaia voina: Novye podkhody, novye dokumenty.* Moscow: Institut vseobshchei istorii RAN, 1995.

Nedobrovo, V. *Zhukovskii: O fil'me i ego sozdateliakh.* Moscow: Goski-noizdat, 1950.

Nedoshivin, German. "O probleme prekrasnogo v sovetskom iskusstve." In *Voprosy teorii sovetskogo izobrazitel'nogo iskusstva: Sbornik statei,* edited by K. A. Sitnik. Moscow: Izd-vo Akademii khudozhestv SSSR, 1950.

———. *Ocherki teorii iskusstva.* Moscow: Iskusstvo, 1953.

Nekrylova, A. F. *Russkie narodnye gorodskie prazdniki, uveseleniia i zre-lishcha.* Leningrad: Iskusstvo, 1988.

Nelson, Amy. *Music for the Revolution: Musicians and Power in Early Soviet Russia.* University Park, PA: Pennsylvania State University Press, 2004.

Neuberger, Joan. *Ivan the Terrible*. London: I. B. Tauris, 2003.

Nezhinskii, L. N., ed. *Sovetskaia vneshniaia politika v gody "kholodnoi voiny" 1945–1985: Novoe prochtenie*. Moscow: Mezhdunarodnye otnosheniia, 1995.

Novikov, Kirill. "Trebuetsia utverdit' odin avtoritet vo vsekh oblastiakh." *Kommersant Vlast*, no. 13 (2007). https://www.kommersant.ru/doc/757011.

Ogurtsov, A. P. "Podavlenie filosofii." In *Filosofiia ne konchaetsia*.

Okhotnikov, Vadim. "Fil'm o velikom izobretatele." *Iskusstvo kino*, no. 3 (1950).

Ostrovitianinov, K. V. "Znachenie truda I. V. Stalina 'Marksizm i voprosy iazykoznaniia' dlia razvitiia ekonomicheskoi i pravovoi nauki." In Sessiia *Otdelenii obshchestvennykh nauk Akademii nauk SSSR*.

Overy, Richard. *Russia's War*. New York: Penguin, 2010.

Palmer, Scott W. "How Memory Was Made: The Construction of the Memorial to the Heroes of Stalingrad." *Russian Review* 68 (July 2009).

Paperno, Irina. *Stories of the Soviet Experience: Memoirs, Diaries, Dreams*. Ithaca, NY: Cornell University Press, 2009.

Parfenov, L., ed. *Zhivye golosa kino: Govoriat vydaiushchiesia mastera otechestvennogo kinoiskusstva (30-e—40-e gody); Iz neopublikovannogo*. Moscow: Belyi bereg, 1999.

Paul, Allen. *Katyn: Stalin's Massacre and the Triumph of Truth*. DeKalb, IL: Northern Illinois University Press, 2010.

Pavlenko, Petr. *Sobranie sochinenii*. Vol. 6: *Stat'i i vospominaniia*. Neopublikovannye *materialy*. Moscow: GIKhL, 1955.

Perrie, Maureen. *The Cult of Ivan the Terrible in Stalin's Russia*. Basingstoke: Palgrave, 2001.

Pervyi vsesoiuznyi s"ezd sovetskikh pisatelei: Stenograficheskii otchet. Moscow: Gos. izd-vo khudozhestvennoi lit-ry, 1934.

Petrov, Vladimir. "Fil'm o geroicheskom srazhenii." *Iskusstvo kino*, no. 3 (1949).

———. "O fil'me 'Przheval'skii. '" *Iskusstvo kino*, no. 3 (1952).

Pipes, Daniel. *Conspiracy: How the Paranoid Style Flourishes and Where It Comes From*. New York: Free Press, 1997.

Platt, Kevin. *Terror and Greatness: Ivan and Peter as Russian Myths*. Ithaca, NY: Cornell University Press, 2011.

Plimak, E. G. "'Nado osnovatel'no prochistit' mozgi' (K 50-letiiu filosofskoi diskussii 1947 goda)." *Voprosy filosofii*, no. 7 (1997).

Plotkin, L. "O pravde zhizni." *Zvezda*, no. 8 (1952).

———. "Propovednik bezideinosti—M. Zoshchenko." In *Protiv bezideinosti v literature*.

———. "Sila sovetskoi literatury." In *Protiv bezideinosti v literature*.

Podoroga, Valerii. "Golos pis'ma i pis'mo vlasti." In *Totalitarizm kak isto-richeskii fenomen*, edited by A. A. Kara-Murza et al. Moscow: Filosof-skoe ob-vo SSSR, 1989.

Pogozheva, L. "Missiia, perestavshaia byt' sekretnoi." *Iskusstvo kino*, no. 5 (1950).

Pokrovskaia, N. V., comp. *Za mir: Poeticheskoe tvorchestvo* trudiashchikh-sia. Moscow: Vsesoiuznyi Dom narodnogo tvorchestva im. N. K. Krup-skoi, 1951.

Poliak, Lidiia. "O 'liricheskom epose' Velikoi Otechestvennoi voiny." *Zna-mia*, nos. 9–10 (1943).

Pollock, Ethan. "From *Partiinost'* to *Nauchnost'* and Not Quite Back Again: Revisiting the Lessons of the Lysenko Affair." *Slavic Review* 68, no. 1 (Spring 2009).

———. *Stalin and the Soviet Science Wars*. Princeton, NJ: Princeton University Press, 2006.

Popov, V. P. *Rossiiskaia derevnia posle voiny (iiun' 1945–mart 1953 gg.): Sbornik dokumentov*. Moscow: Prometei, 1992.

Pospelov, N. S. "Uchenie I. V. Stalina o grammaticheskom stroe iazyka." In *Voprosy iazykoznaniia v svete trudov I. V. Stalina.*

Protiv bezideinosti v literature: Sbornik statei zhurnala "Zvezda." Lenin-grad: Sovetskii pisatel', 1947.

Protiv vul'garizatsii i izvrashcheniia marksizma v iazykoznanii: Sbornik statei. 2 vols. Moscow: Izd-vo Akademii nauk SSSR, 1951–52.

Pudovkin, Vsevolod. "Rabota aktera v kino i sistema Stanislavskogo." In *Voprosy masterstva v sovetskom kinoiskusstve*, compiled by O. Abol'nik. Moscow: Goskinoizdat, 1952.

———. *Sobranie sochinenii*. Moscow: Iskusstvo, 1974–76.

———. "Sovetskii istoricheskii fil'm." In *Sobranie sochinenii*, vol. 2.

Rakhmanova, M. P., ed. and comp. *Sergei Prokof'ev: k 50-letiiu so dnia smerti: vospominaniia, pis'ma, stat'i*. Moscow: Deka-VS, 2004.

Rapoport, Iakov. "Zhivoe veshchestvo i ego konets: Otkrytie O. B. Le-peshinskoi i ego sud'ba." In Iakov Rapoport, *Na rubezhe dvukh epokh: Delo vrachei 1953 goda*. St. Petersburg: Izd-vo Pushkinskogo fonda, 2003.

Ravdin, Boris. "Blokada Leningrada v russkoi podnemetskoi pechati 1941–1945 godov." In *Blokadnye narrativy: Sbornik statei*, compiled and edited by P. Barskova and R. Nikolozi. Moscow: Novoe literaturnoe obozrenie, 2017.

Riurikov, Boris. "Otritsatel'nye obrazy i neprimirimost' pisatelia." *Litera-turnaia gazeta*, July 24, 1952.

———. "'V zhizni tak ne byvaet.'" *Literaturnaia gazeta*, September 11, 1952.

Rodionov, N. "Obrazy fil'ma." *Iskusstvo kino,* no. 3 (1951).

Romm, Mikhail. *Besedy o kino.* Moscow: Iskusstvo, 1964.

Roshal', Grigorii. "Istoriko-biograficheskii fil'm." *Iskusstvo kino,* no. 5 (1949).

———. "Obraz velikogo uchenogo." *Iskusstvo kino,* no. 3 (1949).

Rossiianov, K. O. "Stalin kak redaktor Lysenko." *Voprosy filosofii,* no. 2 (1993).

Rozental', Mark. *Marksistskii dialekticheskii metod.* Moscow: OGIZ, 1947.

Rozhkov, P. *Nuzhna li nam romantika.* Moscow: Sovetskaia literatura, 1934.

Rumii, V. "Otvet odnomu iz talmudistov." *Pod znamenem marksizma,* nos. 8–9 (1923).

Ryklin, Mikhail. *Iskusstvo kak prepiatstvie.* Moscow: Ad Marginem, 1997.

———. *Prostranstva likovaniia: Totalitarizm i razlichie.* Moscow: Logos, 2002.

Ryzhkin, I. Ia., and Z. Safarova. "Sovetskaia muzykal'naia estetika v 30-e gody." In *Iz istorii sovetskogo iskusstvovedeniia i esteticheskoi mysli 1930-kh godov,* edited by V. V. Vanslov and L. F. Denisova. Moscow: Iskusstvo, 1977.

Sadovskii, V. N. "Bonifatii Mikhailovich Kedrov: Chelovek i uchenyi." *Voprosy filosofii,* no. 1 (2004).

Safonov, Vadim. *Pervootkryvateli.* Moscow: Molodaia gvardiia, 1952.

Samoilov, David. *Pamiatnye zapiski.* Moscow: Mezhdunarodnye otnosheniia, 1995.

Samoilov, V. O., and Iu. A. Vinogradov. "Ivan Pavlov i Nikolai Bukharin: Ot konflikta k druzhbe." *Znamia,* no. 10 (1989).

Sandomirskaja, Irina. "Iazyk-Stalin: 'Marksizm i voprosy iazykoznaniia' kak lingvisticheskii povorot vo vselennoi SSSR." In *Landslide of the Norm: Language Culture in Post-Soviet Russia,* edited by Ingunn Lunde and Tine Roesen. Bergen: University of Bergen, 2006.

Sarnov, Benedikt. *Sluchai Zoshchenko: Prishestvie kapitana Lebiadkina.* Moscow: Eksmo, 2005.

Sarnov, Benedikt. *Stalin i pisateli.* Vol. 2. Moscow: Eksmo, 2008.

Saunders, Frances Stonor. *Who Paid the Piper?: The CIA and the Cultural Cold War.* London: Granta Books, 1999.

Schnapp, Jeffrey. *Staging Fascism: 18BL and the Theater of Masses for Masses.* Stanford: Stanford University Press, 1996.

Sergievskii, I. "Ob antinarodnoi poezii A. Akhmatovoi." In *Protiv bezideinosti v literature.*

Sessiia Otdelenii obshchestvennykh nauk Akademii nauk SSSR, posviashchennaia godovshchine opublikovaniia genial'nogo proizvdeniia

I. V. Stalina "Marksizm i voprosy iazykoznaniia": Sbornik materialov. Moscow: Izd-vo AN SSSR, 1951.

Shcheglov, Mark. "Bez muzykal'nogo soprovozhdeniia. . . ." *Novyi mir,* no. 10 (1953).

Shepilov, Dmitrii. *Neprimknuvshii.* Moscow: Vagrius, 2001.

Shkolnikov, Vadim. "The Philosophical Cap of Yegor Fjodorovič or Becoming Belinskij." *Studies in East European Thought* 65, nos. 3–4 (December 2013). Special issue "Hegel in Russia."

Shostakovich, Dmitrii. *D. Shostakovich o vremeni i o sebe, 1926–1975.* Compiled by M. Iakovlev. Moscow: Sovetskii kompozitor, 1980.

———. *Testimony: The Memoirs of Dmitri Shostakovich; as Related to and Edited by Solomon Volkov.* New York: Harper and Row, 1979.

Shtain, G. "Samoe glavnoe." *Teatr,* no. 7 (1948).

Silina, Lada. *Vneshnepoliticheskaia propaganda v SSSR v 1945–1985 gg. (Po materialam Otdela propagandy i agitatsii TsK VKP(b)-KPSS.* Moscow: ROSSPEN, 2011.

Simmons, Ernest J., ed. *Through the Glass of Soviet Literature: Views of Russian Society.* New York: Columbia University Press, 1953.

Simonov, Konstantin. *Glazami cheloveka moego pokoleniia: Razmyshleniia o I. V. Staline.* Moscow: Izd-vo APN, 1988.

———. *Soldatami ne rozhdaiutsia.* Moscow: Sovetskii pisatel', 1964.

Simonov, N. S. *Voenno-promyshlennyi kompleks SSSR v 1920–1950-e gody: Tempy ekonomicheskogo rosta, struktura, organizatsiia proizvodstva i upravlenie.* Moscow: ROSSPEN, 1996.

Smirnova, E. *Aleksei Denisovich Dikii.* Moscow: Goskinoizdat, 1952.

Soifer, Valerii. *Stalin i moshenniki v nauke.* Moscow: Dobrosvet, 2012.

Sokolov, B. M. *Khudozhestvennyi iazyk russkogo lubka.* Moscow: RGGU, 1999.

Sokolov, V. V. "Nekotorye epizody predvoennoi i poslevoennoi filosofskoi zhizni (Iz vospominanii)." *Voprosy filosofii,* no. 1 (2001).

Solov'ev, A. "Puti razvitiia novogo zhanra." *Iskusstvo kino,* no. 4 (1949).

Solov'ev, Vladimir. *Zolotaia chuma (Izmena natsii).* Moscow: Iskusstvo, 1952.

Soveshchanie deiatelei sovetskoi muzyki v TsK VKP(b). Moscow: Pravda, 1948.

Soveshchanie po probleme zhivogo veshchestva i razvitiia kletok: Stenograficheskii otchet. Moscow: Izd-vo Akademii nauk SSSR, 1951.

Stalin, Joseph. Sochineniia. Vol. 1 [XIV: 1934–1940]. Stanford: Hoover Institution, 1967.

———. *Sochineniia.* Vol. 3 [XVI: 1946–1953]. Stanford: Hoover Institution, 1967.

———. *Sochineniia.* Vol. 12. Moscow: Gos. izd-vo polit. lit-ry, 1953.

———. *Sochineniia.* Vol. 16. Moscow: Pisatel', 1997.

———. *Sochineniia.* Vol. 18. Tver': Soiuz, 2006.

Stanchevici, Dmitri. *Stalinist Genetics: The Constitutional Rhetoric of T. D. Lysenko.* London: Routledge, 2011.

Stikhi o mire: Sbornik stikhov Kaluzhskogo oblastnogo literaturnogo ob"edineniia. Kaluga: Izd-vo gazety "Znamia," 1952.

Studitskii, Aleksandr. "Mukholiuby—chelovekonenavistniki." *Ogonek,* no. 11 (1949).

Subotskii, Lev. "Oruzhie pobedy." *Znamia,* no. 5–6 (1945).

Surkov, Aleksei. "Tvorcheskii otchet na zasedanii voennoi komissii SSP 12 iiulia 1943 g." In Anisimov et al., *Sovetskie pisateli na frontakh Velikoi Otechestvennoi voiny.*

Surov, Anatolii. "Nashi zadachi." In *Ideinost' i masterstvo: Sbornik statei sovetskikh pisatelei o dramaturgii (1945–1953),* compiled and edited by Vl. F. Pimenov. Moscow: Iskusstvo, 1953.

Sutyrin, V. "Velikii perelom." *Iskusstvo kino,* no. 1 (1946).

Swayze, Harold. *Soviet Literary Politics, 1946–1956.* Cambridge, MA: Harvard University Press, 1962.

Tarasenkov, Anatolii. *O sovetskoi literature: Sbornik statei.* Moscow: Sovetskii pisatel', 1952.

Thomas, Lawrence. *The Linguistic Theories of N. Ja. Marr.* Berkeley: University of California Press, 1957.

Thompson, Kristin. *Eisenstein's Ivan the Terrible: A Neoformalist Analysis.* Princeton, NJ: Princeton University Press, 1981.

Tikhonov, V. V. *Ideologicheskie kampanii "pozdnego stalinizma" i sovetskaia istoricheskaia nauka (seredina 1940-kh—1953 g.).* St. Petersburg: Nestor-Istoriia, 2016.

Timenchik, Roman. *Anna Akhmatova v 1960-e gody.* Moscow: Vodolei, 2005.

Tiupa, V. I. *Khudozhestvennost' literaturnogo proizvedeniia.* Krasnoiarsk: Izd-vo Krasnoiarskogo un-ta, 1987.

Tomoff, Kiril. *Creative Union: The Professional Organization of Soviet Composers, 1939–1953.* Ithaca, NY: Cornell University Press, 2006.

Trimbach, Sergei. "Vyzhzhenaia zemlia Aleksandra Dovzhenko." *Iskusstvo kino,* no. 9 (1996).

Troshin, D. M. "Marksizm-leninizm ob ob"ektivnom kharaktere zakonov nauki." In *Voprosy dialekticheskogo i istoricheskogo materializma,* vol. 2.

———. "Znachenie truda I. V. Stalina 'Marksizm i voprosy iazykoznaniia' dlia estestvennykh nauk." In *Voprosy dialekticheskogo i istoricheskogo materializma,* vol. 1.

Tsivian, Yuri. *Ivan the Terrible.* London: BFI, 2002.

Tsukerman, Vladislav. "Dvoinaia 'myshelovka,' ili samoubiistvo fil'mom." *Iskusstvo kino,* no. 1 (1991).

Tumarkin, Nina. *The Living and the Dead: The Rise and Fall of the Cult of World War II in Russia.* New York: Basic Books, 1994.

Turovskaia, Maiia. "30–40-e: 'Chastnyi sektor' v epokhu diktatury." *Iskusstvo kino,* no. 2 (1996).

———. "Fil'my 'kholodnoi voiny.'" *Iskusstvo kino,* no. 9 (1996).

Uhlenbruch, Bernd. "The Annexation of History: Eisenstein and the Ivan Grozny Cult of the 1940s." In *The Culture of the Stalin Period,* edited by Hans Gunther. London: Macmillan, 1990.

Urry, John. "How Societies Remember the Past." In *Theorizing Museums: Representing Identity and Diversity in a Changing World,* edited by Sharon Macdonald and Gordon Fyfe. Oxford: Blackwell, 1996.

Vaisfel'd, I. *Epicheskie zhanry v kino.* Moscow: Goskinoizdat, 1949.

Vaiskopf, Mikhail. *Pisatel' Stalin.* Moscow: Novoe literaturnoe obozrenie, 2001.

———. "Stalin glazami Zoshchenko." *Izvestiia AN. Seriia literatury i iazyka* 57, no. 5 (1998).

Vaksberg, Arkadii. *Neraskrytye tainy.* Moscow: Novosti, 1993.

Vasil'ev, V. "Zametki o khudozhestvennom masterstve S. Babaevskogo." *Zvezda,* no. 11 (1951).

Vasil'kov, Ia. V. "Tragediia akademika Marra." *Khristianskii Vostok,* no. 2 (2001).

Vesnik, Evgenii. *Zapiski artista.* 2009. http://www.e-reading.club/book reader.php/1009497/Vesnik_-_Zapiski_artista.html.

Vickery, Walter. "Zhdanovism (1946–53)." In *Literature and Revolution in Soviet Russia 1917–62,* edited by Max Hayward and Leopold Labedz. London: Oxford University Press, 1963.

Vinogradov, Viktor. "Nauchnye zadachi sovetskogo literaturovedeniia." In Egolin et al., *Voprosy literaturovedeniia v svete trudov I. V. Stalina po iazykoznaniiu.*

———. "Razvitie sovetskogo iazykoznaniia v svete ucheniia I. V. Stalina o iazyke." In *Voprosy dialekticheskogo i istoricheskogo materializma,* vol. 1.

———. "Znachenie rabot I. V. Stalina dlia razvitiia sovetskogo iazykoznaniia." In *Voprosy iazykoznaniia v svete trudov I. V. Stalina.*

Vishnevetskii, Igor'. *Sergei Prokof'ev.* Moscow: Molodaia gvardiia, 2009.

Vishnevskii, Vsevolod. "Fil'm 'Ivan Groznyi.'" *Pravda,* January 28, 1945.

———. "Iz dnevnikov 1944–1948 gg." *Kinovedcheskie zapiski,* no. 38 (1998)

———. *Sobranie sochinenii.* Vol. 4. Moscow: GIKhL, 1958.

Vizulis, Izidors. *The Molotov-Ribbentrop Pact of 1939: The Baltic Case.* New York: Praeger, 1990.

Vlasova, Ekaterina. *1948 god v sovetskoi muzyke*. Moscow: Klassika-XXI, 2010.

Volkov, Solomon. *Shostakovich i Stalin: Khudozhnik i Tsar'*. Moscow: Eksmo, 2005.

Volkov, Vitalii. "Za kulisami: Nekotorye kommentarii k odnomu postanovleniiu." *Avrora*, no. 8 (1991).

Volynchik, N. A., ed. *Sovetskoe gosudarstvo i obshchestvo v period pozdnego stalinizma, 1945–1953 gg.: Materialy VII mezhdunarodnoi nauchnoi konferentsii, Tver,' 4–6 dekabria 2014 g.* Moscow: ROSSPEN, 2015.

Voprosy dialekticheskogo i istoricheskogo materializma v trude I. V. Stalina "Marksizm i voprosy iazykoznaniia." 2 vols. Moscow: AN SSSR, 1951–52.

Voprosy iazykoznaniia v svete trudov I. V. Stalina. Moscow: Izd-vo MGU, 1952.

"Voprosy literaturovedeniia v svete trudov tovarishcha Stalina po iazykoznaniiu, 15–19 maia 1951 g." *Izvestiia AN SSSR. Otdelenie literatury i iazyka* 10, no. 3 (1951).

Voprosy teorii i istorii iazyka v svete trudov I. V. Stalina po iazykoznaniiu. Moscow: AN SSSR, 1952.

Voronina, Olga. "'We Started the Cold War': A Hidden Message behind Stalin's Attack on Anna Akhmatova." In *Cold War Cultures: Perspectives on Eastern and Western European Societies*, edited by Annette Vowinckel, Marcus M. Payk, and Thomas Lindenberger. New York: Berghahn Books, 2012.

"Vsesoiuznoe soveshchanie rabotnikov khudozhestvennoi kinematografii po obsuzhdeniiu resheniia TsK VKP(b) o kinofil'me 'Bol'shaia zhizn'" (2 seriia), 14–15 oktiabria 1946 goda." In Parfenov, *Zhivye golosa kino*.

Vtoroi Vsesoiuznyi s"ezd sovetskikh pisatelei. 15–26 dekabria 1954 goda: Stenograficheskii otchet. Moscow: Sovetskii pisatel', 1955.

Vyshinskii, P. E. "Kommunizm i otechestvo." *Voprosy filosofii* 2 (1948).

———. "Sovetskii patriotizm—dvizhushchaia sila razvitiia sovetskogo obshchestva." In *O sovetskom sotsialisticheskom obshchestve*, edited by F. Konstantinov, M. Kammari, and G. Glezerman. Moscow: Gos. izd-vo politicheskoi lit-ry, 1948.

"Vysokaia otvetstvennost' sovetskogo literatora." [Editorial.] *Literaturnaia gazeta*, January 25, 1947.

Wilson, Elizabeth. *Shostakovich: A Life Remembered*. London: Faber and Faber, 2006.

Yakubov, Manashir. "Shostakovich's *Anti-Formalist Rayok*." In *Shostakovich in Context*, edited by Rosamund Bartlett. Oxford: Oxford University Press, 2000.

Yarmolinsky, Avrahm. *Literature under Communism: The Literary Policy of the Communist Party of the Soviet Union from the End of the World War II to the Death of Stalin.* Bloomington: Indiana University Press, 1957.

Yurchak Alexei. *Everything Was Forever until It Was No More: The Last Soviet Generation.* Princeton, NJ: Princeton University Press, 2006.

Zagorianskii, Evgenii. *Sibiriachka.* Moscow and Leningrad: Iskusstvo, 1950.

Zakharenko, Igor' Antonovich. "Istoriia geograficheskogo izucheniia i kartografirovaniia Dal'nevostochnogo prostranstva Rossii i Kitaia." (Author's abstract of dissertation for the Doctorate of Geographical Sciences in the specialty of History.) Moscow: S. I. Vavilov Institute of the History of Natural Science and Technology, Russian Academy of Sciences, 2009. Available at http://cheloveknauka.com/istoriya -geograficheskogo-izucheniya-i-kartografirovaniya-dalnevostochnogo -pogranichnogo-prostranstva-rossii-i-kitaya.

"Zakliuchenie Khudozhestvennogo soveta Ministerstva kinematografii SSSR po fil'mu 'Donetskie shakhtery. '" March 12, 1951. Available at http://www.kino-teatr.ru/kino/history/y1951/429/.

Zalesskaia, L. *O romanticheskom techenii v sovetskoi literature.* Moscow: Nauka, 1973.

"Zasedanie khudozhestvennogo soveta pri komitete po delam kinematografii: Prosmotr i obsuzhdenie vtoroi serii kinokartiny 'Ivan Groznyi' rezhissera S. Eizenshteina. 7 fevralia 1946 goda." In Parfenov, *Zhivye golosa kino.*

Zhabinskii, Vl. *Prosvety: Zametki o sovetskoi literature 1956–1957 gg.* Munich: TsOPE, 1958.

Zhdan, V. "Obraz velikoi bitvy." *Iskusstvo kino,* no. 3 (1949).

Zhdanov, Andrei. *Sovetskaia literatura—samaia ideinaia, samaia peredovaia literatura v mire: Rech' na pervom Vsesoiuznom s"ezde sovetskikh pisatelei.* Moscow: Khudozhestvennaia literatura, 1934.

Zhirnov, Evgenii. "Naznacheny vinovnymi." *Kommersant"-Vlast',* April 14, 2003.

Zholkovskii, Aleksandr. "Novye vin'etki." *Zvezda,* no. 1 (2005).

Zima, V. F. *Golod v SSSR 1946–1947 godov: Proiskhozhdenie i posledstviia.* Moscow: Institut Rossiiskoi istorii RAN, 1996.

Zis', A. Ia. "U istokov zhurnala 'Voprosy filosofii. '" *Voprosy filosofii,* no. 7 (1997).

Zorin, Andrei. *Kormia dvuglavogo orla: Literatura i gosudarstvennaia ideologiia v Rossii v poslednei treti XVIII—pervoi treti XIX veka.* Moscow: Novoe literaturnoe obozrenie, 2004.

Zubkova, E. Iu., et al., comps. *Sovetskaia zhizn', 1945–1953.* Moscow: ROSSPEN, 2003.

Zubkova, Elena. *Poslevoennoe sovetskoe obshchestvo: Politika i povsed-nevnost,' 1945–1953 gg.* Moscow: ROSSPEN, 2000.

Zubok, Vladislav. *Inside the Kremlin's Cold War: From Stalin to Khru-shchev.* Cambridge, MA: Harvard University Press, 1997.

Zvegintsev, V. A. "Poniatie vnutrennikh zakonov razvitiia iazyka v svete rabot I. V. Stalina po iazykoznaniiu." In *Voprosy iazykoznaniia v svete trudov I. V. Stalina.*

Zweerde, Evert van der. *Soviet Philosophy, the Ideology and the Hand-maid: A Historical and Critical Analysis of Soviet Philosophy, with a Case-Study into Soviet History of Philosophy.* Nijmegen, 1994.

Index